Delphi Developer's Guide to XML

Keith Wood

Wordware Publishing, Inc.

Library of Congress Cataloging-in-Publication Data

Wood, Keith, 1961-
    Delphi developer's guide to XML / by Keith Wood.
      p. cm.
    Includes index.
    ISBN 1-55622-812-0 (pbk.)
    1. XML (Document markup language).   2. Delphi (Computer file).   3. Computer software--Development.   I. Title.

QA76.76.H94 W67   2001
005.7'2--dc21   2001026660
                                                                                            CIP

© 2001, Wordware Publishing, Inc.

All Rights Reserved

2320 Los Rios Boulevard
Plano, Texas 75074

No part of this book may be reproduced in any form or by
any means without permission in writing from
Wordware Publishing, Inc.

Printed in the United States of America

ISBN 1-55622-812-0
10 9 8 7 6 5 4 3 2 1
0107

Delphi is a registered trademark of Borland Software Corporation in the United States and other countries. Other products mentioned are used for identification purposes only and may be trademarks of their respective companies.

All inquiries for volume purchases of this book should be addressed to Wordware Publishing, Inc., at the above address. Telephone inquiries may be made by calling:

(972) 423-0090

Contents

Dedication xi
Preface xii
Acknowledgments xiv

Part I: Introduction to XML

Chapter 1: History 3
    XML vs. HTML. 4
    Related Specifications 5
    Extensible Hypertext Markup Language (XHTML) 6
    Mathematical Markup Language (MathML) 8
    Scalable Vector Graphics (SVG) 10
    Synchronized Multimedia Integration Language (SMIL) . . . 13
    Resource Description Framework (RDF) 15
    References 19
    Sample XML 21

Chapter 2: XML Syntax 22
    Elements and Attributes 23
    Name Tokens and Namespaces 24
    Text and White Space 25
    Comments 26
    Processing Instructions 26
    Entities 26
    CDATA Sections 28
    Prolog 29
    Encoding Schemes 29
    XML Processors 31
    Summary 32

Chapter 3: Document Type Definitions 33
    DTD Declarations 35
    Content Model 36
    Attributes 37
    Notations 39
    Entities 39
    Summary 41

Chapter 4:	Extensible Stylesheet Language Transformations	42
	Transformations	42
	Templates and Patterns	43
	Text Content	45
	Building Document Structure	45
	Loops	46
	Conditional Processing	47
	XSLT Sample	48
	Summary	51
Chapter 5:	XLink	52
	Link Definitions	52
	Simple Links	54
	Extended Links	55
	Out-of-Line Links	57
	Summary	57
Chapter 6:	XPath and XPointer	58
	General Form	58
	Axes	59
	Predicates	60
	Locations	61
	Functions	61
	Abbreviated Syntax	63
	Samples	64
	Summary	65
Chapter 7:	XML Schema	66
	Schema Document	67
	Documentation	68
	Simple Types	68
	Complex Types	69
	Attribute Declarations	71
	Element Declarations	72
	Further Abilities of Schemas	73
	Summary	74

Part II: The Document Object Model

Chapter 8:	The Document Object Model (DOM)	77
	DOM Interfaces	77
	DOMException	81
	Node Interface	82
	NodeList Interface	87
	NamedNodeMap Interface	87
	Element Interface	89
	Attr Interface	91

	CharacterData Interface 92
	Text Interface 93
	CDATASection Interface 94
	Comment Interface 94
	ProcessingInstruction Interface 94
	DocumentType Interface 95
	Entity Interface 96
	EntityReference Interface 97
	Notation Interface 97
	DocumentFragment Interface 98
	Document Interface 98
	DOMImplementation Interface 101
	NodeFilter Interface 102
	NodeIterator Interface 103
	TreeWalker Interface 104
	DocumentTraversal Interface 106
	Summary 107
Chapter 9:	Microsoft's Document Object Model 108
	IXMLDOMParseError Interface 110
	IXMLDOMNode Interface 111
	IXMLDOMNodeList Interface 119
	IXMLDOMNamedNodeMap Interface 120
	IXMLDOMElement Interface 122
	IXMLDOMAttribute Interface 124
	IXMLDOMCharacterData Interface 125
	IXMLDOMText Interface 127
	IXMLDOMCDATASection Interface 127
	IXMLDOMComment Interface 128
	IXMLDOMProcessingInstruction Interface 128
	IXMLDOMDocumentType Interface 129
	IXMLDOMEntity Interface 130
	IXMLDOMEntityReference Interface 131
	IXMLDOMNotation Interface 132
	IXMLDOMDocumentFragment Interface 132
	IXMLDOMDocument Interface 133
	IXMLDOMDocument2 Interface 139
	IXMLDOMSchemaCollection Interface 140
	IXMLDOMSelection Interface 141
	IXMLDOMImplementation Interface 143
	Document Traversal 143
	IXSLTemplate Interface 144
	IXSLProcessor Interface 145
	Loading the DOM 147

Contents

    The MS DOM XML Viewer 149
    Viewing Node Details 153
    Threading the DOM 155
    Summary 155

Chapter 10: CUESoft's Document Object Model 157
    TDOMException Exception 158
    TXmlParserError Exception 159
    TXmlNode Class 160
    TXmlNodeList Class 165
    TXmlNamedNodeMap Class 167
    TXmlElement Class 169
    TXmlAttribute Class 172
    TXmlCharacterData Class 172
    TXmlText Class 173
    TXmlCDataSection Class 174
    TXmlComment Class 174
    TXmlProcessingInstruction Class 175
    TXmlDocumentType Class 175
    TXmlEntity Class 176
    TXmlEntityReference Class 177
    TXmlNotation Class 177
    TXmlDocumentFragment Class 178
    TXmlDocument Class 179
    TXmlDomImplementation Class 181
    TXmlObjModel Component 182
    TXmlParser Component 185
    Loading the CUESoft DOM 189
    Summary 194

Chapter 11: Open XML's Document Object Model 195
    EDomException Exception 195
    TdomNode Class 198
    TdomNodeList Class 205
    TdomNamedNodeMap Class 206
    TdomElement Class 208
    TdomAttr Class 211
    TdomCharacterData Class 213
    TdomText Class 214
    TdomCDATASection Class 215
    TdomComment Class 215
    TdomProcessingInstruction Class 216
    TdomDocumentType Class 216
    TdomInternalSubset Class 219
    TdomExternalSubset Class 219

TdomConditionalSection Class 220
TdomEntity Class 221
TdomEntityDeclaration Class 223
TdomEntityReference Class 224
TdomNotation Class 225
TdomNotationDeclaration Class 226
TdomElementTypeDeclaration Class 227
Content Models 228
TdomAttrList Class 230
TdomAttrDefinition Class 231
TdomNametoken Class 232
TdomXmlDeclaration Class 233
TdomTextDeclaration Class 234
TdomDocumentFragment Class 234
TdomDocument Class 235
TdomImplementation Class 244
TdomNodeFilter Class 247
TdomNodeIterator Class 248
TdomTreeWalker Class 250
TXmlToDomParser Class 252
Helper Functions 256
Viewing with the Open XML DOM 261
Summary 268

Part III: Simple API for XML

Chapter 12: Simple API for XML (SAX) 271
Working with SAX 271
SAX Elements 272
SAXException Class 275
SAXParseException Class 276
InputSource Class 277
Locator Interface 279
Attributes Interface 280
ContentHandler Interface 282
DTDHandler Interface 284
EntityResolver Interface 285
ErrorHandler Interface 285
SAX Extensions 286
LexicalHandler Interface 287
DeclHandler Interface 289
XMLReader Interface 290
XMLFilter Interface 291
ParserAdapter and XMLReaderAdapter Classes 292

XMLReaderFactory Class 293
DefaultHandler Class. 293
Summary 294

Chapter 13: Microsoft's SAX Parser 295
IVBSAXLocator Interface 295
IVBSAXAttributes Interface. 296
IVBSAXContentHandler Interface 298
IVBSAXDTDHandler Interface 301
IVBSAXEntityResolver Interface 302
IVBSAXErrorHandler Interface 302
IVBSAXLexicalHandler Interface 303
IVBSAXDeclHandler Interface 305
IVBSAXXMLReader Interface 306
IVBSAXXMLFilter Interface 309
Preparing for SAX Events 309
Responding to the Notifications 314
Summary 316

Chapter 14: SAX in Delphi 317
Conversion to Delphi. 317
ESAXException Class 319
ESAXParseException Class 320
TSAXInputSource Class 321
ISAXLocator Interface 322
ISAXAttributes Interface. 323
ISAXContentHandler Interface 326
ISAXDTDHandler Interface 328
ISAXEntityResolver Interface 329
ISAXErrorHandler Interface 330
SAX Extensions 330
ISAXLexicalHandler Interface. 331
ISAXDeclHandler Interface 333
ISAXXMLReader Interface 334
ISAXXMLFilter Interface 336
TSAXParserAdapter and TSAXXMLReaderAdapter Classes . . . 336
TSAXXMLReaderFactory Class 338
TSAXDefaultHandler Class 340
Building a SAX Reader 341
The SAX XML Viewer. 345
Implementing ISAXContentHandler. 349
Summary 353

Chapter 15: Wrapping External Parsers. 354
Adapting Microsoft's SAX Parser 354
Using CUESoft's Parser 359
Using Open XML's Parser 362
Summary 362

Part IV: Serving XML

Chapter 16: XML is Data 367
Movie-watcher Database 368
Chapter 17: Simple Text. 370
From a Database 370
Summary 375
Chapter 18: Web Modules. 376
Generation 377
TRecordPageProducer 381
Summary 385
Chapter 19: Document Object Model. 386
Microsoft's DOM 386
CUESoft's DOM 391
Open XML's DOM 392
Summary 396
Chapter 20: SAX Generation 397
IMXWriter Interface 397
IMXAttributes Interface 399
Creating a Writer 401
Defining the DTD 403
Adding Content. 404
Summary 406
Chapter 21: Applying XSL Transformations. 407
XSLT Utility 408
Transforming the Document 410
Monolithic HTML Transformation 411
Template-Based HTML Transformation. 413
Comma-Separated Transformation 416
Rich Text Transformation 418
Summary 420
Chapter 22: XML Broker 422
The Data Server 423
InternetExpress 425
The CGI Web Application 426
Using ISAPI 430
XML Usage 430
Summary 434

Part V: Sample Applications

Chapter 23: Mass Electronic Mail-Outs 437
    Loading the Configuration Properties 438
    Mail Message Template 440
    Database Access 443
    Drop It in the Post 445
    Logging and Testing 446
    All Together Now 447
    Summary 449

Chapter 24: A Customized Client 450
    The Client 450
    Information Hiding. 452
    Parsing the XML Documents 453
    Constructing Model Objects 455
    Accumulating Content 457
    Saving Properties. 457
    Client Processing. 459
    Through the Browser. 461
    Summary 463

Chapter 25: Examination XML — Delphi Client 464
    Loading an Exam. 465
    User Tracking 470
    Exam Application 472
    Summary 477

Chapter 26: Examination XML — Web Client 478
    Exam Transformations 478
    Scripting in Transformations. 483
    Web Application Initialization 486
    Applying the Transformations 488
    Finishing Up 492
    Summary 494

Chapter 27: Simple Object Access Protocol 495
    SOAP Introduction 495
    Processing SOAP. 498
    SOAP Server 505
    SOAP Client 507
    Summary 509

Glossary 510
Index 517

Dedication

For Katalin,
who knew I could do it

Preface

This book is designed as an introduction to XML and an examination of how XML can be used in conjunction with Delphi.

XML is a specification that defines a way to describe and process sets of documents that have an inherent structure. An XML document's appearance is similar to HTML (not surprising given its heritage), but it is targeted at describing the meaning of data within the document, rather than the data's presentation as HTML does.

Due to the simple hierarchy of elements within an XML document and the enforcement of certain structural rules, XML documents are easily processed by a variety of parsers. Processors may be written in any language and still handle the same documents.

Given the text-based nature of XML, these documents can be created just with a text editor, through generic XML editors, or automatically from other data sources. Furthermore, the text files are easily transferred between machines over LANs or across the Internet. The target machines can use different operating systems and yet accept the same XML documents.

XML lets you create language- and operating system-independent documents that contain self-describing data. This facilitates the transfer of data and interactions between computers wherever they may be.

Numerous books have been written on XML itself, although these usually deal with Java as the implementation language for any processors. Much of the ongoing work in XML processing also seems to be centered on Java. I felt that Delphi developers should not be left out of this important new standard, and I have written this book to try to fill in some of the gaps in combining the two technologies.

Who is This Book For?

This book is for developers with a working knowledge of Delphi who are interested in learning about XML and its related technologies. No knowledge about XML is assumed.

Some of the topics in the book require the advanced features of the Enterprise editions of Delphi, although basic processing of XML documents can be done with any edition. The code that demonstrates the concepts presented here runs under Delphi 3 through 6. However, due to version differences, there is often a separate Delphi 3 version for each project.

What is in the Book?

Part I introduces the reader to XML, tracing its origins and purpose. Several existing XML applications are presented to show the diversity of uses for XML. The syntax and structure of an XML document is described, along with the corresponding document type definition (DTD). Accompanying standards such as XSLT (XSL Transformations), XLink, XPointer, and XML Schema are also reviewed. XSLT lets you transform XML documents into other formats, typically into HTML for display in a browser. XLink defines how documents can be connected in ways beyond the simple hyperlink of HTML. XPointer describes how to address sections within a document for more focused links. And XML Schema is an alternative to DTDs in describing the structure of XML documents.

Part II shows how to work with XML using Delphi. The Document Object Model (DOM) specification from the World Wide Web Consortium (W3C) is presented, followed by three implementations of it. The DOM is a series of interfaces that provide access to an in-memory structure that represents the XML document. First we discuss Microsoft's DOM as encapsulated in the MSXML v3 library and available to Delphi as COM objects. Next we look at two packages written in Delphi: one from CUESoft and another from the Open XML project.

Part III describes an alternate approach to working with XML: the Simple API for XML (SAX). SAX uses an event-based mechanism for parsing the contents of an XML document, meaning that it does not have to hold the entire document in memory as the DOM does. Again, the basic specification is presented, as developed by David Megginson and the XML-DEV mailing group. Microsoft also has a SAX offering in the MSXML v3 library, which is described in this section. Following that is an implementation of SAX in Delphi and a wrapper around the Microsoft parser that conforms to the Delphi interfaces.

Part IV looks at how XML documents can be generated using Delphi. Starting out with simple text output, the chapters also explore using Delphi's Web modules, the various Document Object Models, and Microsoft's IMXWriter objects. Also examined are XSL Transformations for pre-formatting data and Delphi's XMLBroker for thin-client database interactions.

Part V delves into applications that use XML as one of their building blocks. It provides examples of how XML can be used and how Delphi is brought to bear on the problem. A customizable mass mail-out program is presented, using XML for its configuration file and for the message template. An example of a customized client program for a particular class of XML documents follows, with a description of how to automatically invoke it for appropriate content downloaded from the Internet. The next two chapters present another client program, this time for an examination class of XML documents, and a Web-based application for providing the same content over the Internet. The Web application uses XSLT to help manipulate the XML. Finally, there is a discussion about the Simple Object Access Protocol (SOAP), which is a remote procedure invocation protocol using XML.

Acknowledgments

As is always the case, this book could not have been produced without the support of a team of people.

Thanks to Jim Hill and Wes Beckwith at Wordware for helping me get this book into your hands.

Thanks to Mark Edington of Borland for checking the facts and setting me straight.

Thanks to Dieter Köhler for assistance with the XDOM package from Open XML.

Thanks to Michael Holmes, Trevor de Koekkoek, and Thomas Theobald for feedback early on in the writing process.

Many thanks to my wife, Katalin, for supporting my efforts.

And thanks to the many readers of my Delphi articles who have provided such positive feedback and suggestions for improvements.

Part I
Introduction to XML

XML stands for *Extensible Markup Language*. It is a technology that allows you to describe data in a way that is both human-readable and yet easily processed by computers. It is a standard approved by the World Wide Web Consortium (W3C) and has a great deal of support in the marketplace.

XML documents can be created by simple text editors, through generic XML editors, via customized GUI front ends, or programmatically. This allows almost anyone to generate these documents, and, by following a few simple rules, they are usable by anyone else who knows about XML.

Suites of XML components are available for processing these documents. Generic parsers, editors, and validators are available in just about every language and on every platform. XML support is being built into the latest generation of Web browsers, as well as into databases, application servers, and individual applications.

XML is being used to transfer data from point to point in a platform- and language-independent manner. It can tie together layers in an n-tier architecture. It can manipulate its content with stylesheets to generate a variety of display formats for endusers. It facilitates communications between businesses.

Overall, XML has a bright future, and Delphi users need to be able to use the capabilities that it provides.

Chapter 1: History
Chapter 2: XML Syntax
Chapter 3: Document Type Definitions
Chapter 4: Extensible Stylesheet Language Transformations
Chapter 5: XLink
Chapter 6: XPath and XPointer
Chapter 7: XML Schema

Chapter 1

History

XML is a subset of the *Standard Generalized Markup Language* (SGML) that attempts to provide most of the functionality of the latter, but without all its complexity. As such it is a way of describing classes of documents and their structure through the use of markup (embedded instructions or notations within the content). It was developed in 1996 by the XML Working Group under the aegis of the W3C and the leadership of Jon Bosak. On February 10, 1998, it became a W3C Recommendation.

The World Wide Web Consortium is a collection of over 500 member organizations from around the world. Its purpose is "to lead the World Wide Web to its full potential by developing common protocols that promote its evolution and ensure its interoperability." Proposed ideas and technologies go through a rigorous consensus-building process before they can be assigned the status of "W3C Recommendation."

A specification starts off as a "Working Draft" that generally represents a work in progress and a commitment to pursue work in this area by a Working Group. When the spec is considered ready, it becomes a "Last Call Working Draft," allowing outside review of the document, both within the wider W3C community and by the public. Once accepted, the specification becomes a "Candidate Recommendation"—a published report that invites feedback on implementing the proposal. A "Proposed Recommendation" is the next step, after showing that the spec is workable and incorporating any final changes. The end result of the process is the status of "W3C Recommendation," which indicates that the ideas or technology described in the document are appropriate for widespread deployment and promote the W3C's goals.

SGML has been used for many years to structure documents in a standard way (ISO 8879). It is well suited to the storage and maintenance of long-lived documents, usually from a publishing perspective. However, it provides a great deal of functionality and many options that are infrequently used. This complicates the construction of tools designed to work with the full range of SGML documents.

XML is designed as a simplified subset of SGML to describe and manipulate short-lived documents, and is optimized for the Web environment. Often these documents are dynamically generated and immediately consumed. The design goals for XML, as set out in the XML specification Section 1.1, are as follows:

1. XML shall be straightforwardly usable over the Internet.

2. XML shall support a wide variety of applications.
3. XML shall be compatible with SGML.
4. It shall be easy to write programs which process XML documents.
5. The number of optional features in XML is to be kept to the absolute minimum, ideally zero.
6. XML documents should be human-legible and reasonably clear.
7. The XML design should be prepared quickly.
8. The design of XML shall be formal and concise.
9. XML documents shall be easy to create.
10. Terseness in XML markup is of minimal importance.

Its widespread acceptance and growing use confirm that these goals have been met.

XML vs. HTML

XML is often compared to HTML, frequently as a replacement for it. Both use straight text files for their content. Both include markup in the SGML style using angle brackets (< >). However, whereas HTML has a set of predefined tags that you can use to embellish your content, XML allows you to define an entirely new set of tags and the relationships between them. This definition can then be used to construct a whole series of conforming documents specific to your needs.

HTML allows you to describe the appearance of some data in a device-independent manner, while XML allows you to describe the content of that data in an application- and operating system-independent way.

Compare the following HTML fragment:

```
<h1>Star Wars - The Phantom Menace</h1>
<p>PG, 131 minutes</p>
<p>Directed by George Lucas.</p>
<p>Starring Liam Neeson, Ewan McGregor, Jake Lloyd,
and Natalie Portman</p>
```

and the corresponding XML document fragment:

```
<movie>
  <name>Star Wars - The Phantom Menace</name>
  <rating>PG</rating>
  <length>131</length>
  <director>George Lucas</director>
  <star>Liam Neeson</star>
  <star>Ewan McGregor</star>
  <star>Jake Lloyd</star>
  <star>Natalie Portman</star>
</movie>
```

Both may appear the same in your browser, but just from reading the XML fragment you can immediately see what the content means. In the HTML version you could extract the same elements, but not without an intimate knowledge of the format used. The XML data can be manipulated automatically, such as searching for movies by name or rating, as well as rendering it for display in one or more output formats (including HTML).

In more technical terms, HTML is an SGML application; that is, it is a predefined set of markup tags that deal with the presentation of data. XML, on the other hand, is a subset of SGML, a metalanguage. It allows you to define your own set of tags denoting the meaning of the data and then create documents using them. One of the main ideas behind XML is to separate the data content from its presentation.

XML does not replace HTML; it complements it. XML provides a standard means of describing the meaning of the data, while HTML provides a standard way of presenting that data.

Related Specifications

XML itself is just part of the story—it describes the basic components and structure of a document. Along with this are a number of related specifications that provide further pieces of the puzzle.

Document type definitions (DTDs) provide the templates that define a valid XML document. They detail what elements are allowed and in what context within the document. These are extremely useful when transferring data between different organizations as they impose the necessary structure and consistency on the communications.

Extensible Stylesheet Language (XSL) is a generic way of describing the formatting of XML content for display in a particular graphical medium. An XSL stylesheet is an XML document, allowing it to be created and manipulated in the same way as the actual data that it operates upon.

XSL Transformations (XSLT) is a language for detailing how an XML document should be manipulated to transform its contents into another format. It can reorganize the XML data, select from it, and manipulate it, before wrapping it in whatever formatting instructions are appropriate for the target application. Output can be rendered as HTML, as plain text, as RTF, even as another XML document.

XML Linking Language (XLink) defines how one document can be linked to another. It goes further than normal hyperlinks since it can define multiple links, bi-directional links, and even external links related to a document.

XML Pointer Language (XPointer) extends XLink to allow it to refer to individual parts of a linked document. This could be a single position, like existing HTML named anchors, or a range of elements within the resource.

XML Schema is an alternative way of specifying the content of an XML document, replacing DTDs. It offers the functionality of DTDs while adding data typing for elements and attributes, exact multiplicity (such as between two and four occurrences), and other features. Its major advantage is that the schemas are expressed in XML itself, which allows you to use the same tools on both the data and its description. This specification is still under development.

There are also a number of XML applications already available. The following sections describe some of them. Even though most are not available for use within Delphi, they are presented here to give you a feel for the diversity of applications that XML enables. Although some of the terms used may be unfamiliar to you at this stage, you should get the gist of them from the text while further description is left to the later chapters.

Extensible Hypertext Markup Language (XHTML)

As it states in the specification, this is a reformulation of HTML 4.0 in XML 1.0. The purpose of the specification is to make HTML documents just another XML application, allowing all the tools for XML to be used with them. The semantics of the language do not change from the original HTML 4.0 specification; however, the syntax is tightened up to comply with XML.

XHTML 1.0 is a W3C Recommendation as of January 26, 2000. It defines a set of three document types that cover existing HTML applications. Other guiding principles of the specification include backward compatibility with existing HTML and its current processors (browsers), which allows the Document Object Model to be used with these documents, and providing an extendable framework for future efforts.

The three classes of XHTML documents correspond to the original HTML 4.0 DTDs. These are for strict HTML 4.0, which excludes certain attributes and elements being phased out due to stylesheet usage, for transitional HTML 4.0, which includes those attributes and elements, and for frameset HTML documents, which are identical to the transitional HTML except that the `frameset` element replaces the body one.

XML is stricter than HTML in what is permissible. These sorts of anomalies are corrected in XHTML. All elements must be properly nested, with the `html` element being the top-level one. So, you can no longer have sequences such as:

```
<b>Important news about <i>Delphi</b></i>
```

All element names must be lowercase—XML is case sensitive, while HTML accepts any case. End tags are required for all non-empty elements. For example, under HTML the paragraph tag is optional (and frequently omitted). In XHTML it must always be present.

```
<p>All paragraphs must have end tags.</p><p>XHTML requires it.</p>
```

Similarly, all empty tags must be correctly terminated. This can be done either by adding the slash at the end of the opening tag or by adding the entire closing tag. When using the first technique, you should place a space before the slash at the end of the tag if there are no attributes. This ensures that older browsers still recognize the tag.

```
<img src="bullet.gif"></img><hr />
```

All attributes must be properly quoted in XHTML. In HTML this is only required when the attribute value contains white space or other characters with special meaning. Attributes must have a value specified. Under HTML, some attributes do not have values, such as the checked attribute of a radio button or check box. In XHTML these values must be supplied.

```
<input type="checkbox" name="Delphi 5" checked="checked">Delphi
```

In XHTML, white space in attributes is normalized. This means that leading and trailing white space is removed, and internal sequences of white space are reduced to a single space. Style and

Chapter 1: History

script elements can use CDATA sections (special sections that ignore normal markup) to remove the need to escape certain characters.

Elements are identified through the `id` attribute in XHTML, which is defined to be of type ID (a special attribute type used for names that are unique within the document). The `name` attribute that appears on some elements in HTML is deprecated (phased out) under XHTML.

So, by following a few simple rules, you can easily convert your HTML documents to XHTML documents. Then you can manipulate them using any of the tools designed for XML. Do not forget that XML is extensible, meaning that your XHTML document also gains this ability. Listing 1-1 shows a sample XHTML page fragment. Note the appearance of closing paragraph tags, `</p>`, and that horizontal rules and line breaks are marked as empty, `<hr />`. Otherwise, it is standard HTML.

Listing 1-1: Movie data displayed as XHTML

```
<html>
<head>
<title>Movie Watchers</title>
</head>
<body>
<h1><a name="top">Welcome to Movie Watchers</a></h1>
<p>Your source for local film entertainment.
Have a look at <a href="#movies">what's on</a>,
<a href="#cinemas">where</a> and
<a href="#screenings">when</a>.</p>
<hr />
<h2><a name="movies">Movies</a></h2>
<a name="SW1" href="SW1-site">
  <img src="SW1-logo" alt="Star Wars - The Phantom Menace"/>
</a>
<table border="0" width="100%">
  <tr>
    <th align="left" valign="top" width="15%">Rating:</th>
    <td width="15%">PG</td>
    <th align="left" valign="top" width="15%">Length:</th>
    <td>131 mins</td>
  </tr>
  <tr>
    <th align="left" valign="top">Director:</th>
    <td colspan="3">George Lucas</td>
  </tr>
  <tr>
    <th align="left" valign="top">Starring:</th>
    <td colspan="3">
      Liam Neeson<br />
      Ewan McGregor<br />
      Jake Lloyd<br />
      Natalie Portman<br />
    </td>
  </tr>
  <tr>
    <th align="left" valign="top">Synopsis:</th>
    <td colspan="3">When the evil Trade Federation plots to take over
      the peaceful planet of Naboo, Jedi warrior Qui-Gon Jinn and his
      apprentice Obi-Wan Kenobi embark on an amazing adventure to save
      the planet. With them on their journey is the young queen
      Amidala, Gungan outcast JarJar Binks, and the powerful Captain
```

```
            Panaka, who will all travel to the faraway planets of Tatooine
            and Coruscant in a futile attempt to save their world from Darth
            Sidious, leader of the Trade Federation, and Darth Maul, the
            strongest Dark Lord of the Sith to ever wield a lightsaber.
          </td>
        </tr>
        <tr>
          <th align="left" valign="top">Showing at:</th>
          <td colspan="3">
            <a href="#SW1-MM">
              MovieMania
            </a><br />
            <a href="#SW1-OC">
              Oscar's Cinema
            </a><br />
          </td>
        </tr>
      </table>
        :
      <p>Back to <a href="#top">the top</a>.</p>
      <hr />
        :
      <hr />
      <p>Movie Watcher data supplied by
      <a href="mailto:kbwood@compuserve.com">Keith Wood</a>.</p>
    </body>
</html>
```

Mathematical Markup Language (MathML)

The purpose of MathML is to facilitate the specification and processing of mathematical and scientific content. It encodes mathematical notation in a way that allows you to show it in high-quality displays, present it via audio methods, and manipulate it symbolically via applications.

Eventually, with appropriate stylesheet support, MathML elements will be included as part of a standard XML document and rendered accordingly. Until then, specialized applets and applications allow MathML to be viewed within a browser.

Up to now, mathematical equations were usually presented as images within an HTML page. Although this does provide information for human readers, it is of no use to an application that is interested in the underlying meaning. With the development of MathML, both these purposes can be achieved.

MathML is a W3C Recommendation, with version 1.01 being released on July 7, 1999. Version 2.0 is currently available as a Working Draft. The work with the W3C began in 1994 when a proposal for HTML Math was included in the HTML 3.0 Working Draft. Following numerous discussions, an official Working Group devoted to mathematical markup was formed in March 1997.

The limitations of HTML in rendering mathematical equations was recognized early on. Using images instead was not ideal as these tended to interrupt the flow of the document, and did not align or resize properly. Also, images tend to be of a lower resolution than normal text when printed out, resulting in less than acceptable quality.

Although improvements in HTML layout could solve some of these problems, it would not allow the meaning of the equation to be easily relayed to another application. This is where XML comes in, with its ability to encode the meaning of the data it contains.

The design goals included sufficient richness to encode most equations, recording both notation and meaning; simple conversion between other formats (such as output formats); human legible, yet easily processed by machine; extensible; and allowing application-specific information to be transferred. XML fulfils most of these goals.

MathML elements fall into one of three categories: presentation elements, content elements, or interface elements. *Presentation elements* describe notational structure, such as terms on one line, and sub- and superscripts. *Content elements* denote mathematical objects, such as operators, specific mathematical concepts, or literal values. The one *interface element* is the `math` element, which serves as the top-level tag for a MathML fragment.

For example, the equation:

$$x^2+4x+4=0$$

can be encoded using presentation elements as shown in Listing 1-2, or with content elements as seen in Listing 1-3.

Listing 1-2: MathML presentation elements

```
<math>
  <mrow>
    <mrow>
      <msup>
        <mi>x</mi>
        <mn>2</mn>
      </msup>
      <mo>+</mo>
      <mrow>
        <mn>4</mn>
        <mo>&InvisibleTimes;</mo>
        <mi>x</mi>
      </mrow>
      <mo>+</mo>
      <mn>4</mn>
    </mrow>
    <mo>=</mo>
    <mn>0</mn>
  </mrow>
</math>
```

Listing 1-3: MathML content elements

```
<math>
  <reln>
    <eq/>
    <apply>
      <plus/>
      <apply>
        <power/>
        <ci>x</ci>
        <cn>2</cn>
      </apply>
      <apply>
```

```
            <times/>
            <cn>4</cn>
            <ci>x</ci>
        </apply>
        <cn>4</cn>
    </apply>
    <cn>0</cn>
</reln>
</math>
```

MathML allows these two formats to be combined, either directly or within the `semantics` element. In this latter case, one representation becomes the main format, while the other is included as an annotation, either hinting at how to render the equation or clarifying the meaning of it. MathML offers almost 30 presentation elements, about 75 content ones, and an impressive array of mathematical symbols expressed as entities (named references).

Although MathML is not yet an integrated part of HTML (being rendered in all browsers), it is well on its way to this goal. Editors, viewers, and processors are already available for working with this language.

Scalable Vector Graphics (SVG)

Scalable Vector Graphics is an XML application that describes two-dimensional graphics. It provides three types of graphic objects: vector graphic shapes (such as lines and curves), images, and text. These objects can be grouped, transformed, and styled through the language. Other features include nested transformations, clipping, alpha masks (transparency), filter effects, and templates.

As of August 2, 2000, SVG is a Candidate Recommendation of the W3C. It should be a full recommendation by the time that you read this. It is intended that SVG have its own MIME type, `image/svg-xml`, and it is recommended that all SVG files have an .svg extension.

SVG includes its own Document Object Model, allowing the graphics description to be manipulated through scripting languages. You can embed SVG fragments within an XHTML page and access both from script. It includes a rich set of event handlers providing for interactive sessions with the user.

This specification relies on several others, besides the XML specification itself. It incorporates XLink and XPointer depictions for linking between and within documents. Styling can be achieved through cascading style sheets (CSS) or XSL. Some of its animation features come from the Synchronized Multimedia Integration Language (SMIL). SVG also attempts to remain compatible with HTML and XHTML implementations.

The word "scalable" in the title of this specification means that the encoded graphics can be displayed correctly at any resolution, from a low-resolution computer screen to high-resolution printers. It also means that large numbers of files and large numbers of users can utilize the technology at once. Vector graphics tend to result in smaller encodings of many images (but not photograph-like ones). Using vector graphics allows the image to be rendered at the client, enabling it to make the most of its particular abilities. SVG also includes manipulation of normal rasterized images, as you would find in GIF or JPEG files. The graphics encoded by SVG provide a capability in between straight textual information and standard images, allowing it to be used alone or embedded within another XML application.

SVG documents are made up of graphical objects—paths between points. The more common shapes, such as rectangles and ellipses, are modeled directly, while the generic path element lets you describe other figures. Common symbols can be described and shared between documents. These include items like flowchart elements and electrical symbols. Various raster effects, like blurring and shadowing, can be specified within SVG, while still allowing them to be applied in a scalable fashion. Font elements combine both textual and graphical descriptions, enabling them to be processed either way as necessary.

Listing 1-4 shows a simple SVG document that encodes various basic figures. The output produced by this document looks like Figure 1-1. Note that it includes a reference to the SVG DTD, and starts with the top-level svg element. svg elements can also appear within the body of the document, representing a new viewport or altering the meaning of unit identifiers. When embedded as part of another document, the namespace (language identifier) for the svg elements should be http://www.w3.org/2000/svg.

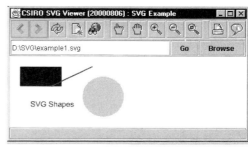

Figure 1-1: The rendered SVG document.

Listing 1-4: A basic SVG document

```
<?xml version="1.0" standalone="no"?>
<!DOCTYPE svg PUBLIC "-//W3C//DTD SVG 20000802//EN"
  "http://www.w3.org/TR/2000/CR-SVG-20000802/DTD/svg-20000802.dtd">
<svg width="6cm" height="5cm">
  <title>SVG Example</title>
  <desc>A sampling of SVG elements</desc>
  <rect x="0.5cm" y="0.5cm" width="2cm" height="1cm"/>
  <circle cx="4.5cm" cy="2cm" r="1cm" style="fill: lightgray"/>
  <line x1="2cm" y1="1.5cm" x2="4cm" y2="0.5cm"
    style="stroke: red; stroke-width: 2"/>
  <text x="1cm" y="2.5cm">SVG Shapes</text>
</svg>
```

Objects are grouped together with the g element, which surrounds its constituent elements. When supplied with an id attribute, these groups can be manipulated as if they were basic shapes. Groupings can be applied to any depth. The defs element is similar to a grouping in that it collects other elements together, but it is only used for defining these elements and is not rendered in the final output.

Containers and graphic objects can have textual descriptions applied to them through the desc and title elements that they encompass. Browsers use these to supply additional information when necessary, such as in a tool tip or in audio renderings of a document. The outermost svg element should always have a title element within it to cater to browsers that cannot deal with the graphics themselves.

The `symbol` element defines template objects, allowing for their reuse elsewhere within the current or in other documents. Like `defs` they are not rendered through normal processing. Instead, you utilize the `use` element to invoke a symbol, a group, an `svg` element, or some other graphical element. Reference to the original element is via an `xlink:href` attribute and refers to the former's `id`. See Listing 1-5 for an example of defining a figure and then reusing it within the image. The corresponding output is shown in Figure 1-2.

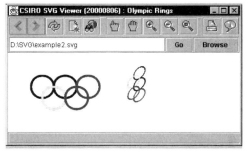

Figure 1-2: Rendering with reuse in SVG.

Listing 1-5: Reuse within SVG

```
<?xml version="1.0" standalone="no"?>
<!DOCTYPE svg PUBLIC "-//W3C//DTD SVG 20000802//EN"
  "http://www.w3.org/TR/2000/CR-SVG-20000802/DTD/svg-20000802.dtd">
<svg width="10cm" height="10cm">
  <title>Olympic Rings</title>
  <desc>The Olympic rings</desc>
  <defs>
    <g id="olympicrings" width="60" height="30"
        style="fill: none; stroke-width: 2">
      <circle cx="10" cy="10" r="10" style="stroke: blue"/>
      <circle cx="30" cy="10" r="10" style="stroke: black"/>
      <circle cx="50" cy="10" r="10" style="stroke: red"/>
      <circle cx="20" cy="20" r="10" style="stroke: yellow"/>
      <circle cx="40" cy="20" r="10" style="stroke: green"/>
    </g>
  </defs>
  <use xlink:href="#olympicrings"
      transform="translate(240,20) rotate(90) skewX(30)"/>
  <use xlink:href="#olympicrings"
      transform="scale(2) translate(20,20)"/>
</svg>
```

As you can see, elements often have a bounding rectangle defined by their `x`, `y`, `width`, and `height` attributes. These are measured in user coordinates (without any units) or in exact distances, such as pixels, points, inches, and centimeters. You can also apply transformations to elements with the `transform` attribute. This takes a list of functions as its value and applies each in turn when rendering the element. Available transformations include translation, rotation, scaling, and skewing. These can be combined to arrive at the desired result.

Elements can have effects such as line thickness and color, and fill colors applied to them. Linear and radial gradients are also available, as are patterns, masks and filters. Each operates on the bounding rectangle for an element.

Existing graphics are included with the `image` element. The referenced document can be in any recognized format, although conforming viewers are only required to deal with PNG, JPEG, and SVG formats.

The `text` element allows for textual display within the rendering. Like other elements, it has a bounding box and may be transformed. The actual content appears within the element as simple character data. To delimit sections of text, you use the `tspan` element, which can have its own set of attributes. Each character can be positioned exactly, or a simple starting position specified. In fact, if you use the `textPath` element, you can have the text wander around curves or shapes. The normal CSS style designations apply to the rendered text, including font selection, color, weight, and decoration.

Drawing the actual characters is left to the SVG viewer. While system fonts are most likely to be used, SVG also provides for the definition of outline fonts for its own use. Descriptions of the individual characters are based on an abstract square, whose height is the intended distance between lines in this font. The `font` element starts a font definition and contains basic measurements within the embedded `font-face` element. Following this are the outlines for the characters, each in its own `glyph` element. SVG fonts are unhinted, and so may not render properly at small sizes.

SVG offers many other abilities and effects. These include filters such as blurs, lighting, blending, and turbulence. Similar to HTML, an a element provides for hyperlinking to other resources (using XLink terminology). Embedded scripts within the document allow actions to be performed in response to events. Animation is also available through the use of SMIL-compatible elements.

Around all of these elements resides a Document Object Model (DOM) that provides access to every section of the document. Through scripting languages you have complete control over the document and its subsequent rendering. Events allow for interaction with the DOM through registered listeners.

Overall, SVG provides a great deal of functionality for rendering graphics. Several test implementations are already available, including the SVG Toolkit from CSIRO in Australia (http://www.cmis.csiro.au/svg) and Jackaroo from the Koala Project in France (http://www.inria.fr/koala/jackaroo). Both of these are written in Java. The ability to render SVG will probably become standard in browsers in the near future.

Synchronized Multimedia Integration Language (SMIL)

The purpose of SMIL (pronounced "smile") is to combine independent multimedia objects into a coordinated presentation. Using this language, you can describe the behavior over time and the positioning of elements within the display, as well as provide hyperlinks from there to other resources.

SMIL 1.0 is a W3C Recommendation that was approved on June 15, 1998. It builds upon XML's base and inherits its syntax, use of namespaces, and extensibility.

The top-level element is, of course, the `smil` element, which serves as the container for the `head` and `body` elements. Within the header, you specify information not related to the temporal nature of the presentation. Included here are any layout specifications for the remaining elements (held in the `layout` element) and any metadata about the document (in the `meta` element). It may also contain a `switch` element, which allows alternate versions of layouts to be defined. The particular one used depends on the capabilities of the display device.

Layout can be defined using SMIL elements or with CSS2 syntax. Named regions are described with their positions, sizes, colors, and depths. Regions may clip or stretch content to their dimensions. These regions are then referred to by other elements within the body of the document.

Individual multimedia elements appear within the body element. The `par` element allows its children to overlap in time (run in parallel). Each may have delays imposed, either as absolute times or when a triggering event occurs. Compare this with the `seq` element, which activates its children one after the other (sequential), with delays if desired.

As children of these elements you can have images, animations, audio tracks, video, and text streams. Each of these elements has attributes that define when it starts and ends (`begin` and `end` or `dur` attributes), where the actual content comes from (`src`), and its type (`type` attribute). All body elements should have a `title` attribute to allow them to be identified in a device that cannot handle their content.

Once more the `switch` element allows you to gracefully degrade the abilities of the document. Each child of the `switch` is evaluated in turn by testing several of its attributes. When a combination is found that the display device can handle, that element is rendered and all other children of the `switch` are ignored. The types of abilities tested for include bit rates, content language, screen size, and color depth. Using these attributes outside of a `switch` element causes that particular element to be included or excluded appropriately, without affecting any surrounding elements.

An example of a multimedia presentation defined using SMIL is shown in Listing 1-6. Here you have a main video component that is always shown. Running alongside that (within the `par` element) is the accompanying audio and an optional subtitle track. Which audio is played depends on the preferred language of the user and whether or not they want dubbed dialog. English, German, and Dutch alternatives are included, with a default of French. Similarly, language-specific subtitles are available if desired.

Listing 1-6: A SMIL movie presentation

```
<!DOCTYPE smil PUBLIC "-//W3C//DTD SMIL 1.0//EN"
  "http://www.w3.org/TR/REC-smil/SMIL10.dtd">
<smil>
  <par>
    <switch>
      <audio src="movie-aud-en.rm" system-language="en"
        system-overdub-or-caption="overdub"/>
      <audio src="movie-aud-de.rm" system-language="de"
        system-overdub-or-caption="overdub"/>
      <audio src="movie-aud-nl.rm" system-language="nl"
        system-overdub-or-caption="overdub"/>
      <!-- French for everyone else -->
      <audio src="movie-aud-fr.rm"/>
    </switch>
    <video src="movie-vid.rm"/>
    <switch>
      <textstream src="movie-caps-en.rtx" system-language="en"
        system-overdub-or-caption="caption"/>
      <textstream src="movie-caps-de.rtx" system-language="de"
        system-overdub-or-caption="caption"/>
```

```
            <textstream src="movie-caps-nl.rtx" system-language="nl"
               system-overdub-or-caption="caption"/>
            <!-- French captions for those that really want them -->
            <textstream src="movie-caps-fr.rtx" system-captions="on"/>
         </switch>
      </par>
   </smil>
```

SMIL sets out the interpretations of the various timing and synchronization issues that arise in attempting to coordinate these different resources. Elements have an implicit begin and end, defined by their position within the object hierarchy. They may also have either or both an explicit begin and end.

Hyperlinks specified within the document allow for navigation to other resources. Basic navigation is provided by the a element, similar to the same tag in HTML. An additional attribute, show, defines how the new resource interacts with the existing one.

However, the a element only attaches a link to an entire media object. For more precise control, use the anchor element. Anchors may be specified to operate temporally, such as during the first five seconds of a video, or spatially, such as when clicking only on the left side of an image. The latter is similar to the image maps used in HTML.

SMIL can be used in standalone documents to orchestrate a presentation, or it can be embedded within another XML document type. In the latter case, the namespace (language identifier) for the fragment should be: http://www.w3.org/TR/REC-smil.

Resource Description Framework (RDF)

The Resource Description Framework is a basis for manipulating metadata about resources available on the Web. Although RDF is an XML application, it can capture information about non-XML documents just as easily. Its purpose is to provide a common way to describe these resources that facilitates their cataloging, categorizing, searching, and retrieval.

The need for RDF grew out of the desire for a standard way of defining Web resources that could easily be processed by automated agents such as Web crawlers. Added to this was a wish to provide additional details about a resource, or indeed an entire site, that did not fit into existing schemes. These details include content rating (such as the Platform for Internet Content Selection (PICS)), privacy policies, and data interchange activities. Of course, extensibility was a big influence on the RDF development, resulting in the abilities to mix and match various RDF specifications and to extend existing ones in new ways.

RDF consists of two parts. The first is the Model and Syntax Specification, which is a W3C Recommendation as of February 22, 1999. This outlines the purpose of RDF and describes the model used to capture the metadata. The second part is the Schema Specification, which is a W3C Candidate Recommendation as of March 27, 2000. This document lays out a syntax and semantics for defining metadata structures (i.e., meta-metadata!).

The RDF model is a syntax-neutral way of representing RDF expressions, or statements about resources. A basic model consists of three parts: the *resource* that is being described, the *property* or aspect of that object being asserted, and the actual *value* of that property. Together these make up an RDF *statement*. The three parts are given the technical names *subject*, *predicate*, and *object* respectively.

For example, you can state that the author of a particular page is a given person. In this case the subject (resource) is the page itself as identified by its URI, the predicate (property) is the author, and the object (value) is the author's name (or some other identifying text). The statement "George Lucas is the director of *Star Wars - The Phantom Menace*" could be expressed using RDF as shown in Listing 1-7.

Listing 1-7: An RDF statement

```
<?xml version="1.0"?>
<rdf:RDF
    xmlns:rdf="http://www.w3.org/1999/02/22-rdf-syntax-ns#"
    xmlns:m="http://movies.org/schema/">
  <rdf:Description
      about="urn:movies:Star Wars - The Phantom Menace">
    <m:Director>George Lucas</m:Director>
  </rdf:Description>
</rdf:RDF>
```

The standard namespace for RDF is shown in this listing, while the m namespace refers to some definition of movie-related objects including the Director tag. The subject of the statement is listed in the about attribute of the Description tag, while the contents of that tag identify the predicate (the element name) and the object (the element content).

RDF also offers an alternate syntax that is a little more compact, as shown in Listing 1-8 below. Here we change sub-elements that only contain text into attributes of the Description element. It also has the advantage that there is no text content within the main RDF element. This allows you to embed RDF statements within HTML documents (among others), without affecting the display of the original document. Normally browsers simply ignore tags that they do not understand, but display all text.

Listing 1-8: Alternate RDF syntax

```
<?xml version="1.0"?>
<rdf:RDF
    xmlns:rdf="http://www.w3.org/1999/02/22-rdf-syntax-ns#"
    xmlns:m="http://movies.org/schema/">
  <rdf:Description
      about="urn:movies:Star Wars - The Phantom Menace"
      m:Director="George Lucas"/>
</rdf:RDF>
```

Frequently, you need to refer to a collection of items within a statement, such as all the documents in a particular site, or a number of people who co-authored a document. For these purposes RDF offers three types of container objects: the *bag*, which is an unordered list of multiple items; the *sequence*, which is an ordered list of multiple items; and the *alternative*, which is a single selection from the list provided. Alternatives are selected on the basis of some testing attribute, such as xml:lang for the content language, in the order in which they appear. A final entry with no test functions as a default selection.

An element that consists of such a collection contains an element of one of these types (rdf:Bag, rdf:Seq, or rdf:Alt) which itself contains the actual items. Each item is listed within an `rdf:li` element (similar to the HTML `li` element). For example, the series of *Star Wars* movies (in order) could be identified as shown in Listing 1-9.

Listing 1-9: An RDF collection

```xml
<?xml version="1.0"?>
<rdf:RDF
    xmlns:rdf="http://www.w3.org/1999/02/22-rdf-syntax-ns#"
    xmlns:m="http://movies.org/schema/">
  <rdf:Description about="urn:movies:Star Wars">
    <rdf:Seq>
      <rdf:li>The Phantom Menace</rdf:li>
      <rdf:li>Episode II</rdf:li>
      <rdf:li>Episode III</rdf:li>
      <rdf:li>A New Hope</rdf:li>
      <rdf:li>The Empire Strikes Back</rdf:li>
      <rdf:li>Return of the Jedi</rdf:li>
    </rdf:Seq>
  </rdf:Description>
</rdf:RDF>
```

You can then make statements about the entire collection. RDF supplies the `aboutEach` attribute to indicate that the statement applies to each item within a collection individually, as if a separate statement had been made for each one. For example, to show that George Lucas produced each of the *Star Wars* movies, you could use the document from Listing 1-10.

Listing 1-10: An statement about a collection

```xml
<?xml version="1.0"?>
<rdf:RDF
    xmlns:rdf="http://www.w3.org/1999/02/22-rdf-syntax-ns#"
    xmlns:m="http://movies.org/schema/">
  <rdf:Seq ID="SW">
    <rdf:li>The Phantom Menace</rdf:li>
    <rdf:li>Episode II</rdf:li>
    <rdf:li>Episode III</rdf:li>
    <rdf:li>A New Hope</rdf:li>
    <rdf:li>The Empire Strikes Back</rdf:li>
    <rdf:li>Return of the Jedi</rdf:li>
  </rdf:Seq>
  <rdf:Description aboutEach="#SW" m:Producer="George Lucas"/>
</rdf:RDF>
```

NOTE If you had used about instead of aboutEach in the example in Listing 1-10, you would be saying that George Lucas produced the collection, not the items listed therein. There is also an aboutEachPrefix attribute that lets you identify a collection of resources by some common prefix, and then apply the statement to each item in that set.

RDF also lets you make statements about other statements. To do this you just refer to the original statement and have an appropriately defined predicate in your new statement. For example, if I assert that George Lucas directed *Freiheit*, I could express it as shown in Listing 1-11. This is not saying that he did direct it (although he did), just that I am saying that he did.

Listing 1-11: An RDF statement about a statement

```xml
<?xml version="1.0"?>
<rdf:RDF
    xmlns:rdf="http://www.w3.org/1999/02/22-rdf-syntax-ns#"
    xmlns:m="http://movies.org/schema/"
    xmlns:a="http://metadata.org/schema/">
  <rdf:Description
      about="urn:movies:Freiheit">
    <m:Director>George Lucas</m:Director>
    <a:attributedTo>Keith Wood</a:attributedTo>
  </rdf:Description>
</rdf:RDF>
```

The schema specification part of RDF allows you to define the elements that make up your metadata. For the previous examples you would create a schema that declared, among others, the `Director` and `Producer` elements, along with their types and meanings. It is important that the intention of these metadata types be explicit since applications rely on that particular meaning for their processing. The use of namespaces allows you to easily identify tags with the same name but with different semantics.

Types within RDF schema are defined as classes, which may then have properties. Following the object-oriented model, these classes can be inherited from and extended by other schema. Use the `rdfs:subClassOf` element within the type definition to identify the parent.

Properties indicate the class that they belong to through the `rdfs:domain` sub-element, and the type of content that they allow through the `rdfs:range` sub-element. Basic types and classes are defined by the RDF Schema specification itself.

Listing 1-12 shows a sample RDF schema that describes the types that make up metadata about search services on the Web. It defines three classes, `SearchQuery`, `SearchResult`, and `SearchService`. `SearchService` simply refers to a resource available on the Web. `SearchQuery` has properties that relate a particular service to a result page, using a query string. `SearchResult` holds a reference to the document with the actual information, along with the title of that document and a rating of its relevance from zero to one.

Listing 1-12: RDF schema example

```xml
<rdf:RDF xml:lang="en"
    xmlns:rdf="http://www.w3.org/1999/02/22-rdf-syntax-ns#"
    xmlns:rdfs="http://www.w3.org/2000/01/rdf-schema#">
  <rdfs:Class rdf:ID="SearchQuery">
    <rdfs:subClassOf
      rdf:resource="http://www.w3.org/2000/01/rdf-schema#Resource"/>
  </rdfs:Class>

  <rdfs:Class rdf:ID="SearchResult">
    <rdfs:subClassOf
      rdf:resource="http://www.w3.org/2000/01/rdf-schema#Resource"/>
  </rdfs:Class>

  <rdfs:Class rdf:ID="SearchService">
    <rdfs:subClassOf rdf:resource=
      "http://www.w3.org/2000/03/example/classes#InternetService"/>
  </rdfs:Class>

  <rdf:Property ID="queryString">
```

```
      <rdfs:domain rdf:resource="#SearchQuery"/>
      <rdfs:range
        rdf:resource="http://www.w3.org/2000/01/rdf-schema#Literal"/>
    </rdf:Property>

    <rdf:Property ID="queryService">
      <rdfs:domain rdf:resource="#SearchQuery"/>
      <rdfs:range rdf:resource="#SearchService"/>
    </rdf:Property>

    <rdf:Property ID="result">
      <rdfs:domain rdf:resource="#SearchQuery"/>
      <rdfs:range rdf:resource="#SearchResult"/>
    </rdf:Property>

    <rdf:Property ID="queryResultPage">
      <rdfs:domain rdf:resource="#SearchResult"/>
      <rdfs:range rdf:resource=
        "http://www.w3.org/2000/03/example/classes#WebPage"/>
    </rdf:Property>

    <rdf:Property ID="queryResultTitle">
      <rdfs:domain rdf:resource="#SearchResult"/>
      <rdfs:range
        rdf:resource="http://www.w3.org/2000/01/rdf-schema#Literal"/>
    </rdf:Property>

    <rdf:Property ID="queryResultRating">
      <rdfs:domain rdf:resource="#SearchResult"/>
      <rdfs:range rdf:resource=
        "http://www.w3.org/2000/03/example/classes#FloatZeroToOne"/>
    </rdf:Property>
</rdf:RDF>
```

RDF offers the promise of providing machine-readable metadata about resources available on the Web. It should facilitate the searching of the Web for relevant documents and supply greater detail about those pages once found. As well as authoring and copyright details, it can provide privacy and content rating information. As with all XML, it can be extended to include whatever additional details are deemed necessary.

References

Further information on XML, related technologies, and the sample applications described above are available from the following sources:

XML Specification

      http://www.w3.org/TR/REC-xml

XSL Specification

      http://www.w3.org/TR/xsl

XSLT Specification

      http://www.w3.org/TR/xslt

XLink Specification
> http://www.w3.org/TR/xlink

XPointer Specification
> http://www.w3.org/TR/xptr

XML Schema Specification
> http://www.w3.org/TR/xmlschema-0

Document Object Model
> http://www.w3.org/DOM

Simple API for XML
> http://www.megginson.com/SAX/

XML.com—a clearinghouse for XML-related items
> http://www.xml.com

XML Software—another clearinghouse for XML
> http://www.xmlsoftware.com

Robin Cover's XML pages at OASIS
> http://www.oasis-open.org/cover/

XHTML Specification
> http://www.w3.org/TR/xhtml1

MathML Specification
> http://www.w3.org/TR/REC-MathML

Scalable Vector Graphics Specification
> http://www.w3.org/TR/SVG

Synchronized Multimedia Integration Language Specification
> http://www.w3.org/TR/REC-smil

Resource Description Framework Model and Syntax Specification
> http://www.w3.org/TR/REC-rdf-syntax

Resource Description Framework Schema Specification
> http://www.w3.org/TR/rdf-schema

Sample XML

Throughout this book I'll be referring to sample XML documents to illustrate various points. Most of these documents contain information on movies that are showing at local theaters, allowing you to find a film for a night's entertainment. Three lists make up each document: one for the movies, one for the cinemas, and one for the screenings that combine these two.

A movie has details such as its name, rating, and length, the names of the director and principal stars, and a brief synopsis of the plot. In addition, a movie can be linked to a suitable graphic and/or Web site for more information.

The name, phone number, and address are the main items for a cinema, with optional directions on how to get there. Further entries detail the facilities available at the theater and the pricing schemes that apply at various times.

Screenings combine the above, defining a particular movie showing at one cinema. Associated with this is an indication of the dates during which the film is running and the actual session times (with links to the appropriate pricing structure). Features of and restrictions on the showing may also be included.

All of this is brought together in a single document under the `movie-watcher` element. Sections of a movie-watcher document can be seen throughout the book, with its DTD appearing in Chapter 3.

Chapter 2
XML Syntax

An XML document is simply a text file, using a standard character set, that is *marked up*, or encoded, by following certain conventions. If you've used HTML at all, you are familiar with the layout of an XML document, although XML enforces some additional restrictions that HTML ignores. Have a look at the XML fragment in Listing 2-1.

Listing 2-1: Sample XML fragment

```xml
<movie id="SW1" rating="PG" logo-url="SW1-logo" url="SW1-site">
  <name>Star Wars - The Phantom Menace</name>
  <length>131</length>
  <director>George Lucas</director>
  <starring>
    <star>Liam Neeson</star>
    <star>Ewan McGregor</star>
    <star>Jake Lloyd</star>
    <star>Natalie Portman</star>
  </starring>
  <synopsis>
    When the evil Trade Federation plots to take over the
    peaceful planet of Naboo, Jedi warrior Qui-Gon Jinn and his
    apprentice Obi-Wan Kenobi embark on an amazing adventure to
    save the planet. With them on their journey is the young
    queen Amidala, Gungan outcast JarJar Binks, and the powerful
    Captain Panaka, who will all travel to the faraway planets of
    Tatooine and Coruscant in a futile attempt to save their
    world from Darth Sidious, leader of the Trade Federation, and
    Darth Maul, the strongest Dark Lord of the Sith to ever wield
    a lightsaber.
  </synopsis>
</movie>
```

This defines data about a movie. From the tags you can immediately see the purpose of each section of content (although the exact meaning of the `length` element may not be entirely clear). This is the intent of XML—human-readable, structured content that is also easily processed by machines.

Elements and Attributes

As in HTML, *tags* are embedded in the XML document to delineate its contents, breaking it up into elements. These tags are enclosed in angle brackets (< >) and contain the name of the element, along with any attributes that it might have. All tags must be terminated with a corresponding closing tag. This is also enclosed in angle brackets, has the same name as the opening tag, and includes a slash (/) immediately before the name.

```
<name>Star Wars - The Phantom Menace</name>
```

In XML, all tags must be closed in the reverse of the sequence in which they were opened. Another way of stating this requirement is that elements must be properly nested within an XML document. Whereas in HTML, examples such as the following are tolerated and generally work as expected, they are not valid in an XML document.

```
<b>This text is <i>very important</b></i>
```

Elements that do not have any content, known as *empty elements*, may be closed in a shortcut fashion by placing the closing slash at the end of the opening tag. Often such elements have attributes to provide additional information, although they can be used just as flags to indicate an item's presence.

```
<candy-bar/>
```

Elements may contain text, additional elements, or combinations of the two. Such nested elements build up a hierarchy within the document. This organization indicates relationships between the data and provides much of the functionality of XML. An XML document must have only a single top-level tag (known as the *document element*), similar to the <html> tag in HTML.

An XML document that has a single top-level element and closes all of its elements in the correct sequence is termed a *well-formed* document. This indicates that it follows the basic conventions of XML and can be successfully processed by standard XML parsers and utilities. If the document is well-formed, claims to follow the dictates of a particular DTD (see the next chapter), and indeed does so, it is known as a *valid* document.

Attributes of an element are identified by name within its opening tag and are followed by an equal sign (=) and their value. The closing tag for an element never has attributes specified for it. All attribute values must be enclosed by either single (') or double quotes (") in XML, while in HTML quotes are only required when the value contains certain restricted characters, such as spaces.

```
<movie id="SW1" logo-url="SW1-logo" url="SW1-site">
   :
</movie>
```

Attributes may be mandatory or optional, may have a set of valid values, and may have a default value. They may identify an element or refer to another element. All of this is specified in the DTD as described in the next chapter.

The decision to make a particular data value an attribute or a sub-element is purely subjective. In general, sub-elements contain data that are displayed when the document is presented, whereas attributes hold supplementary data that is often not shown. Sometimes one way makes more sense than the other. Feel free to use whichever way works for you.

Name Tokens and Namespaces

Names of elements and attributes within XML must begin with a letter or an underscore (_). This may be followed by any combination of letters, numbers, underscores, hyphens (-), colons (:), or periods (.). However, names cannot begin with the letters xml (upper- and/or lowercase) as these are reserved for future use by XML itself.

Colons have a special meaning in names as they are used to delimit namespace references from their local names. Namespaces allow for differentiation between elements that would otherwise be identical. In Delphi terms, this is similar to prefixing a procedure or function call with the name of the unit containing it, separated by a period.

For example, in the movie-watcher documents you have the star element that refers to an actor within a movie. It is possible that there are other types of documents that also have star elements, though they may assign a different meaning to them (such as stellar bodies). If you were to combine these two documents, you might not be able to distinguish between the two based on the element name alone. Namespaces are used to identify different sources (and meanings) and associate a short name with each. This prefix is then combined with the element name to uniquely identify it.

The declaration of a namespace can occur on any element and applies to that element and to all of its children. A reserved attribute name is used for the declaration: xmlns. This is followed by a colon and the prefix used within this document to refer to that namespace. A namespace declaration may specify no prefix, and so defines the *default namespace* used for all elements that have no prefix.

The value of the namespace is just something that distinguishes it from any other namespace, although the use of URIs is encouraged. For several XML technologies, a particular URI is expected for certain namespaces, and the application will generate an error if it is not exactly as specified.

As an example, the fragment below declares three namespaces on the combined element. The first is the default namespace and applies to the combined element itself (since it has no prefix). The other two help to differentiate the two distinct star elements.

```
<combined xmlns="http://www.combined.com"
    xmlns:mv="http://www.movies.com/"
    xmlns:as="http://www.astronomy.com/stellar">
  <mv:star>Liam Neeson</mv:star>
  <as:star>Alpha Centauri</as:star>
</combined>
```

In the name mv:star, the mv part is the namespace prefix, the star part is the local name, and the whole thing is a qualified name.

The names of elements and their attributes are case-sensitive within XML, whereas HTML happily accepts any combination. Hence, movie, Movie, and MOVIE are all different elements in

XML. This can be a source of errors when coming from the Delphi world where case is ignored. I suggest that you stick to one case when creating your documents to reduce possible problems.

Text and White Space

Anything outside of the markup is text or data—the content of the XML document. Generally an XML processor does not touch this text, passing it straight through to the calling application. Exceptions to this are entity references, which are described later.

XML allows most of the characters from the Unicode character set as valid text. Unicode is a 16-bit encoding scheme that covers many of the world's written scripts. Characters that cannot be written directly may be encoded using the following format: &#xhhhh;, where hhhh is the hexadecimal encoding for the required character.

White space between XML elements is generally not significant, whereas white space within data may be. In XML, white space is defined as any of the following characters: space (Unicode/ASCII 32), tab (Unicode/ASCII 9), line feed (Unicode/ASCII 10), and carriage return (Unicode/ASCII 13). For human readability, the tags are often indented to indicate their position within the hierarchy.

XML processors must pass all characters that are not markup through to the application. Validating processors must identify which of these characters appear within element content and which may be safely ignored as separators between tags.

Breaks between lines within the XML document are *normalized* during processing. A single line feed replaces any combination of carriage return and line feed characters.

The xml:space attribute may be added to any element to indicate how white space within it and its descendants is to be treated. It is set to either default or preserve. The default handling allows the application to treat white space in whatever way it normally does, while the alternative asks that all spacing be retained as it appears. The setting may be overridden at a lower level in the hierarchy through another instance of the attribute. In a valid document, this attribute must be declared just like any other.

Another special attribute, xml:lang, allows you to identify the natural language of the contents of an element. The value of this attribute is one of the standard language codes defined by ISO 639, such as en-GB, a language registered with the Internet Assigned Numbers Authority (IANA), like i-navajo, or a user-defined language name of the format x-mydialect. As before, this attribute applies to the element where it is specified and all its descendants, unless overridden by another instance. It must also be declared if documents containing it are to be validated.

Both the xml:space and xml:lang attributes may be defined in the DTD for the documents as having default values, just like any other attribute. This allows them to be set without requiring their presence within a particular document itself.

Comments

As with HTML, comments can be included in an XML document for the enlightenment of prospective readers. These follow the same syntax as HTML as shown below:

```
<!-- Comment -->
```

Comments can contain almost anything (except the sequence -- and, of course, the terminating string -->) and can appear just about anywhere within a document. However, they cannot be placed within element tags, within declarations, or inside other comments.

Comments are designed for authors to add further explanation to their documents. They should not contain information concerning the manipulation of the document since parsers may strip them out and ignore them. For this purpose, use processing instructions instead.

Processing Instructions

To include additional information for automatic handling of the document you may include processing instructions within it. These appear enclosed within the strings <? and ?> as shown below:

```
<?target instructions?>
```

The first token within the delimiters identifies the target application that this instruction is destined for, followed by the actual command. No structure is implied within the instruction data by the XML specification, leaving it up to the target program to interpret its meaning. The name of the target application cannot start with the characters xml, in any combination of upper- or lowercase, as these are reserved for use by XML itself.

These instructions can be picked up by a target application after parsing the XML, and then be decoded and applied to the document. They might define specific formatting instructions (although one of the tenets of XML is to separate content from presentation) or configuration parameters for the program. Applications can safely ignore processing instructions for other target programs.

The targets of processing instructions may be formally declared through the notation mechanism described later.

Entities

XML allows for the declaration of *entities* within a document. These are named strings of characters for substitution throughout the document. Once defined, through the !ENTITY tag, you can incorporate their content by using the entity name, preceded by an ampersand (&) and followed by a semicolon (;). This sequence is known as an *entity reference*. Remember that the names are case-sensitive. Entity declarations appear within the DOCTYPE specification at the start of an XML document.

```
<!DOCTYPE example [
<!ENTITY xml "Extensible Markup Language">
]>
    :
XML stands for &xml;.
```

In order to include the metacharacters used by XML within a document's content, you can use one of the predefined entities shown in Table 2-1. This allows for the placement of these characters in the body of the document without them being misinterpreted as control characters. Again, these are the same as in HTML.

XML tags appear between the < and > signs.

Table 2-1: Predefined entities

Entity Reference	Value
&amp;	&
&lt;	<
&gt;	>
&apos;	'
&quot;	"

In addition, any character in the Unicode set can be represented by a *character reference*. This consists of the entity delimiters surrounding a hash sign (#) and the numeric code for that character. The numeric code is decimal by default, but can be hexadecimal if preceded by an x. In this way, you can easily refer to characters that are outside your document's encoding scheme, or that are not easily entered from your keyboard.

```
This content is copyright &#169;.
```

would appear as the following:

```
This content is copyright ©.
```

XML allows for entities to be defined within the document or external to it. To retrieve the content of another file as the value of an entity, you must declare the entity and identify its source, as either a logical (*public*) or physical (*system*) location. These external entities are then included in the original document wherever their entity name is invoked. In this way you can break a large document up into separate pieces, such as chapters, and then combine them all into a coherent whole. Entities that are incorporated into the XML document are known as *parsed* entities, and may be *internal* or *external* depending on where they reside.

```
<!DOCTYPE example [
<!ENTITY chap01 SYSTEM "http://www.mysite.com/book1/chap01.xml">
]>
    :
&chap01;
```

Parsed entities must be defined before they are used and, if they contain XML markup, must be well-formed to be included in the document. They may not contain recursive references to themselves, either directly or indirectly. External parsed entities may use different encoding schemes than the original document; however, such schemes must be declared at the start of the entity in a format similar to the normal XML prolog.

Entities are also used to identify other items that are not part of the XML document, such as images, audio, video, or Web links. Such entities are not retrieved as part of the XML parsing process (they are *unparsed*), but may be manipulated by the application that uses the XML document. These entities are designated as not being part of the XML document through a type declaration following the NDATA keyword.

```
<!DOCTYPE example [
<!ENTITY SW1-site SYSTEM "http://www.starwars.com/episode-i/"
  NDATA HTML>
<!ENTITY SW1-logo SYSTEM
  "http://www.starwars.com/episode-i/palpatine/img/top_logo.gif"
  NDATA GIF>
]>
  :
<movie id="SW1" logo-url="SW1-logo" url="SW1-site">
  :
</movie>
```

TIP More information on declaring entities, of all types, is provided in the following chapter on the document type definition.

CDATA Sections

An alternative to using the predefined entities in your content is to mark sections as only containing character data, in other words no markup. Therefore, any reserved characters you encounter should be treated simply as their text equivalents. These sections are denoted by a special syntax:

```
<![CDATA[...]]>
```

For example:

```
<![CDATA[Ignore any markup characters such as < and >.]]>
```

The body of this tag can contain any text (except for the terminating combination of]]>). This makes it very easy to talk about XML within an XML document. Trying to achieve the same thing in HTML, talking about HTML, involves a great deal of extra work.

CDATA sections only affect the interpretation of the XML source and are generally converted to the equivalent text within an XML processor. Thus, they can appear simply as textual content to the final application.

Prolog

All XML documents should include an XML identifier at the start of the document to define the file type. This is enclosed within angle brackets and question marks with a tag name of xml. The version of XML being used (currently 1.0) must be included as an attribute. Additional attributes can identify the character encoding in use, and whether or not the document can be used without reference to anything else. If these attributes are specified they must appear in this order:

```
<?xml version="1.0" encoding="UTF-8" standalone="yes"?>
```

Thus, every XML document should have at least the following at its beginning:

```
<?xml version="1.0"?>
```

The current version of XML is 1.0, but this does not imply a commitment to any future versions of the specification, nor to any particular numbering scheme. However, XML processors should check the declared version within a document and raise an error if it does not recognize the given value. This protects against changes in the future that may alter the handling of XML documents.

A *standalone* document is one that contains no markup declarations that affect the interpretation of the XML document and that are external to that document. This does not include references to external entities, provided that they are declared internally. The declaration in the prolog must specify either yes or no, with the latter applying if no declaration is present.

Documents that have any of the following in external parsed entities must not have a standalone declaration set to yes:

- Attributes with default values, if elements appear without those attributes specifically set
- Entities other than the standard ones, if references to those entities are used
- Attributes with values subject to normalization, where values are specified that change because of this
- Element types with element content, if any instance of them contains white space

The syntax for this prolog is the same as that for processing instructions as described earlier. In fact, the prolog could be seen as an instruction to an XML parser defining how this document is to be treated.

Encoding Schemes

XML processors need to be able to deal with a variety of encoding schemes for the documents. All processors must recognize and handle the UTF-8 and UTF-16 encodings. Additional schemes may also be available through specific processors. Documents that are not in one of the two standard formats must include an encoding declaration in the XML prolog.

The common encoding schemes and transformations are described below:

ASCII
: The standard 7-bit encoding used on many computers.

ISO-8859-1
: An 8-bit encoding that extends ASCII to include those accented characters that make up most of the common Western European languages, including French, German, Spanish, and Italian. This is the first of a collection of encodings that enhance basic ASCII.

ISO-8859-2
: Like ISO-8859-1 but for Eastern European languages.

ISO-8859-3
: Like ISO-8859-1 but for Southern European languages.

ISO-8859-4
: Like ISO-8859-1 but for Northern European languages.

ISO-8859-5
: Like ISO-8859-1 but for Cyrillic languages.

ISO-8859-6
: Like ISO-8859-1 but for Arabic languages.

ISO-8859-7
: Like ISO-8859-1 but for the Greek language.

ISO-8859-8
: Like ISO-8859-1 but for Hebrew languages.

ISO-8859-9
: Like ISO-8859-1 but for Turkish languages.

ISO-8859-10
: Like ISO-8859-1 but for Nordic languages.

UNICODE
: A 16-bit encoding that provides access to most of the characters from languages world-wide. The first 128 characters correspond to the ASCII codes. It is defined by the Unicode Consortium (www.unicode.org) and is becoming a standard in many computing environments.

UCS-2
: The Universal Character Set. Another 16-bit encoding that covers most of the world's languages and is effectively equivalent to Unicode.

UCS-4
: An extended form of UCS-2 that uses 32-bit encodings. So far, the first (and only) section defined is equivalent to UCS-2 with additional null bytes to make up the 32 bits.

UTF-8
: A Unicode (or UCS) Transformation Format that maps these encodings to a byte stream. It overcomes the problem of just using the straight 16-bit values whereby the stream has many embedded null bytes, which are often interpreted in programs as the end of a string. To achieve this, and to offer the greatest compatibility with existing systems that use ASCII (remember that the first part of Unicode is ASCII), it uses a variable number of bytes for each character. Normal ASCII is encoded in a single byte, characters from x0080 to x07FF are encoded in two bytes, and characters x0800 to xFFFF are encoded in three bytes. Further encodings are defined for UCS-4 type characters, but these are not currently used. Hence, any standard ASCII file is also a valid UTF-8 file, which is very convenient.

UTF-16   Another transformation for Unicode (or UCS) that maps the characters to 16-bit values. It comes in two flavors: UTF-16BE and UTF-16LE. The first is for *big-endian* byte order, which means that the most significant byte appears first, while the other is for *little-endian* byte order, where the least significant byte comes first. These types are signaled through the presence of a known byte sequence at the start of the file. For BE it is xFEFF and for LE it is xFFFE.

Although the document prolog allows you to specify the encoding scheme used for the document, how do you know which scheme to use to read that declaration? Fortunately, the XML specification identifies ways around this problem. It states that any document not using either the UTF-8 or UTF-16 encoding schemes must have a prolog to indicate the scheme to be used. Furthermore, this prolog must appear at the start of the document and must only contain ASCII characters. This allows a processor to read the first few bytes to determine which family of schemes is in use, then read the rest of the prolog to discover the exact format for the remainder of the document.

For more information on encoding schemes, you can check out these sites:

W3C Internationalization/Localization

> http://www.w3.org/International/O-charset.html

Lycos: Computers/Software/Globalization/Character Encoding

> http://dir.hotbot.lycos.com/Computers/Software/Globalization/Character_Encoding/

Lycos: Computers/Data Formats/Markup Languages/XML/Encoding

> http://dir.hotbot.lycos.com/Computers/Data_Formats/Markup_Languages/XML/Encoding/

XML Processors

The XML specification also defines the capabilities of software modules that can handle XML documents. Collectively, these modules are known as *XML processors*. Typically a processor reads the document and provides access to its content through some mechanism. Another module, the application, calls the processor and makes use of its results.

Processors fall into two main groups: validating and non-validating. Both types must report errors when they encounter constructs that violate the well-formedness constraint of XML. *Validating* processors must also report conflicts between the document and its associated document type definition. To achieve this, these processors must retrieve and decode the entire DTD and any external parsed entities that are referenced. *Non-validating* processors need only handle an internal DTD for well-formedness and for supplying attribute defaults and entity definitions.

The behavior of an XML processor is intended to be highly predictable, allowing you to easily swap between different versions without requiring major changes to your application.

Summary

In this chapter you've been introduced to the syntax of XML and have been shown its major features. This should be enough to construct most documents for normal use. By following the simple rules presented here you can produce well-formed XML documents that can be happily processed by an XML parser. To ensure that a particular document meets the guidelines set out for its class of documents, you need to define a DTD, as described in the next chapter.

Chapter 3
Document Type Definitions

Although XML documents can be used standalone, a great deal of their potential benefit comes from having standard formats that facilitate the transfer of information from one platform or application to another. One way to enforce a particular format is through the use of a document description in the form of a document type definition (DTD).

A DTD specifies, for a particular type of document, what the layout of valid elements can be. Listing 3-1 shows the DTD for the movie-watcher documents. The DTD lists what elements are valid within these documents and what sub-elements or content may appear within each of them. For each element, there can also appear a list of the attributes applicable to it, along with their types and whether or not they are required.

Listing 3-1: DTD for movie-watchers

```
<!-- Data about movies and when and where they are showing
     Developed by Keith Wood, 28 May 1999 -->
<!ELEMENT movie-watcher (movies, cinemas, screenings)>

<!ELEMENT movies (movie+)>

<!-- Information about the movies -->
<!ELEMENT movie (name, length?, director?, starring?, synopsis?)>
<!ATTLIST movie id ID #REQUIRED
                rating (NR | G | PG | PG-13 | R) #REQUIRED
                logo-url ENTITY #IMPLIED
                url ENTITY #IMPLIED>

<!ELEMENT name (#PCDATA)>
<!-- Length as minutes -->
<!ELEMENT length (#PCDATA)>
<!ELEMENT director (#PCDATA)>
<!ELEMENT starring (star+)>
<!ELEMENT star (#PCDATA)>
<!ELEMENT synopsis (#PCDATA | emph)*>
<!ELEMENT emph (#PCDATA)>

<!ELEMENT cinemas (cinema+)>

<!-- Details about the cinemas -->
<!ELEMENT cinema
    (name, phone, address, directions?, facilities?, pricing)>
```

```
<!ATTLIST cinema id ID #REQUIRED
                 logo-url ENTITY #IMPLIED
                 url ENTITY #IMPLIED>

<!ELEMENT phone (#PCDATA)>
<!ELEMENT address (#PCDATA)>
<!ELEMENT directions (#PCDATA)>

<!ELEMENT facilities (candy-bar?, disabled-access?)>

<!ELEMENT candy-bar EMPTY>
<!ELEMENT disabled-access EMPTY>

<!-- List of pricing schemes -->
<!ELEMENT pricing (prices+)>

<!ELEMENT prices (name, period, adult, child, discount?)>
<!ATTLIST prices id ID #REQUIRED>

<!-- When do these prices apply? -->
<!ELEMENT period (#PCDATA)>
<!-- Actual prices in dollars -->
<!ELEMENT adult (#PCDATA)>
<!ELEMENT child (#PCDATA)>
<!ELEMENT discount (#PCDATA)>

<!ELEMENT screenings (screening+)>

<!-- Where and when is a movie showing? -->
<!ELEMENT screening
  (start-date, end-date, features?, restrictions?, sessions)>
<!-- Which movie and cinema? -->
<!ATTLIST screening movie-id IDREF #REQUIRED
                    cinema-id IDREF #REQUIRED>

<!-- Which dates does this apply to? (format mm/dd/yyyy) -->
<!ELEMENT start-date (#PCDATA)>
<!ELEMENT end-date (#PCDATA)>

<!ELEMENT features (digital-sound?)>

<!ELEMENT digital-sound (#PCDATA)>

<!ELEMENT restrictions (no-passes?)>

<!ELEMENT no-passes EMPTY>

<!ELEMENT sessions (session+)>
<!-- Session value is the start time hh:mmam/pm -->
<!ELEMENT session (#PCDATA)>
<!-- Which price schedule to use? -->
<!ATTLIST session price-id IDREF #REQUIRED>
```

DTD Declarations

The DTD for a document can be included directly within that document, following the XML prolog. This is called an *internal subset*. It appears within the DOCTYPE declaration, which specifies the top-level element for the document, and has the element definitions located between the symbols [and]>. A movie-watcher document with its DTD may appear like the following:

```
<?xml version="1.0" encoding="UTF-8" standalone="yes"?>
<!DOCTYPE movie-watcher [
  DTD from above
]>
Rest of movie-watcher document
```

Alternately, the DTD can be stored in a separate document that is referred to by each XML document that claims to conform to it. These DTDs are known as *external subsets*. This allows the definition to be shared by any number of documents and is the basis of a common communication language using XML. Again, the DTD entry appears after the XML prolog and includes either a public or system declaration that lists the (logical or physical) location of the DTD document. The public identifier is designed to be some generally accepted name for a particular DTD, which is then mapped onto an actual document.

```
<?xml version="1.0" encoding="UTF-8"?>
<!DOCTYPE movie-watcher SYSTEM "movie-watcher.dtd">
Rest of movie-watcher document
```

Referring to an external document and then following it with some inline declarations lets you extend a DTD. Typically the inline section refers to entities that are only relevant to the current document, as either internal or external abbreviations (parsed entities), or external document references (unparsed). This technique is used in the movie-watcher documents to point to Web sites and graphics, as shown below:

```
<?xml version="1.0" encoding="UTF-8"?>
<!DOCTYPE movie-watcher SYSTEM "movie-watcher.dtd" [
  <!ENTITY SW1-site SYSTEM "http://www.starwars.com/episode-i/"
    NDATA HTML>
  <!ENTITY SW1-logo SYSTEM
    "http://www.starwars.com/episode-i/palpatine/img/top_logo.gif"
    NDATA GIF>
  <!ENTITY PV "Pleasantville">
]>
Rest of movie-watcher document
```

An XML document that claims to conform to a particular DTD must include a reference to that DTD within itself. If the document is well-formed and does indeed follow the DTD specification, it is regarded as a *valid* document. Documents can quite happily be well-formed without being valid, and are still usable as such.

Content Model

Individual elements within the definition are declared with the <!ELEMENT string, followed by the element's name. Remember that these declaration tags are case-sensitive and must be entered as shown. However, you are free to use whatever case you wish for your own elements. Just remember to use the same case when constructing your documents if you want them to be valid.

The final part of the element definition lists the valid content for that element. Items that do not contain anything are noted as such by having the keyword EMPTY as their only content, such as the candy-bar and disabled-access elements in the example DTD. Elements that can contain anything use the keyword ANY. This is rarely done since the idea of the DTD is to prescribe the structure of the document in a meaningful way.

```
<!ELEMENT disabled-access EMPTY>
```

Most often the content for an element consists of sub-elements or free text. In both cases the model is enclosed within parentheses. The first option lists the name(s) of the valid lower-level elements.

Separating options with vertical bars (|) specifies alternate content at the same position. Sequential content is listed separated by commas (,). Elements from a sequential list must appear in the specified order in the XML document for it to be valid. Parentheses may be used at any point to group items together, and white space can be used to make the text more readable.

For example, the following declaration states that a movie-structure element must contain an opening-title element, followed by any number of either close-up or wide-angle elements, followed by a closing-title element.

```
<!ELEMENT movie-structure
    (opening-title, (close-up | wide-angle)*, closing-title)>
```

Free text content models are also known as *mixed content*. For free text alone the model consists solely of the text #PCDATA. Such an element can contain any valid characters, but no other markup. Characters that have meaning to XML must be replaced by character references, specifically < for < and & for &.

```
<!ELEMENT emph (#PCDATA)>
```

If the element can contain both free text and other elements, then the first entry in the model must be #PCDATA as above. This may be followed by any number of element names, each separated by a vertical bar (|). An asterisk (*) must follow the closing parenthesis. In this combined case you can constrain which child elements may appear, but have no control over their order or the number of times that they are used. Each sub-element may only be listed once, but it may be used within a document many times.

```
<!ELEMENT synopsis (#PCDATA | emph)*>
```

For each content item or group, including the entire content list, you can also indicate its occurrences using the characters shown in Table 3-1. By default, an element must appear exactly once. From the following sample you can see that a movie element must contain a single name entry, followed optionally by length, director, starring, and synopsis elements in this order. The synopsis element above can contain zero or more (*) occurrences of either (|) free text

(#PCDATA) or an emphasis element (emph). Mixed content must always include the zero or more indicator. The emph element can only contain free text.

```
<!ELEMENT movie (name, length?, director?, starring?, synopsis?)>
```

Table 3-1: Occurrence indicators

Indicator	Occurrences
nothing	Content must appear once (mandatory)
?	Content may appear once (optional)
*	Content may appear zero or more times
+	Content must appear one or more times

Content models should be *deterministic*. This means that there should be only one possible path through the DTD for each sequence of elements within a document. You should not have to look ahead within a model to determine which path to follow. XML processors may raise an error if they cannot decide which element within the content model to match with.

Attributes

Attributes are additional information that can be attached to an element. As noted earlier, the choice of making this extra data an attribute or a sub-element is largely a matter of personal taste. Generally, attributes supply details that are not essential to the element under consideration, but are useful in some circumstances. One exception to this is an ID attribute, which serves to uniquely identify an element.

To define an attribute for an element you enter a declaration that begins with the <!ATTLIST string. This is followed by the name of the element to which it applies and a list of the attributes themselves. Each attribute provides its name, its type, and its default declaration. Although the attributes for an element can appear anywhere within the DTD, it is usual to place them directly after the element's declaration.

Multiple attributes for the same element may be listed separately, each within its own ATTLIST declaration, or they may be combined into a single declaration by omitting the ATTLIST text and the element name before the second and subsequent attributes.

If more than one definition for a particular element and attribute combination is encountered, only the first one is used, with any others being ignored. Note that this is not an error. This ability does allow you to override an attribute inherited from an external DTD by re-specifying it within the internal subset in the document itself. An external DTD is read and processed following any internal definitions.

The type of an attribute is usually free text, denoted by CDATA, or a list of literal values (an *enumerated* type). For example, the rating of a movie is declared as an attribute that must be set to one of the listed values (and no others) with the following:

```
<!ATTLIST movie rating (NR | G | PG | PG-13 | R) #REQUIRED>
```

Listing a value at the end of the declaration sets that as the default value for each attribute. In this case, if the attribute is not specified within an appropriate element in a document, it automatically takes the given value. If it does appear in the document, the supplied value is used and the default is ignored. Alternately, you can nominate the presence or absence of the attribute with the #REQUIRED (mandatory) or #IMPLIED (optional) keywords.

Another option is to supply a default value and specify the attribute as #FIXED, or unchangeable. Such attributes automatically take on the given value. You may assign the attribute a value within the document itself; however, this generates an error if that value does not match the fixed one.

Fixed attributes can be used to provide common roles across a number of DTDs, allowing such elements to be processed in a standard way, regardless of where they originate. For example, name elements could be declared to have a title-element attribute with a fixed value. An automated search tool could then find these elements, along with title-element attributes from other XML documents containing book details, and handle them all in the same manner, regardless of the actual names of those elements. These attributes would be fixed so that a document author could not change them, nor forget to include them.

```
<!ATTLIST name title-element CDATA #FIXED "movie">
```

Other specialized attribute types are available, as shown in Table 3-2. The ID and IDREF types are very useful in establishing links between different elements within your documents. Each ID value must be a valid name within XML and no element may have more than one ID type attribute. The default value for an ID type attribute must be either #IMPLIED or #REQUIRED. For example, in the movie-watcher documents, movies and cinemas each have ID attributes, while screenings have two IDREF attributes that link the other elements together. Although it is not necessary to name an attribute of type ID as ID, it is common to do so, or to at least include this as part of the name.

Table 3-2: Attribute types

Attribute Type	Content
ENTITY	An unparsed entity's name
ENTITIES	A list of unparsed entities' names (separated by white space)
ID	A unique identifier within the document
IDREF	Another element's unique identifier
IDREFS	A list of other elements' unique identifiers (separated by white space)
NMTOKEN	Free text but restricted to an identifier format
NMTOKENS	A list of NMTOKENs (separated by white space)
NOTATION	Must be a declared notation

The NOTATION type for an attribute enables us to refer to one or more external type definitions to further restrict the possible valid values for it. An example of this is a date reference. Each NOTATION type must be declared elsewhere within the DTD.

ENTITY types refer to external documents that XML does not manipulate directly. The entities must be defined elsewhere in the DTD, or in the XML document itself, as unparsed entities. Examples of these types of attributes appear in the DTD extract shown below:

```
<!ATTLIST movie id ID #REQUIRED
                rating (NR | G | PG | PG-13 | R) #REQUIRED
                logo-url ENTITY #IMPLIED
                url ENTITY #IMPLIED>
```

An XML processor normalizes attribute values before being passed off to the application. Character and entity references are resolved as the first step. All white space characters are then replaced with spaces. Finally, if the attribute type is not CDATA, leading and trailing spaces are removed, and internal sequences of spaces are replaced by a single space. If the DTD is not available or is not processed, then all attributes are treated as though they were of type CDATA.

Notations

Notations describe the data content of various other items. Each one needs to be declared within the DTD or the XML document where it is used. In attribute declarations a notation defines the range of possible values that can be entered for that attribute. For external entities, a NOTATION declaration indicates a formal specification for a data type or a helper application that can handle that type.

A typical use for notations in attribute declarations is the specification of date formats. The NOTATION declarations refer to the appropriate specification resource:

```
<!NOTATION ISODATE SYSTEM "http://www.iso.ch/date_specification">
```

These notations could then be used on an attribute as follows:

```
<!ELEMENT screening (sessions)>
<!ATTLIST screening start-date NOTATION (ISODATE) #REQUIRED
                    end-date NOTATION (ISODATE) #REQUIRED>
```

Multiple notations may be specified, separated by vertical bars (|), indicating that the attribute value must conform to one of those formats.

Notations declared for use with external entities define the public (logical) or system (physical) location of the format's specification or of a helper program:

```
<!NOTATION HTML PUBLIC "-//W3C//DTD HTML 4.0 Transitional//EN">
```

Entities

An entity within XML is a reference to some other content, either simple text or an entire document held externally. They appear following the string <!ENTITY.

Several standard entities were described in Chapter 2, covering the metacharacters used by XML. Character references were also described there, which allow you to include characters that are outside the current encoding or that cannot be entered directly through the keyboard. Recall that these have the format `&#nnn;` or `&#xhhhh;`, where `nnn` is the decimal encoding for the required character and `hhhh` is its hexadecimal encoding.

For simple substitutions, entities can be defined as abbreviations for the desired text. In addition to the predefined entities, you can define your own entries. These items are expanded within your document by denoting them as *entity references*, i.e., preceding the name with an ampersand (&) and following it with a semicolon (;). Although entities can contain additional markup, there are several restrictions on their use in this way—specifically that the content must be properly nested.

```
<!ENTITY PV "Pleasantville">
:
<address>1234 Main St, &PV;</address>
```

Larger substitutions can be achieved by linking the entity name to an external document containing either text or XML. The `PUBLIC` or `SYSTEM` keyword is used to indicate that a logical or physical location follows. As with simple entities, the contents of the referenced object are included in the current document by entering the appropriate entity reference.

Both of these types of entities are known as *parsed entities* since their content is incorporated into the document and processed as XML. The inline specifications are *internal* entities, while file references are *external* entities.

Another class of entity is the *unparsed entity*. This is an external reference to a document that should not be included in the current document. Typically, these are used for non-text documents such as images, audio, and video, but they can also be hyperlinks to information that is additional to that contained within the current document. These unparsed entities are denoted by the inclusion of the document's type, in the form of a notation name following the keyword `NDATA`, within its declaration:

```
<!ENTITY SW1-logo SYSTEM
  "http://www.starwars.com/episode-i/palpatine/img/top_logo.gif"
  NDATA GIF>
```

One final class of entities exists—*parameter* entities. Parameter entities can be internal or external but are always parsed. They are differentiated from normal entity declarations by having a percent sign (%) before the name. To refer to a parameter entity, you prefix the name with a percent sign and follow it with a semicolon. These entities are only valid within the DTD itself. Often parameter entities are used to include common sequences within the DTD. In this case they must contain both the opening and closing parentheses of any content model groups that they define.

Parameter entities are also used to control the inclusion or exclusion of parts of a DTD through the use of conditional sections. A *conditional section* starts with the text `<![xxx[` and continues until it reaches `]]>`. The `xxx` here is replaced by the keyword `INCLUDE` to process the section normally, or `IGNORE` to bypass it. By using parameter entities, these sections can be turned on and off just by changing the value of that one parameter. Valid conditional sections may contain any combination of complete declarations, comments, processing instructions, or white space. The definitions below would add a `format` attribute to the `movie` element:

```
<!ENTITY % extended "INCLUDE">
<![%extended;[
<!ATTLIST movie format CDATA #IMPLIED>
]]>
```

Conditional sections may be nested. However, once a section is bypassed because its keyword is set to IGNORE, all of its content is also ignored regardless of any embedded conditional sections.

Recall that entity values in an external DTD can be overridden by specifying them in the internal subset of a document. If the external DTD is set up with appropriate conditional sections, these can be turned on or off for each document by simply redefining the controlling entity.

Summary

DTDs consist mainly of the list of valid elements that may appear within an XML document that claims to conform to it. You define what each element may contain—other elements, straight text, or a combination of the two. Attributes can also be specified for each element, along with their types and whether or not they are required.

DTDs may also list standard entities, either parsed or unparsed, internal or external. These may be used in documents referring to the DTD.

XML documents claim conformance with a particular DTD by including the DOCTYPE declaration within their header. This lists the top-level element for the document and where the DTD can be found. DTDs can be included inline in the XML or can be located in external files for sharing among a number of documents. Valid documents are those that refer to a DTD and follow its specification.

This has been a very quick look at XML DTDs, hopefully providing enough information to enable you to create your own basic definitions. For more information you should refer to one of the many books on XML itself. An alternative to DTDs as a means of specifying the legal content of a document is to use an XML Schema, which is covered in Chapter 7.

Chapter 4
Extensible Stylesheet Language Transformations

As we have already seen, XML is a technology for encoding the meaning of data within a document, as opposed to HTML, which describes the presentation of that data. The Extensible Stylesheet Language (XSL) is the link between the two. It provides a language to define the transformation of the plain data into an output format suitable for display on some device.

XSL consist of two main parts: the style language that describes how to format different portions of the document (sometimes known as XSL Formatting) and a transformation language (XSLT) for converting a tree structure.

The style language is an XML format and allows you to define how the various portions of the document are to be displayed. It includes the usual font specifications, colors, and alignments, as well as more advanced features such as flow control, numbering, footnotes, and tables. However, the language is still in its early stages and formatters that know how to deal with such a document are not readily available. The most current implementation available is known as FOP (Formatting Objects to PDF). It is a free Java program from James Tauber that takes an XSL document and generates a PDF file from it. Due to the lack of widespread use of XSL, it is not covered in this book.

Transformations

The XSL Transformation language (XSLT) allows you to manipulate an XML document, extract parts, rearrange sections, and format the results for further consumption. Often the output from the transformation is HTML, allowing the data to be easily accessed over the Internet. However, other document types can also be produced, such as plain text, rich text, audio input, or even other XML documents.

A transformation stylesheet is actually an XML document itself. All the processing is encoded within elements that have a tag starting with `xsl:` (a de facto standard), while the remaining elements are output to the final document. The document element of the stylesheet is the `xsl:stylesheet` element. This requires a version attribute, currently 1.0, and a namespace definition for the `xsl:` elements (which should be exactly as shown below).

```
<?xml version="1.0" encoding="UTF-8"?>
<xsl:stylesheet version="1.0"
    xmlns:xsl="http://www.w3.org/1999/XSL/Transform">
  <xsl:output method="html"/>
    :
</xsl:stylesheet>
```

XSLT is designed to be extensible, allowing for the inclusion of any set of formatting instructions. Each set must be identified by its own namespace with a reference to its definitions. The namespaces are specified within the `xsl:stylesheet` element as additional `xmlns:` attributes. Within the stylesheet the namespaces are used with a colon (:) to denote their scope.

The `xsl:output` element identifies the destination format for the results of the transformation. It should be one of the values `html`, `xml`, or `text`. If no output method is specified it is assumed to be `xml`, unless the first tag generated is `<html>`, in which case the output method becomes `html`. Other values are possible, but are not defined by the specification.

Templates and Patterns

The XSLT stylesheet uses a system of *templates* to match up with portions of the XML document and to specify how they are manipulated. Once a template is matched to an element, the contents of that template are applied to it. At least one template is required to initiate the process, matching with the XML document as a whole.

```
<xsl:template match="/">
  formatting commands for this document as a whole
</xsl:template>
```

Subsequent templates may be set up to match on only parts of the XML document hierarchy. To determine which elements a particular template targets, you use the `match` attribute with a pattern specification. Elements and attributes are identified by name, with attributes being prefixed by an at symbol (@). A slash (/) separates elements at different levels, while the asterisk (*) is a wildcard, matching with anything. The description of the patterns is itself an XML-related specification—XML Path Language (XPath).

Conditions may appear with square brackets ([ ]) following the element to which they apply. Various function-like names identify particular nodes either by their type, by their unique ID attribute, or as the current node of interest. Unless a pattern starts with a slash, making it an absolute reference, all patterns are within the context of the current node. Some sample patterns are shown in Table 4-1.

Part I: Introduction to XML

Table 4-1: XSLT patterns

Pattern	Matches
/	The root node of the XML document
*	Any element
.	The current node
movie	Any movie element
director | star	Any director or any star element
movie/name	Any name element with a movie element parent
movies//name	Any name element with a movies element ancestor
text()	Any text node
node()	Any node other than the root node or an attribute node
id("SW1")	The element with SW1 as its unique ID
context()	The current node (that contains the expression)
star[1]	Any star element that is the first child of its parent
star[last()=1]	Any star element that is the only child of its parent
@url	The url attribute within an element
@*	Any attribute within an element
movie[@rating="PG"]	Any movie element that has a rating attribute of PG
//screening[@movie-id=current()/@id]/start-date	The start date of the screening element whose movie-id attribute is equal to the id of the current node (presumably a movie)

These pattern specifications are used throughout a transformation stylesheet to identify nodes or attributes for subsequent processing. For example, in the `xsl:sort` element they determine the criteria for ordering nodes. In the `xsl:for-each` element they select the subset of nodes to process within a loop.

Within the main template you can invoke other templates through the use of the `xsl:apply-templates` element. When used without a `select` attribute, this tag applies to all the child nodes of the current one. Specifying a pattern within the `select` attribute causes only the matching nodes to be processed through their templates. The following line affects all the `movie` elements within the `movie-watcher/movies` hierarchy.

```
<xsl:apply-templates select="movie-watcher/movies/movie"/>
```

TIP I suggest that you make use of the template structure of XSLT wherever possible. This allows you to make the stylesheet more modular, similar to using procedures in Delphi. You can update each template separately from any other and call it from a number of different points within the stylesheet. Furthermore, using templates allows you to apply specific transformations to particular nodes within an XML document, without having to process the entire thing. Chapter 21 shows how to achieve this.

XSLT has a number of built-in templates that provide basic functionality. One of these continues the recursive application of templates when no specific match is found. Another one automatically copies all text and attribute nodes straight across to the output. One more that matches processing instructions and comments does nothing with them, effectively removing them from the output.

Generally there is only one template for each node type within the XML document. However, by using *named templates*, it is possible to process the same node in different ways at different times. The `name` attribute on the template tag identifies the template. Thereafter, the `xsl:call-template` element can be used to invoke it by specifying that same name.

An alternative approach is to use *modes*. A template can have a `mode` attribute specified as part of its declaration. If this same mode is supplied in the `apply-templates` tag, then only the corresponding template is used. The following example displays only the names of each section within the table of contents:

```
<xsl:apply-templates select="section" mode="contents"/>

<xsl:template match="section" mode="contents">
  <li><xsl:value-of select="name"/></li>
</xsl:template>
```

Text Content

Text from the stylesheet is generally copied across to the resulting document as is. Nodes that contain only white space are stripped from the document during processing. To ensure that these text nodes are retained, you can enclose them within an `xsl:text` element.

```
This appears in the output,
<xsl:text>as  does  this.</xsl:text>
```

To include the content of an element or attribute in the text stream you can use the `xsl:value-of` element. This element's `select` attribute is a pattern that determines what is written out. Use the "." pattern to retrieve the contents of the current node.

```
<xsl:value-of select="@rating"/>
<xsl:value-of select="length"/> mins
```

Building Document Structure

Any elements in the template that do not belong to the XSLT namespace, nor to an extension namespace, are copied directly across to the output document. In this way, it is easy to create HTML pages using XSLT just by including the HTML tags within a template. However, there are times when the tags or their attributes need to be more dynamic. XSLT provides the `xsl:element` and `xsl:attribute` elements for just these purposes.

To create an output element with a computed name, use the `xsl:element` tag and set its `name` attribute. Enclose references to elements or attributes in the name calculation within braces ({ }) to denote it as an expression.

```
<xsl:element name="h{@level}">
  Element content
</xsl:element>
```

Similarly, attributes can have computed names or values through the use of the `xsl:attribute` tag. This tag must appear within the bounds of the element to which it refers.

```
<a>
  <xsl:attribute name="name">
    <xsl:value-of select="@id"/>
  </xsl:attribute>
  Anchor contents
</a>
```

Attribute values may also be created directly within the element using the expression technique described above.

```
<a name="{@id}">
  Anchor contents
</a>
```

Processing instructions and comments are created within the output document in a similar manner with the `xsl:processing-instruction` and `xsl:comment` tags. These elements cannot be transferred directly from the XSL stylesheet since it is an XML document, and so would interpret or ignore these as part of its own processing.

```
<xsl:processing-instruction name="xml">
  version="1.0" encoding="UTF-8"
</xsl:processing-instruction>
<xsl:comment>Comment within the output document</xsl:comment>
```

To transfer an existing node from the source XML to the output document you use the `xsl:copy` tag. However, this does not transfer the attributes nor the child elements of this node. These must be copied manually.

Loops

The `xsl:for-each` tag provides a looping mechanism within XSLT. It applies its contents to each node selected by the expression in its `select` attribute.

```
<xsl:for-each select="starring/star">
  <xsl:value-of select="."/><br />
</xsl:for-each>
```

Ordering of the selected nodes is achieved through the `xsl:sort` element, which is placed as a child of the looping element. Its `select` attribute specifies the values to be used for the ordering. Multiple sorting tags allow for primary and secondary sort keys to be supplied. Additional attributes can be used to determine ascending or descending sorts, the language to be used, and the data type (text, numeric, or other).

```
<xsl:for-each select="movie">
  <xsl:sort select="name"/>
  Movie content
</xsl:for-each>
```

NOTE Earlier versions of the XSLT engine within Internet Explorer seem to reject these sorting tags, preferring instead an order-by attribute, with the same pattern as for the sorting tag.

```
<xsl:for-each select="movie" order-by="name"/>
  Movie content
</xsl:for-each>
```

Conditional Processing

XSL also includes two ways of making decisions within the template. The first is the `xsl:if` tag, which provides a simple "if" test around its contents. You use the `test` attribute to supply the expression to be evaluated. If this expression refers to an element or an attribute, this item's presence is being tested and the contents are applied if the item exists. Otherwise, the expression must evaluate to a true or false value. The following fragment adds an `href` attribute to the output with the value of the source node's `url` attribute as its target, but only if the latter exists.

```
<xsl:if test="@url">
  <xsl:attribute name="href">
    <xsl:value-of select="@url"/>
  </xsl:attribute>
</xsl:if>
```

For an if-then-else or a case statement type of test, you need to use the `xsl:choose` tag. This tag has no attributes itself, but contains a number of `xsl:when` tags and an optional `xsl:otherwise` tag. Each `when` tag acts like the `if` tag above, specifying an expression to be evaluated in its `test` attribute. There may be several `when` tags within `choose`, each testing a different condition. The `otherwise` tag can be added to process any nodes that did not get caught by one of the `when` tags (similar to the else clause in a case statement). The following fragment tests for the existence of a `logo-url` attribute on the current node and inserts an `img` element if it is found. If not, the name is added within a header element.

```
<xsl:choose>
  <xsl:when test="@logo-url">
    <img>
      <xsl:attribute name="src">
        <xsl:value-of select="@logo-url"/>
      </xsl:attribute>
      <xsl:attribute name="alt">
        <xsl:value-of select="name"/>
      </xsl:attribute>
    </img>
  </xsl:when>
  <xsl:otherwise>
    <h3><xsl:value-of select="name"/></h3>
  </xsl:otherwise>
</xsl:choose>
```

XSLT Sample

To bring all of these pieces together, have a look at the XSLT stylesheet fragment in Listing 4-1. This fragment transforms the XML data for a movie into HTML suitable for display on the Web. You can see the HTML tags embedded within the XSL processing. Note that the <img> tag in HTML does not have a closing tag, nor does it have the XML shorthand for closing (a trailing slash). However, within this stylesheet document, which is XML, one of these must be present.

Listing 4-1: Transforming a movie-watcher document into HTML

```xml
<?xml version="1.0" encoding="UTF-8"?>
<!-- HTML style sheet for movie-watcher XML (monolithic format)
     Written by Keith Wood, 4 June 1999 -->
<xsl:stylesheet version="1.0"
    xmlns:xsl="http://www.w3.org/1999/XSL/Transform">
  <xsl:output method="html"/>

  <!-- Match the entire document -->
  <xsl:template match="/">
    <html>
      <head>
        <title>Movie Watchers</title>
      </head>
      <body>
        <h1><a name="top">Welcome to Movie Watchers</a></h1>
        <p>Your source for local film entertainment.
          Have a look at <a href="#movies">what's on</a>,
          <a href="#cinemas">where</a> and
          <a href="#screenings">when</a>.</p>
        <hr/>
        <h2><a name="movies">Movies</a></h2>
        <xsl:for-each select="//movie">
          <xsl:sort select="name"/>
          <!-- Provide link target and optional web link -->
          <a name="{@id}">
            <xsl:if test="@url">
              <xsl:attribute name="href">
                <xsl:value-of select="@url"/>
              </xsl:attribute>
            </xsl:if>
            <xsl:choose>
              <xsl:when test="@logo-url">
                <img src="{@logo-url}" alt="{name}"/>
              </xsl:when>
              <xsl:otherwise>
                <h3><xsl:value-of select="name"/></h3>
              </xsl:otherwise>
            </xsl:choose>
          </a>
          <table border="0" width="100%">
            <tr>
              <th align="left" valign="top" width="15%">Rating:</th>
              <td width="15%"><xsl:value-of select="@rating"/></td>
              <th align="left" valign="top" width="15%">Length:</th>
              <td><xsl:value-of select="length"/> mins</td>
            </tr>
            <tr>
```

```xml
            <th align="left" valign="top">Director:</th>
            <td colspan="3"><xsl:value-of select="director"/></td>
          </tr>
          <tr>
            <th align="left" valign="top">Starring:</th>
            <td colspan="3">
              <xsl:for-each select="starring/star">
                <xsl:value-of select="."/><br/>
              </xsl:for-each>
            </td>
          </tr>
          <tr>
            <th align="left" valign="top">Synopsis:</th>
            <td colspan="3"><xsl:value-of select="synopsis"/></td>
          </tr>
          <tr>
            <th align="left" valign="top">Showing at:</th>
            <td colspan="3">
              <xsl:for-each
                  select="//screening[@movie-id=current()/@id]">
                <a href="#{@movie-id}-{@cinema-id}">
                  <xsl:value-of select="id(@cinema-id)/name"/>
                </a><br/>
              </xsl:for-each>
            </td>
          </tr>
        </table>
      </xsl:for-each>
      <p>Back to <a href="#top">the top</a>.</p>
      :
      :
      <hr/>
      <p>Movie Watcher data supplied by
        <a href="mailto:kbwood@compuserve.com">Keith Wood</a>.</p>
    </body>
  </html>
</xsl:template>
</xsl:stylesheet>
```

The stylesheet contains a single template that matches with the root of the XML document. Within this, it sets up the HTML header block and starts the body of the output HTML. Static links to other sections within the page appear in the introduction, allowing for easy navigation around it. The title for the movies section follows, surrounded by a target anchor for one of the earlier links.

Each movie from the XML document is dealt with in turn by using the `xsl:for-each` loop construct. The `xsl:sort` element sorts them alphabetically. A movie is identified by an image, if one is specified in the XML, or by its name. In either case, this heading is set up as the target for other links within the document through an encompassing anchor tag. The anchor also provides an outward link to a related Web site, but only if it is present in the XML. Note the use of the `xsl:attribute` elements to supply dynamic content for some of the attributes of the resulting HTML.

After the movie's name is a table that allows you to format the remaining details nicely. Values are inserted with the `xsl:value-of` elements. Recall that elements and attributes are identified by their name, with attributes being preceded by an at sign (@). The references are relative to the current node, the `movie` element selected in the for loop, since they do not start with a slash.

Finally, there is a list of the cinemas that are showing the movie. To create this, you need to find the `screening` elements that have this movie's `id` value as one of their attributes.

```
<xsl:for-each select="//screening[@movie-id=current()/@id]">
```

Looping through these with the `<xsl:for-each>` tag, you then want to traverse to the cinema node that corresponds to that screening and retrieve its name for display.

```
<xsl:value-of select="id(@cinema-id)/name"/>
```

Further processing (not shown) within the stylesheet transforms the cinema and screening information into HTML in a similar manner. At the end of the stylesheet you add any closing comments and finish up the HTML document. The results of the transformation are shown in Figure 4-1.

Figure 4-1: XML transformed to HTML.

Summary

This chapter has introduced you to XSL and XSL Transformations. XSL provides an XML syntax to describe complex formatting, although its abilities are not in widespread use yet. XSLT is readily available and allows you to manipulate an XML document tree, extracting, rearranging, and filtering it into another document tree that can then be displayed or processed further. Typically it is used to wrap XML data in HTML for presentation on the Web.

XSLT has several additional abilities that are beyond the scope of this book. These include the following:

- Extension tags, allowing you to creating your own formatting instructions
- Combining and overriding stylesheets
- Variables and parameters for passing values around the stylesheet
- Multiple source documents
- Additional functions

For more information, refer to the XSLT specification at http://www.w3.org/TR/xslt.

Further discussions of XSLT and its use from Delphi appear in Chapter 21—"Applying XSL Transformations" and Chapter 26—"Examination XML—Web Client."

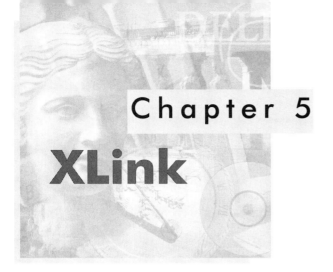

Chapter 5
XLink

XLink, which is part of the Extensible Linking Language (XLL), describes how documents can be linked to each other. Each link points to a resource through its URI (currently just a URL). The related specification, XPointer, defines how to reference parts within a document.

HTML already has linking elements such as the mainstay anchor tags, as well as images and objects. Why have a new specification that duplicates this? One reason is that the links in HTML are hard coded. Only an anchor tag provides a hypertext link to another document. You cannot add a link to another tag, such as a citation. Secondly, the links in HTML are only single links. What if you want to link to different versions of a document, perhaps in different languages, from the one reference? You cannot do this in HTML. Also, the links from HTML are one-way only, from your anchor to the related document. There is no way to create bi-directional links, especially if you do not control the resource at the other end.

XLL is designed to overcome these problems, and to provide an extensible way of describing and using links within a variety of documents. This technology is still being developed, and as yet there are no major implementations of it. Other than this brief introduction to XLink and XPointer, the topic is not covered further in this book.

XLink is defined in the document at http://www.w3.org/TR/xlink. As yet, the XLink specification is not finalized, so the following discussion is based on the Proposed Recommendation of December 20, 2000. The namespace declaration for XLink should be:

```
xmlns:xlink="http://www.w3.org/1999/xlink"
```

Although the defined prefix for XLink could be anything, it is customary to use "xlink." The examples throughout the rest of this chapter assume that the above namespace declaration has been made at an appropriate point earlier in their documents.

Link Definitions

Links are defined in terms of attributes that belong to the XLink namespace. These can then be added to elements in any XML document, with their meaning carrying over from XLink. Other attributes can happily co-exist with the XLink ones. However, all attributes must be properly declared in the DTD for a document to be valid.

The type of link is identified by the `xlink:type` attribute, which is the one XLink attribute that must be present. It must have one of the values shown in Table 5-1, with the associated meanings. Note that the DTD in which this attribute is declared need not provide for all of these types, but those allowed must come from this list. Links are often referred to based on their type, such as simple links and locator-type links. In each case this means the element to which the appropriate type attribute belongs.

Table 5-1: XLink link types

Type	Purpose
simple	An inline unidirectional link
extended	A link that includes other data
locator	A reference to a remote resource
arc	A connection between two resources
resource	A reference to a local resource
title	A human-readable label for a link
none	All XLink attributes are ignored in this element

The actual target of the link is specified in the `xlink:href` attribute, which must refer to a URI.

To define the purpose of the link, you use the `xlink:role` attribute. The role must be a qualified name as defined in some namespace that is in scope at the time of the definition. The `xlink:arcrole` attribute can be attached to arc-type elements, and is used to connect to an external repository of links.

A human-readable description of the link can be supplied with the `xlink:title` attribute. A link processor may display this value in help text, may create a table of links, or use it in whatever way seems appropriate.

The behavior of the link is established by the `xlink:show` and `xlink:actuate` attributes. `show` specifies where the content of the link appears. If it is not one of the values in Table 5-2, and not a recognized qualified name, then the behavior is treated as undefined.

Table 5-2: XLink show values

Type	Purpose
new	A new window is used to display the resource
replace	The resource replaces the current one
embed	The resource appears within the current resource
other	No XLink semantics apply, although other attributes should supply clues to its use
none	No XLink semantics apply, and no other attributes are available to assist

`actuate` defines when the link is activated. As for the previous attribute, it should be one of the values in Table 5-3 or a qualified name. Otherwise, the value is treated as undefined.

Table 5-3: XLink actuate values

Type	Purpose
onLoad	Load the resource immediately
onRequest	The resource is loaded in response to some external event, such as a mouse click
other	No XLink semantics apply, although other attributes should supply clues to its use
none	No XLink semantics apply, and no other attributes are available to assist

The `xlink:from` attribute is used in arc-type links to specify the starting point for the link. Similarly the `xlink:to` attribute indicates the resource to be loaded. The `xlink:label` attribute identifies the elements involved in the arc-type link.

Attributes from the XLink specification can be combined within an element as shown in Table 5-4.

Table 5-4: XLink attribute usage patterns

Attribute	Type					
	simple	extended	locator	arc	resource	title
type	Required	Required	Required	Required	Required	Required
href	Optional		Required			
role	Optional	Optional	Optional		Optional	
arcrole	Optional			Optional		
title	Optional	Optional	Optional	Optional	Optional	
show	Optional			Optional		
actuate	Optional			Optional		
label			Optional		Optional	
from				Optional		
to				Optional		

Simple Links

The links built into HTML, such as a and img, are simple links. They provide one-way inline links. Under XLink an anchor element's definition might appear like that in Listing 5-1. This encodes the current behavior of an anchor that specifies a simple unidirectional link that is activated when the user clicks on it, with the target resource replacing the current page.

Listing 5-1: HTML anchor as an XLink

```
<!ELEMENT a (...)*>
<!ATTLIST a
  xlink:type (simple) #FIXED "simple"
  xlink:href CDATA #REQUIRED
  xlink:title CDATA #IMPLIED
  xlink:show (replace) #FIXED "replace"
  xlink:actuate (onRequest) #FIXED "onRequest">
```

An actual anchor would then look like this:

```
<a xlink:href="http://www.dest.com/newpage.html" xlink:title="A simple link">Link from
here</a>
```

Similarly, an image element's definition might be like the one in Listing 5-2. As before, it is a simple unidirectional link, but it loads immediately and appears within the original document. Note that you can still have `height` and `width` attributes that are unrelated to the XLink mechanism.

Listing 5-2: HTML image as an XLink

```
<!ELEMENT img EMPTY>
<!ATTLIST img
  width CDATA #IMPLIED
  height CDATA #IMPLIED
  xlink:type (simple) #FIXED "simple"
  xlink:href CDATA #REQUIRED
  xlink:title CDATA #IMPLIED
  xlink:show (embed) #FIXED "embed"
  xlink:actuate (onLoad) #FIXED "onLoad">
```

An image element could then be declared as:

```
<img xlink:href="http://www.dest.com/picture.jpeg" xlink:title="A lovely picture" width="100"
height="100"/>
```

These attributes can be applied to any element in any XML document to implement a linking mechanism with defined semantics. You are not restricted to certain elements as you are with HTML. Simple-type linking elements have no XLink defined child elements. Everything they require is specified in the attributes. To take advantage of the main benefits of XLink, you need to use an extended-type link instead.

Extended Links

Going beyond the simple links that you are used to from HTML, extended links allow you to specify multidirectional links, multiple titles, and even out-of-line links.

An extended link is really a container element for a number of other XLink enhanced elements. Within this container can appear locator-type and resource-type elements that identify the remote or local resources involved in the links. A set of arc-type elements then defines the traversal paths from one resource to another. Note that arcs are one-way only. To allow bi-directional traversal you need to specify both directions separately.

Multiple titles can also appear within an extended link element. These are useful when different versions of the title are supplied, such as in different languages, or when the title itself contains other markup.

As an example, you could set up links to a series of related films using an extended link, as shown in Listing 5-3. A browser might, when the user clicks on the linking text, pop up a menu showing the titles of all the related links, allowing the user to select one to view.

Part I: Introduction to XML

Listing 5-3: An extended link

```
The <movie-series>Star Wars series
<movie xlink:href="http://www.starwars.com/episode-i"
  xlink:title="The Phantom Menace"/>
<movie xlink:href="http://www.starwars.com/episode-iv"
  xlink:title="A New Hope"/>
<movie xlink:href="http://www.starwars.com/episode-v"
  xlink:title="The Empire Strikes Back"/>
<movie xlink:href="http://www.starwars.com/episode-vi"
  xlink:title="Return of the Jedi"/>
<linkto xlink:from="movie-series" xlink:to="movie"/>
</movie-series> continually expands the possibilities
of special effects.
```

The DTD for these elements may look like the one in Listing 5-4. Here the movie-series element is the extended link container (using a fixed attribute). Within it can appear text that is displayed as part of the normal content of this document.

Listing 5-4: Extended link elements DTD

```
<!ELEMENT movie-series (#PCDATA | movie | linkto)*>
<!ATTLIST movie-series
  xlink:type (extended) #FIXED "extended"
  xlink:role CDATA #FIXED "http://www.movies.com/movie-series"
  xlink:title CDATA #IMPLIED
  xlink:label NMTOKEN #FIXED "movie-series">
<!ELEMENT movie EMPTY>
<!ATTLIST movie
  xlink:type (locator) #FIXED locator"
  xlink:href CDATA #REQUIRED
  xlink:role CDATA #FIXED "http://www.movies.com/movie"
  xlink:title CDATA #IMPLIED
  xlink:label NMTOKEN #FIXED "movie">
<!ELEMENT linkto EMPTY>
<!ATTLIST linkto
  xlink:type (arc) #FIXED "arc"
  xlink:from NMTOKEN #IMPLIED
  xlink:to NMTOKEN #IMPLIED
  xlink:show (new) #FIXED "new"
  xlink:actuate (onRequest) #FIXED "onRequest">
```

The links are identified through the movie elements, each of which points to a remote resource and has an associated title. Finally, the navigation is specified by the linkto element, which allows you to nominate the starting and ending points for the links from among the listed resources. The links are activated only when initiated by the user, and then produce a new window showing the selected resource. As seen in the XML fragment in Listing 5-3 and the DTD in Listing 5-4, the values for the from and to attributes are taken from the labels of the other elements. If either or both of these attributes is omitted, it instead refers to all elements within the extended link.

Out-of-Line Links

In some cases the resource that serves as the starting point for a link cannot be updated to include the linking information. This may be because the document is not under your control, because it is too expensive to modify and maintain such links inline, or because the resource is in another format altogether.

Even so, you want to be able to provide links to and from such a resource. Out-of-line links are the answer. Such links exist in a document separate from the resources referred to—all the resources for the links are remote. Out-of-line links are always extended links, with locator-type elements to identify the resources and arc-type links to define paths between them.

Additional data can be associated with a set of links, simply by defining appropriate elements within the external link set.

For example, movie-related resources, typically under someone else's control, could be linked with out-of-line links, producing a document similar to that shown in Listing 5-5.

Listing 5-5: Out-of-line links

```
<movie-links>
  <clip xlink:href="http://www.movie-studio.com/blockbuster.avi"
    xlink:title="Blockbuster Trailer"/>
  <script xlink:href="http://www.movie-studio.com/blockbuster.rtf"
    xlink:title="Script for Blockbuster"/>
  <review xlink:href="http://www.reviews.net/reviews?film=blockbuster"
    xlink:title="Reviews of Blockbuster"/>
  <go/>
</movie-links>
```

Since these links are not directly available within the resources to which they refer, there needs to be some mechanism for finding them when browsing such resources. The establishment of link databases is an area of active work in this field and awaits further development.

Summary

XLink is part of the Extensible Linking Language, providing an extensible way to specify links between two or more resources. It does this through the definition of a number of attributes, and their associated semantics, which can be attached to any XML element.

As of yet, the XLink specification is not finalized, and no implementations are widely available to work with these links.

XLink allows you to refer to another resource in a consistent manner. To delve into that resource and pick out individual parts of it, you can use XPointer as described in the next chapter.

Chapter 6
XPath and XPointer

XPointer is the other part of the Extensible Linking Language (XLL), along with XLink. Whereas XLink gets you to another document, XPointer allows you to refer to locations, or ranges of items, within that document.

Again, why duplicate something that already exists in HTML? Currently, you can add an internal location to a URL following a hash sign (#) which typically results in the document being opened and positioned at this point. But what if the spot you wanted to reference does not have a named anchor? If you do not control that document, you cannot just go in and add one. Also, these locations only refer to a single spot within the target document. There is no way of referencing a range of paragraphs, or an entire table.

XPointer is designed to provide these abilities and more. Its specification is available on the accompanying CD-ROM or at http://www.w3.org/TR/xptr. Like XLink, the XPointer specification is not finalized, so the following discussion is based on the Last Call Working Draft of the spec (January 8, 2001).

XPointer is built upon the XML Path Language (XPath), which is also used in XSL Transformations. To this it adds the ability to refer to points (locations between nodes and/or characters) and ranges of nodes, rather than just a single node. It can also find information through string matching. It is used with XLink to provide finer granularity in identifying resources of interest. As such, it only works with XML documents and fragments, not with other types of documents that may be referenced.

XPath is a W3C Recommendation as of November 16, 1999. This specification is also on the CD-ROM, while the online version is found at http://www.w3.org/TR/xpath.

General Form

XPointer references select a part or parts of an XML document by operating on the tree structure that represents it. Selection is done through axes, predicates, and functions. An *axis* defines a set of candidates that are found within the tree. *Predicates* then test those candidates for further processing. And finally, *functions* can operate on the results to transform them or to generate new candidates. For example, you may look at all the child nodes of a particular node (the axis), using only those that have a particular attribute value (the predicate), and then retrieve their first child (the function).

XPointer identifiers have a long form spelled out in the specification, as well as a short form. The two forms are identical as far as their processing is concerned. For example, to find a node with a particular id value you could use the long form:

```
#xpointer(id("SW1"))
```

which can be shortened to:

```
#SW1
```

Note that this latter format matches the existing HTML equivalent of internal references. The intention of the short form is to encourage the use of IDs within documents, as well as to provide compatibility with HTML sections embedded in XML documents.

The xpointer reference identifies the scheme to be used (similar to a namespace). Currently, this is the only scheme defined and it is assumed if omitted.

Another shorthand form provides access down through the hierarchy by referring to a node's position within its parent. The start of the sequence is a node identified by an ID reference as shown above, or by the string /1 which refers to the document element. Following this is a list of integers separated by slashes (/) indicating the required child element's position at each level. Only elements can be referenced in this manner. For example, the following sequence refers to the director element for "Star Wars" in the movie-watcher document.

```
/1/1/2/3
```

NOTE Using indexes to locate particular elements requires a detailed knowledge of the document and thus is very fragile. A simple change to the structure can render it useless. For this reason, the use of IDs is much preferred.

Axes

In general a location reference is made up of an axis, followed by ::, a node name, and any number of predicates within square brackets ([ ]). A string of such references can be concatenated with slashes (/) to further refine or expand the selection. The reference starts from the current context, either the root of an identified document, or a node selected in some previous manner.

An axis defines the collection of nodes, with respect to the current location, that is considered in determining the actual selection. As can be seen from the possibilities in Table 6-1, the axes refer to the hierarchical structure of the tree that represents an XML document. If no axis is specified, it defaults to child.

Table 6-1: XPointer axes

Name	Purpose
child	Locates direct children of the current node (includes text, processing instructions, and comments, but not attributes)
descendant	Locates all nodes contained within the current node

Name	Purpose
descendant-or-self	Like descendant plus the current node itself
parent	Locates the node that contains the current one
ancestor	Collects all the nodes in the parent chain
ancestor-or-self	Like ancestor plus the current node itself
preceding-sibling	Locates nodes with the same parent but appearing before the current node within that parent
following-sibling	Locates nodes with the same parent but appearing after the current node within that parent
preceding	Collects all nodes before the current one within the entire document, including all ancestors
following	Collects all nodes after the current one within the entire document, excluding all ancestors
self	The current node
attribute	The attributes of the current node
namespace	The namespace nodes of the current node (empty if the current node is not an element)

The node name following the axis specifier serves to identify which types of nodes from it are selected. As well as a literal element name, such as `movie`, you can use an asterisk (`*`) for any node, or a function to identify the type of node, like `comment()`.

Predicates

Once the collection of potential candidate nodes is selected, the use of predicates prunes it further. A *predicate* is a simple Boolean test, with the node being retained when it evaluates to true. The predicate expression is evaluated in the context of each candidate node. These tests appear within square brackets (`[ ]`) following the axis and node name. Multiple tests can be combined with `or` or `and` to derive the final result.

If the test expression evaluates to a number, it is tested against the candidate node's position, returning true if it is equal. Results other than numbers and Boolean values have an implicit call to the boolean function to convert them into a usable format.

When testing for position, the current node is used as the reference point with candidate nodes starting at position one. Note that the order of nodes within an axis depends on its type. The `ancestor`, `ancestor-or-self`, `preceding`, and `preceding-sibling` axes are known as reverse axes, with their nodes placed in the reverse order of their appearance within the document. All other axes are forward ones, having nodes in the same order as the document.

Locations

XPointer extends XPath to provide support for locations that are partial nodes or a range of nodes. The new locations are defined to be a point, a range, or an XPath node.

Points are positions between characters within the document. A reference to a container node and a non-negative offset from its beginning identify the point. Since points have no content, they also have no string value. Points come in two versions: *node points* in container nodes that have children (indicating positions between those nodes) and *character points* in containers without child nodes (denoting positions between characters).

Ranges are defined by two points and consist of all the content and XML structure between them. It is possible for nodes to be only partially included in a range. If the starting and ending points of a range are the same, it is said to be a *collapsed* range. To describe a range as an XPointer expression, just identify the two delimiting points and join them with the `range-to` function.

Functions

Several core functions are defined as part of XPath. Use these and the ones specifically from XPointer within expressions to find just the right items. The signatures in Table 6-2 show the function's return type, followed by its name and the types of any parameters. A trailing question mark (?) denotes an optional argument, while an asterisk (*) indicates a repeatable argument. In each case the context node is the candidate node found by a previous axis and node test.

Table 6-2: XPath functions

Function	Purpose
number position()	Retrieve the node's position within the evaluation context starting at one.
number last()	Get the number of items in the evaluation context.
number count(node-set)	Returns the number of nodes in the supplied node-set.
node-set id(object)	Obtain the node(s) with the specified ID(s).
string name(node-set?)	Returns the qualified name of the first node, in document order, from the supplied set. If no parameter is provided, it operates on the context node instead.
string namespace-uri(node-set?)	Similarly, you can obtain the namespace URI of the first node in the set, or from the context node.
string local-name(node-set?)	Completing the set, retrieve the local name of the context node or the first node in the supplied set.
string string(object?)	Convert the supplied object to a string value. For a node-set, this returns the string value of its first node in document order. It operates on the context node if no parameter is given.
string concat(string, string, string*)	Provides the concatenation of all its string arguments.

Function	Purpose
boolean starts-with(string, string)	Returns true if the first string starts with the second string, and false otherwise.
boolean contains(string, string)	Returns true if the first string contains the second string, and false otherwise.
string substring-before(string, string)	Retrieve the substring of the first argument that precedes the first occurrence of the second argument, or an empty string if the second argument does not appear at all.
string substring-after(string, string)	Conversely, get the following substring with this function.
string substring(string, number, number?)	Extract the substring from the supplied value that extends from the first numeric argument (starting at one) for the number of characters equal to the second argument. If the latter is omitted, it extends through to the end of the original string.
number string-length(string?)	Obtain the length of the supplied string, or the context node's string value if no parameter is passed.
string normalize-space(string)	Normalizes white space in the given string (or the context node if none is supplied) and returns the result.
string translate(string, string, string)	Returns the first parameter, with occurrences of characters from the second parameter replaced by the corresponding characters (by position) from the third parameter.
boolean boolean(object)	Convert the given object to a Boolean value. A number is true if it is neither positive or negative zero, nor NaN (not a number). A node-set is true if it is non-empty. A string is true if its length is greater than zero.
boolean not(boolean)	Negates the supplied value.
boolean true()	Returns the corresponding Boolean value.
boolean false()	Returns the corresponding Boolean value.
boolean lang(string)	Test whether the context node's language (based on the xml:lang attribute) is the same as or a sub-language of the supplied value.
number number(object?)	Convert the supplied value, or the context node if none present, to a number. A Boolean true returns 1, while false returns 0. Node-sets operate on the string value of the first node.
number sum(node-set)	Sum the values from the node-set after converting their string values to numbers.
number floor(number)	Returns the largest integer not greater than the supplied value.
number ceiling(number)	Conversely, this returns the smallest integer not less than the value.

Function	Purpose
number round(number)	Returns the closest integer to the given value, with halves rounding up.

The following functions are extensions defined in the XPointer specification.

Table 6-3: XPointer functions

Function	Purpose
location-set here()	Obtain the element node that directly contains the XPointer being evaluated.
location-set origin()	Used in conjunction with out-of-line links, this returns the element from which the link traversal began.
location-set range-to(location-set)	Returns ranges extending from the start-point of the current context to the ends of each of the locations in the supplied set.
location-set range(location-set)	Returns ranges covering the locations in the supplied set.
location-set range-inside(location-set)	Returns ranges covering the contents of the locations in the supplied set.
location-set start-point(location-set)	Retrieves the starting points of the supplied locations as a set.
location-set end-point(location-set)	Retrieves the ending points of the given locations.
location-set string-range(location-set, string, number?, number?)	From the supplied location-set, search for occurrences of the given string and return these as the result. The third argument specifies the offset from the start of the string to match to become the first position in any result, while the last parameter provides the number of characters from that point to include in the return values.

Abbreviated Syntax

Several forms of abbreviated syntax are defined in the XPath specification. These are shown in Table 6-4.

Table 6-4: XPath abbreviations

Shorthand	Full Version	Meaning
xxx	child::xxx	The child element xxx
//	/descendant-or-self::node()/	Any descendant
.	self::node()	The current node
..	parent::node()	The parent node
@	attribute::	An attribute
[n]	[position()=n]	The nth item

Samples

Example paths from the movie-watcher document are shown in Table 6-5. Recall that all are based from the current context node, which has been selected in some other manner. These would probably be used within an XSLT document to select nodes for transformation (see Chapter 4).

Table 6-5: Sample paths

XPath	Retrieves (from the context node)
/	The root node of the XML document
*	All the element children
.	The context node itself
movie	All movie element children
director|star	All director or star child elements
//movie/name	Any name element with a movie element parent
//movies//name	Any name element with a movies element ancestor
text()	All text node children
node()	All child nodes other than attributes
id("SW1")	The element with SW1 as its unique ID
star[1]	The first star child element
star[last()=1]	The star element that is the only child
@url	The url attribute
@*	All attributes
movie[@rating="PG"]	All movie element children that have a rating attribute of PG
//screening[@movie-id=context()/@id]	The screening element whose movie-id attribute is equal to the current node's ID
id(@cinema-id)/name	The name child of the element with an ID equal to the cinema-id attribute of the current node (presumably a screening)

Table 6-6 shows example pointers for the movie-watcher documents. References would likely be used in conjunction with an XLink to identify a portion of a resource. Thus they would be of the form:

```
xlink:href="http://www.movies-online.com/current.xml#xpointer(…)"
```

where the ellipsis is replaced by one of the terms from the table.

Table 6-6: Sample pointers

XPointer	Identifies
`id("SW1")`	The element with SW1 as its unique ID
`descendant::movie[rating="G"]`	All movie elements with a rating of G
`//cinema[2]/name`	The name of the second cinema element
`//text()`	All text nodes in the document
`id("SW1")//star[1]/range-to (following-sibling::star[1])`	The first two stars for the element with an ID of SW1
`id("ENT")/start-point(range-inside (synopsis))/range-to(string-range (synopsis, "."))[1])`	The first sentence (up to a period) of the synopsis for the element with the ID ENT

Summary

XPointer is complementary to XLink, providing for the identification of a resource to continue down into a document to individual nodes or ranges of nodes. It is based on the XPath specification that is also used in XSL Transformations for selecting nodes, and is designed to work only with XML documents.

While XPath is a W3C Recommendation, the XPointer specification is still in draft, and no commercial products are using it yet. Examples of XPath usage appear in Chapter 21, which looks at using XSL Transformations for formatting XML documents, and in Chapter 26, which uses XSLT.

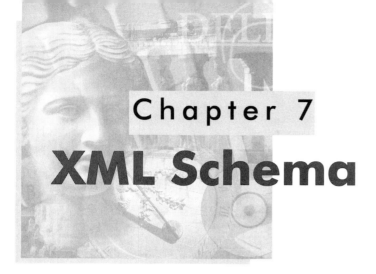

Chapter 7
XML Schema

In Chapter 3 you saw how document type definitions (DTDs) are constructed. These let you spell out what constitutes a valid document for a particular application. You specify each element that may appear within the document. A content model in each declaration defines what may be contained within that element—other elements, text, a combination, or nothing. The multiplicity of each sub-element forms part of that model. Each element also describes the attributes that it may use. Attributes declare a type and have an indication of whether or not they are required.

Together these declarations define what elements may appear and how they are structured within a document that claims conformance to the DTD. Some control over their number and content is provided.

Unfortunately, DTDs fall short in some areas. You have no control over the textual content of an element—it is just text. If you want to have a field that should contain a numeric value, or one that holds a date, then the best that you can do is to add some comments to the DTD to state this intention, and leave it to an application that knows about these documents to enforce those rules. However, the documents could also be written or updated by hand or through a generic XML editor that knows nothing about these requirements. The result is that your documents are not as standard as you would like.

Although DTDs allow you to specify the multiplicity of a sub-element within a content model, this specification is fairly basic. You either have one or none of an element, or many of them. There is no (easy) way to indicate exact numbers of occurrences that are required, such as an element having two to four repeats of a particular sub-element.

NOTE You can achieve the desired outcome of explicit numbers of sub-elements through laying out all the possible combinations as separate content models and then stringing them together as alternatives. However, this can produce a non-deterministic content model—one that cannot tell which option is being used without looking ahead—that may be rejected by some XML processors.

Furthermore, the format for DTDs is quite different from the rest of an XML document. This means that additional complexity and functionality must be built into processors to deal with this variation. Viewing and editing a DTD may require an alternate package to that for the documents that conform to it.

In an effort to overcome these problems, an alternative manner of defining the valid contents of XML documents was defined. Known as XML Schema, it lets you declare the types for the content of text nodes. It also enables you to specify the number, or range of numbers, of times that a sub-element must appear. And lastly, it is itself an XML application, meaning that the same tools can be used to define a document and then to populate it correctly.

The XML Schema specification comes in two parts: the definition of structures for declaring content models and the definition of data types for elements and attributes. Both parts are W3C Recommendations as of May 2, 2001.

NOTE Microsoft has developed and supports a similar standard called XML Data Reduced. This is a subset of the XML Data proposal that was presented to the W3C, and which contributed to the development of XML Schema. There are several differences to the W3C specification. For further information, see http://msdn.microsoft.com/xml.

Schema Document

An XML Schema document is itself an XML document. It must follow the standard for schemas if it is to be considered valid. Hence, there is an XML Schema that defines the layout for XML Schemas available at http://www.w3.org/2000/10/XMLSchema.xsd. A second schema defines the standard data types at http://www.w3.org/2000/10/XMLSchema-datatypes.xsd. (There are also DTD versions of each of these for those on the fence. They are available at http://www.w3.org/2000/10/XMLSchema.dtd and http://www.w3.org/2000/10/datatypes.dtd.)

The meta-XML Schema states that a schema contains a `schema` element at its topmost level. Attributes of this element declare the version of XML Schema being followed and the namespace associated with documents that claim conformance to this new schema. An example of a schema declaration is shown in Listing 7-1. Here you also see the reference to the DTD, so that the schema can be validated, and the definition of the default namespace for schema elements themselves.

Listing 7-1: An XML Schema skeleton

```
<?xml version="1.0" encoding="UTF-8"?>
<!DOCTYPE schema PUBLIC "-//W3C//DTD XMLSCHEMA 200010//EN"
  "http://www.w3.org/2000/10/XMLSchema.dtd" [
<schema xmlns="http://www.w3.org/2000/10/XMLSchema"
    targetNamespace="urn:kbwood/movie-watcher" version="1.0">
    :
</schema>
```

Within the `schema` element appear further tags that provide documentation on the schema, declarations of types of element content, and the definitions of the elements and attributes themselves.

Schemas usually exist in files of their own to allow them to be shared between conforming documents. Such files typically have an `.xsd` suffix. The standard prefix for schema tags is `xs` and its corresponding namespace URI is `http://www.w3.org/2000/10/XMLSchema`. In Listing 7-1 the default namespace for the document is set to this value, meaning that you do not have to supply a prefix for each element.

To attach a schema to an XML document so that it can be validated, you add an attribute to its document element. This attribute comes from another namespace related to XML Schemas (XMLSchema-instance) which must first be defined within a namespace attribute (xmlns). By convention, the xsi prefix is used for instance declarations, with the attribute name being schemaLocation if the XML document has a target namespace, or noNamespaceSchemaLocation if it has no target namespace. For the movie-watcher documents, the schema reference may look like the following:

```
<movie-watcher xmlns:xsi="http://www.w3.org/2000/10/XMLSchema-instance"
    xsi:noNamespaceSchemaLocation="movie-watcher.xsd">
  :
</movie-watcher>
```

Documentation

Although normal XML comments can be used to document the schema, another method is available that promotes the reuse of the embedded descriptions. The annotation element can appear at the beginning of most schema elements and anywhere at the top level of the schema. An annotation consists of either or both of the documentation or appinfo elements, each of which contains text and possibly other tags. The former is intended for human consumption, while the latter is for automated processing. An example is shown in Listing 7-2. This appears following the opening schema tag defined above.

Listing 7-2: Embedded documentation

```
<annotation>
  <documentation>
    Movie-watcher schema.
    Data about movies and when and where they are showing.
    Written by Keith Wood, 7 August, 2000.
  </documentation>
</annotation>
```

Simple Types

The definition of the parts of the document starts at the most basic level with simple types. These are the fundamental types present in most programming languages and database systems. They include the usual string, boolean, integer, long, short, float (32-bit), double (64-bit), date, and time formats all expressed as straight text. Variations on these are available, such as positiveInteger, unsignedLong, month, year, and century. More exotic formats also exist, like recurringDate, recurringDay, timeDuration, and uriReference.

The standard XML attribute types from the DTD specification can be used as well, including ID, IDREF, ENTITY, NOTATION, and NMTOKEN. New types are introduced to cover other XML formats, such as Name, QName (a qualified name), NCName (a QName without the prefix or colon), and language.

All these types are built into the schema specification. From them you can derive additional simple types by applying constraints or *facets*. For example, the `minInclusive` and `maxInclusive` facets let you restrict valid values to a given range. The `pattern` facet provides a regular expression that defines the layout of the expected values, while the `enumeration` facet lists individual values that are allowed. A total of 15 facets are defined in the specification, although not all of these pertain to all base types.

To apply facets to a type you include a `simpleType` element in your schema, with an embedded `restriction` element and its `base` attribute indicating the fundamental type being constrained. If you wish to refer to this type from elsewhere in the document, you must set its name attribute. The alternative is to declare it directly within the item to which it applies using an anonymous `simpleType` element. Within the `restriction` element you list the facets and their values. Listing 7-3 shows an enumerated type to be used for the `rating` attribute in the movie-watcher documents.

Listing 7-3: Enumerating a simple type

```
<simpleType>
  <restriction base="string">
    <enumeration value="NR"/>
    <enumeration value="G"/>
    <enumeration value="PG"/>
    <enumeration value="PG-13"/>
    <enumeration value="R"/>
  </restriction>
</simpleType>
```

Complex Types

More involved types are built from the simple types defined above. As before, these types can be defined at the top level of the schema and given a name. The declarations that rely on these types then refer to them by name. In this way, types can be reused within, and even between, documents. Alternately, anonymous complex types can be declared directly within the elements to which they apply.

Content models are one of the main uses for complex types, since simple types do not have any children. An example of this for the content of the `movie-watcher` element is shown in Listing 7-4, along with samples for the following descriptions. Elements may be declared inline or may reference a declaration defined elsewhere as illustrated here.

Listing 7-4: Building more complex types

```
<complexType>
  <sequence>
    <element ref="movies"/>
    <element ref="cinemas"/>
    <element ref="screenings"/>
  </sequence>
</complexType>
<complexType mixed="true">
  <choice minOccurs="0" maxOccurs="unbounded">
    <element name="emph" type="string"/>
```

```
        </choice>
    </complexType>
```

Various other schema tags let you build more elaborate content models. The `choice` element surrounds a list of other elements from which you may select only one, whereas the `sequence` element specifies that its constituent elements must appear in the listed order. Use the `group` element to collect child elements together for treatment as a single entity.

Alternately, the `all` element says that its contained elements may appear once or not at all, but may do so in any order. This can only be applied to the top-level element in the schema and all of its children must be individual elements. One last option places no restriction on the element types that can appear. The `any` element has no children itself, but permits any type of child element within the document. A namespace can be applied to the any element to limit the valid elements.

Mixed content, a combination of normal text and other elements, is denoted by the presence of the `mixed` attribute on the type declaration with a value of `True`. The order and number of tags appearing in the document must match what is defined in the type declaration. This is different from DTDs, which place no restrictions on embedded tags, other than limiting their types.

Each element or model tag may have its cardinality specified through the `minOccurs` and `maxOccurs` attributes. Both are optional and default to one. The minimum must be a non-negative value, while the maximum must be a greater value or unbounded.

Simple types cannot have attributes. So, whenever an element has an attribute, you must declare a complex type to define it. Within the type tag you list the allowed attributes, giving their name, type, and any other characteristics. The example in Listing 7-5 shows the type for the `session` element in a movie-watcher document. Note that the base content of the type for the element is defined as a `time` value, which is then extended by adding an attribute that refers back to the ID of another element.

Listing 7-5: Adding attributes to an element

```
<complexType>
  <simpleContent>
    <extension base="time">
      <attribute name="price-id" type="IDREF" use="required"/>
    </extension>
  </simpleContent>
</complexType>
```

Complex types let you combine element and attribute declarations within the one definition if it is appropriate. They may be embedded within each other to construct whatever hierarchy is required. Types can also inherit from other complex types and extend or restrict that previous definition.

To define an empty type, you basically declare a complex type that only allows elements as its content and then provide no elements. This works because a complex type without any content specification automatically derives from `anyType`, which allows only elements. The following is shorthand for an empty element without any attributes.

```
<complexType/>
```

If you want no content but do want attributes, just expand this to encapsulate them.

```
<complexType>
  <attribute name="id" type="ID" use="required"/>
</complexType>
```

Attribute Declarations

Now that you have the types laid out, you can apply them to elements and attributes within the schema. To declare an attribute for an element, you need to define a complex type for that element. At the end of the type definition you use the `attribute` tag to specify the attribute itself.

Along with the attribute name you supply its type, which is either one of the predefined basic types or a user-defined extension or restriction of one of them. Optionally, you can also include usage information (`optional` (the default), `required`, `prohibited`, `default`, or `fixed`) and any default or fixed value. Attribute tags may contain a `simpleType` element that defines further facets of the type of data allowed within them.

Listing 7-6 shows two attributes with types corresponding to those available in DTDs. It also includes the `rating` attribute, which uses an anonymous enumeration based on string values for its type.

Listing 7-6: Defining attributes

```
<attribute name="id" type="ID" use="required"/>
<attribute name="logo-url" type="ENTITY"/>
<attribute name="rating" use="required">
  <simpleType>
    <restriction base="string">
      <enumeration value="NR"/>
      <enumeration value="G"/>
      <enumeration value="PG"/>
      <enumeration value="PG-13"/>
      <enumeration value="R"/>
    </restriction>
  </simpleType>
</attribute>
```

Attribute groups let you collect attributes together and manage them as one unit. The `attributeGroup` tag contains a list of the individual attributes, as they would appear within a normal type declaration. See Listing 7-7 for an example.

Listing 7-7: Grouping attributes for ease of reuse

```
<attributeGroup name="commonAttrs">
  <annotation>
    <documentation>
      Attributes common to both movies and cinemas
    </documentation>
  </annotation>
  <attribute name="id" type="ID" use="required"/>
  <attribute name="logo-url" type="ENTITY"/>
  <attribute name="url" type="ENTITY"/>
</attributeGroup>
```

A name serves to identify the group and is used to refer to it from the element definitions that actually have these attributes. In this way, the group can appear in several declarations, providing for its reuse similar to parameter entities within DTDs. This aids in the maintainability of the schema. Groups can also be used to improve the readability of the document by extracting the attributes from the element definitions.

Element Declarations

Whereas in DTDs the textual content of elements cannot be constrained (other than through comments in the DTD itself), in schemas you can apply any of the simple predefined or user-defined types to an element. Thus, you can state that an element should only contain a number or a date. Just specify the required format in the type attribute of the element tag. You must supply a name for each element and may also provide additional facets to control its appearance within a document, such as it cannot be longer than 10 characters.

Listing 7-8 shows a selection of simple element declarations. These range from a simple string element (the only option for a DTD specification), through an optional positive integer, an optional string, and an optional decimal value, to one that requires a date as its content.

Listing 7-8: Simple element definitions

```
<element name="name" type="string"/>
<element name="length" type="positiveInteger" minOccurs="0">
<element name="directions" type="string" minOccurs="0"/>
<element name="discount" type="decimal" minOccurs="0"/>
<element name="start-date" type="date"/>
```

For content other than straight text, you create an element with a complex type. This can be defined inline as an anonymous type, which is useful for one-off combinations, or as a separate named type definition that is referred to by the element. The latter option lets you reuse that element as part of another's content throughout the schema.

As described earlier, the element can use the sequence, choice, group, any, and all tags to define its internal structure. Each child may occur as an inline named element, as an element with its own embedded structure, or as a reference to an element defined elsewhere. Any attributes, either as individual entries or as references to previously defined groups, must appear at the end of the type definition.

Listing 7-9 shows the definition for the movie element from the movie-watcher documents, along with all of its children. It makes use of an anonymous type definition for the movie itself since its composition is unique. Within that definition appear both inline child declarations as well as references to other elements. These are declared externally to promote their reuse or to define their own internal structure without cluttering up the current definition.

Listing 7-9: Elements with content other than text

```
<element name="movie">
  <annotation>
    <documentation>Details about a single movie</documentation>
  </annotation>
  <complexType>
```

```
    <sequence>
      <element ref="name"/>
      <element name="length" type="positiveInteger" minOccurs="0">
        <annotation>
          <documentation>Length of movie in minutes</documentation>
        </annotation>
      </element>
      <element name="director" type="string" minOccurs="0"/>
      <element ref="starring" minOccurs="0"/>
      <element ref="synopsis" minOccurs="0"/>
    </sequence>
    <attributeGroup ref="commonAttrs"/>
    <attribute name="rating" use="required">
      <simpleType>
        <restriction base="string">
          <enumeration value="NR"/>
          <enumeration value="G"/>
          <enumeration value="PG"/>
          <enumeration value="PG-13"/>
          <enumeration value="R"/>
        </restriction>
      </simpleType>
    </attribute>
  </complexType>
</element>

<element name="name" type="string"/>
<element name="starring">
  <complexType>
    <sequence>
      <element name="star" type="string"
        minOccurs="1" maxOccurs="unbounded"/>
    </sequence>
  </complexType>
</element>
<element name="synopsis">
  <complexType mixed="true">
    <choice minOccurs="0" maxOccurs="unbounded">
      <element name="emph" type="string"/>
    </choice>
  </complexType>
</element>
```

The attributes for the `movie` element also reuse external items through the `commonAttrs` group. Since the `rating` attribute only appears in this element, it is defined inline.

Further Abilities of Schemas

The schema specification includes much more than is shown in this chapter. It also provides a section on how namespaces affect and interact with a schema definition. All schema documents have a W3C namespace that defines the tags described above, while the document being declared has its own target namespace.

Type definitions can be constructed in a hierarchical fashion, inheriting content from earlier types and then extending or restricting it. Mechanisms exist to limit what can be altered in a derived declaration, along with descriptions of how changes in the new type interact with those of the parent.

Types can be declared to be equivalent to each other at the top level of the schema via the `substitutionGroup` attribute. Referring to the group class in a content model allows any of these related classes to appear in that position.

Schemas expand on the notion of IDs and IDREFs from the DTD specification by letting you define unique attributes (and even content or combinations of these) throughout the entire document or within given elements. Declaring these items as a key indicates that they must always be present, non-null, and unique.

Several additional content particles exist to allow for the inclusion of any child element while restricting it to a particular namespace or to a namespace other than the current one. Attributes can be similarly constrained.

The datatypes section of the specification goes into great detail about types in general, defining, among other things, their *value spaces* (the actual values, such as 100) as opposed to their *lexical spaces* (the representation of that value, like 100, 1E2, or 100.00). It describes the generic facets that can be applied to the types to constrain their sets of valid values. Each basic datatype is then examined in turn, explaining how these aspects affect them.

Summary

XML Schemas provide an alternative to DTDs for the definition of the valid contents of an XML document. They provide additional functionality over DTDs including type declarations for text content and attribute values, and greater specificity for the number of occurrences of a sub-element. Moreover, one of their biggest advantages is that XML Schemas are defined as XML documents, allowing you to use the same tools for defining the schema as you do for populating documents that conform to it.

The first part of the specification tells you how to define types that can be applied to elements and attributes within a document. Then you apply those types to individual elements while laying out the valid content for each one. Simple types include straight text and numbers, while complex types let you build complicated combinations of sub-elements and attributes.

The second part of the specification details how data types are declared. The basic types are defined within the spec, and these can be extended, restricted, and combined to create new types.

Unfortunately, XML Schema is still only a Candidate Recommendation from the W3C, and so is not widely used yet to validate documents. This situation should change as the benefits of XML Schema over DTDs become more apparent.

Part II
The Document Object Model

Parsing a document involves reading it in, interpreting its structure, and then using the results in an application to provide some useful functionality. XML's simple hierarchical structure was designed to facilitate the parsing of documents by such programs, as well as to ease the processing of the resulting output.

Two main approaches to parsing XML have arisen. The first is the Document Object Model (DOM), which constructs a series of related objects in memory that corresponds to the structure and content of the original document. The second is the Simple API for XML (SAX) that offers an event-based approach, triggering actions as each element or section of content is encountered.

This section looks in detail at the DOM. Chapter 8 describes the DOM specification as presented by the W3C, including some of the enhancements appearing in the second version of this spec. Chapter 9 details Microsoft's implementation of the DOM as COM interfaces. Version 3 of their XML DOM package comes as a set of three DLLs, which can be easily used from Delphi through an imported type library.

Chapter 10 examines a native Delphi implementation of the DOM as produced by CUESoft.com Inc. This commercial product offers tighter integration with your application due to its Delphi source. Chapter 11 describes another native Delphi DOM implementation, this one an open source offering from the Open XML project called XDOM. Again, you have a DOM that compiles into your code, but this time you also have access to the source. XDOM provides extensive support for modeling the DTD section of an XML document, something the other DOMs bypass (as does the DOM specification).

Chapter 8: The Document Object Model (DOM)
Chapter 9: Microsoft's Document Object Model
Chapter 10: CUESoft's Document Object Model
Chapter 11: Open XML's Document Object Model

Chapter 8
The Document Object Model (DOM)

The Document Object Model constructs a hierarchy of objects in memory that represents an XML document. Reasons for developing the DOM include a desire to define a platform- and language-neutral interface that allows applications to access and manipulate the content, style, and structure of a document. It is a recommendation of the W3C, with the latest version being available at http://www.w3.org/DOM.

Version 1 of the DOM became a W3C Recommendation on October 1, 1998. It defined the basic requirements for representing the object model, and appears in two parts. The first part is the core of the DOM and provides sufficient functionality to work with structured documents in general and XML documents in particular. Part 2 extends the core to provide additional abilities suitable for manipulating HTML documents. Version 2 became a Recommendation on November 13, 2000 (except for the HTML section that reverted to being a Working Draft). It primarily adds support for namespaces, as well as methods for creating documents themselves.

DOM Interfaces

The DOM is specified as a series of interfaces, allowing it to be implemented in various ways in different languages. The basis upon which the entire DOM is built is the Node interface. This provides the fundamental abilities of a node within the model structure: a name, a value, attributes, a parent, and possible child nodes. More specific node types derive from this interface with added functionality. See Table 8-1 for a list of the items specified by the DOM core, and the new Traversal section. The Level column indicates when the item was introduced.

Table 8-1: Document Object Model specifications

DOM Item	Type	Level	Purpose
Attr	Interface	I	An attribute of an element
CDATASection	Interface	I	An extended text section that ignores markup characters
CharacterData	Interface	I	Base interface for all text type nodes

DOM Item	Type	Level	Purpose
Comment	Interface	1	An embedded comment
Document	Interface	1	Top level in the model representing the entire document
DocumentFragment	Interface	1	A snippet of a DOM not attached to the main model
DocumentType	Interface	1	Information about the DTD including entities and notations
DOMException	Exception	1	Describes errors encountered during DOM processing
DOMImplementation	Interface	1	Functionality that is independent of an instance of the DOM
DOMString	Type	1	The type for all DOM strings (16-bit UNICODE)
DOMTimeStamp	Type	2	A number of milliseconds
Element	Interface	1	Standard element—the most common node in a document
Entity	Interface	1	Details about an entity (parsed or unparsed) declared in the DTD
EntityReference	Interface	1	An occurrence of a parsed entity in the body of the document
NamedNodeMap	Interface	1	Handle collections of nodes that can be accessed by name, such as attributes
Node	Interface	1	The basic structural element within the DOM, most other interfaces derive from this one
NodeFilter	Interface	2	Accept or reject nodes for a selection
NodeIterator	Interface	2	Handle a collection of selected nodes in sequential order
NodeList	Interface	1	Handle ordered collections of nodes, such as child nodes
Notation	Interface	1	Details about a notation declared in the DTD
ProcessingInstruction	Interface	1	An instruction for a target application
Text	Interface	1	The textual content of an element or attribute
TreeWalker	Interface	2	Handle a collection of selected nodes in a tree structure

NOTE Although there are eight parts to the DOM Level 2 specification (Core, HTML, Views, Stylesheets, CSS, Events, Traversal, and Range), only the Core and Traversal sections are covered here. The remaining sections do not deal with XML or are not widely implemented as yet.

The DOMString type defined by the DOM corresponds to a 16-bit character set, UTF-16. All string values within the DOM use this format.

As an example, the XML document in Listing 8-1 is represented by the DOM shown in Figure 8-1. At the topmost level is the `Document` node, which provides access to all the other nodes. Beneath this appear a `ProcessingInstruction` node for the XML declaration, a `DocumentType` node for the DTD declaration, a `Comment` node, another `ProcessingInstruction` node for the stylesheet reference, and an `Element` node that is the document element.

Listing 8-1: XML fragment

```xml
<?xml version="1.0" encoding="UTF-8"?>
<!DOCTYPE movie-watcher SYSTEM "movie-watcher.dtd" [
  <!NOTATION HTML PUBLIC "-//W3C//DTD HTML 4.0 Transitional//EN">
  <!NOTATION GIF SYSTEM "iview.exe">
  <!ENTITY SW1-site SYSTEM "http://www.starwars.com/episode-i/" NDATA HTML>
  <!ENTITY SW1-logo SYSTEM "http://www.starwars.com/episode-i/palpatine/img/top_logo.gif" NDATA GIF>
  <!ENTITY PV "Pleasantville">
]>
<!-- Sample XML document with data about movies
     and when and where they are showing
     Developed by Keith Wood, 28 May 1999 -->
<?xml:stylesheet type="text/xsl" href="movie-watcher.xsl"?>
<movie-watcher>
  <movies>
    <movie id="SW1" rating="PG" logo-url="SW1-logo" url="SW1-site">
      <name>Star Wars - The Phantom Menace</name>
      <length>131</length>
      <director>George Lucas</director>
      <starring>
        <star>Liam Neeson</star>
        <star>Ewan McGregor</star>
        <star>Jake Lloyd</star>
        <star>Natalie Portman</star>
      </starring>
      <synopsis>When the evil Trade Federation plots to take over the
        peaceful planet of Naboo, Jedi warrior Qui-Gon Jinn and his
        apprentice Obi-Wan Kenobi embark on an amazing adventure to
        save the planet. With them on their journey is the young queen
        Amidala, Gungan outcast JarJar Binks, and the powerful Captain
        Panaka, who will all travel to the faraway planets of Tatooine
        and Coruscant in a futile attempt to save their world from
        Darth Sidious, leader of the Trade Federation, and Darth Maul,
        the strongest Dark Lord of the Sith to ever wield a lightsaber.
      </synopsis>
    </movie>
  </movies>
</movie-watcher>
```

Within the `DocumentType` node are `Notation` nodes representing the notations declared in the internal DTD for this document, and `Entity` nodes for the internal and external entities declared there. Internal entities have their content in `Text` nodes as children.

NOTE The DOM specification does not model the DTD itself, i.e., the element and attribute declarations. However, some implementations of the DOM do provide this extra functionality. See Chapter 11 for information on the Open XML DOM and its DTD representation.

The document element (`movie-watcher`) has further `Element` children for each node in the document hierarchy. At the bottom of the tree are more `Text` nodes that contain the content.

Figure 8-1: DOM representing the document from Listing 8-1.

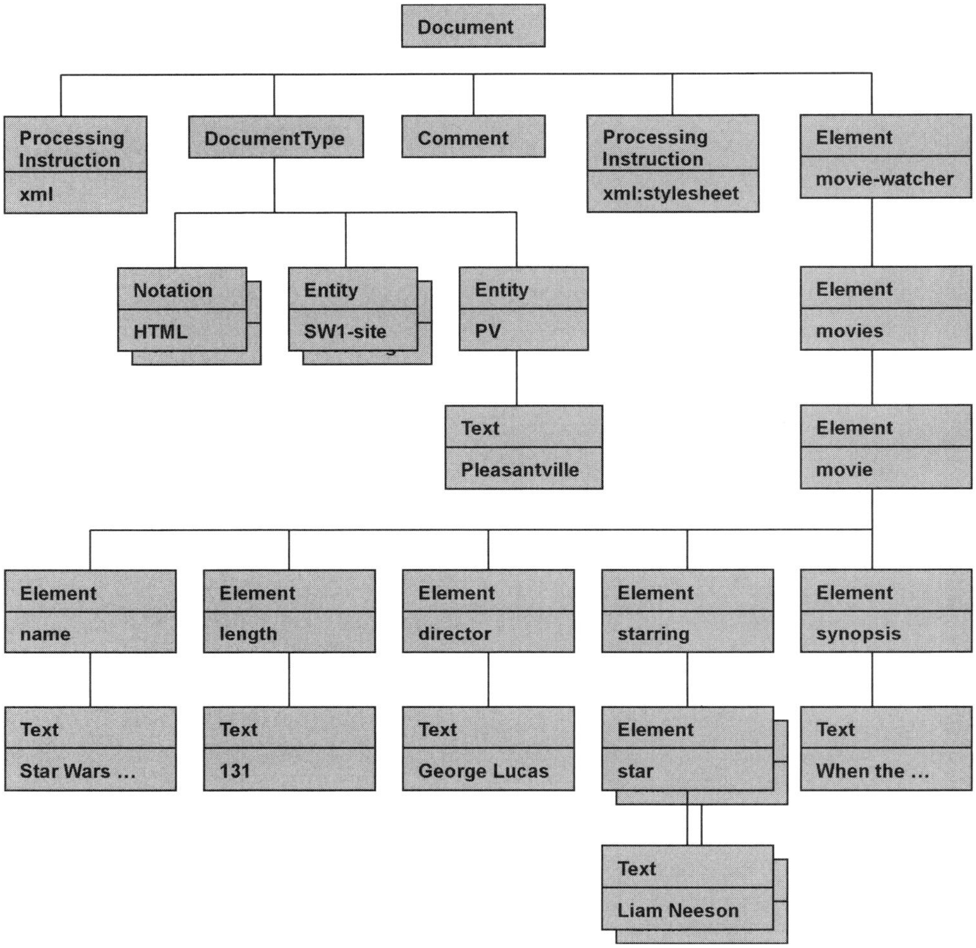

As you can see, the entire document structure is captured within the model (except for the DTD information). Each node can be reached by navigating from the document node down through a series of child nodes, or via one of a number of selection methods from the document or an Element node.

The rest of this chapter goes on to describe each interface and exception in greater detail. Definitions for the interfaces come from the DOM specification and are expressed in Interface Definition Language (IDL) as described by the Object Management Group (OMG). This format is language-neutral and can be mapped onto a number of different languages for implementation purposes.

DOMException

DOMException (see Listing 8-2) is designed to notify you of errors that occur during the processing of a document. In languages that support exceptions (like Delphi) a new exception type should be defined and raised when necessary. The specification defines a number of errors and identifying codes. Occasions when these errors are generated are identified throughout the specification. Although the code is included in the exception here, this may not be necessary in implementations where the type can be identified through other means (such as by subclassing the exception).

Listing 8-2: The DOMException exception

```
exception DOMException {
  unsigned short   code;
};

// ExceptionCode
const unsigned short    INDEX_SIZE_ERR              = 1;
const unsigned short    DOMSTRING_SIZE_ERR          = 2;
const unsigned short    HIERARCHY_REQUEST_ERR       = 3;
const unsigned short    WRONG_DOCUMENT_ERR          = 4;
const unsigned short    INVALID_CHARACTER_ERR       = 5;
const unsigned short    NO_DATA_ALLOWED_ERR         = 6;
const unsigned short    NO_MODIFICATION_ALLOWED_ERR = 7;
const unsigned short    NOT_FOUND_ERR               = 8;
const unsigned short    NOT_SUPPORTED_ERR           = 9;
const unsigned short    INUSE_ATTRIBUTE_ERR         = 10;
// Introduced in DOM Level 2:
const unsigned short    INVALID_STATE_ERR           = 11;
// Introduced in DOM Level 2:
const unsigned short    SYNTAX_ERR                  = 12;
// Introduced in DOM Level 2:
const unsigned short    INVALID_MODIFICATION_ERR    = 13;
// Introduced in DOM Level 2:
const unsigned short    NAMESPACE_ERR               = 14;
// Introduced in DOM Level 2:
const unsigned short    INVALID_ACCESS_ERR          = 15;
```

NOTE The conditions that generate these exceptions occur during the manipulations of the DOM once it is loaded. The specification does not indicate how documents are loaded from or saved to persistent storage. Any errors that arise from reading, parsing, or writing DOMs are produced by the implementing application in a manner specific to that product.

Typical causes of these errors are described below:

INDEX_SIZE_ERR
    An index or size value is negative or greater than the allowed maximum.

DOMSTRING_SIZE_ERR
    A specified range of text does not fit in a DOMString value.

HIERARCHY_REQUEST_ERR
    An attempt is made to insert a node somewhere that it does not belong.

WRONG_DOCUMENT_ERR
    A node is used within a document that did not create it.

INVALID_CHARACTER_ERR
: An invalid character has been used, for example, within an element name.

NO_DATA_ALLOWED_ERR
: A node value is set for a node that does not support values, such as an Element node.

NO_MODIFICATION_ALLOWED_ERR
: An attempt is made to modify a read-only node.

NOT_FOUND_ERR
: An attempt is made to refer to a node that does not exist, for example, when inserting child nodes.

NOT_SUPPORTED_ERR
: The implementation does not support the type of object requested.

INUSE_ATTRIBUTE_ERR
: An attempt is made to add an attribute already in use elsewhere.

INVALID_STATE_ERR
: An attempt is made to use an object that is no longer usable.

SYNTAX_ERR
: An invalid or illegal string is used.

INVALID_MODIFICATION_ERR
: An attempt is made to alter the type of the object.

NAMESPACE_ERR
: An attempt is made to alter the object that is incompatible with namespace usage.

INVALID_ACCESS_ERR
: The object does not support a parameter or an operation.

Node Interface

As mentioned earlier, the Node interface (shown in Listing 8-3) forms the basic unit of the DOM structure. Extensions to this interface may add convenience names for the basic properties, or entirely new abilities, based on their purpose. You do not add a simple node directly to the DOM, but instead use one of its extensions. However, the properties and methods defined here let all nodes be treated identically at a basic level.

Listing 8-3: The Node interface

```
interface Node {
  // NodeType
  const unsigned short   ELEMENT_NODE                = 1;
  const unsigned short   ATTRIBUTE_NODE              = 2;
  const unsigned short   TEXT_NODE                   = 3;
  const unsigned short   CDATA_SECTION_NODE          = 4;
  const unsigned short   ENTITY_REFERENCE_NODE       = 5;
  const unsigned short   ENTITY_NODE                 = 6;
  const unsigned short   PROCESSING_INSTRUCTION_NODE = 7;
  const unsigned short   COMMENT_NODE                = 8;
```

```
        const unsigned short   DOCUMENT_NODE            = 9;
        const unsigned short   DOCUMENT_TYPE_NODE       = 10;
        const unsigned short   DOCUMENT_FRAGMENT_NODE   = 11;
        const unsigned short   NOTATION_NODE            = 12;

        readonly attribute  DOMString       nodeName;
                 attribute  DOMString       nodeValue;
                 // raises(DOMException) on setting
                 // raises(DOMException) on retrieval
        readonly attribute  unsigned short  nodeType;
        readonly attribute  Node            parentNode;
        readonly attribute  NodeList        childNodes;
        readonly attribute  Node            firstChild;
        readonly attribute  Node            lastChild;
        readonly attribute  Node            previousSibling;
        readonly attribute  Node            nextSibling;
        readonly attribute  NamedNodeMap    attributes;
        // Modified in DOM Level 2:
        readonly attribute  Document        ownerDocument;
        Node                insertBefore(in Node newChild,
                              in Node refChild)
                              raises(DOMException);
        Node                replaceChild(in Node newChild,
                              in Node oldChild)
                              raises(DOMException);
        Node                removeChild(in Node oldChild)
                              raises(DOMException);
        Node                appendChild(in Node newChild)
                              raises(DOMException);
        boolean             hasChildNodes();
        Node                cloneNode(in boolean deep);
        // Modified in DOM Level 2:
        void                normalize();
        // Introduced in DOM Level 2:
        boolean             isSupported(in DOMString feature,
                              in DOMString version);
        // Introduced in DOM Level 2:
        readonly attribute DOMString        namespaceURI;
        // Introduced in DOM Level 2:
                 attribute DOMString        prefix;
                 // raises(DOMException) on setting

        // Introduced in DOM Level 2:
        readonly attribute DOMString        localName;
        // Introduced in DOM Level 2:
        boolean             hasAttributes();
};
```

The properties and methods of a Node are described below:

`readonly attribute unsigned short nodeType;`

> Identifies the specific subclass of Node that this object represents. It must be one of the constants listed in the interface, and these correspond to extended interfaces for each type. The contents of the nodeName, nodeValue, and attribute properties also depend on the node type, as shown in Table 8-2.

Table 8-2: Property meanings by node type

Node Type	Node Name	Node Value	Attributes
Attr	attribute name	attribute value	null
CDATASection	#cdata-section	content of CDATA section	null
Comment	#comment	content of the comment	null
Document	#document	null	null
DocumentFragment	#document-fragment	null	null
DocumentType	document type name	null	null
Element	tag name	null	list of attributes
Entity	entity name	null	null
EntityReference	name of referenced entity	null	null
Notation	notation name	null	null
ProcessingInstruction	target	all content excluding the target	null
Text	#text	content of text node	null

readonly attribute DOMString nodeName;
> The name for this node. It is either a name specified in the XML document, such as an element or attribute name, or is one of a set of predefined literals for nodes that have no real name, such as text nodes. See Table 8-2 for the meaning based on the node type.

readonly attribute DOMString localName;
> Introduced in DOM Level 2, this property returns the local part of the qualified name of the node, i.e., the part after any namespace prefix. For nodes other than Element and Attr, and for nodes created with a Level 1 call, it always returns null. A null is also returned if no namespace applies to this node. For example, given the qualified name math:plus, this attribute returns plus.

attribute DOMString prefix;
> Complementary to localName, this property is also introduced in DOM Level 2 and returns the prefix part of the qualified name of the node. For nodes other than Element and Attr, and for nodes created with a Level 1 call, it always returns null. It also returns null if no namespace applies to this node. Given the qualified name math:plus, this attribute returns the math part.

readonly attribute DOMString namespaceURI;
> Also arriving in DOM Level 2, this is the full namespace associated with the node, based on the prefix. As before, for nodes other than Element and Attr, and for nodes created with a Level 1 call, it always returns null. It also returns null if no namespace applies to this node.
> For example, given the namespace declaration:
> ```
> xmlns:math="http://www.w3.org/www.w3.org/TR/REC-MathML"
> ```

and the qualified name math:plus, this attribute returns the value:

http://www.w3.org/www.w3.org/TR/REC-MathML

attribute DOMString nodeValue;

Many nodes such as the text nodes, have an inherent value. Where appropriate, this property returns that value. For the remainder it returns a null value. See Table 8-2 for the meaning of this value based on the node type.

readonly attribute NamedNodeMap attributes;

Only the element nodes have attributes, which are available through this property. Entries are retrieved through a NamedNodeMap that provides access via their names. All other node types return a null.

NOTE Only attributes that have values defined in the XML document itself are guaranteed to appear in this list. If the parser loads any external DTD or schema it can also add those attributes with default or fixed values.

readonly attribute Document ownerDocument;

This is a reference to the Document that created the node. For a Document node itself, or for a DocumentType node not yet associated with a Document, this returns null. Nodes may only be used with the document that created them.

readonly attribute Node parentNode;

Most nodes have a parent, providing navigation up through the document hierarchy. Document, DocumentFragment, and Attr nodes do not have parents. Furthermore, other node types may not have a parent until they are placed into the document structure.

readonly attribute NodeList childNodes;

Many nodes also have children contained within them. These are accessible through this property, which returns a NodeList as described below. If there are no children, the list still exists but has no entries. All NodeList objects have an implied ordering of the nodes they manage. All the nodes returned through this list are "live." This means that any changes to them are made to the real node within the hierarchy. Similarly, adding and removing child nodes immediately affects the contents of the list.

boolean hasChildNodes();

This function returns True if any children exist for the current node, and False otherwise. Alternately, you can check for the length of the childNodes list being non-zero.

readonly attribute Node firstChild;

A convenience property for accessing the first child node. It returns null if there are no children.

readonly attribute Node lastChild;

Similar to firstChild but for the last child node. It also returns null if there are no children.

`readonly attribute Node previousSibling;`
: This property returns the node immediately before the current one in the latter's parent's list of children. It returns `null` if there is no previous node in the parent.

`readonly attribute Node nextSibling;`
: Same as `previousSibling`, but it returns the following node in the parent's list. It returns `null` if there is no next node in the parent.

`Node insertBefore(in Node newChild, in Node refChild) raises(DOMException);`
: Use this method to add a new child node to the current node. The new node is placed immediately before the nominated node in the list, unless the reference parameter is `null`, in which case the new node is added at the end. A reference to the new node is returned by the function. An exception is raised if the new node is not an appropriate child of the current node, if the new node is an ancestor of the current node, if the new node was created by another document, if the current node is read-only, or if the reference node is not found.

`Node replaceChild(in Node newChild, in Node oldChild) raises(DOMException);`
: Use this method to overwrite a child node. The old node specified is removed and becomes the return value of the function. The new node is added in its place. An exception is raised if any of the error conditions for the `insertBefore` method apply.

`Node removeChild(in Node oldChild) raises(DOMException);`
: Child nodes are deleted from the list with this method. A reference to the node removed is returned. If the current node is read-only or if the old node cannot be found, an exception is raised.

`Node appendChild(in Node newChild) raises(DOMException);`
: Adds the supplied node to the end of the list of child nodes. If the node is already in the DOM tree, it is first removed. The return value of the function is a reference to the new node. Exceptions occur under the same circumstances as for the `insertBefore` method.

`Node cloneNode(in boolean deep);`
: This function returns a copy of the current node. Attributes of the node are also copied. However, child nodes are not duplicated unless the supplied parameter is set to `True`. In this case, all descendant nodes are copied. The new node has no parent until it is placed into a document.

`void normalize();`
: Added in DOM Level 2, this method scans the subtree below this node, removes empty `Text` nodes, and combines any adjacent `Text` nodes. CDATAsections are not combined or otherwise affected. This processing is useful when dealing with XPointers, and similar operations, that depend on a standardized tree structure. Following the loading of a new document, the DOM is already in a normalized state.

`boolean isSupported(in DOMString feature, in DOMString version);`
: Also introduced in DOM Level 2, this method tests for a particular feature of the DOM and its version. See the `DOMImplementation` interface for accepted values.

```
boolean hasAttributes();
```
New in DOM Level 2, you use this method to see if the node has any attributes.

NodeList Interface

A node list provides access to an ordered collection of nodes (see Listing 8-4). It is used for the children of a node and as the return value from the getElementsByTagName method that retrieves nodes by name. Nodes returned through the list are "live," meaning that changes made to them are made to the actual nodes within the DOM structure. Similarly, adding nodes to or removing nodes from the list immediately affects the hierarchy.

Listing 8-4: The NodeList interface

```
interface NodeList {
  readonly attribute  unsigned long  length;
  Node        item(in unsigned long index);
};
```

The properties and methods of a NodeList are as follows:

```
readonly attribute unsigned long length;
```
The number of items in the list.

```
Node item(in unsigned long index);
```
This method retrieves a particular entry from the list, given its position. If the index is out of range, a null is returned instead. Numbering starts at zero.

NamedNodeMap Interface

Named node maps (see Listing 8-5) are also collections of nodes, however, they have no inherent order and are primarily accessible by the names of the contained nodes.

Listing 8-5: The NamedNodeMap interface

```
interface NamedNodeMap {
  readonly attribute  unsigned long  length;
  Node        getNamedItem(in DOMString name);
  Node        setNamedItem(in Node arg) raises(DOMException);
  Node        removeNamedItem(in DOMString name)
                raises(DOMException);
  Node        item(in unsigned long index);
  // Introduced in DOM Level 2:
  Node        getNamedItemNS(in DOMString namespaceURI,
                in DOMString localName);
  // Introduced in DOM Level 2:
  Node        setNamedItemNS(in Node arg) raises(DOMException);
  // Introduced in DOM Level 2:
  Node        removeNamedItemNS(in DOMString namespaceURI,
                in DOMString localName) raises(DOMException);
};
```

A `NamedNodeMap`'s properties and methods are described below:

`readonly attribute unsigned long length;`
> The number of items in the list.

`Node getNamedItem(in DOMString name);`
> Retrieve a node from the list via its name with this method. If no matching node is found in the list, a `null` results.

`Node setNamedItem(in Node arg) raises(DOMException);`
> This method adds a new node to the list, using its name as the key. If the name matches an existing node in the list, the new node replaces it and the old node becomes the return value of the method. Otherwise, the method returns a `null`. An exception is raised if the node was created by a different document than the list, if the list is read-only, or if the node is an attribute that already belongs to another element.

`Node removeNamedItem(in DOMString name) raises(DOMException);`
> Delete a node from the list, based on its name, with this method. Attribute nodes deleted through this method may automatically reappear if they are known to have a default value. If the list is read-only or if the named node does not appear in the list, an exception is generated.

`Node item(in unsigned long index);`
> Although the named node map has no inherent order, this method provides sequential access to all the held nodes through their index. This does not impose any particular ordering on the nodes, and merely serves to enumerate all the contained nodes. If the index is out of range, the function returns a `null`. Numbering starts at zero.

`Node getNamedItemNS(in DOMString namespaceURI, in DOMString localName);`
> Introduced in DOM Level 2, this method functions as does `getNamedItem`, but allows a fully qualified name to be used. A `null` results if no matching node is found.

`Node setNamedItemNS(in Node arg) raises(DOMException);`
> Also in DOM Level 2, this method adds a new node to the list, using its fully qualified name as the key. Exceptions occur under the same conditions as for the `setNamedItem` method.

`Node removeNamedItemNS(in DOMString namespaceURI, in DOMString localName) raises (DOMException);`
> New in Level 2, you can delete a node from the list with this method based on its full name. See the `removeNamedItem` method for error conditions.

Element Interface

Elements are the primary nodes found in XML documents. Based on the Node interface, the Element interface (see Listing 8-6) adds better methods for accessing attributes, and other methods for searching its descendants for certain nodes.

Listing 8-6: The Element interface

```
interface Element : Node {
  readonly attribute  DOMString  tagName;
  DOMString   getAttribute(in DOMString name);
  void        setAttribute(in DOMString name, in DOMString value)
                  raises(DOMException);
  void        removeAttribute(in DOMString name)
                  raises(DOMException);
  Attr        getAttributeNode(in DOMString name);
  Attr        setAttributeNode(in Attr newAttr)
                  raises(DOMException);
  Attr        removeAttributeNode(in Attr oldAttr)
                  raises(DOMException);
  NodeList    getElementsByTagName(in DOMString name);
  // Introduced in DOM Level 2:
  DOMString   getAttributeNS(in DOMString namespaceURI,
                  in DOMString localName);
  // Introduced in DOM Level 2:
  void        setAttributeNS(in DOMString namespaceURI,
                  in DOMString qualifiedName, in DOMString value)
                  raises(DOMException);
  // Introduced in DOM Level 2:
  void        removeAttributeNS(in DOMString namespaceURI,
                  in DOMString localName) raises(DOMException);
  // Introduced in DOM Level 2:
  Attr        getAttributeNodeNS(in DOMString namespaceURI,
                  in DOMString localName);
  // Introduced in DOM Level 2:
  Attr        setAttributeNodeNS(in Attr newAttr)
                  raises(DOMException);
  // Introduced in DOM Level 2:
  NodeList    getElementsByTagNameNS(in DOMString namespaceURI,
                  in DOMString localName);
  // Introduced in DOM Level 2:
  boolean     hasAttribute(in DOMString name);
  // Introduced in DOM Level 2:
  boolean     hasAttributeNS(in DOMString namespaceURI,
                  in DOMString localName);
};
```

The properties and methods of the Element node are as follows:

`readonly attribute DOMString tagName;`
    Mapping onto the inherited nodeName property, this is merely a convenience.

`DOMString getAttribute(in DOMString name);`
    This method returns the string value of the named attribute, or an empty string if it does not exist.

void setAttribute(in DOMString name, in DOMString value) raises(DOMException);
: The complement of the previous method, this allows you to set the (string) value of the named attribute. Any existing attribute with that name is overwritten. The value is not parsed or interpreted in any way. An exception occurs if the name contains an illegal character or if the element is read-only.

void removeAttribute(in DOMString name) raises(DOMException);
: Delete an attribute from this node, given its name. If the attribute is known to have a default value (from the DTD or schema), it is immediately added again with that value. If the element is read-only, an exception is raised.

DOMString getAttributeNS(in DOMString namespaceURI, in DOMString localName);
: Introduced in DOM Level 2, this method works just like getAttribute, except that it takes a namespace URI and a local name to identify the attribute.

void setAttributeNS(in DOMString namespaceURI, in DOMString qualifiedName, in DOMString value) raises(DOMException);
: New in DOM Level 2, this method specifies the attribute through its namespace URI and local name. Otherwise, it functions just like setAttribute. An exception occurs if the name contains an illegal character, if the element is read-only, or if the qualified name is malformed. A name is malformed if it has a prefix but no namespace, or if the prefix is xml or xmlns and the namespace is not the corresponding accepted value.

void removeAttributeNS(in DOMString namespaceURI, in DOMString localName) raises(DOMException);
: Also new in DOM Level 2, this method works like removeAttribute, but takes a namespace URI and a local name to select the attribute. If the element is read-only, an exception is raised.

Attr getAttributeNode(in DOMString name);
: Similar to the getAttribute method, this one allows you to retrieve the entire Attr node given its name. This is useful when the attribute contains entity references, since these appear as child nodes of that attribute. A null is returned if the attribute cannot be found.

Attr setAttributeNode(in Attr newAttr) raises(DOMException);
: Add a new attribute based on the node passed to this call. This allows for entity references within an attribute, appearing as children of the attribute node. If an existing attribute is replaced, a reference to the old attribute is returned. Otherwise, the function returns null. Exceptions occur if the attribute was created by another document, if the element is read-only, or if the attribute already belongs to another element.

Attr removeAttributeNode(in Attr oldAttr) raises(DOMException);
: Try to match an attribute of the element with the supplied one, and remove it if found, returning a reference to the deleted node. As before, if the attribute has a default value it automatically reappears with that value. If the element is read-only or if the supplied attribute is not found, an exception is raised.

`Attr getAttributeNodeNS(in DOMString namespaceURI, in DOMString localName);`
: Introduced in DOM Level 2, this method works just like `getAttributeNode`, except that it takes a namespace URI and a local name to identify the attribute.

`Attr setAttributeNodeNS(in Attr newAttr) raises(DOMException);`
: New in DOM Level 2, this method uses the attribute's namespace URI and local name for identification. Otherwise, it functions just like `setAttributeNode`, including raising exceptions.

`NodeList getElementsByTagName(in DOMString name);`
: Given the name of an element, this method walks the descendants of the current node and compiles a list of matching elements. The order within the list is that of a pre-order traversal of the subtree (the same order that elements appear within the text document). As with child nodes, the nodes returned are "live." Use a name of * to match with all tag names.

`NodeList getElementsByTagNameNS(in DOMString namespaceURI, in DOMString localName);`
: Introduced in DOM Level 2, this method works just like `getElementsByTagName`, except that it selects elements by their namespace URI and local name.

`boolean hasAttribute(in DOMString name);`
: Introduced in DOM Level 2, this method returns `True` if the named attribute exists within this node, due to its value being specified in the XML document or as a default value from the DTD or schema. Otherwise, it returns `False`.

`boolean hasAttributeNS(in DOMString namespaceURI, in DOMString localName);`
: New in DOM Level 2, this method uses an attribute's namespace URI and local name to determine its presence. Otherwise, it functions just like `hasAttribute`.

Attr Interface

This interface (shown in Listing 8-7) represents an attribute of an element. The attribute nodes do not appear within the normal DOM hierarchy, only within the `attributes` property of an `Element` node. For this reason their `parentNode`, `previousSibling`, and `nextSibling` properties all return `null`.

Listing 8-7: The Attr interface

```
interface Attr : Node {
  readonly attribute  DOMString  name;
  readonly attribute  boolean    specified;
           attribute  DOMString  value;
           // raises(DOMException) on setting
  // Introduced in DOM Level 2:
  readonly attribute  Element    ownerElement;
};
```

An attribute's value may come from the XML document directly, where it appears as part of the element tag. For documents that have DTDs or schemas, the value may also come from a default or fixed value specified therein. If neither of these situations applies, the attribute does not appear at all in the DOM.

NOTE Deleting an attribute that has a default value set in the DTD or schema causes that attribute to be immediately added again with that default value.

Attributes usually have a single Text node child. However, they may also contain a combination of Text and EntityReference nodes representing their contents.

An Attribute node's properties are described below:

readonly attribute DOMString name;
> The name of the attribute. This is a synonym for the inherited nodeName property.

attribute DOMString value;
> The string value of the attribute. This is a synonym for the inherited nodeValue property. It is the text value of the entire attribute, with any entity references expanded out. Setting this attribute creates a single Text node beneath the attribute, replacing any earlier children. The supplied text is not parsed at all, ignoring anything that otherwise is considered markup. An exception occurs if the node is read-only.

readonly attribute boolean specified;
> This property is True if the attribute's value was explicitly set in the XML document. It is False if the value derived from a default or fixed value in the DTD or schema. Setting the value attribute also sets this attribute to True.

readonly attribute Element ownerElement;
> Introduced in DOM Level 2, this property refers back to the Element that owns this node. It returns null if the attribute is not in use.

CharacterData Interface

The CharacterData interface (see Listing 8-8) extends Node and defines basic functionality for all nodes that contain text. Nodes of this particular type do not appear within the DOM; subclasses of this type are used instead. All offsets within the interface start at zero.

Listing 8-8: The CharacterData interface

```
interface CharacterData : Node {
        attribute DOMString     data;
        // raises(DOMException) on setting
        // raises(DOMException) on retrieval
    readonly attribute  unsigned long   length;
    DOMString   substringData(in unsigned long offset,
            in unsigned long count) raises(DOMException);
    void        appendData(in DOMString arg) raises(DOMException);
    void        insertData(in unsigned long offset,
            in DOMString arg) raises(DOMException);
    void        deleteData(in unsigned long offset,
```

```
                    in unsigned long count) raises(DOMException);
    void            replaceData(in unsigned long offset,
                        in unsigned long count, in DOMString arg)
                        raises(DOMException);
};
```

The properties and methods of a `CharacterData` node are as follows:

`attribute DOMString data;`
> The actual content of the node, equivalent to the `nodeValue` property. An exception occurs if the value is set when the node is read-only or if the value is read but is too large for a `DOMString`. In the latter case, you can use the `substringData` method to retrieve portions of the text. Furthermore, being too large is an implementation-specific problem and may not arise in some processors.

`readonly attribute unsigned long length;`
> The number of characters in the node. This may be zero.

`DOMString substringData(in unsigned long offset, in unsigned long count) raises(DOMException);`
> Retrieves a range of characters from the node. If the `offset` is out of range or if the `count` is negative, an exception occurs. Reading a section too large for a `DOMString` also triggers an exception.

`void appendData(in DOMString arg) raises(DOMException);`
> Adds new text to the end of the existing value. An exception is raised if the node is read-only.

`void insertData(in unsigned long offset, in DOMString arg) raises(DOMException);`
> Adds new text at the specified position within the existing text. Content after that position is pushed along. Exceptions occur if the `offset` is out of range or if the node is read-only.

`void deleteData(in unsigned long offset, in unsigned long count) raises(DOMException);`
> Remove the nominated characters from the content. Subsequent characters move up to fill the gap. If the `offset` is out of range, if the `count` is negative, or if the node is read-only, an exception is generated.

`void replaceData(in unsigned long offset, in unsigned long count, in DOMString arg) raises(DOMException);`
> Combines the previous two operations: removes the specified characters, then adds the new text in its place. The combined error conditions apply.

Text Interface

Derived from `CharacterData`, this interface (shown in Listing 8-9) represents the actual textual content of an XML document. These nodes have no children, with their contents available through the inherited data property. When first loaded, there is only one `Text` node for each block of text in the document. Subsequent operations may add other `Text` nodes. The `normalize` method of a parent node serves to combine adjacent Text nodes, as if the document had been saved and reloaded. This may be necessary for some operations that expect a certain structure.

Listing 8-9: The Text interface

```
interface Text : CharacterData {
  Text        splitText(in unsigned long offset)
              raises(DOMException);
};
```

A Text node's methods are described below:

Text splitText(in unsigned long offset) raises(DOMException);
> Breaks the current text node into two pieces at the specified offset. The original node retains all the text up to that point, while the new node, inserted immediately after the original within its parent, holds the rest. A reference to the new node is returned by the function. If the offset is out of range or if the node is read-only, an exception occurs.

CDATASection Interface

CDATA sections allow you to place characters that would otherwise have to be escaped into the document. This interface is part of the extended core specification for the DOM. If you were only dealing with HTML documents, you would not use the node types in this extension. Since XML is the focus of this book, they are included here.

This interface (see Listing 8-10) extends Text, but adds nothing new to it. As such, it is simply a flagging interface, serving to distinguish straight text from these special sections.

Listing 8-10: The CDATASection interface

```
interface CDATASection : Text {
};
```

Comment Interface

Like the CDATA section, the Comment interface (see Listing 8-11) is just another flagging interface. It extends CharacterData, but adds nothing new. The text of the comment is available from the inherited nodeValue attribute.

Listing 8-11: The Comment interface

```
interface Comment : CharacterData {
};
```

ProcessingInstruction Interface

ProcessingInstruction (shown in Listing 8-12) is another of the extended interfaces of the core DOM. They allow additional commands for specific applications to be passed through the XML in a generalized manner.

Listing 8-12: The `ProcessingInstruction` *interface*

```
interface ProcessingInstruction : Node {
  readonly attribute  DOMString   target;
           attribute  DOMString   data;
           // raises(DOMException) on setting
};
```

The properties of a `ProcessingInstruction` node are as follows:

`readonly attribute DOMString target;`
> This property denotes the audience that will know how to deal with the commands in the rest of the tag. Often, it identifies a particular program. It consists of all text from the start of the tag up to the first white space character. The `nodeName` property holds the same value.

`attribute DOMString data;`
> The remainder of the tag, from the first non-white space character following the target through to the character immediately before the closing sequence, contains the commands destined for the target application. This is a synonym for the `nodeValue` property. No structure is imposed on the data from XML's point of view. The target of the command may expect certain formats, however.

DocumentType Interface

The DTD declaration is encapsulated by the `DocumentType` interface (see Listing 8-13). This is another extended code interface, since HTML does not support this functionality. Under DOM Level 2, `DocumentType` nodes (and their children) cannot be altered.

Listing 8-13: The `DocumentType` *interface*

```
interface DocumentType : Node {
  readonly attribute  DOMString     name;
  readonly attribute  NamedNodeMap  entities;
  readonly attribute  NamedNodeMap  notations;
  // Introduced in DOM Level 2:
  readonly attribute  DOMString     publicId;
  // Introduced in DOM Level 2:
  readonly attribute  DOMString     systemId;
  // Introduced in DOM Level 2:
  readonly attribute  DOMString     internalSubset;
};
```

A `DocumentType` node's properties are described below:

`readonly attribute DOMString name;`
> This property contains the name of the document element. The `nodeName` property holds the same value.

`readonly attribute NamedNodeMap entities;`
> A list of all the entities declared within the document is available through this property. Parameter entities are not included, but both internal and external entities are. Duplicate entity definitions are ignored. As it returns a `NamedNodeMap`, you can retrieve entities by name. Each item within the list implements the `Entity` interface shown below.

readonly attribute NamedNodeMap notations;
> Similarly, all notations from the document are available here. Duplicate definitions are again ignored. As for entities, you can retrieve them by name from the list. The Notation interface returns further details for each item.

readonly attribute DOMString publicId;
> The public (logical) identifier for any external DTD or schema is held in this property. This is new in DOM Level 2.

readonly attribute DOMString systemId;
> This property holds the physical address of the external DTD or schema, usually as a URL. As for the publicId, this property is new to DOM Level 2.

readonly attribute DOMString internalSubset;
> The text value of the internal subset of the DTD is returned by this property. It was introduced as part of DOM Level 2.

Entity Interface

The Entity interface (shown in Listing 8-14) models the entities (parsed and unparsed) in a document, and is another extended core interface. Child nodes represent the contents of the entity, which may include sections of markup. This interface holds details about the entities themselves, but says nothing about the declarations from which they were extracted. Future versions of the DOM will address this issue.

Listing 8-14: The Entity interface

```
interface Entity : Node {
  readonly attribute  DOMString  publicId;
  readonly attribute  DOMString  systemId;
  readonly attribute  DOMString  notationName;
};
```

Entities from an external DTD may not appear in the DOM if the parser does not resolve external references, which is often the case for non-validating parsers.

Entity definitions are only available through the DocumentType interface, and do not form part of the normal tree. Thus, Entity objects have no parent node. Furthermore, these nodes and all their descendants are read-only.

The properties of an Entity node are as follows:

readonly attribute DOMString nodeName;
> This inherited attribute holds the entity's name.

readonly attribute DOMString publicId;
> The public (logical) identifier for the entity is held in this property. It is null if no public identifier is specified.

`readonly attribute DOMString systemId;`
> This property holds the physical address of the entity, usually as a URL. Again, it is `null` if no system identifier is supplied.

`readonly attribute DOMString notationName;`
> The format of an unparsed entity is provided through this property. It must match up with one of the notations declared in the document. For parsed entities this value is `null`.

EntityReference Interface

At the points that entities appear within the body of the document you may find `EntityReference` nodes (see Listing 8-15), yet another extended core interface. These references may not appear if the processor expands them during parsing and replaces them with their contents. When they do appear, they contain copies of the structure beneath the corresponding entity. As for entities, entity reference nodes and their descendants are read-only.

Listing 8-15: The `EntityReference` interface
```
interface EntityReference : Node {
};
```

The interface itself adds no new functionality, merely serving to identify the original source of the content. Read the inherited `nodeName` attribute to retrieve the name of the entity whose contents are used.

Notation Interface

Another extended core interface, `Notation` (see Listing 8-16) provides details about formats for external entities and about processing instruction targets. They are only accessible from the `Notations` property of the `DocumentType` node, and have no parent. Under DOM Level 2 they are read-only.

Listing 8-16: The `Notation` interface
```
interface Notation : Node {
  readonly attribute  DOMString  publicId;
  readonly attribute  DOMString  systemId;
};
```

A `Notation` node's properties are described below:

`readonly attribute DOMString nodeName;`
> This inherited attribute holds the notation's name.

`readonly attribute DOMString publicId;`
> The public (logical) identifier for the notation is held in this property. It returns `null` if no public identifier is specified.

```
readonly attribute DOMString systemId;
```
This property holds the physical address of the notation, usually as a URL. It may refer to a specification for that format, or it may be a reference to a program that can manipulate the format. Again, a `null` is returned if no system identifier is supplied.

DocumentFragment Interface

A document fragment (shown in Listing 8-17) serves to hold and manage a subtree of nodes before adding them to a document. When placed into the document hierarchy, the Document-Fragment node itself is not added. All of its child nodes are instead placed where the fragment would have gone. These nodes never appear within a DOM document structure.

Listing 8-17: The DocumentFragment interface
```
interface DocumentFragment : Node {
};
```

Its interface simply serves as a marker to identify its purpose. All of its abilities are inherited from the basic Node.

Document Interface

Bringing all the other nodes together is the Document interface (see Listing 8-18). As well as serving as the manager and container for each document, it provides numerous factory methods to create the different types of nodes. Nodes should only be generated in this manner, since it guarantees that the document and its child nodes work together properly. All newly instantiated nodes are not part of the document and have no parent until they are explicitly added to another node.

Listing 8-18: The Document interface
```
interface Document : Node {
  readonly attribute DocumentType      doctype;
  readonly attribute DOMImplementation implementation;
  readonly attribute Element           documentElement;
  Element                createElement(in DOMString tagName)
                             raises(DOMException);
  DocumentFragment       createDocumentFragment();
  Text                   createTextNode(in DOMString data);
  Comment                createComment(in DOMString data);
  CDATASection           createCDATASection(in DOMString data)
                             raises(DOMException);
  ProcessingInstruction  createProcessingInstruction(
                             in DOMString target,
                             in DOMString data)
                             raises(DOMException);
  Attr                   createAttribute(in DOMString name)
                             raises(DOMException);
  EntityReference        createEntityReference(in DOMString name)
                             raises(DOMException);
  NodeList               getElementsByTagName(
                             in DOMString tagname);
```

```
           // Introduced in DOM Level 2:
           Node                importNode(in Node importedNode,
                                  in boolean deep) raises(DOMException);
           // Introduced in DOM Level 2:
           Element             createElementNS(
                                  in DOMString namespaceURI,
                                  in DOMString qualifiedName)
                                  raises(DOMException);
           // Introduced in DOM Level 2:
           Attr                createAttributeNS(
                                  in DOMString namespaceURI,
                                  in DOMString qualifiedName)
                                  raises(DOMException);
           // Introduced in DOM Level 2:
           NodeList            getElementsByTagNameNS(
                                  in DOMString namespaceURI,
                                  in DOMString localName);
           // Introduced in DOM Level 2:
           Element             getElementById(in DOMString elementId);
       };
```

The properties and methods of a Document node are as follows:

`readonly attribute DOMImplementation implementation;`
> A pointer to the `DOMImplementation` that supports this document. See below for further details about this interface.

`readonly attribute DocumentType doctype;`
> A reference to the `DocumentType` node for this document, or `null` if there is none. The document type declaration cannot be changed in any way under DOM Level 2.

`readonly attribute Element documentElement;`
> As a convenience, this property points to the single top-level element of the document. This element could also be found by stepping through the child nodes of the document.

`Element createElement(in DOMString tagName) raises(DOMException);`
> A factory method for generating `Element` nodes for use within this document. Nodes cannot be used in documents other than the one in which they were created. Specify the tag name of the element when calling it. An exception occurs if the supplied name contains illegal characters.

`DocumentFragment createDocumentFragment();`
> Produce new `DocumentFragment` nodes with this method.

`Text createTextNode(in DOMString data);`
> Instantiate new `Text` nodes for this document. Pass the contents of the node as a parameter.

`Comment createComment(in DOMString data);`
> Generate new `Comment` nodes. The text of the comment is passed in.

`CDATASection createCDATASection(in DOMString data) raises(DOMException);`
> Produce new `CDATASection` nodes. Text for the CDATA section is provided, and may contain characters that would normally need to be escaped. An exception is generated if this method is used within an HTML DOM.

```
ProcessingInstruction createProcessingInstruction(in DOMString target, in
    DOMString data) raises(DOMException);
```
Instantiate a new `ProcessingInstruction` node. Specify the target application and the command line as you create it. Calling this within an HTML DOM raises an exception, as does supplying a `target` value with an illegal character.

```
Attr createAttribute(in DOMString name) raises(DOMException);
```
Generate a new `Attribute` node to add to an element. Although the name of the attribute may be passed in, you still need to set its value. An exception occurs if the attribute name contains an illegal character.

```
EntityReference createEntityReference(in DOMString name) raises(DOMException);
```
Produce a new `EntityReference` node to mark the position of an `Entity` within the document. Specify the name of the entity to refer to. Exceptions are raised if the name has an illegal character or if it is called within an HTML DOM.

NOTE Since the `DocumentType` node for a document cannot be altered, including the objects it manages, there are no methods to create `Entity` and `Notation` nodes. These must come from a DTD as it is loaded.

```
NodeList getElementsByTagName(in DOMString tagname);
```
Retrieve a list of `Element` nodes that have the specified name from the document. The entries appear in the order in which they are encountered during a pre-order traversal of the tree. Note that the nodes in the list are "live," meaning that any changes made to them affect the actual nodes within the hierarchy. Use a name of * to obtain all elements.

```
Node importNode(in Node importedNode, in boolean deep) raises(DOMException);
```
Return a copy of a node from another document. Recursively include all of its child nodes if the deep parameter is set to `True`. The new node has its `parentNode` set to null until it is placed in the new document. Some special cases apply to various node types as listed below:
   `Document` and `DocumentType` nodes cannot be imported.
   `Element` nodes copy only their specified attributes, although they may acquire new default ones based on the new DTD. The attributes are copied regardless of the deep value.
   `Attribute` nodes always copy their descendants regardless of the deep setting, and their `specified` flag is set to `True`.
   `Entity` and `Notation` nodes can be imported, but they cannot currently be added to the document's `DocumentType` node.
   `EntityReference` nodes never copy their descendants, although they do acquire the descendants of the same named entity in the new document.

```
Element createElementNS(in DOMString namespaceURI, in DOMString qualifiedName)
    raises(DOMException);
```
Generate a new `Element` node with the specified namespace URI and qualified name. This method was added in DOM Level 2. An exception arises if the qualified name contains an illegal character or if it is malformed (it has a prefix but no namespace is supplied or the prefix is xml or xmlns without the namespace being the correct corresponding value).

`Attr createAttributeNS(in DOMString namespaceURI, in DOMString qualifiedName)`
`raises(DOMException);`
: Produce a new `Attribute` node with the given namespace URI and qualified name. This method was added in DOM Level 2. If the qualified name has an illegal character or is malformed, an exception occurs.

`NodeList getElementsByTagNameNS(in DOMString namespaceURI, in DOMString localName);`
: This functions the same as the `getElementsByTagName` method, but takes a namespace URI and a local name as parameters. Either part can be * to match with all values. It was added as part of DOM Level 2.

`Element getElementById(in DOMString elementId);`
: New in DOM Level 2, this method returns the single `Element` node with the specified ID value, or `null` if none can be found. For this method to function, the document must have information that defines which attributes contain ID type values (an attached DTD or schema). If that information is not available, the function returns `null`.

DOMImplementation Interface

Finally, the `DOMImplementation` interface (shown in Listing 8-19) defines functionality that exists outside the scope of any one document.

Listing 8-19: The *DOMImplementation* interface

```
interface DOMImplementation {
    boolean     hasFeature(in DOMString feature,
                    in DOMString version);
    // Introduced in DOM Level 2:
    DocumentType createDocumentType(in DOMString qualifiedName,
                    in DOMString publicId, in DOMString systemId)
                    raises(DOMException);
    // Introduced in DOM Level 2:
    Document    createDocument(in DOMString namespaceURI,
                    in DOMString qualifiedName,
                    in DocumentType doctype) raises(DOMException);
};
```

A `DOMImplementation`'s methods are described below:

`boolean hasFeature(in DOMString feature, in DOMString version);`
: To allow for extension to the DOM in a robust way, this function tests whether a particular feature is supported and at what level. The basic core functionality is always available in any DOM. For the extended core capabilities, you use the feature name XML. Use HTML for the additional HTML node types defined in the DOM (but not covered here). Versions may be tested for explicitly, in which case DOM Level 1 corresponds to version 1.0 and Level 2 is 2.0. If no version is specified, then any supported version returns True.

DocumentType createDocumentType(in DOMString qualifiedName, in DOMString publicId, in DOMString systemId) raises(DOMException);
: Generate an empty DocumentType node with the specified values. Under DOM Level 2 this node is read-only, so entities and notations cannot be added to it (which makes it fairly useless). Future versions of the DOM will probably allow for modification of the DTD. This method was added as part of DOM Level 2. If the qualified name has an illegal character or is malformed, an exception occurs.

Document createDocument(in DOMString namespaceURI, in DOMString qualifiedName, in DocumentType doctype) raises(DOMException);
: Produce a new Document object to work with. Set the document element and document type with the supplied values. Prior to DOM Level 2, when this method was added, the manner in which a document was initially obtained was not specified. It was left to the implementations to provide an appropriate mechanism. Exceptions arise if the names contain an illegal character, if the qualified name is malformed, or if the document type node is already in use or was created by another implementation.

NodeFilter Interface

In addition to the enhancements to the DOM Core, DOM Level 2 added specifications for navigating the model, or a selection of nodes from it. These extra abilities are described below and form the Traversal section of DOM Level 2. The NodeFilter interface (see in Listing 8-20) defines a way to decide whether or not a node is chosen. Objects that implement this interface are used within the NodeIterator and TreeWalker interfaces below to modify the set of nodes extracted from the DOM.

Listing 8-20: The NodeFilter interface

```
// Introduced in DOM Level 2:
interface NodeFilter {
  // Constants returned by acceptNode
  const short           FILTER_ACCEPT = 1;
  const short           FILTER_REJECT = 2;
  const short           FILTER_SKIP   = 3;
  // Constants for whatToShow
  const unsigned long   SHOW_ALL                     = 0xFFFFFFFF;
  const unsigned long   SHOW_ELEMENT                 = 0x00000001;
  const unsigned long   SHOW_ATTRIBUTE               = 0x00000002;
  const unsigned long   SHOW_TEXT                    = 0x00000004;
  const unsigned long   SHOW_CDATA_SECTION           = 0x00000008;
  const unsigned long   SHOW_ENTITY_REFERENCE        = 0x00000010;
  const unsigned long   SHOW_ENTITY                  = 0x00000020;
  const unsigned long   SHOW_PROCESSING_INSTRUCTION  = 0x00000040;
  const unsigned long   SHOW_COMMENT                 = 0x00000080;
  const unsigned long   SHOW_DOCUMENT                = 0x00000100;
  const unsigned long   SHOW_DOCUMENT_TYPE           = 0x00000200;
  const unsigned long   SHOW_DOCUMENT_FRAGMENT       = 0x00000400;
  const unsigned long   SHOW_NOTATION                = 0x00000800;
  short         acceptNode(in Node n);
};
```

The methods of a `NodeFilter` are as follows:

`short acceptNode(in Node n);`
> Given a node, this method returns a flag indicating what its fate is to be. The returned value is one of the FILTER_* constants, which have the following meanings. FILTER_ACCEPT adds the node to the list being compiled, with processing continuing with its descendants (in the case of a `TreeWalker`). FILTER_REJECT discards the node from the list (including all of its descendants for `TreeWalker`). FILTER_SKIP does not add the current node to the list, but does process any descendants to see whether they qualify. Within the implementation of this method, any possible test can be applied to the node.

The SHOW_* constants combine to allow for simple filtering when selecting nodes. Values are added or OR'd together before being passed in as the `whatToShow` parameter during the creation of an iterator or walker in the `DocumentTraversal` interface below. The intent of each constant is obvious from its name. However, attribute, entity, and notation nodes only appear when they are at the root of the tree being searched, since they are not part of the normal DOM tree structure.

NodeIterator Interface

The `NodeIterator` interface, introduced in DOM Level 2 Traversal and shown in Listing 8-21, provides access to a collection of nodes selected from the DOM. Nodes are retrieved in a sequential manner from the iterator, without regard to their original positions within the hierarchy (other than their order which reflects a pre-order walk through the tree).

Listing 8-21: The `NodeIterator` interface

```
// Introduced in DOM Level 2:
interface NodeIterator {
    readonly attribute Node           root;
    readonly attribute unsigned long  whatToShow;
    readonly attribute NodeFilter     filter;
    readonly attribute boolean        expandEntityReferences;

    Node            nextNode() raises(DOMException);
    Node            previousNode() raises(DOMException);
    void            detach();
};
```

The list of nodes accessible through an iterator is "live." Thus, the methods must take into account the current state of the specified subtree and respond accordingly as nodes are added or deleted.

The `NodeIterator`'s properties and methods are described below:

`readonly attribute Node root;`
> The node at the base of the subtree from which the nodes in the list are selected. This is set when the iterator is created and cannot be changed thereafter.

`readonly attribute unsigned long whatToShow;`
> For an initial filter you can specify which types of nodes to select. Use the constants from the `NodeFilter` interface and add or OR them together. These values take precedence over any filter that may be supplied. As for `root`, this set of nodes is specified when the iterator is created and is then read-only.

`readonly attribute NodeFilter filter;`
> For more complex selections you supply an instance of the `NodeFilter` interface that performs whatever testing on individual nodes is required. Once more, the filter is established on creation and cannot be altered.

`readonly attribute boolean expandEntityReferences;`
> This flag determines whether or not child nodes of any entity references within the subtree are provided to the iterator. When set to `False`, the content of these reference nodes is skipped. To hide the entity reference nodes themselves but retain all their descendants, set this flag to `True` and use the `whatToShow` property to exclude entity reference nodes.

`Node nextNode() raises(DOMException);`
> Retrieve the next node in the list with this method, and move the position pointer forward. After the iterator is initially created, this call returns the first node in the list. At the end of the list, the return value is `null`. An exception occurs if the iterator has been detached.

`Node previousNode() raises(DOMException);`
> Return the previous node in the list with this method, and move the current pointer backward. Stepping back from the beginning of the list returns a value of `null`. Calling this on a detached iterator generates an exception.

`void detach();`
> Once the iterator has been used, its resources can be released with this call. Having performed this step, further calls to `nextNode` or `previousNode` result in an invalid state exception being raised.

TreeWalker Interface

The `TreeWalker` interface, part of DOM Level 2 Traversal and shown in Listing 8-22, also provides a view onto the nodes in the DOM. It differs from the `NodeIterator` in that it retains any applicable tree structure. From any particular node (the *current* node), you can navigate through the hierarchy extracted by the walker. Note that the returned tree may be substantially different from the original DOM. This depends on what selection criteria were applied, which nodes were found, and their relationships to each other.

Listing 8-22: The TreeWalker interface

```
// Introduced in DOM Level 2:
interface TreeWalker {
  readonly attribute Node            root;
  readonly attribute unsigned long   whatToShow;
  readonly attribute NodeFilter      filter;
  readonly attribute boolean         expandEntityReferences;
```

```
                attribute Node          currentNode;
                // raises(DOMException) on setting
        Node    parentNode();
        Node    firstChild();
        Node    lastChild();
        Node    previousSibling();
        Node    nextSibling();
        Node    previousNode();
        Node    nextNode();
};
```

Again, the tree walker acts upon a "live" subtree in the document. As nodes are inserted or removed, the walker always takes this into consideration when navigating through its selected nodes. Although the current node may be deleted or set outside the filtered set, the result of a movement always returns a node from the filtered set, or `null` if no such movement could be made.

The properties and methods of a `TreeWalker` are as follows:

readonly attribute Node root;
readonly attribute unsigned long whatToShow;
readonly attribute NodeFilter filter;
readonly attribute boolean expandEntityReferences;

    The above properties all function the same as for the `NodeIterator` interface.

attribute Node currentNode;

    Retrieve the current position within the walker structure with this property. You can also set the node to be used for future navigation through this property. Note that the node specified need not be one of those selected by the walker. In fact, it need not even be in the subtree based at root.

Node parentNode();

    Move to the closest ancestor within the selected nodes. If this steps up past the root node, then it returns `null`. Make the returned node the current one.

Node firstChild();

    Return the first selected child of the current node, or `null` if there are no children. The child node becomes the current node for future calls.

Node lastChild();

    Same as for `firstChild`, but returns the last selected child and moves the current node pointer here.

Node previousSibling();

    Retrieve the preceding sibling of the current node, and return it. If there is no previous sibling, return `null`. Move the current pointer here.

Node nextSibling();

    Same as for `previousSibling`, but returns the following sibling, if there is one.

`Node previousNode();`
: Move to the preceding selected node in document (pre-order) order. Returns `null` if there is no previous node. As always, move the current node to the new node.

`Node nextNode();`
: Same as for `previousNode`, but returns the following node.

DocumentTraversal Interface

To allow you to use the navigation aids defined in DOM Level 2 Traversal, the `DocumentTraversal` interface (see Listing 8-23) specifies how they are created. In each case, you define the selection criteria and the root node to operate from. These values are saved within the resulting object, but cannot be altered there. The construction of `NodeFilter` objects is left to the user, since these are very specific to the application's requirements.

Listing 8-23: The DocumentTraversal interface

```
// Introduced in DOM Level 2:
interface DocumentTraversal {
    NodeIterator  createNodeIterator(in Node root,
                in unsigned long whatToShow,
                in NodeFilter filter,
                in boolean entityReferenceExpansion)
                raises(DOMException);
    TreeWalker   createTreeWalker(in Node root,
                in unsigned long whatToShow,
                in NodeFilter filter,
                in boolean entityReferenceExpansion)
                raises(DOMException);
};
```

The ability of a DOM implementation to support these navigation objects is available through its `hasFeature` method. If the `Traversal` feature returns `True` from this method, you can expect all these abilities to be present.

A `DocumentTraversal`'s methods are described below:

`NodeIterator createNodeIterator(in Node root, in unsigned long whatToShow, in NodeFilter filter, in boolean entityReferenceExpansion) raises(DOMException);`
: Given the node from which to start, the node type selection criteria, an optional filter, and the entity reference flag, create an instance of a `NodeIterator` and return a reference to it. An exception is raised if the root node is `null`.

`TreeWalker createTreeWalker(in Node root, in unsigned long whatToShow, in NodeFilter filter, in boolean entityReferenceExpansion) raises(DOMException);`
: Generate an instance of a `TreeWalker`, given the node from which to start, the node type selection criteria, an optional filter, and the entity reference flag, and return a reference to it. If the root node is `null`, an exception occurs.

Summary

The DOM specification defines a standard way of accessing and manipulating structured documents (particularly XML documents).

The Core specification identifies the functionality necessary for basic document operations, and provides extended coverage for various XML-specific constructs. The HTML specification builds on the core to lay out interfaces for working with HTML documents and their specific node types.

DOM Level 2 has added additional functionality in the form of namespace support and document creation. An extension feature, document traversal, provides ways of selecting a subset of the nodes within a DOM and navigating through them. Other extensions are defined, but these do not yet exist in available DOM implementations and so have not been covered.

In the following chapters you'll see how various parties implement the DOM in ways that can be utilized from Delphi. First, we discuss Microsoft's DOM and parser from their MSXML3.dll package. Then follow two packages that provide Delphi native components for the DOM: a commercial suite from CUESoft and an open source version from Open XML.

Chapter 9
Microsoft's Document Object Model

Microsoft has implemented the DOM specification under Windows in its XML parser package. Originally this was available as msxml.dll, which came with the latest version of Internet Explorer, or could be obtained from the Microsoft Web site. In October 2000, Microsoft released a new version (v3) of its XML DOM package. Three DLLs now make up the package: msxml3.dll, msxml3a.dll, and msxml3r.dll. As well as enhancements to the original DOM implementation, the latest version includes a SAX2-compliant parser and definitions for the associated handlers.

You can obtain the latest XML package from the Microsoft Web site at http://msdn.microsoft.com/xml. Version 3 of the MSXML package is installed alongside any existing MSXML package and both can coexist on your system. Existing applications that use the package continue to use the original version, but you can ask for an instance of the newer version in your programs.

Microsoft also provides a utility, xmlinst.exe, that lets you run the newer version in replace mode. When invoked, this tool modifies entries in the registry to redirect calls for the original version to the newer version. Be warned, however, that this may adversely affect some applications using the older version. Fortunately, the tool also lets you uninstall version 3 as a replacement. This utility is available from the Microsoft Web site as well.

NOTE The use of MSXML version 3 is assumed throughout the rest of the book. This version is the one incorporated into all the demonstration projects.

NOTE The Microsoft DOM implementation does not support all of the abilities described in the DOM Level 2 discussion in the previous chapter. It does support namespace usage, but not the Traversal extension.

Microsoft's DOM is implemented as a series of COM objects. To gain access to the DOM in Delphi, you need to import the type library for it.

1. Choose the **Project | Import Type Library** menu options.
2. Select **Microsoft XML, v3.0 (Version 3.0)** from the list of available objects at the top. Note that there may be multiple versions of the XML package registered. If it does not appear in the list, press the **Add** button and locate the appropriate DLL.

3. Check the **Unit dir name** field to see where the wrapper appears.
4. Press the **Create Unit** button to generate the type library in that directory. It is called MSXML2_tlb.pas. This is the unit that you include in your uses clause to access the package.

Looking through the Pascal version of the type library, you see interfaces declared that correspond with those defined by the DOM specification. In each case the string IXMLDOM prefixes the original name. See Figure 9-1 for the hierarchy of interfaces defined by Microsoft.

Figure 9-1: The Microsoft DOM hierarchy.

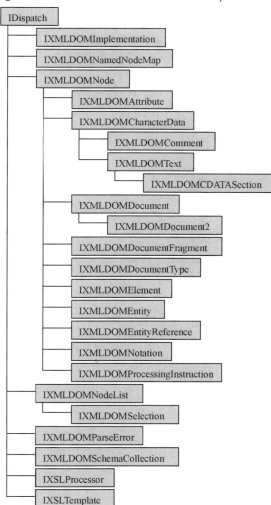

NOTE Within Microsoft's DOM, all string values from the XML document are `WideString` types. These are dynamically allocated strings of 16-bit Unicode characters. Since XML is defined to work with Unicode, this is expected. The Delphi online Help notes that this format is less efficient than the more usual `AnsiString` because it does not use reference counting and copy-on-write semantics.

IXMLDOMParseError Interface

The IXMLDOMParseError interface (as shown in Listing 9-1) is used to report errors during the loading and parsing of a document into the DOM structures. It is thus outside the coverage of the DOM specification.

Listing 9-1: The IXMLDOMParseError interface

```
//******************************************************************//
// Interface: IXMLDOMParseError
// Flags:     (4544) Dual NonExtensible OleAutomation Dispatchable
// GUID:      {3EFAA426-272F-11D2-836F-0000F87A7782}
//******************************************************************//
IXMLDOMParseError = interface(IDispatch)
  ['{3EFAA426-272F-11D2-836F-0000F87A7782}']
  function Get_errorCode: Integer; safecall;
  function Get_url: WideString; safecall;
  function Get_reason: WideString; safecall;
  function Get_srcText: WideString; safecall;
  function Get_line: Integer; safecall;
  function Get_linepos: Integer; safecall;
  function Get_filepos: Integer; safecall;
  property errorCode: Integer read Get_errorCode;
  property url: WideString read Get_url;
  property reason: WideString read Get_reason;
  property srcText: WideString read Get_srcText;
  property line: Integer read Get_line;
  property linepos: Integer read Get_linepos;
  property filepos: Integer read Get_filepos;
end;
```

When an error occurs during the parse process, it returns a `False` flag from that method call. You can then examine the document's `parseError` property, which returns an object of this type, to determine the cause of the problem.

An IXMLDOMParseError's properties are described below. All are read-only.

`property errorCode: Integer read Get_errorCode;`
   This property returns a value indicating the type of error encountered.

`property reason: WideString read Get_reason;`
   A text explanation of the error is returned by this property. This is of much more use to the user than the `errorCode` above. Validation errors include in their description the URL of the schema and the node within it that caused the error.

`property line: Integer read Get_line;`
   The line number (starting from one) in the XML document where the error was detected is available through this property.

property linepos: Integer read Get_linepos;
: Complementing the line property, this one provides the column number within that line (again starting from one) where the error was found.

property filepos: Integer read Get_filepos;
: The location of the error as the character position from the start of the file is returned by this property. Do not forget to take into account the carriage return and line feed characters at the ends of the lines in locating this position.

property srcText: WideString read Get_srcText;
: This property tries to identify the offending section of text by returning the full line where the error is detected. If the error is due to a violation of the well-formedness constraint and cannot be assigned to a particular line, then an empty string is returned.

property url: WideString read Get_url;
: The document that produced the error is available through this property.

Other errors that occur during manipulations of the DOM structure appear as an EOleException. These correspond to the error conditions noted in the DOM specification. Although EOleException has an ErrorCode property, this does not match up with the error codes from the spec.

IXMLDOMNode Interface

The fundamental building block of the DOM is represented by the Node interface. In Microsoft's version this appears as the IXMLDOMNode interface as shown in Listing 9-2. It provides the basic properties of each node in the structure that is the DOM. Various subclasses extend this base, adding functionality specific to their purpose.

Listing 9-2: The IXMLDOMNode interface

```
// *********************************************************************//
// Interface: IXMLDOMNode
// Flags:    (4544) Dual NonExtensible OleAutomation Dispatchable
// GUID:     {2933BF80-7B36-11D2-B20E-00C04F983E60}
// *********************************************************************//
IXMLDOMNode = interface(IDispatch)
  ['{2933BF80-7B36-11D2-B20E-00C04F983E60}']
  function Get_nodeName: WideString; safecall;
  function Get_nodeValue: OleVariant; safecall;
  procedure Set_nodeValue(value: OleVariant); safecall;
  function Get_nodeType: DOMNodeType; safecall;
  function Get_parentNode: IXMLDOMNode; safecall;
  function Get_childNodes: IXMLDOMNodeList; safecall;
  function Get_firstChild: IXMLDOMNode; safecall;
  function Get_lastChild: IXMLDOMNode; safecall;
  function Get_previousSibling: IXMLDOMNode; safecall;
  function Get_nextSibling: IXMLDOMNode; safecall;
  function Get_attributes: IXMLDOMNamedNodeMap; safecall;
  function insertBefore(const newChild: IXMLDOMNode;
    refChild: OleVariant): IXMLDOMNode; safecall;
  function replaceChild(const newChild: IXMLDOMNode;
```

```
    const oldChild: IXMLDOMNode): IXMLDOMNode; safecall;
  function removeChild(const childNode: IXMLDOMNode): IXMLDOMNode;
    safecall;
  function appendChild(const newChild: IXMLDOMNode): IXMLDOMNode;
    safecall;
  function hasChildNodes: WordBool; safecall;
  function Get_ownerDocument: IXMLDOMDocument; safecall;
  function cloneNode(deep: WordBool): IXMLDOMNode; safecall;
  function Get_nodeTypeString: WideString; safecall;
  function Get_text: WideString; safecall;
  procedure Set_text(const text: WideString); safecall;
  function Get_specified: WordBool; safecall;
  function Get_definition: IXMLDOMNode; safecall;
  function Get_nodeTypedValue: OleVariant; safecall;
  procedure Set_nodeTypedValue(typedValue: OleVariant); safecall;
  function Get_dataType: OleVariant; safecall;
  procedure Set_dataType(const dataTypeName: WideString); safecall;
  function Get_xml: WideString; safecall;
  function transformNode(const stylesheet: IXMLDOMNode): WideString;
    safecall;
  function selectNodes(const queryString: WideString): IXMLDOMNodeList;
    safecall;
  function selectSingleNode(const queryString: WideString):
    IXMLDOMNode; safecall;
  function Get_parsed: WordBool; safecall;
  function Get_namespaceURI: WideString; safecall;
  function Get_prefix: WideString; safecall;
  function Get_baseName: WideString; safecall;
  procedure transformNodeToObject(const stylesheet: IXMLDOMNode;
    outputObject: OleVariant); safecall;
  property nodeName: WideString read Get_nodeName;
  property nodeValue: OleVariant read Get_nodeValue
    write Set_nodeValue;
  property nodeType: DOMNodeType read Get_nodeType;
  property parentNode: IXMLDOMNode read Get_parentNode;
  property childNodes: IXMLDOMNodeList read Get_childNodes;
  property firstChild: IXMLDOMNode read Get_firstChild;
  property lastChild: IXMLDOMNode read Get_lastChild;
  property previousSibling: IXMLDOMNode read Get_previousSibling;
  property nextSibling: IXMLDOMNode read Get_nextSibling;
  property attributes: IXMLDOMNamedNodeMap read Get_attributes;
  property ownerDocument: IXMLDOMDocument read Get_ownerDocument;
  property nodeTypeString: WideString read Get_nodeTypeString;
  property text: WideString read Get_text write Set_text;
  property specified: WordBool read Get_specified;
  property definition: IXMLDOMNode read Get_definition;
  property nodeTypedValue: OleVariant read Get_nodeTypedValue
    write Set_nodeTypedValue;
  property xml: WideString read Get_xml;
  property parsed: WordBool read Get_parsed;
  property namespaceURI: WideString read Get_namespaceURI;
  property prefix: WideString read Get_prefix;
  property baseName: WideString read Get_baseName;
end;
```

You do not find IXMLDOMNode objects themselves in the hierarchy, just a descendant. However, this interface allows you to treat them all in a standard manner while obtaining basic information about them. Although this interface provides properties and methods for working with child nodes, not all node types within the DOM may have children. Similarly, the `attributes` property of a node only applies to elements, entities, and notations.

The properties and methods of an `IXMLDOMNode` are shown below. Most of these follow the DOM specification, with any differences highlighted.

property nodeType: DOMNodeType read Get_nodeType;

This property identifies what kind of node you are dealing with. It contains one of the values shown in Listing 9-3. Set during construction of the node, this property cannot be changed at a later stage. Checking this property allows you to safely cast the node into its correct subclass, thus gaining access to its particular abilities. The applicability of certain other properties and methods also depends on this value. For example, the `nodeValue` property does not apply to documents, elements, entities, and notations.

Listing 9-3: Node types in Microsoft's DOM

```
const
    NODE_INVALID                 = $00000000;
    NODE_ELEMENT                 = $00000001;
    NODE_ATTRIBUTE               = $00000002;
    NODE_TEXT                    = $00000003;
    NODE_CDATA_SECTION           = $00000004;
    NODE_ENTITY_REFERENCE        = $00000005;
    NODE_ENTITY                  = $00000006;
    NODE_PROCESSING_INSTRUCTION  = $00000007;
    NODE_COMMENT                 = $00000008;
    NODE_DOCUMENT                = $00000009;
    NODE_DOCUMENT_TYPE           = $0000000A;
    NODE_DOCUMENT_FRAGMENT       = $0000000B;
    NODE_NOTATION                = $0000000C;
```

property nodeTypeString: WideString read Get_nodeTypeString;

This property contains the node type as a string value—the name of the node subclass without the leading IXMLDOM, all in lowercase. Again, this value is set during instantiation of the node and cannot be changed. This is an extension to the original DOM specification.

property nodeName: WideString read Get_nodeName;

Return the name of the node with this read-only property. It always returns some value, never an empty string. For nodes that do not have a real name in the document, certain standard names are used. For example, the node for the document as a whole is named `#document`, comments are labeled `#comment`, text nodes are named `#text`, and CDATA sections are labeled `#cdata-section`.

Element, attribute, entity, and notation nodes each return the qualified name (including any namespace prefix) of their respective entries. Entity reference nodes supply the name of the entity to which they refer, excluding the leading ampersand (&) and trailing semicolon (;). Processing instruction nodes return the target of the instruction, while document type nodes supply the name of the top-level element in the document.

property namespaceURI: WideString read Get_namespaceURI;

Find the full URI that identifies the namespace for this node through this read-only property. For example, given the namespace declaration `xmlns:math="http://www.w3.org/TR/`

REC-MathML" and the qualified name math:plus, this property returns http://www.w3.org/TR/REC-MathML.

property prefix: WideString read Get_prefix;

This read-only property returns the shorthand identifier for the namespace as specified in the name of this node (up to the colon). An empty string is supplied if no prefix applies to the current name.

property baseName: WideString read Get_baseName;

The local name of the element is available through this read-only property (after any colon in the name). It always returns a non-empty string.

NOTE The baseName property is named differently in the DOM specification, which defines it as localName.

property nodeValue: OleVariant read Get_nodeValue write Set_nodeValue;

Some nodes also have a value associated with them, held in this property. Text, CDATASection, and Comment nodes store their contents here, while ProcessingInstruction nodes use it for the instruction data. For Attr nodes, it contains a string corresponding to the full value of the attribute, including expanding out any entity references held therein. Setting this property on an attribute causes any children it has to be deleted and be replaced by a single text node with this value. The remaining node types, for which it has no meaning, return nil.

property text: WideString read Get_text write Set_text;

This property contains the entire textual contents of this node and all of its children, concatenated together. In other words, it includes the content of all the Text and CDATASection nodes, including expanded entity references, that are descendants of this node strung together. White space from text nodes is normalized before concatenation—converting all white space characters to spaces, compressing multiple spaces down to one, and removing leading and trailing spaces—unless overridden with the xml:space attribute and preserveWhiteSpace switch on the parser. CDATA sections always retain their original spacing.

For Text, CDATASection, Comment, and ProcessingInstruction nodes themselves, this property holds the text content, just like the nodeValue property. Entity reference nodes return the content of the entity referred to. An empty string is returned from DocumentType, UnparsedEntity, and Notation nodes.

Setting the text property causes all child nodes to be removed and be replaced by a single text node with the supplied value.

property xml: WideString read Get_xml;

This read-only property retrieves the node and all its sub-nodes as formatted XML. It always returns a Unicode string, regardless of the original encoding of the document. Use the save method to retain the original encoding. Typically, this property is used as the final step in generating a document using the DOM.

Document fragment nodes do not include themselves in the XML returned by this property, only their descendants. For DocumentType nodes, you get the <!DOCTYPE...> declaration, including any internal subset that is specified. EntityReference nodes return the reference itself, rather than the contents of any children that they may have.

NOTE The text and xml properties of the Microsoft DOM have no counterpart in the official DOM specification. However, they are quite useful in the real world of XML processing, especially in generating XML documents or fragments on the fly. See Chapter 19 for further details on creating documents with the DOM.

The properties dataType, nodeTypedValue, and definition are also extensions to the official DOM specification.

```
function Get_dataType: OleVariant; safecall;
procedure Set_dataType(const dataTypeName: WideString); safecall;
```
These methods together represent the type of this node, as declared in the schema for this document. The function returns the value from that schema for attribute, element, and entity reference nodes, or nil if it is not available. For all other nodes it has the value string. Only element and attribute nodes may have this value set. All other nodes ignore the Set_dataType call.

NOTE Although dataType should be a property of an IXMLDOMNode, the differing types in the getter and setter (OleVariant vs. WideString) cause it not to be recognized as such. You need to refer to the underlying methods themselves.

```
property nodeTypedValue: OleVariant read Get_nodeTypedValue write
    Set_nodeTypedValue;
```
Retrieve node data in the dataType format through this property. Attribute nodes return the data of the appropriate type when it is specified in the schema. If not specified, this property returns a string value identical to the nodeValue property. When setting this property, an error occurs if the value cannot be converted into the appropriate type.

Element nodes return the type specified in the schema, or overridden by the dt:dt attribute in the document itself. Like attributes, they return strings if no type is specified. Text nodes provide data of the type of their containing element, or a string if that element is not typed.

Entity reference nodes supply data typed as the entity to which they refer, or a string if the type is not specified. The remaining node types return a string value the same as the nodeValue property since they do not have types.

```
property definition: IXMLDOMNode read Get_definition;
```
This read-only property refers you back to the declaration for a particular node. For entity reference nodes it points to the corresponding entity, for unparsed entities it refers to the notation, and for attributes and elements it contains the schema declaration. All other nodes return a value of nil, as do attributes and elements if no schema is present.

property attributes: IXMLDOMNamedNodeMap read Get_attributes;
: The attributes of an element are accessed through this read-only property. It returns a named node map, which is discussed in more detail below. For element, entity, and notation nodes, a list is always returned, although it may have no entries in it. Other node types return a null from this property. Attributes on the entity and notation nodes encode just the public and system identifiers, and the data type (if applicable).

property specified: WordBool read Get_specified;
: If the node represents an attribute, then this read-only property informs you whether or not the value came from the document itself (True), or was a default value coming from the DTD or schema (False). All other node types return True.

NOTE In the official DOM specification, specified is a property only of Attr nodes.

property ownerDocument: IXMLDOMDocument read Get_ownerDocument;
: All nodes belong to the document that created them. This read-only property provides access to that document. It is set during the creation of the nodes through the appropriate factory methods of the document.

property parentNode: IXMLDOMNode read Get_parentNode;
: Navigating through the DOM is accomplished via this and the following properties and methods. This read-only property returns a reference to the parent of the current node. Attribute, document, and document fragment nodes have no parent, and so always return nil, as do newly created nodes before they are added to the hierarchy and nodes removed from the tree. Entity and notation nodes refer back to the document type node that contains them, while the document type node points back to the document itself.

property childNodes: IXMLDOMNodeList read Get_childNodes;
: Child nodes are held in a node list (covered next) that is accessed via this read-only property. All nodes have a child node list, although that list is empty for any node type that does not have children.

function hasChildNodes: WordBool; safecall;
: Use this function to determine whether or not a node has any children. Alternately, you can check the number of items in the childNodes list. Obviously, it always returns False for nodes that cannot have children.

property firstChild: IXMLDOMNode read Get_firstChild;
: This read-only property returns the first child node of the current one or nil if there are no children. This is a convenience property and the same result could be achieved through the childNodes property.

property lastChild: IXMLDOMNode read Get_lastChild;
: Similarly, this read-only property returns the last child node of the current one, or nil if there are no children. It is a convenience property.

property previousSibling: IXMLDOMNode read Get_previousSibling;
> Retrieve the preceding node in this node's parent's list of children with this read-only property, or `nil` if there is none. This is easier than navigating through the hierarchy yourself. Attribute, document, and document fragment nodes always return `nil` from this property since they have no parent.

property nextSibling: IXMLDOMNode read Get_nextSibling;
> Conversely, this read-only property retrieves the following node in the node's parent's list of children, or `nil` if there is none. Similar comments apply as for the previousSibling property.

function insertBefore(const newChild: IXMLDOMNode; refChild: OleVariant): IXMLDOMNode; safecall;
> Add a new node immediately before the specified one in this node's list of children. If the reference node is `nil`, then the new node is added at the end. A pointer to the new node is returned. Nodes being inserted are first removed from the tree if they are already present. An error occurs if the reference child cannot be found.
>
> When a document fragment is inserted into the hierarchy, it is not added itself. Instead, all of its children are inserted in turn and are removed from the fragment. A pointer to the document fragment is still returned by the function.

NOTE The DOM specification expects an error to be generated if the node being inserted comes from a different document. However, Microsoft's DOM allows the transferring of nodes between documents. Be aware that the nodes may have an altered meaning within the new document due to differences in schemas between the two. This may even lead to parsing failures following the insertion.

function replaceChild(const newChild: IXMLDOMNode; const oldChild: IXMLDOMNode): IXMLDOMNode; safecall;
> Remove an existing child node and replace it with the new one supplied. A reference to the old node is returned. If the new node is specified as `nil`, the old node is simply deleted. Referring to an old node that does not exist as a child causes an error. Attempting to replace a child with a node of an inappropriate type also generates an error.

function removeChild(const childNode: IXMLDOMNode): IXMLDOMNode; safecall;
> Delete the specified node from this node's list of children. An exception is raised if the node does not exist. A pointer to the deleted node is returned.

function appendChild(const newChild: IXMLDOMNode): IXMLDOMNode; safecall;
> Add a new node at the end of the list of child nodes. Return a reference to that node. This is the same as calling `insertBefore(newChild, nil)`. The same comments apply as they did for the insert method.

TIP The use of these methods described above in creating a DOM structure is covered in greater detail in Chapter 19.

function cloneNode(deep: WordBool): IXMLDOMNode; safecall;
> To create a copy of a node, use this method. If the parameter passed to this call is True, then a copy of the entire subtree rooted at the current node is made. Otherwise, just the current node is duplicated. The following properties are duplicated: nodeType, nodeName, nodeValue, ownerDocument, parentNode, and attributes. Copying of the childNodes property depends on the deep setting.

NOTE The remaining methods and properties are extensions to the W3C DOM specification.

function selectNodes(const queryString: WideString): IXMLDOMNodeList; safecall;
> Return a list of those nodes that match the XSL or XPath query provided, based on the subtree rooted at the current node, through this function. Setting the SelectionLanguage property of the document (only available in the IXMLDOMDocument2 interface and defaulting to XSLPattern for backward compatibility) determines which of the query types is used. Finding no matching nodes returns an empty list. See Chapter 4 for more information on XSL and XPath queries.

function selectSingleNode(const queryString: WideString): IXMLDOMNode; safecall;
> This function acts the same as selectNodes, but only returns the first node in the list. nil is returned if no nodes match the query.

function transformNode(const stylesheet: IXMLDOMNode): WideString; safecall;
> Converting one DOM or document fragment into another can be achieved with this method. It takes an XSLT stylesheet reference (as another DOM or part thereof) and applies it to the current node, returning the straight text representation of the resulting tree. Navigation outside of the subtree based on the current node is allowed as the stylesheet processes.

procedure transformNodeToObject(const stylesheet: IXMLDOMNode; outputObject: OleVariant); safecall;
> Similar to transformNode, this method performs the transformation and returns the resulting DOM. Output arrives as either a new DOM structure, if the outputObject is a DOMDocument object, or is sent directly to a stream, if outputObject is such a reference. Getting the result back as another DOM allows for further processing on it.

TIP Using XSL Transformations is covered in greater detail in Chapter 21, which discusses a utility for examining transformations, and in Chapter 26, which uses XSLT to generate Web pages.

property parsed: WordBool read Get_parsed;
> This read-only property informs you whether or not the current node and all of its descendants have been fully parsed and instantiated yet. Usually this is only an issue when performing the parse asynchronously. It returns True if the current subtree has been completed, and False otherwise.

NOTE Missing from the DOM Level 2 specification are the `normalize`, `hasAttributes`, and `isSupported` methods. Under DOM Level 1, `normalize` was attached to an `Element` node, before being moved up the hierarchy in DOM Level 2. Indeed, this is where it is found in Microsoft's implementation, in `IXMLDOMElement`. The functionality of `hasAttributes` can be duplicated through checking the `attributes` property. Use the `IXMLDOMImplementation` class's `hasFeature` method instead of `isSupported`.

IXMLDOMNodeList Interface

Providing the links between the various levels within the DOM, the node list interface defines access to a list of nodes in a particular sequence. Microsoft's implementation is shown in Listing 9-4 and closely follows the official definition. The list is used when retrieving nodes from the DOM, either by tag or via a query string, as well as for the children of each node.

Listing 9-4: The IXMLDOMNodeList interface

```
// *********************************************************************//
// Interface: IXMLDOMNodeList
// Flags:     (4544) Dual NonExtensible OleAutomation Dispatchable
// GUID:      {2933BF82-7B36-11D2-B20E-00C04F983E60}
// *********************************************************************//
IXMLDOMNodeList = interface(IDispatch)
   ['{2933BF82-7B36-11D2-B20E-00C04F983E60}']
   function Get_item(index: Integer): IXMLDOMNode; safecall;
   function Get_length: Integer; safecall;
   function nextNode: IXMLDOMNode; safecall;
   procedure reset; safecall;
   function Get__newEnum: IUnknown; safecall;
   property item[index: Integer]: IXMLDOMNode read Get_item; default;
   property length: Integer read Get_length;
   property _newEnum: IUnknown read Get__newEnum;
end;
```

Recall that a node list is "live," i.e., that changes made to the list affect the DOM itself. This includes adding or removing nodes that are part of the list. Consequently, two references to a node by the same index may return different objects.

An `IXMLDOMNodeList`'s properties and methods are described below:

`property length: Integer read Get_length;`
   Retrieve the number of entries in the list with this read-only property. The value may be zero for lists that do not have any entries.

`property item[index: Integer]: IXMLDOMNode read Get_item; default;`
   Access individual entries via their index (starting from zero) with this read-only property. You are returned an `IXMLDOMNode` object to work with as described in the previous section. After determining its type through the `nodeType` property, you can cast it to that type for full access to its abilities. If the supplied index is out of range, a `nil` is returned.

```
for index := 0 to NodeList.Length - 1 do
  with NodeList.Item[index] do
    { Operate on the node };
```

TIP Item is the default property of a node list, which means that you can omit its name and just use the square brackets to access the entries. For example:
```
Node := Node.ChildNodes.Item[0];
```
can also be expressed as
```
Node := Node.ChildNodes[0];
```

`function nextNode: IXMLDOMNode; safecall;`

> Alternately, the nodes can be stepped through with this function, which returns `nil` when it reaches the end of the list. Initially, you are before the first node in the list, so a call to this returns that first entry. If the current node is removed from the list, subsequent calls to this function return `nil`.

```
NodeList.reset;
repeat
  Node := NodeList.NextNode;
  if Assigned(Node) then
    { Operate on the node }
until not Assigned(Node);
```

`procedure reset; safecall;`

> This procedure returns you to the start of the list for another enumeration using `nextNode`.

 NOTE These last two methods are not part of the official DOM specification, but provide another way of accessing the nodes within the list.

IXMLDOMNamedNodeMap Interface

This interface is similar to the node list, but also allows access to the nodes via their names. The implementation with this DOM is shown in Listing 9-5. It is used for the attributes of a node, as well as the entities and notations that belong to a document.

Listing 9-5: The *IXMLDOMNamedNodeMap* interface

```
// *******************************************************************//
// Interface: IXMLDOMNamedNodeMap
// Flags:     (4544) Dual NonExtensible OleAutomation Dispatchable
// GUID:      {2933BF83-7B36-11D2-B20E-00C04F983E60}
// *******************************************************************//
IXMLDOMNamedNodeMap = interface(IDispatch)
  ['{2933BF83-7B36-11D2-B20E-00C04F983E60}']
  function getNamedItem(const name: WideString): IXMLDOMNode; safecall;
  function setNamedItem(const newItem: IXMLDOMNode): IXMLDOMNode;
    safecall;
  function removeNamedItem(const name: WideString): IXMLDOMNode;
    safecall;
  function Get_item(index: Integer): IXMLDOMNode; safecall;
  function Get_length: Integer; safecall;
  function getQualifiedItem(const baseName: WideString;
    const namespaceURI: WideString): IXMLDOMNode; safecall;
  function removeQualifiedItem(const baseName: WideString;
    const namespaceURI: WideString): IXMLDOMNode; safecall;
  function nextNode: IXMLDOMNode; safecall;
  procedure reset; safecall;
```

```
    function Get__newEnum: IUnknown; safecall;
    property item[index: Integer]: IXMLDOMNode read Get_item; default;
    property length: Integer read Get_length;
    property _newEnum: IUnknown read Get__newEnum;
  end;
```

The entries in the list are not constrained to any particular order, although access via a sequential index is supported to allow the entire collection to be easily traversed. Microsoft adds the entries in the order found in the original document except for attributes that define namespaces. If the element uses a namespace that is declared in this tag, that namespace declaration appears as the first item in the list. Namespace declarations for other attributes appear immediately before the first use of that namespace qualifier.

As for the normal node list, entries in a named node list are "live," so adding and removing entries can alter their count and order. If an attribute is removed from an element's list, but it has a default value defined in the DTD or schema, it is immediately added back into the list with that value.

The properties and methods of IXMLDOMNamedNodeMap are shown below:

function getNamedItem(const name: WideString): IXMLDOMNode; safecall;

    Retrieve an entry from the list using its name with this method. A nil is returned if a matching item cannot be found.

function setNamedItem(const newItem: IXMLDOMNode): IXMLDOMNode; safecall;

    Add a node into the list using this method. The name of the supplied node is extracted and used as the index for later retrieval. Items are automatically updated or added as necessary when calling this routine, overwriting any previous object with the same name. Only lists of attributes belonging to an element may be modified. Attempts to change the lists of entities and notations in the document type object result in an error as they are read-only.

function removeNamedItem(const name: WideString): IXMLDOMNode; safecall;

    Use this method to delete an entry from the list using its name. A reference to the deleted node is returned by the function, unless it could not be found, in which case a nil is returned. Only lists of attributes for elements can be modified. Trying to remove entries from other lists generates an error.

NOTE The following two methods duplicate functionality from the DOM Level 2 specification: getNamedItemNS and removeNamedItemNS. However, the order of parameters to them has been reversed. Furthermore, there is no equivalent of the setNamedItemNS method in Microsoft's implementation since this functionality is available through the setNamedItem method anyway. If the node has a qualified name it is used, otherwise it is not.

function getQualifiedItem(const baseName: WideString; const namespaceURI: WideString): IXMLDOMNode; safecall;

    This method retrieves a named entry from the list based on its namespace URI and local name. If a matching node cannot be found, a nil is returned.

function removeQualifiedItem(const baseName: WideString; const namespaceURI:
    WideString): IXMLDOMNode; safecall;
: To delete an entry based on its namespace URI and local name use this method. The function returns a reference to the deleted node. If no match is found, it returns `nil`.

property length: Integer read Get_length;
: Return the number of entries in the list with this read-only property. The value may be zero if there are no entries in the list.

property item[index: Integer]: IXMLDOMNode read Get_item; default;
: Retrieve entries from the list based on their position (starting from zero). Again, this is the default property of the interface, and so can be omitted when referring to list entries. A `nil` is returned if the index is out of range.

NOTE The following two methods are not part of the DOM Level 2 specification.

function nextNode: IXMLDOMNode; safecall;
: Step through the nodes in the list as an enumeration. `nil` is returned at the end of the list. Removing the current node from the list causes subsequent calls to this function to return `nil` also.

procedure reset; safecall;
: Reposition the current pointer to the start of the list for another traversal with the `nextNode` method.

IXMLDOMElement Interface

Building on the basic DOM node are many of the remaining interfaces defined in the DOM. The first of these is for an element, as shown in Listing 9-6, adding only a few extra abilities. These are mostly involved with manipulating the attributes that belong to the element. Recall that the `attributes` property inherited from IXMLDOMNode provides access to the attached attribute nodes.

Listing 9-6: The IXMLDOMElement interface

```
// *******************************************************************//
// Interface: IXMLDOMElement
// Flags:    (4544) Dual NonExtensible OleAutomation Dispatchable
// GUID:     {2933BF86-7B36-11D2-B20E-00C04F983E60}
// *******************************************************************//
IXMLDOMElement = interface(IXMLDOMNode)
  ['{2933BF86-7B36-11D2-B20E-00C04F983E60}']
  function Get_tagName: WideString; safecall;
  function getAttribute(const name: WideString): OleVariant; safecall;
  procedure setAttribute(const name: WideString; value: OleVariant);
    safecall;
  procedure removeAttribute(const name: WideString); safecall;
  function getAttributeNode(const name: WideString): IXMLDOMAttribute;
    safecall;
  function setAttributeNode(const DOMAttribute: IXMLDOMAttribute):
    IXMLDOMAttribute; safecall;
  function removeAttributeNode(const DOMAttribute: IXMLDOMAttribute):
```

```
        IXMLDOMAttribute; safecall;
    function getElementsByTagName(const tagName: WideString):
        IXMLDOMNodeList; safecall;
    procedure normalize; safecall;
    property tagName: WideString read Get_tagName;
end;
```

IXMLDOMElement's properties and methods are described below:

`property tagName: WideString read Get_tagName;`
> The node name can also be retrieved via this property. It is merely a convenience since it maps directly onto the underlying nodeName.

`function getAttribute(const name: WideString): OleVariant; safecall;`
> Retrieve the string value of a named attribute with this method. All attributes must necessarily appear as string values within the XML document. However, they may be interpreted as other types within a processor. The function returns an empty string if the attribute's value was not specified and did not have a default, or if the attribute does not exist in the first place.

`procedure setAttribute(const name: WideString; value: OleVariant); safecall;`
> To store an attribute's value, use this method. It accepts the name of the attribute and its value. Any existing attribute with the same name is replaced, while a new attribute node is created if not already present. The supplied string value is not interpreted in any way; it is simply stored as a text node. For more extensive structure you must create the subtree first before passing it to the setAttributeNode method.

`procedure removeAttribute(const name: WideString); safecall;`
> Delete an attribute from this element given its name. Recall that if the DTD or schema for the document is available and specifies a default value for the attribute, then it immediately reappears with that value.

`function getAttributeNode(const name: WideString): IXMLDOMAttribute; safecall;`
> Similar to getAttribute, this method returns the entire attribute node rather than just the value. This is useful when the attribute contains entity references, or when using some of Microsoft's extensions to the DOM. A nil is returned if a matching attribute cannot be found.

`function setAttributeNode(const DOMAttribute: IXMLDOMAttribute): IXMLDOMAttribute; safecall;`
> To store an attribute with other than a simple string value, you can use this method. For example, an attribute that refers to an entity has an IXMLDOMEntityReference node as one of its children. Build the required structure before passing it to this method. If the new node replaces an existing attribute with the same name, a reference to the replaced node is returned. Otherwise, the method returns nil.

`function removeAttributeNode(const DOMAttribute: IXMLDOMAttribute): IXMLDOMAttribute; safecall;`
> Finally, you can delete an attribute given a reference to its node with this method. This reference is returned by the function as well.

```
function getElementsByTagName(const tagName: WideString): IXMLDOMNodeList;
    safecall;
```
Obtain a list of sub-elements with a specified name through this method. Use the string * to retrieve all descendant elements. The list can then be processed as described earlier under the `IXMLDOMNodeList` interface. Elements in the list appear in the order of a pre-order traversal of the current node's subtree. Although a list is always returned by this method, it may be empty.

```
procedure normalize; safecall;
```
This method tidies up the node tree beneath this element, combining adjacent text nodes where possible (but excluding CDATA nodes).

NOTES In the DOM Level 2 specification, the `normalize` method has been moved to the Node interface, making it more widely available.

Other methods present in the DOM Level 2 specification but missing from Microsoft's implementation are the namespace-aware versions of several routines: `getAttributeNS`, `setAttributeNS`, `removeAttributeNS`, `getAttributeNodeNS`, `setAttributeNodeNS`, and `getElementsByTagNameNS`. The methods listed that deal with attributes can be duplicated through processing the `attributes` property of the element. Also missing altogether are the `hasAttribute` and `hasAttributeNS` methods from the DOM specification. Again, their functionality can be achieved in other ways.

IXMLDOMAttribute Interface

The settings for an attribute of an element are described in the `IXMLDOMAttribute` interface, as shown in Listing 9-7. It simply adds the `name` and `value` properties, which directly mirror the `nodeName` and `nodeValue` properties of its superclass.

Listing 9-7: The IXMLDOMAttribute interface

```
// *********************************************************************//
// Interface: IXMLDOMAttribute
// Flags:     (4544) Dual NonExtensible OleAutomation Dispatchable
// GUID:      {2933BF85-7B36-11D2-B20E-00C04F983E60}
// *********************************************************************//
IXMLDOMAttribute = interface(IXMLDOMNode)
  ['{2933BF85-7B36-11D2-B20E-00C04F983E60}']
  function Get_name: WideString; safecall;
  function Get_value: OleVariant; safecall;
  procedure Set_value(attributeValue: OleVariant); safecall;
  property name: WideString read Get_name;
  property value: OleVariant read Get_value write Set_value;
end;
```

Attribute nodes are not really part of the normal DOM structure. They are considered properties of their owning element, and so only appear under that element's `attributes` property. Attributes have no parent, and so also have no next or previous siblings. Hence, all these inherited properties return `nil`.

When loading a document, attribute nodes are created for all those attributes explicitly declared in the document. Additional attribute nodes are appended for attributes that have not been specified explicitly, but that have default values defined in the DTD or schema for the document.

Recall that several inherited properties apply to attributes: `dataType` gives the type of the value, `nodeTypedValue` returns the value as that type, and `specified` tells us where the value came from (the document or the DTD).

The properties of an IXMLDOMAttribute node are shown below:

property name: WideString read Get_name;

> Retrieve the attribute's name from this read-only property. This is the same as the `nodeName` property.

property value: OleVariant read Get_value write Set_value;

> Obtain or set the string value of the attribute using this property. For a standard attribute with a simple string value, the attribute node has a single text node child, and that value is returned by the property. If an attribute has an entity reference as part of its content, its child node list contains a mixture of text and entity reference nodes, with this property returning the concatenated value of them all after expanding entity references.
>
> Setting the attribute value through this property causes any existing children to be removed and be replaced by a single text node with the supplied value. The content of the value parameter is not parsed or interpreted in any way.

TIP Under the DOM specification the attribute's value is always a string. However, with Microsoft's implementation it can be of any type. When this ability is combined with an appropriate schema, the values are available in their native format.

property specified: WordBool read Get_specified;

> This inherited read-only property indicates how the attribute's value was set. When it returns `True`, the value appeared directly in the XML document. When it is `False`, the value came from the default defined in the DTD or schema for the document.

NOTE Microsoft's implementation provides no way of retrieving the element that owns an attribute. In the DOM Level 2 specification this is embodied in the `ownerElement` property.

IXMLDOMCharacterData Interface

The interfaces for straight text within the XML document are based on `IXMLDOMCharacterData` (see Listing 9-8), which provides common functionality between the different types of text. Recall that this interface is not implemented directly, and only appears within the DOM as one of its subclasses.

Part II: The Document Object Model

Listing 9-8: The `IXMLDOMCharacterData` *interface*

```
// *********************************************************************//
// Interface: IXMLDOMCharacterData
// Flags:     (4544) Dual NonExtensible OleAutomation Dispatchable
// GUID:      {2933BF84-7B36-11D2-B20E-00C04F983E60}
// *********************************************************************//
IXMLDOMCharacterData = interface(IXMLDOMNode)
  ['{2933BF84-7B36-11D2-B20E-00C04F983E60}']
  function Get_data: WideString; safecall;
  procedure Set_data(const data: WideString); safecall;
  function Get_length: Integer; safecall;
  function substringData(offset: Integer; count: Integer): WideString;
    safecall;
  procedure appendData(const data: WideString); safecall;
  procedure insertData(offset: Integer; const data: WideString);
    safecall;
  procedure deleteData(offset: Integer; count: Integer); safecall;
  procedure replaceData(offset: Integer; count: Integer;
    const data: WideString); safecall;
  property data: WideString read Get_data write Set_data;
  property length: Integer read Get_length;
end;
```

IXMLDOMCharacterData's properties and methods are described below. All offsets start at zero.

`property data: WideString read Get_data write Set_data;`
   This property returns the actual text of the node and is simply a renaming of the `nodeValue` property.

`property length: Integer read Get_length;`
   Determine the size of the data with this read-only property. It is measured as number of characters (recall that `WideString` values use 2 bytes per character).

`function substringData(offset: Integer; count: Integer): WideString; safecall;`
   Extract sections of the node's text contents with this function, as specified by the starting position (`offset`) and length (`count`). If the starting position plus the count of characters extends past the end of the data, only that portion up to the end is returned. An error is generated if the offset or length is out of range.

`procedure appendData(const data: WideString); safecall;`
   Add additional text to the node with this method. The new data is placed at the end of any existing content.

`procedure insertData(offset: Integer; const data: WideString); safecall;`
   Place text at any point in the existing contents through this method. Just specify the offset for the addition and any existing text past that point is shifted along to make room. Using an offset or length that is out of range produces an error.

`procedure deleteData(offset: Integer; count: Integer); safecall;`
   Remove sections of text with this method, which takes the starting offset and number of characters to delete as parameters. If the offset plus the count is more than the length of the data, all the text through the end of the string is removed. An error occurs if the offset or length is out of range.

```
procedure replaceData(offset: Integer; count: Integer; const data: WideString);
    safecall;
```
This routine combines the previous two methods, deleting text from the offset for a given number of characters, then inserting the new text in its place. An offset or length that is out of range causes an error.

IXMLDOMText Interface

From the basic character data interface comes one for real textual nodes, IXMLDOMText, as shown in Listing 9-9. Within these nodes appear the actual content of the XML document, as opposed to the surrounding markup. Most of its abilities are inherited from the IXMLDOMCharacterData interface.

Listing 9-9: The IXMLDOMText interface

```
// *******************************************************************//
// Interface: IXMLDOMText
// Flags:     (4544) Dual NonExtensible OleAutomation Dispatchable
// GUID:      {2933BF87-7B36-11D2-B20E-00C04F983E60}
// *******************************************************************//
IXMLDOMText = interface(IXMLDOMCharacterData)
  ['{2933BF87-7B36-11D2-B20E-00C04F983E60}']
  function splitText(offset: Integer): IXMLDOMText; safecall;
end;
```

> **TIP** When a document is first loaded, all its text nodes are normalized. This means that no text node is adjacent to another text node. Some type of markup node surrounds each one. Using the normalize method of the IXMLDOMNode interface restores this format. Certain processes, such as using XPath identifiers, assume that the hierarchy is in this state.

Text nodes do not have any children. Using the inherited methods or properties to attempt to access or alter them results in errors or empty values as appropriate.

The method of an IXMLDOMText node is shown below:

```
function splitText(offset: Integer): IXMLDOMText; safecall;
```
This function cuts the current text node into two text nodes at the specified offset (starting at zero). The original node now contains text up to the offset, while the new node contains the remainder. A reference to the new node is the return value of the function. Using an offset or length that is out of range generates an error.

IXMLDOMCDATASection Interface

CDATA sections within an XML document are denoted by their own interface, IXMLDOMCDATASection (as seen in Listing 9-10). It inherits all the abilities of the basic character data and text data nodes, but adds nothing new. Hence, it serves merely as a flag to indicate the origins of its contained text within the document. Furthermore, CDATA sections are not affected when normalizing the DOM, i.e., when combining adjacent text nodes.

Listing 9-10: The IXMLDOMCDATASection interface

```
// *******************************************************************//
// Interface: IXMLDOMCDATASection
// Flags:     (4544) Dual NonExtensible OleAutomation Dispatchable
// GUID:      {2933BF8A-7B36-11D2-B20E-00C04F983E60}
// *******************************************************************//
IXMLDOMCDATASection = interface(IXMLDOMText)
  ['{2933BF8A-7B36-11D2-B20E-00C04F983E60}']
end;
```

Recall that CDATA sections can contain characters that would normally need to be escaped. Also, CDATA section nodes do not have children, just like text nodes. Inherited properties and methods that deal with child nodes return appropriate empty values or generate errors if used.

IXMLDOMComment Interface

Comments within the document are encapsulated by the IXMLDOMComment interface (see Listing 9-11) that builds on the character data definition. Note that this interface is just another flagging interface, adding no new functionality.

Listing 9-11: The IXMLDOMComment interface

```
// *******************************************************************//
// Interface: IXMLDOMComment
// Flags:     (4544) Dual NonExtensible OleAutomation Dispatchable
// GUID:      {2933BF88-7B36-11D2-B20E-00C04F983E60}
// *******************************************************************//
IXMLDOMComment = interface(IXMLDOMCharacterData)
  ['{2933BF88-7B36-11D2-B20E-00C04F983E60}']
end;
```

All the text between the opening and closing sequences (<!-- and -->) in the XML document makes up the content of the comment. Use the inherited nodeValue property to retrieve that text. Comment nodes do not have any children. Trying to refer to them or add new ones returns an appropriate empty value or an error.

IXMLDOMProcessingInstruction Interface

Embedded commands for processing an XML document appear through the IXMLDOMProcessingInstruction interface (see Listing 9-12). Processing instructions are the way to transmit commands through the XML document for prospective readers. Comments, which may be stripped from the DOM during processing, should not contain such information.

Listing 9-12: The IXMLDOMProcessingInstruction interface

```
// *******************************************************************//
// Interface: IXMLDOMProcessingInstruction
// Flags:     (4544) Dual NonExtensible OleAutomation Dispatchable
// GUID:      {2933BF89-7B36-11D2-B20E-00C04F983E60}
// *******************************************************************//
IXMLDOMProcessingInstruction = interface(IXMLDOMNode)
  ['{2933BF89-7B36-11D2-B20E-00C04F983E60}']
```

```
      function Get_target: WideString; safecall;
      function Get_data: WideString; safecall;
      procedure Set_data(const value: WideString); safecall;
      property target: WideString read Get_target;
      property data: WideString read Get_data write Set_data;
    end;
```

Processing instruction nodes do not have children. Although the properties and methods inherited from `IXMLDOMNode` let you interact with or manipulate child nodes, they return `nil` values or raise errors if attempts are made to use them.

An `IXMLDOMProcessingInstruction`'s properties are described below:

property target: WideString read Get_target;
> An identifier for the application that knows how to interpret the following command is available through this read-only property. It consists of the first token within the processing instruction tag. The same value is returned by the `nodeName` property.

property data: WideString read Get_data write Set_data;
> The actual command is retrieved through this property. Again, it is a simple renaming of an inherited property, `nodeValue`. XML imposes no structure on the content of the command, though the target program is sure to. All the text within the tag, from the first non-white space character following the target up to the character immediately preceding the terminating ?>, is returned as its data.

IXMLDOMDocumentType Interface

Some information from the DTD for a document is available through the `IXMLDOMDocumentType` interface (see Listing 9-13). Its abilities were intentionally limited since several related issues were not fully resolved when the DOM was specified. The `IXMLDOMDocument` object refers to a node of this type through its `DocType` property. If no DTD is available, this property returns `nil`.

Listing 9-13: The IXMLDOMDocumentType interface

```
// *********************************************************************//
// Interface: IXMLDOMDocumentType
// Flags:     (4544) Dual NonExtensible OleAutomation Dispatchable
// GUID:      {2933BF8B-7B36-11D2-B20E-00C04F983E60}
// *********************************************************************//
IXMLDOMDocumentType = interface(IXMLDOMNode)
  ['{2933BF8B-7B36-11D2-B20E-00C04F983E60}']
  function Get_name: WideString; safecall;
  function Get_entities: IXMLDOMNamedNodeMap; safecall;
  function Get_notations: IXMLDOMNamedNodeMap; safecall;
  property name: WideString read Get_name;
  property entities: IXMLDOMNamedNodeMap read Get_entities;
  property notations: IXMLDOMNamedNodeMap read Get_notations;
end;
```

The properties of an `IXMLDOMDocumentType` node are shown below:

property name: WideString read Get_name;
> Retrieve the name of the document element through this read-only property.

property entities: IXMLDOMNamedNodeMap read Get_entities;
  Access to a list of the entities (excluding parameter entities) declared in the document is provided by this read-only property. The list is returned as an IXMLDOMNamedNodeMap, allowing you to retrieve entries by their names. Items returned from the list are instances of IXMLDOMEntity, whose abilities are described below.

property notations: IXMLDOMNamedNodeMap read Get_notations;
  Similarly, access to the notations declared in the document is gained through this property. The list is also an IXMLDOMNamedNodeMap, although the underlying entries are instances of IXMLDOMNotation, also covered below.

NOTES The name, entities, and notations that come from the DTD for a document are not modifiable under Microsoft's DOM (nor in the DOM specification). They can only be set when loading a document. Any attempt to alter them generates an error.
  The additional DOM Level 2 properties for a document type node—publicId, systemId, or internalSubset—are not available through Microsoft's DOM.

IXMLDOMEntity Interface

The IXMLDOMEntity interface, as shown in Listing 9-14, models entities declared within the XML document. It does not model the declaration itself, merely the representation of that entity within the document. They are available through the entities property of the document type node of the document object. However, all entity nodes and their descendants are read-only, being set up when the document is loaded.

Listing 9-14: The IXMLDOMEntity interface

```
// *******************************************************************//
// Interface: IXMLDOMEntity
// Flags:     (4544) Dual NonExtensible OleAutomation Dispatchable
// GUID:      {2933BF8D-7B36-11D2-B20E-00C04F983E60}
// *******************************************************************//
IXMLDOMEntity = interface(IXMLDOMNode)
    ['{2933BF8D-7B36-11D2-B20E-00C04F983E60}']
    function Get_publicId: OleVariant; safecall;
    function Get_systemId: OleVariant; safecall;
    function Get_notationName: WideString; safecall;
    property publicId: OleVariant read Get_publicId;
    property systemId: OleVariant read Get_systemId;
    property notationName: WideString read Get_notationName;
  end;
```

When the Microsoft parser is in validation mode, it expands external parsed entities. This means that their internal structures are present as children of this node. An entity reference has the same structure beneath it as the entity node with the same name. Although the entity reference node itself may be inserted and deleted, its children are read-only.
  If the Microsoft parser is not validating documents, the external entities are not expanded.

An `IXMLDOMEntity`'s properties are described below:

`property nodeName: WideString read Get_nodeName;`
> The name of the entity appears in this inherited read-only property.

`property publicId: OleVariant read Get_publicId;`
> Retrieve the public (logical) identifier for the DTD or schema attached to the current document using this read-only property. For an internal entity, or an external entity without this value specified, the property returns an empty string.

`property systemId: OleVariant read Get_systemId;`
> Obtain the system (physical) identifier for the DTD or schema through this read-only property. Again, internal entities return an empty string.

`property notationName: WideString read Get_notationName;`
> For unparsed entities, this read-only property holds the type of that resource. It should refer to one of the notations also declared in the DTD. Parsed entities return an empty string for this property.

IXMLDOMEntityReference Interface

Occurrences of entities within the body of a document are represented by the IXMLDOMEntityReference interface, as shown in Listing 9-15. Another flagging interface, it merely indicates where the entity reference was encountered. Any children of this node must match those of the corresponding IXMLDOMEntity node. Note that an XML parser may expand all entity references before building the DOM, so that no entity reference nodes appear in the final model.

Listing 9-15: The IXMLDOMEntityReference interface

```
// ****************************************************************//
// Interface: IXMLDOMEntityReference
// Flags:     (4544) Dual NonExtensible OleAutomation Dispatchable
// GUID:      {2933BF8E-7B36-11D2-B20E-00C04F983E60}
// ****************************************************************//
IXMLDOMEntityReference = interface(IXMLDOMNode)
    ['{2933BF8E-7B36-11D2-B20E-00C04F983E60}']
end;
```

This interface adds no new functionality, again acting as a flag to indicate the original source of the contained nodes. The name of the entity being included is available in the inherited nodeName property.

If the parser is not validating documents, it is not required to expand external entities. In this case, the contents of the entity reference may not be available. Character entity references are automatically expanded and appear as parts of text nodes only; they do not have parent entity reference nodes.

IXMLDOMNotation Interface

Declarations of notations within the DTD of the document appear as `IXMLDOMNotation` interface objects (see Listing 9-16) and are accessible through the `notations` property of the document's document type node. These nodes represent the types of unparsed entities, attributes, and processing instruction targets.

Listing 9-16: The `IXMLDOMNotation` interface

```
// *********************************************************************//
// Interface: IXMLDOMNotation
// Flags:     (4544) Dual NonExtensible OleAutomation Dispatchable
// GUID:      {2933BF8C-7B36-11D2-B20E-00C04F983E60}
// *********************************************************************//
IXMLDOMNotation = interface(IXMLDOMNode)
  ['{2933BF8C-7B36-11D2-B20E-00C04F983E60}']
  function Get_publicId: OleVariant; safecall;
  function Get_systemId: OleVariant; safecall;
  property publicId: OleVariant read Get_publicId;
  property systemId: OleVariant read Get_systemId;
end;
```

As with the `IXMLDOMEntity` objects, these nodes model the notation itself, and not the declaration of that notation within the DTD. Notation nodes cannot be changed once the document is loaded.

The properties of an `IXMLDOMNotation` node are shown below:

`property nodeName: WideString read Get_nodeName;`
  The name of the notation appears in this inherited read-only property.

`property publicId: OleVariant read Get_publicId;`
  Retrieve the public (logical) identifier for the notation through this read-only property. If not specified, this returns an empty string.

`property systemId: OleVariant read Get_systemId;`
  Obtain the system (physical) identifier for the notation from this read-only property. Again, if not specified, it returns an empty string.

IXMLDOMDocumentFragment Interface

Being able to manipulate fragments of a document, or subtrees within the hierarchy, is a useful ability, one that is provided through the `IXMLDOMDocumentFragment` interface as shown in Listing 9-17. Document fragments never form part of the DOM beneath a document node.

Listing 9-17: The `IXMLDOMDocumentFragment` interface

```
// *********************************************************************//
// Interface: IXMLDOMDocumentFragment
// Flags:     (4544) Dual NonExtensible OleAutomation Dispatchable
// GUID:      {3EFAA413-272F-11D2-836F-0000F87A7782}
// *********************************************************************//
IXMLDOMDocumentFragment = interface(IXMLDOMNode)
  ['{3EFAA413-272F-11D2-836F-0000F87A7782}']
end;
```

This is another flagging interface which adds no new functionality to the basic node definition. Its use is in building up sub-structures and moving sections of the tree around. When a document fragment is added to an existing document, the fragment node itself is not added, only its children and descendants. The contents of a document fragment do not need to be a well-formed XML document as a whole. However, each child node should be well-formed on its own (or be a text node).

IXMLDOMDocument Interface

Representing the entire XML document is the IXMLDOMDocument interface as shown in Listing 9-18. This is the primary entry point for creating and navigating the document model. An object of this type is the only one created directly. Thereafter you should use the factory methods provided by this class to correctly instantiate any other nodes that build up the document. Each such node must exist within the context of a document, and so has its ownerDocument property set to the creating object.

Listing 9-18: The IXMLDOMDocument interface

```
// *****************************************************************//
// Interface: IXMLDOMDocument
// Flags:     (4544) Dual NonExtensible OleAutomation Dispatchable
// GUID:      {2933BF81-7B36-11D2-B20E-00C04F983E60}
// *****************************************************************//
IXMLDOMDocument = interface(IXMLDOMNode)
  ['{2933BF81-7B36-11D2-B20E-00C04F983E60}']
  function Get_doctype: IXMLDOMDocumentType; safecall;
  function Get_implementation_: IXMLDOMImplementation; safecall;
  function Get_documentElement: IXMLDOMElement; safecall;
  procedure Set_documentElement(const DOMElement: IXMLDOMElement);
    safecall;
  function createElement(const tagName: WideString): IXMLDOMElement;
    safecall;
  function createDocumentFragment: IXMLDOMDocumentFragment; safecall;
  function createTextNode(const data: WideString): IXMLDOMText;
    safecall;
  function createComment(const data: WideString): IXMLDOMComment;
    safecall;
  function createCDATASection(const data: WideString):
    IXMLDOMCDATASection; safecall;
  function createProcessingInstruction(const target: WideString;
    const data: WideString): IXMLDOMProcessingInstruction; safecall;
  function createAttribute(const name: WideString): IXMLDOMAttribute;
    safecall;
  function createEntityReference(const name: WideString):
    IXMLDOMEntityReference; safecall;
  function getElementsByTagName(const tagName: WideString):
    IXMLDOMNodeList; safecall;
  function createNode(type_: OleVariant; const name: WideString;
    const namespaceURI: WideString): IXMLDOMNode; safecall;
  function nodeFromID(const idString: WideString): IXMLDOMNode;
    safecall;
  function load(xmlSource: OleVariant): WordBool; safecall;
  function Get_readyState: Integer; safecall;
  function Get_parseError: IXMLDOMParseError; safecall;
  function Get_url: WideString; safecall;
```

```
    function Get_async: WordBool; safecall;
    procedure Set_async(isAsync: WordBool); safecall;
    procedure abort; safecall;
    function loadXML(const bstrXML: WideString): WordBool; safecall;
    procedure save(destination: OleVariant); safecall;
    function Get_validateOnParse: WordBool; safecall;
    procedure Set_validateOnParse(isValidating: WordBool); safecall;
    function Get_resolveExternals: WordBool; safecall;
    procedure Set_resolveExternals(isResolving: WordBool); safecall;
    function Get_preserveWhiteSpace: WordBool; safecall;
    procedure Set_preserveWhiteSpace(isPreserving: WordBool); safecall;
    procedure Set_onreadystatechange(Param1: OleVariant); safecall;
    procedure Set_ondataavailable(Param1: OleVariant); safecall;
    procedure Set_ontransformnode(Param1: OleVariant); safecall;
    property doctype: IXMLDOMDocumentType read Get_doctype;
    property implementation_: IXMLDOMImplementation
      read Get_implementation_;
    property documentElement: IXMLDOMElement
      read Get_documentElement write Set_documentElement;
    property readyState: Integer read Get_readyState;
    property parseError: IXMLDOMParseError read Get_parseError;
    property url: WideString read Get_url;
    property async: WordBool read Get_async write Set_async;
    property validateOnParse: WordBool read Get_validateOnParse
      write Set_validateOnParse;
    property resolveExternals: WordBool read Get_resolveExternals
      write Set_resolveExternals;
    property preserveWhiteSpace: WordBool
      read Get_preserveWhiteSpace write Set_preserveWhiteSpace;
    property onreadystatechange: OleVariant write Set_onreadystatechange;
    property ondataavailable: OleVariant write Set_ondataavailable;
    property ontransformnode: OleVariant write Set_ontransformnode;
  end;
```

The IXMLDOMDocument's properties and methods are described below:

property implementation_: IXMLDOMImplementation read Get_implementation_;
   This read-only property leads to an interface that allows you to inspect implementation details outside the scope of any one document. See the IXMLDOMImplementation interface section for more details.

NOTE In the Microsoft DOM package the previous property is called implementation, as it is in the DOM specification. However, since this is a reserved word in Delphi, its name changes to implementation_ as part of the importing process for the type library.

property doctype: IXMLDOMDocumentType read Get_doctype;
   This read-only property returns the node that holds the lists of entities and notations defined for the document, as a result of parsing the DTD. See the IXMLDOMDocumentType interface for more details. It returns a nil for XML documents that do not specify a DTD.

property documentElement: IXMLDOMElement read Get_documentElement write Set_documentElement;
   Retrieve a reference to the single top-level element node within the document with this property. This node could be reached by stepping through the child nodes of the document,

but this property makes access much easier. Recall that there can only be one top-level node in a well-formed XML document. A nil is returned if the document has no root yet.

function createElement(const tagName: WideString): IXMLDOMElement; safecall;
Generate a new IXMLDOMElement node for use within the document. The name of the element is passed as a parameter. A namespace-qualified element cannot be created with this method—the namespaceURI property of the resulting node is always set to an empty string. You must use the createNode method instead for namespace-qualified nodes.

The newly created node has its ownerDocument property set to this document, but it does not automatically become part of the document. You must insert or append it as the child of the document or one of its existing children. The node's nodeType is set to NODE_ELEMENT.

function createDocumentFragment: IXMLDOMDocumentFragment; safecall;
Produces a new IXMLDOMDocumentFragment node for building up a sub-structure. Its nodeType is set to NODE_DOCUMENT_FRAGMENT. These nodes are not added to the main DOM structure.

function createTextNode(const data: WideString): IXMLDOMText; safecall;
Creates a new IXMLDOMText node for use within the document. The content of the node is passed as a parameter, with its nodeType being set to NODE_TEXT. As with an element, the newly constructed text node must still be added to the DOM as the child of an existing node.

function createComment(const data: WideString): IXMLDOMComment; safecall;
Generates a new IXMLDOMComment node for adding to the document, setting its nodeType property to NODE_COMMENT. Text for the comment is passed as a parameter. Following creation you must add the new node to the DOM before it becomes part of the document.

function createCDATASection(const data: WideString): IXMLDOMCDATASection; safecall;
Produces a new IXMLDOMCDATASection node for use within the document. The content of the section is passed as a parameter, with the nodeType property being set to NODE_CDATA_SECTION. Add the new node to the DOM as the child of an existing node.

function createProcessingInstruction(const target: WideString; const data: WideString): IXMLDOMProcessingInstruction; safecall;
Generates a new IXMLDOMProcessingInstruction node for adding to the document, setting its nodeType property to NODE_PROCESSING_INSTRUCTION. The target of and data for the instruction are passed as parameters. After construction, add the new instruction to the DOM.

function createAttribute(const name: WideString): IXMLDOMAttribute; safecall;
Create a new IXMLDOMAttribute node for attaching to an element. The name of the attribute is passed as a parameter, with the nodeType property being set to NODE_ATTRIBUTE. However, the value of that attribute must be set separately. To be useful, the new attribute must be added to an element node.

You cannot create a namespace-qualified attribute using this method—the `namespaceURI` property of the resulting node is always set to an empty string. Use the `createNode` method instead for namespace-qualified attributes.

`function createEntityReference(const name: WideString): IXMLDOMEntityReference; safecall;`

Produce a new IXMLDOMEntityReference node for use within the document. The name of the entity to be included is passed as a parameter, while its nodeType is set to NODE_ENTITY_REFERENCE. Following construction, add the new node to the DOM under an existing node. Recall, however, that you cannot create new entities for your document as these are read-only under DOM Level 2.

`function getElementsByTagName(const tagName: WideString): IXMLDOMNodeList; safecall;`

As for element nodes, this returns a list of element nodes with a particular name. Use a name of * to match with all element names. These nodes may come from anywhere within the entire hierarchy of the document. Their order in the list reflects their order in a pre-order traversal of the original structure. Pre-order means that the node itself is visited first, followed by each of its children in turn from left to right. The resulting list is "live," with updates affecting the DOM directly. For more complex selection criteria, use the `selectNodes` method instead.

`function nodeFromID(const idString: WideString): IXMLDOMNode; safecall;`

Retrieve a particular node based on the value of its ID attribute. The definition of an attribute as an ID type may not be available if the document's DTD or schema cannot be loaded. In this case the function returns `nil`.

NOTE The nodeFromID method corresponds to the getElementById method defined in the DOM specification. All the remaining properties and methods are value-added enhancements provided by Microsoft, although some of them would be expected in any implementation of the DOM. Missing methods from the DOM specification include createElementNS and createAttributeNS, which can be duplicated by the createNode method below, and getElementsByTagNameNS.

`function createNode(type_ : OleVariant; const name: WideString; const namespaceURI: WideString): IXMLDOMNode; safecall;`

Construct a generic node with the given type and names. Note that the other node construction methods do not allow you to specify a namespace URI for the node. In fact, since the `namespaceURI` property of a node is read-only, this is the only way to create a node with an attached namespace. The type of the node must be one of the enumerated values from Listing 9-3 as either its numeric or string value. For node types that do not have names, you should pass an empty string for the name and namespace parameters. An error is generated if a qualified name is supplied, but no namespace URI is given.

TIP When you generate a new element through the createNode method and supply a qualified name and a namespace URI, the DOM automatically includes the corresponding namespace declaration in that element when it is output as XML.

property validateOnParse: WordBool read Get_validateOnParse write Set_validateOnParse;
: This property enables or disables any validation against the DTD or schema for a document. When set to True (the default), any specified DTD or schema is loaded and used to validate the contents of the document. When set to False, the validation is not performed, merely a check for well-formedness.

property resolveExternals: WordBool read Get_resolveExternals write Set_resolveExternals;
: This flag turns on or off the retrieval of external definitions, which include external DTD subsets, external parsed entities, and resolvable namespaces. When set to True (the default), external references are loaded and parsed into the document. When set to False, these entities are not retrieved, which may produce an incomplete document. The setting of this property is independent of the value of the validateOnParse property. However, if externals cannot be resolved when validating a document, an error results. Loading a DTD or schema allows default values for attributes to be obtained, as well as setting the types of attributes and elements.

property preserveWhiteSpace: WordBool read Get_preserveWhiteSpace write Set_preserveWhiteSpace;
: This property controls how white space in the document is handled. When set to True, all white space in the document is retained, regardless of any xml:space attributes that may be set. When it is False (the default), the xml:space attribute settings determine which space is retained and which is not.

function load(xmlSource: OleVariant): WordBool; safecall;
: Create a DOM with this method that takes a URL (including a filename), an IStream object, or an IIS Request object (for scripting purposes) as input, and attempts to retrieve the document at that location and parse it. A return value of True is provided if it succeeds, False otherwise. If it fails, check out the parseError property to determine the cause. Any existing DOM structure in the document is discarded when invoking this method or loadXML.

function loadXML(const bstrXML: WideString): WordBool; safecall;
: This method also creates a DOM but operates on an XML document that is already held in memory as a string, returning the same status values as load. Any existing structure is discarded when called. The supplied string must be in UTF-16 or UCS-2 encodings for this method to work.

property url: WideString read Get_url;
: Which document has been read can be determined by looking at this read-only property. It returns a value following a successful load. An empty string results when a document is being built in memory. The value is not updated when the save method is called.

property parseError: IXMLDOMParseError read Get_parseError;
   If something does go wrong with the parsing, you can find out what by looking at the contents of this read-only property. It refers to an instance of the IXMLDOMParseError interface.

procedure save(destination: OleVariant); safecall;
   Document models can be written to persistent storage with this method, which takes a filename (not a URL), ASP Response object, IXMLDOMDocument reference, or any IStream implementation as a parameter. If necessary, a file is created or any existing file is overwritten when specifying a filename. Using the Response object sends the document back to the client. Saving to another document is the equivalent of saving to a file and then reparsing it, allowing you to verify the persistability of the current document.

   External entity references in the document type, its entities, or notations, are not altered during the save process. The encoding scheme used for the save comes from that specified in the XML declaration in the document. If no scheme is defined, it defaults to UTF-8. No validation is performed during a save, which could result in an invalid document being written out.

property async: WordBool read Get_async write Set_async;
   Parsing can be performed asynchronously by setting this property to True (its default). When True, the load method returns immediately, letting you continue with other processing. The progress of the load is monitored through the readyState property or the onreadystatechange event.

procedure abort; safecall;
   An asynchronous load can be halted with this method. Any structure built so far is discarded. The parseError property then indicates that the download was terminated. If the document is already loaded, this method has no effect.

property readyState: Integer read Get_readyState;
   The status of the parse process is available through this read-only property. Its value is 1 for "Loading," 2 for "Loaded," 3 for "Interactive," or 4 for "Completed." Loading means that the document is still being read from its source location. Loaded indicates that it has all arrived, but has not yet been parsed. Interactive denotes that the parse process is in progress, while Completed means that the entire DOM has been built and is available for use.

property onreadystatechange: OleVariant write Set_onreadystatechange;
   To monitor the progress of an asynchronous operation you can use this write-only property to receive notification of changes to the readyState property.

property ondataavailable: OleVariant write Set_ondataavailable;
   Another event for scripting environments, this write-only property registers an event that triggers as data is read. You can then start processing these chunks, rather than waiting for the entire document.

property ontransformnode: OleVariant write Set_ontransformnode;
> As nodes are processed through an XSL transformation, you can receive events for each node before it is operated on through this write-only property.

IXMLDOMDocument2 Interface

New in the October 2000 release of Microsoft's DOM is the IXMLDOMDocument2 interface (shown in Listing 9-19). This extends the previous IXMLDOMDocument interface and adds new functionality dealing with validation, and namespaces and their associated schema. The entire class is additional to the document functionality laid out in the DOM specification.

Listing 9-19: The IXMLDOMDocument2 interface

```
//*******************************************************************//
// Interface: IXMLDOMDocument2
// Flags:     (4544) Dual NonExtensible OleAutomation Dispatchable
// GUID:      {2933BF95-7B36-11D2-B20E-00C04F983E60}
//*******************************************************************//
IXMLDOMDocument2 = interface(IXMLDOMDocument)
  ['{2933BF95-7B36-11D2-B20E-00C04F983E60}']
  function  Get_namespaces: IXMLDOMSchemaCollection; safecall;
  function  Get_schemas: OleVariant; safecall;
  procedure Set_schemas(otherCollection: OleVariant); safecall;
  function  validate: IXMLDOMParseError; safecall;
  procedure setProperty(const name: WideString; value: OleVariant);
    safecall;
  function  getProperty(const name: WideString): OleVariant; safecall;
  property namespaces: IXMLDOMSchemaCollection read Get_namespaces;
  property schemas: OleVariant read Get_schemas write Set_schemas;
end;
```

The properties and methods of the IXMLDOMImplementation object are described below:

property namespaces: IXMLDOMSchemaCollection read Get_namespaces;
> This read-only property returns a list of the namespaces used in the document. Each distinct namespace has one entry in the list, returning the read-only IXMLDOMNode object that is the top of the corresponding schema structure. The order of the items in the list does not necessarily match their appearance in the document. Loading a new document clears this list. If there are no namespaces defined in the document, an empty list is returned.

property schemas: OleVariant read Get_schemas write Set_schemas;
> This property lets you associate preloaded schemas with particular namespaces. You can also override the schemas used by the document you are about to load. New schemas read during a document load are not automatically added to this list. Setting a schema collection disables any DTD processing since DTDs and schemas cannot be mixed. Restoring this property to nil enables DTDs again.

function getProperty(const name: WideString): OleVariant; safecall;
> Retrieve the current setting for the named document property with this method. See below for property names.

procedure setProperty(const name: WideString; value: OleVariant); safecall;
: Set a particular document property with this method. The current properties are listed below:
: `SelectionLanguage` lets you control the language used in calls to the `selectNodes` or `selectSingleNode` methods. Its value is either `XPath` or `XSLQuery` (the default).
: `ServerHTTPRequest` is set to `True` to use the server-safe `ServerXMLHTTP` component when loading documents.
: `SelectionNamespaces` is a list of space-delimited namespace declarations, like `xmlns:math="http://www.w3.org/TR/REC-MathML"`. Once set, these namespaces can be used in the context of the `selectNodes` and `selectSingleNode` methods.

function validate: IXMLDOMParseError; safecall;
: Invoke the validation processing on the current document with this method. It returns a parse error object that is separate from that found in the `parseError` property, with only the `errorCode` and `reason` properties filled in. This method requires that a DTD or schema be present for the document; it cannot just check well-formedness. It does not import new schemas, but may use those in an existing cache. If a namespace has no schema attached, its elements are not validated.

function selectNodes(const queryString: WideString): IXMLDOMSelection; safecall;
: This method is redefined in IXMLDOMDocument2 to return an IXMLDOMSelection list, rather than an IXMLDOMNodeList.

IXMLDOMSchemaCollection Interface

Also added to the October 2000 release of Microsoft's DOM, and not part of the DOM specification, is the IXMLDOMSchemaCollection interface (shown in Listing 9-20). Schemas may be cached through this interface and then made available to documents for their reuse, which results in faster loading. Instances of this object are created with the CoXMLSchemaCache class.

Listing 9-20: The *IXMLDOMSchemaCollection* interface

```
// ******************************************************************//
// Interface: IXMLDOMSchemaCollection
// Flags:     (4544) Dual NonExtensible OleAutomation Dispatchable
// GUID:      {373984C8-B845-449B-91E7-45AC83036ADE}
// ******************************************************************//
IXMLDOMSchemaCollection = interface(IDispatch)
  ['{373984C8-B845-449B-91E7-45AC83036ADE}']
  procedure add(const namespaceURI: WideString; var_: OleVariant);
    safecall;
  function  get(const namespaceURI: WideString): IXMLDOMNode; safecall;
  procedure remove(const namespaceURI: WideString); safecall;
  function  Get_length: Integer; safecall;
  function  Get_namespaceURI(index: Integer): WideString; safecall;
  procedure addCollection(const otherCollection:
    IXMLDOMSchemaCollection); safecall;
  function  Get__newEnum: IUnknown; safecall;
  property length: Integer read Get_length;
  property namespaceURI[index: Integer]: WideString
```

```
    read Get_namespaceURI; default;
  property _newEnum: IUnknown read Get__newEnum;
end;
```

NOTE Microsoft supports schemas based on XML Data Reduced, which differs from the W3C XML Schema specification.

Schema documents must be free-threaded (see the section titled "Threading the DOM" later in this chapter) to be included in a cache. The cache can be shared between a number of documents, and a single schema document can belong to many caches. To utilize the cache, set the schemas property of the document (after its creation, but before loading) to point to the cache.

An IXMLDOMSchemaCollection object's properties and methods are detailed below:

`property length: Integer read Get_length;`
   The number of schemas in the collection is returned by this read-only property.

`property namespaceURI[index: Integer]: WideString read Get_namespaceURI; default;`
   Step through the schemas and retrieve their associated namespace URIs with this read-only property. Note that this is the default property of the object, and thus it can be referenced just with the brackets, omitting the property name.

`function get(const namespaceURI: WideString): IXMLDOMNode; safecall;`
   This function returns a reference to the read-only node that contains the schema element for the specified namespace URI.

`procedure add(const namespaceURI: WideString; var_: OleVariant); safecall;`
   Add a new schema to the cache with this method, specifying its associated namespace URI. An empty string as the namespace URI denotes the default namespace. The schema reference can be its actual URI, in which case it is loaded synchronously with validation and external resolution turned off, an existing DOM document, or a DOM node representing an inline schema. Setting the schema reference to nil removes any schema for the supplied namespace URI.

`procedure addCollection(const otherCollection: IXMLDOMSchemaCollection); safecall;`
   Add all the schemas from another cache into the current one. Existing schemas with names matching those being added are overwritten.

`procedure remove(const namespaceURI: WideString); safecall;`
   Delete the schema attached to the given namespace URI from the cache.

IXMLDOMSelection Interface

Another addition in the October 2000 release of Microsoft's DOM is the IXMLDOMSelection interface (shown in Listing 9-21), also not part of the DOM specification. This list represents the nodes that match a given XSL query or XPath expression, as returned by the selectNodes method of the IXMLDOMDocument2 interface.

Part II: The Document Object Model

Listing 9-21: The IXMLDOMSelection interface

```
// *********************************************************************//
// Interface: IXMLDOMSelection
// Flags:     (4544) Dual NonExtensible OleAutomation Dispatchable
// GUID:      {AA634FC7-5888-44A7-A257-3A47150D3A0E}
// *********************************************************************//
  IXMLDOMSelection = interface(IXMLDOMNodeList)
    ['{AA634FC7-5888-44A7-A257-3A47150D3A0E}']
    function  Get_expr: WideString; safecall;
    procedure Set_expr(const expression: WideString); safecall;
    function  Get_context: IXMLDOMNode; safecall;
    procedure Set_context(const ppNode: IXMLDOMNode); safecall;
    function  peekNode: IXMLDOMNode; safecall;
    function  matches(const pNode: IXMLDOMNode): IXMLDOMNode; safecall;
    function  removeNext: IXMLDOMNode; safecall;
    procedure removeAll; safecall;
    function  clone: IXMLDOMSelection; safecall;
    function  getProperty(const name: WideString): OleVariant; safecall;
    procedure setProperty(const name: WideString; value: OleVariant);
      safecall;
    property expr: WideString read Get_expr write Set_expr;
    property context: IXMLDOMNode read Get_context write Set_context;
  end;
```

The properties and methods of the IXMLDOMSelection object are shown below:

property context: IXMLDOMNode read Get_context write Set_context;

> This property returns or establishes the root node for the selection. Setting it resets the state of the selection so that it can be stepped through again.

property expr: WideString read Get_expr write Set_expr;

> Retrieve or set the XPath expression with this property. Setting it executes the query and resets the selection state to the beginning of the list. If the expression is invalid, an error results. Use the inherited length and item properties, or the reset and nextNode methods, to traverse the list sequentially.

function peekNode: IXMLDOMNode; safecall;

> Look at the next node without advancing the current position through this function. It returns nil if there is no next node.

function matches(const pNode: IXMLDOMNode): IXMLDOMNode; safecall;

> This function determines whether or not a given node exists in the selection. It returns the node that, if set as the context of the query, would include the supplied node in its results. If no such node exists, it returns nil.

function getProperty(const name: WideString): OleVariant; safecall;
procedure setProperty(const name: WideString; value: OleVariant); safecall;

> These methods let you set or retrieve the value of the named property. The property name would be SelectionLanguage to determine whether XSL or XPath syntax is currently in effect.

function removeNext: IXMLDOMNode; safecall;

> Delete the next node in the list with this function. It returns a reference to that node.

```
procedure removeAll; safecall;
```
Delete all the nodes in the collection through this method.

```
function clone: IXMLDOMSelection; safecall;
```
This function returns an exact copy of the collection, including its current position and context.

IXMLDOMImplementation Interface

The IXMLDOMImplementation interface (see Listing 9-22) provides access to features and abilities outside the scope of a single document.

Listing 9-22: The *IXMLDOMImplementation* interface

```
// ********************************************************************//
// Interface: IXMLDOMImplementation
// Flags:      (4544) Dual NonExtensible OleAutomation Dispatchable
// GUID:       {2933BF8F-7B36-11D2-B20E-00C04F983E60}
// ********************************************************************//
IXMLDOMImplementation = interface(IDispatch)
  ['{2933BF8F-7B36-11D2-B20E-00C04F983E60}']
  function hasFeature(const feature: WideString;
    const version: WideString): WordBool; safecall;
end;
```

The IXMLDOMImplementation object's methods are described below:

```
function hasFeature(const feature: WideString; const version: WideString):
    WordBool; safecall;
```
This method lets you determine what abilities this implementation of the DOM has. Given a feature name and an optional version, it returns a simple flag that indicates whether that feature can be used. The current implementation only recognizes the following features: XML, DOM, and MS-DOM—and only version 1.0 for each.

NOTE The createDocument and createDocumentType methods from the DOM Level 2 specification do not appear in Microsoft's DOM. The package does provide alternate ways to generate new documents, as shown later.

Document Traversal

The document traversal interfaces, also part of the DOM Level 2 specification, are not included in Microsoft's implementation.

The selectNodes method of the IXMLDOMNode interface provides somewhat similar functionality to the NodeIterator from the DOM Level 2. Through the XSL query passed to this method you can select types of nodes, equivalent to the whatToShow property of a NodeIterator. Some NodeFilter operations can be duplicated through predicates on the XSL query.

There is no equivalent of the TreeWalker interface within the Microsoft package.

IXSLTemplate Interface

Support for XSL Transformations also comes in the Microsoft DOM package (another extension beyond the DOM specification). In the IXMLDOMNode interface, there are transformNode and transformNodeToObject methods that apply a given stylesheet to the current node. These take the stylesheet as a hierarchy of nodes and must step through both that structure and the current node's to create the output tree.

The IXSLTemplate interface (shown in Listing 9-23) lets you prepare for transformations by precompiling the stylesheet and caching the result. Processors for the stylesheet are then applied to nodes as necessary, resulting in better performance.

Listing 9-23: The IXSLTemplate interface

```
// *********************************************************//
// Interface: IXSLTemplate
// Flags:     (4544) Dual NonExtensible OleAutomation Dispatchable
// GUID:      {2933BF93-7B36-11D2-B20E-00C04F983E60}
// *********************************************************//
IXSLTemplate = interface(IDispatch)
  ['{2933BF93-7B36-11D2-B20E-00C04F983E60}']
    procedure Set_stylesheet(const stylesheet: IXMLDOMNode); safecall;
    function  Get_stylesheet: IXMLDOMNode; safecall;
    function  createProcessor: IXSLProcessor; safecall;
    property stylesheet: IXMLDOMNode read Get_stylesheet
      write Set_stylesheet;
end;
```

Use the CoXSLTemplate class (for the latest version, or CoXSLTemplate26 or CoXSLTemplate30 for specific versions) to create an instance of the template cache. Supply it with the structure for the stylesheet and construct the required processors later.

The properties and methods of an IXSLTemplate object are shown below:

property stylesheet: IXMLDOMNode read Get_stylesheet write Set_stylesheet;

    This property initializes the template object with the stylesheet to be applied later. Set it to the node that is at the root of the stylesheet document. Thereafter that document is read-only, until no longer used by the template.

function createProcessor: IXSLProcessor; safecall;

    Create an apartment-threading model IXSLProcessor object with this method, based on the template referenced by the stylesheet property. Multiple processors can be created from the one template.

    Each processor is a snapshot of the stylesheet document at the time it is created. The processor can only be updated to reflect changes to a stylesheet by creating a new one.

IXSLProcessor Interface

Having cached the compile stylesheet with the IXSLTemplate interface, you create an IXSLProcessor object (see Listing 9-24) from it for application to a particular node. These processors are apartment-threaded and store the state for a single transformation call.

Listing 9-24: The IXSLProcessor interface

```
//*******************************************************************//
// Interface: IXSLProcessor
// Flags:     (4544) Dual NonExtensible OleAutomation Dispatchable
// GUID:      {2933BF92-7B36-11D2-B20E-00C04F983E60}
//*******************************************************************//
IXSLProcessor = interface(IDispatch)
  ['{2933BF92-7B36-11D2-B20E-00C04F983E60}']
  procedure Set_input(pVar: OleVariant); safecall;
  function  Get_input: OleVariant; safecall;
  function  Get_ownerTemplate: IXSLTemplate; safecall;
  procedure setStartMode(const mode: WideString;
    const namespaceURI: WideString); safecall;
  function  Get_startMode: WideString; safecall;
  function  Get_startModeURI: WideString; safecall;
  procedure Set_output(pOutput: OleVariant); safecall;
  function  Get_output: OleVariant; safecall;
  function  transform: WordBool; safecall;
  procedure reset; safecall;
  function  Get_readyState: Integer; safecall;
  procedure addParameter(const baseName: WideString;
    parameter: OleVariant; const namespaceURI: WideString); safecall;
  procedure addObject(const obj: IDispatch;
    const namespaceURI: WideString); safecall;
  function  Get_stylesheet: IXMLDOMNode; safecall;
  property input: OleVariant read Get_input write Set_input;
  property ownerTemplate: IXSLTemplate read Get_ownerTemplate;
  property startMode: WideString read Get_startMode;
  property startModeURI: WideString read Get_startModeURI;
  property output: OleVariant read Get_output write Set_output;
  property readyState: Integer read Get_readyState;
  property stylesheet: IXMLDOMNode read Get_stylesheet;
end;
```

The IXSLProcessor object's properties and methods are detailed below:

property stylesheet: IXMLDOMNode read Get_stylesheet;
> Gain access to the node hierarchy for the stylesheet through this read-only property. This is the same structure that the IXSLTemplate object returns through its stylesheet property at the time the processor is created, although the template may have been subsequently changed.

property ownerTemplate: IXSLTemplate read Get_ownerTemplate;
> This read-only property gets you back to the template that created this processor.

property input: OleVariant read Get_input write Set_input;
> The nodes to be transformed are set through this property, passing a reference to an IXMLDOMNode.

```
property output: OleVariant read Get_output write Set_output;
```
The results of the transformation are sent to the destination designated by this property. It may be an `IXMLDOMDocument` node, an ASP `Response` object, or any object that implements the `IStream` interface. Setting it to one of these objects causes the transformed tree to be written out to it in an appropriate format. The document's encoding is determined by the corresponding attribute on the `xsl:output` element in the stylesheet.

Alternately, the property can be left unspecified prior to the transformation. Thereafter, reading this property value returns a string representing the output of the process. In an asynchronous transformation, only the next chunk of the output is returned each time it is referenced. String output is always created with the Unicode encoding, regardless of the `xsl:output` setting.

```
procedure setStartMode(const mode: WideString; const namespaceURI: WideString);
    safecall;
```
Use this method to set the starting mode for the transformation. Modes in stylesheets allow different types of transformations to be applied to the same set of nodes—for example, one mode for a table of contents, another for the body of the document. See http://www.w3.org/TR/WD-xslt#modes for more information.

```
property startMode: WideString read Get_startMode;
```
This read-only property returns the base name part of the start mode set above, with a default of an empty string.

```
property startModeURI: WideString read Get_startModeURI;
```
Retrieve the namespace URI part of the start mode set above through this read-only property, again defaulting to an empty string.

```
property readyState: Integer read Get_readyState;
```
During processing, this read-only property returns the current state of the transformation. The value is one of `READYSTATE_UNINITIALIZED` (0), which indicates that some required parameters still need to be set, `READYSTATE_LOADING` (1), not currently used, `READYSTATE_LOADED` (2), where all required properties are set and the transformation can begin, `READYSTATE_INTERACTIVE` (3), when the transformation is proceeding, or `READYSTATE_COMPLETE` (4), when it is all over. You can monitor this value during an asynchronous transformation.

```
procedure addParameter(const baseName: WideString; parameter: OleVariant; const
    namespaceURI: WideString); safecall;
```
Parameter values for use within the transformation (through `xsl:param` elements) are set with this method. Supply the base name of the parameter, its value (as a simple value or as an `IXMLDOMNodeList` or `IXMLDOMNode`, with the latter being converted into a node list with a single entry), and an optional namespace URI. In the stylesheet these parameter values can affect the way the transformation progresses. For asynchronous processing, a parameter value may be updated in callbacks, with the new value taking immediate effect.

```
procedure addObject(const obj: IDispatch; const namespaceURI: WideString);
  safecall;
```
Entire objects are passed to the stylesheet with this method. The object itself is supplied along with its full namespace URI. Within the stylesheet you refer to this namespace when invoking methods on the object.

```
function transform: WordBool; safecall;
```
The heart of the entire transformation, this method starts or resumes the process, returning `True` if successful and `False` otherwise. Certain properties must be set before the transformation can be started, specifically `input`.

```
procedure reset; safecall;
```
Calling this method restores the processor to the state it was in just before invoking `transform`. Property values set previously are not affected by this call.

TIP Chapter 26 "Examination XML—Web Client" demonstrates the use of these transformation interfaces. The application described there delivers content from XML documents as HTML over the Web. XSLT provides the formatting capabilities.

Loading the DOM

Before you can access any of the abilities of the DOM, you need to create an instance of the COM object that implements it. Although the DOM Level 2 specification describes how to create instances of a document, Microsoft does not follow this level of the DOM. Instead, you have several other options with Microsoft's version. Since it is a COM interface you can use `CreateOleObject` from the `ComObj` unit:

```
var
  XMLDoc: OleVariant
XMLDoc := CreateOleObject('MSXML');
if Assigned(XMLDoc) then
  :
```

or you can use `CoCreateInstance` from the `ActiveX` unit:

```
var
  XMLDoc: IXMLDOMDocument;
  hRes: HResult;
hRes := CoCreateInstance(CLASS_DOMDocument, nil,
  CLSCTX_INPROC_SERVER, IID_IXMLDOMDocument, XMLDoc);
if hRes = S_OK then
  :
```

or (probably the easiest) use the `CoDOMDocument` class generated within the MSXML type library:

```
var
  XMLDoc: IXMLDOMDocument;
XMLDoc := CoDOMDocument.Create;
  :
```

The first version creates a late-bound object, and so provides no checking of method names, etc., at compile time. Since the other versions declare the document as type `IXMLDOMDocument`, they can verify all interactions with the object during compilation. In each case you should free up the associated resources when you have finished with them by setting your reference to `VarNull` (for the first version) or `nil` (although they are also freed automatically when the variable goes out of scope).

In this example, a generic viewer of XML documents, the last option is used. For this you must include the `ActiveX` and `MSXML2_tlb` units (for version 3 of Microsoft's DOM) in the uses clause of your project to import the appropriate definitions. The DOM is created to read in an XML document and to display its contents in a viewer that strives to exercise most of the node types.

When you are ready to use the DOM, declare a variable of type `IXMLDOMDocument`, and instantiate it with a call to `CoDOMDocument.Create` (supplied by the type library conversion) as shown in Listing 9-25. The various flags controlling the operation of the parser are set up as menu items within the viewer. Each is a check menu item whose state is transferred directly to the corresponding properties of the parser.

Listing 9-25: Using the Microsoft DOM

```
{ Load an XML document }
procedure TfrmXMLViewer.LoadDoc(Filename: string);
var
  XMLDoc: IXMLDOMDocument;
begin
  pgcDetails.ActivePage := tshDocument;
  { Initialize document-wide details for display }
  InitDocumentDetails;
  { Load the source document }
  memSource.Lines.LoadFromFile(Filename);
  dlgOpen.Filename := Filename;
  { Instantiate the DOM }
  XMLDoc := CoDOMDocument.Create;
  trvXML.Items.BeginUpdate;
  try
    { Parse the document }
    XMLDoc.PreserveWhitespace := mniPreserveWhitespace.Checked;
    XMLDoc.ResolveExternals   := mniResolveExternals.Checked;
    XMLDoc.ValidateOnParse    := mniValidateOnParse.Checked;
    if not XMLDoc.Load(Filename) then
      raise Exception.Create(Format(NoLoadError,
        [XMLDoc.ParseError.Line, XMLDoc.ParseError.LinePos,
        XMLDoc.ParseError.Reason]));
    edtSystemId.Text := XMLDoc.URL;
    { Add the structure to the tree view }
    AddElementToTree(XMLDoc, nil);
    trvXML.Items[0].Expand(False);
  finally
    trvXML.Items.EndUpdate;
    { Release the DOM }
    XMLDoc := nil;
  end;
end;
```

TIP If you use the `CoDOMDocument` class to instantiate your document, you always get an object that reflects the latest version of the `IXMLDOMDocument` interface. If you need to tie your application to a particular version, you can use the `CoDOMDocument26` or `CoDOMDocument30` classes to create specific implementations.

Once you have a reference to the DOM object, you ask it to parse a document by invoking its Load method. As noted earlier, the DOM specification does not describe how a document model is created from an existing document. In fact, until DOM Level 2, the specification did not even define how to create a new document object, although once you have a document instance you can generate other nodes from it.

Another extension to the DOM specification is the ParseError property of the document object. If something goes wrong during the parse process, this property provides useful information in identifying the problem. The main details you want are the explanation of the problem, Reason, and the line and column number of the offending characters within the document, Line and LinePos. Microsoft's implementation does not define a DOM exception, so you can raise a standard one or define your own DOM-specific version.

Now that the document has been successfully parsed, you may access its contents through the properties of the document object. The items encountered within the document are available through its ChildNodes property, although you can go directly to the top-level element via the DocumentElement property.

The MS DOM XML Viewer

As an example of using the Microsoft DOM to parse a document you can build an XML viewer application to show the contents of any XML document. The viewer's form contains a tree view to show the structure of the entire document, with details about each item in the tree appearing on the right-hand side as they are selected (see Figure 9-2).

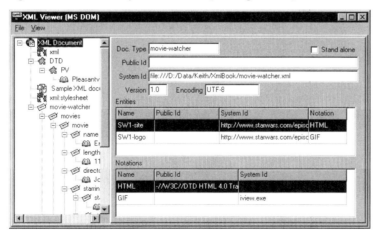

Figure 9-2: The XML viewer showing document details.

The document to parse can be specified through the command line, or by selecting the File | Open menu items.

To build up the structure in the tree view, you work your way through the DOM in memory. At each level, starting with the document itself, you add a tree node for the current DOM node and then call the routine recursively to process each of that node's children (see Listing 9-26). The current DOM node and the parent tree node are passed as parameters to each call.

Listing 9-26: Filling a tree view from the DOM

```
{ Add a TXMLElement to the tree view }
function AddElement(Parent: TTreeNode; Name: string;
  Element: TXMLElement): TTreeNode;
begin
  FList.Add(Element);
  Result := trvXML.Items.AddChildObject(Parent, Name, Element);
  with Result do
  begin
    ImageIndex    := Ord(Element.ElementType);
    SelectedIndex := ImageIndex;
  end;
end;
{ Add current element to the treeview and
  then recurse through children }
procedure AddElementToTree(Node: IXMLDOMNode;
  TreeParent: TTreeNode);
var
  Index: Integer;
  DisplayName: string;
  NewNode: TTreeNode;
  Attribs: TStringList;
  Attrib: IXMLDOMAttribute;
begin
  { Generate name for display in the tree }
  if Node.NodeType in
    [NODE_TEXT, NODE_COMMENT, NODE_CDATA_SECTION] then
  begin
    if Length(Node.NodeValue) > 20 then
      DisplayName := Copy(Node.NodeValue, 1, 17) + '...'
    else
      DisplayName := Node.NodeValue;
  end
  else
    DisplayName := Node.NodeName;
  { Create storage for later display of node values }
  case Node.NodeType of
    NODE_ELEMENT:
      begin
        Attribs := TStringList.Create;
        try
          for Index := 0 to Node.Attributes.Length - 1 do
            with Node.Attributes.Item[Index] do
              Attribs.Values[NodeName] := NodeValue;
          NewNode := AddElement(TreeParent, DisplayName,
            TXMLElement.Create(xtElement, Node.NodeName,
            Node.NamespaceURI, Node.BaseName, '', Attribs));
        finally
          Attribs.Free;
        end;
      end;
    NODE_TEXT:
      with Node as IXMLDOMText do
        NewNode := AddElement(TreeParent, DisplayName,
          TXMLElement.Create(xtText, '', '', '', Data, nil));
    NODE_CDATA_SECTION:
```

```
      with Node as IXMLDOMCDATASection do
        NewNode := AddElement(TreeParent, DisplayName,
          TXMLElement.Create(xtCData, '', '', '', Data, nil));
    NODE_ENTITY_REFERENCE:
      NewNode := AddElement(TreeParent, DisplayName,
        TXMLElement.Create(xtEntityRef, Node.NodeName, '', '',
        '', nil));
    NODE_PROCESSING_INSTRUCTION:
      with Node as IXMLDOMProcessingInstruction do
      begin
        NewNode := AddElement(TreeParent, DisplayName,
          TXMLElement.Create(xtInstruction, Target, '', '',
          Data, nil));
        if UpperCase(Target) = XMLValue then
        begin
          { Special handling for the XML declaration }
          edtVersion.Text :=
            Node.Attributes.GetNamedItem(VersionAttr).NodeValue;
          Attrib := Node.Attributes.GetNamedItem(EncodingAttr) as
            IXMLDOMAttribute;
          if Assigned(Attrib) then
            edtEncoding.Text := Attrib.NodeValue;
          Attrib := Node.Attributes.GetNamedItem(StandAloneAttr) as
            IXMLDOMAttribute;
          if Assigned(Attrib) then
            cbxStandAlone.Checked :=
              (UpperCase(Attrib.NodeValue) = YesValue);
          Attrib := nil;
        end;
      end;
    NODE_COMMENT:
      with Node as IXMLDOMComment do
        NewNode := AddElement(TreeParent, DisplayName,
          TXMLElement.Create(xtComment, '', '', '', Data, nil));
    NODE_DOCUMENT:
      NewNode := AddElement(TreeParent, XMLDocDesc,
        TXMLElement.Create(xtDocument, XMLDocDesc, '', '',
        '', nil));
    NODE_DOCUMENT_TYPE:
      with Node as IXMLDOMDocumentType do
      begin
        edtDocType.Text := Name;
        NewNode := AddElement(TreeParent, DTDDesc,
          TXMLElement.Create(xtvEntityRef, DTDDesc, '', '',
          '', nil));
      end;
    NODE_ENTITY:
      with (Node as IXMLDOMEntity), stgEntities do
        if NotationName <> '' then
        begin
          { Unparsed entity }
          if Cells[0, RowCount - 1] <> '' then
            RowCount := RowCount + 1;
          Cells[0, RowCount - 1] := NodeName;
          Cells[1, RowCount - 1] := PublicId;
          Cells[2, RowCount - 1] := SystemId;
          Cells[3, RowCount - 1] := NotationName;
        end
        else
          { Parsed entity }
```

```
          NewNode := AddElement(TreeParent, DisplayName,
            TXMLElement.Create(xtEntityRef, NodeName,
            '', '', '', nil));
    NODE_NOTATION:
      with (Node as IXMLDOMNotation), stgNotations do
      begin
        if Cells[0, RowCount - 1] <> '' then
          RowCount := RowCount + 1;
        Cells[0, RowCount - 1] := NodeName;
        Cells[1, RowCount - 1] := PublicId;
        Cells[2, RowCount - 1] := SystemId;
      end;
  end;
  { And recurse through any children }
  if Node.HasChildNodes then
    for Index := 0 to Node.ChildNodes.Length - 1 do
      AddElementToTree(Node.ChildNodes[Index], NewNode);
end;
```

Since all the nodes in the DOM ultimately derive from `IXMLDOMNode`, you can treat them generically at this level. The `nodeType` property indicates what sort of node you are dealing with, and dictates how it is processed (through a `case` statement). The `nodeName` and `nodeValue` properties provide basic details about each node, with further information depending on its type.

In constructing the tree view, you need to save additional data about each node so that it can be retrieved for later display on the right-hand side of the form. Although you could save references to the objects within the DOM itself, simpler `TXMLElement` objects hold the basic details. This class provides storage for a node's type, name(s), value, and attributes. The DOM and associated resources can then be discarded after it has been loaded.

The text displayed in the tree view generally comes from the name of each node. For non-text-type nodes this contains a meaningful value such as the element name or processing instruction target application. However, for text type nodes the DOM supplies standard names such as `#text` or `#comment`. To make the tree view more useful, you can extract the first 20 characters for these types of nodes and display them instead. This is what happens at the start of the `AddElementToTree` method with the `DisplayName` variable.

Then you look at the node type to determine how the node is to be interpreted. Generally, you add a node to the tree with the name selected above, and attach a newly created `TXMLElement` object with its values set appropriately. For Element-Type nodes this means extracting the attribute values from the DOM and

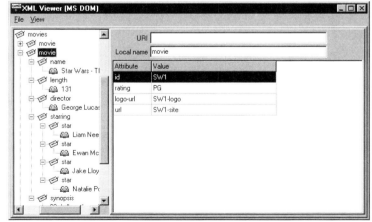

Figure 9-3: Element details displayed within the viewer.

transferring them to a string list for their later display. Figure 9-3 shows the viewer displaying an element's details.

Attribute nodes are handled as part of the processing for an element, and are thus not encountered while traversing the normal DOM hierarchy.

Text type nodes show up with truncated text in the tree view, while their full content appears on the right. See Figure 9-4 for an example.

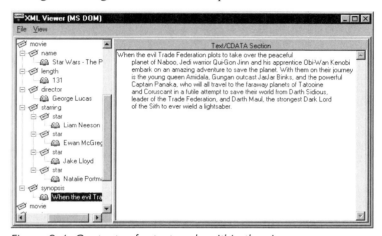

Figure 9-4: Contents of a text node within the viewer.

The processing instruction that contains the XML prolog is singled out to extract further details about the document itself. Otherwise, these appear like text nodes with their target showing in the tree view and their command in the text pane.

Nodes containing DTD information—document type, entity, and notation nodes—are not added to the growing tree view, but are added to controls found on the page for the document as a whole. Only external unparsed entities are treated this way. Parsed entities are treated normally, being added directly beneath the document node in the tree. Their content also appears in the body of the document where they have been referred to.

Finally, in all cases, each child node is processed in the same way through a recursive call. Thus, you work your way down through the document hierarchy, handling each node as it is encountered.

Viewing Node Details

Once the DOM has been processed into the tree view and other controls, the program expands the topmost node in the tree—the document node—and displays the associated document information (see Figure 9-2). As each node is selected within the tree view, its corresponding details are displayed in the right panel.

The code for this is shown in Listing 9-27. Each selection retrieves the TXMLElement object for that node and examines it. Its type determines which detail page is shown and what values are used to fill the controls upon it.

Listing 9-27: Showing details of a selected node

```
{ Display details for the selected XML element }
procedure TfrmXMLViewer.trvXMLChange(Sender: TObject;
  Node: TTreeNode);
var
  Index: Integer;
begin
  with TXMLElement(trvXML.Selected.Data) do
    case ElementType of
      xtDocument:
        { Show document details, including entities
          and notations }
        pgcDetails.ActivePage := tshDocument;
      xtElement:
        begin
          { Show element details, including attributes }
          pgcDetails.ActivePage := tshElement;
          edtURI.Text          := NamespaceURI;
          edtLocalName.Text    := LocalName;
          with stgAttributes do
          begin
            if Attributes.Count = 0 then
              RowCount := 2
            else
              RowCount := Attributes.Count + 1;
            Rows[1].Clear;
            for Index := 0 to Attributes.Count - 1 do
            begin
              Cells[0, Index + 1] := Attributes.Names[Index];
              Cells[1, Index + 1] :=
                Attributes.Values[Attributes.Names[Index]];
            end;
          end;
        end;
      else
        begin
          { Show details for other nodes - text type }
          pgcDetails.ActivePage := tshText;
          memText.Lines.Text    := Value;
          case ElementType of
            xtComment:     lblNodeType.Caption := CommentDesc;
            xtInstruction: lblNodeType.Caption :=
                             InstructionDesc;
            xtEntityRef:   lblNodeType.Caption := EntityRefDesc;
            else           lblNodeType.Caption := TextDesc;
          end;
        end;
    end;
end;
```

Selecting the View | View source menu options allows you to see the underlying XML document for comparison with the extracted structure. Figure 9-5 shows its contents.

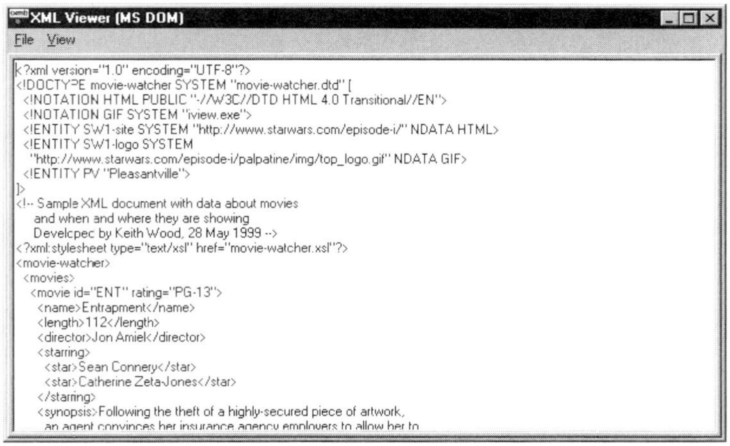

```
XML Viewer (MS DOM)
File View
<?xml version="1.0" encoding="UTF-8"?>
<!DOCTYPE movie-watcher SYSTEM "movie-watcher.dtd" [
  <!NOTATION HTML PUBLIC "-//W3C//DTD HTML 4.0 Transitional//EN">
  <!NOTATION GIF SYSTEM "iview.exe">
  <!ENTITY SW1-site SYSTEM "http://www.starwars.com/episode-i/" NDATA HTML>
  <!ENTITY SW1-logo SYSTEM
    "http://www.starwars.com/episode-i/palpatine/img/top_logo.gif" NDATA GIF>
  <!ENTITY PV "Pleasantville">
]>
<!-- Sample XML document with data about movies
     and when and where they are showing
     Develcpec by Keith Wood, 28 May 1999 -->
<?xml:stylesheet type="text/xsl" href="movie-watcher.xsl"?>
<movie-watcher>
  <movies>
    <movie id="ENT" rating="PG-13">
      <name>Entrapment</name>
      <length>112</length>
      <director>Jon Amiel</director>
      <starring>
        <star>Sean Connery</star>
        <star>Catherine Zeta-Jones</star>
      </starring>
      <synopsis>Following the theft of a highly-secured piece of artwork,
        an agent convinces her insurance agency employers to allow her to
```

Figure 9-5: Compare with the original XML document.

Threading the DOM

The Microsoft implementation of the DOM provides different versions to deal with different threading models. By default (using the `CoDOMDocument` and related classes), an apartment-threaded DOM is created. Although the behavior of the two versions is identical, apartment-threaded documents show better performance since the parser does not have to worry about concurrent access.

If you want a free-threaded document instead, you can use the `CoFreeThreadedDOMDocument` class to create it. As before, this constructs a latest-version object, with `CoFreeThreadedDOMDocument26` and `CoFreeThreadedDOMDocument30` providing the specific versions. Free-threaded documents are required for use with the schema cache.

Documents or nodes created with one threading model cannot be combined with those created under the other model.

Summary

This chapter has examined the Document Object Model as implemented by Microsoft in its MSXML.dll or MSXML3.dll. These versions follow the DOM Level 1 specification fairly closely, providing added functionality where necessary (notably in the `IXMLDOMDocument` interface). Unfortunately, Microsoft does not yet support the full DOM Level 2 functionality. Some aspects appear already, often with different names, but others do not.

Microsoft has added additional abilities in the areas of working with schemas and XSL transformations. You can cache both of these to increase performance. Unfortunately, both support the Microsoft versions of these standards, which have some differences from the W3C version.

Following a look at each of the interfaces that make up Microsoft's offering, you saw how they are used in creating an application that displays the contents and structure of any XML document.

Further abilities of the Microsoft DOM are described in Chapter 19, which takes a look at using the DOM to generate XML; in Chapter 21, where XML documents are transformed using XSL Transformations; and in some of the application examples in Part V, notably Chapter 26 on using XSLT.

Chapter 10
CUESoft's Document Object Model

CUESoft.com has also implemented the DOM specification under Windows, this time as a set of native Delphi objects. The advantage of having native objects is that the parser and DOM can be compiled directly into your program, with no need to worry about mismatched DLLs.

The W3C DOM interfaces are implemented as classes in the CUEXml Delphi package, with the class hierarchy shown in Figure 10-1. CUESoft.com follows the DOM Level 1 specification very closely, although they also have several extensions for increased functionality and usability. They do have some support for namespaces, but handle only string values, not the expected WideStrings.

The CUESoft DOM is a commercial product. You can obtain the source for an additional fee. If you have the source you can compile it into any 32-bit version of Delphi. Otherwise, there are prepackaged libraries available for Delphi versions 3 through 5. In general, all you have to do to install the package is as follows:

1. Unpack the files from CUESoft into an appropriate directory.
2. Select **Component | Install Packages...** from the Delphi menu.
3. Click the **Add** button.
4. Change the file type to **Package collection (*.dpc)**, and browse to the directory where you unpacked the files.
5. Select **cuexml2_X.dpc** (where X is your version of Delphi) and click **OK**.
6. Click **Finish** on the package installation dialog and **OK** on the package dialog. The two components in the package appear on the CUESoft tab in the component palette.

Each of the classes is described in further detail below. Differences from the DOM specification are noted as they are encountered. Unless otherwise noted, all these classes appear in the XmlObjModel unit.

Figure 10-1: The CUESoft DOM class hierarchy.

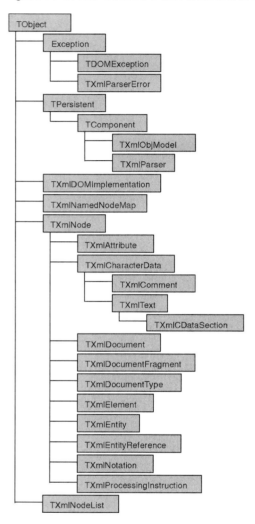

TDOMException Exception

General errors that occur during DOM processing within the CUESoft package are notified as TDOMExceptions (see Listing 10-1). Following the DOM specification, it adds only a single numeric code to denote which type of problem arose.

Listing 10-1: The TDOMException exception

```
TDOMException = class(Exception)
public
  constructor CreateCode(oCode: EExceptionCode);
  property Code: EExceptionCode read FCode;
end;
```

The properties and methods of a TDOMException object are described below:

constructor CreateCode(oCode: EExceptionCode);

> This constructor generates a new exception passing in the type of error encountered. Typically you would not create these exceptions yourself, but would react to those raised by the DOM during its processing.

property Code: EExceptionCode read FCode;

> This read-only property indicates what type of problem arose. Its value is one of those shown in Table 10-1. As you can see, these follow the DOM specification.

Table 10-1: CUESoft error codes

Error Code	Meaning
ecNone	No error
ecIndexSizeErr	An index or size is negative or greater than allowed.
ecWStringSizeErr	The text does not fit into a WideString.
ecHierarchyRequestErr	A node is inserted somewhere it does not belong.
ecWrongDocumentErr	A node from another document is used.
ecInvalidNameErr	An invalid name is used (usually containing an illegal character).
ecNoDataAllowedErr	Data is specified for a node that does not support data.
ecNoModificationAllowedErr	Attempting to modify a read-only node.
ecNotFoundErr	The specified node cannot be found in this context.
ecNotSupportedErr	The action specified for the object is not supported under this implementation.
ecInuseAttributeErr	An attribute already belonging to one element is being added to another.
ecInvalidParamErr	An invalid parameter is passed to a method.

TXmlParserError Exception

Errors arising from the parsing of a document are indicated through a TXmlParserError exception (see Listing 10-2). These include further details about the reason for and position of the error. This class appears in the XmlParser unit.

Listing 10-2: The `TXmlParserError` *exception*

```
TXmlParserError = class(Exception)
public
  constructor CreateParseError(oFilePos, oLine, oLinePos: Integer;
    oUrl, oReason: string);
  property Reason: string read FReason;
  property Line: Integer read FLine;
  property LinePos: Integer read FLinePos;
  property FilePos: Integer read FFilePos;
  property Url: string read FUrl;
end;
```

A `TXmlParserError` object's properties and methods are listed below:

`constructor CreateParseError(oFilePos, oLine, oLinePos: Integer; oUrl, oReason: string);`

Build a new exception during the parse process with this constructor. The parameters set all the properties for this exception. Generally the parser itself raises these errors, and you only need to respond to them.

`property Reason: string read FReason;`

Retrieve a text description of the problem through this read-only property.

`property Line: Integer read FLine;`

This read-only property returns the line number in the XML document where the error was detected.

`property LinePos: Integer read FLinePos;`

The character position within that line is given by this read-only property.

`property FilePos: Integer read FFilePos;`

Find the offset into the XML document as a whole with this read-only property.

`property Url: string read FUrl;`

This read-only property returns the source name of the XML document in error.

TXmlNode Class

All nodes within the DOM structure derive from a common class that provides the basic functionality used by most of them. The `TXmlNode` class (shown in Listing 10-3) embodies this in the CUESoft package.

Listing 10-3: The `TXmlNode` *declaration*

```
TXmlNode = class
protected
  FNodeId: Integer;
  FNodeName: string;
  FNodeType: Integer;
  FNodeValue: string;
  function GetNodeStringType: string;
public
  constructor Create;
  destructor Destroy; override;
```

```
    property Attributes: TXmlNamedNodeMap read FAttributes;
    property BaseName: string read GetBaseName;
    property ChildNodes: TXmlNodeList read FChildNodes;
    property FirstChild: TXmlNode read GetFirstChild;
    property LastChild: TXmlNode read GetLastChild;
    property LevelCode: string read GetLevelCode;
    property Namespace: string read GetNamespace;
    property NextSibling: TXmlNode read GetNextSibling;
    property NodeId: Integer read FNodeId write FNodeId;
    property NodeName: string read FNodeName write FNodeName;
    property NodeStringType: string read GetNodeStringType;
    property NodeType: Integer read FNodeType;
    property NodeValue: string read FNodeValue write FNodeValue;
    property OwnerDocument: TXmlDocument read GetOwnerDocument;
    property ParentNode: TXmlNode read FParentNode;
    property Prefix: string read GetPrefix;
    property PreviousSibling: TXmlNode read GetPreviousSibling;
    property Text: string read GetText;
    property XmlDocument: string read GetXmlDocument;
    procedure AddRef;
    procedure AppendChild(oNewChild: TXmlNode);
    function CloneNode(bDeep: Boolean = True): TXmlNode;
    procedure ForceOwnerDocument(oNode: TXmlNode);
    function GetChildNodesByNodeType(wType: Integer): TXmlNodeList;
    function GetNodesByNodeType(wType: Integer): TXmlNodeList;
    function HasAttributes: Boolean;
    function HasChildNodes: Boolean;
    procedure InsertBefore(oNewChild, oRefChild: TXmlNode);
    function IsAfter(oNode: TXmlNode): Boolean;
    procedure Release;
    procedure RemoveAll;
    function RemoveChild(oRefChild: TXmlNode): TXmlNode;
    function ReplaceChild(oNewChild, oRefChild: TXmlNode): TXmlNode;
  end;
```

Using functionality from the basic node when it is not applicable results in an exception being thrown—for example, attempting to add child nodes to a text node. Simple properties return an empty string or nil if they do not apply to the current node type.

The properties and methods of a TXmlNode object are detailed below:

constructor Create;

> Do not create TXmlNodes directly. They are only used within the DOM hierarchy as one of TXmlNodes' subclasses.

property NodeType: Integer read FNodeType;

> This read-only property identifies the type of node represented by this object, allowing it to be safely cast to that type to access its additional abilities. The value is one of those shown in Table 10-2.

Table 10-2: Node types

Node Type	Implementing Class
ELEMENT_NODE	TXmlElement
ATTRIBUTE_NODE	TXmlAttribute
TEXT_NODE	TXmlText

Node Type	Implementing Class
CDATA_SECTION_NODE	TXmlCDataSection
ENTITY_REFERENCE_NODE	TXmlEntityReference
ENTITY_NODE	TXmlEntity
PROCESSING_INSTRUCTION_NODE	TXmlProcessingInstruction
COMMENT_NODE	TXmlComment
DOCUMENT_NODE	TXmlDocument
DOCUMENT_TYPE_NODE	TXmlDocumentType
DOCUMENT_FRAGMENT_NODE	TXmlDocumentFragment
NOTATION_NODE	TXmlNotation

```
property NodeStringType: string read GetNodeStringType;
```
This read-only property retrieves the node's type as a string value. It returns the node types from Table 10-2 as text.

NOTE The NodeStringType property is an extension to the W3C DOM specification.

```
property NodeName: string read FNodeName write FNodeName;
```
The name of the node is given by this property. For some nodes this is a predefined value. See Table 10-3 for the meaning of this property based on the node's type.

Table 10-3: Node name and value by node type

Node Type	Node Name	Node Value
ELEMENT_NODE	Name of element	" (Empty string)
ATTRIBUTE_NODE	Name of attribute	Attribute value
TEXT_NODE	#text	Content of text
CDATA_SECTION_NODE	#cdata-section	Content of CDATA section
ENTITY_REFERENCE_NODE	Name of entity	"
ENTITY_NODE	Name of entity	"
PROCESSING_INSTRUCTION_NODE	Target of instruction	Content excluding target
COMMENT_NODE	#comment	Content of comment
DOCUMENT_NODE	#document	"
DOCUMENT_TYPE_NODE	Name of document type	"
DOCUMENT_FRAGMENT_NODE	#document-fragment	"
NOTATION_NODE	Name of notation	"

```
property BaseName: string read GetBaseName;
```
Retrieve the local part of the node's name—the part after any namespace prefix—through this read-only property.

NOTE In the W3C DOM Specification, the local part of the node's name is given by the localName attribute.

property Prefix: string read GetPrefix;
: This read-only property returns the namespace prefix—the part up to the colon (:)—from the node's name, or an empty string if there is no prefix.

property Namespace: string read GetNamespace;
: The namespace descriptor for the node comes from this read-only property. It is blank if no namespace applies to the node. Namespaces are declared through xmlns prefixed attributes.

NOTE In the W3C DOM Specification, the namespace for the node is given by the namespaceURI attribute.

property NodeValue: string read FNodeValue write FNodeValue;
: Retrieve or set the text value of the node through this property. Many node types do not use this property, as shown in Table 10-3.

property Attributes: TXmlNamedNodeMap read FAttributes;
: Access the attributes of a node with this read-only property. It returns a named node map containing TXmlAttribute objects. Although it is defined on all nodes, only element nodes use attributes. All other types return nil.

property OwnerDocument: TXmlDocument read GetOwnerDocument;
: All nodes contain a reference to the document that created them, which is available through this read-only property. For document nodes this returns nil.

property ParentNode: TXmlNode read FParentNode;
: Once placed into a DOM structure, this read-only property lets you reach the parent of the node. The parent is nil for attribute, document, and document fragment nodes, as well as for other nodes that have not yet been added to the tree.

property ChildNodes: TXmlNodeList read FChildNodes;
: Moving the other way through the tree uses this read-only property. It returns a "live" list of ordered nodes, meaning that any changes to the nodes in the list immediately update the main structure, and vice versa. If a node has no children, this property still returns a valid list, but that list has no entries in it.

property FirstChild: TXmlNode read GetFirstChild;
: This convenience property returns the first entry in the ChildNodes list or nil if there are no children.

property LastChild: TXmlNode read GetLastChild;
: Similarly, this property returns the last entry in the ChildNodes list, or nil if none.

property NextSibling: TXmlNode read GetNextSibling;
: Another convenience property, this one retrieves the node after the current one in its parent's list of children. Again, a nil is returned if there is no following node.

property PreviousSibling: TXmlNode read GetPreviousSibling;
: Conversely, this property retrieves the node before this one in its parent's list. nil is returned if there is no previous node.

```
procedure AppendChild(oNewChild: TXmlNode);
```
Adds the specified node to the end of this node's list of children. If the supplied node is already in the structure, it is first removed. Adding a document fragment node adds all of its children instead.

```
procedure InsertBefore(oNewChild, oRefChild: TXmlNode);
```
Place the new node immediately before the specified reference node within this node's list of children. If the reference node is nil, the new node is placed at the end of the list. A new node already in the tree is first removed. Inserting a document fragment node adds all of its children instead.

```
function RemoveChild(oRefChild: TXmlNode): TXmlNode;
```
Removes the specified node from this node's list of children. A reference to that node is returned. The old node should be released once the method is finished.

```
function ReplaceChild(oNewChild, oRefChild: TXmlNode): TXmlNode;
```
Remove the specified reference node and insert the new node in its place. The function returns a pointer to the node that is removed.

```
function CloneNode(bDeep: Boolean = True): TXmlNode;
```
Create a copy of the node through this method, including any attributes and their values. Attributes resulting from default values in the DTD are also duplicated. If the bDeep parameter is False, the process stops there. If it is True, all the descendants of this node are also cloned under the copy. The new duplicate has no parent until it is placed back into the DOM hierarchy.

```
function HasChildNodes: Boolean;
```
A convenience function, this returns True when there are child nodes in the list and False when it is empty.

```
function HasAttributes: Boolean;
```
This method returns True when there are entries in the attributes list and False when there are none.

NOTE Although the CUESoft package does not explicitly support DOM Level 2, it does include several properties dealing with namespaces. Missing from the DOM Level 2 spec are the normalize and isSupported methods. normalize does appear in the TXmlElement class in CUESoft's package, while isSupported is duplicated by the HasFeature method of the TXmlDomImplementation class. The following properties and methods are extensions to the DOM specification.

```
property NodeId: Integer read FNodeId write FNodeId;
```
Use this property to define your own ID for each node, separate from any that may be defined in the document itself.

```
property LevelCode: string read GetLevelCode;
```
This read-only property returns the node's location within the DOM hierarchy as a sequence of numbers separated by periods. Each number represents the position of the node's ancestors within their parent's list of children (although counting here starts at one). For example,

4.1.2 is the node at the second position in the node at the first position in the node at the fourth position in the document.

property Text: string read GetText;
: Retrieve all the text from this node and its descendants concatenated together via this read-only property.

property XmlDocument: string read GetXmlDocument;
: Extract the XML fragment that corresponds to this node and all of its descendants from this read-only property.

procedure RemoveAll;
: Delete all child nodes from the list and destroy the node objects.

function IsAfter(oNode: TXmlNode): Boolean;
: This function returns True if the current node appears after the given node in a pre-order traversal of the hierarchy, and False if it does not. For example, a node is after its parent and any previous sibling, but it is not after any next sibling, nor any child nodes.

function GetChildNodesByNodeType(wType: Integer): TXmlNodeList;
: Retrieve a node list containing all the immediate child nodes of a given type. The types are specified using the values shown in Table 10-2.

function GetNodesByNodeType(wType: Integer): TXmlNodeList;
: Similarly, this method returns a list of all descendants of the specified type.

procedure ForceOwnerDocument(oNode: TXmlNode);
: Set the OwnerDocument property for the supplied node and all its descendants to be the same as the current node. This lets you transfer nodes from one document to another.

procedure AddRef;
: Add a reference count to this node. Use Release to decrement the count. This method is automatically called when the node is created, and again when it is added to the tree.

procedure Release;
: Decrement the reference count for this node. When the count reaches zero, the object is destroyed. Be sure to call this method once you are finished with the node after adding it to the tree.

TXmlNodeList Class

The TXmlNodeList class (see Listing 10-4) encapsulates an ordered collection of nodes. It is the object returned by the ChildNodes property of a node, as well as by the various GetNode methods. Items within the list are accessed sequentially by their position.

Listing 10-4: The TXmlNodeList declaration

```
TXmlNodeList = class
public
  constructor Create;
  destructor Destroy; override;
```

```
    property Length: Integer read GetLength;
    property XmlDocument: string read GetXmlDocument;
    procedure Add(oNode: TXmlNode);
    procedure Delete(wIndex: Integer);
    procedure Empty;
    function Exchange(wSrc, wDest: Integer): Boolean;
    function IndexOf(oNode: TXmlNode): Integer;
    procedure Insert(wIndex: Integer; oNode: TXmlNode);
    function Item(wIndex: Integer): TXmlNode;
    function Move(wSrc, wDest: Integer): Boolean;
    procedure Replace(wIndex: Integer; oNode: TXmlNode);
    procedure Sort(sAttribute: string = ''; wOrder: Integer = 0);
  end;
```

The TXmlNodeList object's properties and methods are shown below:

constructor Create;
> Lists are automatically created for you as the result of a query, or through a node's ChildNodes property.

property Length: Integer read GetLength;
> Find the number of entries in the list through this read-only property. Access the individual items with indexes in the range zero to Length −1.

function Item(wIndex: Integer): TXmlNode;
> Access each entry in the list with this function, giving the item's position within the list. If the index value is out of range, the function returns nil.

NOTE All the remaining properties and methods are extensions to the DOM Level 2 specification. The spec intentionally left out methods for manipulating the node list, other than reading items out.

property XmlDocument: string read GetXmlDocument;
> This read-only property returns all the items in the list as a formatted XML fragment. It is not well-formed XML unless there is a single element type node in the list.

procedure Add(oNode: TXmlNode);
> Add the given node to the end of the list.

procedure Insert(wIndex: Integer; oNode: TXmlNode);
> Places the specified node at the given position in the list.

procedure Replace(wIndex: Integer; oNode: TXmlNode);
> Removes the item currently at the nominated index and put the new node in its place.

function Move(wSrc, wDest: Integer): Boolean;
> Moves an item in the list from its source position to its new destination location. The function returns True if the move succeeds, and False otherwise.

function Exchange(wSrc, wDest: Integer): Boolean;
> Swaps the positions of two entries in the list, given their locations. A True value returns if the exchange succeeds, and a False returns otherwise.

`function IndexOf(oNode: TXmlNode): Integer;`
    Finds the position of the specified node within the list. A −1 value is returned if the node cannot be found.

`procedure Sort(sAttribute: string = ''; wOrder: Integer = 0);`
    Order the nodes in the list with this method. If an attribute name is supplied, the nodes sort by the value of that attribute. If the attribute name is left blank, the nodes appear in order of their text content. Use the last parameter to sort in ascending (0, the default) or descending (1) order.

    If the node list is the `ChildNodes` of an element, then sorting physically reorders the actual nodes within the DOM. For other lists, only that list is sorted, without affecting the DOM hierarchy.

`procedure Delete(wIndex: Integer);`
    Removes the indicated node from the list.

`procedure Empty;`
    Deletes all the nodes from the list.

TXmlNamedNodeMap Class

The `TXmlNamedNodeMap` class (see Listing 10-5) also manages a list of nodes, but provides primary access to them via their names. Although you can also retrieve items by their position, this is merely a convenience and does not imply any particular ordering of the nodes.

Listing 10-5: The `TXmlNamedNodeMap` declaration

```
TXmlNamedNodeMap = class
public
  constructor Create;
  destructor Destroy; override;
  property Length: Integer read GetLength;
  procedure Add(oNode: TXmlNode);
  procedure Delete(wIndex: Integer);
  procedure Empty;
  function GetNamedItem(sName: string): TXmlNode;
  function IndexOf(oNode: TXmlNode): Integer;
  procedure Insert(wIndex: Integer; oNode: TXmlNode);
  function Item(wIndex: Integer): TXmlNode;
  function RemoveNamedNode(sName: string): TXmlNode;
  procedure Replace(wIndex: Integer; oNode: TXmlNode);
  function SetNamedItem(oNode: TXmlNode): TXmlNode;
end;
```

The properties and methods of the `TXmlNamedNodeMap` object are described below:

`constructor Create;`
    As for node lists, these node maps are automatically created for you. The `Attributes` property of the `TXmlNode` class and the `Entities` and `Notations` properties of the `TXmlDocumentType` class all return node maps containing their respective node types.

`function GetNamedItem(sName: string): TXmlNode;`
> Retrieves the node from the mapping that has the given name. A `nil` is returned if no node matches this name. The resulting node can be cast to its appropriate subclass to access its specific abilities.

`function SetNamedItem(oNode: TXmlNode): TXmlNode;`
> Adds the given node to the mapping, using its `NodeName` as the index. If an entry already exists with that name, the new node replaces it and a reference to the deleted node is returned. Otherwise, the return value is `nil`.

`function RemoveNamedNode(sName: string): TXmlNode;`
> Find the node in the mapping with the given name and remove it from the list. A reference to that node is returned. If no matching node is found, return a `nil` instead.

`property Length: Integer read GetLength;`
> Return the number of entries in the map through this read-only property.

`function Item(wIndex: Integer): TXmlNode;`
> Access the entries in the list via their position. If the supplied index is out of range, a `nil` is returned.

NOTE The remaining methods are all extensions to the DOM Level 2 specification. The spec does not define how node maps are maintained, so as not to restrict how they are implemented. Missing from that spec are the namespace-aware versions of the Get/Set/RemoveNamedItem methods above.

`procedure Add(oNode: TXmlNode);`
> Add the specified node to the list.

`procedure Insert(wIndex: Integer; oNode: TXmlNode);`
> Place the new node at a particular position within the list. If the index is out of range, an error occurs.

`procedure Replace(wIndex: Integer; oNode: TXmlNode);`
> Delete the node currently in the specified position and insert the new node in its place. An error is raised if the index is out of range.

`procedure Delete(wIndex: Integer);`
> Remove the node at the given position from the list. An out of range index is ignored.

`procedure Empty;`
> Remove all the nodes from the list.

`function IndexOf(oNode: TXmlNode): Integer;`
> Return the position of the given node in the list. If the node is not found, the function returns −1.

TXmlElement Class

Most of the nodes in the DOM will be `TXmlElement` objects (as shown in Listing 10-6). These represent the elements from the XML document, and typically have attributes and child nodes attached to them.

Listing 10-6: The TXmlElement declaration

```
TXmlElement = class(TXmlNode)
public
  constructor Create;
  destructor Destroy; override;
  property ElementText: string read GetElementText;
  property FullEndTag: Boolean read FFullEndTag write FFullEndTag;
  property IgnoreEndTag: Boolean read FIgnoreEndTag
    write FIgnoreEndTag;
  property TagName: string read FNodeName write FNodeName;
  function CreateChildCDataSection(sText: string): TXmlCDataSection;
  function CreateChildElement(sElem: string): TXmlElement;
  function CreateChildText(sText: string): TXmlText;
  function FindElement(sName: string): TXmlElement;
  function GetAttribute(sName: string): string;
  function GetAttributeNode(sName: string): TXmlAttribute;
  function GetChildElementsByTagName(sName: string): TXmlNodeList;
  function GetElementsByTagName(sName: string): TXmlNodeList;
  function GetElementsByTagNameWithAttribute(
    sName, sAttr, sValue: string): TXmlNodeList;
  function MatchExpression(sTerm: string): TXmlNodeList;
  procedure Normalize(bAddSpace: Boolean = False);
  procedure RemoveAttribute(sName: string);
  function RemoveAttributeNode(oOldAttr: TXmlAttribute): TXmlAttribute;
  function SelectNodes(sQuery: string): TXmlNodeList;
  function SelectSingleNode(sQuery: string): TXmlElement;
  procedure SetAttribute(sName, sValue: string);
  function SetAttributeNode(oNewAttr: TXmlAttribute): TXmlAttribute;
end;
```

The `TXmlElement` object's properties and methods are listed below:

`constructor Create;`

Element nodes should not be created directly. Instead, use the `CreateElement` method on the document object or the `CreateChildElement` method described later.

`property TagName: string read FNodeName write FNodeName;`

Set or retrieve the name of the element through this property. It maps directly onto the inherited `NodeName` property.

`function GetAttribute(sName: string): string;`

Although you could use the `Attributes` property to deal with an element's attributes, there are several convenience methods to assist you. This one returns the string value of the named attribute, or an empty string if it cannot be found.

`procedure SetAttribute(sName, sValue: string);`

Set the value of an attribute with this method. Any existing attribute with the same name has its contents overwritten by the new value. The value supplied is not parsed at all.

```
procedure RemoveAttribute(sName: string);
```
Remove the attribute with the given name using this method. Nothing happens if a matching node is not found.

```
function GetAttributeNode(sName: string): TXmlAttribute;
```
Access the entire attribute node by name with this method. If the attribute cannot be found, it returns `nil`.

```
function SetAttributeNode(oNewAttr: TXmlAttribute): TXmlAttribute;
```
Use this method to add attributes that have internal structure beyond a simple string value. Build your attribute node and attach its children before calling this method. The new one replaces any existing attribute with the same name. In this case, a reference to the deleted node is returned. Otherwise, it returns `nil`.

```
function RemoveAttributeNode(oOldAttr: TXmlAttribute): TXmlAttribute;
```
Remove the specified attribute from the element's list through this method. A reference to that node is returned. If the given node is not an attribute of the element, nothing happens.

```
function GetElementsByTagName(sName: string): TXmlNodeList;
```
Obtain a list of all the elements with a given name that are descendants of this node with this function. Use a name of * to get all elements in the subtree. The entries in the list appear in the same order as a pre-order traversal of the subtree.

NOTE The following properties and methods are not part of the DOM Level 2 specification for elements. Missing abilities include the namespace-aware versions of the methods above. Also, the `hasAttribute` and `hasAttributeNS` methods are not implemented, although the `IndexOf` method of the `Attributes` node map provides similar information.

```
property ElementText: string read GetElementText;
```
This read-only property returns the value of the single text node child of this element. If there is no single text child, it returns an empty string.

```
property FullEndTag: Boolean read FFullEndTag write FFullEndTag;
```
Set this property to `True` to force the output of a full closing tag when generating XML. When `False` (the default), an element that has no children uses the shorthand syntax available in XML (placing a slash at the end of the opening tag). This property can be used to maintain compatibility with some existing applications (specifically HTML).

```
property IgnoreEndTag: Boolean read FIgnoreEndTag write FIgnoreEndTag;
```
Setting this property to `True` causes the end tag to be omitted entirely if the element has no children. By default, it is `False`, which always generates an end tag. Again, this is intended for use with generating HTML, but should not be used in any true XML document.

```
function CreateChildCDataSection(sText: string): TXmlCDataSection;
```
This function creates a new CDATASection node and appends it to the element, returning a reference to the new node. You can achieve the same thing through the `CreateCDATA-Section` method on the document object, followed by an `AppendChild` call on this node.

```
function CreateChildElement(sElem: string): TXmlElement;
```
Similarly, this function adds a newly created element node to the current element, and returns a pointer to it.

```
function CreateChildText(sText: string): TXmlText;
```
Lastly, you can easily create and add a child text node with this method. Again, you receive a reference to the new node as the return value.

```
function FindElement(sName: string): TXmlElement;
```
Find the first descendant element node with the given tag name through this method. The subtree is searched in a pre-order traversal. If no matching node is found, a `nil` is returned.

```
function GetChildElementsByTagName(sName: string): TXmlNodeList;
```
Similar to the `GetElementsByTagName` method, this one only searches the immediate children of the element.

```
function   GetElementsByTagNameWithAttribute(sName,    sAttr,    sValue:    string):
TXmlNodeList;
```
Another variation on the `GetElementsByTagName` method, this one looks through all descendants, returning those elements that have the given name and also an attribute with the specified name and value.

```
function MatchExpression(sTerm: string): TXmlNodeList;
```
This method searches the descendants of the element for nodes that match the given expression, and returns those found as a list. Their order in the list matches their order in a pre-order traversal of the hierarchy.

```
procedure Normalize(bAddSpace: Boolean = False);
```
Combine adjacent text nodes in the entire subtree beneath this element. Setting the bAddSpace parameter to True causes an extra space character to be placed between the contents of text nodes that are concatenated. Doing this is not standard DOM functionality. However, the parameter has a default value of False and can safely be omitted.

 NOTE In the DOM Level 2 specification, the Normalize functionality is moved to the Node interface.

```
function SelectNodes(sQuery: string): TXmlNodeList;
```
Retrieves a list of all the nodes that match the given XPath expression. The current node acts as the starting point for relative references. An empty list is returned if no matching nodes are found.

```
function SelectSingleNode(sQuery: string): TXmlElement;
```
This method acts like the previous one, but returns only the first element found, or `nil` if there are none.

TXmlAttribute Class

Attributes are attached to elements and are available through the `Attributes` property on the `TXmlElement` nodes. Other than appearing in these lists, they do not form a part of the normal DOM hierarchy. They have no parent and no siblings, so the corresponding properties return `nil`. Their CUESoft definition is shown in Listing 10-7.

Listing 10-7: The *TXmlAttribute* declaration

```
TXmlAttribute = class(TXmlNode)
public
  constructor Create; override;
  destructor Destroy; override;
  property Name: string read FNodeName write FNodeName;
  property Specified: Boolean read FSpecified write FSpecified;
  property Value: string read GetNodeValue write SetNodeValue;
  function CloneNode(bDeep: Boolean = True): TXmlNode; override;
end;
```

The properties and methods of the `TXmlAttribute` object are discussed below:

`constructor Create;`
   As for elements, use the `CreateAttribute` factory method on the document object instead of creating attributes yourself. You can also instantiate them through the `SetAttribute` method of an element object.

`property Name: string read FNodeName write FNodeName;`
   Retrieve or set the name of the attribute through this property. It maps directly onto the inherited `NodeName` property.

`property Value: string read GetNodeValue write SetNodeValue;`
   Read or write the string value of the attribute with this property. The inherited `NodeValue` property has the same effect. Setting this value causes any children of the attribute to be discarded and to be replaced with just the supplied text. The value is not parsed at all, so any embedded entity references are ignored.

`property Specified: Boolean read FSpecified write FSpecified;`
   This property returns `True` if the value for the attribute came from the body of the XML document itself or was set through the `Value` property, and `False` if the value derives from a default specified for this attribute in the DTD.

TXmlCharacterData Class

The `TXmlCharacterData` class (see Listing 10-8) is the basis of all textual nodes within the DOM. It supplies common functionality for the various subclasses. The base class itself does not appear in the hierarchy.

Listing 10-8: The *TXmlCharacterData* declaration

```
TXmlCharacterData = class(TXmlNode)
public
```

```
    property Data: string read FNodeValue write FNodeValue;
    property Length: Integer read GetLength;
    procedure AppendData(sData: string);
    procedure DeleteData(wOffset, wCount: Integer);
    procedure InsertData(wOffset: Integer; sData: string);
    procedure ReplaceData(wOffset, wCount: Integer; sData: string);
    function SubStringData(wOffset, wCount: Integer): string;
  end;
```

The `TXmlCharacterData` object's properties and methods are listed below. As for the other implementations, all offsets start at zero.

`property Data: string read FNodeValue write FNodeValue;`
Retrieve or set the text content of the node through this property.

`property Length: Integer read GetLength;`
Find the number of characters in the `Data` property, which may be zero.

`procedure AppendData(sData: string);`
Add the supplied text to the end of the existing value. Retrieve the combined text from the `Data` property.

`procedure DeleteData(wOffset, wCount: Integer);`
Remove the text starting from the given offset, for the given number of characters.

`procedure InsertData(wOffset: Integer; sData: string);`
Insert the supplied text into any existing value at the specified offset.

`procedure ReplaceData(wOffset, wCount: Integer; sData: string);`
Delete the substring starting at the nominated offset and extending for the given number of characters, then replace it with the supplied text.

`function SubStringData(wOffset, wCount: Integer): string;`
Extract the section of text from the specified offset, for the given number of characters.

TXmlText Class

Inheriting from the base character data node, the `TXmlText` class (as shown in Listing 10-9) holds the actual content of the XML document within the DOM. When a document is first loaded, some other node type separates all text nodes from each other; contiguous sections of text in the document are placed into a single text node. This state is restored by the `Normalize` method of the element object.

Listing 10-9: The TXmlText declaration

```
TXmlText = class(TXmlCharacterData)
public
  constructor Create;
  function SplitText(wOffset: Integer): TXmlText;
  function CloneNode(bDeep: Boolean = True): TXmlNode; override;
end;
```

The properties and methods of the `TXmlText` object are described below:

constructor Create;
>   Generate text nodes through the `CreateTextNode` method on the document object, or the `CreateChildText` method on an element. Do not construct text nodes directly.

function SplitText(wOffset: Integer): TXmlText;
>   Create a new text node containing all the text from the current node past the specified offset, and return a reference to that node. The current text node has that text deleted. The new node becomes the immediately following sibling of the original node.

TXmlCDataSection Class

Textual content containing characters that would normally be treated as markup can be flagged as just straight text through CDATA sections. Within the DOM these appear as `TXmlCDataSection` objects (as shown in Listing 10-10). This class inherits all the abilities of a normal text node and simply serves as an indicator of its data's origin.

Listing 10-10: The `TXmlCDataSection` declaration

```
TXmlCDataSection = class(TXmlText)
public
  constructor Create; override;
  function CloneNode(bDeep: Boolean = True): TXmlNode; override;
end;
```

The `TXmlCDataSection` object's methods are shown below:

constructor Create;
>   Do not construct CDATA section nodes directly. Use the `CreateCDataSection` method on the document object or the `CreateChildCDataSection` method of an element instead.

TXmlComment Class

Comments usually contain additional, non-essential information about a document. Within the DOM they appear as `TXmlComment` objects (see Listing 10-11). Another text-based node type, all of its abilities are inherited.

Listing 10-11: The `TXmlComment` declaration

```
TXmlComment = class(TXmlCharacterData)
public
  constructor Create; override;
  function CloneNode(bDeep: Boolean = True): TXmlNode; override;
end;
```

The methods of the `TXmlComment` object are discussed below:

constructor Create;
>   Build comments with the `CreateComment` method of the document object. Do not create them directly with this constructor.

TXmlProcessingInstruction Class

Processing instructions are designed to carry information through the document for use by applications using those documents. The TXmlProcessingInstruction class (shown in Listing 10-12) lets you access their contents.

Listing 10-12: The *TXmlProcessingInstruction* declaration

```
TXmlProcessingInstruction = class(TXmlNode)
public
  constructor Create; override;
  property Data: string read FNodeValue write FNodeValue;
  property Target: string read FNodeName write FNodeName;
  function CloneNode(bDeep: Boolean = True): TXmlNode; override;
end;
```

A TXmlProcessingInstruction object's properties and methods are listed below:

constructor Create;
> Use the document object's CreateProcessingInstruction method to instantiate these nodes, rather than this constructor.

property Target: string read FNodeName write FNodeName;
> Retrieve or set the target application for the instruction with this property.

property Data: string read FNodeValue write FNodeValue;
> The remainder of the tag's content appears in this property, from the first non-white space character following the target through to the character immediately before the closing ?>.

TXmlDocumentType Class

The TXmlDocumentType class (see Listing 10-13) encapsulates the declaration of the document type for a document. It appears as the DocType property of the document, although this may be nil. Within it are references to the entities and notations defined within the document.

Listing 10-13: The *TXmlDocumentType* declaration

```
TXmlDocumentType = class(TXmlNode)
public
  constructor Create; override;
  destructor Destroy; override;
  property Entities: TXmlNamedNodeMap read FEntities;
  property Name: string read FNodeName write FNodeName;
  property Notations: TXmlNamedNodeMap read FNotations;
  function CloneNode(bDeep: Boolean = True): TXmlNode; override;
end;
```

The properties and methods of the TXmlDocumentType object are shown below:

constructor Create;
> Normally, a document type node is automatically created as a document is loaded. Even if you did create one of these nodes, you cannot attach it to a document since the DocType property is read-only.

property Name: string read FNodeName write FNodeName;
: Retrieve the name of the document type from this property. This corresponds to the name of the single top-level element in the document.

property Entities: TXmlNamedNodeMap read FEntities;
: Obtain access to a list of the external entities defined within the document through this read-only property. This does not include internal entities, which are automatically expanded, nor parameter entities. Each item in the list is a TXmlEntity object.

property Notations: TXmlNamedNodeMap read FNotations;
: Access the notations defined in the document's DTD with this read-only property. Items in the list are all TXmlNotation objects.

TXmlEntity Class

The TXmlEntity class (see Listing 10-14) supplies the definitions of external entities read from the document's DTD. Access them via the Entities property of the document type node. No parameter or internal entities appear in this list since these are automatically expanded and their value included in the DOM. Only the definition of the entity is modeled, not the declaration itself.

Listing 10-14: The TXmlEntity declaration

```
TXmlEntity = class(TXmlNode)
public
  constructor Create; override;
  property NotationName: string read FNodeName write FNodeName;
  property PublicId: string read FPublicId write FPublicId;
  property SystemId: string read FSystemId write FSystemId;
  function CloneNode(bDeep: Boolean = True): TXmlNode; override;
end;
```

The TXmlEntity object's properties and methods are discussed below:

constructor Create;
: Entity nodes are automatically created when a document is first loaded. They cannot be added to a document type node thereafter.

property NodeName: string read FNodeName write FNodeName;
: This inherited property provides the name of the entity.

NOTE Unfortunately, the current version of CUESoft's DOM returns the name of the entity's notation through the NodeName property, rather than the name of the entity itself. There is no way to retrieve the entity's name unless you go to the underlying parser and its OnEntityDecl event.

property PublicId: string read FPublicId write FPublicId;
: Retrieve or set the public identifier for the entity from this property. If no public identifier is specified, an empty string results.

property SystemId: string read FSystemId write FSystemId;
: This property reads or writes the system identifier for the entity. Again, it returns an empty string if no system identifier is available.

property NotationName: string read FNodeName write FNodeName;
: Unparsed entities return the name of their notation type through this property. For parsed entities, it returns an empty string.

NOTE Although the `NotationName` property is mapped onto the node name field, it does return the correct value. However, the node name field should hold the name of the entity itself.

TXmlEntityReference Class

References to parsed entities are placed into the DOM with the TXmlEntityReference class (as shown in Listing 10-15). The children of this reference duplicate those of the named entity node (if available).

Listing 10-15: The TXmlEntityReference declaration

```
TXmlEntityReference = class(TXmlNode)
public
  constructor Create; override;
  function CloneNode(bDeep: Boolean = True): TXmlNode; override;
end;
```

NOTE The CUESoft parser always expands entity references within the body of the document. So, when you load in a document, no entity reference nodes appear within the DOM, only their corresponding entity's subtree. Also, the contents of entities declared in external subsets may not be available.

The properties and methods of the TXmlEntityReference object are described below:

constructor Create;
: As before, do not build these objects directly. Instead, use the CreateEntityReference method of the document object.

property NodeName: string read FNodeName write FNodeName;
: This inherited property provides the name of the referenced entity.

TXmlNotation Class

Notations can describe the format of unparsed entities, of attributes, and of target applications for processing instructions. They are represented by the TXmlNotation class (see Listing 10-16) and are retrieved from the Notations property of the document type node.

Listing 10-16: The TXmlNotation declaration

```
TXmlNotation = class(TXmlNode)
public
```

```
    constructor Create; override;
    property PublicId: string read FPublicId write FPublicId;
    property SystemId: string read FSystemId write FSystemId;
    function CloneNode(bDeep: Boolean = True): TXmlNode; override;
end;
```

The TXmlNotation object's properties and methods are listed below:

constructor Create;
> Use the document object's CreateNotation method to build new notation nodes.

property NodeName: string read FNodeName write FNodeName;
> The name of the notation is found in this inherited property.

property PublicId: string read FPublicId write FPublicId;
> Retrieve the public identifier for this notation from this property, or an empty string if none is specified.

property SystemId: string read FSystemId write FSystemId;
> This property provides the system identifier for the notation, or an empty string if none is supplied.

TXmlDocumentFragment Class

A document fragment never appears in the main DOM structure. Its purpose is to manage subtrees of nodes outside of the document itself, allowing them to be constructed or extracted before adding them back into the hierarchy. The TXmlDocumentFragment class (see Listing 10-17) provides this functionality. It derives from the basic node without adding any new abilities.

Listing 10-17: The *TXmlDocumentFragment* declaration

```
TXmlDocumentFragment = class(TXmlNode)
public
    constructor Create; override;
    function CloneNode(bDeep: Boolean = True): TXmlNode; override;
end;
```

When a document fragment is added to the main DOM, it is not inserted itself. Instead, all of its child nodes are placed into the hierarchy in its place.

The methods of a TXmlDocumentFragment object are shown below:

constructor Create;
> Build document fragment nodes with the CreateDocumentFragment method of the document object.

TXmlDocument Class

The primary access to the DOM is via the document object, as represented by the TXmlDocument class (shown in Listing 10-18). Another important function of this class is to create new nodes to add to the DOM. Using the factory methods provided here ensures that the nodes are compatible with the document and each other.

Listing 10-18: The TXmlDocument declaration

```
TXmlDocument = class (TXmlNode)
public
  constructor Create; override;
  destructor Destroy; override;
  property ActualCDATA: Boolean read FActualCDATA write FActualCDATA;
  property DocType: TXmlDocumentType read FDocType;
  property DocumentElement: TXmlElement read GetDocumentElement;
  property DomImplementation: TXmlDomImplementation
    read FDomImplementation;
  property FormattedOutput: Boolean read FFormattedOutput
    write FFormattedOutput;
  property IdAttribute: string read FIdAttribute write FIdAttribute;
  property IgnoreCase: Boolean read FIgnoreCase write FIgnoreCase;
  function CloneNode(bDeep: Boolean = True): TXmlNode; override;
  function CreateAttribute(sName: string): TXmlAttribute;
  function CreateComment(sData: string = ''): TXmlComment;
  function CreateCDataSection(sData: string = ''): TXmlCDataSection;
  function CreateDocumentFragment: TXmlDocumentFragment;
  function CreateElement(sTagName: string): TXmlElement;
  function CreateEntityReference(sName: string): TXmlEntityReference;
  function CreateProcessingInstruction(sTarget: string;
    sData: string = ''): TXmlProcessingInstruction;
  function CreateTextNode(sData: string = ''): TXmlText;
  function GetElementsByTagName(sName: string): TXmlNodeList;
  procedure RemoveAll;
end;
```

The TXmlDocument object's properties and methods are discussed below:

constructor Create;
> Documents are created as the result of loading an XML document through the LoadDataSource or LoadMemory methods of the TXmlObjModel class. An empty document node exists initially in the object model class that can be used to generate a new document. All access should be through the Document property of the object model class.

property DomImplementation: TxmlDomImplementation read FDomImplementation;
> Access the DOM implementation for this document through this read-only property.

NOTE Since implementation is a reserved word in Delphi, this W3C DOM attribute is renamed DomImplementation in the CUESoft package.

property DocType: TXmlDocumentType read FDocType;
> If a DTD exists for a loaded XML document, this read-only property returns the corresponding TXmlDocumentType node. If no DTD is specified, and for HTML documents, it returns nil.

TIP You cannot create a document type declaration for a new document in memory since this field property is read-only.

property DocumentElement: TXmlElement read GetDocumentElement;
: Retrieve the single, top-level element in the document with this read-only property. You can also reach it via the ChildNodes property of the document, but this property is more convenient.

function CreateAttribute(sName: string): TXmlAttribute;
: Build a new TXmlAttribute node using this method, by passing in the name of the new attribute. The resulting node still needs to be added to an element to become part of the DOM. Use the element's SetAttributeNode method.

function CreateComment(sData: string = ''): TXmlComment;
: Generate a new TXmlComment node with the supplied text through this method. Add the new node to an existing one as one of its children.

function CreateCDataSection(sData: string = ''): TXmlCDataSection;
: This method produces a new TXmlCDataSection node for adding to the DOM. Specify the text content of the node when it is called. You can also use the CreateChildCDataSection method of an element.

function CreateDocumentFragment: TXmlDocumentFragment;
: Obtain a new TXmlDocumentFragment node with this method. Document fragments are not added to the main DOM hierarchy, but are used instead to manage nodes outside of that structure.

function CreateElement(sTagName: string): TXmlElement;
: A new TXmlElement node is created by this method, passing in the element's name. Add it to the DOM as a child of another node. If placed as the child of the document node itself, it also becomes the value of the DocumentElement property. A new child element is automatically added with the CreateChildElement method of an element node.

function CreateEntityReference(sName: string): TXmlEntityReference;
: Build a new TXmlEntityReference node using this method. Specify the name of the entity to be inserted, and add the new node to the DOM at the required position.

function CreateProcessingInstruction(sTarget: string; sData: string = ''): XmlProcessingInstruction;
: Generate a new TXmlProcessingInstruction node via this method, passing in the name of the target application and its command. Again, add the new node to the DOM structure as the child of an existing node.

function CreateTextNode(sData: string = ''): TXmlText;
: This method produces a new TXmlText node, with the specified content, for adding to the DOM. Alternately, you can use the CreateChildText method of an element to quickly add text to an element.

```
function GetElementsByTagName(sName: string): TXmlNodeList;
```
Find all the elements that are descendants of the document and that have the given name. Use a name of * to retrieve all nodes. The nodes appear in the order of a pre-order traversal through the document tree. If no matching nodes are found, an empty list is returned.

```
function CloneNode(bDeep: Boolean = True): TXmlNode; override;
```
Copy the document node and, if bDeep is True, all of its children to create a new document.

NOTE Missing from the W3C DOM Level 2 specification are the importNode method (whose functionality can be duplicated through the ForceOwnerDocument method of the TXmlNode class), the getElementById method, and the namespace-aware versions of the CreateElement, CreateAttribute, and GetElementsByTagName methods. The following properties and methods are extensions of the W3C specification.

```
property ActualCDATA: Boolean read FActualCDATA write FActualCDATA;
```
Set this property to True to output CDATA sections within the DOM as plain text instead of surrounding them with the normal CDATA tags. Leave it as False (the default) to use the CDATA syntax.

```
property FormattedOutput: Boolean read FFormattedOutput write FFormattedOutput;
```
When True, this property causes the XML generated by the DOM to be formatted for readability. This involves adding line feeds and indentation surrounding the elements and text. When False (the default), the output appears as a single string with no breaks.

```
property IdAttribute: string read FIdAttribute write FIdAttribute;
```
Specify a default attribute to be used as the elements' IDs when querying with XSL and XQL (XML Query Language) expressions.

```
property IgnoreCase: Boolean read FIgnoreCase write FIgnoreCase;
```
This property controls matching through the GetElementsByTagName and SelectNodes methods. If set to True, matches are case-insensitive, whereas setting it to False (the default) enforces matching on case.

```
procedure RemoveAll;
```
Completely empty the document of all its children with this method.

TXmlDomImplementation Class

The TXmlDomImplementation class (see Listing 10-19) provides functions outside of any document. You access its abilities through the DOMImplementation property of a document.

Listing 10-19: The TXmlDomImplementation declaration

```
TXmlDomImplementation = class
public
  function HasFeature(sFeature, sVersion: string): Boolean;
end;
```

The methods of the `TXmlDomImplementation` object are listed below:

`function HasFeature(sFeature, sVersion: string): Boolean;`
> Determine whether this DOM implementation supports certain features with this method. Given a particular feature name and required version, it returns `True` if that functionality is available and `False` otherwise. The version parameter may be left blank to match on any supported version. This implementation currently recognizes the features `XML` and `HTML` (case-insensitive), and version `1.0` of each.

TXmlObjModel Component

Since the DOM Level 1 specification, which is the level supported by this implementation, defines no way of creating a document, it is left to the designers to provide this functionality. In the CUESoft package, the `TXmlObjModel` component (shown in Listing 10-20) performs this necessary task. Consequently, this entire class is an extension to the W3C DOM specification (at least at Level 1).

Listing 10-20: The `TXmlObjModel` declaration

```
TPreserveSpaceEvent = procedure(oOwner: TObject;
  sElementName: string; var bPreserve: Boolean) of object;
TResolveEntityEvent = function (oOwner: TObject;
  sName, sPublicId, sSystemId: string): string of object;

TXmlObjModel = class(TComponent)
protected
  function GetErrorCount: Integer;
  function GetOnPreserveSpace: TPreserveSpaceEvent;
  procedure SetOnPreserveSpace(PreserveSpace: TPreserveSpaceEvent);
public
  constructor Create(AOwner: TComponent); override;
  destructor Destroy; override;
  property Document:   read FDocument;
  property ErrorCount: Integer read GetErrorCount;
  property Errors: TStringList read FErrors;
  property XmlDocument: string read GetXmlDocument;
  procedure ClearDocument;
  function GetErrorMsg(wIdx: Integer): String;
  function LoadDataSource(sSource: String): Boolean;
  function LoadMemory(cpMem: PChar): Boolean;
  function SaveToFile(sFile: string): Boolean;
published
  property FormattedOutput: Boolean read GetFormattedOutput
    write SetFormattedOutput;
  property IdAttribute: string read GetIdAttribute
    write SetIdAttribute;
  property IgnoreCase: Boolean read GetIgnoreCase write SetIgnoreCase;
  property NormalizeData: Boolean read FNormalizeData
    write FNormalizeData
  property OnPreserveSpace: TPreserveSpaceEvent read GetOnPreserveSpace
    write SetOnPreserveSpace;
  property OnResolveEntity: TResolveEntityEvent read FOnResolveEntity
    write SetOnResolveEntity;
  property Password: string read GetPassword write SetPassword;
```

```
    property RaiseErrors: Boolean read FRaiseErrors write FRaiseErrors;
    property UserName: string read GetUserName write SetUserName;
  end;
```

Since this class derives from TComponent, it can appear on the component palette and be dropped onto a form when required. Then set its properties and load the required document in code. Alternately, you can instantiate a copy entirely in code.

A TXmlObjModel component's properties and methods are listed below:

constructor Create(AOwner: TComponent); override;
> If you drag the component from the palette, you do not have to create an instance yourself. Otherwise, use this constructor to generate an object model for your use.

destructor Destroy; override;
> If you create the object model yourself, remember to free it up when you are finished. Objects are automatically destroyed when you drop the component onto the form from the component palette.

property Document: read FDocument;
> This read-only property provides access to the document in memory and all its abilities. You should only use the document through this mechanism.

property ErrorCount: Integer read GetErrorCount;
> Find the number of errors that occurred during a parse through this read-only property.

property Errors: TStringList read FErrors;
> Retrieve each error from the parse in turn with this read-only property.

property FormattedOutput: Boolean read GetFormattedOutput write SetFormattedOutput;
> Duplicating the same property on the document object, this property controls the formatting of any XML generated from the DOM. When True, indentation and line breaks are added to make the text more legible. When False (the default), the text is just one long string.

property IdAttribute: string read GetIdAttribute write SetIdAttribute;
> Also replicating a property on the document object, this one determines what attribute is treated as the ID attribute for searches within the hierarchy.

property IgnoreCase: Boolean read GetIgnoreCase write SetIgnoreCase;
> Another property copied from the document object. When True, this property causes case to be ignored in matches using XSL and XQL queries. When False (the default), case is used in determining a match.

property NormalizeData: Boolean read FNormalizeData write FNormalizeData
> Setting this property to True results in extra white space being stripped from character data in the parse process. Otherwise, all text data is sent through as is (the default).

property OnPreserveSpace: TPreserveSpaceEvent read GetOnPreserveSpace write SetOnPreserveSpace;
> This event triggers once for each element encountered in the parse process. It supplies the name of that element and the current space preservation setting, based on the Normalize-

Data property and any xml:space attributes. An attached event handler may alter the preservation flag.

property OnResolveEntity: TResolveEntityEvent read FOnResolveEntity write SetOnResolveEntity;
External references can be resolved through this event. It passes across the name of the entity, along with its public and system identifiers. Using these you can adjust the actual path to the resource and send it back to the parser as the result of the handler function.

property Password: string read GetPassword write SetPassword;
When reading an XML file from an FTP site, this property establishes the password used to gain access to that site.

property RaiseErrors: Boolean read FRaiseErrors write FRaiseErrors;
Set this property to True to have the parser pass TXmlParserError exceptions through to the application. Otherwise, they are trapped by this component (the default).

property UserName: string read GetUserName write SetUserName;
Complementing the Password property, this one sets the user ID for retrieving documents from FTP sites. If not set, anonymous is used.

property XmlDocument: string read GetXmlDocument;
Generate an XML document from the DOM in memory with this read-only property.

procedure ClearDocument;
Delete the entire DOM with this method. A new document can then be constructed.

function GetErrorMsg(wIdx: Integer): String;
Retrieve individual error messages from the parse process with this method. Duplicating the abilities of the Error property, the index ranges from zero to ErrorCount –1.

function LoadDataSource(sSource: String): Boolean;
The heart of the process, this method invokes the parser on the specified document. Files are identified either as local filenames, or as HTTP or FTP URLs. A return value of True results if the document is successfully loaded and False is returned if problems are encountered. In the latter case, check the Errors property for the reason(s).

function LoadMemory(cpMem: PChar): Boolean;
Similar to the previous method, this one parses a document held in memory at the supplied location. Again, it returns True if successful and False if not.

function SaveToFile(sFile: string): Boolean;
Having created your DOM in memory, use this method to write it to a file. The document type declaration is not included in the document, although the remainder is well-formed XML. You can specify either a local filename or an FTP site to write to. The function returns True if it succeeded and False if a problem arose.

TXmlParser Component

The CUESoft.com package relies on a built-in parser to process XML documents into the DOM structure. CUESoft.com's parser is non-validating, although it does check for well-formed documents. You can access the parser yourself and use it to do your own processing by registering event handlers with it. The TXmlParser component (see Listing 10-21) can also dwell on the component palette, making it easy to incorporate into your project. This class appears in the XmlParser unit.

Listing 10-21: The TXmlParser declaration

```
    TAttributeEvent = procedure (oOwner: TObject;
      sName, sValue: string; bSpecified: Boolean) of object;
    TDocTypeDeclEvent = procedure (oOwner: TObject;
      sDecl, sId0, sId1: string) of object;
    TEntityDeclEvent = procedure (oOwner: TObject;
      sEntityName, sPublicId, sSystemId, sNotationName: string) of object;
    TNonXMLEntityEvent = procedure (oOwner: TObject;
      sEntityName, sPublicId, sSystemId, sNotationName: string) of object;
    TNotationDeclEvent = procedure (oOwner: TObject;
      sNotationName, sPublicId, sSystemId: string) of object;
    TPreserveSpaceEvent = procedure (oOwner: TObject;
      sElementName: string; var bPreserve: Boolean) of object;
    TProcessInstrEvent = procedure (oOwner: TObject;
      sName, sValue: string) of object;
    TResolveEntityEvent = function (oOwner: TObject;
      sName, sPublicId, sSystemId: string): string of object;
    TValueEvent = procedure (oOwner: TObject; sValue: string) of object;

    TXmlParser = class(TComponent)
    protected
      property OnIgnorableWhitespace: TValueEvent
        read FOnIgnorableWhitespace write FOnIgnorableWhitespace;
    public
      constructor Create(oOwner: TComponent);
      destructor Destroy; override;
      property ErrorCount: Integer read GetErrorCount;
      property Errors: TStringList read FErrors;
      function GetErrorMsg(wIdx: Integer): string;
      function ParseDataSource(sSource: string): Boolean;
      function ParseMemory(cpMem: PChar): Boolean;
    published
      property NormalizeData: Boolean read FNormalizeData
        write FNormalizeData;
      property OnAttribute: TAttributeEvent read FOnAttribute
        write FOnAttribute;
      property OnCDATASection: TValueEvent read FOnCDATASection
        write FOnCDATASection;
      property OnCharData: TValueEvent read FOnCharData write FOnCharData;
      property OnComment: TValueEvent read FOnComment write FOnComment;
      property OnDocTypeDecl: TDocTypeDeclEvent read FOnDocTypeDecl
        write FOnDocTypeDecl;
      property OnEndDocument: TNotifyEvent read FOnEndDocument
        write FOnEndDocument;
      property OnEndElement: TValueEvent read FOnEndElement
        write FOnEndElement;
      property OnEntityDecl: TEntityDeclEvent read FOnEntityDecl
```

```
        write FOnEntityDecl;
    property OnNonXMLEntity: TNonXMLEntityEvent read FOnNonXMLEntity
        write FOnNonXMLEntity;
    property OnNotationDecl: TNotationDeclEvent read FOnNotationDecl
        write FOnNotationDecl;
    property OnPreserveSpace: TPreserveSpaceEvent read FOnPreserveSpace
        write FOnPreserveSpace;
    property OnProcessingInstruction: TProcessInstrEvent
        read FOnProcessingInstruction write FOnProcessingInstruction;
    property OnResolveEntity: TResolveEntityEvent read FOnResolveEntity
        write FOnResolveEntity;
    property OnStartDocument: TNotifyEvent read FOnStartDocument
        write FOnStartDocument;
    property OnStartElement: TValueEvent read FOnStartElement
        write FOnStartElement;
    property Password: string read FPassword write FPassword;
    property RaiseErrors: Boolean read FRaiseErrors write FRaiseErrors;
    property UserName: string read FUserName write FUserName;
end;
```

> **TIP** To see CUESoft's parser in action, look at the SAX1 demonstration in Chapter 15. The project contains a SAX1-compatible parser using the CUESoft offering.

The properties and methods of a TXmlParser component are shown below (most of which correspond directly with those in the TXmlObjModel class):

constructor Create(oOwner: TComponent);
> For easiest use, drag-and-drop one of these components from the palette, then set its properties at design time. Otherwise, use this constructor to build a parser in code for your use.

destructor Destroy; override;
> If you create the parser yourself, do not forget to release its resources when finished.

property ErrorCount: Integer read GetErrorCount;
> Find the number of errors from the parse process with this read-only property.

property Errors: TStringList read FErrors;
> Retrieve all the reasons for errors during the parse through this read-only property.

property NormalizeData: Boolean read FNormalizeData write FNormalizeData;
> Strip out extra white space from the document when this property is set to True. Otherwise, all text is passed through unchanged to the OnCharData event (the default). CDATA sections are not affected by this property.

property OnAttribute: TAttributeEvent read FOnAttribute write FOnAttribute;
> Respond to attributes encountered in the document through this event, which fires before the OnStartElement event for their containing element. The attribute name and value, and a flag indicating the origin of that value, are passed to the event handler.

property OnCDATASection: TValueEvent read FOnCDATASection write FOnCDATASection;
> CDATA sections from the document trigger this event, which receives the entire contents of that section.

`property OnCharData: TValueEvent read FOnCharData write FOnCharData;`
   Normal textual content causes this event to fire. Each contiguous section of text appears in one event through the supplied parameter.

`property OnComment: TValueEvent read FOnComment write FOnComment;`
   The entire content of a comment from the document is available within a handler attached to this event.

`property OnDocTypeDecl: TDocTypeDeclEvent read FOnDocTypeDecl write FOnDocTypeDecl;`
   Encountering the document type declaration in the document causes this event to trigger. The name of the document type, and its public and system identifiers are passed across to the event handler. Note that unparsed entities and notations declared in the DTD are notified in events that occur before this one.

`property OnEndDocument: TNotifyEvent read FOnEndDocument write FOnEndDocument;`
   Once the entire document has been processed, this event fires. Use this to complete your processing and to release any resources no longer required.

`property OnEndElement: TValueEvent read FOnEndElement write FOnEndElement;`
   Receive notification of the end tag for an element through this event. The name of the element is supplied. All the content of that element appears as events between this one and its corresponding `OnStartElement`.

`property OnEntityDecl: TEntityDeclEvent read FOnEntityDecl write FOnEntityDecl;`
   Unparsed entity declarations within the document type declaration trigger this event. Save the entity's name, public and system identifiers, and notation name from the parameters passed in. These events occur before the `OnDocTypeDecl` event to which they apply.

`property OnIgnorableWhitespace: TValueEvent read FOnIgnorableWhitespace write FOnIgnorableWhitespace;`
   White space outside of normal text content is notified through this event. However, the fact that it can be ignored is only available if the document is validated against a DTD. Hence, this event is not currently available and appears as a protected property on the parser.

`property OnNonXMLEntity: TNonXMLEntityEvent read FOnNonXMLEntity write FOnNonXMLEntity;`
   This event is triggered when a non-XML entity is encountered in the document. The callback lets you respond to this and perhaps provide some level of support for the entity within your application.

`property OnNotationDecl: TNotationDeclEvent read FOnNotationDecl write FOnNotationDecl;`
   The notations used by entities and processing instructions trigger this event. Save the name, public, and system identifiers for later use. These events arrive before the event for the document type declaration to which they belong.

property OnPreserveSpace: TPreserveSpaceEvent read FOnPreserveSpace write FOnPreserveSpace;
: Fired for each element encountered, this event lets you override the preservation flag setting. Check the element name and current setting, and update the flag if required.

property OnProcessingInstruction: TProcessInstrEvent read FOnProcessingInstruction write FOnProcessingInstruction;
: Each processing instruction found in the document triggers this event. The target application and the actual command are supplied as parameters.

property OnResolveEntity: TResolveEntityEvent read FOnResolveEntity write FOnResolveEntity;
: You can perform resolution for external entities through this event. Given the entity's name and its public and system identifiers, you should return the name of the actual resource to reference.

property OnStartDocument: TNotifyEvent read FOnStartDocument write FOnStartDocument;
: Fired once at the start of the parse process, use this event to initialize your application in preparation for a new document.

property OnStartElement: TValueEvent read FOnStartElement write FOnStartElement;
: The opening tag for each element triggers this event, supplying the name of the element encountered. Recall that the attributes for that element have already appeared in OnAttribute events prior to their containing element.

property Password: string read FPassword write FPassword;
: Set this property to supply a password when accessing documents at FTP sites.

property RaiseErrors: Boolean read FRaiseErrors write FRaiseErrors;
: When set to True, this property causes parse errors (TXmlParserError exceptions) to be sent directly to the application. Otherwise, they are trapped internally and end the parse process in error (the default).

property UserName: string read FUserName write FUserName;
: For accessing FTP sites, specify a user ID to give with this property. If not set, it defaults to anonymous.

function GetErrorMsg(wIdx: Integer): string;
: Retrieve individual error messages through this function. The index ranges from zero to ErrorCount −1.

function ParseDataSource(sSource: string): Boolean;
: Retrieve the document specified and parse its contents, invoking the appropriate events as necessary. The source specification may be either a local filename, or an HTTP or FTP URL. A True results if the parse succeeds and a False if it fails. Check the Errors property in the latter case for the reason(s) it failed.

```
function ParseMemory(cpMem: PChar): Boolean;
```
Similarly, this method parses a document in memory, returning `True` on success and `False` on failure.

Loading the CUESoft DOM

For comparison purposes, you can build the same XML viewer from Chapter 9, but using the CUESoft DOM. The `TXmlObjModel` class is the main entry point into the package. Since this is a Delphi component you can drag it from the component palette, or create it in code, as shown in Listing 10-22. Do not forget to free it after use.

Listing 10-22: Loading the document

```
{ Load an XML document }
procedure TfrmXMLViewer.LoadDoc(Filename: string);
var
  XMLDOM: TXmlObjModel;
begin
  pgcDetails.ActivePage := tshDocument;
  { Initialize document-wide details for display }
  InitDocumentDetails;
  { Load the source document }
  memSource.Lines.LoadFromFile(Filename);
  dlgOpen.Filename := Filename;
  { Instantiate the DOM }
  XMLDOM := TXmlObjModel.Create(nil);
  trvXML.Items.BeginUpdate;
  try
    { Suppress white space? }
    XMLDOM.NormalizeData := mniSuppressWhitespace.Checked;
    { Parse the document }
    if not XMLDOM.LoadDataSource(Filename) then
      raise Exception.Create(
        Format(NoLoadError, [XMLDOM.Errors.Text]));

    edtSystemId.Text := Filename;
    { Add the structure to the tree view }
    AddElementToTree(XMLDOM.Document, nil);
    trvXML.Items[0].Expand(False);
  finally
    trvXML.Items.EndUpdate;
    { Release the DOM }
    XMLDOM.Free;
  end;
end;
```

An item on the menu in the viewer lets you suppress text nodes that contain only white space. This value is transferred directly to the `NormalizeData` property of the DOM. Calling the `LoadDataSource` method on the object model class then loads and parses the specified document, returning a `False` value if it fails. In that case you can raise an exception with the list of problems from the `Errors` property. Otherwise, pass the newly created document, accessed through the `Document` property, to the routine that builds up the tree view on the page.

Like the previous example, the construction of the tree view relies on recursive calls to the AddElementToTree routine (see Listing 10-23). Initially the nodes can be treated in a generic manner to extract a meaningful display value for them. Thereafter, the node type determines what additional information is required and how to retrieve it. Each type is cast to its appropriate subclass before accessing its attributes.

Listing 10-23: Reading the nodes

```
{ Add a TXMLElement to the tree view }
function AddElement(Parent: TTreeNode; Name: string;
  Element: TXMLElement): TTreeNode;
begin
  FList.Add(Element);
  Result := trvXML.Items.AddChildObject(Parent, Name, Element);
  with Result do
  begin
    ImageIndex    := Ord(Element.ElementType);
    SelectedIndex := ImageIndex;
  end;
end;

{ Add current element to the treeview and
  then recurse through children }
procedure AddElementToTree(Node: TXmlNode; TreeParent: TTreeNode);
var
  Index: Integer;
  DisplayName: string;
  NewNode: TTreeNode;
  Attribs: TStringList;

  { Extract an attribute value from a string }
  function GetPseudoAttr(const Name, Data: string): string;
  var
    PosStart, PosEnd: Integer;
  begin
    Result   := '';
    PosStart := Pos(Name, Data);
    if PosStart = 0 then
      Exit;

    PosStart := PosStart + Length(Name) + 1;
    PosEnd   := Pos(Data[PosStart],
      Copy(Data, PosStart + 1, Length(Data)));
    if PosEnd = 0 then
      Result := ''
    else
      Result := Copy(Data, PosStart + 1, PosEnd - 1);
  end;

begin
  { Generate name for display in the tree }
  if Node.NodeType in
    [TEXT_NODE, COMMENT_NODE, CDATA_SECTION_NODE] then
  begin
    if Length(Node.NodeValue) > 20 then
      DisplayName := Copy(Node.NodeValue, 1, 17) + '...'
    else
      DisplayName := Node.NodeValue;
  end
```

```
    else
      DisplayName := Node.NodeName;
    { Create storage for later display of node values }
    case Node.NodeType of
      ELEMENT_NODE:
        with Node as XmlObjModel.TXmlElement do
        begin
          Attribs := TStringList.Create;
          try
            if HasAttributes then
              for Index := 0 to Attributes.Length - 1 do
                with Attributes.Item(Index) do
                  Attribs.Values[NodeName] := NodeValue;
            NewNode := AddElement(TreeParent, DisplayName,
              TXMLElement.Create(xtElement, NodeName,
              Namespace, BaseName, '', Attribs));
          finally
            Attribs.Free;
          end;
        end;
      TEXT_NODE:
        with Node as TXmlText do
          NewNode := AddElement(TreeParent, DisplayName,
            TXMLElement.Create(xtText, '', '', '', Data, nil));
      CDATA_SECTION_NODE:
        with Node as TXmlCDATASection do
          NewNode := AddElement(TreeParent, DisplayName,
            TXMLElement.Create(xtCData, '', '', '', Data, nil));
      ENTITY_REFERENCE_NODE:
        NewNode := AddElement(TreeParent, DisplayName,
          TXMLElement.Create(xtEntityRef, Node.NodeName,
          '', '', '', nil));
      PROCESSING_INSTRUCTION_NODE:
        with Node as TXmlProcessingInstruction do
        begin
          NewNode := AddElement(TreeParent, DisplayName,
            TXMLElement.Create(xtInstruction, Target,
            '', '', Data, nil));
          if UpperCase(Target) = XMLValue then
          begin
            { Special handling for the XML declaration }
            edtVersion.Text     := GetPseudoAttr(VersionAttr, Data);
            edtEncoding.Text    := GetPseudoAttr(EncodingAttr, Data);
            cbxStandAlone.Checked := (UpperCase(GetPseudoAttr(
              StandAloneAttr, Data)) = YesValue);
          end;
        end;
      COMMENT_NODE:
        with Node as TXmlComment do
          NewNode := AddElement(TreeParent, DisplayName,
            TXMLElement.Create(xtComment, '', '', '', Data, nil));
      DOCUMENT_NODE:
        with Node as TXmlDocument do
        begin
          NewNode := AddElement(TreeParent, XMLDocDesc,
            TXMLElement.Create(xtDocument, XMLDocDesc, '', '', '', nil));
          AddElementToTree(DocType, NewNode);
        end;
      DOCUMENT_TYPE_NODE:
        with Node as TXmlDocumentType do
```

```
    begin
      edtDocType.Text := Name;
      NewNode := AddElement(TreeParent, DTDDesc,
        TXMLElement.Create(xtEntityRef, DTDDesc, '', '', '', nil));
      for Index := 0 to Entities.Length - 1 do
        AddElementToTree(Entities.Item(Index), NewNode);
      for Index := 0 to Notations.Length - 1 do
        AddElementToTree(Notations.Item(Index), NewNode);
    end;
  ENTITY_NODE:
    with (Node as TXmlEntity), stgEntities do
      if NotationName <> '' then
      begin
        { Unparsed entity }
        if Cells[0, RowCount - 1] <> '' then
          RowCount := RowCount + 1;
        Cells[0, RowCount - 1] := NodeName;
        Cells[1, RowCount - 1] := PublicId;
        Cells[2, RowCount - 1] := SystemId;
        Cells[3, RowCount - 1] := NotationName;
      end
      else
        { Parsed entity }
        NewNode := AddElement(TreeParent, DisplayName,
          TXMLElement.Create(xtEntityRef, NodeName,
          '', '', '', nil));
  NOTATION_NODE:
    with (Node as TXmlNotation), stgNotations do
    begin
      if Cells[0, RowCount - 1] <> '' then
        RowCount := RowCount + 1;
      Cells[0, RowCount - 1] := NodeName;
      Cells[1, RowCount - 1] := PublicId;
      Cells[2, RowCount - 1] := SystemId;
    end;
  end;
  { And recurse through any children }
  if Node.HasChildNodes then
    for Index := 0 to Node.ChildNodes.Length - 1 do
      AddElementToTree(Node.ChildNodes.Item(Index), NewNode);
end;
```

Elements have their attributes converted into a string list before saving all the details in a `TXmlElement` object. Note that this is a local class defined in the viewer unit, and does not refer to the `TXmlElement` class of the CUESoft package. The local definition replaces the external one, so all references to this class use the internal one. To access the original class, you must prefix it with

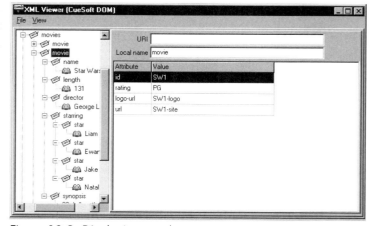

Figure 10-2: Displaying an element.

the name of its unit, `XmlObjModel.TXmlElement`. The results of processing an element are seen in Figure 10-2.

Text type nodes, including CDATA sections and comments, simply copy their content into the corresponding field in the `TXmlElement` for later use. An example of these is shown in Figure 10-3. Processing instructions follow a similar path, placing their command content in the data field of the storage object. A special case exists for the XML declaration whereby its pseudo-properties are extracted and transferred to particular fields on the document page of the viewer.

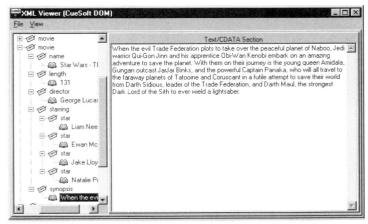

Figure 10-3: Text content within the viewer.

The rest of the information for the document page comes from the document type node, and its entity and notation properties. The latter are not actually children of the document type node in the CUESoft DOM, so you must step through them within their lists and manually invoke the next level of node processing. Thereafter, the notation and unparsed entity nodes get added to the grids on the document page. The document type node also supplies the name of the top-level element for the document. Figure 10-4 shows all this information on the document page in the viewer.

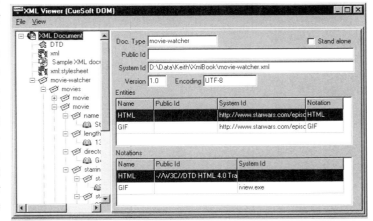

Figure 10-4: The document page in the viewer

Entity references do not appear within the CUESoft DOM since it expands all such references during the parse process. Only the results of the expansion are passed along. Similarly, parsed entities do not appear within the document type node's list of entities.

Finally, each child of the current node is processed in turn through a recursive call. The newly created `TTreeNode` is passed along to provide the context for any additions to the view.

Summary

The CUESoft DOM implements the W3C DOM Level 1 specification very closely, and includes a few elements of the Level 2 spec. However, it does not provide full support for namespaces, which limits its usefulness in some situations.

Having the DOM available as Delphi components and classes makes it very simple to use within your application. The initial steps can be performed without any coding by dragging the TXmlObjModel component from the palette onto your form, then setting its properties in the inspector. Once compiled, the parser and DOM become part of your executable, making it easier to distribute.

The parser in this package can be used on its own without building the associated DOM. Include the XmlParser unit in your project and create an instance of the TXmlParser component, or drag one from the component palette and drop it on your form. By registering event handlers with the parser, you can respond to the items within the XML document as they are encountered. See the SAX demonstration project in Chapter 15 for an example of its use.

NOTE Soon after writing this, CUESoft.com sold its XML technologies to TurboPower. A re-worked version of the package should be available from them by the time you read this.

Chapter 11
Open XML's Document Object Model

The Open XML project includes another implementation of the DOM specification under Windows, also as a set of native Delphi objects. The XDOM package was written by Dieter Köhler and is available from http://www.philo.de/xml/ and on the CD-ROM accompanying this book. It is freely available, including the full source code.

The package conforms very closely to the Document Object Model (Core) Level 1 specification from the W3C. Modifications and enhancements as described in the DOM Level 2 specification (the Candidate Recommendation as of March 7, 2000) have also been implemented. Although the code was designed for Delphi 3, it runs just as well with later versions. The version of XDOM discussed here is 2.2.12a.

Along with the standard DOM implementation, XDOM provides many extensions, especially in the area of modeling DTDs. Many additional classes let you step through all the declarations in the DTD (elements and attributes included), or create your own DTD within the document in memory.

XDOM follows the same pattern as the other DOM packages, with classes corresponding to the items in the DOM specification. The class hierarchy of the XDOM package is contained in the XDOM.pas unit and is shown in Figure 11-1. Like CUESoft's implementation, it is made up of classes rather than interfaces. All string values within XDOM are WideStrings, and all string comparisons are case-sensitive.

EDomException Exception

Errors within the XDOM package show up as exceptions, all of which derive from EDomException. This class adds nothing to the basic Exception, but simply serves as a marker for all errors related to the XML operations. Whereas the DOM specification uses an integer flag within its exception to indicate the cause of the problem, XDOM defines each error type as a different subclass of EDomException. Listing 11-1 contains the full range of declared exceptions. As usual, you can handle all DOM errors by trapping at the topmost level or by drilling down to a subclass for increased precision.

Figure 11-1: Class hierarchy for Open XML's DOM.

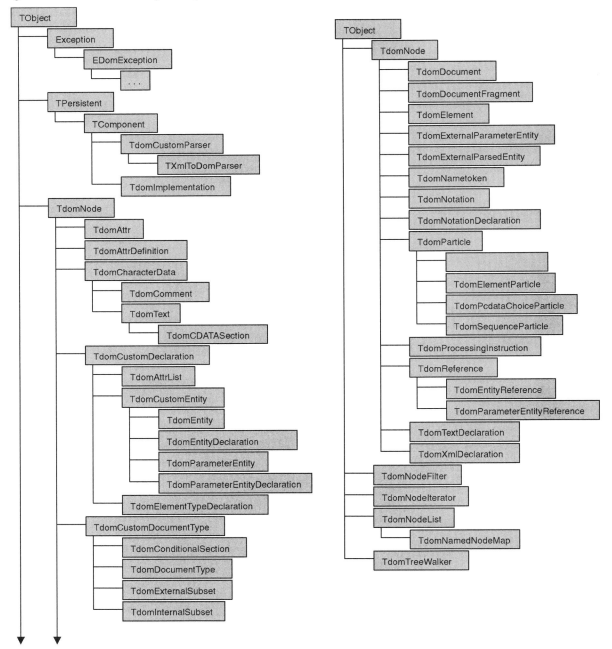

Listing 11-1: The XDOM exceptions

```
    EDomException = class(Exception);

    EIndex_Size_Err = class(EdomException);
    EDomstring_Size_Err = class(EdomException);
    EHierarchy_Request_Err = class(EdomException);
    EWrong_Document_Err = class(EdomException);
    EInvalid_Character_Err = class(EdomException);
    ENo_Data_Allowed_Err = class(EdomException);
    ENo_Modification_Allowed_Err = class(EdomException);
    ENot_Found_Err = class(EdomException);
    ENot_Supported_Err = class(EdomException);
    EInuse_Attribute_Err = class(EdomException);
    EInvalid_State_Err = class(EdomException);
    ESyntax_Err = class(EdomException);
    EInvalid_Modification_Err = class(EdomException);
    ENamespace_Err = class(EdomException);
    EInvalid_Access_Err = class(EdomException);
    EInuse_Node_Err = class(EdomException);
    EInuse_AttributeDefinition_Err = class(EdomException);
    ENo_External_Entity_Allowed_Err = class(EdomException);
    EInvalid_Entity_Reference_Err = class(EdomException);
    EUnknown_Document_Format_Err = class(EdomException);

    EParserException = class(Exception);

    EInternalParserException = class(EParserException);

    EParserFatalError = class(EParserException);
    EParserError = class(EParserException);
    EParserWarning = class(EParserException);

    EParserMissingWhiteSpace_Err = class(EParserFatalError);
    EParserMissingQuotationMark_Err = class(EParserFatalError);
    EParserMissingEqualitySign_Err = class(EParserFatalError);
    EParserDoubleEqualitySign_Err = class(EParserFatalError);
    EParserInvalidElementName_Err = class(EParserFatalError);
    EParserInvalidAttributeName_Err = class(EParserFatalError);
    EParserInvalidAttributeValue_Err = class(EParserFatalError);
    EParserDoubleAttributeName_Err = class(EParserFatalError);
    EParserInvalidEntityName_Err = class(EParserFatalError);
    EParserInvalidProcessingInstruction_Err = class(EParserFatalError);
    EParserInvalidXmlDeclaration_Err = class(EParserFatalError);
    EParserInvalidCharRef_Err = class(EParserFatalError);
    EParserMissingStartTag_Err = class(EParserFatalError);
    EParserMissingEndTag_Err = class(EParserFatalError);
    EParserInvalidEndTag_Err = class(EParserFatalError);
    EParserInvalidCharacter_Err = class(EParserFatalError);
    EParserNotInRoot_Err = class(EParserFatalError);
    EParserDoubleRootElement_Err = class(EParserFatalError);
    EParserRootNotFound_Err = class(EParserFatalError);
    EParserWrongOrder_Err = class(EParserFatalError);
    EParserInvalidDoctype_Err = class(EParserFatalError);
    EParserInvalidTextDeclaration_Err = class(EParserFatalError);

    EParserDoubleDoctype_Err = class(EParserInvalidDoctype_Err);
    EParserUnknownDeclarationType_Err = class(EParserInvalidDoctype_Err);
    EParserInvalidEntityDeclaration_Err = class(EParserInvalidDoctype_Err);
    EParserInvalidElementDeclaration_Err =
      class(EParserInvalidDoctype_Err);
```

```
    EParserInvalidAttributeDeclaration_Err =
      class(EParserInvalidDoctype_Err);
    EParserInvalidNotationDeclaration_Err =
      class(EParserInvalidDoctype_Err);
    EParserInvalidConditionalSection_Err =
      class(EParserInvalidDoctype_Err);

    EParserDouble_Entity_Decl_Warning = class(EParserWarning);
    EParserDouble_Parameter_Entity_Decl_Warning = class(EParserWarning);
    EParserDouble_Notation_Decl_Warning = class(EParserWarning);
    EParserUnusable_Entity_Decl_Warning = class(EParserWarning);
```

TdomNode Class

As in the previous DOM implementations, TdomNode is the base for all the nodes that appear within the object model. This class allows nodes to be treated in a generic way, without having to cast them to their appropriate subclasses. However, not all of the properties and methods apply to all of the possible descendants. For example, although TdomNode has methods for accessing child nodes, attempting to add one to a TdomText node results in an exception since Text nodes do not have children.

The public interface of the TdomNode class is shown in Listing 11-2. Note that many of the properties are read-only, their values being initialized upon creation of the node.

Listing 11-2: The TdomNode declaration

```
    TdomNode = class
    public
      constructor Create(const AOwner: TdomDocument);
      destructor Destroy; override;
      procedure Clear; virtual;
      function InsertBefore(const newChild, refChild: TdomNode):
        TdomNode; virtual;
      function ReplaceChild(const newChild, oldChild: TdomNode):
        TdomNode; virtual;
      function RemoveChild(const oldChild: TdomNode): TdomNode;
        virtual;
      function AppendChild(const newChild: TdomNode): TdomNode;
        virtual;
      function HasChildNodes: boolean; virtual;
      function CloneNode(const deep: boolean): TdomNode; virtual;
      function IsAncestor(const AncestorNode: TdomNode): boolean;
        virtual;
      procedure GetLiteralAsNodes(const RefNode: TdomNode); virtual;
      procedure normalize; virtual;
      function supports(const feature, version: WideString): boolean;
        virtual;
    published
      property Attributes:      TdomNamedNodeMap read GetAttributes;
      property ChildNodes:      TdomNodeList     read GetChildNodes;
      property Code:            WideString       read GetCode;
      property FirstChild:      TdomNode         read GetFirstChild;
      property LastChild:       TdomNode         read GetLastChild;
      property LocalName:       WideString       read GetLocalName;
      property NamespaceURI:    WideString       read GetNamespaceURI;
      property NextSibling:     TdomNode         read GetNextSibling;
```

```
        property NodeName:         WideString        read GetNodeName;
        property NodeType:         TdomNodeType      read GetNodeType;
        property NodeValue:        WideString        read GetNodeValue;
          write SetNodeValue;
        property OwnerDocument:    TdomDocument      read GetDocument;
        property ParentNode:       TdomNode          read GetParentNode;
        property PreviousSibling:  TdomNode          read GetPreviousSibling;
        property Prefix:           WideString        read GetPrefix
          write SetPrefix;
    end;
```

The TdomNode's properties and methods are described below:

constructor Create(const AOwner: TdomDocument);

> You should not call this constructor directly. Instead use the appropriate method provided by the TdomDocument class. The owning document of the node is passed in as a parameter.

property NodeType: TdomNodeType read GetNodeType;

> The particular type of subclass derived from TdomNode is identified by this read-only property. Its value is one of the constants listed in the TDomNodeType type. See Table 11-1 for the correspondence between the node types and the implementing classes.

Table 11-1: XDOM node types

Node Type	Subclass
ntUnknown	-
ntElement_Node	TdomElement
ntAttribute_Node	TdomAttr
ntText_Node	TdomText
ntCDATA_Section_Node	TdomCDATASection
ntEntity_Reference_Node	TdomEntityReference
ntEntity_Node	TdomEntity
ntProcessing_Instruction_Node	TdomProcessingInstruction
ntComment_Node	TdomComment
ntDocument_Node	TdomDocument
ntDocument_Type_Node	TdomDocumentType
ntDocument_Fragment_Node	TdomDocumentFragment
ntNotation_Node	TdomNotation
ntXml_Declaration_Node	TdomXmlDeclaration
ntConditional_Section_Node	TdomConditionalSection
ntParameter_Entity_Reference_Node	TdomParameterEntityReference
ntParameter_Entity_Node	TdomParameterEntity
ntEntity_Declaration_Node	TdomEntityDeclaration
ntParameter_Entity_Declaration_Node	TdomParameterEntityDeclaration
ntElement_Type_Declaration_Node	TdomElementTypeDeclaration
ntSequence_Particle_Node	TdomSequenceParticle

Node Type	Subclass
ntChoice_Particle_Node	TdomChoiceParticle
ntPcdata_Choice_Particle_Node	TdomPcdataChoiceParticle
ntElement_Particle_Node	TdomElementParticle
ntAttribute_List_Node	TdomAttrList
ntAttribute_Definition_Node	TdomAttrDefinition
ntNametoken_Node	TdomNametoken
ntText_Declaration_Node	TdomTextDeclaration
ntNotation_Declaration_Node	TdomNotationDeclaration
ntExternal_Parsed_Entity_Node	TdomExternalParsedEntity
ntExternal_Parameter_Entity_Node	TdomExternalParameterEntity
ntExternal_Subset_Node	TdomExternalSubset
ntInternal_Subset_Node	TdomInternalSubset

Once the type of node is determined, the node can be cast to the correct subclass to gain access to its unique abilities. The meaning of the NodeName and NodeValue properties depends on the node type as shown in Table 11-2.

Table 11-2: NodeName and NodeValue meanings based on node type

Node Type	NodeName	NodeValue
ntAttribute_Definition_Node	Name of attribute	Default value of attribute
ntAttribute_List_Node	Name of element	" (Empty string)
ntAttribute_Node	Name of attribute	Value of attribute
ntCDATA_Section_Node	#cdata-section	Content of the CDATA section
ntChoice_Particle_Node	#choice-particle	"
ntComment_Node	#comment	Content of the comment
ntConditional_Section_Node	#conditional-section	"
ntDocument_Fragment_Node	#document-fragment	"
ntDocument_Node	#document	"
ntDocument_Type_Node	Document type name	Entire content excluding name and external ID
ntElement_Node	Name of element	"
ntElement_Particle_Node	Name of element	"
ntElement_Type_Declaration_Node	Name of element	Value of declaration
ntEntity_Declaration_Node	Name of entity	Value of entity
ntEntity_Node	Name of entity	Value of entity
ntEntity_Reference_Node	Name of entity	"
ntExternal_Parameter_Entity_Node	#external-parameter-entity	"

Node Type	NodeName	NodeValue
ntExternal_Parsed_Entity_Node	#external-parsed-entity	"
ntExternal_Subset_Node	#external-subset	"
ntInternal_Subset_Node	#internal-subset	"
ntNametoken_Node	Name of name token	"
ntNotation_Declaration_Node	Name of notation	"
ntNotation_Node	Name of notation	"
ntParameter_Entity_Declaration_Node	Name of parameter entity	Value of parameter entity
ntParameter_Entity_Node	Name of parameter entity	Value of parameter entity
ntParameter_Entity_Reference_Node	Name of parameter entity	"
ntPcdata_Choice_Particle_Node	#pcdata-choice-particle	"
ntProcessing_Instruction_Node	Name of target	Entire content excluding the target
ntSequence_Particle_Node	#sequence-particle	"
ntText_Declaration_Node	#text-declaration	"
ntText_Node	#text	Content of the text
ntUnknown	–	–
ntXml_Declaration_Node	#xml-declaration	"

property NodeName: WideString read GetNodeName;

>   This read-only property returns the name of the node. The actual value depends on the type of the node, as shown in Table 11-2. For nodes within a namespace, this value includes the associated prefix.

property NamespaceURI: WideString read GetNamespaceURI;

>   This read-only property finds the full URI that identifies the namespace for this node. If no namespace applies to the node, an empty string is returned.

property Prefix: WideString read GetPrefix write SetPrefix;

>   The shorthand identifier for the above namespace (up to the colon) is returned by this property. An empty string results if no namespace is applicable. Setting this value also updates the NodeName property, as well as the TagName property of element nodes, and the Name property of attribute nodes. An exception arises if the new value contains illegal characters, the prefix is malformed, the NamespaceURI property is an empty string, or the prefix is a reserved XML one without the corresponding namespace being specified.

property LocalName: WideString read GetLocalName;

>   The rest of the node's name (after the colon) is retrieved through this read-only property. For a node that does not belong to a namespace, this is the same as the NodeName property.

property NodeValue: WideString read GetNodeValue write SetNodeValue;
: This property contains the text value of the node, if applicable. For a text node, this is the actual text, while a processing instruction node places its command data here. The value is an empty string for those nodes that do not have a value. See Table 11-2 for the exact meaning based on the node type. Attempting to alter this value on a read-only node results in an exception being raised.

property Code: WideString read GetCode;
: Use this read-only property to retrieve the XML text that corresponds to this node and all of its children. When generating a document or document fragment with the DOM, you extract the resulting XML from here before saving it to a file or sending it on to another process.

NOTE As with the previous DOMs, the Code property is an extension to the DOM specification, but a necessary one for creating XML documents on the fly.

property Attributes: TdomNamedNodeMap read GetAttributes;
: Access the attributes of an element node through this read-only property. For all other node types the property returns nil. As in the specification, the result is a named node map, which is covered in a later section.

property OwnerDocument: TdomDocument read GetDocument;
: Traverse to the document that created the node via this read-only property. Nodes belong to their creating document and cannot be moved between documents. For document nodes and for document type nodes when not yet attached to a document, this property returns nil.

property ParentNode: TdomNode read GetParentNode;
: The next node up in the DOM hierarchy is available via this read-only property. From the root of the structure, a document or document fragment node, this returns nil. Attribute, attribute definition, entity, and notation nodes also do not have a parent, nor does a newly created node before it is added to a tree.

property ChildNodes: TdomNodeList read GetChildNodes;
: Use this read-only property to move down through the DOM hierarchy. It returns a node list, which is described in more detail below. If there are no children, this property still returns a node list but it has no entries in it.

function HasChildNodes: boolean; virtual;
: As a convenience, this function returns a flag indicating the presence or absence of children on this node. You can also check the length of the ChildNodes list property.

property FirstChild: TdomNode read GetFirstChild;
: This convenience property (read-only) returns the first child node of the current node, or nil if there are no children. You could achieve the same result through the ChildNodes property.

property LastChild: TdomNode read GetLastChild;
: Similarly, this read-only property provides access to the last child in the current node's list, or nil if there are no children.

property PreviousSibling: TdomNode read GetPreviousSibling;
: This read-only property returns the preceding node in this node's parent's list of children, the current node's sibling. If there is no node before this one at that level, a nil is returned.

property NextSibling: TdomNode read GetNextSibling;
: Conversely, this read-only property provides access to the next node in the parent's child list. Again, nil is returned if there is no following node at that level.

function InsertBefore(const newChild, refChild: TdomNode): TdomNode; virtual;
: Add children to a node using this method. The new node passed in as a parameter is placed immediately before the supplied reference node. If the latter is nil, the new node is placed at the end of the list of children. A pointer to the new node is returned by the function. If the new node is already present in the tree, it is first removed. An exception occurs if the node does not allow children of the new node's type, if the new node is already an ancestor of the current node, if the new node was created by another document, if the current or new node's parent is read-only, or if the reference node is not a child of the current node.

function ReplaceChild(const newChild, oldChild: TdomNode): TdomNode; virtual;
: Insert a new node in place of an existing one with this method. This time a reference to the node being replaced is returned by the function. Exceptions arise if the existing node cannot be found as a child, if the current node is read-only, if the new node was created by another document, if the new node is an ancestor of the current node, or if the new node type is not allowed as a child of the current node. If the new node was already present in the DOM, it is removed from that point before being inserted in its new spot.

function RemoveChild(const oldChild: TdomNode): TdomNode; virtual;
: Delete a particular child node with this method. A reference to the deleted node is returned by the function. An exception occurs if the node to be deleted cannot be found as a child or if the current node is read-only.

function AppendChild(const newChild: TdomNode): TdomNode; virtual;
: Add a new node at the end of this node's child list using this method. A pointer to the new node is returned by the function. The node is removed from the DOM if it is already present. Exceptions are raised for the same reasons as the InsertChild method. In fact, InsertChild can provide the same functionality as this method when its reference node is set to nil.

TIP When adding a document fragment to a DOM, that node is not inserted directly. Instead, all the children of that fragment are inserted in turn. This allows you to transfer nodes or subtrees between sections of the document easily.

```
function CloneNode(const deep: boolean): TdomNode; virtual;
```
Create a copy of the current node using this method and return a reference to it. This new node has no parent until it is placed into the main DOM or a document fragment. If the deep parameter is set to True, then all the nodes below the current one are also copied and placed below its duplicate. Otherwise, only the single current node is replicated.

An element node always has its attributes copied, regardless of the deep setting, but any text within it is only reproduced on a deep copy. Cloning a document type node also duplicates its entity and notation nodes automatically. When a read-only node is copied, the resulting node can be altered. This does not apply to entity and entity reference nodes whose contents remain read-only.

```
procedure normalize; virtual;
```
Normalizing a node causes any adjacent text nodes within the subtree below it to be combined. Thus there are only markup nodes (elements, comments, CDATA sections, entity references, and processing instructions) surrounding text nodes. Note that CDATA sections are not combined with text nodes. Performing this operation ensures that the DOM is in a consistent state for either saving or for working with other technologies such as XPointer.

```
function supports(const feature, version: WideString): boolean; virtual;
```
Test whether or not a particular ability is supported by this DOM implementation through this method. Given a feature name and required version, it returns True if those capabilities are present and False otherwise.

NOTE In the DOM specification, the supports method is named isSupported. Missing from the DOM spec is the hasAttributes method; however, looking at the Attributes property can duplicate its functionality. The remaining methods are not part of the standard DOM.

```
procedure Clear; virtual;
```
Remove all children from this node using this method, except for those that are read-only. An exception arises if the node itself is read-only. You can use this to prepare a node for a new set of children.

```
function IsAncestor(const AncestorNode: TdomNode): boolean; virtual;
```
This convenience method returns True if the supplied node is an ancestor of the current node, and False if it is not.

```
procedure GetLiteralAsNodes(const RefNode: TdomNode); virtual;
```
The functionality for this method has not yet been fully implemented.

TdomNodeList Class

Node lists provide the structure within the DOM. Each node has a `ChildNodes` property that returns an object of this type. Using this you can traverse down through the hierarchy and process the entire XML document.

Listing 11-3 shows the public and protected declarations for `TdomNodeList`. These follow the DOM specification very closely.

Listing 11-3: The TdomNodeList declaration

```
TdomNodeList = class
protected
  function IndexOf(const Node: TdomNode): integer; virtual;
public
  constructor Create(const NodeList: TList);
  property Length: integer read GetLength;
  function Item(const index: integer): TdomNode; virtual;
end;
```

The properties and methods of `TdomNodeList` are detailed below:

`constructor Create(const NodeList: TList);`
> Generate a new node list object, passing in the `TList` of nodes to be managed. Usually these node lists are created automatically for you.

`property Length: integer read GetLength;`
> Retrieve the number of entries in the list with this read-only property.

`function Item(const index: integer): TdomNode; virtual;`
> Access each entry in the list via its index (starting from zero) using this function. If the index is not valid, a `nil` is returned.

`function IndexOf(const Node: TdomNode): integer; virtual;`
> This protected function returns the index of a given node within its list. If the specified node is not in the list, a value of −1 is returned. Note that this method is only available when subclassing the `TdomNodeList` class.

Various specialized node lists are also defined within the XDOM package, all deriving from the basic node list. The `TdomElementsNodeList` provides an ordered collection of nodes from the document based on a tag name passed into its constructor. `TdomElementsNodeListNS` is a namespace-aware version of the previous class. Similarly, the `TdomSpecialNodeList` gives access to an ordered collection of nodes of one or more specified node types, selecting from a list of nodes passed in as a parameter. These classes are used internally and you see them only as a normal `TdomNodeList` outside the XDOM package.

TdomNamedNodeMap Class

The named node map provides access to a list of nodes, just like the node list above, but primarily does so through the nodes' names, rather than their location within the list. Listing 11-4 shows the declaration for the TdomNamedNodeMap class. It inherits the abilities of the normal node list, before adding its own functionality. Although the parent class provides sequential access to the list entries, this does not imply any particular order in their retrieval within this subclass.

Listing 11-4: The TdomNamedNodeMap declaration

```
TdomNamedNodeMap = class(TdomNodeList)
protected
  function RemoveItem(const Arg: TdomNode): TdomNode; virtual;
  function GetNamedIndex(const Name: WideString): integer;
    virtual;
public
  constructor Create(const AOwner, AOwnerNode: TdomNode;
    const NodeList: TList; const AllowedNTs: TDomNodeTypeSet);
    virtual;
  function GetNamedItem(const Name: WideString): TdomNode;
    virtual;
  function SetNamedItem(const Arg: TdomNode): TdomNode; virtual;
  function RemoveNamedItem(const Name: WideString): TdomNode;
    virtual;
  function GetNamedItemNS(const namespaceURI, LocalName:
    WideString): TdomNode; virtual;
  function SetNamedItemNS(const Arg: TdomNode): TdomNode;
    virtual;
  function RemoveNamedItemNS(const namespaceURI, LocalName:
    WideString): TdomNode; virtual;
published
  property ownerNode: TdomNode read GetOwnerNode;
  property namespaceAware: boolean read GetNamespaceAware
    write SetNamespaceAware;
end;
```

TdomNamedNodeMap's properties and methods are detailed below:

`constructor Create(const AOwner, AOwnerNode: TdomNode; const NodeList: TList; const AllowedNTs: TDomNodeTypeSet); virtual;`
Build a new named node map for your use. The node that creates the map and the one that uses the map (or `nil` if not used by a node) are passed in as parameters. Also supplied is a `TList` of nodes to be managed by the map. Normally these lists are created for you automatically.

`property ownerNode: TdomNode read GetOwnerNode;`
Find the node to which this map is attached with this read-only property, or return `nil` if there is no such node.

`property namespaceAware: boolean read GetNamespaceAware write SetNamespaceAware;`
By default this property is set to `False`, indicating that the non-namespace versions of the following methods should be used. When set to `True`, the namespace version must be used (those with `NS` in their names). The value may be altered so long as there are no entries in the

list. If you attempt to access the wrong version of the remaining methods, an exception is raised.

`function GetNamedItem(const Name: WideString): TdomNode; virtual;`
> This function retrieves a node from the list, given its name. If the node cannot be found, a `nil` is returned instead. If the `namespaceAware` property is set to `True`, an exception occurs when calling this method.

`function SetNamedItem(const Arg: TdomNode): TdomNode; virtual;`
> This property adds a new node to the list using its name as the key. An exception is raised if the new node was created by another document, if this list is read-only, if a node is supplied that already exists within the document, or if the `namespaceAware` property is set to `True` when calling this method.

`function RemoveNamedItem(const Name: WideString): TdomNode; virtual;`
> Delete the specified node from the list based on its name. An exception occurs if the node cannot be found, if this list is read-only, or if the `namespaceAware` property is set to `True` when calling this method.

NOTE If an attribute is removed from an element's list, but that attribute has a default value specified in the DTD, it should immediately reappear with that default value. This functionality is not yet implemented in the XDOM package.

`function GetNamedItemNS(const namespaceURI, LocalName: WideString): TdomNode; virtual;`
> This method is the namespace-aware version of `GetNamedItem`. It works just like the original except that it raises an exception if the `namespaceAware` property is set to `False` when it is invoked.

`function SetNamedItemNS(const Arg: TdomNode): TdomNode; virtual;`
> Similarly, this method is the namespace-aware version of `SetNamedItem`, with the opposite behavior of the `namespaceAware` property.

`function RemoveNamedItemNS(const namespaceURI, LocalName: WideString): TdomNode; virtual;`
> Another namespace-aware method, this time for `removeNamedItem`. As above, it only works when the `namespaceAware` property is set to `True`.

`function RemoveItem(const Arg: TdomNode): TdomNode; virtual;`
> This protected method deletes an entry from the list.

NOTE The replacement of deleted attribute nodes which have default values is not yet implemented.

`function GetNamedIndex(const Name: WideString): integer; virtual;`
> Given the name of a node, this method returns its index within the list, or -1 if it does not appear at all. An exception is raised if the `namespaceAware` property is `True`. This method is also protected.

Internally the list of entities for a document is held (in the document type object) in a customized subclass of TdomNamedNodeMap. However, the additional functionality is not used outside of the XDOM package and the list can be treated just like an ordinary node map.

TdomElement Class

Most of the nodes within a DOM are of this type which represents an Element node. The declaration for TdomElement is shown in Listing 11-5.

Listing 11-5: The TdomElement declaration

```
TdomElement = class (TdomNode)
public
  constructor Create(const AOwner: TdomDocument;
    const NamespaceURI, TagName: WideString); virtual;
  destructor Destroy; override;
  function GetTagName: WideString; virtual;
  function GetAttributes: TdomNamedNodeMap; override;
  function GetAttribute(const Name: WideString): WideString;
    virtual;
  function SetAttribute(const Name, Value: WideString): TdomAttr;
    virtual;
  function RemoveAttribute(const Name: WideString): TdomAttr;
    virtual;
  function GetAttributeNode(const Name: WideString): TdomAttr;
    virtual;
  function SetAttributeNode(const NewAttr: TdomAttr): TdomAttr;
    virtual;
  function RemoveAttributeNode(const OldAttr: TdomAttr):
    TdomAttr; virtual;
  function GetElementsByTagName(const Name: WideString):
    TdomNodeList; virtual;
  function GetAttributeNS(const namespaceURI, localName:
    WideString): WideString; virtual;
  function SetAttributeNS(const namespaceURI, qualifiedName,
    value: WideString): TdomAttr; virtual;
  function RemoveAttributeNS(const namespaceURI, localName:
    WideString): TdomAttr; virtual;
  function GetAttributeNodeNS(const namespaceURI, localName:
    WideString): TdomAttr; virtual;
  function SetAttributeNodeNS(const NewAttr: TdomAttr): TdomAttr;
    virtual;
  function GetElementsByTagNameNS(const namespaceURI, localName:
    WideString): TdomNodeList; virtual;
  function hasAttribute(const name: WideString): boolean;
    virtual;
  function hasAttributeNS(const namespaceURI, localName:
    WideString): boolean; virtual;
  procedure normalize; override;
published
  property TagName: WideString read GetTagName;
end;
```

The properties and methods of `TdomElement` are detailed below:

`constructor Create(const AOwner: TdomDocument; const NamespaceURI, TagName: WideString); virtual;`
： As for `TdomNode`, this constructor should not be directly invoked. Ask a `TdomDocument` object for a new element instead with its `CreateElement` or `CreateElementNS` methods. This ensures that the new node is correctly set up.

`property TagName: WideString read GetTagName;`
： Retrieve the name of the element through this property. This is the same value as returned by the `NodeName` property. The name is read-only, having been set during the construction of the element node.

`function GetAttributes: TdomNamedNodeMap; override;`
： This function is overridden here to return a reference to the `TdomNamedNodeMap` object that manages the attributes of this element. Although you could access the attributes in this manner, there are numerous convenience methods defined on the element class to manipulate them. See their definitions below.

`function hasAttribute(const name: WideString): boolean; virtual;`
： Determine whether or not an attribute exists using this function. It returns `True` if the named attribute is present and `False` otherwise. If the attribute list's `namespaceAware` property is set to `True`, this method raises an exception. Use the `hasAttributeNS` method in this case.

`function GetAttribute(const Name: WideString): WideString; virtual;`
： Find the text value of a named attribute with this function. If the attribute does not exist on this element, an empty string is returned. An exception occurs if the `namespaceAware` property of the attributes is set to `True` when this method is invoked. In this case you should use the `GetAttributeNS` method instead.

`function SetAttribute(const Name, Value: WideString): TdomAttr; virtual;`
： Add an attribute with a particular value using this method. The name of the attribute and its value are passed in, and a reference to the newly created `TdomAttr` object is returned. If an attribute by the given name is already present, its value is changed to be the new one. An exception occurs if an invalid character is specified as part of the name, or if the attribute list's `namespaceAware` property is set to `True`. In the latter case you should use the `SetAttributeNS` method instead.

： This method only allows you to set a straight textual value for an attribute. If you need one that contains entity references you must build it up yourself before attaching it to the element with the `SetAttributeNode` method.

`function RemoveAttribute(const Name: WideString): TdomAttr; virtual;`
： Deletes an attribute with a given name. The function returns a reference to the deleted node. Not finding the attribute or having the `namespaceAware` property of the attributes set to `True` raises an exception. For namespace-defined attributes you should use the `RemoveAttributeNS` method.

NOTE If the attribute is deleted but has a default value specified in the DTD, it should immediately reappear on the element with that default value. However, this behavior is not yet implemented in the XDOM package.

`function GetAttributeNode(const Name: WideString): TdomAttr; virtual;`
> Instead of retrieving the text value of an attribute given its name, you can obtain a reference to the entire node with this method. This allows you to examine other properties of the attribute node, and to manipulate any child nodes it has. A `nil` is returned if the attribute cannot be found. Using this method when the `namespaceAware` property of the attribute list is `True` raises an exception. In this case you should use the `GetAttributeNodeNS` method instead.

`function SetAttributeNode(const NewAttr: TdomAttr): TdomAttr; virtual;`
> Use this function to add a new attribute to the element, having previously constructed it yourself. If an attribute with that name already exists, the new one replaces it. When this happens, a reference to the replaced attribute is returned by the function. Otherwise it returns `nil`. An exception occurs if the attribute was created by another document, if the attribute already belongs to another element, or if the attribute list is namespace aware. In the latter case you can use the `SetAttributeNodeNS` method.

`function RemoveAttributeNode(const OldAttr: TdomAttr): TdomAttr; virtual;`
> Deletes an attribute when given a reference to it. A reference to the removed node is returned. An exception is raised if the attribute is not found within this element.

 NOTE As for `RemoveAttribute`, the attribute should immediately reappear on the element with a default value if one is specified. However, this behavior is not yet implemented in the XDOM package.

`function GetAttributeNS(const namespaceURI, localName: WideString): WideString; virtual;`
`function SetAttributeNS(const namespaceURI, qualifiedName, value: WideString): TdomAttr; virtual;`
`function RemoveAttributeNS(const namespaceURI, localName: WideString): TdomAttr; virtual;`
`function GetAttributeNodeNS(const namespaceURI, localName: WideString): TdomAttr; virtual;`
`function SetAttributeNodeNS(const NewAttr: TdomAttr): TdomAttr; virtual;`
`function hasAttributeNS(const namespaceURI, localName: WideString): boolean; virtual;`
> All of these methods function the same as their counterparts without the NS suffix. However, they only work with namespace-defined attributes. The `namespaceAware` property of the attribute list needs to be set to `True` for them to function. If set to `False`, calling any of these methods generates an exception.

function GetElementsByTagName(const Name: WideString): TdomNodeList; virtual;
: Given the name of an element, this method retrieves a list (TdomNodeList) of such elements from within the subtree beneath this node. The nodes appear in the list in the order that they are encountered during a pre-order traversal of the tree (the same order as you would read them within the XML document). Nodes within the list are "live"—any changes to them also affect the original nodes within the subtree. You can access all the elements in the current element's subtree by passing the name *.

TIP The TdomNodeList created by the GetElementsByTagName method is only freed when the element itself is released. Calling the function many times for different tag names results in increasing memory usage. A better strategy is to use a node iterator or a tree walker instead (see the corresponding sections below).

Furthermore, the requirement for "live" nodes means that the list must be traversed from the beginning each time an item is referenced. This imposes a performance hit on the application. Again, using a node iterator or a tree walker should be faster.

The same considerations apply to the namespace-aware version, GetElementsByTagNameNS.

function GetElementsByTagNameNS(const namespaceURI, localName: WideString): TdomNodeList; virtual;
: This method works like the GetElementsByTagName function but searches for namespace defined elements. Pass in the full namespace URI and the local name to find the required elements. As before, use * to match with all possible values.

procedure normalize; override;
: As for the TdomNode class, this method combines adjacent text nodes within the element's subtree. This produces a standard tree for saving or other processing.

TdomAttr Class

Attributes are a special type of node. They do not sit within the normal DOM hierarchy, but are instead managed by a named node map belonging to an element. Due to this, their ParentNode, PreviousSibling, and NextSibling properties all return nil. Attribute nodes are accessible via the Attributes property of an element, which returns the node map itself, or through one of the numerous convenience methods in the element class that deal with attributes.

Attributes do derive from the standard TdomNode class, and thus possess the same basic properties and abilities as other nodes. The definition of XDOM's attribute class is shown in Listing 11-6.

Listing 11-6: The TdomAttr declaration

```
TdomAttr = class (TdomNode)
public
  constructor Create(const AOwner: TdomDocument;
    const NamespaceURI, Name: WideString; const Spcfd: boolean);
    virtual;
  procedure normalize; override;
```

```
published
  property Name: WideString read GetName;
  property Specified: boolean read GetSpecified default false;
  property Value: WideString read GetValue write SetValue;
  property OwnerElement: TdomElement read GetOwnerElement;
end;
```

Most attributes have a simple text string as their value. For these, a single text node is sufficient to hold that value. However, for attributes that contain entity references, their content must be specified through a combination of text nodes and entity reference nodes that make up the attribute's value as children.

TdomAttr's properties and methods are detailed below:

constructor Create(const AOwner: TdomDocument; const NamespaceURI, Name: WideString; const Spcfd: boolean); virtual;

Use the CreateAttribute or CreateAttributeNS methods of the TdomDocument class to construct a new attribute node, rather than calling this constructor directly. The parameters set the document that created the node, the namespace URI for the attribute along with its local name, and a flag indicating where the attribute's value came from. Alternately, have an element create one automatically by calling the SetAttribute or SetAttributeNS methods and supplying the attribute's name and value.

property Name: WideString read GetName;

A renaming of the inherited NodeName property, this read-only property returns the attribute's qualified name.

property Value: WideString read GetValue write SetValue;

This property retrieves the text equivalent of the attribute's value. Any character and entity references are replaced with their values and are combined with any text before being returned. Setting this property removes all child nodes from the attribute and replaces them with a single child text node containing the supplied value. Attempting to modify a read-only attribute raises an exception, as does reading one that contains an unknown entity reference.

property Specified: boolean read GetSpecified default false;

This read-only flag indicates the source of the attribute's value. When True, the value comes directly from the XML document as a listed attribute on that element. When False, the value derives from a default or fixed value specified in the DTD for the document. If the attribute is not listed in the document and does not have a default value specified, then no attribute node for it appears within the DOM. This value is set when processing the document and cannot be changed directly. However, setting the Value property of the attribute does change this flag to True.

property OwnerElement: TdomElement read GetOwnerElement;

This property returns a reference to the element node that owns the attribute. It is set when the attribute is added to an element and cannot be altered directly.

procedure normalize; override;
> As before, this method combines adjacent text nodes within the element's subtree, creating a standardized hierarchy.

TdomCharacterData Class

All textual data within the DOM have certain common abilities. These are encapsulated in the `TdomCharacterData` class, which is then subclassed for the actual node types in the document. Instances of this class itself do not appear in the DOM. The declaration for the class is shown in Listing 11-7.

Listing 11-7: The `TdomCharacterData` *declaration*

```
TdomCharacterData = class (TdomNode)
public
  constructor Create(const AOwner: TdomDocument); virtual;
  function SubstringData(const offset, count: integer):
    WideString; virtual;
  procedure AppendData(const arg: WideString); virtual;
  procedure InsertData(const offset: integer;
    const arg: WideString); virtual;
  procedure DeleteData(const offset, count: integer); virtual;
  procedure ReplaceData(const offset, count: integer;
    const arg: WideString); virtual;
published
  property Data: WideString read GetData write SetData;
  property length: integer read GetLength;
end;
```

The properties and methods of the `TdomCharacterData` object are detailed below. Remember that all offset values start from zero at the beginning of the text.

constructor Create(const AOwner: TdomDocument); virtual;
> As this class is a base class for all text type nodes, it should never be instantiated on its own. Subclasses call this constructor as necessary as part of their own initialization.

property Data: WideString read GetData write SetData;
> This property returns the actual textual content of the node. It is a read-only property since the initial value is set on creation, and other methods provide for manipulating the text. The inherited `NodeValue` property holds the same value.

property length: integer read GetLength;
> Find the length of the contained text (in characters) with this read-only property. The returned value may be zero, indicating an empty node.

function SubstringData(const offset, count: integer): WideString; virtual;
> Extract a portion of the text using this function, specifying the starting offset and the number of characters desired. If the total of the offset and count are greater than the length of the text, then all the text up to the end is returned. If the offset is negative or greater than the length of the string, or if the count is negative, an exception occurs.

`procedure AppendData(const arg: WideString); virtual;`
> Add the specified text to the end of the current data value. Retrieve the concatenated value with the `Data` property.

`procedure InsertData(const offset: integer; const arg: WideString); virtual;`
> Add new text within the body of the current data value. The offset parameter indicates the starting point, and text beyond that is shifted along to make room. An offset that is negative or greater than the length of the current text produces an exception.

`procedure DeleteData(const offset, count: integer); virtual;`
> Remove a portion of the current text using this method. Specify the characters to delete with the offset and count parameters. A count extending past the end of the current text removes all text up to the end. As before, invalid offset or count values raise an exception.

`procedure ReplaceData(const offset, count: integer; const arg: WideString); virtual;`
> Combine the functionality of the previous two methods to remove text and then insert new data in its place. As before, an exception occurs for invalid offset or count values.

TdomText Class

Text nodes contain the actual content of the document. When initially loaded, a single text node encapsulates each contiguous section of text. You may then add other text nodes, or split the existing ones. Adjacent text nodes do not persist between instances of the DOM and may be automatically combined through the `normalize` method of the `TdomNode` class.

Text nodes inherit all the abilities of the `TdomCharacterData` class, adding only one new method. The declaration for a text node is shown in Listing 11-8.

Listing 11-8: The TdomText declaration

```
TdomText = class (TdomCharacterData)
  public
    constructor Create(const AOwner: TdomDocument); override;
    function SplitText(const offset: integer): TdomText; virtual;
  end;
```

The `TdomText` object's methods are detailed below:

`constructor Create(const AOwner: TdomDocument); override;`
> As before, you should not instantiate a text node directly. Instead, use the `CreateTextNode` method on the `TdomDocument` class.

`function SplitText(const offset: integer): TdomText; virtual;`
> This method breaks a text node into two parts at the specified offset (starting from zero). The two nodes then exist as siblings beneath the parent of the original text node. Characters up to the offset remain in the original node, while those after the offset are transferred to the new node. The method returns a reference to the newly created node. If the offset is out of range, an exception occurs.

TdomCDATASection Class

CDATA sections are just like text nodes except that any metacharacters are ignored. This means that what would normally be regarded as markup (tags and entity references) is left as normal text. A `TdomCDATASection` node inherits all of its functionality from the normal text node and adds nothing. Thus, it simply serves as a marker to indicate the different treatment of the contained characters.

The declaration for a CDATA section node is shown in Listing 11-9.

Listing 11-9: The `TdomCDATASection` *declaration*

```
TdomCDATASection = class (TdomText)
public
  constructor Create(const AOwner: TdomDocument); override;
end;
```

The methods of a `TdomCDATASection` object are shown below:

constructor Create(const AOwner: TdomDocument); override;
> Do not instantiate these nodes directly. Instead use the `TdomDocument` class's `CreateCDATASection` method.

TdomComment Class

The `TdomComment` class (shown in Listing 11-10) represents comments within the DOM. Similar to the CDATA section nodes, this class simply flags that the encapsulated text is treated differently while inheriting all its abilities from the base character data class.

Listing 11-10: The `TdomComment` *declaration*

```
TdomComment = class (TdomCharacterData)
public
  constructor Create(const AOwner: TdomDocument); override;
end;
```

The methods of a `TdomComment` object are detailed below:

constructor Create(const AOwner: TdomDocument); override;
> Generate comment nodes with the `TdomDocument` class's `CreateComment` method rather than using this constructor directly.

TdomProcessingInstruction Class

Instructions for applications handling the document can be passed through processing instruction nodes. Recall that XML imposes no structure on the data part of the instruction, assuming that the target program understands it all. See Listing 11-11 for the declaration of the processing instruction node.

Listing 11-11: The `TdomProcessingInstruction` *declaration*

```
TdomProcessingInstruction = class (TdomNode)
public
  constructor Create(const AOwner: TdomDocument;
    const Targ: WideString); virtual;
published
  property Target: WideString read GetTarget;
  property Data: WideString read GetData write SetData;
end;
```

The `TdomProcessingInstruction` object's properties and methods are described below:

`constructor Create(const AOwner: TdomDocument; const Targ: WideString); virtual;`
Use the `CreateProcessingInstruction` method of the `TdomDocument` class to generate these nodes, rather than calling this constructor directly.

`property Target: WideString read GetTarget;`
Retrieve the identifier for the application that knows how to use the following instruction. This value cannot be altered once set during creation. The returned value corresponds to the inherited `NodeName` property.

`property Data: WideString read GetData write SetData;`
Read or update the actual command for the target application through this property. When an instruction is parsed out of a document, this property contains all the text from the first non-white space character following the target, up to the character immediately before the closing ?>. Validating any syntax requirements for the data when setting its value is the responsibility of the calling program. The inherited `NodeValue` property contains the same value as this property.

TdomDocumentType Class

This node type represents the document type declaration within an XML document (the one that starts with <!DOCTYPE). Such nodes are read-only, having their main properties set at the time of creation. They have only two child nodes: one each of an internal (`TdomInternalSubset`) and an external subset (`TdomExternalSubset`). These children are not read-only and contain the declarations for the owning document.

NOTE XDOM's document type node differs quite a bit from the DOM specification. This is due to the former's extensive support for DTDs within the DOM. According to the spec, document type nodes may be created during parsing of a document, but cannot be altered during normal processing of the hierarchy.

Document type nodes are created through the `TdomImplementation` or `TdomDocument` classes and their `CreateDocumentType` or `CreateDocumentTypeNS` methods. They derive from the `TdomCustomDocumentType` class (see Listing 11-12), which provides some common functionality among different document types. The declaration for the `TdomDocumentType` class itself is shown in Listing 11-13.

NOTE The DOM specification only provides for the creation of document type nodes through the `Implementation` class.

Listing 11-12: The `TdomCustomDocumentType` declaration

```
TdomCustomDocumentType = class (TdomNode)
public
  constructor Create(const AOwner: TdomDocument);
  destructor Destroy; override;
published
  property AttributeLists: TdomNamedNodeMap read GetAttributeLists;
  property ParameterEntities: TdomNamedNodeMap
    read GetParameterEntities;
end;
```

Listing 11-13: The `TdomDocumentType` declaration

```
TdomDocumentType = class (TdomCustomDocumentType)
protected
  procedure detectUnusableEntities; virtual;
public
  constructor Create(const AOwner: TdomDocument; const Name,
    PubId, SysId: WideString); virtual;
  destructor destroy; override;
published
  property Entities: TdomEntitiesNamedNodeMap read GetEntities;
  property ExternalSubsetNode: TdomExternalSubset
    read GetExternalSubsetNode;
  property InternalSubset: WideString read GetInternalSubset;
  property InternalSubsetNode: TdomInternalSubset
    read GetInternalSubsetNode;
  property Name: WideString read GetName;
  property Notations: TdomNamedNodeMap read GetNotations;
  property PublicId: WideString read GetPublicId;
  property SystemId: WideString read GetSystemId;
end;
```

The TdomDocumentType object's properties and methods (including those of `TdomCustomDocumentType`) are described below:

`constructor Create(const AOwner: TdomDocument; const Name, PubId, SysId: WideString); virtual;`

Specify the top-level element name and optional references to an external DTD when constructing a document type node. These values cannot be altered later. As with other nodes, you should use the factory methods of the `TdomImplementation` or `TdomDocument` classes instead of creating these directly.

property Name: WideString read GetName;
Retrieve the name of the top-level element for this DTD through this read-only property. It cannot be changed after creation.

property PublicId: WideString read GetPublicId;
This property returns the public identifier for an external DTD. A public identifier is a well-known name for a resource, which can then be mapped to an actual instance of the document. Once set during instantiation, this value cannot be altered. It returns an empty string if no public identifier is specified.

property SystemId: WideString read GetSystemId;
Retrieve the system identifier for an external DTD with this property. A system identifier is the actual URI that locates the resource to be used. The value cannot be changed after creation of the node. Again, an empty string results if no system identifier is supplied.

property Entities: TdomEntitiesNamedNodeMap read GetEntities;
This read-only node list property (TdomNamedNodeMap) provides access to the general entities (not parameter entities) declared within the DTD, returning each as a `TdomEntity`. Each new document type object automatically has five nodes in this list. These correspond to the five default XML entities: lt, gt, amp, quot, and apos.

property Notations: TdomNamedNodeMap read GetNotations;
Another node list (TdomNamedNodeMap), this read-only property returns the notations declared in the DTD as `TdomNotation` objects.

property InternalSubset: WideString read GetInternalSubset;
Obtain the entire subset of the DTD specified within the XML document as a wide string value using this read-only property. The internal subset cannot be updated via this property.

NOTE The remaining properties are extensions within XDOM and are not part of the DOM specification.

property ExternalSubsetNode: TdomExternalSubset read GetExternalSubsetNode;
Get a reference to the child node that contains the external declarations from this read-only property. This is a convenience property since you could find the node among the children of the document type node.

property InternalSubsetNode: TdomInternalSubset read GetInternalSubsetNode;
Another convenience property, this read-only property returns a reference to the child node that holds the internal declarations.

property ParameterEntities: TdomNamedNodeMap read GetParameterEntities;
All the parameter entities from the document reside in this read-only node list. They are returned as `TdomParameterEntity` objects.

property AttributeLists: TdomNamedNodeMap read GetAttributeLists;
: Lists of attributes declared in the DTD are found in this read-only node list property. It is indexed by the element name, and each entry is a TdomAttrList object.

TdomInternalSubset Class

The part of the document type declaration within the XML document itself is called the internal subset. Modeling this in the XDOM package is the TdomInternalSubset class (see Listing 11-14). It is a child of the document type node and cannot be removed. All the type declarations within the document appear as children of this node.

Listing 11-14: The TdomInternalSubset declaration

```
TdomInternalSubset = class (TdomCustomDocumentType)
public
  constructor Create(const AOwner: TdomDocument); virtual;
end;
```

NOTE This class has no equivalent within the DOM specification.

This class derives from the TdomCustomDocumentType class (see Listing 11-12) which also forms the basis for the normal document type node. No new functionality is added in this class, although it does make use of some inherited abilities. It mainly serves to delineate the origin of the declarations that it contains.

The properties and methods of the TdomInternalSubset object are detailed below:

constructor Create(const AOwner: TdomDocument); virtual;
: A node of this type is created automatically when the document type node is constructed. You should never create one yourself.

property AttributeLists: TdomNamedNodeMap read GetAttributeLists;
: Lists of attributes declared in the internal subset are found in this read-only node list property. It is indexed by the element name, and each entry is a TdomAttrList object.

property ParameterEntities: TdomNamedNodeMap read GetParameterEntities;
: All the parameter entities from the internal subset reside in this read-only node list. They are returned as TdomParameterEntity objects.

TdomExternalSubset Class

Complementing the internal subset above, any type declarations loaded from an external DTD appear beneath a TdomExternalSubset node (see Listing 11-15), which is the other child of the document type node.

Listing 11-15: The TdomExternalSubset declaration

```
TdomExternalSubset = class (TdomCustomDocumentType)
public
  constructor Create(const AOwner: TdomDocument); virtual;
```

```
    function CloneNode(const deep: boolean): TdomNode; override;
end;
```

NOTE This class has no equivalent within the DOM specification.

This class derives from the `TdomCustomDocumentType` class (see Listing 11-12), inheriting most abilities and overriding one. Its main purpose, though, is to manage the nodes resulting from the type declarations in the external DTD.

The `TdomExternalSubset` object's properties and methods are described below:

constructor Create(const AOwner: TdomDocument); virtual;
> When the document type node is created, a node of this type is automatically constructed as one of its children. You should never create these nodes directly.

property AttributeLists: TdomNamedNodeMap read GetAttributeLists;
> This read-only node list property holds the lists of attributes declared in the external subset. They are indexed by the element name, and each entry is a `TdomAttrList` object.

property ParameterEntities: TdomNamedNodeMap read GetParameterEntities;
> This read-only node list contains all the parameter entities from the external subset. They are returned as `TdomParameterEntity` objects.

function CloneNode(const deep: boolean): TdomNode; override;
> The external subset node overrides this method to ensure that all its children are set to be read-only.

TdomConditionalSection Class

The `TdomConditionalSection` class (shown in Listing 11-16) represents a conditional section in an external subset. It also derives from `TdomCustomDocumentType`, which can be found in Listing 11-12. Its children are only used if the value of its `Included` property is equal to INCLUDE.

Listing 11-16: The `TdomConditionalSection` declaration

```
TdomConditionalSection = class(TdomCustomDocumentType)
protected
  function SetIncluded(const node: TdomNode): TdomNode; virtual;
public
  constructor Create(const AOwner: TdomDocument;
    const IncludeStmt: WideString); virtual;
published
  property Included: TdomNode read GetIncluded;
end;
```

NOTE This class has no equivalent within the DOM specification.

The properties and methods of the `TdomConditionalSection` object are listed below:

`constructor Create(const AOwner: TdomDocument; const IncludeStmt: WideString); virtual;`

Build a conditional section in a DTD subset with this constructor. The second parameter must be either the text `INCLUDE` or `IGNORE`, or the name of a parameter entity that evaluates to one of these. An exception occurs if the `IncludeStmt` value does not match the expected text. As usual, these nodes should not be created directly. Use the `CreateConditionalSection` method on the `TdomDocument` class instead.

`property Included: TdomNode read GetIncluded;`

Having been set during construction of this node, this read-only property refers to either a text node with the value `INCLUDE` or `IGNORE`, or a parameter entity node containing such a text node.

`function SetIncluded(const node: TdomNode): TdomNode; virtual;`

You can set the value of the `Included` property through this protected method, but only within a subclass.

`property AttributeLists: TdomNamedNodeMap read GetAttributeLists;`

Lists of attributes declared in the conditional section are found in this read-only node list property. It is indexed by the element name, and each entry is a `TdomAttrList` object.

`property ParameterEntities: TdomNamedNodeMap read GetParameterEntities;`

All the parameter entities from the conditional section reside in this read-only node list. They are returned as `TdomParameterEntity` objects.

TdomEntity Class

Entities refer to sections of the document that may appear in several places or that are held externally. `TdomEntity` nodes represent these entities within the document type node, and are retrieved through the `Entities` property of the document type node. The `TdomEntityDeclaration` class maintains the declaration of the entity separately.

`TdomEntity` derives from the `TdomCustomDeclaration` (see Listing 11-17) and `TdomCustomEntity` (see Listing 11-18) classes, gaining functionality as it goes. Its own declaration is shown in Listing 11-19.

Listing 11-17: The `TdomCustomDeclaration` declaration

```
TdomCustomDeclaration = class (TdomNode)
public
  constructor Create(const AOwner: TdomDocument;
    const Name: WideString);
published
  property Value: WideString read GetValue write SetValue;
end;
```

Listing 11-18: The `TdomCustomEntity` *declaration*

```
TdomCustomEntity = class (TdomCustomDeclaration)
public
  constructor Create(const AOwner: TdomDocument;
    const Name, PubId, SysId: WideString);
  function InsertBefore(const newChild, refChild: TdomNode): TdomNode;
    override;
  function ReplaceChild(const newChild, oldChild: TdomNode): TdomNode;
    override;
  function AppendChild(const newChild: TdomNode): TdomNode; override;
published
  property PublicId: WideString read GetPublicId;
  property SystemId: WideString read GetSystemId;
  property IsInternalEntity: boolean read GetIsInternalEntity;
end;
```

Listing 11-19: The `TdomEntity` *declaration*

```
TdomEntity = class (TdomCustomEntity)
public
  constructor create(const AOwner: TdomDocument;
    const Name, PubId, SysId, NotaName: WideString); virtual;
  function cloneNode(const deep: boolean): TdomNode; override;
  property isUnusable: boolean read getIsUnusable write SetIsUnusable
    default false;
  property NotationName: WideString read GetNotationName;
end;
```

The `TdomEntity` object's properties and methods (including those of its custom ancestors) are detailed below:

constructor create(const AOwner: TcomDocument; const Name, PubId, SysId, NotaName: WideString); virtual;
    Construct a new entity node with this method. You should use the `CreateEntity` method of the `TdomDocument` class instead to ensure the nodes are initialized properly.

property NodeName: WideString read GetNodeName;
    This inherited read-only property contains the name of the entity.

property PublicId: WideString read GetPublicId;
    External entities return their public identifier through this read-only property. It may be an empty string if no public identifier is defined, or if the entity is internal.

property SystemId: WideString read GetSystemId;
    Retrieve the system identifier for the entity via this read-only property. For internal entities it returns an empty string, as do entities without a system identifier specified.

property NotationName: WideString read GetNotationName;
    For unparsed entities (non-XML external resources), this read-only property holds the name of the format for that data. It is an empty string for all parsed entities.

NOTE The remaining properties are not part of the DOM specification.

property Value: WideString read GetValue write SetValue;
: For an internal entity, this property contains the actual text value of the entity. It is an empty string for external entities.

property IsInternalEntity: boolean read GetIsInternalEntity;
: This read-only property returns True if the entity is declared internally, and False otherwise. An internal entity has no public or system identifier, but does have a value.

property isUnusable: boolean read getIsUnusable write SetIsUnusable default false;
: Monitor this property to determine whether or not the entity has been fully loaded and can be used. It returns True if the other properties are valid, and False if they are not. An entity may not be usable if it is declared externally but the document is not validated, in which case external references are not followed.

function cloneNode(const deep: boolean): TdomNode; override;
: Entities override this method to make sure that all their children are set to be read-only.

TdomEntityDeclaration Class

Whereas the previous class modeled the value of an entity, this one models the type declaration for that entity. Objects of the TdomEntityDeclaration class (see Listing 11-20) appear within an internal or external subset. They are derived from the TdomCustomEntity class (shown in Listing 11-18).

Listing 11-20: The TdomEntityDeclaration declaration

```
TdomEntityDeclaration = class (TdomCustomEntity)
public
  constructor Create(const AOwner: TdomDocument;
    const Name, EntityValue, PubId, SysId, NotaName: WideString);
    virtual;
  property ExtParsedEnt: TdomExternalParsedEntity read GetExtParsedEnt
    write SetExtParsedEnt;
  property NotationName: WideString read GetNotationName;
end;
```

NOTE This class has no equivalent within the DOM specification.

The properties and methods of the TdomEntityDeclaration object are shown below:

constructor Create(const AOwner: TdomDocument; const Name, EntityValue, PubId, SysId, NotaName: WideString); virtual;
: Entity declaration nodes should be created through the CreateEntityDeclaration method of the document object, rather than with this constructor.

property NodeName: WideString read GetNodeName;
: This inherited read-only property returns the name of the entity.

property Value: WideString read GetValue write SetValue;
: For an internal entity, this property contains the actual text value of the entity. It is an empty string for external entities. Setting this property discards any existing children and replaces them with a single text node that has the value given. The contents of this value are not parsed.

property PublicId: WideString read GetPublicId;
: This read-only property returns the public identifier for external entities. An empty string results if no public identifier is defined, or if the entity is internal.

property SystemId: WideString read GetSystemId;
: For external entities this read-only property retrieves the system identifier for the entity. For internal entities it returns an empty string, as do entities without a system identifier specified.

property NotationName: WideString read GetNotationName;
: This read-only property holds the name of the format for the data for unparsed entities (non-XML external resources). It is an empty string for all parsed entities.

property IsInternalEntity: boolean read GetIsInternalEntity;
: This read-only property returns True if the entity is declared internally, and False otherwise. An internal entity has no public or system identifier, but does have a value.

property ExtParsedEnt: TdomExternalParsedEntity read GetExtParsedEnt write SetExtParsedEnt;
: Access the external parsed entity node corresponding to this declaration through this property. For internal entities it is nil. Attempting to set this property for an internal entity generates an error.

TdomEntityReference Class

Placing entities within the body of the document uses the `TdomEntityReference` class. A node of this type is positioned where the replacement text should appear. The class itself derives from `TdomReference` (see Listing 11-21), which provides common base functionality for references. Its declarations are shown in Listing 11-22.

Listing 11-21: The TdomReference declaration

```
TdomReference = class (TdomNode)
public
  constructor Create(const AOwner: TdomDocument; const Name:
    WideString); virtual;
published
  property Declaration: TdomCustomEntity read GetDeclaration;
end;
```

Listing 11-22: The `TdomEntityReference` *declaration*

```
TdomEntityReference = class (TdomReference)
public
  constructor Create(const AOwner: TdomDocument;
    const Name: WideString); override;
  function CloneNode(const deep: boolean): TdomNode; override;
end;
```

The properties and methods of a `TdomEntityReference` object (including those of its ancestors) are described below:

`constructor Create(const AOwner: TdomDocument; const Name: WideString); virtual;`
Use the `CreateEntityReference` method of the `TdomDocument` class rather than this constructor to generate a new entity reference node.

NOTE The remaining properties and methods are not part of the DOM specification.

`property Declaration: TdomCustomEntity read GetDeclaration;`
This read-only property contains a reference to the `TdomEntity` node that defines the entity and its contents.

`function CloneNode(const deep: boolean): TdomNode; override;`
Entity reference nodes override this method to ensure that all its children are made read-only.

TdomNotation Class

The formats for external resources must be declared through notation entries in the DTD. See Listing 11-23 for the definition of the `TdomNotation` class. This class only represents the content of the notation node. Notation declarations are modeled separately through the `TdomNotationDeclaration` class.

Listing 11-23: The `TdomNotation` *declaration*

```
TdomNotation = class (TdomNode)
public
  constructor Create(const AOwner: TdomDocument; const Name,
    PubId, SysId: WideString); virtual;
published
  property PublicId: WideString read GetPublicId;
  property SystemId: WideString read GetSystemId;
end;
```

The `TdomNotation` object's properties and methods are shown below:

`constructor Create(const AOwner: TdomDocument; const Name, PubId, SysId: WideString); virtual;`
Build new notations with the `CreateNotation` method of the `TdomDocument` class rather than this constructor.

`property NodeName: WideString read GetNodeName;`
Retrieve the name of the notation through this inherited read-only property.

property PublicId: WideString read GetPublicId;
: Retrieve the public identifier for this notation through this property. Once the identifier is set during construction of the notation, it cannot be altered. The public identifier is a well-known name for the resource. If no public identifier is specified, an empty string is returned.

property SystemId: WideString read GetSystemId;
: This property provides the system identifier for the notation. Again, it is read-only after being set during construction. The system identifier is an actual location (URI) for the notation, although the resource at that location may be anything (or may not exist at all). An empty string results if the system identifier is not supplied.

TdomNotationDeclaration Class

Modeling the declaration of a notation within the internal or external subset is the purpose of the TdomNotationDeclaration class (see Listing 11-24).

Listing 11-24: The TdomNotationDeclaration *declaration*

```
TdomNotationDeclaration = class (TdomNode)
public
  constructor Create(const AOwner: TdomDocument;
    const Name, PubId, SysId: WideString); virtual;
published
  property PublicId: WideString read GetPublicId;
  property SystemId: WideString read GetSystemId;
end;
```

NOTE This class has no equivalent within the DOM specification.

The properties and methods of a TdomNotationDeclaration object are described below:

constructor Create(const AOwner: TdomDocument; const Name, PubId, SysId: WideString); virtual;
: Use the CreateNotationDeclaration method of the document object to build these objects. Do not instantiate them directly.

property NodeName: WideString read GetNodeName;
: This inherited read-only property returns the name of the notation.

property PublicId: WideString read GetPublicId;
: Retrieve the public identifier for this notation through this read-only property. Its value is established at the time of creation and cannot be changed thereafter. An empty string returns if the value is not set.

property SystemId: WideString read GetSystemId;
: Similarly, the system identifier for the notation is set during construction and is unalterable later. Obtain its value from this read-only property. An empty string returns if it is not set.

TdomElementTypeDeclaration Class

The main part of the DTD is the definition of the elements that make up a valid document. The TdomElementTypeDeclaration class in the XDOM package (shown in Listing 11-25) models these.

Listing 11-25: The TdomElementTypeDeclaration *declaration*

```
TdomElementTypeDeclaration = class (TdomCustomDeclaration)
public
  constructor Create(const AOwner: TdomDocument;
    const Name: WideString; const Contspec: TdomContentspecType);
    virtual;
  function AppendChild(const newChild: TdomNode): TdomNode; override;
  function InsertBefore(const newChild, refChild: TdomNode): TdomNode;
    override;
published
  property Contentspec: TdomContentspecType read GetContentspec;
end;
```

NOTE This class has no equivalent within the DOM specification.

A TdomElementTypeDeclaration object's properties and methods are detailed below:

constructor Create(const AOwner: TdomDocument; const Name: WideString; const Contspec: TdomContentspecType); virtual

As usual, you should not call this constructor directly, but should use the CreateElement-TypeDeclaration method of the document object.

property NodeName: WideString read GetNodeName;

This inherited read-only property returns the name of the element.

property Contentspec: TdomContentspecType read GetContentspec;

This read-only property returns the type of content allowed in this element. Once set during construction it cannot be altered. Its value is one of those shown in Table 11-3. The child of this node (and there can be only one) defines the actual content model, if applicable.

Table 11-3: Element content types

Content Specification	Meaning
ctEmpty	The element cannot have any content. In the DTD the EMPTY keyword denotes this model.
ctAny	Any element may be a child of this one. In the DTD the ANY keyword indicates this model.
ctMixed	The content of the element consists of free text, optionally mixed with other elements. In the DTD this model starts with #PCDATA.
ctChildren	Only the nominated elements may appear within this element, and only in the order and number defined. In the DTD this appears as a list of the specified sub-elements.

```
function AppendChild(const newChild: TdomNode): TdomNode; override;
```
The class overrides this method to add a check regarding the content specification. If you attempt to add a child to a node marked as empty or accepting any content an error is generated. An error also occurs if you try to add more than one child.

```
function InsertBefore(const newChild, refChild: TdomNode): TdomNode; override;
```
Similarly, this method is overridden to apply the same tests as above.

Content Models

An element uses the classes described in this section, collectively known as *particles*, to define its valid content. One of these nodes becomes the child of the element type declaration (unless its content specification is for an empty node or for any content). All except the element particle can then have further children to build up the model hierarchy.

NOTE None of these classes has an equivalent within the DOM specification.

Basic functionality for a particle comes from the `TdomParticle` class shown in Listing 11-26. Objects of this type are not created directly; one of its subclasses is used instead.

Listing 11-26: The TdomParticle declaration

```
TdomParticle = class (TdomNode)
public
  constructor Create(const AOwner: TdomDocument;
    const Freq: WideString);
published
  property Frequency: WideString read GetFrequency;
end;
```

The properties and methods of the `TdomParticle` object are shown below:

```
constructor Create(const AOwner: TdomDocument; const Freq: WideString);
```
Do not create particle objects themselves. Build one of the subclasses instead.

```
property Frequency: WideString read GetFrequency;
```
Retrieve the occurrences applicable to this particle within the content model through this read-only property. Its value is set at creation time, and must be one of those listed in Table 11-4. An error occurs if it is not one of these values.

Table 11-4: Particle frequencies

Frequency	Meaning
'' (an empty string)	This particle must appear once and once only.
?	This particle may appear once or not at all.
+	This particle must appear at least once, but may appear multiple times.
*	This particle may appear multiple times or not at all.

The `TdomSequenceParticle` class (see Listing 11-27) defines a sequence of items within a content specification. In the DTD these items appear separated by a comma (,). The children of this node, themselves other particles, list the set of nodes that must appear in this order.

Listing 11-27: The `TdomSequenceParticle` declaration

```
TdomSequenceParticle = class (TdomParticle)
public
  constructor Create(const AOwner: TdomDocument;
    const Freq: WideString); virtual;
end;
```

The `TdomSequenceParticle` object's methods are listed below:

constructor Create(const AOwner: TdomDocument; const Freq: WideString); virtual;
    Create sequence particles with the `CreateSequenceParticle` method of the document object, rather than through this constructor.

Alternate items in the content specification use the `TdomChoiceParticle` class (shown in Listing 11-28) to define those options. Vertical bars (|) separate these choices in the DTD. The children of this node (more particles) specify the options.

Listing 11-28: The `TdomChoiceParticle` declaration

```
TdomChoiceParticle = class (TdomParticle)
public
  constructor create(const AOwner: TdomDocument;
    const Freq: WideString); virtual;
end;
```

The methods of a `TdomChoiceParticle` object are detailed below:

constructor create(const AOwner: TdomDocument; const Freq: WideString); virtual;
    Do not use this constructor directly. Instead use the `CreateChoiceParticle` method on the document object.

The `TdomPcdataChoiceParticle` class (see Listing 11-29) represents mixed content in the content specification. Use this when the element type node's content is set to `ctMixed`. The children of this node should all be unique element particles. In the DTD they appear separated by vertical bars (|) following an initial #PCDATA.

Listing 11-29: The `TdomPcdataChoiceParticle` declaration

```
TdomPcdataChoiceParticle = class (TdomParticle)
public
  constructor create(const AOwner: TdomDocument;
    const Freq: WideString); virtual;
end;
```

The `TdomPcdataChoiceParticle` object's methods are described below:

constructor create(const AOwner: TdomDocument; const Freq: WideString); virtual;
    Use the `CreatePcdataChoiceParticle` method of the document object to instantiate these objects, not this constructor. Note that the frequency for these nodes must be set to *, with an error occurring if any other value is used.

Finally, individual elements within the content specification appear as `TdomElementParticle` objects (see Listing 11-30). In the DTD they appear as the element name.

Listing 11-30: The *TdomElementParticle* declaration

```
TdomElementParticle = class (TdomParticle)
public
  constructor Create(const AOwner: TdomDocument;
    const Name, Freq: WideString); virtual;
end;
```

The methods of the `TdomElementParticle` object are listed below:

constructor Create(const AOwner: TdomDocument; const Name, Freq: WideString);
    virtual;
    Instead of using this constructor, use the `CreateElementParticle` method on the document object. Specify the name of the element appearing at this location.

property NodeName: WideString read GetNodeName;
    Retrieve the name of the element with this inherited read-only property.

TdomAttrList Class

Definitions for valid attributes also appear in the DTD. In the XDOM package the `TdomAttrList` class (shown in Listing 11-31) represents these, managing the set of attributes for a single element.

Listing 11-31: The *TdomAttrList* declaration

```
TdomAttrList = class(TdomCustomDeclaration)
public
  constructor Create(const AOwner: TdomDocument;
    const Name: WideString); virtual;
  destructor Destroy; override;
  function RemoveAttributeDefinition(const Name: WideString):
    TdomAttrDefinition; virtual;
  function GetAttributeDefinitionNode(const Name: WideString):
    TdomAttrDefinition; virtual;
  function SetAttributeDefinitionNode(
    const NewAttDef: TdomAttrDefinition): boolean; virtual;
  function RemoveAttributeDefinitionNode(
    const OldAttDef: TdomAttrDefinition): TdomAttrDefinition; virtual;
published
  property AttributeDefinitions: TdomNamedNodeMap
    read GetAttributeDefinitions;
end;
```

NOTE This class has no equivalent within the DOM specification.

The `TdomAttrList` object's properties and methods are shown below:

constructor Create(const AOwner: TdomDocument; const Name: WideString); virtual;
    Again, use the `CreateAttributeList` method on the document object instead of this constructor. The name supplied is that of the element to which the contained attributes belong.

property NodeName: WideString read GetNodeName;
: This inherited read-only property returns the name of the element.

property AttributeDefinitions: TdomNamedNodeMap read GetAttributeDefinitions;
: Access the list of attribute definitions for this element through this read-only property. Each item in the list is a TdomAttrDefinition object.

function GetAttributeDefinitionNode(const Name: WideString): TdomAttrDefinition; virtual;
: Retrieve a single attribute definition, given its name, with this method. If a matching attribute cannot be found, nil is returned.

function SetAttributeDefinitionNode(const NewAttDef: TdomAttrDefinition): boolean; virtual;
: Add a new attribute definition with this method. It returns True if the definition is added, and False if an existing attribute already exists under the same name. In the latter case, the new definition is ignored. Attribute definitions cannot be shared between elements.

function RemoveAttributeDefinition(const Name: WideString): TdomAttrDefinition; virtual;
: Delete the named attribute definition from the list through this method. An error occurs if the definition cannot be found.

function RemoveAttributeDefinitionNode(const OldAttDef: TdomAttrDefinition): TdomAttrDefinition; virtual;
: This method duplicates the previous one, but takes a reference to the entire node as its parameter rather than just the attribute's name. Again, an error occurs if the attribute is not found.

TdomAttrDefinition Class

Individual attributes for an element appear as TdomAttrDefinition objects (see Listing 11-32) within the AttributeDefinitions property of the element's attribute list.

Listing 11-32: The TdomAttrDefinition declaration

```
TdomAttrDefinition = class(TdomNode)
public
  constructor Create(const AOwner: TdomDocument;
    const Name, AttType, DefaultDecl, AttValue: WideString); virtual;
published
  property AttributeType: WideString read GetAttributeType;
  property DefaultDeclaration: WideString read GetDefaultDeclaration;
  property Name: WideString read GetName;
  property ParentAttributeList: TdomAttrList
    read GetParentAttributeList;
end;
```

NOTE This class has no equivalent within the DOM specification.

The properties and methods of the `TdomAttrDefinition` object are detailed below:

constructor Create(const AOwner: TdomDocument; const Name, AttType, DefaultDecl, AttValue: WideString); virtual;
Do not use this constructor. Instead, use the `CreateAttributeDefinition` method of the document object. An error occurs if the attribute type or default declaration is invalid, if a default value is defined when the default declaration is `#REQUIRED` or `#IMPLIED`, or the default is missing when the default declaration is `#FIXED` or blank.

property Name: WideString read GetName;
Retrieve the name of the attribute through this read-only property. Set during construction, it cannot be changed later.

property AttributeType: WideString read GetAttributeType;
This read-only property, set during creation, returns the attribute's type. It should be one of the standard XML types, such as `ID`, `IDREF`, `ENTITY`, etc., or `CDATA` for a list of valid enumerated values. These values then appear as `TdomNametoken` children of the definition node.

property DefaultDeclaration: WideString read GetDefaultDeclaration;
Obtain the attribute's default setting with this read-only property. It may be `#REQUIRED`, `#IMPLIED`, `#FIXED`, or blank.

property NodeValue: WideString read GetNodeValue write SetNodeValue;
This inherited property returns the default value for the attribute, or an empty string if no default is specified.

property ParentAttributeList: TdomAttrList read GetParentAttributeList;
Access the owning attribute list through this read-only property.

TdomNametoken Class

The `TdomNametoken` class (see Listing 11-33) holds individual enumerated values for use in attribute definitions for the DTD. These nodes are set as children of a `TdomAttrDefinition` node that has its `AttributeType` set to `CDATA`.

Listing 11-33: The *TdomNametoken* declaration

```
TdomNametoken = class (TdomNode)
public
  constructor Create(const AOwner: TdomDocument;
    const Name: WideString); virtual;
  procedure SetNodeValue(const Value: WideString); override;
end;
```

NOTE This class has no equivalent within the DOM specification.

The TdomNametoken object's methods are shown below:

constructor Create(const AOwner: TdomDocument; const Name: WideString); virtual;
> Use the CreateNametoken method of the document object instead of this constructor.

property NodeName: WideString read GetNodeName;
> Retrieve the name of the token with this inherited read-only property.

procedure SetNodeValue(const Value: WideString); override;
> This method is overridden to force an error if you try to change the node value.

TdomXmlDeclaration Class

The TdomXmlDeclaration class (see Listing 11-34) represents the XML declaration at the start of a document. It must appear as the first child of the document object.

Listing 11-34: The TdomXmlDeclaration declaration

```
TdomXmlDeclaration = class (TdomNode)
public
  constructor Create(const AOwner: TdomDocument;
    const Version, EncDl, SdDl: WideString); virtual;
published
  property VersionNumber: WideString read GetVersionNumber;
  property EncodingDecl: WideString read GetEncodingDecl
    write SetEncodingDecl;
  property SDDecl: WideString read GetStandalone write SetStandalone;
end;
```

NOTE This class has no equivalent within the DOM specification.

The TdomXmlDeclaration object's properties and methods are described below:

constructor Create(const AOwner: TdomDocument; const Version, EncDl, SdDl: WideString); virtual;
> Do not use this constructor; rather use the CreateXmlDeclaration method on the document object. An error occurs if any of the version number, encoding scheme, or standalone declaration is invalid.

property VersionNumber: WideString read GetVersionNumber;
> Retrieve the XML version number through this read-only property, which is set during construction. It should always be 1.0.

property EncodingDecl: WideString read GetEncodingDecl write SetEncodingDecl;
> This property retrieves or updates the encoding scheme used by the document. An error occurs if the encoding is invalid.

property SDDecl: WideString read GetStandalone write SetStandalone;
> Get or set the standalone declaration with this property. If the value is not yes, no, or an empty string, an error is generated.

TdomTextDeclaration Class

Similar to the XML declaration described above, a text declaration may appear at the start of an external entity to define its type and encoding. The `TdomTextDeclaration` class (shown in Listing 11-35) represents this in the XDOM package.

Listing 11-35: The `TdomTextDeclaration` declaration

```
TdomTextDeclaration = class (TdomNode)
public
  constructor Create(const AOwner: TdomDocument;
    const Version, EncDl: WideString); virtual;
published
  property VersionNumber: WideString read GetVersionNumber;
  property EncodingDecl: WideString read GetEncodingDecl
    write SetEncodingDecl;
end;
```

NOTE This class has no equivalent within the DOM specification.

The properties and methods of the `TdomTextDeclaration` object are shown below:

constructor Create(const AOwner: TdomDocument; const Version, EncDl: WideString); virtual;
    Call the `CreateTextDeclaration` method on the document object rather than this constructor. Errors are generated if the version or encoding is invalid.

property VersionNumber: WideString read GetVersionNumber;
    Retrieve the XML version through this read-only property. Again, it should always be 1.0.

property EncodingDecl: WideString read GetEncodingDecl write SetEncodingDecl;
    Obtain or update the encoding scheme with this property. Supplying an invalid encoding generates an error.

TdomDocumentFragment Class

Nodes of this type do not appear within the normal DOM structure. They are intended for use in constructing and transferring subtrees within the normal hierarchy.

The definition of the `TdomDocumentFragment` class (shown in Listing 11-36) adds no new functionality. It simply serves as a marker to restrict the child nodes that may be added to it and to invoke special processing when it is added to a document or one of its nodes. In the latter case, the fragment itself is not added; all of its child nodes are added in its place.

Listing 11-36: The `TdomDocumentFragment` declaration

```
TdomDocumentFragment = class (TdomNode)
public
  constructor Create(const AOwner: TdomDocument); virtual;
end;
```

A fragment may contain any number of child nodes, including elements, compared to a document, which may only have one element node as a child. Thus, fragments might not be well-formed XML. This is acceptable, and indeed useful, while manipulating the DOM. In the end though, fragments are discarded and it is the document node that ends up being used.

The methods of the `TdomDocumentFragment` object are shown below:

`constructor Create(const AOwner: TdomDocument); virtual;`
> Use the factory method of the `TdomDocument` object to build new document fragments rather than this constructor directly.

TdomDocument Class

Managing all the node type objects is the domain of the `TdomDocument` class (shown in Listing 11-37). It provides a number of factory methods that let you create the other nodes as you need them. This ensures that the nodes are correctly registered with their owning document.

Listing 11-37: The `TdomDocument` declaration

```
TdomDocument = class (TdomNode)
protected
  function DuplicateNode(Node: TdomNode): TdomNode; virtual;
  procedure InitDoc(const TagName: wideString); virtual;
  procedure InitDocNS(const NamespaceURI, QualifiedName: WideString);
    virtual;
public
  constructor Create(const AOwner: TDomImplementation); virtual;
  destructor Destroy; override;
  procedure Clear; override;
  procedure ClearInvalidNodeIterators; virtual;
  function CreateElement(const TagName: WideString): TdomElement;
    virtual;
  function CreateElementNS(const NamespaceURI, QualifiedName:
    WideString): TdomElement; virtual;
  function CreateDocumentFragment: TdomDocumentFragment; virtual;
  function CreateTextNode(const Data: WideString): TdomText; virtual;
  function CreateComment(const Data: WideString): TdomComment; virtual;
  function CreateConditionalSection(const IncludeStmt: WideString):
    TdomConditionalSection; virtual;
  function CreateCDATASection(const Data: WideString):
    TdomCDATASection; virtual;
  function CreateProcessingInstruction(const Targ, Data : WideString):
    TdomProcessingInstruction; virtual;
  function CreateXmlDeclaration(const Version, EncDl, SdDl:
    WideString): TdomXmlDeclaration; virtual;
  function CreateAttribute(const Name: WideString): TdomAttr; virtual;
  function CreateAttributeNS(const NamespaceURI, QualifiedName:
    WideString): TdomAttr; virtual;
  function CreateEntityReference(const Name: WideString):
    TdomEntityReference; virtual;
  function CreateParameterEntityReference(const Name: WideString):
    TdomParameterEntityReference; virtual;
  function CreateDocumentType(const Name, PubId, SysId: WideString):
    TdomDocumentType; virtual;
  function CreateNotation(const Name, PubId, SysId: WideString):
    TdomNotation; virtual;
```

```
function CreateNotationDeclaration(const Name, PubId, SysId:
  WideString): TdomNotationDeclaration; virtual;
function CreateEntity(const Name, PubId, SysId, NotaName:
  WideString): TdomEntity; virtual;
function CreateParameterEntity(const Name, PubId, SysId: WideString):
  TdomParameterEntity; virtual;
function CreateEntityDeclaration(const Name, EntityValue, PubId,
  SysId, NotaName: WideString): TdomEntityDeclaration; virtual;
function CreateParameterEntityDeclaration(const Name, EntityValue,
  PubId, SysId: WideString): TdomParameterEntityDeclaration; virtual;
function CreateElementTypeDeclaration(const Name: WideString;
  const Contspec: TdomContentspecType): TdomElementTypeDeclaration;
  virtual;
function CreateSequenceParticle(const Freq: WideString):
  TdomSequenceParticle; virtual;
function CreateChoiceParticle(const Freq: WideString):
  TdomChoiceParticle; virtual;
function CreatePcdataChoiceParticle: TdomPcdataChoiceParticle;
  virtual;
function CreateElementParticle(const Name, Freq: WideString):
  TdomElementParticle; virtual;
function CreateAttributeList(const Name: WideString): TdomAttrList;
  virtual;
function CreateAttributeDefinition(const Name, AttType, DefaultDecl,
  AttValue: WideString) : TdomAttrDefinition; virtual;
function CreateNametoken(const Name: WideString): TdomNametoken;
  virtual;
function CreateTextDeclaration(const Version, EncDl: WideString):
  TdomTextDeclaration; virtual;
function CreateExternalParsedEntity: TdomExternalParsedEntity;
  virtual;
function CreateExternalParameterEntity: TdomExternalParameterEntity;
  virtual;
function CreateExternalSubset: TdomExternalSubset; virtual;
function CreateInternalSubset: TdomInternalSubset; virtual;
procedure FreeAllNodes(const Node: TdomNode); virtual;
procedure FreeTreeWalker(const TreeWalker: TdomTreeWalker); virtual;
function GetElementById(const elementId: WideString): TdomElement;
  virtual;
function GetElementsByTagName(const TagName: WideString):
  TdomNodeList; virtual;
function GetElementsByTagNameNS(const namespaceURI, localName:
  WideString): TdomNodeList; virtual;
function ImportNode(const importedNode: TdomNode;
  const deep: boolean): TdomNode; virtual;
function InsertBefore(const newChild, refChild: TdomNode): TdomNode;
  override;
function ReplaceChild(const newChild, oldChild: TdomNode): TdomNode;
  override;
function AppendChild(const newChild: TdomNode): TdomNode; override;
function CreateNodeIterator(const root: TdomNode;
  whatToShow: TdomWhatToShow; nodeFilter: TdomNodeFilter;
  entityReferenceExpansion: boolean): TdomNodeIterator; virtual;
function CreateTreeWalker(const root: TdomNode;
  whatToShow: TdomWhatToShow; nodeFilter: TdomNodeFilter;
  entityReferenceExpansion: boolean): TdomTreeWalker; virtual;
property codeAsString: string read GetCodeAsString;
property codeAsWideString: WideString read GetCodeAsWideString;
property defaultView: TdomAbstractView read FDefaultView;
property doctype: TdomDocumentType read GetDoctype;
```

```
    property documentElement: TdomElement read GetDocumentElement;
    property domImplementation: TDomImplementation read FDomImpl;
    property filename: TFilename read GetFilename write SetFilename;
    property xmlDeclaration: TdomXmlDeclaration read GetXmlDeclaration;
  end;
```

A document is itself a node, although it is one of the few node types that have no parent. Thus, it has a node name and children as usual. Special properties provide access to particular nodes that only apply to a document, such as the single top-level element and the document type node.

The TdomDocument object's properties and methods are described below:

constructor Create(const AOwner: TDomImplementation); virtual;
> The document itself should be initially generated using the CreateDocument or CreateDocumentNS methods of the TdomImplementation class, rather than through this constructor. Again, this ensures that the document is properly managed by the XDOM package. It also allows for custom documents to be produced based on types registered with the implementation object.

property codeAsString: string read GetCodeAsString;
> Use this read-only property to retrieve a string version of the DOM for this document. The contents are encoded using UTF-8, and this is reflected in any XML declaration for the document. Single line feed characters within the text are replaced by a carriage return/line feed combination.

property codeAsWideString: WideString read GetCodeAsWideString;
> Similar to the previous property, this one (also read-only) returns the entire DOM as a formatted wide string. The encoding is set to UTF-16BE and the text starts with the $FEFF sequence.

property doctype: TdomDocumentType read GetDoctype;
> Gain access to the document type node (TdomDocumentType) for the document through this read-only property. If the document has no type specified it returns nil.

property documentElement: TdomElement read GetDocumentElement;
> Quickly locate the top-level element node with this read-only property. It returns a TdomElement node. You could find the node by stepping through the child nodes of the document, but this property makes it much easier.

property domImplementation: TDomImplementation read FDomImpl;
> Retrieve the DOM implementation that created this document through this read-only property.

NOTE Since implementation is a reserved word in Delphi, the previous property is named domImplementation instead. The following properties, filename and xmlDeclaration, are extensions to the DOM specification.

property filename: TFilename read GetFilename write SetFilename;
> Documents loaded from the local file system set this property to the full name of that file. Otherwise, it returns an empty string.

`property xmlDeclaration: TdomXmlDeclaration read GetXmlDeclaration;`
: Access the XML declaration node for this document through this property. It returns `nil` if there is no declaration associated with the document. Again, you could search through the child nodes for this one if you wanted to.

`function CreateElement(const TagName: WideString): TdomElement; virtual;`
: Construct a new element node (`TdomElement`) for this document with the specified name. Until the element is added to a document or document fragment it has no parent. Providing an invalid name raises an exception.

`function CreateElementNS(const NamespaceURI, QualifiedName: WideString): TdomElement; virtual;`
: The same as the previous method except that it takes a namespace qualified name for the element. Using a malformed name, such as one of the reserved prefixes (xml*) without the corresponding namespace or a prefixed name with no namespace, generates an exception.

`function CreateAttribute(const Name: WideString): TdomAttr; virtual;`
: Build a new attribute node (`TdomAttr`) with the specified name. After setting the attribute's value and other properties, add it to the appropriate element with its `SetAttributeNode` method. Supplying an invalid name raises an exception.

`function CreateAttributeNS(const NamespaceURI, QualifiedName: WideString): TdomAttr; virtual;`
: Create a namespace-aware attribute, then treat it like a normal attribute from above. As for a namespace-aware element, an exception occurs if the name is malformed.

`function CreateDocumentFragment: TdomDocumentFragment; virtual;`
: Produce a document fragment (`TdomDocumentFragment`) node. These nodes can hold structures as they are being worked on, separate from the document. Usually they are inserted into that document at some stage, at which time all the children of the fragment are inserted in turn, but not the fragment itself.

`function CreateText(const Data: WideString): TdomText; virtual;`
: Generate a new text node (`TdomText`), containing the supplied text, to hold the actual content of the document. Text nodes have no children and appear only at the bottommost levels in the DOM hierarchy. The node has no parent until it is added to the document or a fragment.

`function CreateCDATASection(const Data: WideString): TdomCDATASection; virtual;`
: Produce a new CDATA section node (`TdomCDATASection`), containing the supplied text. Characters that would normally denote markup within the text are ignored as such. Like text nodes, these have no children. The node has no parent until it is added to the document or a fragment.

`function CreateComment(const Data: WideString): TdomComment; virtual;`
: Construct a new comment node (`TdomComment`), containing the supplied text. Comments add explanation to the document, but should not be relied upon to carry processing information, as they may be stripped from the document upon loading. Comments have no children.

function CreateProcessingInstruction(const Targ, Data : WideString):
    TdomProcessingInstruction; virtual;
    Build a new processing instruction node (TdomProcessingInstruction) for the specified target application and command sequence. Use these nodes to pass processing details through to a client application. Processing instructions have no children.

function CreateEntityReference(const Name: WideString): TdomEntityReference;
    virtual;
    Generate a new entity reference node (TdomEntityReference) given the entity's name.

function CreateDocumentType(const Name, PubId, SysId: WideString):
    TdomDocumentType; virtual;
    Construct a new document type node (TdomDocumentType) given the name of the top-level element, and the public and/or system identifier for an external DTD.

NOTE The DOM specification creates document type nodes from the Implementation object. However, the XDOM package provides this functionality at the document level instead.

function CreateNotation(const Name, PubId, SysId: WideString): TdomNotation;
    virtual;
    Produce a new notation node (TdomNotation) given its name, and the public and/or system identifier that corresponds to it. Use empty strings for the latter two if the values are not known. These notations are placed within the Notations property of a document type node. They represent the result of parsing the document containing a notation declaration. To generate the declaration itself, you need to use the CreateNotationDeclaration method described below.

function CreateEntity(const Name, PubId, SysId, NotaName: WideString): TdomEntity;
    virtual;
    Build a new entity node (TdomEntity) given its name, the public and/or system identifier that references an external document, and the notation name that specifies its type. For external entities, either or both of the external identifiers must be given (use empty strings for the unknown ones). For unparsed entities, you must supply the notation name. As for notations above, these nodes represent the entities defined in the document, but not the declarations themselves. As such, only unparsed entities appear in the Entities property of the document type node. Use the CreateEntityDeclaration method below to define an entity within the document.

function GetElementById(const elementId: WideString): TdomElement; virtual;
    Return a reference to the node that has the supplied ID value, or nil if none can be found. Results are unpredictable if more than one node has the specified ID value. The DOM must know (through a DTD) which attributes contain ID values before it can match on them, returning nil from this function if that information is unknown.

```
function GetElementsByTagName(const TagName: WideString): TdomNodeList; virtual;
```
Find all the elements with the given tag name and return them in a node list in the order that they appear in the document text. Use a name of * to retrieve all the elements in the document in a flat list.

TIP The `GetElementsByTagName` method creates a new node list for each name given. These lists are not released until the document is destroyed or its `Clear` method is called. This can increase memory usage with many calls to the function with different names. A better method is to create a node iterator or tree walker with a filter instead.

Furthermore, the DOM requirement for a live result set means that the list must be traversed from the beginning for each reference to an indexed item. This is much slower than using an equivalent node iterator or tree walker.

```
function GetElementsByTagNameNS(const namespaceURI, localName: WideString):
    TdomNodeList; virtual;
```
This is the namespace-aware version of the above method. It has the same abilities and limitations.

```
function ImportNode(const importedNode: TdomNode; const deep: boolean): TdomNode;
    virtual;
```
The functionality is identical to the `CloneNode` method, creating a copy of a node, except for the fact that the original node may belong to another document. Attempting to import a document or document type node raises an exception.

NOTE The following two methods appear in the DOM specification under the `DocumentTraversal` interface. In the XDOM package this interface is wrapped into the document, which is the appropriate place for it.

```
function CreateNodeIterator(const root: TdomNode; whatToShow: TdomWhatToShow;
    nodeFilter: TdomNodeFilter; entityReferenceExpansion: boolean):
    TdomNodeIterator; virtual;
```
Construct a new node iterator (`TdomNodeIterator`) over the subtree beneath the specified node. That root node may be included in the selection depending on the filter settings. You can specify what types of nodes are considered, and can apply a filter to them (use `nil` if no filter is used). Setting the appropriate parameter expands entity references. An exception occurs if the root is `nil`.

```
function CreateTreeWalker(const root: TdomNode; whatToShow: TdomWhatToShow;
    nodeFilter: TdomNodeFilter; entityReferenceExpansion: boolean):
    TdomTreeWalker; virtual;
```
Similar to the above method, this one creates a new tree walker (`TdomTreeWalker`) for the specified nodes. Although the parameters are the same, the result of `CreateNodeIterator` is a sequential list of the nodes found, while this method returns the nodes still in a tree structure.

NOTE The following methods are not part of the DOM specification. The Create methods construct the remaining nodes introduced in the XDOM package, mainly to support the definition of a DTD.

function CreateXmlDeclaration(const Version, EncDl, SdDl: WideString):
    TdomXmlDeclaration; virtual;
    Produce a new XML prolog node (TdomXmlDeclaration) to appear at the start of the document. The parameters determine the contents of that node, indicating the version of XML in use (currently 1.0), the encoding scheme used for the document, and whether or not the document can be used standalone (yes, no, or ' '). An exception occurs if any supplied value is invalid. Add the new node to the document as the first child.

function CreateTextDeclaration(const Version, EncDl: WideString):
    TdomTextDeclaration; virtual;
    Generate a new text prolog node (TdomTextDeclaration) for an external entity. It accepts the same version and encoding parameters as the XML prolog above.

function CreateExternalSubset: TdomExternalSubset; virtual;
    Construct a new external subset node (TdomExternalSubset) for the document's DTD. You should not have to call this method since an external subset is automatically created as a child of a document type node.

function CreateInternalSubset: TdomInternalSubset; virtual;
    Create a new internal subset node (TdomInternalSubset) for the document's DTD. Like the external subset, a node of this type is automatically created in the document type node, so you should not have to call this method yourself.

function CreateNotationDeclaration(const Name, PubId, SysId: WideString):
    TdomNotationDeclaration; virtual;
    Generate a new notation declaration node (TdomNotationDeclaration) for the document's DTD.

function CreateParameterEntity(const Name, PubId, SysId: WideString):
    TdomParameterEntity; virtual;
    This method builds a new parameter entity node (TdomParameterEntity) given its name, and the public and/or system identifier that references an external document (or empty strings if internally defined).

function CreateParameterEntityReference(const Name: WideString):
    TdomParameterEntityReference; virtual;
    Constructs a new parameter entity reference node (TdomParameterEntityReference) given the entity's name. Use it within the DTD section as shorthand for other content or markup.

function CreateEntityDeclaration(const Name, EntityValue, PubId, SysId, NotaName:
    WideString): TdomEntityDeclaration; virtual;
    Builds a new entity declaration node (TdomEntityDeclaration) given its name, and value or public and/or system identifier. Internal entities have a value only (the external identifiers are empty strings). External entities have no value, but either or both of the identifiers.

Unparsed entities also have their notation specified. These entities appear within the context of the DTD within the document, and produce appropriate declarations when the DOM is output.

function CreateParameterEntityDeclaration(const Name, EntityValue, PubId, SysId: WideString): TdomParameterEntityDeclaration; virtual;

Similar to the above method, this one instead creates a new parameter entity declaration node (TdomParameterEntityDeclaration). As before, internal entities have a value only (the external identifiers are empty strings), while external entities have no value, but either or both of the identifiers. Again, these entities belong within an internal subset within the document, and generate declarations when output.

function CreateConditionalSection(const IncludeStmt: WideString): TdomConditionalSection; virtual;

Generates a new conditional section node (TdomConditionalSection) for use in the DTD section of the document. The supplied text must be INCLUDE, IGNORE, or the name of a parameter entity reference that refers to one of these strings.

function CreateElementTypeDeclaration(const Name: WideString; const Contspec: TdomContentspecType): TdomElementTypeDeclaration; virtual;

Builds an element definition node (TdomElementTypeDeclaration) for the document's DTD. The method takes the element's name and an indication of its content: ctEmpty, ctAny, ctMixed, or ctChildren. Add the new node to the DTD of the document.

function CreateSequenceParticle(const Freq: WideString): TdomSequenceParticle; virtual;

Constructs a particle definition node (TdomSequenceParticle) for an element's content model. Elements of type ctMixed or ctChildren may use these particles to build up their model hierarchy. Children of this particle must appear as the element's children in the same order for the element to be valid. Specify the occurrences of the sequence with the required parameter: '' for once only, ? for zero or once, + for once or more, or * for zero or more. An exception occurs if it is not one of these values.

function CreateChoiceParticle(const Freq: WideString): TdomChoiceParticle; virtual;

Produces a particle definition node (TdomChoiceParticle) for an element's content model. Any of this particle's children can match with an element's next child for the document to be valid. Only elements of type ctMixed or ctChildren may use these particles. Supply the occurrences as for the sequence particle above. Again, an invalid value raises an exception.

function CreatePcdataChoiceParticle: TdomPcdataChoiceParticle; virtual;

Generates a particle definition node (TdomPcdataChoiceParticle) that represents mixed content (type ctMixed). The occurrences value is automatically set to * (for zero or more entries). Straight text or one of the children of this node must match the element's children to be valid.

function CreateElementParticle(const Name, Freq: WideString): TdomElementParticle;
   virtual;
   Builds a particle definition node (TdomElementParticle) that represents a single element. Generally these are placed as children of one of the other particle node types. An exact match between this node and the element's next child makes it valid. Specify occurrences as described above.
function CreateAttributeList(const Name: WideString): TdomAttrList; virtual;
   Constructs a new list for attributes declarations (TdomAttrList) of a specified element. Attach the actual declarations to the list within the DOM.
function CreateAttributeDefinition(const Name, AttType, DefaultDecl, AttValue: WideString): TdomAttrDefinition; virtual;
   Produces a new attribute declaration (TdomAttrDefinition) for the document's DTD. Specify its name, its type (as text, like (yes | no) or ID), its default declaration (#REQUIRED, #IMPLIED, #FIXED, or ''), and its default value. Place this definition within the corresponding attribute list.
function CreateNametoken(const Name: WideString): TdomNametoken; virtual;
   Generates a new nametoken node (TdomNametoken) for use as an attribute's value when it has an enumerated type. Add it to the appropriate attribute definition.
function CreateExternalParsedEntity: TdomExternalParsedEntity; virtual;
   Builds a new external parsed entity node (TdomExternalParsedEntity), which is referred to by an entity declaration object.
function CreateExternalParameterEntity: TdomExternalParameterEntity; virtual;
   Constructs a new external parameter entity node (TdomExternalParameterEntity), which is referenced by a parameter entity declaration object.
procedure Clear; override;
   Releases all nodes, node lists, node iterators, and tree walkers belonging to this document. You can then start building a new document.
procedure FreeAllNodes(const Node: TdomNode); virtual;
   Releases the specified node (created by this document) and all of its children. The target node must be removed from any document or fragment in which it appears before it can be freed. Exceptions appear if the node belongs to another document, if the node is the document itself, or if the node is still attached to the DOM.
procedure ClearInvalidNodeIterators; virtual;
   Frees all node iterators that have a state of invalid (those that have been detached).
procedure FreeTreeWalker(const TreeWalker: TdomTreeWalker); virtual;
   Releases the supplied tree walker. If the tree walker was created by another document, an exception occurs.
function DuplicateNode(Node: TdomNode): TdomNode; virtual;
   Create a copy of a node internally with this protected method. All the attributes of an

element are copied during this process, as are any entities and notations attached to a document type node. Other node types just return a straight copy of that one node.

procedure InitDoc(const TagName: wideString); virtual;
> Given a tag name, this method initializes the document by creating the top-level element node for the hierarchy. The CreateDocument methods of the TdomImplementation class call this method as part of that process. Subclasses of TdomDocument may override this protected method to perform their own initialization. Calling this procedure on a document that already has a document element results in an exception, as does calling it with an invalid tag name.

procedure InitDocNS(const NamespaceURI, QualifiedName: WideString); virtual;
> Similar to the previous method, this one creates a document element node that belongs to a specified namespace. Otherwise, it functions just like the normal version. An exception occurs if this procedure is called with a malformed name, such as using a reserved prefix without the corresponding namespace or specifying a prefixed name but no namespace.

TdomImplementation Class

To access functionality that is outside of any one document you use the TdomImplementation class (whose declaration appears in Listing 11-38). It allows you to create documents to fill with content nodes, and to determine what abilities are available within this implementation of the DOM.

Listing 11-38: The TdomImplementation declaration

```
TdomImplementation = class (TComponent)
public
  constructor Create(aOwner: TComponent); override;
  destructor Destroy; override;
  procedure Clear; virtual;
  procedure FreeDocument(const doc: TdomDocument); virtual;
  procedure FreeDocumentType(const docType: TdomDocumentType); virtual;
  function hasFeature(const feature, version: WideString): boolean;
    virtual;
  function createDocument(const name: WideString;
    doctype: TdomDocumentType): TdomDocument; virtual;
  function createDocumentNS(const namespaceURI, qualifiedName:
    WideString; doctype: TdomDocumentType): TdomDocument; virtual;

{
  The following two methods have been removed from this version of
  the XDOM, but will be reintroduced in a further release.

  function createDocumentType(const name, publicId, systemId:
    WideString): TdomDocumentType; virtual;
  function createDocumentTypeNS(const qualifiedName, publicId,
    systemId: WideString): TdomDocumentType; virtual;
}

  function GetDocumentClass(const aNamespaceUri, aQualifiedName:
    wideString): TdomDocumentClass; virtual;
  class procedure RegisterDocumentFormat(const aNamespaceUri,
    aQualifiedName: wideString; aDocumentClass: TdomDocumentClass);
```

```
      virtual;
    function SupportsDocumentFormat(const aNamespaceUri, aQualifiedName:
      wideString): boolean; virtual;
    class procedure UnregisterDocumentClass(const aDocumentClass:
      TdomDocumentClass); virtual;
    property documents: TdomNodeList read getDocuments;
    property documentTypes: TdomNodeList read getDocumentTypes;
  end;
```

The properties and methods of the `TdomImplementation` object are described below:

constructor Create(aOwner: TComponent); override;

> As you can see, this class derives from TComponent, allowing you to select the Tdom-Implementation component from the component palette and drop it onto a form. Alternately, you can call this constructor directly to gain access to the DOM implementation through code.

function hasFeature(const feature, version: WideString): boolean; virtual;

> You can determine which parts of the DOM specification are supported using this function. If you pass in the feature name, such as XML or HTML, and the desired version, only 1.0 or 2.0 so far, you will receive a Boolean flag indicating its presence (True) or absence (False).

function createDocument(const name: WideString; doctype: TdomDocumentType): TdomDocument; virtual;

> Generate a new document and its top-level element, using the name specified, with this method. You may also pass in a reference to a document type node, created elsewhere. Use nil if no document type applies to the document. Passing an invalid element name, or a document type node that was created by another implementation or is already in use in another document raises an exception.
>
> The new document is by default a TdomDocument object. However, by registering a subclass of this as a new format and referring to it with the qualified element name, you can obtain an instance of that subclass instead.

function createDocumentNS(const namespaceURI, qualifiedName: WideString; doctype: TdomDocumentType): TdomDocument; virtual;

> This method is a namespace-aware version of the previous one. It functions as its counterpart, with the addition that a malformed namespace produces an exception. Namespaces are malformed if a prefix is specified but no namespace is provided, or if a reserved XML namespace is used without the corresponding namespace.

NOTE The following two methods to create document type nodes have been removed from the TdomImplementation object in version 2.2.12a of the XDOM package. You can use the same methods on the document object itself. They are intended for replacement in a later version.

function createDocumentType(const name, publicId, systemId: WideString): TdomDocumentType; virtual;
> Build a new document type node with this method. The name of the top-level element, and public and system identifiers for an external DTD are provided as parameters. Leave the latter two as empty strings if there is no external DTD. The new node is added to the documentTypes list until such time as it is associated with a document.

function createDocumentTypeNS(const qualifiedName, publicId, systemId: WideString): TdomDocumentType; virtual;
> For namespace-aware document types, use this method rather than createDocumentType. It functions just like the latter, with the addition that a malformed namespace produces an exception. Namespaces are malformed if a prefix is specified but no namespace is provided, or if a reserved namespace is used without the corresponding namespace.

NOTE The remaining properties and methods do not form part of the DOM specification, but are extensions in the XDOM package.

property documents: TdomNodeList read getDocuments;
> Retrieves a list of all the documents created by this object. The returned value is a TdomNodeList, with each entry being a TdomDocument object.

property documentTypes: TdomNodeList read getDocumentTypes;
> Similarly, you obtain a list through this property of all the document type nodes generated by this object. Only those nodes not yet attached to a document appear in the list. As above, you get a TdomNodeList returned, but the entries this time are all TdomDocumentType objects.

class procedure RegisterDocumentFormat(const aNamespaceUri, aQualifiedName: wideString; DocumentClass: TdomDocumentClass); virtual;
> For added functionality, you can create your own subclasses of TdomDocument, adding whatever behavior you require, then register them with the XDOM package using this method. The namespace and qualified name passed to this call serve to identify the associated subclass. Thereafter, creating a document with an element that matches one of these formats results in the creation of an instance of that subclass.
>
> A match occurs if the namespace and qualified name for the top-level element in the CreateDocumentNS call match exactly with the corresponding registered values. For non-namespace-aware documents, the element's name must match with the registered entry, while namespace-aware documents namespaces must be blank.
>
> For example, you could create a movie-watcher subclass that provided factory methods for movie and cinema elements.
>
> The list of registered formats is global. This means that all TdomImplementation objects in the application share it.

```
class procedure UnregisterDocumentClass(const aDocumentClass: TdomDocumentClass);
  virtual;
```
Conversely, this method removes the specified document class from the list of those registered.

```
function SupportsDocumentFormat(const aNamespaceUri, aQualifiedName: wideString):
  boolean; virtual;
```
Determine whether or not a document format is supported with this function. Given a namespace URI and a qualified element name, it searches the list of registered formats and returns True if a match is found. Otherwise, it returns False.

```
function GetDocumentClass(const aNamespaceUri, aQualifiedName: wideString):
  TdomDocumentClass; virtual;
```
Retrieves a reference to the last document class registered under the given namespace URI and qualified name. These classes must be registered with the implementation prior to this call. Finding no match results in an exception.

```
procedure Clear; virtual;
```
Frees all the documents and document type nodes created by this object (accessible through its documents and documentTypes properties). Any objects owned by these items are also released.

```
procedure FreeDocument(const doc: TdomDocument); virtual;
```
Use this method to free the specified document and remove it from the document list. Nodes, node iterators, and tree walkers that it owns are also released. An exception occurs if the document cannot be found in the implementation's list.

```
procedure FreeDocumentType(const docType: TdomDocumentType); virtual;
```
Similarly, free an unattached document type and delete it from the documentTypes list with this method. If the node cannot be found, an exception occurs.

TdomNodeFilter Class

A filter is part of the DOM Level 2 Traversal specification, and it allows you to select which nodes presented to it are accepted and which are rejected. Filters work in conjunction with the node iterator and tree walker objects, providing greater specificity in returning nodes. The definition for the TdomNodeFilter class is shown in Listing 11-39. This class is abstract, as the XDOM package knows nothing about how you want to select your nodes. You must derive a new class from this one, overriding the acceptNode method to perform your particular selection. This is one of the few classes in this package that you do create yourself.

Listing 11-39: The TdomNodeFilter declaration

```
TdomNodeFilter = class
public
  function acceptNode(const node: TdomNode): TdomFilterResult; virtual;
    abstract;
end;
```

The `TdomNodeFilter` object's methods are listed below:

`function acceptNode(const node: TcomNode): TdomFilterResult; virtual; abstract;`
Given a single node from either a node iterator or a tree walker, you can perform whatever operations on it that you wish to determine whether or not to accept it for further processing. You do not have to worry about where the node comes from nor how it is stored, just check it for inclusion. The return value must be one of the values shown in Table 11-5.

Table 11-5: Node filter return values

Frequency	Meaning
`filter_accept`	Accept the node. It is included in those returned through the node iterator or tree walker objects.
`filter_reject`	Reject the node. It is not included in those returned through the node iterator or tree walker objects. Furthermore, in the tree walker, none of this node's children are returned either.
`filter_skip`	Skip the node. It is not included in those returned by the node iterator or tree walker objects. However, the tree walker continues to process any children of this node, which may in turn be accepted, rejected, or skipped.

TdomNodeIterator Class

Another part of the DOM Level 2 Traversal specification, node iterators let you step through a sequential list of nodes in an implementation-independent manner. These nodes appear in the list in the same order that they appear in the document. The definition of the `TdomNodeIterator` class is shown in Listing 11-40.

Listing 11-40: The `TdomNodeIterator` declaration

```
TdomNodeIterator = class
public
  constructor create(const Root: TdomNode;
    const WhatToShow: TdomWhatToShow; const NodeFilter: TdomNodeFilter;
    const EntityReferenceExpansion: boolean); virtual;
  procedure detach; virtual;
  function NextNode: TdomNode; virtual;
  function PreviousNode: TdomNode; virtual;
  property expandEntityReferences: boolean
    read GetExpandEntityReferences;
  property filter: TdomNodeFilter read GetFilter;
  property root: TdomNode read GetRoot;
  property whatToShow: TdomWhatToShow read GetWhatToShow;
end;
```

Node iterators are live objects. They continue to return sensible results even when the structure on which they are based is altered. All movements are based on the current position within the list, generally before a particular node. If that node is removed from the subtree altogether, the current position moves back to the first node that remains.

The properties and methods of the `TdomNodeIterator` object are detailed below:

`constructor create(const Root: TdomNode; const WhatToShow: TdomWhatToShow; const NodeFilter: TdomNodeFilter; const EntityReferenceExpansion: boolean); virtual;`
   Obtain node iterators through the `CreateNodeIterator` method of the document object instead of using this constructor. On creation, you specify the root node from which to select, the set of node types to select, any node filter to apply, and a flag indicating whether or not entity references are expanded and included in the search. The entire subtree based at the specified root is scanned in order, matched by type, filtered out, and then included in the iterator if they remain.

`property root: TdomNode read GetRoot;`
   This read-only property returns a reference to the root node of the subtree scanned by the iterator.

`property whatToShow: TdomWhatToShow read GetWhatToShow;`
   Retrieve the set of node types initially selected through this read-only property.

`property filter: TdomNodeFilter read GetFilter;`
   The filter used to screen nodes is returned by this read-only property. It returns `nil` if no filter is used.

`property expandEntityReferences: boolean read GetExpandEntityReferences;`
   This read-only property returns the flag indicating whether or not the iterator returns descendants of entity reference nodes. When set to `True` (during creation of the iterator), the child nodes are processed. When set to `False`, they are totally ignored. This setting overrides any node types given in the `whatToShow` property.

`function NextNode: TdomNode; virtual;`
   Returns a reference to the next node in the list and advances the current position. After an iterator is created, this method returns the first node in the list. It returns `nil` if at the end of the list.

`function PreviousNode: TdomNode; virtual;`
   Similarly, this method returns a reference to the previous node in the list and moves the position backwards. A `nil` is returned if at the start of the list.

`procedure detach; virtual;`
   When you finish with a node iterator, you should call this method to notify the DOM, allowing its resources to be reclaimed. The iterator is placed into an `invalid` state. Calling the `NextNode` or `PreviousNode` methods at this time generates an error. Use the `ClearInvalidNodeIterators` method of the document object to totally dispose of iterators in this state.

TdomTreeWalker Class

More of the DOM Level 2 Traversal specification, tree walkers are similar to node iterators in that they manage collections of nodes. However, tree walkers maintain the original tree structure, as much as possible, of the subtree that they are based upon. See Listing 11-41 for the definition of the `TdomTreeWalker` class.

Listing 11-41: The TdomTreeWalker declaration

```
TdomTreeWalker = class
public
  constructor create(const Root: TdomNode;
    const WhatToShow: TdomWhatToShow; const NodeFilter: TdomNodeFilter;
    const EntityReferenceExpansion: boolean); virtual;
  function parentNode: TdomNode; virtual;
  function firstChild: TdomNode; virtual;
  function lastChild: TdomNode; virtual;
  function previousSibling: TdomNode; virtual;
  function nextSibling: TdomNode; virtual;
  function NextNode: TdomNode; virtual;
  function PreviousNode: TdomNode; virtual;
  property currentNode: TdomNode read GetCurrentNode
    write SetCurrentNode;
  property expandEntityReferences: boolean
    read GetExpandEntityReferences;
  property filter: TdomNodeFilter read GetFilter;
  property root: TdomNode read GetRoot;
  property whatToShow: TdomWhatToShow read GetWhatToShow;
end;
```

Tree walkers are also live structures—they reflect any changes made to the DOM on the fly. A sensible approach to insertions and deletions is taken, with any movements through the tree walker returning to a valid selected node based on its current position.

A TdomTreeWalker object's properties and methods are described below:

constructor create(const Root: TdomNode; const WhatToShow: TdomWhatToShow; const NodeFilter: TdomNodeFilter; const EntityReferenceExpansion: boolean); virtual;

Do not use this constructor to build tree walkers. Instead, use the CreateTreeWalker method of the document object. The parameters are the same as for a node iterator: the root of the subtree, the set of node types to select initially, any filter to apply to those nodes, and a flag denoting the expansion of entity reference nodes.

property root: TdomNode read GetRoot;

Retrieve the node at the root of the subtree scanned by the tree walker through this read-only property.

property whatToShow: TdomWhatToShow read GetWhatToShow;

This read-only property returns the set of node types included in the initial selection. Omitting particular node types can drastically alter the shape of the subtree as seen through the tree walker. For example, only selecting text nodes causes them all to appear as direct children of the root node, regardless of their original depths.

property filter: TdomNodeFilter read GetFilter;
   Obtain a reference to any filter applied to the selected node through this read-only property. A `nil` results if no filter is used.

property expandEntityReferences: boolean read GetExpandEntityReferences;
   As for the node iterator, this read-only property determines whether or not the descendants of entity reference nodes are included in those returned by the tree walker. If `True`, these child nodes are processed, but when `False`, they are all ignored. This setting overrides any node types specified in the `whatToShow` property.

property currentNode: TdomNode read GetCurrentNode write SetCurrentNode;
   Retrieve or set the current node within the tree walker's structure through this property. It is possible to set the current node to any node at all, even outside of the subtree being scanned, or to a node rejected because of the `whatToShow` or `filter` properties. In these cases, further movements within the tree walker start from that node and return the appropriate node from within the selected set. An error occurs if an attempt is made to set this value to `nil`.

function parentNode: TdomNode; virtual;
   This method returns the closest visible ancestor of the current node, the first one that is accepted by the node type setting and any filter. Move the current node pointer to the node found. A `nil` is returned if attempting to move upward from the root node. In this case, the current node pointer remains where it was.

function firstChild: TdomNode; virtual;
   Returns the first visible child of the current node, and resets the current node to refer to it. If no such node exists, the current node remains where it is, and the function returns `nil`.

function lastChild: TdomNode; virtual;
   Similarly, this method returns the last visible child of the current node and moves the current pointer here. Again, it returns `nil` if no such node exists.

function previousSibling: TdomNode; virtual;
   Obtains the node immediately before the current one in its parent's list of children. Move the current pointer here if found, and return a `nil` if not found.

function nextSibling: TdomNode; virtual;
   Conversely, finds the node immediately following this one at the same level. It returns `nil` if no such node exists.

function NextNode: TdomNode; virtual;
   Retrieve the next node in document order relative to the current one though this method. This may traverse up or down the hierarchy. Move the current node pointer if found. If there is no next node, it returns a `nil`.

function PreviousNode: TdomNode; virtual;
   Similarly, this method finds the previous node in document order, returning `nil` if there is none.

TXmlToDomParser Class

The actual loading of a document is performed by the XDOM parser as encapsulated in the TXmlToDomParser class (see Listing 11-43), which derives from the TdomCustomParser class (see Listing 11-42). This class ultimately derives from TComponent, allowing it to be dropped onto a form from the component palette. You can then attach it to a DOM implementation object and create an external subset handler if desired. Alternately, you can create a parser in code—just remember to free it when you are finished.

Listing 11-42: The TdomCustomParser *declaration*

```
TdomCustomParser = class (TComponent)
protected
  procedure parseDtd(const locator: TdomStandardLocator;
    const name, pubId, sysId, data: WideString); virtual; abstract;
end;
```

Listing 11-43: The TXmlToDomParser *declaration*

```
TParserEvent = procedure(Sender: TObject; const PublicId,
  SystemId: WideString; var extSubset: WideString) of object;

TXmlToDomParser = class (TdomCustomParser)
protected
  FDocBuilder: TdomStandardDocBuilder;  FDocXMLReader: TdomStandardDocXMLReader;  FErrorHandler: TdomStandardErrorHandler;
  FExtDtdBuilder: TdomStandardExtSubsetBuilder;
  FExtDtdReader: TdomStandardExtSubsetXMLReader;
  FIntDtdBuilder: TdomStandardIntSubsetBuilder;
  FIntDtdReader: TdomStandardIntSubsetXMLReader;
  procedure Notification(AComponent: TComponent;
    Operation: TOperation); override;
  procedure parseDtd(const locator: TdomStandardLocator;
    const name, pubId, sysId, data: WideString); override;
public
  constructor Create(aOwner: TComponent); override;
  destructor destroy; override;
  procedure DocMemoryToDom(const Ptr: Pointer; const Size: Longint;
    const pubId, sysId: wideString; const RefNode: TdomNode); virtual;
  procedure DocSourceCodeToDom(const DocSourceCode: TXmlSourceCode;
    const pubId, sysId: wideString; const RefNode: TdomNode); virtual;
  procedure DocStreamToDom(const Stream: TStream;
    const pubId, sysId: wideString; const RefNode: TdomNode); virtual;
  procedure DocStringToDom(const Str: string;
    const pubId, sysId: wideString; const RefNode: TdomNode); virtual;
  procedure DocWideStringToDom(Str: WideString;
    const pubId, sysId: wideString; const RefNode: TdomNode); virtual;
  procedure ExtDtdMemoryToDom(const Ptr: Pointer; const Size: Longint;
    const pubId, sysId: wideString; const RefNode: TdomNode); virtual;
  procedure ExtDtdSourceCodeToDom(
    const ExtDtdSourceCode: TXmlSourceCode;
    const pubId, sysId: wideString; const RefNode: TdomNode); virtual;
  procedure ExtDtdStreamToDom(const Stream: TStream;
    const pubId, sysId: wideString; const RefNode: TdomNode); virtual;
  procedure ExtDtdStringToDom(const Str: string;
    const pubId, sysId: wideString; const RefNode: TdomNode); virtual;
  procedure ExtDtdWideStringToDom(Str: WideString;
```

```
        const pubId, sysId: wideString; const RefNode: TdomNode); virtual;
      procedure IntDtdMemoryToDom(const Ptr: Pointer; const Size: Longint;
        const pubId, sysId: wideString; const RefNode: TdomNode); virtual;
      procedure IntDtdSourceCodeToDom(
        const IntDtdSourceCode: TXmlSourceCode;
        const pubId, sysId: wideString; const RefNode: TdomNode); virtual;
      procedure IntDtdStreamToDom(const Stream: TStream;
        const pubId, sysId: wideString; const RefNode: TdomNode); virtual;
      procedure IntDtdStringToDom(const Str: string;
        const pubId, sysId: wideString; const RefNode: TdomNode); virtual;
      procedure IntDtdWideStringToDom(Str: WideString;
        const pubId, sysId: wideString; const RefNode: TdomNode); virtual;
      function fileToDom(const filename: TFileName): TdomDocument; virtual;
      function memoryToDom(const Ptr: Pointer; const Size: Longint): TdomDocument; virtual;
      function sourceCodeToDom(const IntDtdSourceCode: TXmlSourceCode): TdomDocument; virtual;
      function streamToDom(const Stream: TStream): TdomDocument; virtual;
      function stringToDom(const Str: String): TdomDocument; virtual;
      function wideStringToDom(Str: WideString): TdomDocument; virtual;
      property DocBuilder: TdomStandardDocBuilder read FDocBuilder;
      property DocXMLReader: TdomStandardDocXMLReader read FDocXMLReader;
      property ErrorHandler: TdomStandardErrorHandler read FErrorHandler;
      property ExtDtdBuilder: TdomStandardExtSubsetBuilder
        read FExtDtdBuilder;
      property ExtDtdReader: TdomStandardExtSubsetXMLReader
        read FExtDtdReader;
      property IntDtdBuilder: TdomStandardIntSubsetBuilder
        read FIntDtdBuilder;
      property IntDtdReader: TdomStandardIntSubsetXMLReader
        read FIntDtdReader;
    published
      property DOMImpl: TDomImplementation read GetDomImpl
        write SetDomImpl;
      property OnExternalSubset: TParserEvent read FOnExternalSubset
        write FOnExternalSubset;
    end;
```

Once a parse is finished it returns a document object that contains the new DOM. The parser currently supports the following encoding schemes: UTF-8, UTF-16BE, UTF-16LE, ISO-8859-1 through ISO-8859-10, ISO-8859-13 through ISO-8859-15, KOI8-R, cp10000_MacRoman, and cp1251.

The properties and methods of a TXmlToDomParser object are listed below:

`constructor Create(aOwner: TComponent); override;`

Use this method to instantiate a parser object, supplying an owning component if desired. If you drop the parser onto your form from the palette, it is automatically created for you.

`destructor destroy; override;`

If you created the parser yourself, do not forget to free it when you are finished.

`property DOMImpl: TDomImplementation read GetDomImpl write SetDomImpl;`

Use this method to retrieve or set the implementation object used during construction of a DOM during parsing with the `fileToDom` method.

Part II: The Document Object Model

property OnExternalSubset: TParserEvent read FOnExternalSubset write
    FOnExternalSubset;
    Attach a handler to this event to supply an external DTD subset to the document during parsing. The signature for the event is shown above. It passes across the public and system identifiers for the external DTD, and expects back a WideString value, encoded as UTF-16BE, representing the contents of that reference. Any nodes resulting from the parsing of this string are placed under the external subset node of the document type, and are all made read-only.

property DocBuilder: TdomStandardDocBuilder read FDocBuilder;
    Access the internal TdomStandardDocBuilder object used to build the DOM structure through this read-only property.

property DocXMLReader: TdomStandardDocXMLReader read FDocXMLReader;
    Retrieve the internal TdomStandardDocXmlReader used to parse the XML document through this read-only property.

property ErrorHandler: TdomStandardErrorHandler read FErrorHandler;
    This read-only property lets you reference the internal TdomStandardErrorHandler that deals with parsing errors.

property ExtDtdBuilder: TdomStandardExtSubsetBuilder read FExtDtdBuilder;
    The internal TdomStandardExtSubsetBuilder object that constructs the external subset is available through this read-only property.

property ExtDtdReader: TdomStandardExtSubsetXMLReader read FExtDtdReader;
    Access the internal TdomStandardExtSubsetXMLReader object used to parse the external subset through this read-only property.

property IntDtdBuilder: TdomStandardIntSubsetBuilder read FIntDtdBuilder;
    This read-only property returns a reference to the internal TdomStandardIntSubsetBuilder object that generates the internal subset.

property IntDtdReader: TdomStandardIntSubsetXMLReader read FIntDtdReader;
    Retrieve the internal TdomStandardIntSubsetXMLReader object used to process the internal subset through this read-only property.

function fileToDom(const filename: TFileName): TdomDocument; virtual;
    This method is the heart of the parse process. It loads the specified XML document from a file and parses its contents into a DOM structure. The OnExternalSubset event is triggered if an external DTD reference is encountered, and any text returned from that call is incorporated into the document as read-only nodes. The return value of the function is a reference to the new DOM hierarchy.

    Errors occur if the DOMImpl property is nil or if an invalid filename is supplied. Other errors are generated by documents that are not well-formed. Check the contents of the ErrorHandler's errorList property to determine the cause of the problem.

NOTE The XDOM parser is a non-validating parser, although it does read and process the external subset of the DTD if this is provided through the OnExternalSubset event.

```
function memoryToDom(const Ptr: Pointer; const Size: Longint): TdomDocument;
    virtual;
procedure DocMemoryToDom(const Ptr: Pointer; const Size: Longint; const pubId,
    sysId: wideString; const RefNode: TdomNode); virtual;
```
  If you already have the XML document in memory, you can use these methods to create the corresponding DOM structure. Supply a pointer to the start of the document, which is assumed to be in UTF-16BE encoding if it starts with $FEFF, in UTF-16LE if it starts with $FFFE, and in UTF-8 encoding otherwise, and the length of the document in bytes. The function version returns a reference to the DOM, while the procedure (also accepting the public and system identifiers if available) takes a reference to a node where the resulting subtree is inserted. An error occurs if the document is not well-formed.

```
function sourceCodeToDom(const IntDtdSourceCode: TXmlSourceCode): TdomDocument;
    virtual;
procedure DocSourceCodeToDom(const DocSourceCode: TXmlSourceCode; const pubId,
    sysId: wideString; const RefNode: TdomNode); virtual;
```
  Similar to the previous methods, these two work from a sequence of TXmlSourceCodePiece objects to construct the DOM. As before, the function returns the DOM itself, while the procedure inserts the DOM under the supplied node.

```
function streamToDom(const Stream: TStream): TdomDocument; virtual;
procedure DocStreamToDom(const Stream: TStream; const pubId, sysId: wideString;
    const RefNode: TdomNode); virtual;
```
  These methods are just like the memoryToDom and DocMemoryToDom ones, except that they read from a stream rather than memory. The same encodings are assumed. Once more, the function returns a reference to the DOM, whereas the procedure inserts the new hierarchy beneath the specified node.

```
function stringToDom(const Str: String): TdomDocument; virtual;
procedure DocStringToDom(const Str: string; const pubId, sysId: wideString; const
    RefNode: TdomNode); virtual;
```
  Further methods like memoryToDom and DomMemoryToDom, however these start with a string value, which only contains valid ASCII XML characters. Get the complete DOM from the function version, or have it inserted beneath the given node with the procedure.

```
function wideStringToDom(Str: WideString): TdomDocument; virtual;
procedure DocWideStringToDom(Str: WideString; const pubId, sysId: wideString;
    const RefNode: TdomNode); virtual;
```
  The last in the series, these methods read from a WideString value encoded with UTF-16BE to produce the DOM. The function returns the DOM itself, while the procedure inserts the new nodes beneath the specified one.

```
procedure ExtDtdMemoryToDom(const Ptr: Pointer; const Size: Longint; const pubId,
    sysId: wideString; const RefNode: TdomNode); virtual;
```
  Parse the contents of an external DTD subset through this method, reading the document from memory. The resulting DOM structure is inserted into the supplied node. The XDOM

package does not follow the XML specification exactly here, only resolving parameter entities in places where they might appear in an internal subset.

procedure ExtDtdSourceCodeToDom(const ExtDtdSourceCode: TXmlSourceCode; const pubId, sysId: wideString; const RefNode: TdomNode); virtual;
Similar to `ExtDtdMemoryToDom` except that the document comes from a sequence of `TXmlSourceCodePiece` objects.

procedure ExtDtdStreamToDom(const Stream: TStream; const pubId, sysId: wideString; const RefNode: TdomNode); virtual;
Another version, reading from a stream to create the external subset.

procedure ExtDtdStringToDom(const Str: string; const pubId, sysId: wideString; const RefNode: TdomNode); virtual;
Process the supplied string value to extract the external subset.

procedure ExtDtdWideStringToDom(Str: WideString; const pubId, sysId: wideString; const RefNode: TdomNode); virtual;
Generate the external subset from the supplied `WideString` value.

procedure IntDtdMemoryToDom(const Ptr: Pointer; const Size: Longint; const pubId, sysId: wideString; const RefNode: TdomNode); virtual;
This method processes the indicated memory to derive an internal DTD subset and inserts it into the specified node.

procedure IntDtdSourceCodeToDom(const IntDtdSourceCode: TXmlSourceCode; const pubId, sysId: wideString; const RefNode: TdomNode); virtual;
Build the internal subset from the sequence of `TXmlSourceCodePiece` objects supplied.

procedure IntDtdStreamToDom(const Stream: TStream; const pubId, sysId: wideString; const RefNode: TdomNode); virtual;
Read the stream specified and generate the internal subset from it.

procedure IntDtdStringToDom(const Str: string; const pubId, sysId: wideString; const RefNode: TdomNode); virtual;
Use the supplied string value to construct the internal subset.

procedure IntDtdWideStringToDom(Str: WideString; const pubId, sysId: wideString; const RefNode: TdomNode); virtual;
This method builds the internal subset from the contents of the given `WideString`.

Helper Functions

A large number of helper functions are defined in the XDOM package that you can use in your own code.

function XMLExtractPrefix(const qualifiedName: wideString): wideString;
Extract the prefix from a qualified name with this function. For example, it returns the `math` part of the name `math:plus`. An exception occurs if the supplied name is malformed.

```
function XMLExtractLocalName(const qualifiedName: wideString): wideString;
```
Conversely, retrieve the local part of a qualified name with this function. For example, it returns the plus part of the name math:plus. An exception occurs if the supplied name is malformed.

The following functions test whether or not the given character is of a particular type as defined by the XML specification. Each returns True if the character is in the appropriate set, and False otherwise.

```
function IsXmlChar(const S: WideChar): boolean;
function IsXmlWhiteSpace(const S: WideChar): boolean;
function IsXmlLetter(const S: WideChar): boolean;
function IsXmlBaseChar(const S: WideChar): boolean;
function IsXmlIdeographic(const S: WideChar): boolean;
function IsXmlCombiningChar(const S: WideChar): boolean;
function IsXmlDigit(const S: WideChar): boolean;
function IsXmlExtender(const S: WideChar): boolean;
function IsXmlNameChar(const S: WideChar): boolean;
function IsXmlPubidChar(const S: WideChar): boolean;
```

The next set of functions check whether a particular string conforms to the various formats defined in the XML specification. Each returns True if the string matches the appropriate definition, and False otherwise.

```
function IsXmlS(const S: WideString): boolean;
function IsXmlName(const S: WideString): boolean;
function IsXmlNames(const S: WideString): boolean;
function IsXmlNmtoken(const S: WideString): boolean;
function IsXmlNmtokens(const S: WideString): boolean;
function IsXmlCharRef(const S: WideString): boolean;
function IsXmlEntityRef(const S: WideString): boolean;
function IsXmlPEReference(const S: WideString): boolean;
function IsXmlReference(const S: WideString): boolean;
function IsXmlEntityValue(const S: WideString): boolean;
function IsXmlAttValue(const S: WideString): boolean;
function IsXmlSystemLiteral(const S: WideString): boolean;
function IsXmlPubidLiteral(const S: WideString): boolean;
function IsXmlCData(const S: WideString): boolean;
function IsXmlCharData(const S: WideString): boolean;
function IsXmlPITarget(const S: WideString): boolean;
function IsXmlVersionNum(const S: WideString): boolean;
function IsXmlEncName(const S: WideString): boolean;
function IsXmlStringType(const S: WideString): boolean;
function IsXmlTokenizedType(const S: WideString): boolean;
```

Similar to the previous functions, this set tests a string's conformance to the named XML-namespace types, as defined in the XML specification. Each returns True if the string matches the specification, and False otherwise.

```
function IsXmlNCNameChar(const s: WideChar): boolean;
function IsXmlNCName(const S: WideString): boolean;
function IsXmlDefaultAttName(const S: WideString): boolean;
function IsXmlPrefixedAttName(const S: WideString): boolean;
function IsXmlNSAttName(const S: WideString): boolean;
function IsXmlLocalPart(const S: WideString): boolean;
function IsXmlPrefix(const S: WideString): boolean;
function IsXmlQName(const S: WideString): boolean;
```

The following functions provide conversion abilities.

`function ResolveCharRefs(const S: WideString): wideString;`
Given a string containing character entity references, the returned string has these replaced by their actual characters. An error occurs if the string contains a malformed reference or an invalid character.

`function XmlIntToCharRef(const value: integer): wideString;`
Convert an integer value into the corresponding character reference.

`function XmlCharRefToInt(const S: WideString): integer;`
Extract the equivalent integer value from a character reference, &#n; or &#xhh;. If the character reference is invalid, an error occurs.

`function XmlCharRefToStr(const S: WideString): WideString;`
Convert the given character reference to its corresponding string value. An error occurs if the character reference is invalid.

`function XmlStrToCharRef(const S: WideString): WideString;`
Return the sequence of character references that equate to the supplied string value. If an invalid character is encountered, an error occurs.

The following functions convert from the named character set to UTF-16 encoding. Either a single character or an entire string is transformed. Errors occur if invalid sequences in the original encoding are encountered.

```
function Iso8859_1ToUTF16Char(const P: Char):WideChar;
function Iso8859_2ToUTF16Char(const P: Char):WideChar;
function Iso8859_3ToUTF16Char(const P: Char):WideChar;
function Iso8859_4ToUTF16Char(const P: Char):WideChar;
function Iso8859_5ToUTF16Char(const P: Char):WideChar;
function Iso8859_6ToUTF16Char(const P: Char):WideChar;
function Iso8859_7ToUTF16Char(const P: Char):WideChar;
function Iso8859_8ToUTF16Char(const P: Char):WideChar;
function Iso8859_9ToUTF16Char(const P: Char):WideChar;
function Iso8859_10ToUTF16Char(const P: Char):WideChar;
function Iso8859_13ToUTF16Char(const P: Char):WideChar;
function Iso8859_14ToUTF16Char(const P: Char):WideChar;
function Iso8859_15ToUTF16Char(const P: Char):WideChar;
function KOI8_RToUTF16Char(const P: Char):WideChar;
function cp10000_MacRomanToUTF16Char(const P: Char):WideChar;
function cp1251ToUTF16Char(const P: Char):WideChar;
function Iso8859_1ToUTF16Str(const s: string):WideString;
function Iso8859_2ToUTF16Str(const s: string):WideString;
function Iso8859_3ToUTF16Str(const s: string):WideString;
function Iso8859_4ToUTF16Str(const s: string):WideString;
function Iso8859_5ToUTF16Str(const s: string):WideString;
function Iso8859_6ToUTF16Str(const s: string):WideString;
function Iso8859_7ToUTF16Str(const s: string):WideString;
function Iso8859_8ToUTF16Str(const s: string):WideString;
function Iso8859_9ToUTF16Str(const s: string):WideString;
function Iso8859_10ToUTF16Str(const s: string):WideString;
function Iso8859_13ToUTF16Str(const s: string):WideString;
function Iso8859_14ToUTF16Str(const s: string):WideString;
function Iso8859_15ToUTF16Str(const s: string):WideString;
function KOI8_RToUTF16Str(const s: string):WideString;
function cp10000_MacRomanToUTF16Str(const s: string):WideString;
```

function UTF8ToUTF16BEStr(const s: string): WideString;
: Convert from a UTF-8 encoded string to UTF-16BE encoding. An error occurs if an invalid UTF-8 sequence is found.

function UTF16BEToUTF8Str(const ws: WideString; const expandLF: boolean): string;
: Going the opposite way, return the UTF-8 equivalent to the supplied UTF-16BE string, expanding line feeds to the combination of carriage returns and line feeds if the `expandLF` parameter is `True`. If the original string contains an invalid UTF-16BE sequence, an error occurs.

function Utf16HighSurrogate(const value: integer): WideChar;
: Retrieve the high surrogate character for the given code (in the range $10000 to $10FFFF). This allows for the encoding of characters in this range in UTF-16BE. An error occurs if the value is outside the nominated range.

function Utf16LowSurrogate(const value: integer): WideChar;
: Similar to the above function, this returns the low surrogate character. It has the same restrictions as above.

function Utf16SurrogateToInt(const highSurrogate, lowSurrogate: WideChar): integer;
: Going back the other way, this function converts from the high and low surrogate characters to the original code value. If the surrogates are not in their respective ranges ($D800 to $DBFF for the high one, $DC00 to $DFFF for the low), an error occurs.

function IsUtf16HighSurrogate(const S: WideChar): boolean;
: Test whether a character is a high surrogate with this function. It returns `True` if the character is in the appropriate range, and `False` otherwise.

function IsUtf16LowSurrogate(const S: WideChar): boolean;
: Similarly, this function tests for the low surrogate range.

function XMLNormalizeLineBreaks(const source :WideString): WideString;
: Convert carriage returns, or carriage returns and line feeds, into single line feeds with this function.

procedure XMLAnalyzePCDATA(Source: widestring; var Lines: TStringList);
: This procedure parses the supplied string and returns a string list where each entry contains either all white space characters, or all non-white space characters.

procedure XMLAnalyzeTag(const Source: WideString; var TagName, AttribSequence: WideString);
: This procedure retrieves the tag name and set of attributes from the supplied string. The tag name is all the text from the start of the string to the first white space character (or the end of the string). The attributes comprise the remainder of the string (if any), stripped of leading and trailing white space.

procedure XMLAnalyseEntityDef(Source: WideString; var EntityValue, SystemLiteral,
    PubidLiteral, NDataName: WideString; var Error: boolean);
    Parse out the contents of an entity definition, returning the entity value, or its system and public identifiers, and optional data type. The Error parameter returns True if the definition is malformed, and False if everything is OK.

procedure XMLAnalyseNotationDecl(const Decl: WideString; var SystemLiteral,
    PubidLiteral: WideString; var Error: boolean);
    This procedure parses out a notation definition, returning the system and public identifiers, and a flag indicating any errors.

procedure XMLIsolateQuote(Source: WideString; var content, rest: WideString; var
    QuoteType: WideChar; var Error: boolean);
    After stripping off leading white space, this procedure expects to see a single (') or double quote ("), returning this as QuoteType. It then searches for the corresponding closing quote, and returns the intervening characters as content. Any remaining characters in the string appear in rest. An error is signaled if no quote is found at the beginning, if there is no matching end quote, or if the end quote is followed by a non-white space character.

function XMLTrunc(const Source: WideString): WideString;
    This function removes leading and trailing white space.

procedure XMLTruncAngularBrackets(const Source: WideString; var content:
    WideString; var Error: boolean);
    After removing leading or trailing white space, this procedure then strips off a set of leading and trailing square brackets ([ ]). An error is signaled if both brackets are not found.

procedure XMLTruncRoundBrackets(const Source: WideString; var content: WideString;
    var Error: boolean);
    Similar to the previous procedure, this one expects parentheses. Again, an error is flagged if they are not present.

function XMLAnalysePubSysId(const PublicId, SystemId, NotaName: WideString):
    WideString;
    This function validates the formats of the supplied identifiers and notation name, before returning the formatted definition using these values, such as SYSTEM "http://www.starwars.com/episode-i/" NDATA HTML. Errors occur if the values are invalid.

Viewing with the Open XML DOM

For a comparison with the other DOM implementations, you can write the same XML document viewer that you saw earlier using the XDOM package. Since this package is written in Delphi, obtaining and using the necessary objects is very straightforward. The steps to take are:

1. Create an instance of the parser `TXmlToDomParser`.

2. Create an instance of the DOM implementation `TDomImplementation`.

3. Attach the implementation object to the parser so that the latter can construct an appropriate document, followed by the necessary node types.

4. Parse the XML document by using the `FileToDOM` method, supplying the filename to be loaded.

5. Work with the resulting DOM returned by the parse process. From here you can navigate down through the hierarchy to reach all the nodes generated from the text document.

6. When you have finished, free up the implementation and parser.

All of this is shown in the `LoadDoc` method from the viewer (see Listing 11-44). The remainder of the code here initializes the viewer GUI and loads the DOM structure into a tree view for you.

Listing 11-44: Loading a document with the Open XML DOM

```
{ Load an XML document }
procedure TfrmXMLViewer.LoadDoc(Filename: string);
var
  XMLParser: TXmlToDomParser;
  XMLImpl: TDomImplementation;
begin
  pgcDetails.ActivePage := tshDocument;
  { Initialise document-wide details for display }
  InitDocumentDetails;
  { Load the source document }
  memSource.Lines.LoadFromFile(Filename);
  dlgOpen.Filename := Filename;
  { Instantiate the DOM }
  XMLParser          := TXmlToDomParser.Create(Self);
  XMLImpl            := TDomImplementation.Create(Self);
  trvXML.Items.BeginUpdate;
  try
    XMLParser.DomImpl          := XMLImpl;
    XMLParser.OnExternalSubset := ExternalSubset;
    { Parse the document and add the structure to the tree view }
    AddElementToTree(XMLParser.FileToDOM(Filename), nil);
    trvXML.Items[0].Expand(False);
  finally
    trvXML.Items.EndUpdate;
    XMLParser.Free;
    XMLImpl.Free;
  end;
end;
```

You will notice that a handler is attached to the parser's `OnExternalSubset` event. This lets you retrieve an external DTD and return it to the parser. The parser then incorporates its contents into the DOM under the `ExternalSubset` node of the document type node. See Listing 11-45 for the implementation of this handler. It receives the system identifier for the DTD (a filename) and uses this to read the contents of that file into the `extSubset` parameter, which returns to the caller.

Listing 11-45: Retrieving an external DTD

```
{ Supply the external DTD }
procedure TfrmXMLViewer.ExternalSubset(Sender: TObject;
  const PublicId, SystemId: WideString; var extSubset: WideString);
var
  stmDTD: TFileStream;
  stmString: TStringStream;
begin
  stmDTD    := TFileStream.Create(SystemId, fmOpenRead);
  stmString := TStringStream.Create('');
  try
    stmString.CopyFrom(stmDTD, 0);
    extSubset := stmString.DataString;
  finally
    stmString.Free;
    stmDTD.Free;
  end;
end;
```

NOTE Even though the XDOM parser loads the external DTD, it does not validate XML documents. It simply tests them for being well-formed.

The main part of the viewer is the `AddElementToTree` procedure that recursively steps down through the DOM hierarchy and adds the nodes it encounters to a tree view component, matching the original structure. It is first invoked with the document node and a `nil` representing the root of the tree view. This routine and its supporting ones are shown in Listing 11-46.

Listing 11-46: Processing the Open XML DOM

```
{ Add a TXMLElement to the tree view }
function AddElement(Parent: TTreeNode; Name: string;
  Element: TXMLElement): TTreeNode;
begin
  FList.Add(Element);
  Result := trvXML.Items.AddChildObject(Parent, Name, Element);
  with Result do
  begin
    ImageIndex    := Ord(Element.ElementType);
    SelectedIndex := ImageIndex;
  end;
end;
{ Return true if text is all whitespace, false otherwise }
function SkipWhiteSpace(Text: string): Boolean;
var
  Index: Integer;
begin
  Result := mniSuppressWhitespace.Checked;
  if not Result then
    Exit;
```

```
      for Index := 1 to Length(Text) do
        if not (Text[Index] in [#0..#32]) then
        begin
          Result := False;
          Exit;
        end;
    end;

    { Add current element to the treeview and
      then recurse through children }
    procedure AddElementToTree(Node: TdomNode; TreeParent: TTreeNode);
    var
      Index, Index2: Integer;
      DisplayName, DisplayValue: string;
      NewNode: TTreeNode;
      Attribs: TStringList;
    begin
      { Generate name for display in the tree }
      if Node.NodeType in
        [ntText_Node, ntComment_Node, ntCDATA_Section_Node] then
      begin
        if Length(Node.NodeValue) > 20 then
          DisplayName := Copy(Node.NodeValue, 1, 17) + '...'
        else
          DisplayName := Node.NodeValue;
      end
      else
        DisplayName := Node.NodeName;
      { Create storage for later display of node values }
      case Node.NodeType of
        ntElement_Node:
          with Node as TdomElement do
          begin
            Attribs := TStringList.Create;
            try
              for Index := 0 to Node.Attributes.Length - 1 do
                with Node.Attributes.Item(Index) do
                  Attribs.Values[NodeName] := NodeValue;
              NewNode := AddElement(TreeParent, DisplayName,
                TXMLElement.Create(xtElement, TagName, NamespaceURI,
                LocalName, '', Attribs));
            finally
              Attribs.Free;
            end;
          end;
        ntText_Node:
          with Node as TdomText do
            if not SkipWhiteSpace(Data) then
              NewNode := AddElement(TreeParent, DisplayName,
                TXMLElement.Create(xtText, '', '', '', Data, nil));
        ntCDATA_Section_Node:
          with Node as TdomCDATASection do
            if not SkipWhiteSpace(Data) then
              NewNode := AddElement(TreeParent, DisplayName,
                TXMLElement.Create(xtCData, '', '', '', Data, nil));
        ntEntity_Reference_Node:
          with Node as TdomEntityReference do
          begin
            if Assigned(Declaration) then
            begin
```

```
          if Declaration.IsInternalEntity then
            DisplayValue := Declaration.NodeValue
          else
            DisplayValue := Declaration.Value;
        end
        else
          DisplayValue := '';
        NewNode := AddElement(TreeParent, DisplayName,
          TXMLElement.Create(xtEntityRef, NodeName, '', '',
          DisplayValue, nil));
      end;
    ntProcessing_Instruction_Node:
      with Node as TdomProcessingInstruction do
        NewNode := AddElement(TreeParent, DisplayName,
          TXMLElement.Create(xtInstruction, Target, '', '',
          Data, nil));
    ntComment_Node:
      with Node as TdomComment do
        NewNode := AddElement(TreeParent, DisplayName,
          TXMLElement.Create(xtComment, '', '', '', Data, nil));
    ntDocument_Node:
      with Node as TdomDocument do
      begin
        edtSystemId.Text := FileName;
        NewNode := AddElement(TreeParent, XMLDocDesc,
          TXMLElement.Create(xtDocument, XMLDocDesc, '', '',
          '', nil));
      end;
    ntXML_Declaration_Node:
      with Node as TdomXmlDeclaration do
      begin
        edtVersion.Text      := VersionNumber;
        edtEncoding.Text     := EncodingDecl;
        cbxStandAlone.Checked := (UpperCase(SDDecl) = YesValue);
        DisplayValue         := 'versior="' + VersionNumber + '"';
        if EncodingDecl <> '' then
          DisplayValue := DisplayValue + ' encoding="' +
            EncodingDecl + '"';
        if UpperCase(SDDecl) = YesValue then
          DisplayValue := DisplayValue + ' standalone="' +
            SDDecl + '"';
        NewNode := AddElement(TreeParent, 'xml', TXMLElement.Create(
          xtInstruction, 'xml', '', '', DisplayValue, nil));
      end;
    ntDocument_Type_Node:
      with Node as TdomDocumentType do
      begin
        edtDocType.Text := Name;
        NewNode := AddElement(TreeParent, DTDDesc,
          TXMLElement.Create(xtDTD, DTDDesc, '', '', Name, nil));
      end;
    ntInternal_Subset_Node, ntExternal_Subset_Node:
      NewNode := AddElement(TreeParent, Node.NodeName,
        TXMLElement.Create(xtEntityRef, Node.NodeName, '', '',
        '', nil));
    ntEntity_Declaration_Node:
      with Node as TdomEntityDeclaration, stgEntities do
        if NotationName <> '' then
        begin
          if Cells[0, RowCount - 1] <> '' then
```

```
            RowCount := RowCount + 1;
        Cells[0, RowCount - 1] := NodeName;
        Cells[1, RowCount - 1] := PublicId;
        Cells[2, RowCount - 1] := SystemId;
        Cells[3, RowCount - 1] := NotationName;
      end
      else
      begin
        if IsInternalEntity then
          DisplayValue := NodeValue
        else
          DisplayValue := Value;
        NewNode := AddElement(TreeParent, DisplayName,
          TXMLElement.Create(xtEntityRef, NodeName, '', '',
          DisplayValue, nil));
      end;
ntNotation_Declaration_Node:
  with Node as TdomNotationDeclaration, stgNotations do
  begin
    if Cells[0, RowCount - 1] <> '' then
      RowCount := RowCount + 1;
    Cells[0, RowCount - 1] := NodeName;
    Cells[1, RowCount - 1] := PublicId;
    Cells[2, RowCount - 1] := SystemId;
  end;
ntElement_Type_Declaration_Node:
  with Node as TdomElementTypeDeclaration do
    NewNode := AddElement(TreeParent, DisplayName,
      TXMLElement.Create(xtElementDecl, NodeName, '', '',
      Value, nil));
ntAttribute_List_Node:
  with Node as TdomAttrList do
  begin
    Attribs := TStringList.Create;
    try
      for Index := 0 to AttributeDefinitions.Length - 1 do
        with AttributeDefinitions.Item(Index) as
          TdomAttrDefinition do
          begin
            if HasChildNodes then
            begin
              DisplayValue := '';
              for Index2 := 0 to ChildNodes.Length - 1 do
                DisplayValue := DisplayValue + '|' +
                  ChildNodes.Item(Index2).Code;
              DisplayValue := '(' + Copy(DisplayValue, 2,
                Length(DisplayValue) - 1) + ')';
            end
            else
              DisplayValue := AttributeType;
            Attribs.Values[Name] := DisplayValue + ' ' +
              DefaultDeclaration;
          end;
      NewNode := AddElement(TreeParent, DisplayName,
        TXMLElement.Create(xtAttributeDecl, NodeName, '', '',
        '', Attribs));
    finally
      Attribs.Free;
    end;
  end;
```

```
      else
      begin
        NewNode := TreeParent;
        OutputDebugString(PChar(DisplayName + ' ' +
          IntToStr(Ord(Node.NodeType)) + ' ' +
          IntToStr(Node.ChildNodes.Length)));
      end;
    end;
    { And recurse through children }
    if Node.HasChildNodes then
      for Index := 0 to Node.ChildNodes.Length - 1 do
        AddElementToTree(Node.ChildNodes.Item(Index), NewNode);
  end;
```

As with the previous viewers, the first step is to build a displayable name for the node being processed. For text type nodes, up to 20 characters from the text itself are used, whereas for the other nodes you retrieve the full node name. Then you use the node type to determine what other processing needs to be performed on it.

Elements have their attributes extracted and placed into a string list, indexed by their names. This list is added to a TXMLElement object along with the original element's name (in all forms) and a flag denoting it as an element node. The TXMLElement object is used internally in the viewer to hold details about nodes for later viewing when selected from the tree view (see Figure 11-2).

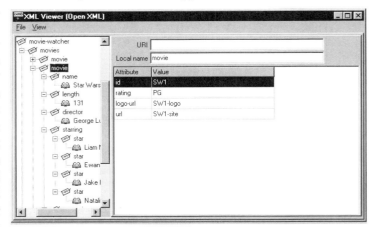

Figure 11-2: An element's details in the viewer.

Text, CDATA section, and comment nodes carry only their text content over to the TXMLElement object, plus a flag indicating their node type. See Figure 11-3 for an example of a text node following loading. Processing instruction nodes supply these values and add the target of the command. Entity reference nodes retrieve the value of that entity through their Declaration properties, before adding it to the tree with

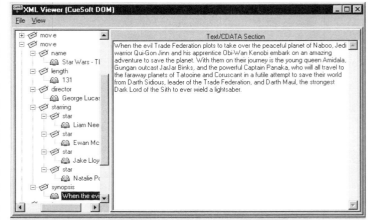

Figure 11-3: The contents of a text node.

the entity name. Note how each node is cast to its actual type, allowing you access to its specific properties.

The document node itself creates a tree node with a predefined name, XML Document. Various details about the document overall appear on the information page displayed when the document node is selected in the tree view (see Figure 11-4). Similarly, the document type node also has a preset name, DTD, while its internal and external subset nodes use the names given by the DOM. The XML declaration node supplies values to various fields on the document details page of the viewer, as well as becoming an "instruction" entry in the tree.

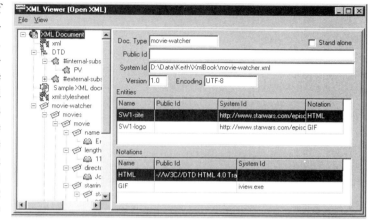

Figure 11-4: The document details in the viewer.

The content of the DTD comes from the following nodes:

- Entity declarations are checked to determine whether or not they are unparsed entities. If unparsed, their details are directed to the grid on the document page of the viewer. Parsed entities appear in the body of the tree, with their value set as the text to be displayed.

- Notation declarations are also sent to the grid on the document page.

- Element declarations appear beneath the internal or external subset nodes with their name and their content model as data, the latter coming from the Value property. Attribute declarations arrive within an attribute list node, from which you retrieve the element name. You then step through all of the node's children to retrieve the attributes themselves. The attribute type comes from the AttributeType property, or from children of the attribute itself if an enumerated value is specified. Each attribute's details are accumulated into a string list, indexed by the

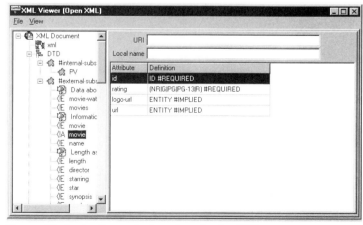

Figure 11-5: Attribute declarations in the DTD.

attribute name. This list then is attached to the TXMLElement node for the entire attribute list for that element (as shown in Figure 11-5).

Any remaining node types are ignored for this application, but are noted in the debugging output log by their name, node type, and number of children.

Finally, all the child nodes of the current one are processed in turn, handing them off to this same routine. Note that the tree node passed to this recursive call is the one just created for the parent node, thus maintaining the DOM structure within the tree view.

Summary

The XDOM package is an open source, native Delphi implementation of the DOM specification. It follows the DOM Level 2 spec very closely with additions where necessary to make the suite more usable.

Its biggest difference from the other DOMs described previously is its extensive support for the document type node and its internal and external subsets. With this package you can retrieve or create the entire document, including the DTD sections omitted from the other DOMs, and the XML specification itself.

Being written in Delphi means that you can compile it directly into your program without having to worry about the availability of external DLLs. Having the source with the package lets you trace through it, if necessary, to follow the processing of your documents.

The underlying parser for the XDOM package is SAX-like and can be used on its own or wrapped in the SAX interfaces. (This is left as an exercise for the reader.)

Future developments for XDOM include support for document validation and separating the DTD content models from the rest of the tree. Quite possibly these will have been implemented by the time you read this. Check it out at the Open XML Web site.

Part III
Simple API for XML

The Document Object Model discussed in Part II presents the XML document as a hierarchy of nodes in memory. You can instantly navigate to any node within the tree and work with it. The model can be updated by adding new nodes or deleting existing ones. New documents can be built from scratch. All this requires is the DOM to load in the entire document and have it available on request.

To reduce memory usage, you can use the Simple API for XML instead. It presents the XML document as a series of events to which you can respond. Thus, it only needs resources for a single node at a time. For large documents this can be a great saving. It is also useful if you are only interested in a small portion of the document, such as one subtree or only one type of element. SAX lets you easily focus on just these parts and work with them.

The DOM lets you alter the document structure in memory and most implementations let you write out the new document. SAX, however, creates no such structure and only lets you read the document (or parts thereof), though you could create handlers to do these things.

Chapter 12 looks at the SAX specification itself. It describes each of the interfaces and classes that make up the functionality. By defining SAX as interfaces only, their implementation is left open. Although the reference version of SAX is written in Java, other languages can also be used, such as Delphi.

Chapter 13 examines Microsoft's SAX offering. As part of the latest MSXML package you get a SAX2-compliant parser. You can then write whatever handlers you desire to interact with it.

Chapter 14 presents a native Delphi implementation of SAX. As well as translating the interfaces into Delphi, you can build a simple parser and an application that uses it.

Chapter 15 combines these two versions by wrapping the Microsoft SAX parser in the Delphi interfaces. This lets you easily swap between the two implementations with a single line of code, demonstrating one of the tenets of SAX in that you do not have to rewrite your application to take advantage of different versions.

Chapter 12: Simple API for XML (SAX)
Chapter 13: Microsoft's SAX Parser
Chapter 14: SAX in Delphi
Chapter 15: Wrapping External Parsers

Chapter 12
Simple API for XML (SAX)

An alternate method of processing XML documents was developed by the XML-DEV mailing list under the leadership of David Megginson. Instead of constructing an object model that corresponds to the entire structure within a document, they proposed an event-based approach that triggered certain actions whenever a new element or piece of content was encountered in parsing the document. Details of the standard and a Java implementation are available at http://www.megginson.com/SAX/ and are included on the CD-ROM that accompanies this book.

One of the main benefits of this approach is that you do not have to build the entire object model in memory. This can be very important for large documents, especially when only a small portion of the document is actually required for processing.

Since the original release of SAX in May 1998, the specification has been revised and enhanced, with version 2 being released in May 2000. Several of the original interfaces have been discontinued (deprecated) in favor of newer offerings with more functionality. The main additions to the design have been support for namespaces within the document, and extra events for lexical elements such as the DTD, comments, and CDATA sections.

Working with SAX

When working with SAX, you typically already have a compliant parser (called a *reader* in SAX2 since it implements the `XMLReader` interface) supplied by a third party, along with implementations of the basic helper classes defined in SAX. Given an XML document, the reader scans it to extract the various text tokens that make it up, such as entity declarations, element tags, text, and comments. As it does this, it makes callbacks to a number of registered *handlers*, similar to the way event handlers work in Delphi. In fact, each callback is known as an *event*.

The abilities of these handlers are defined by a number of interfaces. To react to the events that the reader produces, you would usually write your own class that implements the `ContentHandler` interface (which deals with basic elements and text). After registering this with the reader, you would parse the document and receive event notifications through method calls to your class. For example, for each block of text encountered, the `characters` method is invoked.

In many circumstances you would also write a class that implements the `ErrorHandler` interface to deal with any problems that arise during the parse process. To receive more details about the document, you could create and register classes that implement the `DTDHandler`, `DeclHandler`, and/or `LexicalHandler` interfaces. Since these are all interfaces, you could write just the one class that implements them all, and register it with the reader under each category.

SAX Elements

SAX defines several interfaces to encapsulate its functionality, along with a few classes and exceptions. Specifying only an interface makes it much easier to provide alternate implementations of the API. This is important since you usually implement at least one of the interfaces that responds to the SAX events for each application.

Furthermore, restricting the interactions to an interface allows the different parts of the implementation to be decoupled; each part's knowledge of the other parts is limited so that each can evolve independently. This allows you to create a handler that works with one compliant parser, and expect to have it work, without any changes, with another compliant parser. As new technologies appear you can replace the appropriate pieces without breaking the rest of the application. Once you have a suitable parser, you can easily write any number of handlers to respond to it. You may even be able to reuse handlers across a number of projects.

All the definitions that make up SAX are shown in Table 12-1, along with the version in which they are defined (version 1, version 2, or extensions to version 2).

Table 12-1: SAX definitions

SAX Item	Type	Vers.	Purpose
AttributeList	Interface	1	Provide access to a list of attribute details (deprecated in favor of Attributes)
Attributes	Interface	2	Provide access to a list of attribute details, including support for namespaces
ContentHandler	Interface	2	Process elements and content from the document as they are encountered
DeclHandler	Interface	2x	Provide notification of additional declarations within the document's DTD (a SAX2 extension)
DefaultHandler	Class	2	Provide a default implementation of the handler interfaces
DocumentHandler	Interface	1	Process elements and content from the document as they are encountered (deprecated in favor of ContentHandler)
DTDHandler	Interface	1	Deal with unparsed entities and notations from the DTD
EntityResolver	Interface	1	Resolve references to external entities

SAX Item	Type	Vers.	Purpose
ErrorHandler	Interface	1	Deal with errors that may arise during processing
HandlerBase	Class	1	Provide a default implementation of the handler interfaces (deprecated in favor of DefaultHandler)
InputSource	Class	1	Encapsulate the retrieval and supply of a resource
LexicalHandler	Interface	2x	Provide notification of additional lexical constructions within the document (a SAX2 extension)
Locator	Interface	1	Provide details on the current position within the document while parsing
Parser	Interface	1	Perform the parsing process and interact with the handler interfaces as necessary (deprecated in favor of XMLReader)
ParserAdapter	Class	2	Wrap a SAX1 Parser to make it act like a SAX2 XMLReader
ParserFactory	Class	1	Create instances of a default or named parser
SAXException	Exception	1	A general exception to flag all problems during SAX operations
SAXNotRecognizedException	Exception	2	Flag an unknown feature or property of the XML reader
SAXNotSupportedException	Exception	2	Flag a known feature or property that is not supported
SAXParseException	Exception	1	Flag an error during the parse process that includes location information
XMLFilter	Interface	2	Filter events from an XMLReader before passing them on to a handler
XMLReader	Interface	2	Perform the parsing process and interact with the handler interfaces as necessary
XMLReaderAdapter	Class	2	Wrap a SAX2 XMLReader to make it act like a SAX1 Parser

As an example, processing of the document shown in Listing 12-1 through a SAX reader may result in the stream of events shown in Listing 12-2. Having each handler method respond to the event by writing out the method name and its parameters could produce this output.

Listing 12-1: A sample XML document

```
<?xml version="1.0" encoding="UTF-8"?>
<!DOCTYPE movie-watcher SYSTEM "movie-watcher.dtd" [
  <!NOTATION HTML PUBLIC "-//W3C//DTD HTML 4.0 Transitional//EN">
  <!NOTATION GIF SYSTEM "iview.exe">
  <!ENTITY SW1-site SYSTEM "http://www.starwars.com/episode-i/"
    NDATA HTML>
```

```
    <!ENTITY SW1-logo SYSTEM
      "http://www.starwars.com/episode-i/palpatine/img/top_logo.gif"
      NDATA GIF>
    <!ENTITY PV "Pleasantville">
]>
<!-- Sample XML document with data about movies
     and when and where they are showing
     Developed by Keith Wood, 28 May 1999 -->
<?xml:stylesheet type="text/xsl" href="movie-watcher.xsl"?>
<movie-watcher>
  <movies>
    <movie id="SW1" rating="PG" logo-url="SW1-logo" url="SW1-site">
      <name>Star Wars-The Phantom Menace</name>
      <length>131</length>
      <director>George Lucas</director>
      <starring>
        <star>Liam Neeson</star>
        <star>Ewan McGregor</star>
        <star>Jake Lloyd</star>
        <star>Natalie Portman</star>
      </starring>
      <synopsis>When the evil Trade Federation plots to take over the
        peaceful planet of Naboo, Jedi warrior Qui-Gon Jinn and his
        apprentice Obi-Wan Kenobi embark on an amazing adventure to
        save the planet. With them on their journey is the young queen
        Amidala, Gungan outcast JarJar Binks, and the powerful Captain
        Panaka, who will all travel to the faraway planets of Tatooine
        and Coruscant in a futile attempt to save their world from
        Darth Sidious, leader of the Trade Federation, and Darth Maul,
        the strongest Dark Lord of the Sith to ever wield a lightsaber.
      </synopsis>
    </movie>
  </movies>
</movie-watcher>
```

Listing 12-2: SAX events from parsing the XML document

```
Start document
Start DTD
Notation declaration    - HTML
Notation declaration    - GIF
Unparsed entity         - SW1-site
Unparsed entity         - SW1-logo
Internal entity         - PV
End DTD
Comment
Processing instruction - xml:stylesheet
Start element          - movie-watcher
Characters             - white space
Start element          - movies
Characters             - white space
Start element          - movie
Characters             - white space
Start element          - name
Characters             - Star Wars...
End element            - name
Characters             - white space
Start element          - length
Characters             - 131
End element            - length
Characters             - white space
```

```
        Start element       - director
        Characters          - George Lucas
        End element         - director
        Characters          - white space
        Start element       - starring
        Characters          - white space
        Start element       - star
        Characters          - Liam Neeson
        End element         - star
        Characters          - white space
        Start element       - star
        Characters          - Ewan McGregor
        End element         - star
        Characters          - white space
        Start element       - star
        Characters          - Jake Lloyd
        End element         - star
        Characters          - white space
        Start element       - star
        Characters          - Natalie Portman
        End element         - star
        Characters          - white space
        End element         - starring
        Characters          - white space
        Start element       - synopsis
        Characters          - When the evil Trade Federation...
        End element         - synopsis
        Characters          - white space
        End element         - movie
        Characters          - white space
        End element         - movies
        Characters          - white space
        End element         - movie-watcher
        End document
```

Further discussions of these interfaces, classes, and exceptions follow. Items that are defined in SAX1 but that have been replaced in SAX2 are not described. The remaining items from SAX1 are discussed as they are still used under the newer version. The reference SAX implementation is written in Java and the declarations shown below come from that package.

SAXException Class

The `SAXException` class enables you to easily identify all those errors arising from processing with SAX. Error handlers can look for this type of error and process them accordingly.

This exception extends the base `Exception` class and adds the ability to wrap a "normal" exception, one that is not derived from `SAXException`. Doing this allows you to identify these errors as having been generated by the parsing activity, while retaining the details of the underlying problem.

The definition of this class appears in Listing 12-3. It provides the abilities described above, as well as several overloaded constructors that accept the various error components.

Listing 12-3: The SAXException class

```
public class SAXException extends Exception {
  public SAXException (String message);
  public SAXException (Exception e);
  public SAXException (String message, Exception e);
  public String getMessage ();
  public Exception getException ();
  public String toString ();
}
```

A description of the SAXException class's methods follows:

public SAXException (String message);
public SAXException (Exception e);
public SAXException (String message, Exception e);

> The constructors for this class allow you to create an exception with only a message, one wrapping another exception, or one that wraps an exception but supplies a different message.

public String getMessage ();

> This method retrieves the text description of the exception. It returns the specific message for this exception, if one was supplied, or the message from an embedded exception otherwise.

public Exception getException ();

> If this exception wraps another one, this method returns that embedded exception. Otherwise it returns null.

public String toString ();

> The standard Java method that returns some description of the class.

SAX2 introduces two new defined exceptions: SAXNotRecognizedException and SAXNotSupportedException. Both are used when dealing with features and properties of XML readers. If the reader does not know about a feature or property, the first exception is raised. If the feature or property is known but cannot be handled by the reader, it raises the second exception. Both of these are derived directly from SAXException and add no other functionality.

SAXParseException Class

The SAXParseException class extends the basic SAX exception to provide location information within the document. The definition of this class appears in Listing 12-4. It provides the abilities described above, as well as numerous overloaded constructors that accept the various error components.

Listing 12-4: The SAXParseException class

```
public class SAXParseException extends SAXException {
  public SAXParseException (String message, Locator locator);
  public SAXParseException (String message, Locator locator,
    Exception e);
  public SAXParseException (String message, String publicId,
```

```
         String systemId, int lineNumber, int columnNumber);
    public SAXParseException (String message, String publicId,
         String systemId, int lineNumber, int columnNumber, Exception e);
    public String getPublicId ();
    public String getSystemId ();
    public int getLineNumber ();
    public int getColumnNumber ();
}
```

The methods of the SAXParseException class are described below:

```
public SAXParseException (String message, Locator locator);
public SAXParseException (String message, Locator locator, Exception e);
public SAXParseException (String message, String publicId, String systemId, int
    lineNumber, int columnNumber);
public SAXParseException (String message, String publicId, String systemId, int
    lineNumber, int columnNumber, Exception e);
```
> The constructors for the class let you specify the message and/or wrapped exception (just like SAXException), along with positional information in the form of a Locator or the document identifiers and line and column numbers.

`public String getPublicId ();`
> Returns the public identifier for the document in which the error occurred. If no identifier is available it returns null.

`public String getSystemId ();`
> Finds the system identifier for the document in which the error occurred. A null is returned if no identifier is available.

`public int getLineNumber ();`
> Retrieves the number of the line on which the error occurred or –1 if it is unknown.

`public int getColumnNumber ();`
> Returns the column number within that line at which the error occurred or –1 if unknown.

Exceptions of this type appear in calls to the various ErrorHandler methods (see below). Hopefully, this allows you to identify the problem in the original XML document and correct it.

InputSource Class

The InputSource class (see its Java definition in Listing 12-5) is a helper class within SAX. Its purpose is to do the actual locating and loading of an external entity and to present it as a stream. This class knows how to deal with the Internet (at least using HTTP) to allow for the loading of remote documents. Input sources are used as the result of the EntityResolver.resolveEntity method and as the input for the XMLReader.parse method.

Listing 12-5: The InputSource class declaration

```
public class InputSource {
    public InputSource ();
    public InputSource (String systemId);
    public InputSource (InputStream byteStream);
```

```
    public InputSource (Reader characterStream);
    public void setPublicId (String publicId);
    public String getPublicId ();
    public void setSystemId (String systemId);
    public String getSystemId ();
    public void setByteStream (InputStream byteStream);
    public InputStream getByteStream ();
    public void setEncoding (String encoding);
    public String getEncoding ();
    public void setCharacterStream (Reader characterStream);
    public Reader getCharacterStream ();
}
```

The SAX readers use an InputSource object to determine how to read XML input. If there is a stream available, the reader reads that stream directly; if not, it attempts to open a URL connection to the resource identified by the system identifier. The reader should never modify an InputSource object since it belongs to the application.

A description of the InputSource class's methods follows:

```
public InputSource ();
public InputSource (String systemId);
public InputSource (InputStream byteStream);
public InputSource (Reader characterStream);
```
> The constructors for this class allow you to create an empty source, or one that takes its input from a named resource or a stream.

```
public void setPublicId (String publicId);
public String getPublicId ();
```
> These methods store and retrieve the public (logical) identifier for the document encapsulated by the source object. This value should be set manually after creating the object.

```
public void setSystemId (String systemId);
public String getSystemId ();
```
> The system (physical) identifier for the wrapped document is saved or read by these methods. Again, this should be set manually after construction.

```
public void setByteStream (InputStream byteStream);
public InputStream getByteStream ();
```
> These methods let you store and retrieve the contents of the source as a stream.

```
public void setEncoding (String encoding);
public String getEncoding ();
```
> The encoding, or format, of the embedded stream is available through these methods.

```
public void setCharacterStream (Reader characterStream);
public Reader getCharacterStream ();
```
> An alternative to the byte stream, these methods provide access to the content as an encoded stream.

Locator Interface

The Locator interface, shown in Listing 12-6, defines how to determine the current character position when parsing an XML document. A locator object is passed to a content handler at the start of the parse process. The handler may then refer back to that locator whenever it needs to find the current character position.

Listing 12-6: The Locator interface

```
public interface Locator {
  public abstract String getPublicId ();
  public abstract String getSystemId ();
  public abstract int getLineNumber ();
  public abstract int getColumnNumber ();
}
```

NOTE The results returned by the Locator object are only valid during the scope of each content handler method; the application receives unpredictable results if it attempts to use the locator at any other time.

SAX readers are not required to supply a locator, but they are very strongly encouraged to do so. If the reader supplies a locator, it must do so before reporting any other document events. If no locator has been set by the time the StartDocument event occurs, the application should assume that a locator is not available.

Most often the reader and content handler use the locator object to assist in reporting errors. For example, the content handler may impose further type restrictions on the incoming data than can be specified in XML alone. If the text does not conform, the handler could raise a parse exception and provide to it the location within the document that produced the error. This helps the problem to be traced and resolved by the user.

Frequently, the reader itself implements the Locator interface. Since it already has intimate knowledge of the document under consideration, this is a natural place for it to appear.

The methods of the Locator interface are described below:

public abstract String getPublicId ();
> This method returns the public (logical) identifier for the current document. If the location is not available, it returns a null.

public abstract String getSystemId ();
> The system (physical) identifier for the current document is returned by this method. A null is returned if the location is not available.

public abstract int getLineNumber ();
> Find the current line position within the document with this method. If the information is not available it returns −1.

public abstract int getColumnNumber ();
> Complementing the previous method, this one returns the character position within the line, or −1 if the position is unknown.

Attributes Interface

The `Attributes` interface provides access to a list of the attributes for an element. It is used to pass attribute information to a content handler through the `startElement` event. Details are provided only for attributes that have been set or that have default values (for a validating reader). Attributes that are implied but not specified do not appear.

This interface is defined in SAX2 and replaces the `AttributeList` one from the SAX1 specification. It adds support for namespaces within attributes, as well as retrieving properties by name in addition to using an index. The SAX specification defines two features that control the functioning of namespace values. The first is denoted by the following name:

> `http://xml.org/sax/features/namespaces`

If this feature is `False` (it defaults to `True`), then access by namespace-qualified names may not be available. The second feature is denoted by the name:

> `http://xml.org/sax/features/namespace-prefixes`

If this feature is `False` (its default value), then namespace declarations within an element are not passed back as attributes.

TIP See the section titled "SAX Extensions" later in this chapter for more information about querying and setting features in SAX.

The interface serves to hide the implementation details of the list from the rest of the application. Its definition is shown in Listing 12-7.

Listing 12-7: The `Attributes` interface

```
public interface Attributes {
  public abstract int getLength ();
  public abstract String getURI (int index);
  public abstract String getLocalName (int index);
  public abstract String getQName (int index);
  public abstract String getType (int index);
  public abstract String getValue (int index);
  public int getIndex (String uri, String localPart);
  public int getIndex (String qName);
  public abstract String getType (String uri, String localName);
  public abstract String getType (String qName);
  public abstract String getValue (String uri, String localName);
  public abstract String getValue (String qName);
}
```

A description of the `Attributes` interface's methods follows:

`public abstract int getLength ();`

> The number of attributes in the list is returned by this method.

`public abstract String getURI (int index);`

> Retrieve the full namespace URI of the attribute via this method, using its position in the list. An empty string is returned if the attribute has no namespace, while a `null` is returned if the index is out of range.

```
public abstract String getLocalName (int index);
```
   Find the local name of the attribute (the part following any colon) with this method. The attribute's position in the list is passed in. As for the namespace URI, an empty string or a `null` may be returned.

```
public abstract String getQName (int index);
```
   The qualified name of the attribute is found using this method. A qualified name includes any prefix (shorthand for the namespace URI), a colon, and the local name. If namespaces are not used, just the local name appears here. The index position of the attribute identifies the required one. Also, an empty string or a `null` is returned when the name is not available or the index is out of range.

```
public abstract String getType (int index);
public abstract String getType (String uri, String localName);
public abstract String getType (String qName);
```
   Retrieve the type of the attribute with these methods. The value returned is one of those defined by the XML specification, such as `ID`, `NMTOKEN`, or `ENTITY`. Enumerations appear as `NMTOKEN` or `NOTATION`, depending on their purpose. If the type is unknown (the DTD was not read) then the type must be returned as `CDATA`. To get an attribute's type you can supply either its position within the list, its qualified name, or its namespace URI and local name. A `null` is returned for an unknown index, or missing name.

```
public abstract String getValue (int index);
public abstract String getValue (String uri, String localName);
public abstract String getValue (String qName);
```
   Find the string value of the attribute through these methods. Again, you can identify the attribute via its position in the list, its qualified name, or its namespace URI and local name. You get a `null` back if the index is out of range or if the name does not exist.

```
public int getIndex (String uri, String localPart);
public int getIndex (String qName);
```
   An attribute's position in the list is returned by this method. Specify either the qualified name of the attribute, or its namespace URI and local name. If the name is not found, the method returns –1.

A standard implementation of this interface is usually provided with a SAX package. This default class is due to the simple nature of the list. Its abilities are not likely to change greatly from one project to the next, unlike some of the other interfaces. Thus, a basic but functional implementation is available for use whenever it is required. Developers are able, indeed encouraged, to create more efficient implementations as necessary.

ContentHandler Interface

The `ContentHandler` interface is the one most users of XML documents are interested in, because it allows you to respond to the sections of the document as they are encountered. It is this interface that is usually implemented by each application so that it can deal with a particular document type. An object expressing this interface is supplied to the reader, which then invokes the appropriate methods within it as it steps through the document.

`ContentHandler` is defined as part of SAX2 and replaces the `DocumentHandler` interface of SAX1. It adds support for namespaces on elements and notifies the handler of entities that are skipped (in a non-validating reader). The definition of this interface is shown in Listing 12-8.

Listing 12-8: The `ContentHandler` interface

```java
public interface ContentHandler {
  public void setDocumentLocator (Locator locator);
  public void startDocument () throws SAXException;
  public void endDocument() throws SAXException;
  public void startPrefixMapping (String prefix, String uri)
    throws SAXException;
  public void endPrefixMapping (String prefix)
    throws SAXException;
  public void startElement (String namespaceURI, String localName,
    String qName, Attributes atts) throws SAXException;
  public void endElement (String namespaceURI, String localName,
    String qName) throws SAXException;
  public void characters (char ch[], int start, int length)
    throws SAXException;
  public void ignorableWhitespace (char ch[], int start, int length)
    throws SAXException;
  public void processingInstruction (String target, String data)
    throws SAXException;
  public void skippedEntity (String name) throws SAXException;
}
```

The methods of the `ContentHandler` interface are described below:

`public void setDocumentLocator (Locator locator);`
> This method allows the content handler to tie into the parse process and to find out where in the source document you are. It means that the content handler can perform further validations on the data, such as verifying date or numeric formats, etc., and report any violations while indicating the characters in error. If the reader supplies a locator, this method is called by it before any others during the parse process.

`public void startDocument () throws SAXException;`
`public void endDocument() throws SAXException;`
> When the reader calls the `startDocument` method, it signifies the beginning of a new XML document which allows the handler to perform any necessary initializations, such as emptying a DOM structure or creating a new output file.
>
> The `endDocument` method is called by the reader to terminate the document and to release any held resources. Here the DOM structure can be normalized or an output file closed. These methods are the first and last events triggered during a normal parse process.

```
public void startPrefixMapping (String prefix, String uri) throws SAXException;
public void endPrefixMapping (String prefix) throws SAXException;
```
To deal with namespace declarations within elements, the `startPrefixMapping` method informs you that a new mapping has been encountered, supplying the shorthand prefix and the full namespace URI. The mapping applies until the corresponding `endPrefixMapping` method is called. These two calls always envelop the element notifications to which they refer.

```
public void startElement (String namespaceURI, String localName, String qName,
    Attributes atts) throws SAXException;
public void endElement (String namespaceURI, String localName, String qName) throws
    SAXException;
```
As elements are read from the XML document, the `startElement` method notifies you of their presence, passing their name(s) and list of attributes. All the content of each tag is then processed through further calls before the corresponding `endElement` method is invoked. Even for an empty tag, both of these routines are called.

```
public void characters (char ch[], int start, int length) throws SAXException;
```
This method denotes text data from the document. It is called between the start and end calls for its owning element.

> **TIP** Text from CDATA sections also appears through the `characters` call. You can tell which is which through the `LexicalHandler` extension described later.

```
public void ignorableWhitespace (char ch[], int start, int length) throws
    SAXException;
```
All white space between tags that is insignificant (according to the XML specification) is sent through this method. However, this only happens in validating readers that can determine which elements contain significant text. Otherwise, all these separators appear through the `characters` method.

```
public void processingInstruction (String target, String data) throws
    SAXException;
```
Obviously, embedded instructions are identified by this method. Although the XML declaration at the start of each document appears as a processing instruction, it is not reported to the handler.

```
public void skippedEntity (String name) throws SAXException;
```
This method informs you that an entity reference was ignored. This happens in a non-validating reader that does not load any external DTD or entities. It can also happen when the reader is configured through various features.

The actions taken by each of these methods depend entirely on your application. You could write details about each event to a file. You could also count the number of each type of element and display the results at the end. Or you could create your own document model based on the items encountered by the reader.

Additional parts of the XML document are available as extensions to the SAX specification. These include comments and CDATA sections, which are discussed in the LexicalHandler and DeclHandler sections below.

DTDHandler Interface

The DTDHandler interface provides information on the notations and unparsed entities declared within an XML document. An object expressing this interface can be passed to a reader, which then calls its methods at the appropriate times as the document is processed.

Calls are made as the reader encounters notation declarations and unparsed external entities. Note that parsed entities should be handled by the reader and incorporated into the current document. The calls to these methods may appear in any order, not necessarily that of the document, but all such calls must arrive after the content handler's startDocument call and before the first startElement call.

By saving these details, you can possibly provide some level of support for these items within your application.

Listing 12-9 displays the definition for this interface.

Listing 12-9: The DTDHandler interface

```
public interface DTDHandler {
    public abstract void notationDecl (String name, String publicId,
      String systemId) throws SAXException;
    public abstract void unparsedEntityDecl (String name,
      String publicId, String systemId, String notationName)
      throws SAXException;
}
```

A description of the DTDHandler interface's methods follows:

public abstract void notationDecl (String name, String publicId, String systemId) throws SAXException;

This method informs you of a notation name defined in the DTD.

public abstract void unparsedEntityDecl (String name, String publicId, String systemId, String notationName) throws SAXException;

Unparsed entities defined in the DTD trigger this method. Parsed entities are incorporated into the body of the document, or are skipped (see the ContentHandler.skippedEntity method).

Recall that some XML documents may be usable without reference to their DTDs, whereas others may require the DTD to supply default attribute values or standard entity and notation references. Therefore, you may not be informed of all the notations and unparsed entities for a document, especially in a non-validating reader.

TIP Additional parts of the DTD are available as extensions to the SAX specification, including the DTD declaration itself, and element and attribute declarations. These are discussed in the LexicalHandler and DeclHandler sections below.

EntityResolver Interface

The `EntityResolver` interface allows you to redirect searches for entities. A single method comprises the interface, accepting the public and system identifiers for an entity and returning an `InputSource` that provides its content. If the entities are not being redirected, the method returns a `null` value and the reader uses its normal methods for obtaining them.

An object expressing this interface can be supplied to the reader for its use. Then, whenever it needs to access an external document, the reader passes the appropriate identifiers to the `resolveEntity` method and expects the contents at that location to be returned as a stream, encapsulated by the `InputSource` class.

Implementing this interface enables you to translate a public or system identifier for an entity into an actual location. For example, you could retrieve the entity from a database rather than across the Internet, or you could supply a new version of an entity during testing. Readers know how to obtain documents from HTTP URLs, through the `InputSource` class, but may require a custom resolver if an alternate protocol is used.

The definition of the interface is shown in Listing 12-10.

Listing 12-10: The `EntityResolver` interface

```
public interface EntityResolver
  {public abstract InputSource resolveEntity (String publicId,
     String systemId) throws SAXException, IOException;
}
```

The methods of the `EntityResolver` interface are described below:

`public abstract InputSource resolveEntity (String publicId, String systemId)`
    `throws SAXException, IOException;`
    This method allows you to trap and redirect references to entities from within an XML document. If you wish to supply content for the specified entity, you must compile that document from whatever source, before wrapping it in an `InputSource` object. To retain the standard handling of external entities, just return a `null`.

The default implementation of this interface, as supplied by the `DefaultHandler` class, simply returns `null`, causing the reader to obtain any entities through the normal channels based on their public and/or system identifiers.

ErrorHandler Interface

The `ErrorHandler` interface provides notification of errors that occur during the SAX parsing process. Errors in SAX come in three levels of severity: *warnings* that you should be aware of but that do not compromise the accuracy of the document, *errors* that are more severe but still do not destroy the usefulness of the document, and *fatal errors* that invalidate the current document but may allow continued processing to reveal further errors.

These are represented by the three methods in this interface (see the definition in Listing 12-11). Each is passed a `SAXParseException` that encapsulates the error condition and its location.

Listing 12-11: The ErrorHandler *interface*

```
public interface ErrorHandler {
  public abstract void warning (SAXParseException exception)
    throws SAXException;
  public abstract void error (SAXParseException exception)
    throws SAXException;
  public abstract void fatalError (SAXParseException exception)
    throws SAXException;
}
```

A description of the ErrorHandler interface's methods follows:

public abstract void warning (SAXParseException exception) throws SAXException;
: Minor violations of the parsing process are denoted by this method. Processing of the document continues and should still be usable following this call.

public abstract void error (SAXParseException exception) throws SAXException;
: A recoverable error during the parsing process causes this method to trigger. For example, violating a validity constraint may invoke this action. Processing of the document continues and should still be usable following this call.

public abstract void fatalError (SAXParseException exception) throws SAXException;
: Major errors are identified by this method, such as violating the well-formedness constraint. The document being parsed is no longer usable by the application, but the reader may continue if it wants to report any further errors.

The default implementation of this interface, from the DefaultHandler class, does nothing for warnings and errors, but raises fatal errors as an exception to be processed elsewhere in the application. You can use this class as a base from which to derive your own error handler, letting you only override those methods that you wish to respond to.

SAX Extensions

There were several areas lacking in the original SAX1 specification, primarily of interest to application writers that were developing tools for creating XML documents, rather than end-consumers of those documents. With SAX2 there is a specification for how SAX can be extended beyond its core abilities in a generic fashion.

XML readers now expose setFeature and setProperty methods that allow you to enhance or customize their behavior. Each feature or property is identified by a name based on a particular URI. Features are simple flags that are read to determine whether an ability is currently in force, and are set to enable or disable that ability.

Properties let you supply any object as a named value. Using this you can attach additional handlers to the reader. As long as the reader knows how to deal with that object it accepts it and makes use of it.

For both these attributes, if the reader does not understand the name supplied, it raises a SAXNotRecognizedException to alert you to this fact. If it knows the name but cannot make use of it, it raises SAXNotSupportedException.

Several standard features are defined, of which the first two must be recognized by every SAX reader.

`http://xml.org/sax/features/namespaces`
> Determines whether or not namespace URIs replace defined prefixes on elements and attributes. It defaults to `True`, and performs the replacement.

`http://xml.org/sax/features/namespace-prefixes`
> Determines whether or not qualified names are returned for elements and attributes. This feature also controls the passing back of namespace declaration attributes (with names like `xmlns:xxx`). It defaults to `False`, which makes the supply of qualified names optional and suppresses namespace declarations from attribute lists.

`http://xml.org/sax/features/validation`
> Controls whether the reader performs validations on the documents processed. Set it to `True` to validate against a DTD.

`http://xml.org/sax/features/external-general-entities`
> Determines whether or not external general entities may be skipped.

`http://xml.org/sax/features/external-parameter-entities`
> Determines whether or not external parameter entities may be skipped.

LexicalHandler Interface

The `LexicalHandler` interface provides additional notifications of lexical items within the XML document. It is one of the standard extensions defined in SAX2 and informs you about comments, and the start and end of the DTD declaration, CDATA sections, and entity references. The definition is shown in Listing 12-12.

Listing 12-12: The LexicalHandler interface

```
public interface LexicalHandler {
  public abstract void startDTD (String name, String publicId,
    String systemId) throws SAXException;
  public abstract void endDTD () throws SAXException;
  public abstract void startEntity (String name) throws SAXException;
  public abstract void endEntity (String name) throws SAXException;
  public abstract void startCDATA () throws SAXException;
  public abstract void endCDATA () throws SAXException;
  public abstract void comment (char ch[], int start, int length)
    throws SAXException;
}
```

The methods of the `LexicalHandler` interface are described below:

```
public abstract void startDTD (String name, String publicId, String systemId)
    throws SAXException;
public abstract void endDTD () throws SAXException;
```
> The DTD declaration, if one appears, is passed to the handler as a matched set of `startDTD` and `endDTD` calls. Between these two are notifications of all the references within that DTD. Notations and unparsed entities are supplied through the appropriate methods of the

DTDHandler interface. Element and attribute declarations and parsed entities are notified through the methods of the DeclHandler interface defined below. The latter is another extension to SAX, and so cannot be relied upon from any given reader. Any comments or processing instructions encountered within the DTD declaration are passed on through the usual methods.

`public abstract void startEntity (String name) throws SAXException;`
`public abstract void endEntity (String name) throws SAXException;`

Entity references found in the DTD of the document were quietly resolved and processed under SAX1. With the startEntity and endEntity methods you can be informed of their presence (possibly including parameter entities). All events arising from the contents of an entity must appear between these two calls. An external DTD also appears as an entity under this scheme, and has the name [dtd] assigned to it. Reporting of an external DTD and parameter entities by the reader is optional.

NOTE Parameter entities are denoted by their names beginning with a percent sign (%). Whether or not they are reported depends on the setting of the following feature (a setting of true informs you):
  http://xml.org/sax/features/lexical-handler/parameter-entities

Any entities that are subsequently skipped are notified to you through the skippedEntity method of the content handler.

`public abstract void startCDATA () throws SAXException;`
`public abstract void endCDATA () throws SAXException;`

Although the text content of a CDATA section was passed on in the original SAX1 specification, the fact that it came from such a section was not. In this extension, the actual text is still supplied via the characters method of the ContentHandler interface, but this call is now wrapped in a startCDATA and endCDATA pair.

`public abstract void comment (char ch[], int start, int length) throws SAXException;`

Comments are identified by this method. These entries are generally only of interest to applications that are constructing or reviewing entire XML documents, rather than manipulating the content of those documents. Comments should not be relied upon to contain useful information, and may not be supplied at all by some readers. If this information is necessary, then using a processing instruction would be a better option.

If you are interested in receiving notification of the events encapsulated by this interface, you need to implement it within a class and register that class with the XML reader. A lexical handler is registered with the reader using its Properties property with the following name:
  http://xml.org/sax/properties/lexical-handler

DeclHandler Interface

The `DeclHandler` interface is the second standard extension to SAX and provides additional notifications on declarations within the DTD part of the document. It informs you about element and attribute declarations, along with declarations for parsed entities. All the calls from this extension occur between the `startDTD` and `endDTD` notifications of the `LexicalHandler` interface (if this is in use). See Listing 12-13 for its declaration.

Listing 12-13: The DeclHandler interface

```
public interface DeclHandler {
  public abstract void elementDecl (String name, String model)
    throws SAXException;
  public abstract void attributeDecl (String eName, String aName,
    String type, String valueDefault, String value)
    throws SAXException;
  public abstract void internalEntityDecl (String name, String value)
    throws SAXException;
  public abstract void externalEntityDecl (String name,
    String publicId, String systemId) throws SAXException;
}
```

A description of the `DeclHandler` interface's methods follows:

`public abstract void elementDecl (String name, String model) throws SAXException;`
> Each element declaration is identified by this method, passing the element's name and its content model (as a string value).

`public abstract void attributeDecl (String eName, String aName, String type, String valueDefault, String value) throws SAXException;`
> Similarly, the appearance of each attribute declaration produces a call to this method. Along with the element and attribute names come the value default (#IMPLIED, #REQUIRED, #FIXED, or null), any default value, and the attribute's type, such as ID, IDREF, ENTITY, or CDATA. The type consists of the full token list for enumerated and notation types, separated by vertical bars (|) and with all white space removed.

`public abstract void internalEntityDecl (String name, String value) throws SAXException;`
> This method informs you of an internal parsed entity declaration. It supplies the name of that entity and its replacement value.

`public abstract void externalEntityDecl (String name, String publicId, String systemId) throws SAXException;`
> External parsed entity declarations also trigger a notification. Along with the name of the entity you receive its public and system identifiers.

Like the `LexicalHandler`, a declaration handler is also registered with the reader using its Properties property, but with the following name:

```
http://xml.org/sax/properties/declaration-handler
```

XMLReader Interface

The XMLReader interface defines how an XML parser communicates with the various handlers. All SAX readers must implement this basic interface, which replaces the SAX1 Parser one and provides support for the new ContentHandler.

SAX readers are reusable but not re-entrant; the application may reuse a reader object (possibly with a different input source) once the first parse has completed successfully, but it may not invoke the parse methods recursively within a parse.

The reader provides for the registering of a content handler, a DTD handler, an entity resolver, and/or an error handler. Additional functionality is requested or provided through the features and properties methods of the reader. When the parse method is invoked, it calls routines in the registered handlers at appropriate times as it parses the document.

See Listing 12-14 for the definition of this interface. Implementations of XMLReader can be parsers, validating or not, written from scratch. Or they can be wrappers around existing parsers.

Listing 12-14: The XMLReader interface

```java
public interface XMLReader {
  public boolean getFeature (String name)
    throws SAXNotRecognizedException, SAXNotSupportedException;
  public void setFeature (String name, boolean value)
    throws SAXNotRecognizedException, SAXNotSupportedException;
  public Object getProperty (String name)
    throws SAXNotRecognizedException, SAXNotSupportedException;
  public void setProperty (String name, Object value)
    throws SAXNotRecognizedException, SAXNotSupportedException;
  public void setEntityResolver (EntityResolver resolver);
  public EntityResolver getEntityResolver ();
  public void setDTDHandler (DTDHandler handler);
  public DTDHandler getDTDHandler ();
  public void setContentHandler (ContentHandler handler);
  public ContentHandler getContentHandler ();
  public void setErrorHandler (ErrorHandler handler);
  public ErrorHandler getErrorHandler ();
  public void parse (InputSource input)
    throws IOException, SAXException;
  public void parse (String systemId)
    throws IOException, SAXException;
}
```

The methods of the XMLReader interface are described below:

public boolean getFeature (String name) throws SAXNotRecognizedException, SAXNotSupportedException;
public void setFeature (String name, boolean value) throws SAXNotRecognized-Exception, SAXNotSupportedException;

Allowing SAX functionality to be extended and controlled, these methods let you discover which abilities are available and allow you to control their application. Feature names are based on URIs, and can be defined by anyone. Several standard features are defined (two of which are required). Unknown and unimplemented features raise exceptions.

```
public Object getProperty (String name) throws SAXNotRecognizedException,
    SAXNotSupportedException;
public void setProperty (String name, Object value) throws
    SAXNotRecognizedException, SAXNotSupportedException;
```
> Also extending SAX functionality, these methods let you supply and read extension objects from the reader. Property names are also based on URIs. Two standard extensions are defined. Unknown and unimplemented properties raise exceptions.

```
public void setEntityResolver (EntityResolver resolver);
public EntityResolver getEntityResolver ();
```
> To redirect external entity references you need to use these methods. As external objects are required, your EntityResolver is invoked to determine where to find their content.

```
public void setDTDHandler (DTDHandler handler);
public DTDHandler getDTDHandler ();
```
> Registering or retrieving a DTDHandler with the reader is done through these methods. Methods in the handler are called in response to tokens found in the XML document.

```
public void setContentHandler (ContentHandler handler);
public ContentHandler getContentHandler ();
```
> These methods let you register or retrieve a ContentHandler with the reader. As the reader works through the document, it calls the appropriate methods from the handler. Setting a content handler for a parse is most likely done in every application using SAX.

```
public void setErrorHandler (ErrorHandler handler);
public ErrorHandler getErrorHandler ();
```
> Although you do not want to have any errors occur, these methods let you find out about the ones that do. Errors in the parse process trigger the methods in an ErrorHandler registered in this way.

```
public void parse (InputSource input) throws IOException, SAXException;
public void parse (String systemId) throws IOException, SAXException;
```
> The heart of the process, these methods start the parsing of the named or supplied XML document. As the tokens are encountered, they trigger methods in the various handlers that are registered with the reader. Once the parse process has begun, it must complete before another one can be invoked.

XMLFilter Interface

Occasionally it is useful to be able to modify the results of a parse operation before the final processing of the results. The XMLFilter interface (shown in Listing 12-15) defines this ability. It appears like an XMLReader, since it extends that interface, but itself responds to events from another reader.

Listing 12-15: The XMLFilter interface

```
public interface XMLFilter extends XMLReader {
  public abstract void setParent (XMLReader parent);
  public abstract XMLReader getParent ();
}
```

A description of the XMLFilter interface's methods follows:

public abstract void setParent (XMLReader parent);
public abstract XMLReader getParent ();

> These methods let you store and read the XMLReader on which this filter relies for its parsing. Events from that source (which may be another filter) can be intercepted by the filter and altered as it sees fit. Generally, it would pass the events on to the consumers registered with it for final processing.

To use a filter you implement the XMLFilter interface and one or more of the handler interfaces, such as ContentHandler. You then register the filter with the specified parent reader as the handler for those interfaces. The filter may manipulate any events received from the parent before calling the corresponding event on any handlers registered with it.

A default implementation of the filter interface is usually available (the XMLFilterImpl class). All it does is pass parse requests up to its parent reader, and events back down to its registered handlers. Using this as a base, you can quickly implement a real filter by overriding only those requests or events of interest.

ParserAdapter and XMLReaderAdapter Classes

To facilitate the uptake of SAX2 and assist in porting legacy SAX1 code, two classes are defined in SAX to allow interoperation between SAX1 and SAX2 parsers/readers and handlers.

The ParserAdapter class wraps a SAX1 Parser to make it appear like a SAX2 XMLReader. It implements the reader interface, passing DTD, entity, and error handler events directly through from the parser. It also implements the SAX1 DocumentHandler interface, which it converts into ContentHandler events for the final consumer. Obviously, some events and abilities of SAX2 cannot be reproduced from a SAX1 parser; however, the basic functionality is immediately available.

Conversely, XMLReaderAdapter wraps a SAX2 XMLReader to make it act like a SAX1 Parser. Similar to the parser adapter, this one passes through whatever events it can, while converting content handler events into document handler events. The extra functionality of SAX2 is basically ignored and discarded.

XMLReaderFactory Class

To make it easier to create readers for use in parsing documents, SAX includes factory classes. These let you identify a reader by name and have it instantiated within the program. In this way the actual reader can be determined at run time, possibly from an initialization file or a command line parameter.

The declaration of the XMLReaderFactory is shown in Listing 12-16. It replaces the ParserFactory class of SAX1.

Listing 12-16: The XMLReaderFactory class

```
final public class XMLReaderFactory {
  public static XMLReader createXMLReader ()
    throws SAXException
  public static XMLReader createXMLReader (String className)
    throws SAXException
}
```

A description of the XMLReaderFactory class's methods follows:

public static XMLReader createXMLReader () throws SAXException
public static XMLReader createXMLReader (String className) throws SAXException

The factory provides two methods for obtaining a reader: one that returns a default implementation and one that returns a reader by name. The default reader is identified through some parameter to the application's environment. In Java this is done through system properties.

DefaultHandler Class

The DefaultHandler class provides a default implementation of the various handler interfaces. This class serves two purposes: as a base class for customized handlers and as a possible default for a SAX reader when no other handler is specified. Defined in SAX2, this class replaces the HandlerBase class of SAX1.

In most cases this class does nothing as a result of the calls made to it. The one exception is the fatalError method of the error handler, which raises the exception to the application.

Since this class already provides do-nothing implementations of all the methods for each handler interface, you only need to override those methods that you are interested in when deriving a custom handler. The remaining methods inherit the abilities of the base class and happily ignore any other calls.

Summary

This chapter has introduced you to the Simple API for XML (SAX). You have seen that it is an event-based API, as opposed to the structure-based API inherent in the DOM. This has advantages in that you do not need to have the entire document in memory at any one time. Instead you can read through the elements, processing the ones of interest as they are encountered. This is especially useful for large documents, and also where only a small fraction of the nodes are required for the processing.

However, SAX only lets you process a document sequentially, and does not inherently provide for the manipulation of that document and its subsequent output. The filter mechanism lets you write code that alters the events as they come in before passing them along to another handler, giving some opportunity for modification. Also, Microsoft has included a SAX writer in its MSXML v3 package, which outputs a document in response to SAX events sent to it. See Chapter 20 for further discussion on this topic.

The original SAX specification was updated in May 2000 to provide additional support for namespaces within XML documents, as well as to add missing functionality from the earlier version. Also included is a way to extend the abilities of SAX readers in a consistent manner. Two extensions are already available as add-ons to the basic specification.

In the following chapters you see how this specification is implemented: first by Microsoft in its MSXML package, and then in Delphi as native interfaces and classes, and finally by wrapping the MSXML package in the Delphi interfaces.

Chapter 13
Microsoft's SAX Parser

With version 3.0 of Microsoft's XML offering comes a built in SAX2-compliant reader. Also included are definitions for the various interfaces that interact with the reader.

When you import the MSXML type library from the MSXML3.dll, as described in Chapter 9 on Microsoft's DOM, you also get the SAX interfaces. These come in two versions: one for use with C/C++ (prefixed by ISAX) and one for use with Visual Basic (prefixed by IVBSAX). The VB versions are easier to work with from Delphi since they use the WideString type for their string-type parameters, rather than the pointer references of the C versions.

Microsoft only supports version 2 of the SAX specification. Deprecated interfaces, such as DocumentHandler, are not defined.

Several aspects of the SAX specification are not present in the Microsoft implementation. There are no SAX exceptions defined. Instead, the information usually carried by those objects is passed across as separate fields to the error handler. Other processing errors are raised as EOleExceptions.

Also, there is no equivalent of the InputSource class. In its place, the reader accepts a wide variety of sources, as described in the IVBSAXXMLReader section, and handles all processing itself through these sources.

All string parameters for the handler methods are WideStrings and are passed by reference. The latter is for performance reasons since the contents then do not have to be copied locally. However, you should not alter their values.

IVBSAXLocator Interface

The IVBSAXLocator interface (see Listing 13-1) provides information on the current position within the document during the parse process. You obtain a reference to the locator for a document through the documentLocator property of the IVBSAXContentHandler interface. When available, this property is set by the reader before any calls are made to the other content handler methods. If a locator is not supplied by the time the startDocument method fires, no position information is provided.

Listing 13-1: The IVBSAXLocator interface

```
// *********************************************************************//
// Interface: IVBSAXLocator
// Flags:     (4544) Dual NonExtensible OleAutomation Dispatchable
// GUID:      {796E7AC5-5AA2-4EFF-ACAD-3FAAF01A3288}
// *********************************************************************//
IVBSAXLocator = interface(IDispatch)
  ['{796E7AC5-5AA2-4EFF-ACAD-3FAAF01A3288}']
  function  Get_columnNumber: SYSINT; safecall;
  function  Get_lineNumber: SYSINT; safecall;
  function  Get_publicId: WideString; safecall;
  function  Get_systemId: WideString; safecall;
  property columnNumber: SYSINT read Get_columnNumber;
  property lineNumber: SYSINT read Get_lineNumber;
  property publicId: WideString read Get_publicId;
  property systemId: WideString read Get_systemId;
end;
```

Information from the locator is only valid during one of the handler callbacks. Using a supplied locator at other times gives unpredictable results.

The properties of the IVBSAXLocator interface are listed below:

property publicId: WideString read Get_publicId;
property systemId: WideString read Get_systemId;

> Retrieve the public and system identifiers for the document through these read-only properties. An empty string is returned if the value is unknown.

property lineNumber: SYSINT read Get_lineNumber;
property columnNumber: SYSINT read Get_columnNumber;

> These read-only properties return the current position within the document. Generally, this is at the first location following the text that was just parsed. If the location is unknown, –1 is returned.

IVBSAXAttributes Interface

The attributes attached to an element are made available through the IVBSAXAttributes interface (shown in Listing 13-2). An object expressing this interface is supplied in the startElement method of the IVBSAXContentHandler interface.

Listing 13-2: The IVBSAXAttributes interface

```
// *********************************************************************//
// Interface: IVBSAXAttributes
// Flags:     (4544) Dual NonExtensible OleAutomation Dispatchable
// GUID:      {10DC0586-132B-4CAC-8BB3-DB00AC8B7EE0}
// *********************************************************************//
IVBSAXAttributes = interface(IDispatch)
  ['{10DC0586-132B-4CAC-8BB3-DB00AC8B7EE0}']
  function  Get_length: SYSINT; safecall;
  function  getURI(nIndex: SYSINT): WideString; safecall;
  function  getLocalName(nIndex: SYSINT): WideString; safecall;
  function  getQName(nIndex: SYSINT): WideString; safecall;
  function  getIndexFromName(const strURI: WideString;
    const strLocalName: WideString): SYSINT; safecall;
```

```
    function getIndexFromQName(const strQName: WideString): SYSINT;
      safecall;
    function getType(nIndex: SYSINT): WideString; safecall;
    function getTypeFromName(const strURI: WideString;
      const strLocalName: WideString): WideString; safecall;
    function getTypeFromQName(const strQName: WideString): WideString;
      safecall;
    function getValue(nIndex: SYSINT): WideString; safecall;
    function getValueFromName(const strURI: WideString;
      const strLocalName: WideString): WideString; safecall;
    function getValueFromQName(const strQName: WideString): WideString;
      safecall;
    property length: SYSINT read Get_length;
  end;
```

Attributes only appear if they are explicitly assigned values in the XML document, or have a default value set through the DTD. Namespace declarations that appear as attributes (those starting with xmlns:) are not included unless the http://xml.org/sax/features/namespace-prefixes property is set to True. If this feature is False (its default value), access by qualified name may not be possible. Similarly, if the http://xml.org/sax/features/namespaces feature is False, access by qualified name may not be available.

A description of the properties and methods of the IVBSAXAttributes interface follows:

property length: SYSINT read Get_length;
: This read-only property supplies the number of attributes in the collection. They are indexed from zero to length −1.

function getURI(nIndex: SYSINT): WideString; safecall;
: Retrieve the namespace URI for an attribute, given its position in the list, with this method. If the attribute has no namespace, this returns an empty string. If the index is out of range, an error occurs.

function getLocalName(nIndex: SYSINT): WideString; safecall;
: Given an attribute's position in the list, this method returns its local name. Like the previous method, an index out of range generates an error.

function getQName(nIndex: SYSINT): WideString; safecall;
: This method returns the qualified name of the specified attribute or an error if the index is out of range.

function getIndexFromName(const strURI: WideString; const strLocalName: WideString): SYSINT; safecall;
function getIndexFromQName(const strQName: WideString): SYSINT; safecall;
: Use these methods to find the position of an attribute in the list given its namespace URI and local name or its qualified name. For ambiguous names, it returns the lowest index that matches. An error occurs if the attribute cannot be found.

```
function getType(nIndex: SYSINT): WideString; safecall;
function getTypeFromName(const strURI: WideString; const strLocalName:
    WideString): WideString; safecall;
function getTypeFromQName(const strQName: WideString): WideString; safecall;
```
> Retrieve the type of an attribute (ID, ENTITY, etc.) from the DTD or schema through these methods. The attribute is identified by its position in the list or by its name(s). If there is no DTD or schema information available, these functions return CDATA. For ambiguous names, the type of the first one found is returned. An error occurs if the attribute cannot be found.

```
function getValue(nIndex: SYSINT): WideString; safecall;
function getValueFromName(const strURI: WideString; const strLocalName:
    WideString): WideString; safecall;
function getValueFromQName(const strQName: WideString): WideString; safecall;
```
> These methods return the text value of the specified attribute, given its position in the list or its name(s). Supplying an ambiguous name results in the value of the first match found. If the attribute cannot be located, an error occurs.

IVBSAXContentHandler Interface

The `IVBSAXContentHandler` interface (shown in Listing 13-3) is the one most commonly used in applications since it responds to the basic items within the XML document: elements and text content. You implement it in whichever class is most appropriate and then register it with the XML reader. During the parse process, the methods in this interface are called at the appropriate times as items are encountered.

Listing 13-3: The *IVBSAXContentHandler* interface

```
// ********************************************************************//
// Interface: IVBSAXContentHandler
// Flags:     (4544) Dual NonExtensible OleAutomation Dispatchable
// GUID:      {2ED7290A-4DD5-4B46-BB26-4E4155E77FAA}
// ********************************************************************//
IVBSAXContentHandler = interface(IDispatch)
  ['{2ED7290A-4DD5-4B46-BB26-4E4155E77FAA}']
  procedure Set_documentLocator(const Param1: IVBSAXLocator); safecall;
  procedure startDocument; safecall;
  procedure endDocument; safecall;
  procedure startPrefixMapping(var strPrefix: WideString;
    var strURI: WideString); safecall;
  procedure endPrefixMapping(var strPrefix: WideString); safecall;
  procedure startElement(var strNamespaceURI: WideString;
    var strLocalName: WideString; var strQName: WideString;
    const oAttributes: IVBSAXAttributes); safecall;
  procedure endElement(var strNamespaceURI: WideString;
    var strLocalName: WideString; var strQName: WideString); safecall;
  procedure characters(var strChars: WideString); safecall;
  procedure ignorableWhitespace(var strChars: WideString); safecall;
  procedure processingInstruction(var strTarget: WideString;
    var strData: WideString); safecall;
  procedure skippedEntity(var strName: WideString); safecall;
  property documentLocator: IVBSAXLocator write Set_documentLocator;
end;
```

The IVBSAXLocator interface's properties and methods are shown below:

procedure Set_documentLocator(const Param1: IVBSAXLocator); safecall;

> If the reader supports a locator, it uses this method to provide the content handler with a reference to it. You can then obtain the current position (the end of the text generating a call) within the XML document through this interface during any of the other handler callbacks. Do not access this interface at any other time, as its values are undefined. If no locator has been supplied before the startDocument call, then none is available.

procedure startDocument; safecall;

> Use this method to initialize your application in preparation for a new XML document. This call is only made once before any other handler calls (except for the setting of the locator).

procedure endDocument; safecall;

> This method lets you tidy up at the end of a document, by running any final processing and releasing any resources used. It is called once after all the other events have fired.

procedure startPrefixMapping(var strPrefix: WideString; var strURI: WideString); safecall;

> Receive notification about the start of a namespace declaration through this method, supplying the prefix and full namespace URI. This call comes before the startElement event in which it appeared. It remains in effect until the corresponding end method.
>
> The reader automatically performs namespace processing for elements and attributes when the http://xml.org/sax/features/namespaces feature is True, which is the default setting. This call lets you obtain the prefixes and their mappings for other uses.

procedure endPrefixMapping(var strPrefix: WideString); safecall;

> The end of a namespace's scope occurs with this call. It happens after the endElement call to which it is attached. Note that prefix mapping calls may not nest properly (the end calls may not necessarily appear in the reverse order of the start calls), but they will all occur.

procedure startElement(var strNamespaceURI: WideString; var strLocalName: WideString; var strQName: WideString; const oAttributes: IVBSAXAttributes); safecall;

> This method informs you of the opening tag for an element in the document. You receive its name parts and any attributes it has. All the content of the element appears through other calls before the corresponding endElement event.
>
> Two features control the appearance of the name parts for an element: When http://xml.org/sax/features/namespaces is True (the default), both the namespace URI and local name are required; otherwise they are optional. When http://xml.org/sax/features/namespace-prefixes is True, the qualified name is required; otherwise it is optional (the default). This latter feature also determines the presence of namespace declarations (those starting with xmlns) within the attributes list. When True, these declarations appear as attributes, and they are not present when it is False.

procedure endElement(var strNamespaceURI: WideString; var strLocalName:
    WideString; var strQName: WideString); safecall;
    Once the element's contents have been provided, this method signifies its end. Note that this event occurs for all elements, even those without any content. The same rules apply to the names here as for the startElement method.

procedure characters(var strChars: WideString); safecall;
    Normal text appears via this method, including that from CDATA sections. Any entity references are expanded out and arrive via other calls, although their text content comes through this one. Contiguous strings of text from the document may appear in a single call, or may be split across several calls. However, each invocation contains text from a single entity so that the locator object provides meaningful information.

procedure ignorableWhitespace(var strChars: WideString); safecall;
    This method notifies you of insignificant white space between tags, which can only be identified if the DTD or schema is loaded and processed. Otherwise, all text content must come through the characters method.

NOTE Since the current SAX reader is non-validating, the ignorableWhitespace method is never called.

procedure processingInstruction(var strTarget: WideString; var strData:
    WideString); safecall;
    Handle processing instructions through this method, receiving its target and command. The XML declaration, although it looks like a processing instruction, is not supplied via any SAX interface.

procedure skippedEntity(var strName: WideString); safecall;
    Entities that are skipped over are notified via this call. These cannot be expanded when their definitions, contained in an external document, are not loaded. Otherwise, you receive startEntity and endEntity events from the IVBSAXLexicalHandler interface that surround the entity's content. This method may also be called for an external DTD reference.
    Two features control the loading of external entities: http://xml.org/sax/features/external-general-entities for normal entities and http://xml.org/sax/features/external-parameter-entities for parameter entities. Set these to True to load the respective entity types. Both default to False. A leading percent sign (%) identifies parameter entities.

IVBSAXDTDHandler Interface

For information on some items from the DTD in an XML document, implement the IVBSAXDTDHandler interface (see Listing 13-4) in your application. Register this object with the XML reader and wait for the corresponding notifications. The calls in this interface do not necessarily arrive in the same order that the declarations are found in the XML document. However, they all appear after the startDocument call and before the first startElement call. If the IVBSAXLexicalHandler interface is also used, these events occur between the startDTD and endDTD methods.

Listing 13-4: The IVBSAXDTDHandler interface

```
// *********************************************************************//
// Interface: IVBSAXDTDHandler
// Flags:     (4544) Dual NonExtensible OleAutomation Dispatchable
// GUID:      {24FB3297-302D-4620-BA39-3A732D850558}
// *********************************************************************//
IVBSAXDTDHandler = interface(IDispatch)
  ['{24FB3297-302D-4620-BA39-3A732D850558}']
  procedure notationDecl(var strName: WideString;
    var strPublicId: WideString; var strSystemId: WideString);
    safecall;
  procedure unparsedEntityDecl(var strName: WideString;
    var strPublicId: WideString; var strSystemId: WideString;
    var strNotationName: WideString); safecall;
end;
```

The methods of the IVBSAXDTDHandler interface are detailed below:

procedure notationDecl(var strName: WideString; var strPublicId: WideString; var strSystemId: WideString); safecall;

> This method informs you of notation declarations found in the DTD, providing the notation's name and whatever public and system identifiers are available. If the latter are URLs, these are fully resolved by the reader before appearing in this call.

procedure unparsedEntityDecl(var strName: WideString; var strPublicId: WideString; var strSystemId: WideString; var strNotationName: WideString); safecall;

> Unparsed entities, those that do not consist of XML or straight text, appear through this method. You receive the entity's name, its public and system identifiers, and the name of the notation describing its contents. The latter should correspond to one of the notations from the previous method. As before, URLs are fully resolved before being passed in.

IVBSAXEntityResolver Interface

External entities defined in the XML document may appear with either or both a public and system identifier. These serve to locate the resource that holds the contents of the entity. System identifiers are actual locations: filenames or URLs. Public identifiers are well-known names that are mapped onto physical resources. The IVBSAXEntityResolver interface (shown in Listing 13-5) lets you perform this mapping, or even redirect system identifiers to alternate locations.

Listing 13-5: The *IVBSAXEntityResolver* interface

```
// *********************************************************************//
// Interface: IVBSAXEntityResolver
// Flags:     (4544) Dual NonExtensible OleAutomation Dispatchable
// GUID:      {0C05D096-F45B-4ACA-AD1A-AA0BC25518DC}
// *********************************************************************//
IVBSAXEntityResolver = interface(IDispatch)
  ['{0C05D096-F45B-4ACA-AD1A-AA0BC25518DC}']
  function  resolveEntity(var strPublicId: WideString;
    var strSystemId: WideString): OleVariant; safecall;
end;
```

NOTE Currently, an entity resolver cannot be registered with the XML reader since it does not resolve external entities.

A description of the method from the IVBSAXEntityResolver interface follows:

function resolveEntity(var strPublicId: WideString; var strSystemId: WideString):
    OleVariant; safecall;
    Given the public and system identifier for the entity, you can retrieve the corresponding contents and supply them back to the reader. This method returns a null to use the normal entity resolution processing.

IVBSAXErrorHandler Interface

When errors occur during a document parse, they appear through the XML reader as method calls into the IVBSAXErrorHandler interface (see Listing 13-6). Errors come in three levels of severity, from minor warnings to show-stopping fatal errors, corresponding to the three methods available.

Listing 13-6: The *IVBSAXErrorHandler* interface

```
// *********************************************************************//
// Interface: IVBSAXErrorHandler
// Flags:     (4544) Dual NonExtensible OleAutomation Dispatchable
// GUID:      {D963D3FE-173C-4862-9095-B92F66995F52}
// *********************************************************************//
IVBSAXErrorHandler = interface(IDispatch)
  ['{D963D3FE-173C-4862-9095-B92F66995F52}']
  procedure error(const oLocator: IVBSAXLocator;
    var strErrorMessage: WideString; nErrorCode: Integer); safecall;
  procedure fatalError(const oLocator: IVBSAXLocator;
    var strErrorMessage: WideString; nErrorCode: Integer); safecall;
  procedure ignorableWarning(const oLocator: IVBSAXLocator;
```

```
        var strErrorMessage: WideString; nErrorCode: Integer); safecall;
    end;
```

NOTE Currently all errors from the parse process are fatal. Thus, the warning and normal error methods are never called.

The IVBSAXErrorHandler interface's methods are described below:

procedure error(const oLocator: IVBSAXLocator; var strErrorMessage: WideString; nErrorCode: Integer); safecall;

These errors are serious, but not enough to halt the parse process. Check the error code and message for the cause of the problem, and use the locator to determine its position within the document.

procedure fatalError(const oLocator: IVBSAXLocator; var strErrorMessage: WideString; nErrorCode: Integer); safecall;

Problems that prohibit parsing the remainder of the document, such as violating the well-formedness constraint of XML, appear through this call. The parameters are as for a normal error.

procedure ignorableWarning(const oLocator: IVBSAXLocator; var strErrorMessage: WideString; nErrorCode: Integer); safecall;

This method informs you of minor problems. Again, the parameters are as for a normal error.

NOTE The SAX specification passes details to these methods encapsulated in a SAXParseException, whereas Microsoft's implementation supplies the individual fields due to differences in the COM implementation of exceptions. Also, under SAX the last method is just called warning rather than ignorableWarning.

IVBSAXLexicalHandler Interface

One of the standard extensions defined under SAX, the IVBSAXLexicalHandler interface (shown in Listing 13-7) provides additional information about the source of certain items from the XML document. Generally, its methods are called before and after the events that make up the content of that particular node type.

Listing 13-7: The IVBSAXLexicalHandler interface

```
// ****************************************************************//
// Interface: IVBSAXLexicalHandler
// Flags:     (4544) Dual NonExtensible OleAutomation Dispatchable
// GUID:      {032AAC35-8C0E-4D9D-979F-E3B702935576}
// ****************************************************************//
IVBSAXLexicalHandler = interface(IDispatch)
  ['{032AAC35-8C0E-4D9D-979F-E3B702935576}']
  procedure startDTD(var strName: WideString;
    var strPublicId: WideString; var strSystemId: WideString);
    safecall;
  procedure endDTD; safecall;
  procedure startEntity(var strName: WideString); safecall;
```

```
    procedure endEntity(var strName: WideString); safecall;
    procedure startCDATA; safecall;
    procedure endCDATA; safecall;
    procedure comment(var strChars: WideString); safecall;
end;
```

An implementer of this interface cannot be directly registered with an XML reader. Instead, you must use the property mechanism of SAX to attach it, as shown below:

```
MySAXReader.putProperty(
    'http://xml.org/sax/properties/lexical-handler', MyLexicalHandler);
```

The methods of the `IVBSAXLexicalHandler` interface are listed below:

```
procedure startDTD(var strName: WideString; var strPublicId: WideString; var
    strSystemId: WideString); safecall;
procedure endDTD; safecall;
```

> These two methods mark the beginning and ending of the DTD declaration within an XML document. They occur after the `startDocument` call but before the first `startElement` one. All notation and entity declaration events appear between them, as do those for any element and attribute declarations. The starting call provides the name of the document (its top-level element) and the public and system identifiers for an external DTD if defined. If there is no DTD defined for the document these methods are not invoked.

```
procedure startEntity(var strName: WideString); safecall;
procedure endEntity(var strName: WideString); safecall;
```

> Entity references within the document are delimited by these two methods, each of which identifies the entity in question. Between them appear calls for the content of that entity. If external entities have not been loaded, then references to them appear as `skippedEntity` calls within the content handler interface.
>
> The report of parameter entities is optional, depending on the setting of the `http://xml.org/sax/features/lexical-handler/parameter-entities` feature. A leading percent sign (%) identifies parameter entities as such. An external DTD is also reported as an entity with the name [dtd]. Character references are not reported, but are quietly expanded.

```
procedure startCDATA; safecall;
procedure endCDATA; safecall;
```

> While the text content of CDATA sections is always passed on, under SAX1 you could not tell that it originated there. With this extension you receive callbacks at the start and end of the section, while the content still shows up through the `characters` method of the content handler.

```
procedure comment(var strChars: WideString); safecall;
```

> This method informs you of comments encountered within the XML document, passing along their text. Comments may appear at any level within the document, including outside of the document element.

IVBSAXDeclHandler Interface

The second standard SAX extension, the IVBSAXDeclHandler interface (see Listing 13-8) notifies you of additional items from the DTD of a document beyond those provided by the IVBSAXDTDHandler interface. When used at the same time as the IVBSAXLexicalHandler interface, all the events defined here occur between the startDTD and endDTD calls.

Listing 13-8: The *IVBSAXDeclHandler* interface

```
//*****************************************************************//
// Interface: IVBSAXDeclHandler
// Flags:     (4544) Dual NonExtensible OleAutomation Dispatchable
// GUID:      {E8917260-7579-4BE1-B5DD-7AFBFA6F077B}
//*****************************************************************//
IVBSAXDeclHandler = interface(IDispatch)
  ['{E8917260-7579-4BE1-B5DD-7AFBFA6F077B}']
  procedure elementDecl(var strName: WideString;
    var strModel: WideString); safecall;
  procedure attributeDecl(var strElementName: WideString;
    var strAttributeName: WideString; var strType: WideString;
    var strValueDefault: WideString; var strValue: WideString);
    safecall;
  procedure internalEntityDecl(var strName: WideString;
    var strValue: WideString); safecall;
  procedure externalEntityDecl(var strName: WideString;
    var strPublicId: WideString; var strSystemId: WideString);
    safecall;
end;
```

Like the lexical handler, implementations of this interface must register themselves with the XML reader through the SAX property mechanism, as shown below:

```
MySAXReader.putProperty(
    "http://xml.org/sax/properties/declaration-handler", MyDeclHandler);
```

A description of the methods of the IVBSAXDeclHandler interface follows:

procedure elementDecl(var strName: WideString; var strModel: WideString); safecall;

The declaration of an element within the DTD appears through this method, supplying its name and content model (as a string). Content models consist of the values EMPTY or ANY, or a group of allowable values enclosed in parentheses and followed by an optional occurrences character. Models are normalized before being passed over. This involves expanding out any parameter entities and removing any white space.

procedure attributeDecl(var strElementName: WideString; var strAttributeName: WideString; var strType: WideString; var strValueDefault: WideString; var strValue: WideString); safecall;

An attribute's declaration arrives through this method. Along with the element and attribute names come the type of the attribute (as a string), its default setting (#REQUIRED, #IMPLIED, #FIXED, or ' '), and any default value. The type may be one of the standard types (ID, IDREF, ENTITY, etc.) or it may be a list of valid values separated by vertical bars (|) and surrounded by parentheses. Notation types follow the latter pattern but are prefixed with the text NOTATION. All white space is removed from these lists.

Although attributes for one element may be declared in a single list, separate calls result for each one. Only the first definition for each attribute is returned, as required by the XML specification.

```
procedure internalEntityDecl(var strName: WideString; var strValue: WideString);
  safecall;
procedure externalEntityDecl(var strName: WideString; var strPublicId: WideString;
  var strSystemId: WideString); safecall;
```

These two methods notify you of parsed entity declarations from the DTD. Both pass along the entity's name and its value (for internal entities), or its public and system identifiers (for external ones). Parameter entities within an internal entity's value are automatically expanded, but general entity references are not. The declarations for parameter entities themselves have a leading percent sign (%) in their names. Only the first declaration for each entity is reported. Unparsed entities appear via the unparsedEntityDecl method of the DTD handler interface.

IVBSAXXMLReader Interface

The IVBSAXXMLReader interface (shown in Listing 13-9) provides the parsing engine of the Microsoft SAX offering. You do not implement this interface in your own application, but create a built-in object that expresses it. After registering your handlers with the reader, you start the parse process and wait for the appropriate events to fire.

Listing 13-9: The *IVBSAXXMLReader* interface

```
// ******************************************************************//
// Interface: IVBSAXXMLReader
// Flags:     (4544) Dual NonExtensible OleAutomation Dispatchable
// GUID:      {8C033CAA-6CD6-4F73-B728-4531AF74945F}
// ******************************************************************//
IVBSAXXMLReader = interface(IDispatch)
  ['{8C033CAA-6CD6-4F73-B728-4531AF74945F}']
  function  getFeature(const strName: WideString): WordBool; safecall;
  procedure putFeature(const strName: WideString; fValue: WordBool);
    safecall;
  function  getProperty(const strName: WideString): OleVariant;
    safecall;
  procedure putProperty(const strName: WideString;
    varValue: OleVariant); safecall;
  function  Get_entityResolver: IVBSAXEntityResolver; safecall;
  procedure Set_entityResolver(const oResolver: IVBSAXEntityResolver);
    safecall;
  function  Get_contentHandler: IVBSAXContentHandler; safecall;
  procedure Set_contentHandler(const oHandler: IVBSAXContentHandler);
    safecall;
  function  Get_dtdHandler: IVBSAXDTDHandler; safecall;
  procedure Set_dtdHandler(const oHandler: IVBSAXDTDHandler); safecall;
  function  Get_errorHandler: IVBSAXErrorHandler; safecall;
  procedure Set_errorHandler(const oHandler: IVBSAXErrorHandler);
```

Chapter 13: Microsoft's SAX Parser

```
      safecall;
    function  Get_baseURL: WideString; safecall;
    procedure Set_baseURL(const strBaseURL: WideString); safecall;
    function  Get_secureBaseURL: WideString; safecall;
    procedure Set_secureBaseURL(const strSecureBaseURL: WideString);
      safecall;
    procedure parse(varInput: OleVariant); safecall;
    procedure parseURL(const strURL: WideString); safecall;
    property entityResolver: IVBSAXEntityResolver read Get_entityResolver
      write Set_entityResolver;
    property contentHandler: IVBSAXContentHandler read Get_contentHandler
      write Set_contentHandler;
    property dtdHandler: IVBSAXDTDHandler read Get_dtdHandler
      write Set_dtdHandler;
    property errorHandler: IVBSAXErrorHandler read Get_errorHandler
      write Set_errorHandler;
    property baseURL: WideString read Get_baseURL write Set_baseURL;
    property secureBaseURL: WideString read Get_secureBaseURL
      write Set_secureBaseURL;
  end;
```

You obtain an object implementing this interface from the CoClass defined in the imported type library as shown in the following code. CoSAXMLReader always returns an instance of the latest reader, while CoSAXXMLReader30 always returns a version 3.0 reader. At this time they are synonymous.

    MySAXReader := CoSAXXMLReader.Create;

The IVBSAXXMLReader interface's properties and methods are listed below:

property entityResolver: IVBSAXEntityResolver read Get_entityResolver write
     Set_entityResolver;
property contentHandler: IVBSAXContentHandler read Get_contentHandler write
     Set_contentHandler;
property dtdHandler: IVBSAXDTDHandler read Get_dtdHandler write Set_dtdHandler;
     property errorHandler: IVBSAXErrorHandler read Get_errorHandler write
     Set_errorHandler;
Register your handler(s) with the XML reader through these properties.

NOTE The entityResolver property is not currently supported since the reader does not resolve external entities. Using it generates a run-time error.

function getFeature(const strName: WideString): WordBool; safecall;
procedure putFeature(const strName: WideString; fValue: WordBool); safecall;
     Read or set features of the reader through these methods, which let you control some of its processing. Features are identified by standard names that appear as URIs and exist as simple Boolean flags. See the section on SAX extensions in Chapter 12 for a list of the common feature names. If a feature is not known or is not supported, an error occurs.

New features supported by the Microsoft reader include:

`normalize-line-breaks`
> Set to True (its default value) CR-LF sequences in text are replaced by a single LF, as required by the XML specification. When False, they are not altered.

`server-http-request`
> If True, the reader uses the server-safe ServerXMLHTTP object for the parseURL method. Otherwise, the WinInet component is used (the default).

NOTE Although the standard http://xml.org/sax/features/validation and http://xml.org/sax/features/string-interning features are recognized by the reader, they cannot be set under the current implementation.

```
function getProperty(const strName: WideString): OleVariant; safecall;
procedure putProperty(const strName: WideString; varValue: OleVariant); safecall;
```
> Similarly, properties of a reader let you expand its abilities by supplying additional interfaces for its use. The names of the two standard extensions are shown in their respective sections above. Again, an error occurs if the property is unknown or not supported.

Besides the extensions noted above, the reader also recognizes the following properties. They are only available after the XML header has been parsed and are empty if there is no XML declaration or if the property is not found.

`xmldecl-version`
> Retrieve the version value from the XML declaration through this property.

`xmldecl-encoding`
> This property returns the encoding value from the XML declaration.

`xmldecl-standalone`
> Determine whether the document is standalone through this property. It returns either yes or no if the declaration exists.

NOTE Because of the naming used for these methods (put instead of set), properties were not automatically generated during the importation of the type library into Delphi.

```
procedure parse(varInput: OleVariant); safecall;
procedure parseURL(const strURL: WideString); safecall;
```
> Having attached your handlers to the reader, you are ready to start the parse process itself. Call one of these methods supplying the document as either a string containing its contents, an implementation of IStream, or its (fully resolved) URL. The parse process is reusable but not re-entrant; you cannot start a second parse while the first is running, but you can once it has finished.

NOTE The following properties are not part of the SAX specification.

`property baseURL: WideString read Get_baseURL write Set_baseURL;`
> Set or retrieve the base URL for the reader through this property.

property secureBaseURL: WideString read Get_secureBaseURL write Set_secureBaseURL;
> This property controls security enforcement for retrieving documents. If not set, full access is allowed. When set, the applicable IE security settings come into effect.

IVBSAXXMLFilter Interface

A mechanism for intercepting SAX events comes from the `IVBSAXXMLFilter` interface (see Listing 13-10). Also implementing the basic reader interface, it mediates between your normal handlers and an actual reader. It may trap some events and not pass them on at all, or it may alter the contents of those events before their eventual use.

Listing 13-10: The `IVBSAXXMLFilter` *interface*

```
// *******************************************************************//
// Interface: IVBSAXXMLFilter
// Flags:     (4544) Dual NonExtensible OleAutomation Dispatchable
// GUID:      {1299EB1B-5B88-433E-82DE-82CA75AD4E04}
// *******************************************************************//
IVBSAXXMLFilter = interface(IDispatch)
  ['{1299EB1B-5B88-433E-82DE-82CA75AD4E04}']
    function Get_parent: IVBSAXXMLReader; safecall;
    procedure Set_parent(const oReader: IVBSAXXMLReader); safecall;
    property parent: IVBSAXXMLReader read Get_parent write Set_parent;
  end;
```

The property of the `IVBSAXXMLFilter` interface is shown below:

property parent: IVBSAXXMLReader read Get_parent write Set_parent;
> Set or retrieve the XML reader that this filter relies upon through this property. Requests for parsing flow up to this reader, while its events pass back down through the filter. Note that the parent may itself be another filter, allowing for chains of processing.

Preparing for SAX Events

To demonstrate how the SAX interfaces function, you can build a document viewer that operates from them, as opposed to the various DOMs used in the previous part of the book. Once more, the viewer has a tree view on the left that shows the structure of the document, with details of selected nodes appearing on the right. Figure 13-1 (on the following page) shows the viewer with the document node selected and the notations and external entities listed on the right.

The first step is to declare the handler interfaces that respond to the SAX events. Being interfaces, you can apply them directly to the viewer form. Listing 13-11 shows the form's type declaration, which is modified to implement the various handlers. The corresponding methods must then be declared within the `public` section of the form.

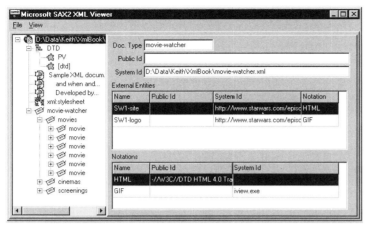

Figure 13-1: Document details via SAX.

Listing 13-11: Declaring the SAX interfaces

```
TfrmSAX2Viewer = class(TForm, IVBSAXEntityResolver, IVBSAXDTDHandler,
    IVBSAXContentHandler, IVBSAXErrorHandler,
    IVBSAXLexicalHandler, IVBSAXDeclHandler)
  pgcMain: TPageControl;
    tshStructure: TTabSheet;
      trvXML: TTreeView;
      pgcDetails: TPageControl;
        tshDocument: TTabSheet;
          Label1: TLabel;
          edtDocType: TEdit;
          Label2: TLabel;
          edtPublicId: TEdit;
          Label3: TLabel;
          edtSystemId: TEdit;
          Label6: TLabel;
          stgEntities: TStringGrid;
          Label7: TLabel;
          stgNotations: TStringGrid;
        tshElement: TTabSheet;
          pnlNames: TPanel;
            Label4: TLabel;
            edtURI: TEdit;
            Label5: TLabel;
            edtLocalName: TEdit;
          stgAttributes: TStringGrid;
          stgPrefixes: TStringGrid;
        tshText: TTabSheet;
          lblNodeType: TLabel;
          memText: TMemo;
    tshSource: TTabSheet;
      memSource: TRichEdit;
  mnuMain: TMainMenu;
    mniFile: TMenuItem;
      mniOpen: TMenuItem;
      mniSep1: TMenuItem;
      mniParserOptions: TMenuItem;
        mniValidation: TMenuItem;
```

```
      mniNamespaces: TMenuItem;
      mniNamespacePrefixes: TMenuItem;
    mniSep2: TMenuItem;
    mniExit: TMenuItem;
  mniView: TMenuItem;
    mniExpandAll: TMenuItem;
    mniCollapseAll: TMenuItem;
    mniSep3: TMenuItem;
    mniViewSource: TMenuItem;
  imlXML: TImageList;
  dlgOpen: TOpenDialog;
  procedure FormCreate(Sender: TObject);
  procedure FormDestroy(Sender: TObject);
  procedure mniOpenClick(Sender: TObject);
  procedure mniExitClick(Sender: TObject);
  procedure mniExpandAllClick(Sender: TObject);
  procedure mniCollapseAllClick(Sender: TObject);
  procedure mniViewSourceClick(Sender: TObject);
  procedure trvXMLChange(Sender: TObject; Node: TTreeNode);
private
  FCharIcon: Integer;
  FCurrent: TTreeNode;
  FLocator: IVBSAXLocator;
  FPrefixes: TStringList;
  FSAXReader: IVBSAXXMLReader;
  procedure ClearTree;
  procedure LoadDoc(Filename: string);
  procedure ShowError(Level: TMsgDlgType;
    const oLocator: IVBSAXLocator;
    const strError: WideString; nErrorCode: Integer);
  function TruncateText(Text: string): string;
public
  { IVBSAXEntityResolver }
  function resolveEntity(var strPublicId: WideString;
    var strSystemId: WideString): OleVariant; safecall;
  { IVBSAXDTDHandler }
  procedure notationDecl(var strName: WideString;
    var strPublicId: WideString; var strSystemId: WideString);
    safecall;
  procedure unparsedEntityDecl(var strName: WideString;
    var strPublicId: WideString; var strSystemId: WideString;
    var strNotationName: WideString); safecall;
  { IVBSAXContentHandler }
  procedure Set_documentLocator(const Param1: IVBSAXLocator); safecall;
  procedure startDocument; safecall;
  procedure endDocument; safecall;
  procedure startPrefixMapping(var strPrefix: WideString;
    var strURI: WideString); safecall;
  procedure endPrefixMapping(var strPrefix: WideString); safecall;
  procedure startElement(var strNamespaceURI: WideString;
    var strLocalName: WideString; var strQName: WideString;
    const oAttributes: IVBSAXAttributes); safecall;
  procedure endElement(var strNamespaceURI: WideString;
    var strLocalName: WideString; var strQName: WideString); safecall;
  procedure characters(var strChars: WideString); safecall;
  procedure ignorableWhitespace(var strChars: WideString); safecall;
  procedure processingInstruction(var strTarget: WideString;
    var strData: WideString); safecall;
  procedure skippedEntity(var strName: WideString); safecall;
  property documentLocator: IVBSAXLocator write Set_documentLocator;
```

```
  { IVBSAXLexicalHandler }
  procedure startDTD(var strName: WideString;
    var strPublicId: WideString; var strSystemId: WideString);
    safecall;
  procedure endDTD; safecall;
  procedure startEntity(var strName: WideString); safecall;
  procedure endEntity(var strName: WideString); safecall;
  procedure startCDATA; safecall;
  procedure endCDATA; safecall;
  procedure comment(var strChars: WideString); safecall;
  { IVBSAXDeclHandler }
  procedure elementDecl(var strName: WideString;
    var strModel: WideString); safecall;
  procedure attributeDecl(var strElementName: WideString;
    var strAttributeName: WideString; var strType: WideString;
    var strValueDefault: WideString; var strValue: WideString);
    safecall;
  procedure internalEntityDecl(var strName: WideString;
    var strValue: WideString); safecall;
  procedure externalEntityDecl(var strName: WideString;
    var strPublicId: WideString; var strSystemId: WideString);
    safecall;
  { IVBSAXErrorHandler }
  procedure error(const oLocator: IVBSAXLocator;
    var strError: WideString; nErrorCode: Integer); safecall;
  procedure fatalError(const oLocator: IVBSAXLocator;
    var strError: WideString; nErrorCode: Integer); safecall;
  procedure ignorableWarning(const oLocator: IVBSAXLocator;
    var strError: WideString; nErrorCode: Integer); safecall;
end;
```

The actual implementation of these methods appears later. Before they are called, though, an XML reader must be created and the handlers registered with it. You can do this in the `FormCreate` event since the reader can be reused. Listing 13-12 shows the necessary processing. Currently, attempting to set an entity resolver generates an error from the XML reader. The setting of the extension interfaces is wrapped in an exception handler to allow for the possibility that they are not supported. In that case, you simply ignore the error and process the remainder of the SAX events.

Listing 13-12: Registering the handlers

```
{ Initialization—load the XML document on start up }
procedure TfrmSAX2Viewer.FormCreate(Sender: TObject);
begin
  :
  { Other initializations }
  :
  { Load XML reader }
  FSAXReader              := CoSAXXMLReader.Create;
  { Set standard handlers }
  FSAXReader.ContentHandler := Self;
  FSAXReader.DTDHandler     := Self;
  FSAXReader.ErrorHandler   := Self;
  { Currently not implemented }
//  FSAXReader.EntityResolver := Self;
  { Set extension handlers }
  try
    FSAXReader.putProperty(LexicalHandlerProperty,
```

```
        IVBSAXLexicalHandler(Self));
    except
      { Ignore }
    end;
    try
      FSAXReader.putProperty(DeclHandlerProperty,
        IVBSAXDeclHandler(Self));
    except
      { Ignore }
    end;
end;
```

Finally, you can start the parse process. In the viewer you indicate the document to read by passing its filename to the `ParseURL` method of the reader (as shown in Listing 13-13). As it steps through the document it triggers the appropriate events through the attached handlers. Prior to starting the parse, an attempt is made to set several features on the reader. These correspond to checked menu options in the viewer. The call for each one is wrapped in an exception handler in case the reader cannot deal with it. If an error occurs, the related menu item is disabled to show that it does not apply.

Listing 13-13: Starting the parse process

```
{ Load an XML document }
procedure TfrmSAX2Viewer.LoadDoc(Filename: string);
begin
  try
    Screen.Cursor        := crHourGlass;
    pgcDetails.ActivePage := tshDocument;
    trvXML.Items.BeginUpdate;
    { Load the source document }
    memSource.Lines.LoadFromFile(Filename);
    dlgOpen.Filename     := Filename;
    { Attempt to set standard features from menu items }
    try
      FSAXReader.PutFeature(ValidationFeature, mniValidation.Checked);
    except
      mniValidation.Enabled := False;
    end;
    try
      FSAXReader.PutFeature(NamespacesFeature, mniNamespaces.Checked);
    except
      mniNamespaces.Enabled := False;
    end;
    try
      FSAXReader.PutFeature(NamespacePrefixesFeature,
        mniNamespacePrefixes.Checked);
    except
      mniNamespacePrefixes.Enabled := False;
    end;
    { Parse the document-form already registered
      with parser as handlers }
    FSAXReader.ParseURL(Filename);
  finally
    trvXML.Items.EndUpdate;
    Screen.Cursor := crDefault;
  end;
end;
```

Responding to the Notifications

The XML reader makes calls back to its attached handlers as it encounters the various parts of the XML document. Notifications about elements arrive through the content handler interface and its `startElement` and `endElement` methods (shown in Listing 13-14).

Listing 13-14: Element notifications

```
{ Note this element as the current node and save its attributes }
procedure TfrmSAX2Viewer.startElement(
  var strNamespaceURI, strLocalName, strQName: WideString;
  const oAttributes: IVBSAXAttributes);
var
  Element: TElement;
  Index: Integer;
begin
  Element := TElement.Create(strNamespaceUri, strLocalName);
  for Index := 0 to oAttributes.Length -1 do
    Element.Attributes.Values[oAttributes.getQName(Index)] :=
      oAttributes.getValue(Index);
  Element.Prefixes.Assign(FPrefixes);
  FPrefixes.Clear;
  FCurrent              :=
    trvXML.Items.AddChildObject(FCurrent, strQName, Element);
  FCurrent.ImageIndex    := ElementIcon;
  FCurrent.SelectedIndex := ElementIcon;
  if edtDocType.Text = '' then
    edtDocType.Text := strQName;
end;

{ Move the current context up the hierarchy when an element ends }
procedure TfrmSAX2Viewer.endElement(
  var strNamespaceURI, strLocalName, strQName: WideString);
begin
  FCurrent := FCurrent.Parent;
end;
```

For the viewer, you first create a `TElement` object to hold the node's details for later display. Then transfer the list of attributes supplied by the call into a normal string list on that object followed by any namespace declarations accumulated from the `startPrefixMapping` events that preceded this call. Lastly, add a new node to the tree view, using the element's qualified name as its display value, and attach the `TElement` to it as data. This new tree node becomes the current one for subsequent additions.

Conversely, when the end of the element arrives, you need to step back up the tree view hierarchy, setting the current node to its parent. Figure 13-2 shows the details for an element within the viewer.

Normal textual content arrives via the `characters` method (see Listing 13-15). Text consisting of all white space is discarded, with the remaining calls creating a new tree node and corresponding `TString` object. The latter simply wraps a single string property, which is needed since strings are not objects themselves. Text nodes do not alter the position of the current node within the tree view since they cannot have children. Figure 13-3 shows textual content in the viewer. Note that this XML reader treats each line of text as a separate item.

Chapter 13: Microsoft's SAX Parser   **315**

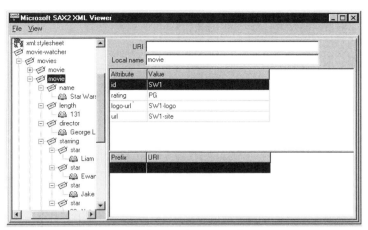

Figure 13-2: The viewer shows element information.

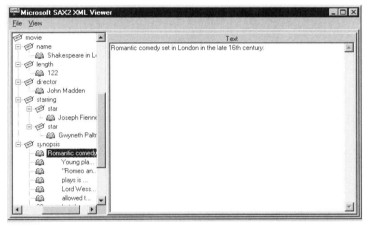

Figure 13-3: Textual content in the viewer.

Listing 13-15: Processing textual content

```
{ Add a text node to the tree }
procedure TfrmSAX2Viewer.characters(var strChars: WideString);
var
  Index: Integer;
  Text: string;
begin
  { Ignore all white space }
  Text := strChars;
  for Index := 1 to Length(Text) do
    if Text[Index] > ' ' then
      Break;
  if Index > Length(Text) then
    Exit;

  with trvXML.Items.AddChildObject(FCurrent, TruncateText(strChars),
    TString.Create(strChars)) do
```

```
    begin
      ImageIndex    := FCharIcon;
      SelectedIndex := FCharIcon;
    end;
end;
```

CDATA sections also send their content through the `characters` method. The difference is that `startCDATA` and `endCDATA` events surround the call. In this viewer, starting a CDATA section merely alters the value of `FCharIcon`, while ending it restores the original value. This variable controls the icon attached to the text in the tree view.

The remaining events generally just add a new tree node representing their content. An example is the `processingInstruction` method in Listing 13-16.

Listing 13-16: Handling a processing instruction

```
{ Add a processing instruction to the tree }
procedure TfrmSAX2Viewer.processingInstruction(
  var strTarget, strData: WideString);
begin
  with trvXML.Items.AddChildObject(
    FCurrent, strTarget, TString.Create(strData)) do
  begin
    ImageIndex    := ProcInstrIcon;
    SelectedIndex := ProcInstrIcon;
  end;
end;
```

By implementing the SAX handler interfaces, the form directly interacts with the XML reader. Once the parse process completes, you can select nodes from the tree view and see their content on the right of the form. The type of data attached to the tree node and the icon that represents that node control this display.

Summary

The SAX functionality provided by version 3.0 of Microsoft's XML package lets you process an XML document by responding to events generated by its various components. This lets you minimize the resources required for large documents compared to the DOM approach.

Once the MSXML type library is imported into Delphi, it is very easy to create your own handlers and hook them up to Microsoft's reader. The viewer described here shows how this is done.

Another feature of Microsoft's offering is the `IMXWriter` interface. Objects obtained through its CoClass implement the various handler interfaces and respond to them by generating an XML document on the fly. Chapter 20 describes this in greater detail.

The next chapter looks at implementing SAX in Delphi as native interfaces and classes. Then, Chapter 15 shows how you can wrap the Microsoft SAX reader in these Delphi interfaces, letting you easily swap between the two by changing only a single line of code.

Chapter 14
SAX in Delphi

The SAX specification defines a number of interfaces and classes that provide the functionality necessary to parse an XML document and work with its contents. Since they are interfaces, it is relatively easy to translate them into Delphi and implement them there. Delphi provides all the required language constructs: interfaces, inheritance, method overloading, and exceptions.

Conversion to Delphi

Converting the interfaces, originally expressed as Java, into Delphi is fairly straightforward. Starting with Delphi 3, the `interface` construct allows you to directly copy most of the API's declarations. Of course, there are some minor changes in keeping with Delphi's naming standards: interfaces start with I, classes with T, and exceptions with E, as well as prefixing each name with SAX as a way of producing unique names within the wider Delphi world. Also, properties were added as appropriate where `get` and/or `set` methods were defined, again maintaining the feel of Delphi.

Each interface is assigned a GUID to allow for its presence to be determined at some later stage. The methods are basically copied from the specification and some types are altered to reflect Delphi's capabilities, such as an enumerated type for the attribute types. A `TSAXString` type is declared as being equivalent to the `WideString` type. Subsequently, using this to define all string variables within the SAX implementation ensures that they are all the correct type.

The Delphi definitions for the basic SAX interfaces and classes are placed into several units, as shown in Table 14-1. These are then imported into the units that implement the various interfaces. Although the SAX1 interfaces and classes are available in these units, those that have been superceded are not described below.

Table 14-1: Delphi units for SAX

Unit	Purpose	Contents
SAX	Basic SAX1 specification	ISAXAttributeList, ISAXDocumentHandler, ISAXDTDHandler, ISAXEntityResolver, ISAXErrorHandler, ISAXLocator, ISAXParser, TSAXInputSource, ESAXException, ESAXParseException
SAXHelper	Common SAX1 implementations	TSAXAttribute, TSAXAttributeList, TSAXCustomParser, TSAXHandlerBase, TSAXLocator, TSAXParserFactory
SAXCue	ISAXParser wrapper (SAX1) for native Delphi XML parser provided by CUESoft	TSAXCuesoftParser
SAXDelphi	Native Delphi XML parser that implements ISAXParser (SAX1)	TSAXDelphiParser
SAXMS	Wrapper (SAX1) for MS XML v3 DOM that implements ISAXParser	TSAXMSParser
SAX2	Basic SAX2 specification	ISAXAttributes, ISAXContentHandler, ISAXXMLFilter, ISAXXMLReader, ESAXNotRecognizedException, ESAXNotSupportedException
SAX2Helper	Common SAX2 implementations	TSAXAttributes, TSAXCustomXMLFilter, TSAXCustomXMLReader, TSAXDefaultHandler, TSAXNamespaceSupport, TSAXParserAdapter, TSAXXMLReaderAdapter, TSAXXMLReaderFactory
SAX2Ext	SAX2 extension specification	ISAXDeclHandler, ISAXLexicalHandler
SAX2Delphi	Native Delphi XML reader that implements ISAXXMLReader (SAX2)	TSAX2DelphiReader
SAX2MS	Wrapper for MS XML 3 SAX2 parser that implements ISAXXMLReader	TSAX2MSReader
ParserXML	The native Delphi XML parser used by the native SAX1 parser and SAX2 reader	TXMLParser

ESAXException Class

The `ESAXException` class enables you to easily identify all those errors arising from processing with SAX. Error handlers can trap this type of error and process them accordingly.

This exception extends the base `Exception` class and adds the ability to wrap a "normal" exception, one that is not derived from `ESAXException`. Thus you can identify these errors as having been generated by the parsing activity, while retaining the details of the underlying problem.

The Delphi version of this class appears in Listing 14-1. It provides the abilities described above, as well as several overloaded constructors that accept the various error components.

Listing 14-1: The ESAXException class

```
ESAXException = class(Exception)
public
  { Create a new SAXException. }
  constructor Create(Message: string); overload;
  constructor Create(WrappedException: Exception); overload;
  constructor Create(Message: string; WrappedException:
    Exception); overload;
  property Message: string read GetMessage;
  property WrappedException: Exception read FException
    write FException;
end;
```

A description of the `ESAXException` class's properties and methods follows:

`constructor Create(Message: string); overload;`
`constructor Create(WrappedException: Exception); overload;`
`constructor Create(Message: string; WrappedException: Exception); overload;`

Generate new SAX exceptions with these constructors. The different versions let you supply whatever details you have about the error—from a simple message to a previous exception (optionally overriding its message). Normally only the SAX classes themselves would raise these errors, leaving you to react to them.

`property Message: string read GetMessage;`

Retrieve the description of the problem from this read-only property. The message of the embedded exception is returned if there is one and it has not been overridden by the normal message of the `ESAXException`.

`property WrappedException: Exception read FException write FException;`

Access any embedded exception through this property. It returns `nil` if there is no such exception.

SAX2 introduced two new defined exceptions: `ESAXNotRecognizedException` and `ESAXNotSupportedException`. Both are used when dealing with features and properties of readers. If the reader does not know about a feature or property, the first exception is raised. If the feature or property is known but cannot be handled by the reader, it raises the second exception. Both of these are derived directly from `ESAXException` and add no other functionality.

ESAXParseException Class

The `ESAXParseException` class extends the basic SAX exception to provide location information within the document. The Delphi version of this class appears in Listing 14-2. It provides the abilities described above, as well as numerous overloaded constructors that accept the various error components.

Listing 14-2: The `ESAXParseException` class

```
ESAXParseException = class(ESAXException)
public
  constructor Create(Message: string; PublicId, SystemId: TSAXString;
    LineNumber, ColumnNumber: Integer); overload;
  constructor Create(Message: string; PublicId, SystemId: TSAXString;
    LineNumber, ColumnNumber: Integer; WrappedException:
    Exception); overload;
  constructor Create(Message: string; Locator: ISAXLocator);
    overload;
  constructor Create(Message: string; Locator: ISAXLocator;
    WrappedException: Exception); overload;
  property ColumnNumber: Integer read FColumnNumber
    write FColumnNumber;
  property LineNumber: Integer read FLineNumber
    write FLineNumber;
  property PublicId: TSAXString read FPublicId write FPublicId;
  property SystemId: TSAXString read FSystemId write FSystemId;
end;
```

The properties and methods of the `ESAXParseException` class are listed below:

`constructor Create(Message: string; PublicId, SystemId: TSAXString; LineNumber, ColumnNumber: Integer); overload;`

`constructor Create(Message: string; PublicId, SystemId: TSAXString; LineNumber, ColumnNumber: Integer; WrappedException: Exception); overload;`

`constructor Create(Message: string; Locator: ISAXLocator); overload;`

`constructor Create(Message: string; Locator: ISAXLocator; WrappedException: Exception); overload;`

These constructors let you produce new parse exceptions while supplying whatever details are available. Information can include the error message, an embedded exception, and positional details in the form of a locator object or the actual line and column numbers. Normally these exceptions are only created by the reader and appear through the `ISAXErrorHandler` interface for you to deal with.

`property LineNumber: Integer read FLineNumber write FLineNumber;`
`property ColumnNumber: Integer read FColumnNumber write FColumnNumber;`

Retrieve or set the line or column within the line where the error is detected through these properties. They return –1 if the position is unknown.

`property PublicId: TSAXString read FPublicId write FPublicId;`

Find the public identifier for the document in error through this property. It returns an empty string if unknown.

property SystemId: TSAXString read FSystemId write FSystemId;
> This property retrieves the system identifier for the document that is in error. When unknown, it returns an empty string.

TSAXInputSource Class

The TSAXInputSource class (see Listing 14-3) is a helper class within SAX. Its purpose is to do the actual locating and loading of an external entity and to present it as a stream. This class knows how to deal with the Internet (at least using HTTP) to allow for the loading of remote documents. Input sources are used as the result of the ISAXEntityResolver.ResolveEntity method and as the input for the ISAXXMLReader.Parse method.

Listing 14-3: The TSAXInputSource class declaration

```
TSAXInputSource = class(TMemoryStream)
public
  constructor Create(Stream: TStream); overload;
  constructor Create(SystemId: TSAXString); overload;
  property Encoding: TSAXString read FEncoding write FEncoding;
  property PublicId: TSAXString read FPublicId write FPublicId;
  property SystemId: TSAXString read FSystemId write FSystemId;
end;
```

SAX readers use a TSAXInputSource object to retrieve the XML input. The Delphi implementation of this class extends TMemoryStream to provide the basic streaming abilities.

The TSAXInputSource class's properties and methods are shown below:

constructor Create(Stream: TStream); overload;
constructor Create(SystemId: TSAXString); overload;
> Generate a new input source from either an existing stream or from its system identifier. For the former, the stream is simply copied into the internal stream.
>
> Otherwise, the reader attempts to open a connection to the resource identified by the system identifier. An initial attempt is made to read the document from local storage and, if that fails, a further attempt is made to find it on the Internet, using the TNMHTTP component.
>
> A TSAXInputSource object belongs to the application; the SAX reader should never modify it in any way.

property Encoding: TSAXString read FEncoding write FEncoding;
> Set or read the encoding for the encapsulated stream with this property. If available, this is set manually following creation of the input source. It returns an empty string if unknown.

property PublicId: TSAXString read FPublicId write FPublicId;
> Specify the public identifier for the input through this property. Again, it should be set once the object is created. Otherwise, it returns an empty string.

```
property SystemId: TSAXString read FSystemId write FSystemId;
```
This property reads or writes the system identifier for the input. When the input is generated based on its system identifier, the value is automatically set. Otherwise, you should initialize it manually if known. It returns an empty string if never set.

ISAXLocator Interface

The `ISAXLocator` interface defines how to determine the current character position when parsing an XML document. A locator object is passed to a content handler at the start of the parse process. The handler may then refer back to that locator whenever it needs to find the current character position.

Note that the results returned by the object are only valid during the scope of each content handler method; the application receives unpredictable results if it attempts to use the locator at any other time.

SAX readers are not required to supply a locator, but they are very strongly encouraged to do so. If the reader does supply a locator, it must do so before reporting any other document events. If no locator has been set by the time the `StartDocument` event occurs, the application should assume that a locator is not available. Often the locator interface is implemented by the reader itself, as is the case for the base implementation in `TSAXCustomXMLReader`. Since it already has intimate knowledge of the document under consideration, this is a natural place for it to appear.

Most often the reader and content handler use the locator object to assist in reporting errors. For example, the content handler may impose further type restrictions on the incoming data than can be specified in XML alone. If the text does not conform, the handler could raise a parse exception and provide to it the location within the document that produced the error. This helps the problem to be traced and resolved by the user.

The Delphi definition of the interface is shown in Listing 14-4.

Listing 14-4: The *ISAXLocator* interface

```
ISAXLocator = interface(IUnknown)
  ['{669D9AA2-3D80-11D4-9ABD-B87D0AF18D62}']
  function GetPublicId: TSAXString;
  function GetSystemId: TSAXString;
  function GetLineNumber: Integer;
  function GetColumnNumber: Integer;
  property PublicId: TSAXString read GetPublicId;
  property SystemId: TSAXString read GetSystemId;
  property LineNumber: Integer read GetLineNumber;
  property ColumnNumber: Integer read GetColumnNumber;
end;
```

A description of the `ISAXLocator` interface's properties follows:

`property PublicId: TSAXString read GetPublicId;`
    Retrieve the public identifier for the document from this read-only property. It returns an empty string if unknown.

`property SystemId: TSAXString read GetSystemId;`
    This read-only property returns the system identifier for the document, or an empty string if not known.

`property LineNumber: Integer read GetLineNumber;`
`property ColumnNumber: Integer read GetColumnNumber;`
    Find the current line and column within the document through these read-only properties. A −1 is returned if the actual location is not known.

The `TSAXLocator` class in the `SAXHelper` unit provides a default implementation of the `ISAXLocator` interface. Normally, only application (handler) writers that want to take a snapshot of the location at a particular point would use this class. Its overloaded constructor allows you to easily copy an existing locator. For parser writers, it is probably more efficient to provide the location information only when requested, rather than constantly updating an instance of this class.

ISAXAttributes Interface

The `ISAXAttributes` interface provides access to a list of the attributes for an element. It passes attribute information to a content handler in the `StartElement` call. Details are provided only for attributes that have been set or that have default values (for a validating reader). Attributes that are implied but not specified do not appear.

The interface serves to hide the implementation details of the list from the rest of the application. Its Delphi definition is shown in Listing 14-5.

Listing 14-5: The `ISAXAttributes` interface

```
ISAXAttributes = interface
  ['{F430E0E0-3B30-11D4-9ABD-98F2DF77D546}']
  function AttrType(Index: Integer): TSAXAttributeType; overload;
  function AttrType(QName: TSAXString): TSAXAttributeType;
    overload;
  function AttrType(URI, LocalName: TSAXString):
    TSAXAttributeType; overload;
  function Index(QName: TSAXString): Integer; overload;
  function Index(URI, LocalName: TSAXString): Integer; overload;
  function Length: Integer;
  function LocalName(Index: Integer): TSAXString;
  function QName(Index: Integer): TSAXString;
  function URI(Index: Integer): TSAXString;
  function Value(Index: Integer): TSAXString; overload;
  function Value(QName: TSAXString): TSAXString; overload;
  function Value(URI, LocalName: TSAXString): TSAXString; overload;
end;
```

The methods of the ISAXAttributes interface are listed below:

```
function AttrType(Index: Integer): TSAXAttributeType; overload;
function AttrType(QName: TSAXString): TSAXAttributeType; overload;
function AttrType(URI, LocalName: TSAXString): TSAXAttributeType; overload;
```

> Get the attribute type from these methods. The attribute is identified by either its position in the collection (from zero to Length −1), its qualified name, or its namespace URI and local name. One of the values from the enumerated type below is returned:
>
> ```
> TSAXAttributeType = (atCData, atId, atIdref, atIdrefs, atNMToken, atNMTokens, atEntity,
>     atEntities, atNotation);
> ```
>
> If the type is unknown (such as when the DTD has not been loaded) it always comes back as atCData. You can obtain the corresponding text name for these types from the AttributeTypeNames array, which is indexed by the values above. Both of these are declared in the SAX unit.

```
function Index(QName: TSAXString): Integer; overload;
function Index(URI, LocalName: TSAXString): Integer; overload;
```

> Given the name of an attribute, either as its qualified name or its namespace URI and local name, these methods return its location within the attribute collection. A −1 comes back if no match is found with the supplied name.

```
function Length: Integer;
```

> Retrieve the number of entries in the collection from this method. Individual items are indexed from zero to this value −1.

```
function LocalName(Index: Integer): TSAXString;
```

> Get the local name for an attribute given its location from this method. If the index is out of bounds, an empty string is returned.

```
function QName(Index: Integer): TSAXString;
```

> Similarly, this method returns the qualified name for the attribute at the specified position, or an empty string if the index is out of bounds.

```
function URI(Index: Integer): TSAXString;
```

> Completing the set, this method retrieves the namespace URI for the attribute given its location. Again, an empty string results if the index is invalid.

```
function Value(Index: Integer): TSAXString; overload;
function Value(QName: TSAXString): TSAXString; overload;
function Value(URI, LocalName: TSAXString): TSAXString; overload;
```

> Use one of these methods to find the text value of an attribute. You can identify the attribute by its position, its qualified name, or its namespace URI and local name. An empty string is returned if the attribute cannot be found.

A standard implementation of this interface is defined in the SAX2Helper unit as the TSAXAttributes class. This default definition is due to the simple nature of the list. Its abilities are not likely to change greatly from one project to the next, unlike some of the other interfaces. Thus, a basic but functional implementation is available for use whenever it is required. Developers are able, indeed encouraged, to create more efficient implementations as necessary.

The attribute list is implemented as a string list within the `TSAXAttributes` class, which allows you to easily refer to the individual attributes either by position or by (qualified) name. Each entry in the string list contains a reference to a `TSAX2Attribute` object, which holds all the name parts, the type, and value of that attribute.

In addition to the functionality required by the interface, the attribute list provides methods to add new attributes, or alter or remove existing ones. These functions are not defined in the SAX specification to allow implementers to provide access in an efficient manner. The declaration for the `TSAXAttributes` class is shown in Listing 14-6.

Listing 14-6: The `TSAXAttributes` class

```
TSAXAttributes = class(TInterfacedObject, ISAXAttributes)
public
  constructor Create; overload;
  constructor Create(Attributes: ISAXAttributes); overload;
  destructor Destroy; override;
  procedure AddAttribute(URI, LocalName, QName, Value: TSAXString;
    AttrType: TSAXAttributeType = atCData);
  procedure Clear;
  procedure RemoveAttribute(Index: Integer);
  procedure SetAttribute(Index: Integer; URI, LocalName, QName, Value:
    TSAXString; AttrType: TSAXAttributeType = atCData);
  procedure SetAttributes(Attributes: ISAXAttributes);
  procedure SetAttrType(Index: Integer; AttrType: TSAXAttributeType);
  procedure SetLocalName(Index: Integer; LocalName: TSAXString);
  procedure SetQName(Index: Integer; QName: TSAXString);
  procedure SetURI(Index: Integer; URI: TSAXString);
  procedure SetValue(Index: Integer; Value: TSAXString);
  { ISAXAttributes }
  function AttrType(Index: Integer): TSAXAttributeType; overload;
  function AttrType(QName: TSAXString): TSAXAttributeType; overload;
  function AttrType(URI, LocalName: TSAXString): TSAXAttributeType;
    overload;
  function Index(QName: TSAXString): Integer; overload;
  function Index(URI, LocalName: TSAXString): Integer; overload;
  function Length: Integer;
  function LocalName(Index: Integer): TSAXString;
  function QName(Index: Integer): TSAXString;
  function URI(Index: Integer): TSAXString;
  function Value(Index: Integer): TSAXString; overload;
  function Value(QName: TSAXString): TSAXString; overload;
  function Value(URI, LocalName: TSAXString): TSAXString; overload;
end;
```

The `TSAXAttributes` class's properties and methods (beyond those for the `ISAXAttributes` interface) are shown below:

`constructor Create; overload;`
`constructor Create(Attributes: ISAXAttributes); overload;`
   Produces a new attribute list, which is initially empty or a copy of another list.

`procedure AddAttribute(URI, LocalName, QName, Value: TSAXString; AttrType:`
   `TSAXAttributeType = atCData);`
   Add a new attribute to the list, setting its properties to the given values. Attribute type defaults to `atCData`, which is the correct value if the DTD is not available and the actual type

is unknown. The list does not check whether an attribute under the given qualified name already exists; it just adds a new entry to the end of the list. The calling program should do any necessary checking.

procedure Clear;
Removes all the entries from the list.

procedure RemoveAttribute(Index: Integer);
Deletes the specified attribute from the list.

procedure SetAttribute(Index: Integer; URI, LocalName, QName, Value: TSAXString; AttrType: TSAXAttributeType = atCData);
Overwrite the properties of the attribute at the specified position with the values supplied here. Again, the attribute type defaults to the correct value if the actual type is unknown.

procedure SetAttributes(Attributes: ISAXAttributes);
Replace any existing contents with a copy of those in the given list.

procedure SetAttrType(Index: Integer; AttrType: TSAXAttributeType);
procedure SetLocalName(Index: Integer; LocalName: TSAXString);
procedure SetQName(Index: Integer; QName: TSAXString);
procedure SetURI(Index: Integer; URI: TSAXString);
procedure SetValue(Index: Integer; Value: TSAXString);
Use these methods to set individual properties on a specified attribute within the list.

ISAXContentHandler Interface

The ISAXContentHandler interface is the one most users of XML documents are interested in, allowing you to respond to the main sections of the document as they are encountered. An object expressing this interface is supplied to the reader, which then invokes the appropriate methods within it as it steps through the document.

ISAXContentHandler is defined as part of SAX2 and replaces the ISAXDocumentHandler interface of SAX1. It adds support for namespaces on elements and notifies the handler of entities that are skipped (in a non-validating reader). The Delphi definition of this interface is shown in Listing 14-7.

Listing 14-7: The ISAXContentHandler interface

```
ISAXContentHandler = interface
['{F430E0E1-3B30-11D4-9ABD-98F2DF77D546}']
procedure SetDocumentLocator(Locator: ISAXLocator);
procedure StartDocument;
procedure EndDocument;
procedure StartPrefixMapping(Prefix, URI: TSAXString);
procedure EndPrefixMapping(Prefix: TSAXString);
procedure StartElement(NamespaceURI, LocalName, QName:
  TSAXString; Attributes: ISAXAttributes);
procedure EndElement(NamespaceURI, LocalName, QName:
  TSAXString);
procedure Characters(Text: TSAXString);
procedure IgnorableWhitespace(Text: TSAXString);
```

```
    procedure ProcessingInstruction(Target, Data: TSAXString);
    procedure SkippedEntity(Name: TSAXString);
  end;
```

A description of the `ISAXContentHandler` interface's methods follows:

procedure SetDocumentLocator(Locator: ISAXLocator);
> This method lets the content handler tie into the parse process and find out where in the source document you are. Hence the content handler can perform further validations on the data, such as verifying date or numeric formats, etc., and report any violations while indicating the characters in error. If the reader supplies a locator, this method is called before any others during the parse process.

procedure StartDocument;
> This method signifies the beginning of a new XML document, allowing the handler to perform any necessary initializations, such as emptying a DOM structure or creating a new output file.

procedure EndDocument;
> Similarly, the reader calling this method terminates the document and lets you release any held resources. Here, the DOM structure could be normalized or the output file closed.

procedure StartPrefixMapping(Prefix, URI: TSAXString);
> To deal with namespace declarations within elements, this method informs you that a new mapping has been encountered. The mapping applies until the corresponding EndPrefix-Mapping method is called. These two calls always envelop the element notifications to which they refer.

procedure EndPrefixMapping(Prefix: TSAXString);
> Receive notification of the end of a namespace mapping through this method.

procedure StartElement(NamespaceURI, LocalName, QName: TSAXString; Attributes: ISAXAttributes);
> As elements are read from the XML document, this method notifies you of their presence. All the content of each tag is then processed through further calls before the corresponding EndElement method is invoked. Even for an empty tag, both of these routines are called.

procedure EndElement(NamespaceURI, LocalName, QName: TSAXString);
> Notification for the end of an element lets you finish up its processing. If you create a DOM from the SAX events you would step back up one level of the hierarchy at this point.

procedure Characters(Text: TSAXString);
> Basic textual content arrives via this method, including that derived from CDATA sections. In the latter case StartCData and EndCData calls (via the ISAXLexicalHandler interface) surround this call.

procedure IgnorableWhitespace(Text: TSAXString);
> White space between and within tags that is not significant is returned through this method. Knowing that white space is not necessary requires reading and processing a DTD for the document, so non-validating readers do not use this method. Instead, all white space comes through the Characters method.

procedure ProcessingInstruction(Target, Data: TSAXString);
: Embedded instructions appear via this method. Although the XML declaration at the start of each document appears like a processing instruction, it is not reported to the handler.

procedure SkippedEntity(Name: TSAXString);
: This method informs you that an entity reference was ignored. This happens in a non-validating reader that does not load external DTDs or entities. It can also happen when the reader is configured through various features.

The default implementation of this interface, as provided by the TSAXDefaultHandler class in the SAX2Helper unit, does nothing with the information provided. You can use this class as a base from which to derive your own content handler, allowing you to only override those methods that you wish to respond to.

Additional parts of the XML document are available as extensions to the SAX specification. These include comments and CDATA sections, which are discussed in the ISAXLexicalHandler and ISAXDeclHandler sections below.

ISAXDTDHandler Interface

The ISAXDTDHandler interface provides information on the notations and unparsed entities declared within an XML document. An object expressing this interface can be passed to a reader, which then calls its methods at the appropriate times as the document is processed.

Calls to these methods may appear in any order, not necessarily that of the document, but all such calls must arrive after the content handler's StartDocument call and before the first StartElement call. By saving these details, you can provide some level of support for these items within your application.

Listing 14-8 displays the Delphi definition for this interface.

Listing 14-8: The ISAXDTDHandler interface

```
ISAXDTDHandler = interface(IUnknown)
  ['{669D9AA1-3D80-11D4-9ABD-B87D0AF18D62}']
  procedure NotationDecl(Name, PublicId, SystemId: TSAXString);
  procedure UnparsedEntityDecl(
    Name, PublicId, SystemId, NotationName: TSAXString);
end;
```

The methods of the ISAXDTDHandler interface are listed below:

procedure NotationDecl(Name, PublicId, SystemId: TSAXString);
: The definition for a notation from the DTD appears through this method.

procedure UnparsedEntityDecl(Name, PublicId, SystemId, NotationName: TSAXString);
: This method informs you of unparsed entity declarations from the DTD. Note that parsed entities should be handled by the reader and incorporated into the current document. With the SAX extensions you can also receive notification of parsed entities through the ISAXDeclHandler interface.

The default implementation of this interface, as provided by the `TSAXDefaultHandler` class in the `SAXHelper` unit, does nothing with the information provided. You can use this class as a base from which to derive your own DTD handler, only allowing you to override those methods that you wish to respond to.

Recall that some XML documents may be usable without reference to their DTDs, whereas others may require the DTD to supply default attribute values or standard entity and notation references. Therefore, you may not be informed of all the notations and entities for a document, especially in a non-validating reader.

Additional parts of the DTD are available as extensions to the SAX specification. These include the DTD declaration itself, and element and attribute declarations. These are discussed in the `ISAXDeclHandler` section below.

ISAXEntityResolver Interface

The `ISAXEntityResolver` interface allows you to redirect searches for entities. An object expressing this interface can be supplied to the reader for its use. Then, whenever it needs to access a document, the reader passes the appropriate identifiers to the `ResolveEntity` method and expects the contents at that location to be returned as a stream, encapsulated by the `TSAXInputSource` class.

Implementing this interface enables you to translate a public or system identifier for an entity into an actual location. For example, you could retrieve the entity from a database rather than across the Internet, or you could supply a new version of an entity during testing. Readers know how to obtain documents from HTTP URLs, through the `TSAXInputSource` class, but may require a custom resolver if an alternate protocol is used.

The Delphi definition of the interface is shown in Listing 14-9.

Listing 14-9: The *ISAXEntityResolver* interface

```
ISAXEntityResolver = interface(IUnknown)
  ['{669D9AA0-3D80-11D4-9ABD-B87D0AF18D62}']
  function ResolveEntity(PublicId, SystemId: TSAXString):
    TSAXInputSource;
end;
```

The `ISAXEntityResolver` interface's method is described below:

function ResolveEntity(PublicId, SystemId: TSAXString): TSAXInputSource;
> This method accepts the public and system identifiers for an entity, and returns an input source that provides its content. If the entity is not being redirected, the method returns a `nil` value and the reader uses its normal methods for obtaining the content.

The default implementation of this interface, as supplied by the `TSAXDefaultHandler` class, simply returns `nil`, causing the reader to obtain any entities through the normal channels based on their public and/or system identifiers.

ISAXErrorHandler Interface

The `ISAXErrorHandler` interface provides notification of errors that occur during the SAX parsing process. Errors in SAX come in three levels of severity: *warnings* that you should be aware of but that do not compromise the accuracy of the document, *errors* that are more severe but still do not destroy the usefulness of the document, and *fatal errors* that invalidate the current document but may allow continued processing to reveal further errors.

These are represented by the three methods in this interface (see the Delphi definition in Listing 14-10). Each is passed an `ESAXParseException` that encapsulates the error condition and its location.

Listing 14-10: The ISAXErrorHandler interface

```
ISAXErrorHandler = interface(IUnknown)
  ['{669D9AA5-3D80-11D4-9ABD-B87D0AF18D62}']
  procedure Error(ParseError: ESAXParseException);
  procedure FatalError(ParseError: ESAXParseException);
  procedure Warning(ParseError: ESAXParseException);
end;
```

A list of the `ISAXErrorHandler` interface's methods follows:

procedure Error(ParseError: ESAXParseException);

  An error has occurred in parsing the document, as described in the exception supplied.

procedure FatalError(ParseError: ESAXParseException);

  A major error has occurred during parsing that may terminate the entire process. The document is no longer usable.

procedure Warning(ParseError: ESAXParseException);

  A warning about a problem in the parse process is notified through this method.

The default implementation of this interface, from the `TSAXDefaultHandler` class, does nothing for warnings and errors, but raises fatal errors as an exception to be processed elsewhere in the application. You can use this class as a base from which to derive you own error handler, allowing you to only override those methods that you wish to respond to.

SAX Extensions

Under SAX2, extensions to the basic SAX abilities are available in a standardized manner. The new `XMLReaders` provide a `Features` and a `Properties` attribute that lets you enhance or customize their behavior. Each extension is identified by a name based on a particular URI.

For both these attributes, if the reader does not understand the name supplied, it raises an `ESAXNotRecognizedException` to alert you to this fact. If it knows the name but cannot make use of it, it raises an `ESAXNotSupportedException`.

Several standard features are defined and are available as constant values in the SAX2 unit. The first two features are required to be recognized by all SAX-compliant XML readers.

`NamespacesFeature = 'http://xml.org/sax/features/namespaces';`
: This feature determines whether or not namespace URIs replace defined prefixes on elements and attributes. It defaults to `True`, which performs the replacement.

`NamespacePrefixesFeature = 'http://xml.org/sax/features/namespace-prefixes';`
: Determine whether or not qualified names are returned for elements and attributes through this feature. This feature also controls the passing back of namespace declaration attributes (with names like `xmlns:xxx`). It defaults to `False`, which makes the supply of qualified names optional and suppresses namespace declarations from attribute lists.

`ValidationFeature = 'http://xml.org/sax/features/validation';`
: This feature controls whether the reader performs validations on the documents processed. Set it to `True` to validate against a DTD.

`ExternalGeneralFeature = 'http://xml.org/sax/features/external-general-entities';`
: Determine whether or not external general entities may be skipped with this feature.

`ExternalParameterFeature = 'http://xml.org/sax/features/external-parameter-entities';`
: Similarly, this feature determines whether or not external parameter entities may be skipped.

ISAXLexicalHandler Interface

Additional notifications of lexical items within the XML document come through the `ISAXLexicalHandler` interface, a SAX extension. It informs you about comments, and the start and end of the DTD declaration, CDATA sections, and entity references. The Delphi definition is shown in Listing 14-11.

Listing 14-11: The *ISAXLexicalHandler* interface

```
ISAXLexicalHandler = interface
  ['{F430E0E5-3B30-11D4-9ABD-98F2DF77D546}']
  procedure Comment(Text: TSAXString);
  procedure StartCData;
  procedure EndCData;
  procedure StartDTD(Name, PublicId, SystemId: TSAXString);
  procedure EndDTD;
  procedure StartEntity(Name: TSAXString);
  procedure EndEntity(Name: TSAXString);
end;
```

The methods of the `ISAXLexicalHandler` interface are shown below:

`procedure Comment(Text: TSAXString);`
: Comments are identified by this method. These entries are generally only of interest to applications that are constructing or reviewing entire XML documents, rather than manipulating the content of those documents. Comments should not be relied upon to contain useful information, and may not be supplied at all by some readers. If this information is necessary, then using a processing instruction would be a better option.

```
procedure StartCData;
procedure EndCData;
```
> Although the text content of a CDATA section is passed on under the original SAX specification, the fact that it came from such a section is not. In this extension, the actual text is still supplied via the Characters method of the ISAXContentHandler interface, but this call is wrapped in a StartCData and EndCData pair to denote its source.

```
procedure StartDTD(Name, PublicId, SystemId: TSAXString);
procedure EndDTD;
```
> The DTD declaration, if one appears, is passed to the handler as a matched set of StartDTD and EndDTD calls. Between these two are notifications of all the references within that DTD. Notations and unparsed entities are supplied through the appropriate methods of the ISAXDTDHandler interface. Element and attribute declarations and parsed entities are notified through the methods of the ISAXDeclHandler interface defined below. The latter is another extension to SAX, and so cannot be relied upon from any given reader. Any comments or processing instructions encountered within the DTD declaration are passed on through the usual methods.

```
procedure StartEntity(Name: TSAXString);
procedure EndEntity(Name: TSAXString);
```
> Entity references found in the DTD of the document were quietly resolved and processed under SAX1. With the StartEntity and EndEntity methods you can be informed of their presence. All events arising from the contents of an entity must appear between these two calls. An external DTD also appears as an entity under this scheme, and has the name [dtd] assigned to it.

Parameter entities can also be reported and are denoted by their names beginning with a percent sign (%). Whether or not they are reported depends on the setting of the following feature (named in the SAX2Ext unit), where a value of True informs you:

```
ParameterEntitiesFeature = 'http://xml.org/sax/features/lexical-handler/
   parameter-entities';
```
> Any entities that are skipped are notified to you through the SkippedEntity method of the content handler.

A lexical handler is registered with the reader using its Properties property with the following name (defined in the SAX2Ext unit):

```
LexicalHandlerProperty =
    'http://xml.org/sax/properties/lexical-handler';
```

Thus the registration may appear like the example below:

```
MyXMLReader.Properties[LexicalHandlerProperty] :=
    MyLexicalHandler.Create;
```

ISAXDeclHandler Interface

Further information from the DTD comes from the ISAXDeclHandler interface, which is the second standard extension to SAX. It notifies you about element and attribute declarations, along with declarations for parsed entities. All the calls from this extension occur between the StartDTD and EndDTD notifications of the ISAXLexicalHandler interface (if this is in use). See Listing 14-12 for the Delphi declaration.

Listing 14-12: The *ISAXDeclHandler* interface

```
ISAXDeclHandler = interface
  ['{F430E0E4-3B30-11D4-9ABD-98F2DF77D546}']
  procedure AttributeDecl(
    EName, AName, AttrType, ValueDefault, Value: TSAXString);
  procedure ElementDecl(Name, Model: TSAXString);
  procedure ExternalEntityDecl(Name, PublicId, SystemId: TSAXString);
  procedure InternalEntityDecl(Name, Value: TSAXString);
end;
```

The ISAXDeclHandler interface's methods are detailed below:

procedure ElementDecl(Name, Model: TSAXString);
> Each element declaration is identified by this method, passing the element's name and its content model (as a string).

procedure AttributeDecl(EName, AName, AttrType, ValueDefault, Value: TSAXString);
> Similarly, the appearance of each attribute produces a call to this method. Along with the element and attribute names come the default declaration (#IMPLIED, #REQUIRED, #FIXED, or blank), any default value, and the attribute's type (as a string). The type includes the full token list for enumerated and notation types, after removing all white space.

procedure ExternalEntityDecl(Name, PublicId, SystemId: TSAXString);
procedure InternalEntityDecl(Name, Value: TSAXString);
> Parsed entities, as well as being used for internal replacement, are also defined to the handler. These methods are invoked depending on the type of entity encountered.

A declaration handler is also registered with the reader using its Properties property, but with the following name (also defined in the SAX2Ext unit):

```
DeclHandlerProperty = 'http://xml.org/sax/properties/declaration-handler';
```

It is then registered like the example below:

```
MyXMLReader.Properties[DeclHandlerProperty] := MyDeclHandler.Create;
```

ISAXXMLReader Interface

The `ISAXXMLReader` interface defines how an XML reader communicates with the various handlers. All SAX2 readers must implement this basic interface, which replaces the SAX1 `ISAXParser` one, providing support for the new `ISAXContentHandler`.

SAX readers are reusable but not re-entrant: the application may reuse a reader object (possibly with a different input source) once the first parse has completed successfully, but it may not invoke the `Parse` methods recursively within a parse.

The reader provides for the registering of a content handler, a DTD handler, an entity resolver, and/or an error handler. Additional functionality is requested or provided through the `Features` and `Properties` of the reader. When the `Parse` method is invoked, it calls routines in the registered handlers at appropriate times as it parses the document.

See Listing 14-13 for the Delphi definition of this interface. Implementations of ISAXXMLReader can be parsers, validating or not, written entirely in Delphi, or they can be wrappers around existing parsers.

Listing 14-13: The *ISAXXMLReader interface*

```
ISAXXMLReader = interface
  ['{F430E0E2-3B30-11D4-9ABD-98F2DF77D546}']
  function GetContentHandler: ISAXContentHandler;
  function GetDTDHandler: ISAXDTDHandler;
  function GetEntityResolver: ISAXEntityResolver;
  function GetErrorHandler: ISAXErrorHandler;
  function GetFeature(Name: TSAXString): Boolean;
  function GetProperty(Name: TSAXString): TObject;
  procedure Parse(Input: TSAXInputSource); overload;
  procedure Parse(SystemId: TSAXString); overload;
  procedure SetContentHandler(
    ContentHandler: ISAXContentHandler);
  procedure SetDTDHandler(DTDHandler: ISAXDTDHandler);
  procedure SetEntityResolver(
    EntityResolver: ISAXEntityResolver);
  procedure SetErrorHandler(ErrorHandler: ISAXErrorHandler);
  procedure SetFeature(Name: TSAXString; Value: Boolean);
  procedure SetProperty(Name: TSAXString; Value: TObject);
  property ContentHandler: ISAXContentHandler
    read GetContentHandler write SetContentHandler;
  property DTDHandler: ISAXDTDHandler
    read GetDTDHandler write SetDTDHandler;
  property EntityResolver: ISAXEntityResolver
    read GetEntityResolver write SetEntityResolver;
  property ErrorHandler: ISAXErrorHandler
    read GetErrorHandler write SetErrorHandler;
  property Features[Name: TSAXString]: Boolean
    read GetFeature write SetFeature;
  property Properties[Name: TSAXString]: TObject
    read GetProperty write SetProperty;
end;
```

A description of the ISAXXMLReader interface's properties and methods follows:

```
property ContentHandler: ISAXContentHandler read GetContentHandler write
    SetContentHandler;
property DTDHandler: ISAXDTDHandler read GetDTDHandler write SetDTDHandler;
property EntityResolver: ISAXEntityResolver read GetEntityResolver write
    SetEntityResolver;
property ErrorHandler: ISAXErrorHandler read GetErrorHandler write
    SetErrorHandler;
```
  Use these properties to set or retrieve the handlers to be invoked by the reader.

```
property Features[Name: TSAXString]: Boolean read GetFeature write SetFeature;
```
  This property reads or writes the setting for a named feature within the reader. Use the constants from the SAX2 and SAX2Ext units when accessing the standard features.

```
property Properties[Name: TSAXString]: TObject read GetProperty write SetProperty;
```
  Set or retrieve objects on the reader through this property. Again, you should use the constants from the SAX2Ext unit for the standard property names.

```
procedure Parse(Input: TSAXInputSource); overload;
procedure Parse(SystemId: TSAXString); overload;
```
  The heart of the SAX framework, these methods start the parse process. As items are encountered within the document, the corresponding methods on the various handlers registered with it are called. Input for the parsing comes from either an existing input source or from an identified resource (subsequently loaded through an input source object).

An abstract base for an ISAXXMLReader is defined as the TSAXCustomXMLReader class in the SAX2Helper unit. It handles the bookkeeping tasks of registering handlers and noting basic features, along with directing both versions of the parse method to a single routine. This protected ParseInput method is abstract, requiring the subclass to fill in how the parse is actually done.

The class also implements the ISAXLocator interface, providing positional feedback to the handlers. Since the reader is the object processing the document, it is in the best position to supply the locator details. The implementation in this class returns the default values, blank strings or –1, but can be easily overridden in subclasses.

Deriving a concrete reader from this base really only requires overriding the ParseInput method. Other enhancements could include returning actual location information, convenience constructors, and implementing additional features or properties.

ISAXXMLFilter Interface

Occasionally, it is useful to be able to modify the results of a parse operation before the final processing of the results. The `ISAXXMLFilter` interface (shown in Listing 14-14) defines this ability. It appears like an `ISAXXMLReader`, since it extends that interface, but responds to events from another source.

Listing 14-14: The ISAXXMLFilter interface

```
ISAXXMLFilter = interface(ISAXXMLReader)
  ['{F430E0E3-3B30-11D4-9ABD-98F2DF77D546}']
  function GetParent: ISAXXMLReader;
  procedure SetParent(Parent: ISAXXMLReader);
  property Parent: ISAXXMLReader read GetParent write SetParent;
end;
```

The one property of the `ISAXXMLFilter` interface is listed below:

`property Parent: ISAXXMLReader read GetParent write SetParent;`
  This property refers to the `ISAXXMLReader` that does the real processing (although this could be another filter in turn).

A default implementation of the filter is available in the `TSAXCustomXMLFilter` class in the `SAX2Helper` unit. All it does is pass parse requests up to its parent reader, and events back down to its registered handlers. Using this as a base, you can quickly implement a real filter by overriding only those requests or events of interest.

TSAXParserAdapter and TSAXXMLReaderAdapter Classes

To facilitate the uptake of SAX2 and to deal with legacy code, two classes are provided in the SAX2Helper unit to allow interoperation between SAX1 and SAX2 parsers and handlers.

The TSAXParserAdapter class (see Listing 14-15) wraps a SAX1 ISAXParser to make it appear like a SAX2 ISAXXMLReader. It implements the reader interface, passing DTD, entity, and error handler events directly through from the parser. It also implements the SAX1 `ISAXDocumentHandler` interface, which it converts into `ISAXContentHandler` events for the final consumer. Obviously, some events and abilities of a SAX2 reader cannot be reproduced from a SAX1 parser; however, the basic functionality is immediately available.

Listing 14-15: The TSAXParserAdapter class

```
TSAXParserAdapter = class(TInterfacedObject,
  ISAXXMLReader, ISAXDocumentHandler)
public
  constructor Create; overload;
  constructor Create(Parser: ISAXParser); overload;
  { ISAXXMLReader }
  procedure Parse(Input: TSAXInputSource); overload;
  procedure Parse(SystemId: TSAXString); overload;
  property ContentHandler: ISAXContentHandler
```

```
      read GetContentHandler write SetContentHandler;
    property DTDHandler: ISAXDTDHandler
      read GetDTDHandler write SetDTDHandler;
    property EntityResolver: ISAXEntityResolver
      read GetEntityResolver write SetEntityResolver;
    property ErrorHandler: ISAXErrorHandler
      read GetErrorHandler write SetErrorHandler;
    { ISAXDocumentHandler }
    procedure Characters(Text: TSAXString);
    procedure EndDocument;
    procedure EndElement(QName: TSAXString);
    procedure IgnorableWhitespace(Text: TSAXString);
    procedure ProcessingInstruction(Target, Data: TSAXString);
    procedure SetDocumentLocator(Locator: ISAXLocator);
    procedure StartDocument;
    procedure StartElement(QName: TSAXString; Attributes: ISAXAttributeList);
  end;
```

The TSAXParserAdapter class's methods are shown below:

```
constructor Create; overload;
constructor Create(Parser: ISAXParser); overload;
```

Produce a new adapter with these constructors. If you specify a parser, it is used to process the documents. Otherwise, a default parser is created through the TSAXParserFactory class.

The adapter's remaining properties and methods duplicate those described in the ISAXXMLReader and ISAXDocumentHandler interfaces.

Conversely, TSAXXMLReaderAdapter wraps a SAX2 ISAXXMLReader to make it act like a SAX1 ISAXParser (see Listing 14-16). Similarly to the parser adapter, this one passes through whatever events it can, while converting content handler events into document handler ones. The extra functionality of SAX2 is basically ignored and discarded.

Listing 14-16: The TSAXXMLReaderAdapter class

```
TSAXXMLReaderAdapter = class(TInterfacedObject,
    ISAXParser, ISAXContentHandler)
  public
    constructor Create; overload;
    constructor Create(XMLReader: ISAXXMLReader); overload;
    destructor Destroy; override;
    { ISAXParser }
    procedure Parse(Input: TSAXInputSource); overload;
    procedure Parse(SystemId: TSAXString); overload;
    property DocumentHandler: ISAXDocumentHandler
      read GetDocumentHandler write SetDocumentHandler;
    property DTDHandler: ISAXDTDHandler
      read GetDTDHandler write SetDTDHandler;
    property EntityResolver: ISAXEntityResolver
      read GetEntityResolver write SetEntityResolver;
    property ErrorHandler: ISAXErrorHandler
      read GetErrorHandler write SetErrorHandler;
    { ISAXContentHandler }
    procedure Characters(Text: TSAXString);
    procedure EndDocument;
    procedure EndElement(NamespaceURI, LocalName, QName: TSAXString);
    procedure EndPrefixMapping(Prefix: TSAXString);
    procedure IgnorableWhitespace(Text: TSAXString);
    procedure ProcessingInstruction(Target, Data: TSAXString);
```

```
    procedure SetDocumentLocator(Locator: ISAXLocator);
    procedure SkippedEntity(Name: TSAXString);
    procedure StartDocument;
    procedure StartElement(NamespaceURI, LocalName, QName: TSAXString;
      Attributes: ISAXAttributes);
    procedure StartPrefixMapping(Prefix, URI: TSAXString);
  end;
```

A listing of the TSAXXMLReaderAdapter class's methods follows:

constructor Create; overload;
constructor Create(XMLReader: ISAXXMLReader); overload;

> Build a new adapter with these constructors. If you do not specify a reader to use, the TSAXXMLReaderFactory class creates a default one.

Again, the adapter's other properties and methods duplicate those discussed elsewhere in the ISAXParser and ISAXContentHandler interfaces.

TSAXXMLReaderFactory Class

To make it easier to create readers for use in parsing documents, SAX includes factory classes. These allow you to identify a reader by name and have it instantiated within the program. In this way, the actual reader can be determined at run time, possibly from an initialization file or the registry.

In Delphi you can make use of one of the abilities of TPersistent to achieve this. Descendants of this class can be registered with the application to allow them to be used with the streaming functionality. Thus, instances of classes can be created, based on their names, as they are encountered within a .dfm file being read in.

The FindClass routine takes a class name as a parameter and returns a reference to the class that it corresponds to. From this class reference you can call Create to build an instance of it. Finally, the resulting class is cast as the required interface and returned for your use.

Since only classes descended from TPersistent can be constructed using this technique, and given that the reader implements one or more interfaces, an appropriate base class is defined in the SAXHelper unit as TInterfacedPersistent. This class is derived from TPersistent and only adds the basic reference counting and interface querying of IUnknown. This class is then used as a base for all the readers in SAX.

Before a class can be found in this manner, it must be registered with the application. The RegisterClass routine does just this, taking the class as its parameter. By making this call in the initialization section of the unit containing the reader, you ensure that it is available whenever the program needs it. The class is unregistered in the finalization section.

```
initialization
  RegisterClass(TSAX2DelphiReader);
finalization
  UnRegisterClass(TSAX2DelphiReader);
end.
```

TSAXXMLReaderFactory (see Listing 14-17) is defined as a static class. All its methods are declared as class methods, meaning that they can be invoked from the class itself, without creating an actual object.

Listing 14-17: The *TSAXXMLReaderFactory* class

```
TSAXXMLReaderFactory = class(TObject)
public
  constructor Create;
  class function CreateXMLReader: ISAXXMLReader; overload;
  class function CreateXMLReader(Name: TSAXString): ISAXXMLReader;
    overload;
end;
```

The methods of the TSAXXMLReaderFactory class are described below:

constructor Create;

The constructor raises an exception since you do not instantiate this class.

class function CreateXMLReader(Name: TSAXString): ISAXXMLReader; overload;

Given the name of a class that implements the ISAXXMLReader interface (and that has registered itself with the system), this method generates an instance of that class (using FindClass) and returns it as a reader. If the specified class cannot be found, an exception occurs.

class function CreateXMLReader: ISAXXMLReader; overload;

Similarly, this method creates and returns an instance of a default class that implements the reader interface. But how can we identify the default reader? Rather than hard-code a particular class or rely on a command line parameter, you can get the name from an environment variable. For SAX2, this variable is called SAX2RDR, which is set to the name of the appropriate class. A line like the following placed in your autoexec.bat establishes the setting:

    SET SAX2RDR=TSAX2DelphiReader

For the TSAXParserFactory class, the default SAX1 parser is obtained from the SAXPSR environment variable. These values can be set up at boot time, or could be added by .bat files or even programmatically.

The implementation of the TSAXXMLReaderFactory is shown in Listing 14-18.

Listing 14-18: Implementing the factory

```
{ Attempt to create an XML reader from an environment variable.
  This method uses the value of the environment variable SAX2RDR
  as the full name of a Delphi class and tries to instantiate
  that class as a SAX2 ISAXXMLReader. This class must have been
  registered with a call to RegisterClass.
}
class function TSAXXMLReaderFactory.CreateXMLReader:
  ISAXXMLReader;
var
  Buffer: array [0..255] of Char;
begin
  GetEnvironmentVariable(EnvReader, Buffer, 255);
  Result := CreateXMLReader(Buffer);
end;
{ Attempt to create an XML reader from a class name.
```

```
    Given a class name, this method attempts to load
    and instantiate the class as an XML reader. This class must
    have been registered with a call to RegisterClass.
  }
  class function TSAXXMLReaderFactory.CreateXMLReader(
    Name: TSAXString): ISAXXMLReader;
  var
    ReaderClass: TInterfacedPersistentClass;
    Reader: TInterfacedPersistent;
  begin
    try
      ReaderClass := TInterfacedPersistentClass(FindClass(Name));
      Reader      := ReaderClass.Create;
      Result      := Reader as ISAXXMLReader;
    except on Exc: Exception do
      raise ESAXException.Create(Format(NoParser, [Name]), Exc);
    end;
  end;
```

TSAXDefaultHandler Class

The `TSAXDefaultHandler` class provides a default implementation of the various basic handler interfaces. This class serves two purposes: firstly as a base class for customized handlers, and secondly as a possible default for a SAX reader when no other handler is specified. Defined in SAX2, this class replaces the `TSAXHandlerBase` class of SAX1.

In most cases this class does nothing as a result of the calls made to it. The one exception is the `FatalError` method of the error handler, which raises the exception to the application.

Since this class already provides do-nothing implementations of all the methods for each handler interface, you only need to override those methods that you are interested in when deriving a custom handler. The remaining methods inherit the abilities of the base class and happily ignore any other calls. All methods are declared as `virtual` to allow for this overriding.

The Delphi declaration of this class is shown in Listing 14-19. It just provides implementations for the four standard handlers defined in SAX.

Listing 14-19: The *TSAXDefaultHandler* class

```
TSAXDefaultHandler = class(TInterfacedObject, ISAXEntityResolver,
  ISAXDTDHandler, ISAXContentHandler, ISAXErrorHandler)
public
  { ISAXEntityResolver }
  function ResolveEntity(PublicId, SystemId: TSAXString):
    TSAXInputSource; virtual;
  { ISAXDTDHandler }
  procedure NotationDeclaration(
    Name, PublicId, SystemId: TSAXString); virtual;
  procedure UnparsedEntityDeclaration(
    Name, PublicId, SystemId, NotationName: TSAXString); virtual;
  { ISAXContentHandler }
  procedure Characters(Text: TSAXString); virtual;
  procedure EndDocument; virtual;
  procedure EndElement(NamespaceURI, LocalName, QName:
    TSAXString); virtual;
  procedure EndPrefixMapping(Prefix: TSAXString); virtual;
  procedure IgnorableWhitespace(Text: TSAXString); virtual;
```

```
    procedure ProcessingInstruction(Target, Data: TSAXString);
      virtual;
    procedure SetDocumentLocator(Locator: ISAXLocator); virtual;
    procedure SkippedEntity(Name: TSAXString); virtual;
    procedure StartDocument; virtual;
    procedure StartElement(NamespaceURI, LocalName, QName:
      TSAXString; Attributes: ISAXAttributes); virtual;
    procedure StartPrefixMapping(Prefix, URI: TSAXString); virtual;
    { ISAXErrorHandler }
    procedure Error(Exception: ESAXParseException); virtual;
    procedure FatalError(Exception: ESAXParseException); virtual;
    procedure Warning(Exception: ESAXParseException); virtual;
  end;
```

Building a SAX Reader

Now that the basic components of SAX have been defined in Delphi, you can construct an actual reader that implements this functionality.

The SAX reader loads a document, interprets its contents, and makes calls to its registered handlers to enable them to process the resulting information. In general, you would write a new content handler for each document type, dealing with the specific tags present therein.

Although this may seem like more work than having a consistent object model to deal with, you would still have to write customized code for each application to extract the information from that model. The big advantage with using SAX is that your handlers can interact with any reader that implements the SAX ISAXXMLReader interface. This allows you to swap readers as new technologies appear without affecting the remainder of the application. Similarly, one reader can be used to supply any number of handlers in a consistent manner.

Both a native Delphi SAX1 parser and a SAX2 reader are implemented in the accompanying package. They each rely on the TXMLParser class (see Listing 14-21) defined in the ParserXML unit, which extends the basic abilities of the TCustomParser class (see Listing 14-20) from the ParserBase unit. The custom parser provides functionality common to many parsers (reading a stream, handling character encodings, and counting lines and columns), while the XML reader knows about XML and returns XML-specific tokens to the caller.

Listing 14-20: The *TCustomParser* class

```
    TCustomParser = class(TObject)
    protected
      FStream: TStream;
      property Column: Integer read FColumn write FColumn;
      property CurChar: WideChar read FCurChar write FCurChar;
      property Encoding: TEncoding read FEncoding write FEncoding;
      property Line: Integer read FLine write FLine;
      property Token: TCustomToken read FToken write FToken;
      property TokenString: WideString read FTokenString
        write FTokenString;
      procedure Error(const Message: string); virtual;
      function ExtractTo(CharSet: WideString; EOFError: string):
        WideString; virtual;
      function NextChar: WideChar; virtual;
      function NextToken: TCustomToken; virtual;
      function PeekChar: WideChar; virtual;
```

```
    function PeekString(Text: WideString): Boolean; virtual;
    procedure SkipBlanks; virtual;
  public
    constructor Create(Stream: TStream); virtual;
  end;
```

The TCustomParser class's properties and methods are discussed below:

constructor Create(Stream: TStream); virtual;

>Produce a new basic parser that operates on the supplied stream. The parser immediately moves to the first token.

property Encoding: TEncoding read FEncoding write FEncoding;

>This property sets or retrieves the encoding scheme used in the stream. Its value must be one of those in Table 14-2. Initially it is set to enUnknown and it is up to the user of the parser to set it correctly.

Table 14-2: Encoding types

Encoding	Description
enUnknown	The scheme is unknown and is treated as straight ASCII (single byte characters).
enUTF8	The scheme is UTF-8, a multi-byte encoding for Unicode that is optimized for ASCII characters.
enUTF16BE	The scheme is UTF-16BE, a 16-bit encoding for Unicode in big-endian ordering.
enUTF16LE	The scheme is UTF-16LE, a 16-bit encoding for Unicode in little-endian ordering.

property Line: Integer read FLine write FLine;
property Column: Integer read FColumn write FColumn;

>Obtain the current line and column number through these properties. Line counts are based on the presence of line feed characters. Both counts start at one.

property CurChar: WideChar read FCurChar write FCurChar;

>This property returns the character most recently read from the stream. Note that this may correspond to one or more bytes based on the encoding used. A null character (EOF) is returned once the end of the stream is reached.

property Token: TCustomToken read FToken write FToken;

>Retrieve the token type just read from this property. At this level it is either toCharacter for a normal character or toEOF at the end of the stream.

property TokenString: WideString read FTokenString write FTokenString;

>At this level, this property simply returns the current character.

function NextChar: WideChar; virtual;

>Extract the next character from the input stream through this method, setting the CurChar property in the process. Based on the current encoding this may consist of more than one byte. It returns EOF if the end of the stream is reached.

function PeekChar: WideChar; virtual;

>This method returns the next character from the stream without actually reading it, giving you a one-character look ahead.

function PeekString(Text: WideString): Boolean; virtual;
Check for the presence of an entire string with this method. It returns True if the string is next in the input stream and advances the stream position to just after that value. Otherwise, it returns False without changing the stream position.

function NextToken: TCustomToken; virtual;
Retrieve the next token from the input stream through this method. It returns toEOF at the end of the stream. Normally, this method controls the loop that steps through the contents of the file.

function ExtractTo(CharSet: WideString; EOFError: string): WideString; virtual;
Given a set of characters to match on, this method compiles and returns characters from the stream up to but not including the delimiter. Each character in the first parameter is looked for individually. If the end of the stream is found before any of the terminating characters, an error is generated using the supplied text.

procedure SkipBlanks; virtual;
Skip over white space characters with this method. The stream is left just before the first non-white space character found.

procedure Error(const Message: string); virtual;
Raise an exception from the parser with this method. It attaches the current line and column numbers to the supplied message before signaling the error.

Listing 14-21: The *TXMLParser* class

```
TXMLParser = class(TCustomParser)
protected
  procedure Error(const Message: string); override;
  function ExtractTo(CharSet: WideString; EOFError: string):
    TSAXString; override;
public
  constructor Create(Stream: TStream); override;
  destructor Destroy; override;
  property Line;
  property Column;
  property Token: TXMLToken read FToken write FToken;
  property TagType: TXMLTagType read FTagType write FTagType;
  property TokenString;
  property Attributes: TStringList read FAttributes;
  function NextToken: TXMLToken;
end;
```

A listing of the TXMLParser class's properties and methods follows. Those not discussed match the corresponding ones from the basic parser.

constructor Create(Stream: TStream); override;
This constructor determines the encoding for the stream (as described in the XML specification) before proceeding with the rest of the processing.

property Token: TXMLToken read FToken write FToken;
Replacing the inherited property, this one returns an indication of the type of XML token encountered. See Table 14-3 for a list of valid values.

Part III: Simple API for XML

Table 14-3: XML token types

Token	Description	TokenString
toEOF	End of stream reached	
toElement	An element	The element name
toComment	A comment	The comment text
toInstruction	A processing instruction	The target
toText	A text node	The text
toCData	A CDATA section	The text
toEntityRef	An entity reference	The entity name
toDTD	The DTD declaration	The DTD name
toEntity	An entity declaration	The entity name
toNotation	A notation declaration	The notation name
toElementDecl	An element declaration	The element name
toAttrDecl	An attribute declaration	The element name

`property TokenString;`

The meaning of this property depends on the token type as shown in Table 14-3.

`property TagType: TXMLTagType read FTagType write FTagType;`

Applicable to element and DTD declaration nodes, this property defines whether it is the start or end of that node. The valid values are shown in Table 14-4.

Table 14-4: XML tag types

Tag Type	Description
ttOpening	This is the start of the node.
ttClosing	This is the end of the node.
ttEmpty	For an element only, this node is empty.

`property Attributes: TStringList read FAttributes;`

This property is overloaded in meaning depending on the token type. See Table 14-5 for a description of its contents.

Table 14-5: Attributes meanings

Token	Attributes
toEOF	Empty
toElement	On the opening tag, contains attribute values accessed through the Values property by name
toComment	Empty
toInstruction	First entry is the data portion of the processing instruction
toText	Empty
toCData	Empty

Token	Attributes
toEntityRef	Empty
toDTD	On the opening tag, contains settings from the DTD declaration accessed through the Values property by the following name constants: PublicAttr and SystemAttr
toEntity	Contains settings from the entity declaration accessed through the Values property by the following name constants: PublicAttr, SystemAttr, NDataAttr, and ValueAttr.
toNotation	Contains settings from the notation declaration accessed through the Values property by the following name constants: PublicAttr and SystemAttr.
toElementDecl	The first entry is the content model for the element.
toAttrDecl	Entries are the (white space delimited) tokens that make up the attribute declaration list for this tag, which may include several attributes.

```
function NextToken: TXMLToken;
```
This method reads the next token from the input stream and returns its type. In the process it establishes the values of the remaining properties.

The SAX XML Viewer

Putting it all together you can build another version of the XML viewer from the DOM section (see Figure 14-1). This time, a SAX reader instead of the DOM does the processing of the document, with the results being shown in the same tree structure.

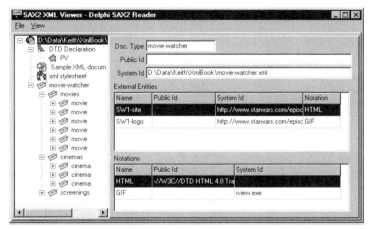

Figure 14-1: The SAX document viewer.

Since the viewer form is the object interested in the contents of the XML document, it can implement the various SAX handler interfaces directly. This is one of the main benefits of using interfaces—any object, regardless of its position in the object hierarchy, can express the necessary functionality. The declaration for the form needs to be altered to reflect these extra abilities. In its type definition, add the SAX handler references as shown in Listing 14-22. Then add all the methods from these interfaces to its `public` section.

Listing 14-22: XML viewer form implementing SAX handler interfaces

```
type
  TfrmSAX2Viewer = class(TForm, ISAXDTDHandler,
      ISAXContentHandler, ISAXErrorHandler,
      ISAXLexicalHandler, ISAXDeclHandler)
    pgcMain: TPageControl;
    tshStructure: TTabSheet;
      trvXML: TTreeView;
      pgcDetails: TPageControl;
        tshDocument: TTabSheet;
          Label1: TLabel;
          edtDocType: TEdit;
          Label2: TLabel;
          edtPublicId: TEdit;
          Label3: TLabel;
          edtSystemId: TEdit;
          Label6: TLabel;
          stgEntities: TStringGrid;
          Label7: TLabel;
          stgNotations: TStringGrid;
        tshElement: TTabSheet;
          pnlNames: TPanel;
            Label4: TLabel;
            edtURI: TEdit;
            Label5: TLabel;
            edtLocalName: TEdit;
          stgAttributes: TStringGrid;
          stgPrefixes: TStringGrid;
        tshText: TTabSheet;
          lblNodeType: TLabel;
          memText: TMemo;
    tshSource: TTabSheet;
      memSource: TRichEdit;
    mnuMain: TMainMenu;
      mniFile: TMenuItem;
        mniOpen: TMenuItem;
        mniSep1: TMenuItem;
        mniParser: TMenuItem;
          mniDelphi2: TMenuItem;
          mniDelphi1: TMenuItem;
          mniMicrosoft2: TMenuItem;
          mniMicrosoft1: TMenuItem;
        mniParserOptions: TMenuItem;
          mniValidation: TMenuItem;
          mniNamespaces: TMenuItem;
          mniNamespacePrefixes: TMenuItem;
        mniSep2: TMenuItem;
        mniExit: TMenuItem;
      mniView: TMenuItem;
        mniExpandAll: TMenuItem;
        mniCollapseAll: TMenuItem;
        mniSep3: TMenuItem;
        mniViewSource: TMenuItem;
    imlXML: TImageList;
    dlgOpen: TOpenDialog;
    procedure FormCreate(Sender: TObject);
```

```delphi
    procedure FormDestroy(Sender: TObject);
    procedure mniOpenClick(Sender: TObject);
    procedure mniParserClick(Sender: TObject);
    procedure mniExitClick(Sender: TObject);
    procedure mniExpandAllClick(Sender: TObject);
    procedure mniCollapseAllClick(Sender: TObject);
    procedure mniViewSourceClick(Sender: TObject);
    procedure trvXMLChange(Sender: TObject; Node: TTreeNode);
  private
    FSAXReader: ISAXXMLReader;
    FLocator: ISAXLocator;
    FCurrent: TTreeNode;
    FCaption: string;
    FCharIcon: Integer;
    FPrefixes: TStringList;
    procedure ClearTree;
    procedure LoadDoc(sFilename: string);
    procedure ShowError(mtLevel: TMsgDlgType; ParseError:
      ESAXParseException);
    function TruncateText(Text: string): string;
  public
    { ISAXDTDHandler }
    procedure NotationDecl(Name, PublicId, SystemId: TSAXString);
    procedure UnparsedEntityDecl(
      Name, PublicId, SystemId, NotationName: TSAXString);
    { ISAXContentHandler }
    procedure Characters(Text: TSAXString);
    procedure EndDocument;
    procedure EndElement(NamespaceURI, LocalName, QName: TSAXString);
    procedure EndPrefixMapping(Prefix: TSAXString);
    procedure IgnorableWhitespace(Text: TSAXString);
    procedure ProcessingInstruction(Target, Data: TSAXString);
    procedure SetDocumentLocator(Locator: ISAXLocator);
    procedure SkippedEntity(Name: TSAXString);
    procedure StartDocument;
    procedure StartElement(NamespaceURI, LocalName, QName:
      TSAXString; Attributes: ISAXAttributes);
    procedure StartPrefixMapping(Prefix, URI: TSAXString);
    { ISAXErrorHandler }
    procedure Error(ParseError: ESAXParseException);
    procedure FatalError(ParseError: ESAXParseException);
    procedure Warning(ParseError: ESAXParseException);
    { ISAXDeclHandler }
    procedure AttributeDecl(
      EName, AName, AttrType, ValueDefault, Value: TSAXString);
    procedure ElementDecl(Name, Model: TSAXString);
    procedure ExternalEntityDecl(Name, PublicId, SystemId:
      TSAXString);
    procedure InternalEntityDecl(Name, Value: TSAXString);
    { ISAXLexicalHandler }
    procedure Comment(Text: TSAXString);
    procedure EndCData;
    procedure EndDTD;
    procedure EndEntity(Name: TSAXString);
    procedure StartCData;
    procedure StartDTD(Name, PublicId, SystemId: TSAXString);
    procedure StartEntity(Name: TSAXString);
  end;
```

Registering the form with the reader lets it respond to the events defined by the handler interfaces. The basic SAX handlers are set directly into the reader through the correspondingly named properties. Extended handlers must be registered through the Properties property. In these cases, you need to trap exceptions that may arise due to that property not being recognized or supported. Listing 14-23 shows the necessary code.

Listing 14-23: Registering handlers with the XML reader

```
FSAXReader.ContentHandler := Self;
FSAXReader.DTDHandler     := Self;
FSAXReader.ErrorHandler   := Self;
try
  FSAXReader.Properties[DeclHandlerProperty] := Self;
except
  { Ignore }
end;
try
  FSAXReader.Properties[LexicalHandlerProperty] := Self;
except
  { Ignore }
end;
```

Various menu items within the viewer let you control some of the standard features of a SAX reader. Within the code these are set immediately before starting the parse process (see Listing 14-24) since they may be updated by the user at any time. As with the properties above, setting a feature may result in an exception if it is unknown or not supported. In that case, the corresponding menu item is disabled indicating that this feature cannot be used on this reader.

Listing 14-24: Setting reader properties and starting the parse process

```
{ Attempt to set various feature }
try
  FSAXReader.Features[ValidationFeature] := mniValidation.Checked;
except on ESAXException do
  mniValidation.Enabled := False;
end;
try
  FSAXReader.Features[NamespacesFeature] := mniNamespaces.Checked;
except on ESAXException do
  mniNamespaces.Enabled := False;
end;
try
  FSAXReader.Features[NamespacePrefixesFeature] :=
    mniNamespacePrefixes.Checked;
except on ESAXException do
  mniNamespacePrefixes.Enabled := False;
end;
{ Parse the document-form already registered
  with parser as handlers }
FSAXReader.Parse(Filename);
```

Implementing ISAXContentHandler

Each of these methods must now be implemented for the viewer to function. The StartDocument method initializes all the display parts of the form in preparation for the parsing of the new document. The tree view is cleared of its current contents, and the root node (for the document as a whole) is added and made current in FCurrent. At the end of the process the EndDocument method opens up the root node in the tree to expose the top-level structure of the document. These routines are shown in Listing 14-25.

Listing 14-25: Starting and ending the document

```
{ Initialization for a new document display }
procedure TfrmSAX2Viewer.StartDocument;
begin
  ClearTree;
  FCurrent := trvXML.Items.AddChild(nil, dlgOpen.FileName);
  FCurrent.ImageIndex    := iDocumentIcon;
  FCurrent.SelectedIndex := iDocumentIcon;
  edtDocType.Text        := '';
  edtPublicId.Text       := '';
  edtSystemId.Text       := dlgOpen.FileName;
  stgEntities.RowCount   := 2;
  stgEntities.Rows[1].Clear;
  stgNotations.RowCount  := 2;
  stgNotations.Rows[1].Clear;
end;
{ Tidy up and expand the top level of the tree }
procedure TfrmSAX2Viewer.EndDocument;
begin
  trvXML.Items[0].Expand(False);
end;
```

As elements are encountered, they are added to the tree view on the form (see the code in Listing 14-26). The StartElement routine collects all the supplied information about the node and places it in a specialized class, TElement. This class is added to the tree view when the node for this element is established, allowing the associated data to be displayed when that element is later selected within the tree. The new node is added as the child of the current node, and is then set as the current node itself. In this way the hierarchy within the document is easily reflected within the tree view. Conversely, the EndDocument method moves the current node pointer back up one level within the tree. The result of saving this information is seen in Figure 14-2.

Listing 14-26: Adding an element to the tree

```
{ Note this element as the current node and save its attributes }
procedure TfrmSAX2Viewer.StartElement(NamespaceURI, LocalName,
  QName: TSAXString; Attributes: ISAXAttributes);
var
  Element: TElement;
  Index: Integer;
begin
  Element := TElement.Create(NamespaceURI, LocalName);
  for Index := 0 to Attributes.Length -1 do
    Element.Attributes.Values[Attributes.QName(Index)] :=
      Attributes.Value(Index);
  Element.Prefixes.Assign(FPrefixes);
```

```
      FPrefixes.Clear;
      FCurrent:= trvXML.Items.AddChildObject(FCurrent, QName, Element);
      FCurrent.ImageIndex    := ElementIcon;
      FCurrent.SelectedIndex := ElementIcon;
      if edtDocType.Text = '' then
        edtDocType.Text := QName;
    end;
    { Move the current context up the hierarchy
      when an element ends }
    procedure TfrmSAX2Viewer.EndElement(
      NamespaceURI, LocalName, QName: TSAXString);
    begin
      FCurrent := FCurrent.Parent;
    end;
```

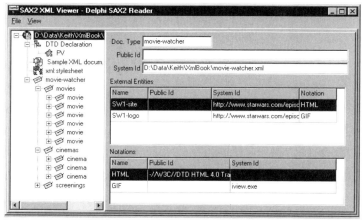

Figure 14-2: Element details displayed in the viewer.

Text is added in a similar manner. When the `Characters` method is called, you add a new node to the tree view, with associated data that is the text itself (see Listing 14-27). A check is made here to discard text that consists solely of white space. Some readers return everything from the XML document, including all the formatting. Next the text is trimmed to provide a shorter name for display in the tree view itself. Finally, the full text is wrapped in an object so that it can be included in the node as associated data. The `TString` class used is merely a class that has a single string property. Figure 14-3 shows a text node in the viewer.

Listing 14-27: Add text to the tree

```
    { Add a text node to the tree }
    procedure TfrmSAX2Viewer.Characters(Text: TSAXString);
    var
      Index: Integer;
    begin
      { Ignore all white space }
      for Index := 1 to Length(Text) do
        if Text[Index] > '' then
          Break;
      if Index > Length(Text) then
        Exit;
      with trvXML.Items.AddChildObject(FCurrent, TruncateText(Text),
```

```
      TString.Create(Text)) do
  begin
    ImageIndex    := FCharIcon;
    SelectedIndex := FCharIcon;
  end;
end;
```

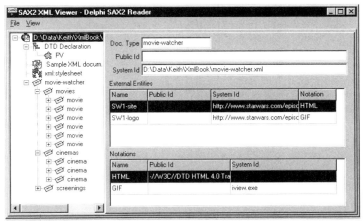

Figure 14-3: The viewer showing a text node.

CDATA sections are also presented to the program as text. However, with SAX and its extensions, you can register an `ISAXLexicalHandler` to be notified of their presence. In this case, all you do is set a variable to refer to the CDATA icon when informed of the start of a CDATA section, and reset it to the normal text icon when the section ends (see Listing 14-28). This variable is the one used in the `Characters` method in Listing 14-27 to control which icon appears for that node in the tree view.

Listing 14-28: Marking CDATA sections

```
{ Note start of CData section }
procedure TfrmSAX2Viewer.StartCData;
begin
  FCharIcon := CDataIcon;
end;
{ Note end of CData section }
procedure TfrmSAX2Viewer.EndCData;
begin
  FCharIcon := TextIcon;
end;
```

Under SAX, you can also receive notification of element and attribute declarations from the DTD. These arrive through the `ISAXDeclHandler` interface. Similar to the text processing above, the calls generate a new node in the tree and store details other than the name as the data. Listing 14-29 shows the handler code, while Figures 14-4 and 14-5 display the result of viewing these nodes once they are loaded.

Listing 14-29: Processing attribute and element declarations

```
{ Add an attribute declaration to the tree }
procedure TfrmSAX2Viewer.AttributeDecl(
  EName, AName, AttrType, ValueDefault, Value: TSAXString);
begin
  with trvXML.Items.AddChildObject(FCurrent, EName + '.' + AName,
    TString.Create(Value + ': ' + AttrType + ' (' + ValueDefault +
    ')')) do
  begin
    ImageIndex    := AttrDeclIcon;
    SelectedIndex := AttrDeclIcon;
  end;
end;
{ Add an element declaration to the tree }
procedure TfrmSAX2Viewer.ElementDecl(Name, Model: TSAXString);
begin
  with trvXML.Items.AddChildObject(FCurrent, Name,
    TString.Create(Model)) do
  begin
    ImageIndex    := ElemDeclIcon;
    SelectedIndex := ElemDeclIcon;
  end;
end;
```

Figure 14-4: SAX2 includes element declarations.

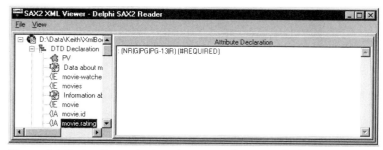

Figure 14-5: Attribute declarations are also provided.

The remaining handler methods follow the patterns described here, building up the tree view with the contents of the document. Once it is completed, you can select any of the nodes from the tree and have its details displayed on the panel to the right.

Summary

Since the SAX definitions appear mainly as interfaces, it is relatively simple to implement them in various languages. This chapter describes how they are translated into Delphi and shows the corresponding declarations. Basic classes from SAX are also implemented in Delphi, including the input source and attribute list classes.

Having defined the SAX functionality in Delphi you saw how to build a native XML parser that supplies tokens to either a SAX1 parser or a SAX2 reader, all written in Delphi. An XML viewer then invokes these objects after registering itself as the destination for each of the SAX handlers. As the events are notified to the viewer, it builds up a tree view corresponding to the document structure.

In the next chapter you look at how to wrap Microsoft's SAX reader in these Delphi interfaces, providing plug-and-play opportunities between the two versions.

Chapter 15
Wrapping External Parsers

One of the main principles behind the design of SAX is to allow different parsers to provide the actual processing, while presenting the results in a standardized manner. The previous chapters show how this is achieved by SAX implementations from Microsoft and in pure Delphi. However, an application written against one version still requires several changes before it can be used with the other. This chapter describes how external readers are wrapped in the Delphi SAX interfaces, allowing you to swap from one reader to the other in a single line of code.

Adapting Microsoft's SAX Parser

Since Microsoft has defined their own version of the SAX specification under Windows, it obviously differs somewhat from the Delphi version of SAX developed in Chapter 14. To be able to use the new reader with the existing framework, you need to employ the Adapter design pattern, interposing a class between Delphi SAX and Microsoft's SAX that knows how to convert between the two. To Delphi it appears as an `ISAXXMLReader`, while to the actual reader it appears as a collection of Microsoft-compatible handlers.

NOTE There are some name conflicts between the Delphi SAX interfaces and those provided by Microsoft. Although the latter's `IVBSAX*` interfaces are the easiest to use from Delphi's point of view, they are basically wrappers around equivalent C++ interfaces with names that start with `ISAX`. This is where the problems arise since these same names are used in the Delphi implementation. The solution is simple—just prefix the affected names with the unit in which they originate, like `SAX2.ISAXContentHandler`. The compiler should let you know if you miss any.

Listing 15-1 shows the declaration for the adapter class. It inherits from `TSAXCustomXMLReader`, which provides the basic bookkeeping abilities for registering handlers, as well as funneling the two versions of `Parse` into a single abstract method. On top of this it implements the Microsoft versions of the SAX handler interfaces. It must also implement the `IDispatch` interface for compatibility with the external reader (although the actual methods do nothing).

Listing 15-1: Declaring the Microsoft SAX adapter

```
{ Adapter for Microsoft's SAX 2 reader as found in MSXML3.dll.
  Since it uses a different set of SAX definitions (that provide
  the same functionality) we need to adapt these to fit with the
  Delphi version of SAX.
  Thus, this class acts as handlers for Microsoft's SAX2 reader,
  while acting as a Delphi SAX2 reader to other parties. Care must
  be taken to reference the correct version of each interface.
}
TSAX2MSReader = class(TSAXCustomXMLReader, IVBSAXContentHandler,
  IVBSAXDTDHandler, IVBSAXEntityResolver, IVBSAXErrorHandler)
private
  FAttributes: SAX2Helper.TSAXAttributes;
  FDeclHandler: TObject;
  FIAttributes: SAX2.ISAXAttributes;
  FLexicalHandler: TObject;
  FLocator: IVBSAXLocator;
  FXMLReader: IVBSAXXMLReader;
protected
  function GetColumnNumber: Integer; override;
  function GetFeature(Name: TSAXString): Boolean; override;
  function GetLineNumber: Integer; override;
  function GetProperty(Name: TSAXString): TObject; override;
  function GetPublicId: TSAXString; override;
  function GetSystemId: TSAXString; override;
  procedure ParseInput(Input: TSAXInputSource); override;
  procedure SetFeature(Name: TSAXString; Value: Boolean); override;
  procedure SetProperty(Name: TSAXString; Value: TObject); override;
public
  constructor Create; overload; override;
  constructor Create(ContentHandler: SAX2.ISAXContentHandler;
    DTDHandler: SAX.ISAXDTDHandler = nil;
    EntityResolver: SAX.ISAXEntityResolver = nil;
    ErrorHandler: SAX.ISAXErrorHandler = nil); overload;
  destructor Destroy; override;
  { IVBSAXContentHandler }
  procedure Set_documentLocator(const Param1: IVBSAXLocator); safecall;
  procedure startDocument; safecall;
  procedure endDocument; safecall;
  procedure startPrefixMapping(var strPrefix: WideString;
    var strURI: WideString); safecall;
  procedure endPrefixMapping(var strPrefix: WideString); safecall;
  procedure startElement(var strNamespaceURI: WideString;
    var strLocalName: WideString; var strQName: WideString;
    const oAttributes: IVBSAXAttributes); safecall;
  procedure endElement(var strNamespaceURI: WideString;
    var strLocalName: WideString; var strQName: WideString); safecall;
  procedure characters(var strChars: WideString); safecall;
  procedure ignorableWhitespace(var strChars: WideString); safecall;
  procedure processingInstruction(var strTarget: WideString;
    var strData: WideString); safecall;
  procedure skippedEntity(var strName: WideString); safecall;
  property documentLocator: IVBSAXLocator write Set_documentLocator;
  { IVBSAXDTDHandler }
  procedure notationDecl(var strName: WideString;
    var strPublicId: WideString; var strSystemId: WideString);
    safecall;
  procedure unparsedEntityDecl(var strName: WideString;
    var strPublicId: WideString; var strSystemId: WideString;
    var strNotationName: WideString); safecall;
```

```
  { IVBSAXEntityResolver }
  function resolveEntity(var strPublicId: WideString;
    var strSystemId: WideString): OleVariant; safecall;
  { IVBSAXErrorHandler }
  procedure error(const oLocator: IVBSAXLocator;
    var strError: WideString; nErrorCode: Integer); safecall;
  procedure fatalError(const oLocator: IVBSAXLocator;
    var strError: WideString; nErrorCode: Integer); safecall;
  procedure ignorableWarning(const oLocator: IVBSAXLocator;
    var strError: WideString; nErrorCode: Integer); safecall;
  { IDispatch }
  function GetTypeInfoCount(out Count: Integer): HResult; stdcall;
  function GetTypeInfo(Index, LocaleID: Integer; out TypeInfo):
    HResult; stdcall;
  function GetIDsOfNames(const IID: TGUID; Names: Pointer;
    NameCount, LocaleID: Integer; DispIDs: Pointer): HResult; stdcall;
  function Invoke(DispID: Integer; const IID: TGUID; LocaleID: Integer;
    Flags: Word; var Params; VarResult, ExcepInfo, ArgErr: Pointer):
    HResult; stdcall;
end;
```

Creating a new adapter automatically creates a new Microsoft reader as well, holding it in the FXMLReader variable for later use. The current class immediately registers itself with the reader as the handler for all of its events (see Listing 15-2). At present, attempting to register an entity resolver generates an error.

Listing 15-2: Creating a new adapter

```
{ Initialize }
constructor TSAX2MSReader.Create;
begin
  inherited Create;
  FAttributes   := SAX2Helper.TSAXAttributes.Create;
  FIAttributes  := FAttributes as SAX2.ISAXAttributes;  { AddRef }
  FLocator      := nil;
  { Instantiate MS SAX reader and register self as handlers }
  FXMLReader                := CoSAXXMLReader.Create;
  FXMLReader.contentHandler := Self;
  FXMLReader.dtdHandler     := Self;
//  FXMLReader.entityResolver := Self;
  FXMLReader.errorHandler   := Self;
end;

{ Initialise and use specified XML handlers }
constructor TSAX2MSReader.Create(
  ContentHandler: SAX2.ISAXContentHandler;
  DTDHandler: SAX.ISAXDTDHandler = nil;
  EntityResolver: SAX.ISAXEntityResolver = nil;
  ErrorHandler: SAX.ISAXErrorHandler = nil);
begin
  Create;
  Self.ContentHandler := ContentHandler;
  Self.DTDHandler     := DTDHandler;
  Self.EntityResolver := EntityResolver;
  Self.ErrorHandler   := ErrorHandler;
end;
```

Requests to parse a document get passed from the adapter up to the embedded parser (see Listing 15-3). You need to override the `ParseInput` method to achieve this. Since the document arrives as a `TSAXInputSource`, which ultimately is a `TStream`, and the parser knows how to deal with `IStream`s, the simplest way to send the document is via the `TStreamAdapter` class. As its name suggests, this class wraps a normal stream to make it look like an `IStream`.

Listing 15-3: Passing along a parse request

```
{ Adapt Delphi SAX parse invocation to MS SAX parse invocation }
procedure TSAX2MSReader.ParseInput(Input: TSAXInputSource);
var
  Stream: IStream;
begin
  Stream := TStreamAdapter.Create(Input);
  try
    FXMLReader.parse(Stream);
  finally
    Stream := nil;
  end;
end;
```

Once the parse process begins, events from it trigger the methods in the adapter class. Generally, all these handlers need to do is send the values received directly along to the corresponding event in the adapter's registered handlers. Listing 15-4 shows a sample of methods from the different handlers that do just this. In the error handling method you must collect all the problem details and wrap them in an `ESAXParseException` before sending them on.

Listing 15-4: Sample adapter methods

```
{ Adapt MS SAX characters event to Delphi SAX characters event }
procedure TSAX2MSReader.characters(var strChars: WideString);
begin
  ContentHandler.Characters(strChars);
end;

{ Adapt MS SAX notation declaration event to Delphi
  SAX notation declaration event }
procedure TSAX2MSReader.notationDecl(var strName: WideString;
  var strPublicId: WideString; var strSystemId: WideString);
begin
  DTDHandler.NotationDecl(strName, strPublicId, strSystemId);
end;

{ Adapt MS SAX fatal error event to Delphi SAX fatal error event }
procedure TSAX2MSReader.fatalError(const oLocator: IVBSAXLocator;
  var strError: WideString; nErrorCode: Integer);
begin
  ErrorHandler.FatalError(ESAXParseException.Create(
    Format(ErrorMsg, [nErrorCode, strError]), oLocator.publicId,
    oLocator.systemId, oLocator.lineNumber, oLocator.columnNumber));
end;
```

The process is a little more complicated when at the start of a new element (see Listing 15-5). Along with the element's name comes a list of its attributes. Although you could write an adapter for the attribute list itself, the approach taken here is to transfer the details into a Delphi attribute list to send on. Instead of creating a new list for each call, a previously defined one is reused.

Listing 15-5: Translating attributes for an element

```
{ Adapt MS SAX start element event to Delphi SAX start element event }
procedure TSAX2MSReader.startElement(var strNamespaceURI: WideString;
  var strLocalName: WideString; var strQName: WideString;
  const oAttributes: IVBSAXAttributes);
var
  Index: Integer;
  AttrType: TSAXAttributeType;
begin
  { Transfer attributes to Delphi interface }
  FAttributes.Clear;
  for Index := 0 to oAttributes.Length -1 do
  begin
    for AttrType := High(TSAXAttributeType) downto
        Succ(Low(TSAXAttributeType)) do
      if AttributeTypeNames[AttrType] = oAttributes.getType(Index) then
        break;
    FAttributes.AddAttribute(oAttributes.getUri(Index),
      oAttributes.getLocalName(Index), oAttributes.getQName(Index),
      oAttributes.getValue(Index), AttrType);
  end;
  ContentHandler.StartElement(
    strNamespaceUri, strLocalName, strQName, FAttributes);
end;
```

Microsoft's reader also supports the two standard SAX extensions. Since these appear separately from the main handlers, they are each provided with their own adapters, which follow the pattern above of simply passing along any events they receive. When an application sets one of these properties, it is wrapped and set on the actual reader (as shown in Listing 15-6). A reference is kept in the adapter so that it can be returned if the property is subsequently read. Unrecognized features generate an error.

Listing 15-6: Handling SAX extensions

```
{ Adapt Delphi SAX property query to MS SAX property query }
function TSAX2MSReader.GetProperty(Name: TSAXString): TObject;
begin
  if Name = LexicalHandlerProperty then
    Result := FLexicalHandler
  else if Name = DeclHandlerProperty then
    Result := FDeclHandler
  else
    raise ESAXNotRecognizedException.Create(Name);
end;

{ Adapt Delphi SAX property setting to MS SAX property setting }
procedure TSAX2MSReader.SetProperty(Name: TSAXString; Value: TObject);
var
  LexicalIntf: SAX2Ext.ISAXLexicalHandler;
  DeclIntf: SAX2Ext.ISAXDeclHandler;
begin
  if Name = LexicalHandlerProperty then
  begin
    FLexicalHandler := Value;
    Value.GetInterface(SAX2Ext.ISAXLexicalHandler, LexicalIntf);
    FXMLReader.putProperty(Name,
      IVBSAXLexicalHandler(TSAX2MSLexicalAdapter.Create(LexicalIntf)));
  end
```

```
    else if Name = DeclHandlerProperty then
    begin
      FDeclHandler := Value;
      Value.GetInterface(SAX2Ext.ISAXDeclHandler, DeclIntf);
      FXMLReader.putProperty(Name,
        IVBSAXDeclHandler(TSAX2MSDeclAdapter.Create(DeclIntf)));
    end
    else
      raise ESAXNotRecognizedException.Create(Name);
  end;
```

To work with the reader factory defined in the Delphi SAX package, the new adapter class must be registered with the system. As before, this is done in the `initialization` section for the unit, ensuring that the reader can always be found when needed. The class is unregistered in the `finalization` section.

```
initialization
  Classes.RegisterClass(TSAX2MSReader);
finalization
  Classes.UnRegisterClass(TSAX2MSReader);
end.
```

Now the Microsoft SAX reader is available through the Delphi interfaces and can be used in place of the native reader with no change to the rest of the application. Just replace the line to generate the Delphi implementation:

```
MySAXReader := TSAX2DelphiReader.Create;
```

with the one for the Microsoft adapter

```
MySAXReader := TSAX2MSReader.Create;
```

Using CUESoft's Parser

Just as you can wrap Microsoft's reader in the Delphi SAX interfaces, you can do the same for CUESoft's offering. Since CUESoft does not support namespaces nor the extensions defined for SAX2, it is best to provide it as just a SAX1 parser.

The `TXmlParser` class (from the `XmlParser` unit) is the heart of CUESoft's parser. It is set up as a component, letting you drop it onto your form at design time. Because of this, you interact with it by setting event handlers corresponding to the tokens from an XML document.

The adapter declaration (shown in Listing 15-7) contains an internal field for the parser and defines methods to use as event handlers with it. Derived from `TSAXCustomParser`, it needs to override the `ParseInput` method to do the actual parsing.

Listing 15-7: CUESoft adapter declaration

```
{ Adapter for CUESoft's SAX parser as found in
  their TXmlParser component.
  Thus, this class acts as handlers for CUESoft's XML parser,
  while acting as a Delphi SAX parser to other parties.
}
TSAXCuesoftParser = class(TSAXCustomParser)
private
  FAttributes: TSAXAttributeList;
```

```
    FIAttributes: ISAXAttributeList;
    FXMLParser: TXmlParser;
  protected
    procedure ParseInput(Input: TSAXInputSource); override;
  public
    constructor Create; overload; override;
    constructor Create(DocumentHandler: ISAXDocumentHandler;
      DTDHandler: ISAXDTDHandler = nil;
      EntityResolver: ISAXEntityResolver = nil;
      ErrorHandler: ISAXErrorHandler = nil); overload;
    destructor Destroy; override;
    procedure DoAttribute(oOwner: TObject; sName, sValue: string;
      bSpecified: Boolean);
    procedure DoCDATASection(oOwner: TObject; sValue: string);
    procedure DoCharData(oOwner: TObject; sValue: string);
    procedure DoComment(oOwner: TObject; sValue: string);
    procedure DoDocTypeDecl(oOwner: TObject; sDecl, sId0, sId1: string);
    procedure DoEndDocument(oOwner: TObject);
    procedure DoEndElement(oOwner: TObject; sValue: string);
    procedure DoEntityDecl(oOwner: TObject;
      sEntityName, sPublicId, sSystemId, sNotationName: string);
    procedure DoIgnorableWhitespace(oOwner: TObject; sValue: string);
    procedure DoNonXMLEntity(oOwner: TObject;
      sEntityName, sPublicId, sSystemId, sNotationName: string);
    procedure DoNotationDecl(oOwner: TObject;
      sNotationName, sPublicId, sSystemId: string);
    procedure DoProcessingInstruction(oOwner: TObject;
      sName, sValue: string);
    function DoResolveEntity(oOwner: TObject;
      sName, sPublicId, sSystemId: string): string;
    procedure DoStartDocument(oOwner: TObject);
    procedure DoStartElement(oOwner: TObject; sValue: string);
  end;
```

As with the Microsoft adapter, creating a CUESoft one also creates a corresponding parser object and establishes handlers for all its events (see Listing 15-8). The OnIgnorableWhitespace property is protected and cannot be assigned a handler. Since CUESoft does not validate documents, this omission is not surprising.

Listing 15-8: Creating the adapter

```
{ Initialize }
constructor TSAXCuesoftParser.Create;
begin
  inherited Create;
  FAttributes  := TSAXAttributeList.Create;
  FIAttributes := FAttributes as ISAXAttributeList;  { AddRef }
  { Instantiate Cuesoft parser and register self as event handlers }
  FXMLParser                   := TXmlParser.Create(nil);
  FXMLParser.OnAttribute       := DoAttribute;
  FXMLParser.OnCDATASection    := DoCDATASection;
  FXMLParser.OnCharData        := DoCharData;
  FXMLParser.OnComment         := DoComment;
  FXMLParser.OnDocTypeDecl     := DoDocTypeDecl;
  FXMLParser.OnEndDocument     := DoEndDocument;
  FXMLParser.OnEndElement      := DoEndElement;
  FXMLParser.OnEntityDecl      := DoEntityDecl;
  { Currently not available }
  { FXMLParser.OnIgnorableWhitespace := DoIgnorableWhitespace; }
  FXMLParser.OnNonXMLEntity    := DoNonXMLEntity;
```

```
    FXMLParser.OnNotationDecl          := DoNotationDecl;
    FXMLParser.OnProcessingInstruction := DoProcessingInstruction;
    FXMLParser.OnResolveEntity         := DoResolveEntity;
    FXMLParser.OnStartDocument         := DoStartDocument;
    FXMLParser.OnStartElement          := DoStartElement;
  end;

{ Initialize and use specified XML handlers }
constructor TSAXCuesoftParser.Create(
  DocumentHandler: ISAXDocumentHandler;
  DTDHandler: ISAXDTDHandler = nil;
  EntityResolver: ISAXEntityResolver = nil;
  ErrorHandler: ISAXErrorHandler = nil);
begin
  Create;
  Self.DocumentHandler := DocumentHandler;
  Self.DTDHandler      := DTDHandler;
  Self.EntityResolver  := EntityResolver;
  Self.ErrorHandler    := ErrorHandler;
end;
```

When a parse request arrives at the adapter, it is passed on to the embedded parser as shown in Listing 15-9. If the input source specifies a system identifier, this is handed off to the `ParseDataSource` method. Otherwise, the contents of the document are sent to the `ParseMemory` method after being converted to a `PChar`. Any errors encountered are transformed into `ESAXParseExceptions`.

Listing 15-9: Starting a parse

```
{ Adapt Delphi SAX parse invocation to Cuesoft parse invocation }
procedure TSAXCuesoftParser.ParseInput(Input: TSAXInputSource);
var
  OK: Boolean;
  Stream: TStringStream;
  Text: string;
begin
  try
    if Input.SystemId <> '' then
      OK := FXMLParser.ParseDataSource(Input.SystemId)
    else
    begin
      Stream := TStringStream.Create('');
      try
        Stream.CopyFrom(Input, 0);
        Text := Stream.DataString;
        OK   := FXMLParser.ParseMemory(PChar(Text));
      finally
        Stream.Free;
      end;
    end;
    if not OK then
      raise ESAXParseException.Create(FXMLParser.Errors.Text);
  except on E: TXmlParserError do
    raise ESAXParseException.Create(
      E.Reason, '', E.Url, E.Line, E.LinePos);
  end;
end;
```

Similar to the Microsoft adapter, most events from the parser are simply passed along to the corresponding SAX handler method. Elements are handled slightly differently since their attributes appear in separate events prior to the element itself. Thus, the attributes are collected into a SAX attribute list and are added to the element details when they arrive (see Listing 15-10).

Listing 15-10: Handling an element notification

```
{ Save Cuesoft attributes for later use with the element }
procedure TSAXCuesoftParser.DoAttribute(oOwner: TObject; sName,
  sValue: string; bSpecified: Boolean);
begin
  FAttributes.AddAttribute(sName, sValue, atCData);
end;

{ Pass on start of element notification }
procedure TSAXCuesoftParser.DoStartElement(oOwner: TObject; sValue: string);
begin
  { Use attributes accumulated previously }
  DocumentHandler.StartElement(sValue, FAttributes);
  FAttributes.Clear;
end;
```

The CUESoft parser can now be accessed through the SAX1 interfaces defined in Delphi. Other than the initial call to create an instance of the parser through its adapter, the application doesn't need to know that it is not using the native Delphi version.

```
MySAXParser := TSAXCuesoftParser.Create;
```

Using Open XML's Parser

Open XML's parser can also be wrapped as a SAX reader. Internally, the `TXMLToDomParser` class creates a `TdomStandardDocXMLReader` to do the actual parsing. This functions like a SAX parser, passing events to its registered `ContertHandler`, `DtdHandler`, and `ErrorHandler`. By deriving your own handlers from the appropriate custom parent classes and registering them with the parser's `DocXMLReader` property, you can respond to the parser events and present them as Delphi SAX events instead. This is left to the reader as an exercise.

Summary

The XML viewer developed in Chapter 14 is extended to incorporate the new adapters and their underlying parsers. An initial form selects either SAX1 or SAX2 implementations. From the subsequent viewer forms you can select which parser to use from the File | Parser menu options (see Figure 15-1).

Chapter 15: Wrapping External Parsers **363**

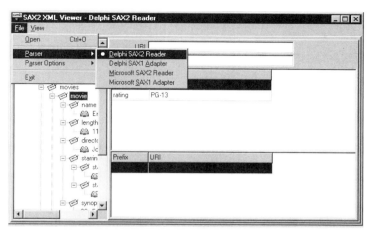

Figure 15-1: Selecting a SAX reader.

Under SAX1 you can use the native Delphi implementation, CUESoft's parser through the adapter described above, or Microsoft's DOM also wrapped in an adapter (however, using the DOM defeats the SAX advantage of not having to load the entire document at once). Under SAX2 you have the option of using the native Delphi version, Microsoft's SAX reader, or the corresponding SAX1 implementations through a TSAXParserAdapter.

Although there are slight differences between the results of parsing the same document with each of these SAX versions, in general, each is interchangeable with the others.

Part IV
Serving XML

In the previous chapters you saw how to read in an XML document using different technologies and manipulate its contents. But where do these XML documents come from? Although you can handcraft each one, it is more likely that you want to generate them automatically on demand. Chapter 16 points out that XML is really data, formatted to be both human- and machine-readable. The source of this data is often a database.

This section describes various ways in which XML can be generated programmatically. You can write it directly as text as shown in Chapter 17 and display or store the document locally. Chapter 18 shows how the documents can be generated from a database, and then be delivered across the Internet with Delphi's Web modules. In Chapter 19 you see how to create documents from within a DOM, while Chapter 20 describes a SAX-based approach using Microsoft's IMXWriter interface.

In addition to serving XML directly, you can manipulate the documents and present them in some other format. Chapter 21 demonstrates how an XSLT stylesheet is applied to an XML document to produce formatted output for further distribution.

Finally, Chapter 22 describes how Delphi uses XML to deliver MIDAS data to a Web-based client, and how it is processed within the browser through JavaScript functions.

Chapter 16: XML is Data
Chapter 17: Simple Text
Chapter 18: Web Modules
Chapter 19: Document Object Model
Chapter 20: SAX Generation
Chapter 21: Applying XSL Transformations
Chapter 22: XML Broker

Chapter 16
XML is Data

XML is a way of describing the meaning of data within the data stream itself. When you are dealing with large amounts of data it is often maintained within a database. Extracting that data and presenting it as XML provides a standardized way in which to transfer information between applications, whether they are on your own computer or across the Internet. Since XML is text-based, it can easily cross platform and operating system boundaries without losing its usefulness.

Mapping a single table from a relational database into XML can be very straightforward. The hierarchy inherent in XML matches the table/record/field structure within the database. Thus, for a given database table, you create an XML document with the upper level tag corresponding to that table. Within this you define an element that delimits each record and place further elements in here representing each field. As a naming convention I suggest you use a plural form of the table name for the outermost element since it is a collection of records. Then, individual records can use the singular form of the table name as their element name. Elements coming from fields can use the field names (allowing for any restrictions imposed on names by XML).

For a more complex situation where you are dealing with multiple tables, you simply extend the XML structure to include an all-encompassing element that parallels the database itself—a collection of tables. Below this you have the table elements as before. Use the database name as the outermost element name in this case.

To allow you to refer to individual records from the original database you should include an ID attribute at the record level and construct its value from the primary key field(s) of that table. Relationships between records, represented by foreign keys within the database, are translated into IDREF attributes in XML. These can then be used to reconstruct the original links. In fact, the transformation power of XSLT can follow these links and retrieve any and all related details, easily combining data from multiple records into a coherent display.

Movie-watcher Database

For demonstration purposes, the data for creating the movie-watcher XML documents is placed into a Paradox database consisting of six tables (see the table definitions in Table 16-1 and the data model in Figure 16-1). You can see how the tables and fields correspond to the elements defined in the DTD for these documents (Listing 3-1).

Table 16-1: Paradox table structures for sample database
P = primary key field, F = foreign key field

Table	Field	Type	Key
Movie.db	Movie_id	Long	P
	Name	Alpha(30)	
	Rating	Alpha(5)	
	Length	Long	
	Director	Alpha(30)	
	Synopsis	Memo(5)	
	URL	Alpha(70)	
	Logo_URL	Alpha(70)	
Stars.db	Star_id	Long	P
	Movie_id	Long	F
	Star	Alpha(30)	
Cinema.db	Cinema_id	Long	P
	Name	Alpha(30)	
	Phone	Alpha(15)	
	Address	Alpha(50)	
	Directions	Memo(1)	
	Candy_bar	Logical	
	Disabled_access	Logical	
Pricing.db	Pricing_id	Long	P
	Cinema_id	Long	F
	Name	Alpha(20)	
	Period	Alpha(30)	
	Adult	Number	
	Child	Number	
	Discount	Number	
Screening.db	Movie_id	Long	P,F
	Cinema_id	Long	P,F
	Start_date	Date	
	End_date	Date	

Table	Field	Type	Key
	Digital_sound	Alpha(5)	
	No_passes	Logical	
Sessions.db	Movie_id	Long	P,F
	Cinema_id	Long	P,F
	Time	Time	P
	Pricing_id	Long	F

Figure 16-1: Data model for movie-watcher database.

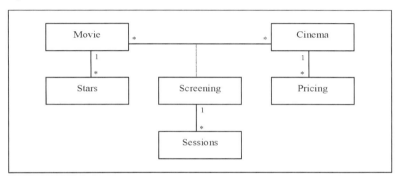

To access the data, you need to set up a database alias for it in the BDE. The following steps show you how:

1. Call up the BDE Administrator program from the Delphi folder under the Start menu.
2. Select **Object | New** from the menu.
3. Leave the database driver name at STANDARD.
4. Enter the new alias's name: movie-watcher.
5. Browse to the directory holding the tables in the Path field.
6. Save the changes by pressing the **Apply** button and pressing **OK** in the confirmation dialog.

All the demonstration programs in this part of the book that access information from the database expect this alias. The following chapters use these tables to provide the content for XML documents. Various methods of generating XML are shown: from straight text, through a Web module, to the different DOMs, and a SAX-based approach. Maintaining the database can also involve XML as used by the XMLBroker technology of Delphi.

Chapter 17
Simple Text

An XML document is just a text file—its format and structure are what make it different and useful. As such, it is very easy to create one programmatically.

All you need to do is to write the expected format for the document and its encapsulated data to that file. For very static documents, you could encode them directly into a string within the program and write that out to the appropriate file.

```
const
  XMLDoc = '<?xml version="1.0"?><response>OK</response>';
begin
  writeln(XMLFile, XMLDoc);
end;
```

For a little more variability you could define the string as a format, noting where the variable sections should go. These are then replaced on the fly using the Format function. Again, the resulting string is written to the output file.

```
const
  XMLDoc = '<?xml version="1.0"?><response>%s</response>';
begin
  writeln(XMLFile, Format(XMLDoc, [Outcome]));
end;
```

In some cases the XML document does not have to be written out to a file. Once created as a string, you can pass this directly to another routine or application that knows how to deal with it.

From a Database

To demonstrate how you can generate an XML document from the database, construct the following program:

1. Open a new project and place a memo field and two buttons on the main form. The memo contains the results of the generation process, allowing you to review the output. One button will enable you to initiate the document creation into the memo, while the other will let you save that text out to a file.

2. Add a series of query components and related datasources for interacting with the database. One query is required for each table (six in all) and they all reference the `movie-watcher` alias (see Chapter 16). Each query selects all the fields from its table, with the three subordinate tables being linked back to their respective parents (through the datasources) in a master-child relationship. For example, the SQL for the query attached to the movie table is:

    ```
    select * from movie
    ```

    whereas the corresponding query for its star performers is:

    ```
    select * from stars
    where movie_id = :movie_id
    ```

3. Define XML snippets for each table, containing embedded fields for use with the `Format` function to include variable content The actual generation process combines snippets of XML for each table into a coherent whole. Each record in the query uses these snippets in turn. Field values are simply retrieved from the records and inserted into the layouts. Listing 17-1 shows XML templates for the document header and the list of movies.

Listing 17-1: XML snippets for generating a document

```
resourcestring
  { XML document fragments }
  DocumentOpening = '<movie-watcher>'#13;
  DocumentClosing = '</movie-watcher>'#13;
  MovieIdFormat   = 'M%d';
  MoviesClosing   = '</movies>'#13;
  MoviesOpening   = '<movies>'#13;
  MovieTag        = '  <movie id="M%d" rating="%s"%s%s>'#13 +
                    '    <name>%s</name>'#13 +
                    '    <length>%d</length>'#13 +
                    '    <director>%s</director>'#13 +
                    '    <starring>%s</starring>'#13 +
                    '    <synopsis>%s</synopsis>'#13 +
                    '  </movie>'#13;
  StarTag         = '<star>%s</star>';
  XMLProlog       = '<?xml %s?>'#13 +
                    '<!DOCTYPE %s SYSTEM "%s" ['#13 +
                    '<!NOTATION HTML PUBLIC "-//W3C//DTD ' +
                    'HTML 4.0 Transitional//EN">'#13 +
                    '<!NOTATION GIF SYSTEM "iview.exe">'#13 +
                    '%s]>'#13 +
                    '<!-- %s -->'#13 +
                    '<?%s %s?>'#13;
```

4. Add code to generate each section of the document in response to activating the Generate button. Listing 17-2 shows the header and movies generation code that uses the snippets above. Code for the cinemas and screenings portions of the resulting document is just like that for the movies and is not shown here.

Listing 17-2: Generating XML as text

```
{ Generate the XML document as text }
procedure TfrmTextXML.btnGenerateClick(Sender: TObject);

  { Compile entities for the movie }
  function GenerateEntities: string;
  begin
```

```delphi
      Result := '';
      with qryMovie do
      begin
        First;
        while not EOF do
        begin
          if FieldByName(LogoURLField).AsString <> '' then
            Result := Result + Format(EntityDecl, [Format(MovieIdFormat,
              [FieldByName(MovieIdField).AsInteger]) + 'Logo',
              FieldByName(LogoURLField).AsString, GIFType]);
          if FieldByName(URLField).AsString <> '' then
            Result := Result + Format(EntityDecl, [Format(MovieIdFormat,
              [FieldByName(MovieIdField).AsInteger]) + 'Url',
              FieldByName(URLField).AsString, HTMLType]);
          Next;
        end;
      end;
    end;

    { Compile elements for the stars of the movie }
    function GenerateStars: string;
    begin
      Result := '';
      with qryStars do
      begin
        First;
        while not EOF do
        begin
          Result := Result +
            Format(StarTag, [FieldByName(StarField).AsString]);
          Next;
        end;
      end;
    end;

    { Generate elements for each movie }
    function GenerateMovies: string;
    var
      MovieId: Integer;
    begin
      Result := MoviesOpening;
      with qryMovie do
      begin
        First;
        while not EOF do
        begin
          MovieId := FieldByName(MovieIdField).AsInteger;
          Result := Result + Format(MovieTag, [MovieId,
            FieldByName(RatingField).AsString,
            GetOptEntityAttr(FieldByName(LogoURLField),
              Format(MovieIdFormat, [MovieId]) + 'Logo'),
            GetOptEntityAttr(FieldByName(URLField),
              Format(MovieIdFormat, [MovieId]) + 'Url'),
            FieldByName(NameField).AsString,
            FieldByName(LengthField).AsInteger,
            FieldByName(DirectorField).AsString,
            GenerateStars, FieldByName(SynopsisField).AsString]);
          Next;
        end;
      end;
```

```
      Result := Result + MoviesClosing;
   end;

   { Code for cinemas and screenings not shown }
begin
   memXML.Lines.Text := Format(XMLProlog,
      [XMLPrologAttrs, MovieWatcherTag, XMLDTDFile,
      GenerateEntities, XMLComment, XMLStyleTag, XMLStyleAttrs]) +
      DocumentOpening + GenerateMovies + GenerateCinemas +
      GenerateScreenings + DocumentClosing;
end;
```

Within the database, movies may have a URL and an image associated with them. These appear in the movie-watcher documents as attributes on the `movie` tag that reference external entities. To provide the actual locations, entity declarations occur in the document type declaration. The `GenerateEntities` function searches for these references in the movies table and generates appropriate entries from their content. Its result is included in the `XMLProlog` string through the `Format` function. Corresponding notations are predefined in this string since they do not change from document to document. Calculated names based on the ID of the record supply the entity names.

For the movie content, the movies table is traversed again in the `GenerateMovies` method. This time each record's details merge into the `MovieTag` format string. ID values for the `movie` elements in the XML document come from the primary key in the database table, ensuring that they are unique. Each one is prefixed with an M to prevent conflicts with IDs for cinemas and pricing schemes.

Since the `url` and `logo_url` attributes of a movie are optional, a helper routine only includes references to the appropriate entities declared previously when they are present. A separate routine compiles the list of stars for each movie, as there are an unknown number of these.

The `GenerateStars` function steps through each star for the current movie and combines their names into the `StarTag` format string. Automatic selection of the appropriate stars for each movie comes from the query component setup, whereby the stars table is connected to the movies table via a parameterized query.

5. Ensure that fields are formatted as required. Specifiers within the format strings handle most formatting requirements. Text fields return their value through the `AsString` method. `%d` or `%f` format specifiers match up with numeric fields that are retrieved via their `AsInteger` or `AsFloat` methods. However, the `Time` field in the sessions query must use the `FormatDateTime` function since dates and times are not dealt with by the normal `Format` routine.

Several helper functions are used for content that is optional and may not appear in the final output at all. `GetOptEntityAttr` creates an attribute entry if the supplied field is not empty, giving it the supplied value. The entity attributes in the `movie` element use this to refer to the previously defined external entities. `GetOptElement` produces an empty tag for logical field types that evaluate to `True` and an empty string if `False`. In each case, the attribute or element name is generated from the field name with the `ModifyName` function. This allows for differences between database and XML naming conventions. Listing 17-3 shows these three functions.

Listing 17-3: Helper functions for text XML generation

```
{ Convert field names to XML names }
function ModifyName(Name: string): string;
begin
  Result :=
    LowerCase(StringReplace(Name, '_', '-', [rfReplaceAll]));
end;

{ Include attribute entity reference only if present }
function GetOptEntityAttr(Sender: TField; Reference: string): string;
begin
  if Sender.AsString <> '' then
    Result := ' ' + ModifyName(Sender.FieldName) +
      '="' + Reference + '"'
  else
    Result := '';
end;

{ Include empty field tag only if flag in DB set }
function GetOptElement(Sender: TField): string;
begin
  if Sender.AsBoolean then
    Result := '<' + ModifyName(Sender.FieldName) + '/>'
  else
    Result := '';
end;
```

6. Add code to save the XML document from the memo to a file (see Listing 17-4). You need to add a `TSaveDialog` component to the form to prompt the user for the filename to use.

Listing 17-4: Save the new XML document

```
{ Save the generated XML }
procedure TfrmTextXML.btnSaveClick(Sender: TObject);
begin
  with dlgSave do
    if Execute then
      memXML.Lines.SaveToFile(Filename);
end;
```

7. Save the program, compile, and run it. Figure 17-1 shows the generated XML document in the memo field.

Once the XML has been generated you can peruse it on screen, before saving the text to a file on disk with the second button. Then, use an appropriate browser or application to view the result.

Figure 17-1: XML generated as text.

Summary

This technique is the simplest way to generate XML documents. Its advantages are that it is very easy to implement and that it has almost no overhead in terms of additional code necessary to produce it. However, it is probably only appropriate for smaller documents and those that can be created sequentially.

Generating text from a database can be used for XML documents that are derived from data held in a database but that do not change often. For a more dynamic approach, consider the following chapter on delivering XML across the Internet.

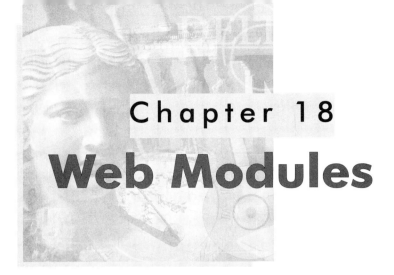

Chapter 18
Web Modules

XML can be delivered across the Internet just as easily as HTML, either as a standalone document or embedded within an HTML page. An XML-aware browser knows how to handle the data and can render the contents in a basic but meaningful way. Furthermore, when the XML is associated with an XSL stylesheet, it can be automatically transformed into beautifully formatted HTML, including such things as a table of contents, hypertext links, and images.

To facilitate the delivery of content across the Internet, Delphi provides a Web Server Application wizard and its key component, the TWebModule. This is a specialized data module that allows non-visual components to be easily managed and manipulated at design time. In conjunction with a protocol-specific wrapper, it automatically forwards HTTP requests from a Web server to an appropriate action within the application.

Each Web action is passed references to the user input, encapsulated in a TWebRequest, and the output, in a TWebResponse, allowing the program to generate its content and pass it back to the client browser easily. Normally you use the TPageProducer component to provide an HTML template, either embedded as text or from an external file, that is output on request. Within that template, special tags are intercepted by the component and presented to the application for replacement. These tags appear in angle brackets (< >) as usual, and start with a pound sign followed by the name of the tag:

```
<#movies>
```

They may optionally have attributes specified in the usual HTML style. Each such tag that is found triggers the OnHTMLTag event on the page producer, providing you with the type of the tag, its name, and any attributes. You respond by using this information to supply the text that replaces the tag in the output document.

Enhancements to the basic page producer provide for the generation of HTML tables directly from a query or other data set.

This process can just as easily be used to generate XML instead of HTML. You simply replace the HTML snippets in the page producers with XML snippets, using the replacement tag mechanism to substitute the values from the database, as in the straight text generation.

Generation

To create the XML dynamically from the database tables described earlier, you follow these steps:

1. Start a new application using the Web Server Application wizard from the New Items dialog box (**File | New** on the menu).
2. Select the CGI option for this example, although there is no reason not to use one of the other types if your Web server supports them.
3. Place table and data source components into the resulting Web module corresponding to the movie-watcher database described above (see Chapter 16). Link them appropriately (with the movie-watcher alias) and activate them.
4. Add several TPageProducer components: one for the overall document and one for each of the tables. Your Web module should now look like the one in Figure 18-1.

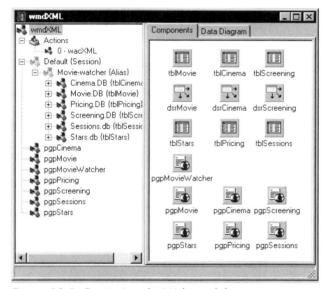

Figure 18-1: Designing the Web module.

5. Enter the XML prolog and the highest level tags—those corresponding to the database and main tables (see Listing 18-1)—into the HTMLDoc property of the main page producer component.

Listing 18-1: Main document outline for XML

```
<?xml version="1.0" encoding="UTF-8"?>
<!DOCTYPE movie-watcher SYSTEM "/movie-watcher.dtd">
<?xml:stylesheet type="text/xsl" href="/movie-watcher.xsl"?>
<movie-watcher>
<movies>
<#movies></movies>
<cinemas>
<#cinemas></cinemas>
```

```
<screenings>
<#screenings></screenings>
</movie-watcher>
```

6. Enter an XML document fragment describing the record structure for each table within their corresponding page producers. The entire snippet is enclosed in a tag indicating the type of record. Following this are the individual fields and an enclosing tag for any dependent tables. Using the field names as the substitution tag names makes the processing simpler during replacement. See the fragment for the `movie` element in Listing 18-2.

Listing 18-2: Document fragment for the movie element

```
<movie id="<#movie_id>" rating="<#rating>"<#logo_url><#url>>
  <name><#name></name>
  <length><#length></length>
  <director><#director></director>
  <starring>
<#stars>   </starring>
  <synopsis><#synopsis></synopsis>
</movie>
```

7. Create an event handler for the main page producer's `OnHTMLTag` event that replaces the contents of the table tags with XML representing the records. For each one it must step through all the records in that table and apply the appropriate template, from another page producer, over and over. The `GetRecords` method performs this task within the application, taking the table and page producer as parameters. See the code in Listing 18-3.

Listing 18-3: Handling tags for the main document

```
{ Cycle through all the records in the table
  and generate the XML snippet }
function TwmdXML.GetRecords(tbl: TTable; pgp: TPageProducer):
  string;
begin
  Result := '';
  with tbl do
  begin
    First;
    while not EOF do
    begin
      Result := Result + pgp.Content;
      Next;
    end;
  end;
end;
{ Generate movie-watcher XML document }
procedure TwmdXML.pgpMovieWatcherHTMLTag(Sender: TObject;
  Tag: TTag; const TagString: string; TagParams: TStrings;
  var ReplaceText: string);
begin
  if TagString = 'movies' then
    ReplaceText := GetRecords(tblMovie, pgpMovie)
  else if TagString = 'cinemas' then
    ReplaceText := GetRecords(tblCinema, pgpCinema)
  else if TagString = 'screenings' then
    ReplaceText := GetRecords(tblScreening, pgpScreening);
end;
```

8. Generate OnHTMLTag event handlers for the page producers associated with each table using the tag name to find a field value from the table, or invoke the GetRecords method for dependent tables. Listing 18-4 show the code for the movie page producer.

Listing 18-4: Substituting fields in the movie element

```
{ Add details for a movie }
procedure TwmdXML.pgpMovieHTMLTag(Sender: TObject; Tag: TTag;
  const TagString: string; TagParams: TStrings;
  var ReplaceText: string);
begin
  if TagString = 'stars' then
    ReplaceText := GetRecords(tblStars, pgpStars)
  else
    ReplaceText := tblMovie.FieldByName(TagString).DisplayText;
end;
```

9. Provide additional formatting for individual fields through the normal Delphi mechanisms: the DisplayFormat property or the OnGetText event on the field itself. The primary key identifiers for each table are made unique by prefixing them with a character corresponding to the table name (document-wide uniqueness is required of XML IDs) through their DisplayFormat properties.

The OnGetText event supplies the text for the display version of each field. Various specialized handlers provide necessary functionality as follows (see Listing 18-5). Some fields are presented as attributes and are not included in the document at all if their values are blank. The AttributeGetText method provides this functionality. Several Boolean fields are indicated by the presence or absence of an empty tag in the final document, which comes from invoking the EmptyFieldGetText method. And finally, the memo fields must provide their actual value, rather than their type, as obtained through the MemoGetText method.

Listing 18-5: Specialized formatting for various fields

```
{ Include attributes only if present }
procedure TwmdXML.AttributeGetText(Sender: TField;
  var Text: string; DisplayText: Boolean);
begin
  if Sender.AsString <> '' then
    Text := ' ' + ModifyName(Sender.FieldName) + '="' +
      Sender.AsString + '"';
end;

{ Include empty field tag only if flag in DB set }
procedure TwmdXML.EmptyFieldGetText(Sender: TField;
  var Text: string; DisplayText: Boolean);
begin
  if Sender.AsBoolean then
    Text := '<' + ModifyName(Sender.FieldName) + '/>';
end;

{ Display longer text }
procedure TwmdXML.MemoGetText(Sender: TField; var Text: string;
  DisplayText: Boolean);
begin
  Text := Sender.AsString;
end;
```

10. Generate the entire XML document by creating a default Web action for the module through the editor for the Actions property of the module. Within the action's handler you set the content type to text/xml and invoke the main page producer to create the actual content (as shown in Listing 18-6). Finally, you indicate that you have supplied the Web response by setting the Handled parameter to True.

Listing 18-6: Generating the entire document as an action

```
{ Main response }
procedure TwmdXML.wmdXMLwacXMLAction(Sender: TObject;
  Request: TWebRequest; Response: TWebResponse; var Handled: Boolean);
begin
  Response.ContentType := 'text/xml';
  Response.Content    := pgpMovieWatcher.Content;
  Handled             := True;
end;
```

11. Save your Web module and project (available as CGIXML.dpr on the CD-ROM) and compile it to create the CGI executable.

Once the application is compiled and placed in your Web server's CGI directory you can call it up and view the results (see Figure 18-2). To do this, you need to have a browser that supports XML and XSL, such as IE 5.

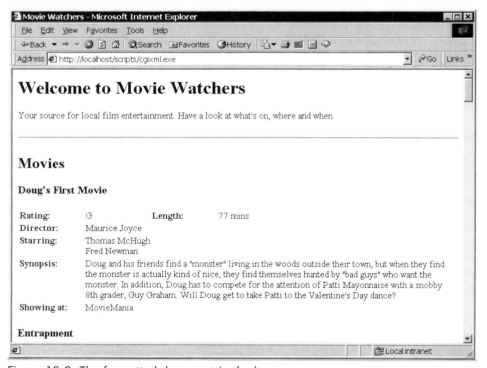

Figure 18-2: The formatted document in the browser.

NOTE To run your new application from a Web server, you need to deploy it in a location known to that server. For a CGI program (as developed above) and Personal Web Server (PWS) or Internet Information Server (IIS), you can use the default scripts directory and place the executable there. Then, reference the application (assuming it is running on the same machine) as http://localhost/scripts/cgixml.exe.

The stylesheet and DTD for the generated XML document also need to go into the scripts directory. You need to configure the Web server to allow these files to be read from this location as well.

TRecordPageProducer

In the previous example you manually cycled through all the records in a table in order to generate the section of the XML document that is derived from it. As you have seen, this process is repeated several times on the different tables, all of which are doing basically the same thing. In true Delphi tradition you can capture that process within a component, making it available for future use with minimal effort.

The TPageProducer component on Delphi's Internet tab allows you to generate a section of a document from a template. The TQueryTableProducer and TDataSetTableProducer components transform the contents of a query or any data set respectively into an HTML table for inclusion in a document. What you want is somewhere in between: being able to process each record in a data set, but without the hard-coded HTML table output.

To achieve this you create your own component, TRecordPageProducer, which generates its section of the document for each record in the attached data set. It builds on the abilities of TPageProducer in that the document fragment can be specified as either embedded text or a file reference, as well as inheriting the substitution operations on fields within the snippet.

1. Create the new component by selecting the **Component | New Component** menu options. Derive it from TPageProducer (its ancestor) and name it TRecordPageProducer. You can place it on the Internet tab in the Component Palette along with the other page producer components.

2. Add the new properties (see Listing 18-7). Obviously, you add one to refer to the attached data set, DataSet, as well as others to allow for the reporting of a lack of data, NoRecsFile and NoRecsDoc.

Listing 18-7: Adding properties to the component

```
type
  TRecordPageProducer = class(TPageProducer)
  private
    FDataSet: TDataSet;
    FNoRecsDoc: TStrings;
    FNoRecsFile: TFileName;
    procedure SetDataSet(DataSet: TDataSet);
    procedure SetNoRecsDoc(Value: TStrings);
    procedure SetNoRecsFile(const Value: TFileName);
  protected
    procedure DoTagEvent(Tag: TTag; const TagString: String;
      TagParams: TStrings; var ReplaceText: String); override;
```

```
    procedure Notification(AComponent: TComponent;
      Operation: TOperation); override;
  public
    constructor Create(AOwner: TComponent); override;
    destructor Destroy; override;
    function ContentFromStream(Stream: TStream): String; override;
  published
    property DataSet: TDataSet read FDataSet write SetDataSet;
    property NoRecsDoc: TStrings read FNoRecsDoc write SetNoRecsDoc;
    property NoRecsFile: TFileName read FNoRecsFile
      write SetNoRecsFile;
  end;
```

3. Override the constructor and destructor to allocate and release the string list used by the NoRecsDoc property, and the Notification method to clear your reference to the data set if it is deleted (see Listing 18-8).

Listing 18-8: Overriding inherited methods

```
{ Initialization }
constructor TRecordPageProducer.Create(AOwner: TComponent);
begin
  inherited Create(AOwner);
  FNoRecsDoc := TStringList.Create;
end;

{ Release resources }
destructor TRecordPageProducer.Destroy;
begin
  FNoRecsDoc.Free;
  inherited Destroy;
end;

{ Clear our reference to the data set if it is deleted }
procedure TRecordPageProducer.Notification(AComponent: TComponent;
  Operation: TOperation);
begin
  inherited Notification(AComponent, Operation);
  if (Operation = opRemove) and Assigned(DataSet) and
      (DataSet = AComponent) then
    DataSet := nil;
end;
```

NOTE When referring to one component from another you should always override the Notification method to clear your pointer to it if it is deleted from the form. Always call the inherited method to invoke any in-built functionality, then match the notifying component to your property and erase it if appropriate.

4. Add the new functionality: cycling through all records and automatically substituting for field references. Browsing through the code for TPageProducer you find that all content requests end up going through the ContentFromStream method. This means that if you override this one method to cycle through each record it works no matter how the content is requested.

In your version of the method you first check to see that the DataSet exists, is open, and actually contains some data. If so, you reposition the data set to the beginning before stepping through each record and applying the template to it (see Listing 18-9). Here you make use of the functionality of the ancestor to perform the processing of the template through the call to the inherited `ContentFromStream`. Note that you must reset the template stream to the beginning each time around the loop as it is processed within the inherited method.

Listing 18-9: Generating a document snippet for each record

```
{ Iterate through the records in the dataset }
function TRecordPageProducer.ContentFromStream(Stream: TStream):
  string;
var
  stmNoRecs: TStream;
begin
  Result := '';
  if Assigned(FDataSet) then
    if FDataSet.Active then
      if FDataSet.RecordCount > 0 then
        { Cycle through all the records }
        with FDataSet do
        begin
          First;
          while not EOF do
          begin
            Stream.Position := 0;
            Result := Result +
              inherited ContentFromStream(Stream);
            Next;
          end;
          Exit;
        end;

  { No data found }
  if FNoRecsFile <> '' then
    stmNoRecs := TFileStream.Create(
      FNoRecsFile, fmOpenRead + fmShareDenyWrite)
  else
    stmNoRecs := TStringStream.Create(FNoRecsDoc.Text);
  if Assigned(stmNoRecs) then
    try
      Result := inherited ContentFromStream(stmNoRecs);
    finally
      stmNoRecs.Free;
    end;
end;
```

If no data exists in the data set, or it is not assigned or not open, then output the contents of the `NoRecsDoc` or `NoRecsFile` properties instead.

5. Automatically substitute field values for tags with their names by overriding another inherited method. Some examination reveals that the `DoTagEvent` routine is the one you want. In `TPageProducer` it simply calls the `OnHTMLTag` event handler if it exists. Instead, you want it to try to match the tag name with a field name, and only call the event handler if that fails (see Listing 18-10). An exception occurs if the data set is not active or if the field does not exist. You trap this and redirect processing to the user event instead.

Part IV: Serving XML

Listing 18-10: Automatically replacing field references

```
{ Replace field references automatically }
procedure TRecordPageProducer.DoTagEvent(Tag: TTag;
  const TagString: string; TagParams: TStrings;
  var ReplaceText: string);
begin
  try
    ReplaceText := FDataSet.FieldByName(TagString).DisplayText;
  except
    inherited DoTagEvent(Tag, TagString, TagParams, ReplaceText);
  end;
end;
```

6. Add the new component to the Component Palette by selecting **Component | Install Component**. Place it in an existing package (such as the default user one) or create your own new package.

Using this new component instead of the basic page producer makes your program code that much simpler. The application presented at the start of this chapter is updated in CGIXML2.dpr to demonstrate the new abilities. Drop TRecordPageProducer components onto the Web module instead of the normal page producers used for each table (six in all) and attach them to the corresponding table components. The content of their HTMLDoc properties remains the same as before.

Code for the action and main page producer does not change. However, the OnHTMLTag event handlers for the new page producers does change. Those for stars, pricing schemes, and sessions disappear altogether since their functionality is subsumed into the new component. The movie, cinema, and screening handlers now only need to deal with the embedded tables (as shown in Listing 18-11); the other fields get substituted automatically (based on their names within the tags).

Listing 18-11: Handling movie tags

```
{ Add details for a movie }
procedure TwmdXML.pgrMovieHTMLTag(Sender: TObject; Tag: TTag;
  const TagString: String; TagParams: TStrings;
  var ReplaceText: String);
begin
  if TagString = 'stars' then
    ReplaceText := pgrStars.Content;
end;
```

NOTE Deploy the new CGI program to your scripts directory on the Web server. The other required files should already be there from the first version. Access it with: http://localhost/scripts/cgixml2.exe.

Summary

The applications presented here demonstrate how to produce an XML document from an existing database on demand. But recall that the Web modules are able to accept additional parameters from the user. These can be used to further customize the output: either by providing a subset of the data in the first place, or by referring to a different stylesheet from within the document. The latter allows for presenting the same XML document in different ways and can include its own selection criteria. In fact, you could generate a customized stylesheet as well as the original XML.

The Internet technologies built into Delphi enable you to quickly generate server-side applications for processing and delivering data. You can use these abilities to produce XML documents, as well as the more usual HTML ones. The full functionality of Delphi can take on the problem, allowing you to access databases and to customize the documents that are produced.

To make the processing of information from data sources easier, you can use the `TRecordPageProducer` component that cycles through each record in its attached data set and applies its HTML/XML template to each one.

Chapter 19
Document Object Model

In addition to its use in parsing an existing document, the DOM can also create and manipulate documents. One of the aims in specifying the DOM is the ability to parse, deconstruct, and reconstruct a document any number of times with no loss of structure or content.

The DOM specification defines a number of factory methods on the Document interface, such as createElement and createTextNode. These let you create all the necessary nodes to place in your new document while ensuring that they are compatible with the rest of the implementation and are linked to their owning document.

However, DOM Level 1 did not specify how the document object is created in the first place. DOM Level 2 filled in this gap by including the createDocument and createDocumentType methods on the DOMImplementation interface. This still leaves the generation of an implementation reference to the specific packages (you have to start somewhere), but once you have this you can produce everything else.

NOTE One major area that is missing in the DOM specification as it stands is the ability to generate the contents of the document type declaration for a document. Although you can specify the document type itself during creation of the document object, you cannot add or alter any entities or notations within that section.

Microsoft's DOM

You can use the Microsoft DOM as implemented in the MSXML v3 library to generate new XML documents. The creation of the type library for this package is described in Chapter 9. Thereafter, you follow these steps to build a new document based on the movie-watcher database.

1. Add the generated type library to your uses clause. Also add the ActiveX unit to allow for initialization of the COM system.

    ```
    uses ..., ActiveX, MSXML2_tlb;
    ```

2. Initialize COM in the initialization section, and free it up in the finalization section.

    ```
    initialization
      CoInitialize(nil);
    ```

```
      finalization
        CoUninitialize;
      end.
```

3. Create a document object. This package does not have a DOM implementation object as such, and lets you create document objects directly through the CoDOMDocument class.

```
var
  XMLDoc: IXMLDOMDocument;
{ Instantiate the DOM }
XMLDoc := CoDOMDocument.Create;
```

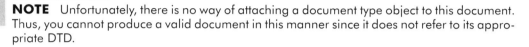

NOTE Unfortunately, there is no way of attaching a document type object to this document. Thus, you cannot produce a valid document in this manner since it does not refer to its appropriate DTD.

4. Add the document's top-level children using its AppendChild method and its factory methods. In the case of a movie-watcher document these may be a comment, a stylesheet reference (as a processing instruction), and the document element itself (which also sets the DocumentElement property of the document). You can include an XML prolog by adding another processing instruction as the first child. The GenerateHeaders method in Listing 19-1 shows the generation of the top-level children.

Listing 19-1: Generating XML via the DOM

```
{ Generate the XML document as text }
procedure TfrmDOMXML.btnGenerateClick(Sender: TObject);
var
  XMLDoc: IXMLDOMDocument;

  { Generate XML prolog, style sheet reference,
    and document element }
  procedure GenerateHeaders;
  begin
    with XMLDoc do
    begin
      AppendChild(CreateProcessingInstruction(
        XMLTag, XMLPrologAttrs));
      AppendChild(CreateComment(XMLComment));
      AppendChild(CreateProcessingInstruction(
        XMLStyleTag, XMLStyleAttrs));
      AppendChild(CreateElement(MovieWatcherTag));
    end;
  end;

  { Compile elements for the stars of the movie }
  procedure GenerateStars(Starring: IXMLDOMElement);
  begin
    with qryStars do
    begin
      First;
      while not EOF do
      begin
        AddSimpleElement(Starring, FieldByName(StarField));
        Next;
      end;
    end;
```

```
    end;

  { Generate elements for each movie }
  procedure GenerateMovies;
  var
    Movies, Movie: IXMLDOMElement;
  begin
    Movies := IXMLDOMElement(XMLDoc.DocumentElement.AppendChild(
      XMLDoc.CreateElement(MoviesTag)));
    with qryMovie do
    begin
      First;
      while not EOF do
      begin
        Movie := IXMLDOMElement(Movies.AppendChild(
          XMLDoc.CreateElement(MovieTag)));
        Movie.SetAttribute(Id,
          FieldByName(MovieIdField).DisplayText);
        Movie.SetAttribute(Rating,
          FieldByName(RatingField).DisplayText);
        AddOptAttribute(Movie, FieldByName(LogoURLField));
        AddOptAttribute(Movie, FieldByName(URLField));
        AddSimpleElement(Movie, FieldByName(NameField));
        AddSimpleElement(Movie, FieldByName(LengthField));
        AddSimpleElement(Movie, FieldByName(DirectorField));
        GenerateStars(IXMLDOMElement(Movie.AppendChild(
          XMLDoc.CreateElement(StarringTag))));
        AddSimpleElement(Movie, FieldByName(SynopsisField),
          True);
        Next;
      end;
    end;
  end;

  { GenerateCinemas and GenerateScreenings are similar
    to the above and are not shown here }

begin
  try
    Screen.Cursor := crHourglass;
    { Instantiate the DOM }
    XMLDoc      := CoDOMDocument.Create;
    { Generate the structure }
    GenerateHeaders;
    GenerateMovies;
    GenerateCinemas;
    GenerateScreenings;
    { And convert to XML }
    memXML.Lines.Text := XMLDoc.XML;
  finally
    { Release the DOM }
    XMLDoc       := nil;
    Screen.Cursor := crDefault;
  end;
end;
```

5. Include the list of movies in the document by adding the movies element as a child of the document element. (See the GenerateMovies method in Listing 19-1). You use the DocumentElement property of the document to refer to the top-level element added in Step

4. Retain a reference to the `movies` element since you need to add several children to it. The `AppendChild` method returns a pointer to the node it just added, which should be cast as an element for later use.

6. Cycle through all the movie records from the associated query and create a child element for each one (see the `GenerateMovies` method in Listing 19-1). Again, a reference to the new node is kept for further processing. On that node you set the values of a couple of attributes with the `SetAttribute` method. Then add the fields from the record as sub-elements with text nodes as children. Values for the ID attribute of each movie are set from the primary key field in the database, which is prefixed by a different character for each table to ensure that IDs are unique across the entire document.

Helper functions handle the details of adding these basic child nodes (`AddSimpleElement`) as well as the situation where you want to add an attribute only if it has an actual value (`AddOptAttribute`) as shown in Listing 19-2. Element and attribute names come from the name of the field being worked upon (after allowing for differences in naming conventions). The former routine also has a flag (defaulting to `False`) that indicates whether or not the text should be wrapped in a CDATA section. In this example, the synopsis field from the database is automatically generated as CDATA to show the use of such sections and their resulting output.

Listing 19-2: Helper functions for DOM XML generation

```
{ Add a simple element that only contains text }
procedure AddSimpleElement(Parent: IXMLDOMElement;
  Field: TField; AsCDATA: Boolean = False);
var
  Internal: IXMLDOMElement;
begin
  Internal := IXMLDOMElement(Parent.AppendChild(
    XMLDoc.CreateElement(ModifyName(Field.FieldName))));
  if AsCDATA then
    Internal.AppendChild(
      XMLDoc.CreateCDATASection(Field.DisplayText))
  else
    Internal.AppendChild(
      XMLDoc.CreateTextNode(Field.DisplayText));
end;

{ Include attributes only if present }
procedure AddOptAttribute(Element: IXMLDOMElement;
  Field: TField);
begin
  if Field.AsString <> '' then
    Element.SetAttribute(ModifyName(Field.FieldName),
      Field.DisplayText);
end;
```

NOTE Since you cannot manipulate the document type node for a generated document, you cannot declare entities and notations within it. This means that the references to the external HTML and GIF resources encoded in the movies table appear as direct URLs rather than as external entity references as required by the DTD. However, as you cannot specify the DTD either, perhaps this does not matter.

7. Generate the embedded `star` elements. Since the stars data comes from another table and has an unknown number of occurrences, a separate routine provides its content (`GenerateStars` in Listing 19-1). Called from the generation of the movie elements, it is provided a reference to the surrounding `starring` element, and steps through each stars record, adding it as a simple, text-filled child.

8. Repeat the process for the cinemas and screenings elements and tables, with their embedded pricing schemes and sessions respectively. Another helper function includes empty tags for Boolean fields only when their value is `True` (see Listing 19-3). An empty tag is simply one that has no children.

Listing 19-3: Creating optional empty elements

```
{ Include empty field tag only if flag in DB set }
procedure AddOptElement(Parent: IXMLDOMElement; Field: TField);
begin
  if Field.AsBoolean then
    Parent.AppendChild(Parent.OwnerDocument.CreateElement(
      ModifyName(Field.FieldName)));
end;
```

9. Convert the document in memory into an XML document through the XML property of the document object. This is not part of the XML specification as defined by the W3C, but is provided by Microsoft's implementation for your benefit. Don't forget to release the DOM object by setting its reference back to `nil` (although Delphi will do this for you when the variable goes out of scope).

As with the text generation example in Chapter 17, the completed document is written into a memo control on the form and can be saved to the disk by pressing the Save button. Figure 19-1 shows the start of the movie-watcher document generated with Microsoft's DOM.

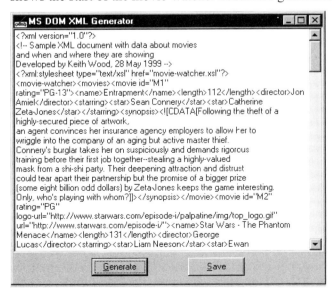

Figure 19-1: Generating with Microsoft's DOM.

CUESoft's DOM

CUESoft's DOM can also produce documents on the fly. It offers basically the same functionality and restrictions as Microsoft's implementation. In fact, the code is almost identical.

Obvious changes are the different names of the DOM objects: Microsoft's start with IXMLDOM while CUESoft's start with TXml. The manner of creating the blank document and extracting the resulting XML also differ. CUESoft's version is shown in Listing 19-4. An object model is initially constructed from which you get the document itself. Upon completion of the generation process you access the XMLDocument property to retrieve the XML output. Setting the FormattedOutput property of the model affects the document's appearance, in this case by adding line feeds at the ends of tags and appropriate indentation.

Listing 19-4: Initializing a CUESoft document object

```
{ Generate the XML document as text }
procedure TfrmDOMXML.btnGenerateClick(Sender: TObject);
var
  XMLModel: TXmlObjModel;
  XMLDoc: TXmlDocument;
begin
  try
    Screen.Cursor := crHourglass;
    { Instantiate the DOM }
    XMLModel := TXmlObjModel.Create(nil);
    XMLDoc   := XMLModel.Document;
    { Generate the structure }
    GenerateHeaders;
    GenerateMovies;
    GenerateCinemas;
    GenerateScreenings;
    { And convert to XML }
    XMLModel.FormattedOutput := True;
    memXML.Lines.Text        := XMLModel.XMLDocument;
  finally
    { Release the DOM }
    XMLModel.Free;
    Screen.Cursor := crDefault;
  end;
end;
```

Another subtle difference is that the AppendChild method in CUESoft's implementation does not return a reference to the new node. Thus, the creation of a new element, assigning it to a variable, and adding it to the DOM cannot be achieved in a single statement as you can do with Microsoft's version. So, instead of the previous:

```
Movie := IXMLDOMElement(Movies.AppendChild(
  XMLDoc.CreateElement(MovieTag)));
```

you must now use:

```
Movie := XMLDoc.CreateElement(MovieTag);
Movies.AppendChild(Movie);
```

As before, a memo field receives the resulting XML for display on the screen. You can copy it to disk with the Save button. Figure 19-2 shows the output from the CUESoft generation process. Like Microsoft's implementation, you cannot add a document type declaration to the document.

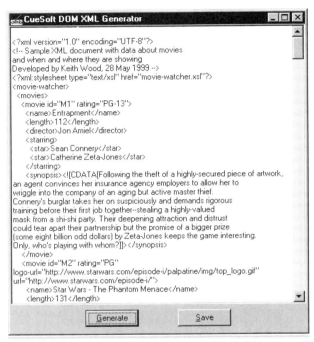

Figure 19-2: Generating with CUESoft's DOM.

Open XML's DOM

Using Open XML's DOM to produce XML documents is quite similar to the previous two. Minor variations occur in naming the classes (Tdom prefix compared to Microsoft's IXMLDOM) and in starting the process by instantiating an implementation object and asking it to generate the actual document (see Listing 19-5). The creation method needs the name of the document element and may take a document type reference. However, in this release, you cannot create a document type object until you have created the document.

Listing 19-5: Creating documents with Open XML

```
{ Generate the XML document as text }
procedure TfrmDOMXML.btnGenerateClick(Sender: TObject);
var
  XMLImpl: TdomImplementation;
  XMLDoc: TdomDocument;
begin
  Screen.Cursor := crHourglass;
  { Instantiate the DOM }
  XMLImpl := TDomImplementation.Create(nil);
```

```
    try
      XMLDoc := XMLImpl.CreateDocument(MovieWatcherTag, nil);
      { Generate the structure }
      GenerateHeaders;
      GenerateMovies;
      GenerateCinemas;
      GenerateScreenings;
      { And convert to XML }
      memXML.Lines.Text := XMLDoc.codeAsString;
    finally
      { Release the DOM }
      XMLImpl.FreeDocument(XMLDoc);
      XMLImpl.Free;
      Screen.Cursor := crDefault;
    end;
  end;
```

The name of the document element prompts a search through the list of document classes registered with the XDOM package. This lets you create specialized documents with added abilities and have them automatically invoked when creating a document of that type. For example, you could write an HTML document class that provided factory methods for all the HTML tags. Once registered with the `RegisterDocumentFormat` method in the `TDomImplementation` class, it is available whenever a document with an `html` document element is requested.

A major difference between Open XML's DOM and the previous versions is its support for the DTD within a document. It lets you completely describe the contents of the DTD, from an external subset to internal entities and notations. Listing 19-6 shows how to generate a header for the movie-watcher document. First up you should add an XML prolog. However, this cannot be done if the document has any children, which it already does due to its creation based on an element name. The workaround is to delete the document element, add the XML prolog, and then replace that element.

Listing 19-6: Generating the document headers

```
  { Generate XML prolog, style sheet reference, and document element }
  procedure GenerateHeaders;
  var
    BaseId: string;
  begin
    with XMLDoc do
    begin
      RemoveChild(DocumentElement);
      AppendChild(CreateXmlDeclaration('1.0', 'UTF-8', 'no'));
      AppendChild(CreateElement(MovieWatcherTag));
      InsertBefore(CreateDocumentType(
        MovieWatcherTag, '', XMLDTDFile), DocumentElement);
      DocType.InternalSubsetNode.AppendChild(
        CreateNotationDeclaration(GIFType, GIFPubId, GIFSysId));
      DocType.InternalSubsetNode.AppendChild(
        CreateNotationDeclaration(HTMLType, HTMLPubId, HTMLSysId));
      with qryMovie do
      begin
        First;
        while not EOF do
        begin
          BaseId := FieldByName(MovieIdField).DisplayText;
          if FieldByName(LogoURLField).AsString <> '' then
```

```
        begin
          DocType.Entities.SetNamedItem(CreateEntity(BaseId + 'Logo',
            '', FieldByName(LogoURLField).DisplayText, GIFType));
          DocType.InternalSubsetNode.AppendChild(
            CreateEntityDeclaration(BaseId + 'Logo', '',
            '', FieldByName(LogoURLField).DisplayText, GIFType));
        end;
        if FieldByName(URLField).AsString <> '' then
        begin
          DocType.Entities.SetNamedItem(CreateEntity(BaseId + 'Url',
            '', FieldByName(URLField).DisplayText, HTMLType));
          DocType.InternalSubsetNode.AppendChild(
            CreateEntityDeclaration(BaseId + 'Url', '',
            '', FieldByName(URLField).DisplayText, HTMLType));
        end;
        Next;
      end;
    end;
    InsertBefore(CreateComment(XMLComment), DocumentElement);
    InsertBefore(CreateProcessingInstruction(
      XMLStyleTag, XMLStyleAttrs), DocumentElement);
  end;
end;
```

The DTD section of the document starts with a document type object added before the document element via the `InsertBefore` method, with a reference to the external DTD being passed along. This automatically creates internal and external subset nodes as children of the document type. To the internal subset you add declarations for the two standard notations for movie-watcher documents. Stepping through the movies database, you add entity declarations for any external references found (again to the internal subset of the DTD). Lastly, the usual comment and stylesheet reference are also added to the document itself.

Content for the document comes from processing each appropriate database record in turn and adding element and text nodes as with the previous DOMs. Listing 19-7 show the code for appending movie information. Note that now the URL and logo attributes of a movie refer to the entities rather than the actual URIs. Cinemas and screenings use a similar approach. As before, the `AddSimpleElement` routine adds a sub-element with a name based on the supplied field and with a single text child holding its data. The synopsis field is saved as a CDATA section just to show how these appear.

Listing 19-7: Adding movies

```
{ Add a simple element that only contains text }
procedure AddSimpleElement(Parent: TdomElement; Field: TField;
  AsCDATA: Boolean = False);
var
  Internal: TdomNode;
begin
  Internal := Parent.AppendChild(
    XMLDoc.CreateElement(ModifyName(Field.FieldName)));
  if AsCDATA then
    Internal.AppendChild(
      XMLDoc.CreateCDATASection(Field.DisplayText))
  else
    Internal.AppendChild(XMLDoc.CreateTextNode(Field.DisplayText));
end;
```

```
{ Compile elements for the stars of the movie }
procedure GenerateStars(Starring: TdomElement);
begin
  with qryStars do
  begin
    First;
    while not EOF do
    begin
      AddSimpleElement(Starring, FieldByName(StarField));
      Next;
    end;
  end;
end;

{ Generate elements for each movie }
procedure GenerateMovies;
var
  Movies, Movie: TdomElement;
  BaseId: string;
begin
  Movies := TdomElement(XMLDoc.DocumentElement.AppendChild(
    XMLDoc.CreateElement(MoviesTag)));
  with qryMovie do
  begin
    First;
    while not EOF do
    begin
      Movie := TdomElement(Movies.AppendChild(
        XMLDoc.CreateElement(MovieTag)));
      BaseId := FieldByName(MovieIdField).DisplayText;
      Movie.SetAttribute(Id, BaseId);
      Movie.SetAttribute(Rating,
        FieldByName(RatingField).DisplayText);
      if FieldByName(LogoURLField).AsString <> '' then
        Movie.SetAttribute(ModifyName(
          FieldByName(LogoURLField).FieldName), BaseId + 'Logo');
      if FieldByName(URLField).AsString <> '' then
        Movie.SetAttribute(ModifyName(
          FieldByName(URLField).FieldName), BaseId + 'Url');
      AddSimpleElement(Movie, FieldByName(NameField));
      AddSimpleElement(Movie, FieldByName(LengthField));
      AddSimpleElement(Movie, FieldByName(DirectorField));
      GenerateStars(TdomElement(Movie.AppendChild(
        XMLDoc.CreateElement(StarringTag))));
      AddSimpleElement(Movie, FieldByName(SynopsisField), True);
      Next;
    end;
  end;
end;
```

Generating XML with this DOM produces a document that matches exactly the DTD defined earlier, including unparsed entity references. The result is shown in Figure 19-3. Save the output as before and view it in your browser.

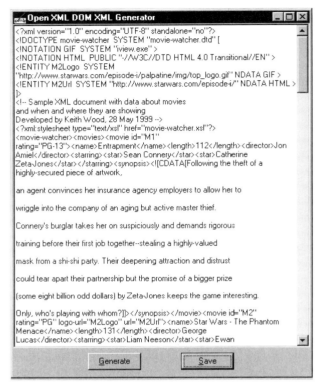

Figure 19-3: Open XML's DOM includes a document type section.

Summary

Producing documents in this manner is more work than using the straight text version. However, it does create the DOM directly in memory, allowing it to be further manipulated by the program. For example, you could create a document, or fragment, and then apply a style sheet to it to transform it into an alternate output. In this way you could use a single transfer medium between various sources and destinations. All you need is a routine to convert the originator into XML, and an appropriate driver to transform the XML into the desired output.

Even though there is a standard DOM specification, the various DOM implementations have different abilities when it comes to supporting the document type part of the model. Open XML provides full support, while Microsoft and CUESoft provide none (which conforms to the current specification). The latter DOMs cannot, therefore, use external entity references and should design DTDs that do not rely on these. But then again, they cannot include references to a DTD anyway. Hopefully, the next version of the DOM addresses this issue, and the various implementations support the changes.

Chapter 20
SAX Generation

A SAX parser breaks the input XML document up into tokens and triggers events on attached handlers for each one. These handlers may process the events in whatever manner they choose, such as looking for particular elements and their contents or building a DOM.

One of the extra abilities included in the Microsoft XML support for SAX is its `IMXWriter` interface. An object created through this interface also expresses each of the other handler interfaces. Invoking handler methods on such an object causes it to generate an XML document that reproduces those events. The result is available through the `Output` property, which may be referenced as a `WideString` value, or may be sent directly to an `IStream` object.

So, instead of instantiating a SAX parser and supplying your own handlers, you generate a document by creating an `IMXWriter` object and calling its handler methods as if you are the parser. An alternative use is to transform an existing XML document by having a SAX parser read it, pass the events through a SAX filter (which does the actual transformation), and direct its output to a writer.

IMXWriter Interface

Objects created through the CoClass for the `IMXWriter` interface also implement the `IVBSAXContentHandler`, `IVBSAXDTDHandler`, `IVBSAXErrorHandler`, `IVBSAXLexicalHandler`, and `IVBSAXDeclHandler` interfaces. You invoke these to generate an XML document. In principle, piping the events from a SAX parser directly to a writer produces exactly the same document on output as on input. However, certain input deemed insignificant by the XML specification may be skipped or generated differently. Also the output encoding may be different to that on input.

The properties specific to the `IMXWriter` interface let you control the appearance of the resulting document. See Listing 20-1 for the interface's declaration.

Listing 20-1: The `IMXWriter` interface

```
// *******************************************************************//
// Interface: IMXWriter
// Flags:     (4544) Dual NonExtensible OleAutomation Dispatchable
// GUID:      {4D7FF4BA-1565-4EA8-94E1-6E724A46F98D}
// *******************************************************************//
IMXWriter = interface(IDispatch)
  ['{4D7FF4BA-1565-4EA8-94E1-6E724A46F98D}']
```

```
    procedure Set_output(varDestination: OleVariant); safecall;
    function  Get_output: OleVariant; safecall;
    procedure Set_encoding(const strEncoding: WideString); safecall;
    function  Get_encoding: WideString; safecall;
    procedure Set_byteOrderMark(fWriteByteOrderMark: WordBool); safecall;
    function  Get_byteOrderMark: WordBool; safecall;
    procedure Set_indent(fIndentMode: WordBool); safecall;
    function  Get_indent: WordBool; safecall;
    procedure Set_standalone(fValue: WordBool); safecall;
    function  Get_standalone: WordBool; safecall;
    procedure Set_omitXMLDeclaration(fValue: WordBool); safecall;
    function  Get_omitXMLDeclaration: WordBool; safecall;
    procedure Set_version(const strVersion: WideString); safecall;
    function  Get_version: WideString; safecall;
    procedure Set_disableOutputEscaping(fValue: WordBool); safecall;
    function  Get_disableOutputEscaping: WordBool; safecall;
    procedure flush; safecall;
    property output: OleVariant read Get_output write Set_output;
    property encoding: WideString read Get_encoding write Set_encoding;
    property byteOrderMark: WordBool read Get_byteOrderMark
      write Set_byteOrderMark;
    property indent: WordBool read Get_indent write Set_indent;
    property standalone: WordBool read Get_standalone
      write Set_standalone;
    property omitXMLDeclaration: WordBool read Get_omitXMLDeclaration
      write Set_omitXMLDeclaration;
    property version: WideString read Get_version write Set_version;
    property disableOutputEscaping: WordBool
      read Get_disableOutputEscaping write Set_disableOutputEscaping;
  end;
```

The IMXWriter's properties and methods are described below:

`property output: OleVariant read Get_output write Set_output;`

Retrieve or redirect the XML document generated by the writer through this property. If assigned an object that implements IStream, the output is sent directly to that stream. If not assigned a value, or if it is assigned an empty string, the output appears as a string value when this property is read. Assigning an empty string also clears the internal buffer in preparation for generating the next section of the document. In this way, the memory requirements of the writer are reduced. The output is also reset whenever a startDocument event occurs.

`property encoding: WideString read Get_encoding write Set_encoding;`

This property sets or returns the encoding scheme used by the writer. If you are retrieving the output as a string value, this setting is ignored since all strings are UTF-16 encoded.

`property byteOrderMark: WordBool read Get_byteOrderMark write Set_byteOrderMark;`

Set this property to True to have the writer generate a byte order mark for appropriate encodings. When False, no byte order mark is included. A byte order mark is never produced when output is retrieved as a string.

`property indent: WordBool read Get_indent write Set_indent;`

When set to True the output document is formatted for improved readability. Each level of elements is indented by one tab and opening tags appear on a new line. If set to False, the XML appears without any breaks.

property standalone: WordBool read Get_standalone write Set_standalone;
> This property controls the appearance of the standalone declaration in the XML prolog. The default is to omit it (a setting of `False`).

property omitXMLDeclaration: WordBool read Get_omitXMLDeclaration write Set_omitXMLDeclaration;
> The entire XML prolog can be excluded by setting this property to `True`. By default it is set to `False`, which includes the prolog.

property version: WideString read Get_version write Set_version;
> Set or retrieve the XML version declaration from the prolog through this property. It defaults to `1.0`.

property disableOutputEscaping: WordBool read Get_disableOutputEscaping write Set_disableOutputEscaping;
> This property determines whether or not text is escaped before being written out. When `True`, text is not escaped, which may result in a malformed document, and when `False`, (the default) the text is escaped, meaning that the standard metacharacters (like <) are replaced by their corresponding entity references (like <).

procedure flush; safecall;
> Flush the internal buffer to its output stream or string. This happens automatically when the `output` property is accessed or when the `endDocument` event occurs.

IMXAttributes Interface

Generating an element requires its attributes (if any) be specified. The `IVBSAXAttributes` interface from SAX defines how to extract information about a set of attributes, but says nothing about how to set up those details in the first place. The `IMXAttributes` interface (see Listing 20-2) provides the necessary functionality. An object that expresses this interface also implements the `IVBSAXAttributes` one, allowing it to be passed directly to the `startElement` call.

Listing 20-2: The IMXAttributes interface

```
//******************************************************************//
// Interface: IMXAttributes
// Flags:     (4544) Dual NonExtensible OleAutomation Dispatchable
// GUID:      {F10D27CC-3EC0-415C-8ED8-77AB1C5E7262}
//******************************************************************//
IMXAttributes = interface(IDispatch)
  ['{F10D27CC-3EC0-415C-8ED8-77AB1C5E7262}']
  procedure addAttribute(const strURI: WideString;
    const strLocalName: WideString; const strQName: WideString;
    const strType: WideString; const strValue: WideString); safecall;
  procedure addAttributeFromIndex(varAtts: OleVariant; nIndex: SYSINT);
    safecall;
  procedure clear; safecall;
  procedure removeAttribute(nIndex: SYSINT); safecall;
  procedure setAttribute(nIndex: SYSINT; const strURI: WideString;
    const strLocalName: WideString; const strQName: WideString;
    const strType: WideString; const strValue: WideString); safecall;
```

```
    procedure setAttributes(varAtts: OleVariant); safecall;
    procedure setLocalName(nIndex: SYSINT;
      const strLocalName: WideString); safecall;
    procedure setQName(nIndex: SYSINT; const strQName: WideString);
      safecall;
    procedure setType(nIndex: SYSINT; const strType: WideString);
      safecall;
    procedure setURI(nIndex: SYSINT; const strURI: WideString); safecall;
    procedure setValue(nIndex: SYSINT; const strValue: WideString);
      safecall;
  end;
```

Create an object of this type through the CoSAXAttributes class's Create method. Using the CoSAXAttributes30 class instead ties the object to this version of the XML package.

The methods of an IMXAttributes object are shown below:

procedure addAttribute(const strURI: WideString; const strLocalName: WideString; const strQName: WideString; const strType: WideString; const strValue: WideString); safecall;

Add an attribute to the end of the list with this method, which takes the name of the attribute, as well as its type and string value. Send a single space if a parameter is not known. No check is made for a pre-existing attribute with the same name. For performance reasons, this is left to the user to implement if necessary.

procedure addAttributeFromIndex(varAtts: OleVariant; nIndex: SYSINT); safecall;

Adds an attribute, whose value is equal to the specified entry from the input object, to the end of the list.

procedure clear; safecall;

This method empties the attribute list, readying it for reuse. It does not free up the associated memory.

procedure removeAttribute(nIndex: SYSINT); safecall;

Delete the specified attribute by index, starting at zero, with this method.

procedure setAttribute(nIndex: SYSINT; const strURI: WideString; const strLocalName: WideString; ccnst strQName: WideString; const strType: WideString; const strValue: WideString); safecall;

Given an attribute's position (starting from zero), set its name and value to the specified arguments through this method.

procedure setAttributes(varAtts: OleVariant); safecall;

Use this method to copy the contents of another attribute collection. It is probably more efficient to reuse an existing object than to generate a copy.

procedure setLocalName(nIndex: SYSINT; const strLocalName: WideString); safecall;

Update the local name for the specified attribute with this method.

procedure setQName(nIndex: SYSINT; const strQName: WideString); safecall;

Similarly, alter the qualified name of the nominated attribute through this method.

procedure setType(nIndex: SYSINT; const strType: WideString); safecall;

Use this method to change the type for the specified attribute.

procedure setURI(nIndex: SYSINT; const strURI: WideString); safecall;
   Modify the nominated attribute's namespace URI with this method.

procedure setValue(nIndex: SYSINT; const strValue: WideString); safecall;
   And, finally, overwrite the specified attribute's value via this method.

Creating a Writer

Obtaining a SAX writer object is easy with the `CoMXXMLWriter` CoClass. Once the `MSXML2_tlb` unit is included in your uses clause, you call on this class to generate a new writer via its `Create` method. Use `CoMXXMLWriter30` instead to always produce an object from this version of the XML package, rather than the latest version returned by the previous CoClass. Although the `IMXWriter` interface derives directly from `IDispatch` and makes no mention of the handler interfaces, the resulting object implements them. The easiest way to refer to them from Delphi is to declare variables for each desired interface and use the as operator to cast the writer accordingly. See Listing 20-3 for the creation code.

Listing 20-3: Creating a SAX writer

```
{ Generate the XML document as text }
procedure TfrmWriterXML.btnGenerateClick(Sender: TObject);
const
  Empty: WideString = '';
  NoValue: WideString = ' ';
var
  XMLDoc: IMXWriter;
  ContentHandler: IVBSAXContentHandler;
  DTDHandler: IVBSAXDTDHandler;
  LexicalHandler: IVBSAXLexicalHandler;
  Attributes: IMXAttributes;
  { Add the document generated so far to the output }
  procedure UpdateOutput;
  begin
    memXML.Lines.Text := memXML.Lines.Text + XMLDoc.Output;
    XMLDoc.Output    := Empty;
  end;
  { Generate XML prolog, style sheet reference, and document element }
  procedure GenerateDocument;
  var
    Wide1, Wide2: WideString;
  begin
    ContentHandler.StartDocument;
    GenerateDTD;
    Wide1 := XMLComment;
    LexicalHandler.Comment(Wide1);
    Wide1 := XMLStyleTag;
    Wide2 := XMLStyleAttrs;
    ContentHandler.ProcessingInstruction(Wide1, Wide2);
    UpdateOutput;
    StartElement(MovieWatcherTag);
    GenerateMovies;
    UpdateOutput;
    GenerateCinemas;
    UpdateOutput;
```

```
      GenerateScreenings;
      EndElement(MovieWatcherTag);
      ContentHandler.EndDocument;
      UpdateOutput;
    end;
  begin
    Screen.Cursor := crHourglass;
    memXML.Lines.Clear;
    { Instantiate the XML writer }
    XMLDoc         := CoMXXMLWriter.Create;
    try
      ContentHandler := XMLDoc as IVBSAXContentHandler;
      DTDHandler     := XMLDoc as IVBSAXDTDHandler;
      LexicalHandler := XMLDoc as IVBSAXLexicalHandler;
      Attributes     := CoSAXAttributes.Create;
      XMLDoc.Indent  := True;
      { Generate the structure }
      GenerateDocument;
    finally
      { Release the XML writer }
      Attributes   := nil;
      XMLDoc       := nil;
      Screen.Cursor := crDefault;
    end;
  end;
```

Also necessary is an instance of the `IMXAttributes` interface, which provides for the writing of attribute values into a storage area. Such objects also implement the `IVBSAXAttributes` interface that lets you retrieve that information. Use this to accumulate attributes for an element that can then be passed into the corresponding `StartElement` call of the content handler.

Generation continues with calls to the appropriate handler methods, beginning with the content handler's `StartDocument` call and finishing with its `EndDocument`. Between these appear other calls to include the DTD, a top-level comment, a stylesheet reference, and the actual content of the document. The latter occurs within the bounds of a `StartElement` and `EndElement` call for the main document element.

NOTE Since the handler methods take `WideStrings` as arguments, all internal values are converted to this format through assignments before being passed across.

To demonstrate the chunking ability of the writer, the `UpdateOutput` method is called after each major section of the document is completed. This routine adds the generated XML to the memo on the screen via the `Output` property and then resets that property ready for the next section. Setting the `Indent` property to `True` prior to any handler calls causes the document to be formatted for improved readability.

Defining the DTD

Since the writer is based on the SAX2 specification, it implements the two standard extensions: IVBSAXLexicalHandler and IVBSAXDeclHandler. The first of these lets you add the DTD declaration itself through its StartDTD method, specifying the document type and its public and system identifiers (see Listing 20-4). Following this call, and before the EndDTD call, you use the DTD handler interface to add any notations and unparsed entities.

Listing 20-4: Generating the DTD

```
{ Generate DTD and contents }
procedure GenerateDTD;
var
  Wide1, Wide2, Wide3: WideString;
  BaseId: string;
begin
  Wide1 := MovieWatcherTag;
  Wide2 := XMLDTDFile;
  LexicalHandler.StartDTD(Wide1, Empty, Wide2);
  Wide1 := GIFType;
  Wide2 := GIFPubId;
  Wide3 := GIFSysId;
  DTDHandler.NotationDecl(Wide1, Wide2, Wide3);
  Wide1 := HTMLType;
  Wide2 := HTMLPubId;
  Wide3 := HTMLSysId;
  DTDHandler.NotationDecl(Wide1, Wide2, Wide3);
  with qryMovie do
  begin
    First;
    while not EOF do
    begin
      BaseId := FieldByName(MovieIdField).DisplayText;
      if FieldByName(LogoURLField).AsString <> '' then
      begin
        Wide1 := BaseId + 'Logo';
        Wide2 := FieldByName(LogoURLField).DisplayText;
        Wide3 := GIFType;
        DTDHandler.UnparsedEntityDecl(Wide1, Empty, Wide2, Wide3);
      end;
      if FieldByName(URLField).AsString <> '' then
      begin
        Wide1 := BaseId + 'URL';
        Wide2 := FieldByName(URLField).DisplayText;
        Wide3 := HTMLType;
        DTDHandler.UnparsedEntityDecl(Wide1, Empty, Wide2, Wide3);
      end;
      Next;
    end;
  end;
  LexicalHandler.EndDTD;
end;
```

You could define the entire DTD internally, including element and attribute declarations, by invoking methods on the IVBSAXDeclHandler interface. Such calls must appear between the start and end DTD calls.

Adding Content

The main information in the generated document comes from calls to the content handler's methods, especially `StartElement/EndElement` and `Characters`. Data for movies in the sample document appears within the confines of the document element. A `movies` element is started prior to stepping through each database record and producing its output. Upon completion, the corresponding closing tag is written. See Listing 20-5 for the generation code.

Listing 20-5: Adding movie content

```
{ Start a new element tag }
procedure StartElement(Name: WideString);
begin
  ContentHandler.StartElement(
    NoValue, NoValue, Name, Attributes as IVBSAXAttributes);
  Attributes.Clear;
end;
{ End an element tag }
procedure EndElement(Name: WideString);
begin
  ContentHandler.EndElement(NoValue, NoValue, Name);
end;
{ Save an attribute for adding to an element }
procedure AddAttribute(Name, Value: WideString);
begin
  Attributes.AddAttribute(NoValue, NoValue, Name, NoValue, Value);
end;
{ Add a simple element that only contains text }
procedure AddSimpleElement(Field: TField; AsCDATA: Boolean = False);
var
  Value: WideString;
begin
  StartElement(ModifyName(Field.FieldName));
  if AsCDATA then
    LexicalHandler.StartCDATA;
  Value := Field.DisplayText;
  if Value = '' then
    Value := NoValue;
  ContentHandler.Characters(Value);
  if AsCDATA then
    LexicalHandler.EndCDATA;
  EndElement(ModifyName(Field.FieldName));
end;
{ Compile elements for the stars of the movie }
procedure GenerateStars;
begin
  with qryStars do
  begin
    StartElement(StarringTag);
    First;
    while not EOF do
    begin
      AddSimpleElement(FieldByName(StarField));
      Next;
    end;
    EndElement(StarringTag);
  end;
```

```
    end;
    { Generate elements for each movie }
    procedure GenerateMovies;
    var
      BaseId: string;
    begin
      StartElement(MoviesTag);
      with qryMovie do
      begin
        First;
        while not EOF do
        begin
          BaseId := FieldByName(MovieIdField).DisplayText;
          AddAttribute(Id, BaseId);
          AddAttribute(Rating, FieldByName(RatingField).DisplayText);
          if FieldByName(LogoURLField).AsString <> '' then
            AddAttribute(ModifyName(FieldByName(LogoURLField).FieldName),
              BaseId + 'Logo');
          if FieldByName(URLField).AsString <> '' then
            AddAttribute(ModifyName(FieldByName(URLField).FieldName),
              BaseId + 'URL');
          StartElement(MovieTag);
          AddSimpleElement(FieldByName(NameField));
          AddSimpleElement(FieldByName(LengthField));
          AddSimpleElement(FieldByName(DirectorField));
          GenerateStars;
          AddSimpleElement(FieldByName(SynopsisField), True);
          EndElement(MovieTag);
          Next;
        end;
      end;
      EndElement(MoviesTag);
    end;
```

Attributes for an element are sent as part of the opening element call. Therefore, they must be accumulated and prepared before that time. The helper routine, AddAttribute, places the specified attribute into the IMXAttributes object created during initialization of the document. The StartElement call then uses this to supply the information to the writer and subsequently clears the list ready for the next element.

TIP Since no namespaces appear in the movie-watcher document, the corresponding parameters in the attribute and element calls should be empty strings. However, sending such value results in an error—The parameter is incorrect. Instead, you must send a string with a single space. This is encapsulated by the NoValue constant within the sample application.

Another helper routine, AddSimpleElement, adds a child element with a single text node body. As in previous chapters, the element name derives from the database field name and the field's value provides the content. A flag indicates whether the text should be treated as a CDATA section, as is the case for the synopsis data (just because you can). The text is always sent via the Characters method, but in the case of a CDATA section, this call appears between the lexical handler's StartCDATA and EndCDATA calls.

Invoke the generation process with the Generate button and the output appears on the screen (see Figure 20-1). To view it within your browser, use the Save button and open the resulting file.

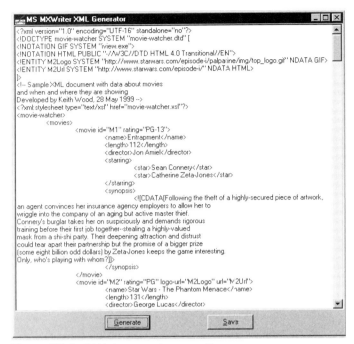

Figure 20-1: SAX document generation.

Summary

Similar in structure to generating a document through one of the DOM offerings, the SAX writer approach offers the usual SAX advantage of reducing memory requirements. Only a single element or text node appears at any one time. Furthermore, this technique lets you create the entire document, including any internal DTD—something that most DOMs do not allow.

Of course, you are generating the output into memory as text. This resource can be reduced through multiple calls to the Output property of the writer. Each time the document is returned, it is cleared for the next section. Thus, you can chunk the document and write out smaller pieces at a time. Alternately, you can set the Output property to an IStream, which then accepts each part as it is created.

The SAX writer is another option to consider when creating XML documents on the fly. It can be used to advantage when the resulting document is too large to comfortably fit in memory and when there is no need to randomly access the nodes within the document.

If you want to use XSLT to alter the appearance of the new document, you need to stay with the DOM approach. The following chapter explores this in greater detail.

Chapter 21
Applying XSL Transformations

Not only can you generate and deliver XML documents directly, you can also preprocess those documents and generate formatted output for further distribution. XSL Transformations, as described in Chapter 4, provide a way of describing the conversion process. The Microsoft XML DOM supplies the means to apply those changes.

Recall that an XSL Transformation is also an XML document, which can be loaded into a DOM in exactly the same way. Once you have both the XML data and the transformation in memory, you can apply the latter to the former with the TransformNode method of a Microsoft DOM node. This produces a string value that contains the results of the modifications, which can then be saved to a file, displayed on the screen, or sent across the Internet. The basic code for this process is shown in Listing 21-1.

Listing 21-1: Applying a transformation

```
var
  XMLDoc: IXMLDOMDocument;
  XSLTDoc: IXMLDOMDocument;
  Output: string;
begin
  { Instantiate the DOMs }
  XMLDoc  := CoDOMDocument.Create;
  XSLTDoc := CoDOMDocument.Create;
  try
    { Load the XML data }
    XMLDoc.Load(edtXML.Text);
    { Load the XSLT stylesheet }
    XSLTDoc.Load(edtXSLT.Text);
    { Combine the two and display the results }
    Output := XMLDoc.TransformNode(XSLTDoc);
  finally
    { Release the DOMs }
    XMLDoc  := nil;
    XSLTDoc := nil;
  end;
end;
```

The transformation does not have to occur for the entire document, nor for the entire stylesheet. Since the TransformNode method operates on any node, and takes a node as its parameter, you can pick out a particular node of interest from the XML DOM and apply the corresponding node from the stylesheet. This only works if you have followed the template model for the stylesheet, such that you have defined a template to match with the node being used as the base. Often you want to pass the entire stylesheet into this routine, since you have templates that rely on other templates that are not within the same subtree in the XSLT DOM.

Remember that the transformation process does not have to produce HTML as the output, though this is probably the most common use. You can also have stylesheets that generate straight text (including comma-separated values files), rich text, or even another XML document.

If you would prefer the results of the transformation as another DOM object, you can use the TransformNodeToObject method of the node instead. This allows you to manipulate the output further, before creating a formatted file, but is really only applicable if you are producing XML or HTML.

XSLT Utility

To demonstrate how the transformation process can be applied to particular nodes within the DOM, and how different stylesheets can produce alternate output from the same source XML, you can create a utility to do the work.

This utility asks for the name of the XML source and XSLT stylesheet documents, loads them into DOMs and displays the contents of each within memo fields. For the XML document, it also parses the DOM to create a corresponding tree view of the contents. From this you can select a particular node to which to apply the transformation. Selecting the root node affects the entire document.

Pressing the Transform button then works the magic of XSLT and displays the resulting output in an appropriate viewer. If the stylesheet generates HTML, a browser control is loaded with the result. Otherwise, it is directed to a rich text edit control. To determine which is used, the utility searches for the text <html> (upper- or lowercase) in the stylesheet, classing it as HTML if found.

The first step in the process is selecting the XML file. This only occurs through the associated Browse button, ensuring that you can load the DOM and parse it as part of the process. The selected file is loaded into the XML memo field, as well as into the DOM. From the latter you recursively step through all the elements in the document and place them into the tree view. Once this is completed, you can expand out the tree and select its root node, corresponding to the document as a whole. See Listing 21-2 for the code that performs this step.

Listing 21-2: Loading and parsing the XML document

```
{ Find an XML source file }
procedure TfrmStylesheets.btnXMLClick(Sender: TObject);
  { Load the DOM elements into a tree view recursively }
  procedure LoadElements(Node: IXMLDOMNode; Parent: TTreeNode);
  var
    Index: Integer;
    Current: TTreeNode;
  begin
    if (Node.NodeType = NODE_ELEMENT) or
       (Node.NodeType = NODE_DOCUMENT) then
    begin
      Current := trvDOM.Items.AddChildObject(Parent,
```

```
            NodeDisplay(Node), TXMLNode.Create(Node));
        for Index := 0 to Node.ChildNodes.Length -1 do
          LoadElements(Node.ChildNodes[Index], Current);
      end;
    end;
begin
  with dlgOpen do
  begin
    Filename := edtXML.Text;
    Filter   := XMLFilter;
    Title    := XMLOpen;
    if Execute then
    begin
      edtXML.Text := Filename;
      memXML.Lines.Clear;
      trvDOM.Items.BeginUpdate;
      try
        ClearTreeView;
        { Load the XML data }
        memXML.Lines.LoadFromFile(edtXML.Text);
        if not XMLDoc.Load(edtXML.Text) then
          with XMLDoc.ParseError do
          begin
            MessageDlg(Reason + ' at ' + IntToStr(Line) + ',' +
              IntToStr(LinePos), mtError, [mbOK], 0);
            Exit;
          end;
        { Load the DOM tree view }
        LoadElements(XMLDoc, nil);
        trvDOM.Items[0].Expand(True);
        trvDOM.TopItem := trvDOM.Items[0];
        trvDOMChange(trvDOM, trvDOM.Items[0]);
      finally
        trvDOM.Items.EndUpdate;
        pgcStylesheets.ActivePage := tabDOM;
      end;
    end;
  end;
end;
```

Although a tree view can hold additional data (a pointer) with each node, using this directly on the DOM nodes causes problems due to the reference counting of the interfaces. Instead, the strategy adopted here is to wrap that reference in a simple object, TXMLNode, and store this with the tree node.

Then, when a node is chosen from the tree view, you can retrieve the associated node as shown in Listing 21-3. You save this element into a variable for later use during the transformation phase. The node's description is displayed on the top of the form for verification.

Listing 21-3: Selecting the current node

```
{ Select the node to operate on }
procedure TfrmStylesheets.trvDOMChange(Sender: TObject; Node: TTreeNode);
begin
  XMLNode := TXMLNode(Node.Data).Node;
  edtElement.Text := NodeDisplay(XMLNode);
end;
```

Loading the XSLT document is very similar, but without the complexity of parsing the DOM. The stylesheet is checked, however, to try to determine whether or not it produces HTML output, as described earlier.

Transforming the Document

Finally, the stylesheet is applied to the selected node as shown in Listing 21-4. The results of the transformation are first inspected to see that the process worked. If the value is blank, then either there was some error or the templates did not match the input elements. In either case, a message is displayed. For HTML output, a blank document is created, since the browser objects to loading completely empty files.

Listing 21-4: Transforming the selected element

```
{ Apply the stylesheet to the data and see the results }
procedure TfrmStylesheets.btnTransformClick(Sender: TObject);
var
  Output: string;
  FileOut: TFileStream;
  StrOut: TStringStream;
  Filename: string;
begin
  Filename := ExtractFilePath(Application.ExeName) + XSLTOutput;
  { Combine the two and display the results }
  Output := XMLNode.TransformNode(XSLTDoc);
  if Output = '' then
  begin
    MessageDlg(NoOutput, mtError, [mbOK], 0);
    if HTMLOutput then
      Output := '<html><body></body></html>';
  end;
  { Save to a temporary file }
  FileOut := TFileStream.Create(Filename, fmCreate);
  StrOut  := TStringStream.Create(Output);
  try
    FileOut.CopyFrom(StrOut, 0);
  finally
    FileOut.Free;
    StrOut.Free;
  end;
  tabHTML.TabVisible := False;
  tabRTF.TabVisible  := False;
  if HTMLOutput then
  begin
    { Load into browser }
    brsOutput.Navigate(Filename);
    tabHTML.TabVisible        := True;
    pgcStylesheets.ActivePage := tabHTML;
  end
  else
  begin
    { Load into rich text memo }
    memOutput.Lines.LoadFromFile(Filename);
    tabRTF.TabVisible        := True;
    pgcStylesheets.ActivePage := tabRTF;
```

```
      end;
    btnSave.Enabled := True;
  end;
```

The output string is saved to a temporary file to facilitate its display within the browser. For HTML, the browser is directed to this file, while other output is sent to the rich text control. The tab corresponding to the display component is made visible and is brought to the front. Also, the Save button is enabled to allow you to save the results to a more permanent location.

Included with the utility are several sample XSLT documents as shown in Table 21-1.

Table 21-1: Sample XSLT documents

Document	Purpose
movie-watcher.xsl	An HTML stylesheet (monolithic)
movie-watcher-tmplt.xsl	An HTML stylesheet (template-based)
movie-watcher-csv.xsl	A comma-separated values (CSV) stylesheet
movie-watcher-rtf.xsl	A rich text stylesheet

Monolithic HTML Transformation

The monolithic HTML stylesheet appears in Listing 21-5. It has a single template that matches the document root and for-each loops that iterate over the child nodes at each level. Note the use of the ID and IDREF attributes within the document to create links between the different sections. Also, note the shorthand syntax (enclosed in braces) used for references that form attribute values in the final output.

Listing 21-5: A monolithic transformation to HTML

```xml
<?xml version="1.0" encoding="UTF-8"?>
<!-- HTML style sheet for movie-watcher XML (monolithic format)
     Written by Keith Wood, 4 June 1999 -->
<xsl:stylesheet version="1.0"
    xmlns:xsl="http://www.w3.org/1999/XSL/Transform">
  <xsl:output method="html"/>
  <!-- Match the entire document -->
  <xsl:template match="/">
    <html>
      <head>
        <title>Movie Watchers</title>
      </head>
      <body>
        <h1><a name="top">Welcome to Movie Watchers</a></h1>
        <p>Your source for local film entertainment.
          Have a look at <a href="#movies">what's on</a>,
          <a href="#cinemas">where</a> and
          <a href="#screenings">when</a>.</p>
        <hr/>
        <h2><a name="movies">Movies</a></h2>
        <xsl:for-each select="//movie">
          <xsl:sort select="name"/>
          <!-- Provide link target and optional web link -->
          <a name="{@id}">
```

```xml
            <xsl:if test="@url">
               <xsl:attribute name="href">
                  <xsl:value-of select="@url"/></xsl:attribute>
            </xsl:if>
            <xsl:choose>
               <xsl:when test="@logo-url">
                  <img src="{@logo-url}" alt="{name}"/>
               </xsl:when>
               <xsl:otherwise>
                  <h3><xsl:value-of select="name"/></h3>
               </xsl:otherwise>
            </xsl:choose>
         </a>
         <table border="0" width="100%">
            <tr>
               <th align="left" valign="top" width="15%">Rating:</th>
               <td width="15%"><xsl:value-of select="@rating"/></td>
               <th align="left" valign="top" width="15%">Length:</th>
               <td><xsl:value-of select="length"/> mins</td>
            </tr>
            <tr>
               <th align="left" valign="top">Director:</th>
               <td colspan="3"><xsl:value-of select="director"/></td>
            </tr>
            <tr>
               <th align="left" valign="top">Starring:</th>
               <td colspan="3">
                  <xsl:for-each select="starring/star">
                     <xsl:value-of select="."/><br/>
                  </xsl:for-each>
               </td>
            </tr>
            <tr>
               <th align="left" valign="top">Synopsis:</th>
               <td colspan="3"><xsl:value-of select="synopsis"/></td>
            </tr>
            <tr>
               <th align="left" valign="top">Showing at:</th>
               <td colspan="3">
                  <xsl:for-each
                     select="//screening[@movie-id=current()/@id]">
                     <a href="#{@movie-id}-{@cinema-id}">
                        <xsl:value-of select="id(@cinema-id)/name"/>
                     </a><br/>
                  </xsl:for-each>
               </td>
            </tr>
         </table>
      </xsl:for-each>
      <p>Back to <a href="#top">the top</a>.</p>
      <hr/>
         : Cinemas and screenings removed
      <hr/>
      <p>Movie Watcher data supplied by
         <a href="mailto:kbwood@compuserve.com">Keith Wood</a>.</p>
     </body>
    </html>
   </xsl:template>
</xsl:stylesheet>
```

Applying the monolithic stylesheet to a node other than the root results in just the plain text from that node and its descendants concatenated together, since its one template does not match with any other element. The result of transforming the entire document is shown in Figure 21-1.

Figure 21-1: HTML output from the movie-watcher document.

Template-Based HTML Transformation

The template version is very similar to the monolithic version above, but it breaks each major element out into its own template. Apply-template calls replace the for-each loops of the earlier version. This stylesheet can be successfully applied to individual movies, cinemas, and screenings, or to the collections of each of these.

Listing 21-6 shows the template-based transformation for the movie element and its descendants. Note the use of a mode on the list of screenings shown at the end of each movie. This lets the same nodes be processed in different ways depending on their location.

Listing 21-6: A template-based transformation to HTML

```
<?xml version="1.0" encoding="UTF-8"?>
<!-- HTML style sheet for movie-watcher XML (template format)
     Written by Keith Wood, 4 June 1999 -->
<xsl:stylesheet version="1.0"
    xmlns:xsl="http://www.w3.org/1999/XSL/Transform">
  <xsl:output method="html"/>
  <!-- Main document template -->
  <xsl:template match="/">
```

```xml
      <html>
        <head>
          <title>Movie Watchers</title>
        </head>
        <body>
          <h1><a name="top">Welcome to Movie Watchers</a></h1>
          <p>Your source for local film entertainment.
            Have a look at <a href="#movies">what's on</a>,
            <a href="#cinemas">where</a> and
            <a href="#screenings">when</a>.</p>
          <hr/>
          <h2><a name="movies">Movies</a></h2>
          <xsl:apply-templates select="//movie">
            <xsl:sort select="name"/>
          </xsl:apply-templates>
          <p>Back to <a href="#top">the top</a>.</p>
          <hr/>
          <h2><a name="cinemas">Cinemas</a></h2>
          <xsl:apply-templates select="//cinema">
            <xsl:sort select="name"/>
          </xsl:apply-templates>
          <p>Back to <a href="#top">the top</a>.</p>
          <hr/>
          <h2><a name="screenings">Screenings</a></h2>
          <xsl:apply-templates select="//screening">
            <xsl:sort select="id(@movie-id)/name"/>
            <xsl:sort select="id(@cinema-id)/name"/>
          </xsl:apply-templates>
          <p>Back to <a href="#top">the top</a>.</p>
          <hr/>
          <p>Movie Watcher data supplied by
            <a href="mailto:kbwood@compuserve.com">Keith Wood</a>.</p>
        </body>
      </html>
</xsl:template>
<!-- Details for one movie -->
<xsl:template match="movie">
  <!-- Provide link target and optional web link -->
  <a name="{@id}">
    <xsl:if test="@url">
      <xsl:attribute name="href">
        <xsl:value-of select="@url"/></xsl:attribute>
    </xsl:if>
    <xsl:choose>
      <xsl:when test="@logo-url">
        <img src="{@logo-url}" alt="{name}"/>
      </xsl:when>
      <xsl:otherwise>
        <h3><xsl:value-of select="name"/></h3>
      </xsl:otherwise>
    </xsl:choose>
  </a>
  <table border="0" width="100%">
    <tr>
      <th align="left" valign="top" width="15%">Rating:</th>
      <td width="15%"><xsl:value-of select="@rating"/></td>
      <th align="left" valign="top" width="15%">Length:</th>
      <td><xsl:value-of select="length"/> mins</td>
    </tr>
    <tr>
```

```
              <th align="left" valign="top">Director:</th>
              <td colspan="3"><xsl:value-of select="director"/></td>
            </tr>
            <tr>
              <th align="left" valign="top">Starring:</th>
              <td colspan="3">
                <xsl:apply-templates select="starring/star"/></td>
            </tr>
            <tr>
              <th align="left" valign="top">Synopsis:</th>
              <td colspan="3"><xsl:value-of select="synopsis"/></td>
            </tr>
            <tr>
              <th align="left" valign="top">Showing at:</th>
              <td colspan="3">
                <xsl:apply-templates
                  select="//screening[@movie-id=current()/@id]"
                  mode="movie"/>
              </td>
            </tr>
          </table>
    </xsl:template>
    <!-- List each star -->
    <xsl:template match="star">
      <xsl:value-of select="."/><br/>
    </xsl:template>
    : Cinema templates removed
    <!-- List a screening from the point of view of a movie -->
    <xsl:template match="screening" mode="movie">
      <a href="#{@movie-id}-{@cinema-id}">
        <xsl:value-of select="id(@cinema-id)/name"/>
      </a><br/>
    </xsl:template>
    <!-- List a screening from the point of view of a cinema -->
    <xsl:template match="screening" mode="cinema">
      <a href="#{@movie-id}-{@cinema-id}">
        <xsl:value-of select="id(@movie-id)/name"/>
      </a><br/>
    </xsl:template>
    <!-- Details for one screening -->
    <xsl:template match="screening">
        : Main screening template removed
    </xsl:template>
</xsl:stylesheet>
```

Although the appearance of the final output is exactly the same as the monolithic version when operating on the entire document, differences become apparent when working with other nodes. This version successfully converts individual movies and cinemas, whereas the previous version did not. Figure 21-2 shows the result of transforming a single cinema node.

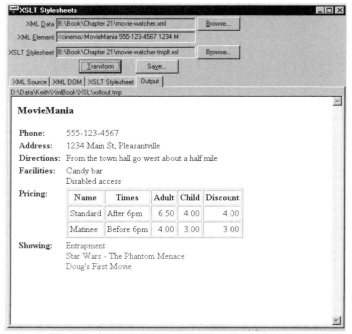

Figure 21-2: Template-based HTML output.

Comma-Separated Transformation

The CSV stylesheet (see Listing 21-7) generates a multi-part CSV file, with one section for each of the movies, cinemas, and screenings. Each section generates a header line before applying a template for the data values. Individual items appear on their own line with each field surrounded by quotes (") and separated by commas (,). Care must be taken with spacing if proper formatting of the output is required.

Listing 21-7: Producing a comma-separated value file

```
<?xml version="1.0" encoding="UTF-8"?>
<!-- Straight text style sheet for movie-watcher XML
     Multiple comma-separated value lists
     Written by Keith Wood, 30 May 2000 -->
<xsl:stylesheet version="1.0"
    xmlns:xsl="http://www.w3.org/1999/XSL/Transform">
  <xsl:output method="text"/>
  <!-- Main document template -->
  <xsl:template
    match="/">"Name","Rating","Length","Director","Stars","Synopsis"
<xsl:apply-templates select="//movie">
  <xsl:sort select="name"/>
</xsl:apply-templates>
----------------------------------------------------------------------
"Name","Phone","Address","Directions","Facilities"
<xsl:apply-templates select="//cinema">
  <xsl:sort select="name"/>
```

```
      </xsl:apply-templates>
------------------------------------------------------------------------
"Movie","Cinema","Dates","Features","Restrictions","Sessions"
<xsl:apply-templates select="//screening">
   <xsl:sort select="id(@movie-id)/name"/>
   <xsl:sort select="id(@cinema-id)/name"/>
</xsl:apply-templates>
    </xsl:template>
    <!-- Details for one movie -->
    <xsl:template match="movie">"<xsl:value-of
      select="name"/>","<xsl:value-of select="@rating"/>","<xsl:value-of
      select="length"/>","<xsl:value-of
      select="director"/>","<xsl:apply-templates
      select="starring/star"/>","<xsl:value-of
      select="translate(synopsis,'&quot;','&quot;'&quot;)"/>"
</xsl:template>
    <!-- Details for each star -->
    <xsl:template match="star"><xsl:value-of select="."/>
      <xsl:if test="position()!=last()">,</xsl:if></xsl:template>
    <!-- Details for one cinema -->
    <xsl:template match="cinema">"<xsl:value-of
      select="name"/>","<xsl:value-of select="phone"/>","<xsl:value-of
      select="address"/>","<xsl:value-of select="directions"/>","<xsl:if
      test="facilities/candy-bar">Candy bar,</xsl:if><xsl:if
      test="facilities/disabled-access">Disabled access</xsl:if>"
</xsl:template>
    <!-- Table of pricing schemes -->
    <xsl:template match="prices">"<xsl:value-of
      select="name"/>","<xsl:value-of select="period"/>","<xsl:value-of
      select="adult"/>","<xsl:value-of select="child"/>","<xsl:value-of
      select="discount"/>"
</xsl:template>
    <!-- Details for one screening -->
    <xsl:template match="screening">"<xsl:value-of
      select="id(@movie-id)/name"/>","<xsl:value-of
      select="id(@cinema-id)/name"/>","<xsl:value-of
      select="start-date"/>-<xsl:value-of select="end-date"/>","<xsl:if
      test="features/digital-sound">Digital sound: <xsl:value-of
      select="features/digital-sound"/></xsl:if>","<xsl:if
      test="restrictions/no-passes">No passes</xsl:if>","
      <xsl:apply-templates select="sessions/session"/>
</xsl:template>
    <!-- Table of session details -->
    <xsl:template match="session"><xsl:value-of select="."/><xsl:if
      test="position()!=last()">,</xsl:if></xsl:template>
</xsl:stylesheet>
```

Note the use of a positional test when compiling a list of sub-items, such as the stars in a movie, to include commas between entries but not at the end of the list.

```
<xsl:if test="position()!=last()">,</xsl:if>
```

To handle embedded quotes within the text fields you can use the `translate` function, which operates on its first parameter, replacing characters from the second parameter with characters in the corresponding positions in the third parameter. With this you can change any double quotes to single quotes. Due to the XSLT selection already being quoted, you must escape all the matching quotes within the translation.

```
<xsl:value-of select="translate(synopsis,'&quot;','&quot;'&quot;)"/>
```

After applying the transformation, the result is shown in a memo field (see Figure 21-3). Since this stylesheet is based on templates you can select individual nodes for separate processing.

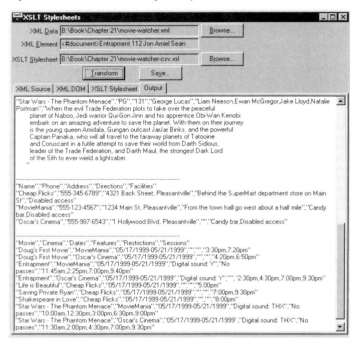

Figure 21-3: Converting to comma-separated values.

Rich Text Transformation

Lastly, the rich text template produces a word-processing document equivalent of the HTML version (without the hyperlinks). The display looks reasonable within the rich edit control, but appears much better within Word. Rich text is fairly easy to generate since it is text based and does not have character counts like PDF requires. Furthermore, it does not use the XML markup characters for its own markup.

To create the rich text template, you can format the final output within Word to appear as you want. Once this is saved as RTF, you can open it in Notepad, which does not interpret the RTF, to see the underlying structure. Cut and paste from this into the XSL stylesheet, adding references to element values as you go. A basic knowledge of RTF certainly helps! You need to be careful about where you place any carriage returns to preserve the required output. It is messy, but it does work.

Listing 21-8 shows the document header and the repeated section for each movie element and its descendants. Basically, RTF commands are grouped by braces ({ }) and delimited by a backslash (\ ). The par or pard commands denote paragraphs. A document starts with the string {\rtf1 to indicate its format.

Listing 21-8: Generating a rich text document

```xml
<?xml version="1.0" encoding="UTF-8"?>
<!-- RTF style sheet for movie-watcher XML
     Written by Keith Wood, 20 May 2000 -->
<xsl:stylesheet version="1.0"
    xmlns:xsl="http://www.w3.org/1999/XSL/Transform">
  <xsl:output method="text"/>
  <!-- Match the entire document -->
  <xsl:template match="/">{\rtf1\ansi\ansicpg1252\uc1
\deff0\deflang1033\deflangfe1033
{\fonttbl{\f0\froman\fcharset0\fprq2{\*\panose 02020603050405020304}Times New
Roman;}{\f1\fswiss\fcharset0\fprq2{\*\panose 020b0604020202020204}Arial;}}
{\colortbl;\red0\green0\blue0;\red0\green0\blue255;\red0\green255\blue255;\red0\green255\blue0;
\red255\green0\blue255;\red255\green0\blue0;\red255\green255\blue0;\red255\green255\blue255;\red0\green
0\blue128;\red0\green128\blue128;\red0\green128\blue0;\red128\green0\blue128;\red128\green0\blue0;\red1
28\green128\blue0;\red128\green128\blue128;
\red192\green192\blue192;}
{\stylesheet{\sb100\sa100\nowidctlpar\adjustright \snext0 Normal;}{\*\cs10 \additive Default Paragraph
Font;}{\s18\sb100\sa100\keepn\nowidctlpar\outlinelevel1\adjustright \b\fs48\kerning36 \sbasedon0
\snext0 H1;}{\s19\sb100\sa100\keepn\nowidctlpar\outlinelevel2\adjustright \b\fs36
\sbasedon0 \snext0 H2;}{\s20\sb100\sa100\keepn\nowidctlpar\outlinelevel3\adjustright \b\fs28 \sbasedon0
\snext0 H3;}}
{\info{\title Movie Watchers}{\author movie-watcher-rtf.xsl}}
\pard\plain \s18\sb100\sa100\keepn\nowidctlpar\outlinelevel0\adjustright \b\fs48\kerning36
{Welcome to Movie Watchers\par}
\pard\plain \sb100\sa100\nowidctlpar\outlinelevel0\adjustright
{Your source for local film entertainment.\par}
\pard\plain \s19\sb100\sa100\keepn\nowidctlpar\outlinelevel0\adjustright \b\fs36 {Movies\par}
<!-- Display each movie's details -->
<xsl:for-each select="//movie">
  <xsl:sort select="name"/>
\pard\plain \s20\sb100\sa100\keepn\nowidctlpar\outlinelevel0\adjustright \b\fs28
{<xsl:value-of select="name"/>\par}
\trowd \clvertalt\cltxlrtb \cellx1520\clvertalc\cltxlrtb \cellx4485\clvertalt\cltxlrtb
\cellx7450\clvertalc\cltxlrtb \cellx9359\pard\plain \qc\sb100\sa100\nowidctlpar\intbl\adjustright {\b
Rating:\cell}
\pard\plain \sb100\sa100\nowidctlpar\intbl\adjustright {<xsl:value-of select="@rating"/>\cell}
\pard \qc\sb100\sa100\nowidctlpar\intbl\adjustright {\b Length:\cell }
\pard\plain \sb100\sa100\nowidctlpar\intbl\adjustright {<xsl:value-of select="length"/> mins\cell}
\pard \nowidctlpar\widctlpar\intbl\adjustright {\row}
\trowd \clvertalt\cltxlrtb \cellx1520\clmgf\clvertalc\cltxlrtb \cellx4485\clmrg\clvertalc\cltxlrtb
\cellx7450 \clmrg\clvertalc\cltxlrtb \cellx9359\pard \qc\sb100\sa100\nowidctlpar\intbl\adjustright {\b
Director:\cell }
\pard \sb100\sa100\nowidctlpar\intbl\adjustright {<xsl:value-of select="director"/>\cell \cell \cell}
\pard \nowidctlpar\widctlpar\intbl\adjustright {\row}\pard
\qc\sb100\sa100\nowidctlpar\intbl\adjustright {\b Starring:\cell}
\pard \sb100\sa100\nowidctlpar\intbl\adjustright {
<xsl:for-each select="starring/star">
<xsl:value-of select="."/><xsl:if test="position()!=last()">,</xsl:if>
</xsl:for-each>
\cell \cell \cell}
\pard \nowidctlpar\widctlpar\intbl\adjustright {\row}
\pard \qc\sb100\sa100\nowidctlpar\intbl\adjustright {\b Synopsis:\cell}
\pard \sb100\sa100\nowidctlpar\intbl\adjustright {<xsl:value-of select="synopsis"/>\cell \cell \cell}
\pard \nowidctlpar\widctlpar\intbl\adjustright {\row}
\trowd \clvertalt\cltxlrtb \cellx1520\clmgf\clvertalc\cltxlrtb \cellx4485\clmrg\clvertalc\cltxlrtb
\cellx7450\clmrg\clvertalc\cltxlrtb \cellx9359
\pard \qc\sb100\sa100\nowidctlpar\intbl\adjustright {\b Showing at:\cell}
\pard \sb100\sa100\nowidctlpar\intbl\adjustright {
<xsl:for-each select="//screening[@movie-id=current()/@id]">
```

```
<xsl:value-of select="id(@cinema-id)/name"/><xsl:if test="position()!=last()">,</xsl:if>
</xsl:for-each>
\cell \cell \cell}
\pard \nowidctlpar\widctlpar\intbl\adjustright {\row}
</xsl:for-each>
\pard\plain \s19\sb100\sa100\keepn\nowidctlpar\outlinelevel0\adjustright \b\fs36 {Cinemas\par}
    : Cinema and screening transformations removed
\pard\plain \sb100\sa100\nowidctlpar\outlinelevel0\adjustright
{Movie Watcher data supplied by Keith Wood (kbwood@compuserve.com)\par}}
</xsl:template>
</xsl:stylesheet>
```

The resulting output is shown in Figure 21-4 after being loaded into Word (much nicer looking than the application version).

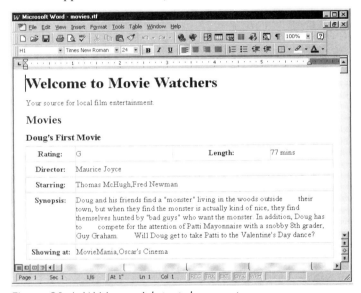

Figure 21-4: Writing a rich text document.

Summary

XSLT lets you reformat an XML document. The transformation description is itself an XML document, letting you edit and process it with the same tools as the original document. A rich query language and template-based matching lets you easily manipulate sections of the document. Output can be in a variety of formats, from HTML to comma-separated text, rich text, or another XML type.

Microsoft's DOM allows you to apply a transformation to an entire document or to a single node. Load both the original XML document and the XSLT stylesheet into memory as DOMs. Then use the `TransformNode` or `TransformNodeToObject` methods on a node in the former to apply the transformation.

The process described in this chapter basically loads the XSLT stylesheet for every transformation. Often a single stylesheet is applied repeatedly to many different documents of the same type. For better performance in this case, Microsoft provides the IXSLTemplate and IXSLProcessor interfaces. The former lets you load a stylesheet into it, which is then compiled and cached for later use. When the transformation is required, you ask the template to create an IXSLProcessor. Set the input and outputs for the processor and start the process to generate the transformation. Because a compiled version of the stylesheet is used, the process is much faster. See Chapter 26 for a demonstration of these interfaces in the delivery of examinations over the Web.

Chapter 22
XML Broker

Starting with Delphi 5, MIDAS clients can receive data packets in XML format from the server, rather than the OleVariants used previously. Combining the XML data with JavaScript functions and Delphi's Web server application support, you can easily build browser-based clients to access back-end databases. Together this forms the InternetExpress framework in Delphi.

The flow through the application starts with a request from the browser that goes through the Web server to a Web application based on MIDAS technology. This client program then makes requests to a server, which actually retrieves the data from the database.

The response is formatted as XML and returned to the Web application. It is then added to an HTML page as embedded XML. This page also references several standard JavaScript libraries that manipulate the data on the client, providing navigation through the data and keeping track of any changes to it. When requested, these changes are sent back to the Web application (again, as XML) to be applied to the database itself. Figure 22-1 shows this flow.

Figure 22-1: A multi-tiered Web-based application using MIDAS.

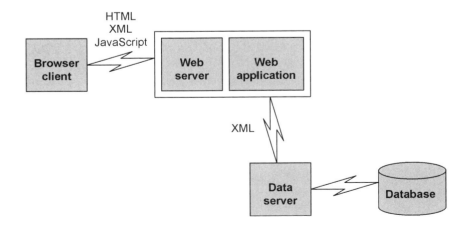

JavaScript is the key to manipulating the XML on the client side. Several libraries of functions are available for use with the HTML generated during design and are automatically included as needed. They appear in the Source\Webmidas directory under your Delphi installation. Table 22-1 lists these libraries and describes their functionality.

Table 22-1: JavaScript libraries

Library	Purpose
xmldb.js	This library manages the XML data and delta packets used during data access.
xmldisp.js	Functions for linking the data access classes above with the HTML controls representing them appear in this library.
xmldom.js	A DOM-compatible XML parser used to process the embedded XML. It is not required in IE5 as this recognizes XML islands and processes them itself.
xmlerrdisp.js	Classes that process reconciliation errors appear in this library.
xmlshow.js	This library contains functions to display the XML data and delta packets.

This architecture lets you deploy a thin client on the browser that requires only HTML and JavaScript support. All database access occurs in the server application, with the Web application acting as mediator. XML travels between the server and the Web application, then on to the browser as part of an HTML page. Changes to the data arrive back as XML to be passed on to the server for updating the database.

The Data Server

First, you need to build the MIDAS server program that extracts the information from the database and makes it available to other applications that are interested in it.

1. Start a plain new application.

2. Set the caption for your server form and resize it as necessary. If you want to, you may add additional controls to the form to monitor the server's workings. For example, you could add labels to display how many connections exist.

3. Add a Remote Data Module to your program from the Multitier tab on the New Items dialog (select **File | New**). Name it **MovieData** and leave the instancing and threading model options at their defaults.

4. Drop the following components on the data module: a TSession, two TQuerys, a TDataSource, and a TDataSetProvider. The first three appear on the Data Access tab on the component palette, while the last one appears on the Midas tab.

5. Set the component properties as shown in Table 22-2. This links the two queries together—one showing movie data and the other showing only those stars for the current movie. When the session's AutoSessionName property is True, a new session name is generated for each instance of the data module. This is necessary to avoid conflicts between multiple instances

created by the various clients. Each request gets its own data module running in a separate thread. The resulting data module should look like the one shown in Figure 22-2.

Table 22-2: Server component properties

Component	Property	Value
TSession	Name	sesMovies
	AutoSessionName	True
TQuery (1)	Name	qryMovies
	DatabaseName	Movie-watcher
	RequestLive	True
	SQL	SELECT * FROM movie
TDataSource	Name	dsrMovies
	DataSet	qryMovies
TQuery (2)	Name	qryStars
	DatabaseName	Movie-watcher
	DataSource	dsrMovies
	RequestLive	True
	SQL	SELECT * FROM starsWHERE movie_id = :movie_id
TDataSetProvider	Name	dspMovies
	DataSet	qryMovies

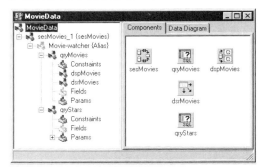

Figure 22-2: The server data module.

6. Add extra functionality to the data module if desired. For example, you could update connection counts on the main server form when the data module is created and destroyed. Pre-generated code takes care of registering the server and its provider, and of creating instances of the module.

7. Compile and run the server. The first time it is run, the server registers itself with COM so that clients may find it. You can then close it down and it restarts automatically when needed.

The server designed here provides access to data from the movie and stars tables in the database. Due to the master/detail relationship between these two query components, the corresponding data from the stars table is encapsulated in a nested table that is returned with each movie record.

InternetExpress

In Delphi 5, InternetExpress is basically the collection of components that appear on the component palette tab of the same name. The two standard components are `TXMLBroker` and `TMidasPageProducer`.

`TXMLBroker` serves as the client-side interface to the server program. It sends and receives data and updates as XML documents. Placed on a Web module, the broker automatically registers itself to receive notification of any incoming HTTP requests. If these contain XML-encoded updates, the broker deals with them directly.

`TMidasPageProducer` derives from `TPageProducer` (through several intermediates) and provides a means of generating a document built around XML for sending back to a client browser. Internally, this component manages a number of sub-components that interact with the XMLBroker to generate HTML for the data coming from the server.

Double-click on the page producer to invoke its Web page editor (or right-click and select Web Page Editor). Here you can add and customize components that encapsulate forms for data entry, grids for rows of data, and navigators for moving through and updating the data. Behind the scenes, the page producer also generates supporting HTML to include JavaScript libraries and embedded XML to contain the actual information from the server.

Before creating the Web server application there are a few InternetExpress add-ons available that enhance its abilities. In the `Demos\Midas\InternetExpress\InetXCustom` directory under your Delphi 5 installation directory, you can find several sample InternetExpress components, including `TReconcilePageProducer`, `TShowXMLButton`, and `TShowDeltaButton`. To add these, do the following:

1. Open the inetxcustom.dpk package project in that location and compile it. This run-time package contains the actual component code.

2. Open the dclinetxcustom.dpk package project, compile, and install it. This design-time package registers the new components with the IDE. `TReconcilePageProducer` appears on the InternetExpress tab on the palette, whereas the remainder are available within the page producer editor.

`TReconcilePageProducer` provides a reconciliation page for handling errors that may occur when a set of changes is applied to the database. It has a pre-generated HTML document embedded in it that displays the record(s) that caused the problem and lets you select what action to take to correct it. Link it into the generation process through the `ReconcileProducer` property on the `TXMLBroker` object.

The two buttons appear as possible children of a data navigator component within a `TMidasPageProducer`. `TShowXMLButton` displays the XML data packet sent with the HTML page, while `TShowDeltaButton` shows the XML delta packet (the set of changes to the information) that gets returned to the Web application. Although you probably do not want these to appear on a finished page, they are very valuable during development to see what is being sent back and forth.

Other components in the package include `TImgDataNavigator`, a navigator that uses graphic buttons instead of real ones, `TQueryHiddenField` and `TQueryPasswordField`, for hidden and password form fields, `TFieldLink` and `TLirkColumn`, for creating URL links, and `TSortTextColumn`, which lets you sort on a column's values in an HTML table.

The CGI Web Application

Now you can develop the Web server application that acts as the go-between for the browser and the server. It accesses the server using DCOM, passing XML back and forth, while providing HTML, JavaScript, and embedded XML to the browser.

1. Start a new application by selecting the Web Server Application icon in the New Items dialog (select **File | New**).

2. Select **CGI** from the next dialog and press **OK** to create the basic application, including its Web module. You could choose any of the Web application types, depending on your Web server's abilities and your performance requirements. CGI is picked here, but later you see how this can easily be altered to an ISAPI extension.

3. Add the following components to the Web module: a `TDCOMConnection`, a `TXMLBroker`, a `TMidasPageProducer`, and a `TReconcilePageProducer`. The first component appears on the Midas tab in the palette, while the remainder come from the InternetExpress tab.

4. Set the component's properties as shown in Table 22-3. These attach the connection with the server created earlier (it should start up automatically if not already running), then tie the XML broker to the server's provider through that connection. The broker is also linked to the reconciliation page for error handling purposes. Both of the page producers need to set the location of the JavaScript libraries that support their functionality. Enter the name of the directory on the Web server where they are held. Figure 22-3 shows the Web module during design, including the page producer components added below.

Table 22-3: Web application component properties

Component	Property	Value
TDCOMConnection	Name	conMovies
	ServerName	MovieServer.MovieData
	Connected	True
TXMLBroker	Name	xbrMovies
	RemoteServer	conMovies
	ProviderName	dspMovies
	ReconcileProducer	rppMovies

Component	Property	Value
TMidasPageProducer	Name	mppMovies
	IncludePathURL	/webmidas/
TReconcilePageProducer	Name	rppMovies
	IncludePathURL	/webmidas/

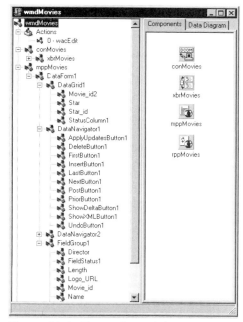

Figure 22-3: The Web module.

5. Double-click on the TMidasPageProducer component to open up its Web Page Editor (or right-click on it and select from the menu).

6. Add a DataForm to the page by pressing the **New Item** button or by right-clicking on the mppMovies node at the top-right and selecting **New Component**. To the data form add a FieldGroup (using the same technique as above) and set its XMLBroker property to xbrMovies. This automatically populates the Web page with the fields from the movies query returned from the server.

7. Customize the movie fields by right-clicking on the FieldGroup and selecting **Add All Fields** from the menu. This creates persistent field objects (similar to persistent fields for DataSets) that correspond to the fields already showing on the Web page. Alter their properties as necessary, such as adjusting their Captions to remove underscores. All fields default to FieldText types. You can replace the Rating field with a FieldSelectOptions object, set its FieldName, and enter its possible values in the Items property. The Synopsis field can be exchanged for a FieldTextArea object, setting its FieldName, DisplayRows, and DisplayWidth properties.

8. Append a data navigator to the form by selecting the `DataForm` node and adding a `DataNavigator` object as described above. If you installed the InternetExpress add-ons, you could select an `ImgDataNavigator` instead. Set the navigator's `XMLComponent` property to the `FieldGroup`. A default set of buttons appears beneath the fields already created.

9. Customize the buttons by adding components to the navigator. Select all the buttons down to `ApplyUpdatesButton`, except for `PriorPageButton` and `NextPageButton`. Add the `ShowXMLButton` and `ShowDeltaButton` (part of the InternetExpress add-ons).

10. Add a `DataGrid` component to the `DataForm`, setting its `XMLBroker` property to `xbrMovies`. Initially, this shows the movie fields in the grid. To display the list of stars for a particular movie, you set the grid's `XMLDataSetField` property to `qryStars`. Customize the data grid fields by selecting **Add All Fields** from the pop-up menu on the grid and then updating the fields' properties.

11. Attach a second data navigator to the `DataForm` and set its `XMLComponent` property to the `DataGrid`. Customize its buttons by adding fields for them. This time you do not need the `ApplyUpdatesButton` nor the Show buttons. Figure 22-4 shows part of the generated Web page in the editor.

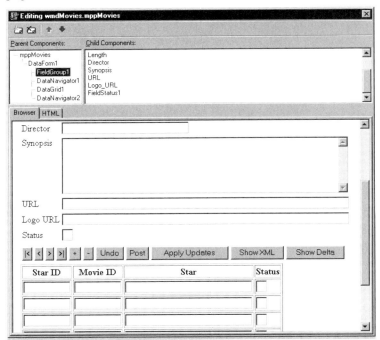

Figure 22-4: Designing the HTML page.

12. Put the finishing touches on the HTML page through the `HTMLDoc` property of the `TMidasPageProducer`. You can add a page title and a heading and footer. Be careful not to disturb the substitution tags (those starting with #) created by the Web page designer.

13. Customize the HTMLDoc property of the TReconcilePageProducer for this application, perhaps adding a title. Again, be careful not to alter the existing document in its treatment of the reconciliation errors.

14. Right-click on the Web module and select **Action Editor** from the pop-up menu. Add a new action, make it the default, and set its Producer property to mppMovies.

15. Save and compile the Web application.

16. Deploy the executable to your CGI program directory on the Web server (usually \inetpub\scripts under PWS and IIS). Also set up the directory that holds the JavaScript libraries used by the resulting HTML pages (/webmidas in this example, which corresponds to \inetpub\wwwroot\webmidas under PWS and IIS) and copy the JavaScript files there. The original libraries are found in the Source\Webmidas directory under your Delphi 5 installation.

Now you can access the application through your JavaScript-enabled browser and view the information from the database. Use the navigation buttons to step through the records. Make changes to the fields as desired and send the new values back to the server with the Apply Updates button. Figure 22-5 shows the application running in the browser. Its URL may look like the following if you are running a local Web server: http://localhost/scripts/movieweb.exe.

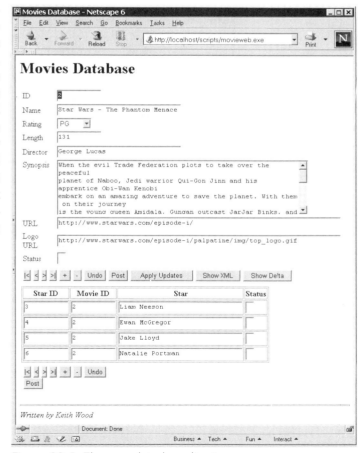

Figure 22-5: The completed application.

Using ISAPI

Providing access through an ISAPI server extension, rather than a CGI application, is extremely easy with Delphi's Web server application support. You can reuse the Web module developed for the CGI version.

1. Start a new application and select **Web Server Application** from the New Items dialog.
2. Select **ISAPI/NSAPI** from the following dialog and press **OK** to generate the project file and Web module unit.
3. Delete the new Web module unit entirely and replace all references to it in the project file with corresponding ones for the existing Web module.
4. Compile and deploy the ISAPI DLL to the `scripts` directory on the Web server. It is that simple!

Listing 22-1 shows the project file for the ISAPI version of the movie-watcher application. Its functionality is exactly the same as the CGI version, demonstrating the power of the Delphi Web application framework and encapsulation.

Listing 22-1: *An ISAPI version of the Web application*

```
library MovieWebI;
uses
  WebBroker,
  ISAPIApp,
  MovieWeb1 in 'MovieWeb1.pas' {wmdMovies: TWebModule};
{$R *.RES}
exports
  GetExtensionVersion,
  HttpExtensionProc,
  TerminateExtension;
begin
  Application.Initialize;
  Application.CreateForm(TwmdMovies, wmdMovies);
  Application.Run;
end.
```

XML Usage

As stated earlier, XML documents are passed back and forth between the browser, Web application, and server to control the workings of the program. The Show XML button on the HTML page displays in a separate window the XML embedded in the page (see Listing 22-2).

Listing 22-2: *The XML data packet sent to the browser*

```
<DATAPACKET Version="2.0" >
  <METADATA>
    <FIELDS>
      <FIELD attrname="Movie_id" fieldtype="i4" required="true" />
      <FIELD attrname="Name" fieldtype="string" required="true"
        WIDTH="30" />
```

```xml
    <FIELD attrname="Rating" fieldtype="string" required="true"
      WIDTH="5" />
    <FIELD attrname="Length" fieldtype="i4" />
    <FIELD attrname="Director" fieldtype="string" WIDTH="30" />
    <FIELD attrname="Synopsis" fieldtype="bin.hex" WIDTH="5"
      SUBTYPE="Text" />
    <FIELD attrname="URL" fieldtype="string" WIDTH="70" />
    <FIELD attrname="Logo_URL" fieldtype="string" WIDTH="70" />
    <FIELD attrname="qryStars" fieldtype="nested" >
      <FIELDS>
        <FIELD attrname="Star_id" fieldtype="i4" />
        <FIELD attrname="Movie_id" fieldtype="i4" />
        <FIELD attrname="Star" fieldtype="string" WIDTH="30" />
      </FIELDS>
      <PARAMS LCID="1033" />
    </FIELD>
  </FIELDS>
  <PARAMS MD_FIELDLINKS="9 1 2" LCID="1033" />
</METADATA>
<ROWDATA>
  <ROW Movie_id="1" Name="Entrapment" Rating="PG-13" Length="112"
    Director="Jon Amiel" Synopsis="Following the theft of a
    highly-secured piece of artwork, an agent convinces her
    insurance agency employers to allow her to wriggle into the
    company of an aging but active master thief. Connery&apos;s
    burglar takes her on suspiciously and demands rigorous training
    before their first job together--stealing a highly-valued mask
    from a shi-shi party. Their deepening attraction and distrust
    could tear apart their partnership but the promise of a bigger
    prize (some eight billion odd dollars) by Zeta-Jones keeps the
    game interesting. Only, who&apos;s playing with whom?" >
    <qryStars>
      <ROWqryStars Star_id="1" Movie_id="1" Star="Sean Connery" />
      <ROWqryStars Star_id="2" Movie_id="1" Star="Catherine
        Zeta-Jones" />
    </qryStars>
  </ROW>
  <ROW Movie_id="2" Name="Star Wars—The Phantom Menace" Rating="PG"
    Length="131" Director="George Lucas" Synopsis="When the evil
    Trade Federation plots to take over the peaceful planet of Naboo,
    Jedi warrior Qui-Gon Jinn and his apprentice Obi-Wan Kenobi
    embark on an amazing adventure to save the planet. With them on
    their journey is the young queen Amidala, Gungan outcast JarJar
    Binks, and the powerful Captain Panaka, who will all travel to
    the faraway planets of Tatooine and Coruscant in a futile attempt
    to save their world from Darth Sidious, leader of the Trade
    Federation, and Darth Maul, the strongest Dark Lord of the Sith
    to ever wield a lightsaber. "
    URL="http://www.starwars.com/episode-i/" Logo_URL=
    "http://www.starwars.com/episode-i/palpatine/img/top_logo.gif" >
    <qryStars>
      <ROWqryStars Star_id="3" Movie_id="2" Star="Liam Neeson" />
      <ROWqryStars Star_id="4" Movie_id="2" Star="Ewan McGregor" />
      <ROWqryStars Star_id="5" Movie_id="2" Star="Jake Lloyd" />
      <ROWqryStars Star_id="6" Movie_id="2" Star="Natalie Portman" />
    </qryStars>
  </ROW>
:
```

```
         Other ROW elements removed
              :
  </ROWDATA>
</DATAPACKET>
```

You can see that it starts with a description of the fields present in the rest of the document in the `FIELDS` element within the `METADATA` element. Each field has its name and type specified (including length where appropriate), along with whether or not it is required to be entered. The stars data for each movie appears as a nested set of fields representing the master/detail relationship between the tables. The final `PARAMS` element holds details about how to link movies and stars—field 9 (`qryStars`) is linked via its parent's field 1 (`Movie_id`) and its own field 2 (`Movie_id`).

Following these definitions are the data themselves. Each record appears in a `ROW` element with its fields showing up as attributes. The nested star details occur within the `qryStars` element as `ROWqryStars` elements with their information stored as attributes.

As changes are made to the data, they are stored internally through JavaScript functions in a collection known as the *delta*. The Status fields on the Web page indicate how records have changed: `I` for inserted, `M` for modified. Deleted records disappear entirely. The Show Delta button on the page displays these changes, again in a separate window. Listing 22-3 shows the delta after adding a URL, a Logo URL, and a new star to one of the movies.

Listing 22-3: An XML document for updates

```
<DATAPACKET Version="2.0" >
  <METADATA>
    <FIELDS>
      <FIELD attrname="Movie_id" fieldtype="i4" required="true" />
      <FIELD attrname="Name" fieldtype="string" required="true"
        WIDTH="30" />
      <FIELD attrname="Rating" fieldtype="string" required="true"
        WIDTH="5" />
      <FIELD attrname="Length" fieldtype="i4" />
      <FIELD attrname="Director" fieldtype="string" WIDTH="30" />
      <FIELD attrname="Synopsis" fieldtype="bin.hex" WIDTH="5"
        SUBTYPE="Text" />
      <FIELD attrname="URL" fieldtype="string" WIDTH="70" />
      <FIELD attrname="Logo_URL" fieldtype="string" WIDTH="70" />
      <FIELD attrname="qryStars" fieldtype="nested" >
        <FIELDS>
          <FIELD attrname="Star_id" fieldtype="i4" />
          <FIELD attrname="Movie_id" fieldtype="i4" />
          <FIELD attrname="Star" fieldtype="string" WIDTH="30" />
        </FIELDS>
        <PARAMS LCID="1033" />
      </FIELD>
    </FIELDS>
    <PARAMS MD_FIELDLINKS="9 1 2" LCID="1033" DATASET_DELTA="1" />
  </METADATA>
  <ROWDATA>
    <ROW Movie_id="1" Name="Entrapment" Rating="PG-13" Length="112"
      Director="Jon Amiel" Synopsis="Following the theft of a
      highly-secured piece of artwork, an agent convinces her
      insurance agency employers to allow her to wriggle into the
      company of an aging but active master thief. Connery&apos;s
      burglar takes her on suspiciously and demands rigorous training
      before their first job together—stealing a highly-valued mask
```

```
            from a shi-shi party. Their deepening attraction and distrust
            could tear apart their partnership but the promise of a bigger
            prize (some eight billion odd dollars) by Zeta-Jones keeps the
            game interesting. Only, who&apos;s playing with whom?"
            RowState="1" >
            <qryStars/>
        </ROW>
        <ROW RowState="8" URL="http://us.imdb.com/Title?0137494"
            Logo_URL="http://posters.imdb.com/Covers/13/74/94.jpg" >
            <qryStars/>
        </ROW>
        <ROW Movie_id="1" Name="Entrapment" Rating="PG-13" Length="112"
            Director="Jon Amiel" Synopsis="Following the theft of a
            highly-secured piece of artwork, an agent convinces her
            insurance agency employers to allow her to wriggle into the
            company of an aging but active master thief. Connery&apos;s
            burglar takes her on suspiciously and demands rigorous training
            before their first job together--stealing a highly-valued mask
            from a shi-shi party. Their deepening attraction and distrust
            could tear apart their partnership but the promise of a bigger
            prize (some eight billion odd dollars) by Zeta-Jones keeps the
            game interesting. Only, who&apos;s playing with whom?"
            RowState="64" URL="http://us.imdb.com/Title?0137494"
            Logo_URL="http://posters.imdb.com/Covers/13/74/94.jpg" >
            <qryStars>
              <ROWqryStars RowState="4" Star_id="16" Movie_id="1"
                Star="Ving Rhames" />
            </qryStars>
        </ROW>
      </ROWDATA>
    </DATAPACKET>
```

The delta still starts with the metadata definition of the contents. However, an additional attribute of the final PARAMS element identifies it as the delta:

```
DATASET_DELTA="1"
```

Instead of a complete list of the records, the delta only contains details about those records that have changed. Before and after snapshots of the data appear since the original values may be needed when locating the old record for an update (its UpdateMode is set to upWhereAll). The RowState attribute on each element indicates what it contains. The meaning of its values is shown in Table 22-4.

Table 22-4: RowState values

RowState	Meaning
1	Original record
2	Deleted record
4	Inserted record
8	Updated record
64	Detail updates

If an error occurs during the updating of the database, it is propagated back to the XML broker, which then invokes its ReconcileProducer component to deal with the problem. Figure 22-6 shows the page returned when a star is added to a movie that does not exist.

Part IV: Serving XML

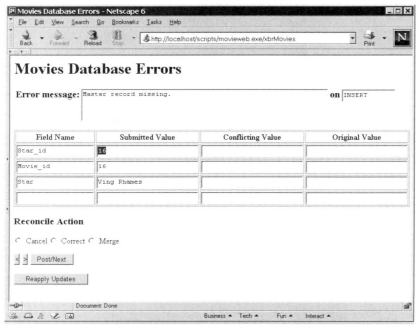

Figure 22-6: Reconciling an error

Summary

Delphi 5 makes use of XML to deliver database functionality to a thin client in a Web browser. XML data packets arrive from a back-end server into a Web application. The Web application then embeds the XML in an HTML page and adds JavaScript to support navigation and updating of the data. When changes are submitted back to the server, another XML document is sent with the updates, via the Web application.

The InternetExpress components let you easily design HTML pages that interact with the data from the XML. You can build lists of fields and grids of data, and add navigation buttons to them. Further components from the demonstration projects supplied with Delphi add a page producer that deals with reconciliation errors, buttons for displaying the XML data or delta packets, and assorted additional fields for use elsewhere in your page.

Part V
Sample Applications

This section explores the development of some applications that make use of XML.

Chapter 23 presents a program that performs mass electronic mail-outs by merging database information with a message template and sending these out using SMTP. XML is used to specify the configuration file as well as the message template, which allows for the embedding of values from database fields within the text. The template also includes the actual SQL query used to obtain the information in the first place. For processing the XML, Microsoft's XML parser is used.

Chapter 24 demonstrates how to process XML documents into a customized client written in Delphi. The movie-watcher documents are used as the example, and are shown in a custom GUI with appropriate navigation links between the sections. A native Delphi SAX1-compliant parser is used to process the XML, demonstrating an implementation of the `ISAXDocumentHandler` interface. As a bonus you see how to set up your browser to automatically open the movie-watcher documents in the new client when they are downloaded.

Chapter 25 contains another customized client in Delphi. This time it is for an examination style of XML document. Questions, possible answers, solutions, and explanations are included in the XML, allowing the client to load and administer the exam. Microsoft's XML package supplies the parsing abilities.

Chapter 26 highlights one of the main principles of XML, the separation of content from presentation, by producing an HTML front-end for the examination documents used in Chapter 25. The generation of these pages is handled by Delphi (of course) through a Web server application. It uses XSLT to generate the required pages and requires the holding of state information on the server. Microsoft again supplies the underlying processing power with its XSLT engine.

Chapter 27 describes an implementation of the Simple Object Access Protocol (SOAP). This protocol specifies how XML can be used to invoke methods on remote objects. In this case, the objects reside in a Web server application and are accessed through HTTP. Open XML's DOM provides the decoding functionality on the server. A specialized Delphi client talks to the SOAP server and interprets the responses.

Chapter 23: Mass Electronic Mail-Outs
Chapter 24: A Customized Client
Chapter 25: Examination XML—Delphi Client
Chapter 26: Examination XML—Web Client
Chapter 27: Simple Object Access Protocol

Chapter 23

Mass Electronic Mail-Outs

The purpose of the mass-mailer program described in this chapter is to perform mass electronic mail-outs based on a document template. Fields within the template are merged with recipient data (extracted from a datasource) to customize the mailings. An additional objective is to make the application as modular as possible, allowing you to easily maintain different parts independently.

To protect the program against future technology changes, it relies on several standards, each of which is encapsulated in a class:

- XML is used for the configuration properties, as well as for the template containing the message to be sent out. The text-based format of XML allows these files to be easily maintained through normal text editors, as well as specialized XML editors. Changes to the message template can be made without affecting the rest of the program, nor requiring a recompile.

- SQL is used to retrieve data from a datasource. Information from here determines where the e-mails are sent and the field values that can be included in the message. Access to the datasource uses a BDE alias. Together, this means that your data can reside in almost any format, since Delphi provides access to several databases natively and many others through ODBC and OLE DB. Using SQL gives you a common method for retrieving the data, freeing you from worrying about how it is actually held. If the data needs to be moved (to a different server and/or to a more powerful database), then all you need to do is update the BDE alias and the program still runs as before.

- The Simple Mail Transfer Protocol (SMTP) is used to communicate with the e-mail server for the dispatch of the messages.

The program works as follows:

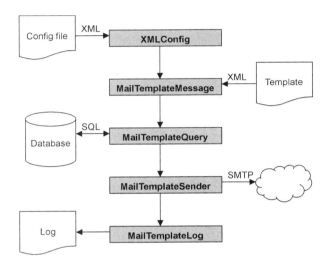

Figure 23-1: Data flow through the program.

1. You read in an XML configuration document that contains the various settings to use in the current run. This file details the SMTP attributes, the database connection, and the name of the file containing the message template to be used.
2. The actual query and the message template are read in from another XML document (as identified in the configuration parameters above).
3. You retrieve your list of recipients from the database, which you access using the BDE alias from the configuration file and the SQL query from the template.
4. For each record retrieved, merge the requested fields from the database into the message template.
5. The merged messages are sent out using SMTP, allowing you to talk to any number of mail servers. For testing purposes the messages are redirected to a log file where they can be reviewed.

Loading the Configuration Properties

The loading of the program properties is accomplished in a generic manner, retrieving them from an XML document. The hierarchy within the XML file determines the names of the properties, compiled from the full element path to the value (separated by periods (.) and ignoring the top-level element), with the property value coming from the actual text content. For example, the XML configuration file in Listing 23-1 results in the accumulation of these properties and values:

```
smtp.host=mail.thingies.com
smtp.user=keith
smtp.from=kbwood@thingies.com
database.alias=mailtemp
settings.pauseTime=2000
settings.template=MailMessage.xml
settings.testing=Y
```

Listing 23-1: Sample XML configuration file

```xml
<?xml version="1.0"?>
<mailTemplate>
  <smtp>
    <host>mail.thingies.com</host>
    <port/>
    <user>keith</user>
    <from>kbwood@thingies.com</from>
  </smtp>
  <database>
    <alias>mailtemp</alias>
    <user/>
    <password/>
  </database>
  <settings>
    <pauseTime>2000</pauseTime>
    <template>MailMessage.xml</template>
    <testing>Y</testing>
  </settings>
</mailTemplate>
```

This layout takes advantage of the structure inherent in XML to group related property values. It also builds on the ability of XML documents to be processed when they are merely well-formed, without requiring conformance to a DTD. In this way, the technique is general enough that it could be reused elsewhere.

NOTE Recall that a well-formed document simply follows the conventions of XML—only one top-level element, all elements have matching end tags in order, etc. If the document claims to follow a DTD and, in fact, does, then it is deemed to be valid. The DTD prescribes which elements and attributes may appear where within the document. In many cases, well-formed documents are sufficient for useful work.

To aid in its reuse, the functionality of the property loading is placed into its own unit, XMLConfig. Property names and values are placed into a string list using its Values property, providing a simple way to retrieve them by name later on. The LoadPropertiesFromXML procedure (see Listing 23-2) takes the name of the file to load and a reference to a string list and fills the latter with the properties found. Just add this unit to another project to reuse its abilities.

Listing 23-2: Configuration properties from XML

```
{ Open the configuration file and then load the properties }
procedure LoadPropertiesFromXML(Filename: string; Props: TStrings);
var
  XMLDoc: IXMLDOMDocument;
  Index: Integer;
  { Recursively read XML document until text leaves are reached.
    Property name is the accumulated tags to this point
```

```
       (separated by periods).
       Property value is the actual text.
       Add these into a string list using its Values property. }
  procedure LoadSubProperties(Element: IXMLDOMNode;
    PropPrefix: string);
  var
    Index: Integer;
  begin
    with Element do
      if (NodeType = NODE_TEXT) or (NodeType = NODE_CDATA_SECTION) then
        Props.Values[Copy(PropPrefix, 2, Length(PropPrefix) -1)] :=
          NodeValue
      else
        for Index := 0 to ChildNodes.Length -1 do
          LoadSubProperties(ChildNodes[Index],
            PropPrefix + '.' + NodeName);
  end;
begin
  XMLDoc := CoDOMDocument.Create;
  Props.Clear;
  try
    XMLDoc.Load(Filename);
    { Read through each second level element and process them }
    with XMLDoc.DocumentElement do
      for Index := 0 to ChildNodes.Length -1 do
        LoadSubProperties(ChildNodes[Index], '');
  finally
    XMLDoc := nil;
  end;
end;
```

The routine itself creates an instance of the Microsoft XML parser, `IXMLDOMDocument`, and asks it to parse the specified document. It then steps through all the child nodes of the main document element and calls the internal procedure, `LoadSubProperties`, on each. This latter routine tests for text-type nodes and creates an entry in the properties list when one is found. The name for the property is built up from the names of the elements leading to the text node, which is achieved through recursive calls to this same routine for embedded child nodes.

TIP Freeing up the DOM in the `finally` clause is not strictly necessary. Delphi automatically decrements the reference count for an interface when its variable goes out of scope.

Mail Message Template

Once the configuration properties have been loaded, you can extract the name of the message template file and load that, too. This file is another XML document that holds the text of the message to be sent, along with the query used to retrieve the recipients and their details. A sample template is shown in Listing 23-3.

Listing 23-3: XML mail-out template

```
<?xml version="1.0"?>
<template>
  <query emailfield="EmailAddress">select * from customer</query>
  <subject>Come visit your new Web site</subject>
```

```
    <message>Dear <field>FirstName</field>,
Our new Web site is up and running at http://www.thingies.com.
As <field>Position</field> of <field>Company</field> we think you
would find something of interest here.
Yours sincerely,
Keith Wood
    </message>
</template>
```

First, the SQL query is specified. The only database field that needs to be specifically identified for the application's use is the recipient's e-mail address, which is done through the `emailfield` attribute of the `query` element. Otherwise, the query can be as complex or as simple as necessary and can retrieve whatever fields it requires for use in the message itself. Recipients can easily be filtered out of the database as a whole for targeted mailings—just include an appropriate `where` clause in the query.

The subject of the e-mail appears in the `subject` element, with the body of the message being specified in the `message` element. Within the latter you can insert values from fields in the database by positioning `field` elements, containing the name of the field to display, at the appropriate points in the text. Any formatting of the field values can be done within the SQL query, so no additional processing should be necessary here.

Using XML means that the templates can be maintained by anyone with a text or XML editor. A minimal knowledge of SQL is required. To hide a complex query, a view could be constructed presenting the necessary values in a simple-to-use format. Having the database query in the document along with the message text ensures that the two remain synchronized. As a security measure, the logon details for the database are not included in the XML message template.

The XML document is loaded and accessed through the `TMailTemplateMessage` class, which resides in its own unit, `MailTemplateMessage`. In its constructor the class creates an instance of the Microsoft XML parser, and requests this to load the specified XML file. Thereafter, you have access to the complete contents of the document. Setting the `PreserveWhiteSpace` property to `True` ensures that your message appears in the e-mail the same way it does in the template. If this property was left at `False`, white space next to the field elements is lost.

```
{ Initialization }
constructor TMailTemplateMessage.Create(Filename: string);
begin
  inherited Create;
  FXMLDoc := CoDOMDocument.Create;
  FXMLDoc.PreserveWhiteSpace := True;
  FXMLDoc.Load(Filename);
end;
```

Two methods provide easy access to the elements and attributes within the document (see Listing 23-4). `NodeValue` returns the text contained within the specified element, or an empty string if the element cannot be found. The routine assumes that there is only one of each type of element in the document, and that it contains only a single text node. `AttributeValue` returns the value of the named attribute of a given element. Again, a single occurrence of the element is assumed, and an empty string is returned if the attribute or node does not exist.

Listing 23-4: Retrieving element and attribute values

```
{ Return the value of the named attribute -
  assumes only one such node }
function TMailTemplateMessage.AttributeValue(
  NodeName, AttrName: string): string;
var
  Elements: IXMLDOMNodeList;
begin
  Elements := FXMLDoc.GetElementsByTagName(NodeName);
  if Elements.Length = 0 then
    Result := ''
  else
    Result :=
      Elements.Item[0].Attributes.GetNamedItem(AttrName).Text;
end;
{ Return the value of the named node -
  assumes only one such node and no children }
function TMailTemplateMessage.NodeValue(NodeName: string):
  string;
var
  Elements: IXMLDOMNodeList;
begin
  Elements := FXMLDoc.GetElementsByTagName(NodeName);
  if Elements.Length = 0 then
    Result := ''
  else
    Result := Elements.Item[0].Text;
end;
```

In both routines you use the `GetElementsByTagName` method of the document to locate and return the required node. Actually, this routine returns a list of nodes, but you only expect a single result. This saves you the process of searching through all the nodes yourself. From the list, it is easy to retrieve the node of interest and then its value or attribute.

The main activity involving the XML document is the processing of the message template and the substitution of field values in marked positions. The `ParseMessage` method provides this functionality (see Listing 23-5), accepting a string list that contains the field mappings for the current record. The mappings are established and accessed using the `Values` property of a string list, which associates a text value with an identifying key.

Listing 23-5: Performing the mail merge

```
{ Parse the message tag and return its value }
function TMailTemplateMessage.ParseMessage(Fields: TStrings):
  string;
var
  Elements: IXMLDOMNodeList;
  FieldValue: string;
  Index: Integer;
begin
  Elements := FXMLDoc.GetElementsByTagName(MessageTag);
  if Elements.Length = 0 then
    raise EMailException.Create(NoMessage)
  Result := '';
  with Elements[0] do
    for Index := 0 to ChildNodes.Length -1 do
      { Add text elements directly }
      if (ChildNodes[Index].NodeType = NODE_TEXT) or
```

```
        (ChildNodes[Index].NodeType = NODE_CDATA_SECTION)
      then
        Result := Result + ChildNodes[Index].Text
      { For 'field' elements get the field value }
      else if (ChildNodes[Index].NodeType = NODE_ELEMENT) and
          (ChildNodes[Index].NodeName = FieldTag) then
      begin
        FieldValue := Fields.Values[ChildNodes[Index].Text];
        if FieldValue = '' then
          { Error if no such field }
          raise EMailException.Create(
            Format(MissingField, [ChildNodes[Index].Text]));
        if FieldValue = Empty then
          { Replace empty field notation with empty string }
          FieldValue := '';
        Result := Result + FieldValue;
      end;
  end;
end;
```

You locate the message element in the document (again using the `GetElementsByTagName` method) and then step through each of its child elements, constructing the message text as you go. The children should only consist of text nodes, which are appended directly to the message, or `field` elements, for which you extract the field name and then append the value of that field from the mapping. Note that the `Text` method of a node returns all the text contained within that node (at any level), so you do not have to traverse down to the actual text node and retrieve its value. An exception occurs if the field does not exist in the record (denoted by an empty string being returned from the mapping).

TIP One special case exists when the field has an empty string value. If you were to try to place this directly in the field list, it would not save the entry (the list automatically returns an empty string for any key that does not have a value set). To let you recognize the difference between a field that does not exist at all, as opposed to one that has an empty value, you must substitute a flagging value for the missing one. This flag, the constant `Empty`, is checked for when the value is retrieved and is then reset to its empty value.

Database Access

In keeping with the modular approach, all the database access is contained within one unit, `MailTemplateQuery`, and managed through the `TMailTemplateQuery` class. An instance of the class is created and initialized by passing to it the configuration properties and the query to be executed (from the message template XML document).

From the configuration details it extracts the BDE alias and logon parameters. It then creates internal instances of a `TDatabase` and a `TQuery`, which are initialized from the passed-in values, before opening the query (see the code in Listing 23-6).

Listing 23-6: Initializing the query and extracting its field values

```
{ Initialization—connect to database and open query }
constructor TMailTemplateQuery.Create(Props: TStrings;
  QuerySQL: string);
begin
```

```
    inherited Create;
    FFields   := TStringList.Create;
    FDatabase := TDatabase.Create(nil);
    with FDatabase do
    begin
      AliasName    := Props.Values[QueryAliasProp];
      DatabaseName := 'MailOut';
      LoginPrompt  := False;
      if Props.Values[QueryUserProp] <> '' then
        Params.Add('username=' + Props.Values[QueryUserProp]);
      if Props.Values[QueryPasswordProp] <> '' then
        Params.Add('password=' + Props.Values[QueryPasswordProp]);
      Connected := True;
    end;
    FQuery := TQuery.Create(nil);
    with FQuery do
    begin
      DatabaseName := FDatabase.DatabaseName;
      SQL.Text     := QuerySQL;
      AfterScroll  := QueryAfterScroll;
      Active       := True;
    end;
end;
{ Set up the list of fields and values }
procedure TMailTemplateQuery.QueryAfterScroll(DataSet: TDataSet);
var
  Index: Integer;
begin
  with FQuery do
    for Index := 0 to FieldCount -1 do
      if Fields[Index].DisplayText = '' then
        { If string value is empty then entry doesn't appear
          in the list, so replace it }
        FFields.Values[Fields[Index].FieldName] := Empty
      else
        FFields.Values[Fields[Index].FieldName] :=
          Fields[Index].DisplayText;
end;
```

Thereafter, the program interacts with the resulting data through the following attributes: the `NextRecord` method to step through each record in turn, the `EOF` property to determine when it has reached the end, and the `Fields` property to access the values from the current record. The field values are held in an associative format in a string list for use by the message substitution routine. This is achieved through the `Values` property of the string list.

To place the field values into the list, you attach an event handler to the `AfterScroll` event of the query (see the code in Listing 23-6). This is called whenever the current record changes, which is ideal for your purposes. You can cycle through each field returned by the query and place its name and value into the list. As mentioned earlier, special processing is required for fields with empty string values.

Drop It in the Post

Once you have constructed the mail message and merged in the fields from the database, you are ready to send it off. Again, make use of open standards by using an SMTP server to post the mail.

Wrap a TNMSMTP component in another object to provide a simple interface for the rest of the program (a Façade design pattern). One advantage of doing this is that you could come back later and replace the underlying mail implementation without affecting the rest of the program. All you must do is retain the existing interface.

NOTE As mentioned before, feel free to replace the TNMSMTP component with your favorite e-mail component. In Delphi 3, you can use the TSMTP component since the TNMSMTP one is not available.

The mailing object, TMailTemplateSender (from the MailTemplateSender unit), is passed the list of configuration properties upon its creation (see Listing 23-7). From this it extracts the ones it requires (the name and port of the SMTP host, and the user account to use) and initializes the SMTP component with them.

Listing 23-7: Interfacing with the SMTP component

```
{ Initialization }
constructor TMailTemplateSender.Create(Props: TStrings);
begin
  inherited Create;
  FSender := TNMSMTP.Create(nil);
  with FSender do
  begin
    Host := Props.Values[MailHostProp];
    try
      Port := StrToInt(Props.Values[MailPortProp]);
    except  { Ignore }
    end;
    UserId := Props.Values[MailUserProp];
    Connect;
  end;
end;
{ Send an e-mail }
procedure TMailTemplateSender.Send(
  FromEmail, ToEmail, Subject, Message: string);
begin
  with FSender.PostMessage do
  begin
    FromAddress    := FromEmail;
    ToAddress.Text := ToEmail;
    Subject        := Subject;
    Body.Text      := Message;
  end;
  FSender.SendMail;
end;
```

Thereafter, the only interaction with the mailer is to request that a completed message be sent. The Send method (also in Listing 23-7) takes the sender's name and the recipient's e-mail addresses, along with the subject and body of the message as parameters. These are parceled up and sent out.

Logging and Testing

To keep an eye on what is happening within your application, generate a log file for each run. This displays the parameters passed to the program and the recipients of the completed messages.

For testing purposes, the log file also captures the entire text of the message, as it would have been sent. This allows you to verify that the merge process is working as expected before sending out your message. A flag in the configuration file determines whether or not you are in test mode.

To continue your goal of modularizing the program, you put the logging functionality into its own object in a separate unit, MailTemplateLog. The TMailTemplateLog object (see Listing 23-8) automatically creates a timestamped log file based on the name of the application when it is itself created. Including the current time within the filename ensures that previous logs are not overwritten (although you must remember to purge the old log files at some stage). The log file is automatically closed when the wrapper object is destroyed. This is another example of the Façade design pattern, hiding several more complex functions behind a simplified interface.

Listing 23-8: Logging your actions

```
{ Open the log file }
constructor TMailTemplateLog.Create;
var
  Filename: string;
begin
  inherited Create;
  Filename := ChangeFileExt(ExtractFileName(ParamStr(0)),
    FormatDateTime(LogFormat, Now) + LogExt);
  AssignFile(FLogFile, Filename);
  Rewrite(FLogFile);
end;
{ Close the log file }
destructor TMailTemplateLog.Destroy;
begin
  CloseFile(FLogFile);
  inherited Destroy;
end;
{ Write an error message }
procedure TMailTemplateLog.Error(Error: Exception);
begin
  Log(Error.Message);
end;
{ Write a log message }
procedure TMailTemplateLog.Log(Message: string);
begin
  Writeln(FLogFile, TimeStamp + Message);
  Flush(FLogFile);
end;
{ Write a testing message }
procedure TMailTemplateLog.LogTest(
  FromEmail, ToEmail, Subject, Message: string);
begin
  Writeln(FLogFile, TestOnly);
  Writeln(FLogFile, LogFrom + FromEmail);
  Writeln(FLogFile, LogTo + ToEmail);
  Writeln(FLogFile, LogSubject + Subject);
  Writeln(FLogFile, LogMessage + Message);
```

```
    { Ensure it gets written out }
    Flush(FLogFile);
  end;
  { Return the current time }
  function TMailTemplateLog.TimeStamp: string;
  begin
    Result := FormatDateTime(TimeFormat, Now);
  end;
```

You then have three methods for interacting with the log file: `Log`, `LogTest`, and `Error`. `Log` adds a simple timestamped message to the file. `LogTest` is a convenience method that records all the details for a message sent while in test mode. Finally, `Error` records any exceptions that are passed to it. All these methods flush the file buffer before they complete, ensuring that you are able to see all the relevant log messages.

All Together Now

Now that you have a set of objects, each performing its own specialized task with minimal interactions between them, you can pull them all together into a coherent whole.

The application has no user interface, so all of the main code appears in the .dpr unit (see Listing 23-9), and is marked as being a console application with the {$APPTYPE CONSOLE} directive.

Listing 23-9: The completed mail-out processing

```
var
  FromEmail, ToEmail, Subject, Message: string;
  QuerySQL, EmailField: string;
  Count: Integer;
  LogFile: TMailTemplateLog;
  Template: TMailTemplateMessage;
  Query: TMailTemplateQuery;
  Sender: TMailTemplateSender;
Begin
  Props    := TStringList.Create;
  LogFile  := nil;
  Template := nil;
  Query    := nil;
  Sender   := nil;
  Count    := 0;
  try
    try
      { Load the program properties }
      LoadMailProperties(Props);
      { Create and open the log file }
      LogFile    := TMailTemplateLog.Create;
      { Open the XML template document }
      Template   :=
        TMailTemplateMessage.Create(Props.Values[TemplateProp]);
      { Extract various parameters }
      FromEmail  := Props.Values[MailFromProp];
      QuerySQL   := Template.NodeValue(QueryTag);
      Subject    := Template.NodeValue(SubjectTag);
      EmailField := Template.AttributeValue(QueryTag, EmailAttr);
      { Query the database }
      Query      := TMailTemplateQuery.Create(Props, QuerySQL);
      { Create an interface to the e-mail system }
```

```
       if not Testing then
         Sender := TMailTemplateSender.Create(Props);
       { Log parameters }
       LogFile.Log(Started);
       LogFile.Log(LogFrom + FromEmail);
       LogFile.Log(LogTemplate + Props.Values[TemplateProp]);
       LogFile.Log(LogSubject + Subject);
       LogFile.Log(LogDatabase + Props.Values[QueryAliasProp]);
       LogFile.Log(LogQuery + QuerySQL);
       { Process each record from the query }
       while not Query.EOF do
       begin
         { Get the recipient }
         ToEmail := Query.Fields.Values[EmailField];
         { Perform the mail merge -
           XML document with query fields }
         Message := Template.ParseMessage(Query.Fields);
         { And output the results }
         if Testing then
           logFile.LogTest(FromEmail, ToEmail, Subject, Message)
         else
         begin
           Sender.Send(FromEmail, ToEmail, Subject, Message);
           LogFile.Log(Format(EmailSent, [ToEmail]));
           { Pause so as not to overwhelm the e-mail server }
           Sleep(PauseTime);
         end;
         Inc(Count);
         Query.NextRecord;
       end;
     except on Error: Exception do
       { Catch any errors and report them }
       LogFile.Error(Error);
     end;
   finally
     LogFile.Log(Format(Finished, [Count]));
     { Tidy up }
     Props.Free;
     LogFile.Free;
     Template.Free;
     Query.Free;
     Sender.Free;
   end;
end.
```

The steps in generating and sending the e-mail messages are as follows:

1. Check for any command-line parameters in `LoadMailProperties`, as these can be used to pass in the name of a configuration file to read instead of the default one. If no file is specified, the program looks for one with the same name as itself but with an .xml extension. From the selected file, the program properties are retrieved into a string list using the `LoadPropertiesFromXML` routine from the `XMLConfig` unit. This list is passed to the other objects for them to extract their necessary values.

2. Create a `TMailTemplateLog` object to record your current session and write initial settings to it.

3. Load the XML template file. Its name is retrieved from the configuration parameters and is passed to a TMailTemplateMessage object.

4. Extract the query to be executed from the template file and pass it, along with the configuration parameters, to a TMailTemplateQuery object.

5. Iterate through all the records returned from the query, performing the mail merge as you go.

6. Send each completed message to a TMailTemplateSender object to mail out, or write it to the log file if only testing. A pause is taken after each message is sent. This reduces the load on the mail server, and is configurable through the properties file.

7. Finalize the log file entries and free up all the objects. Your mail-out is complete. To run the example project, you need to set up the mailtemp database alias with the BDE to point to the supplied customer table.

NOTE The code for this application appears within the .dpr file but not within a procedure or class method. All Pascal programs have their main code in the body of the main unit, between a begin and the final end. In a more typical Delphi program for Windows, you find that the .dpr contains code to initialize the application, create the opening forms, and then set it all going. You are free to add or alter the code that appears there, although most often the standard code is sufficient.

You can use the application as it stands for generating mass mailings from your database of contacts (but only with their permission of course). Just alter the configuration file for your database and server situation, then create the mail template with its embedded query, and away you go. Enhancements to the program could include an attachment element in the template XML document that causes the named file(s) to be sent out with each message. The rest is up to you.

Summary

Using open standards helps to protect your coding investment from future technology changes. This program works with any SQL database and with any SMTP server. Similarly, partitioning the application into several modules/objects, each of which has a well-defined and simple interface, allows you to more easily modify parts of the program with minimal effects on the remainder.

The application described here performs customized electronic mass mail-outs. It retrieves configuration information from an XML document, selects records from a database using SQL, merges fields from these records into a message format held in another XML document, and sends the completed message out into the world using a SMTP server.

Due to the use of XML for the configuration file and message template, these can be easily altered without a detailed knowledge of the program mechanics, and without requiring a recompilation.

Chapter 24
A Customized Client

Since all XML documents follow the rules described in Chapter 2 and have a simple tree structure, it is easy to process them in a generic manner. Applications can display the tree, create new documents based on the DTD, or search through the data for specific values in particular fields. However, generic applications are not always the most user-friendly. You are forced to use the tree structure that XML defines, whereas related data may be better presented in some other format. Hence there is a need for a customized client program, designed specifically to handle a particular document type (those based on one DTD). XML still provides an application-independent transfer mode, allowing the client to easily interoperate with a database serving up the data, or with another application that also knows about this XML type.

To illustrate how to load and process an XML document on the client side, you can use the movie-watcher format described previously. Using Delphi you can produce a program that reads the document, transforms it into domain-specific objects, and then presents a UI to browse through them. Recall that the elements in this document are related to each other through ID and IDREF type attributes, which form the basis of the navigation you provide within the application.

The Client

Your client application extracts all the relevant details from the XML document and places them into three lists: movies, cinemas, and screenings. The main form then displays the details to the user and lets them browse the information. A tab control provides the main access to each of the three lists. As an item is selected from a list, its details are displayed on the right side of the form (see Figures 24-1 through 24-3).

Chapter 24: A Customized Client **451**

Figure 24-1: Select a movie that is showing.

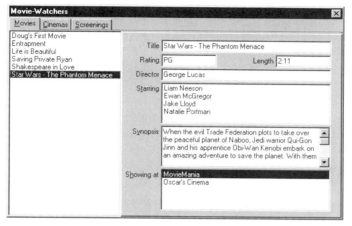

Figure 24-2: Find a time when it is showing.

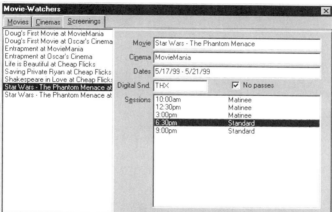

Figure 24-3: See what the cinema has to offer.

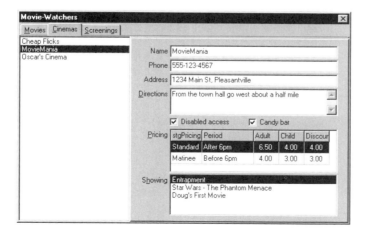

Secondary navigation is provided by double-clicking on linking fields, such as on the list of cinemas on the movie page, or on the movie name on the screening page. In this way you can easily find a movie, select a session, and find out where the cinema is.

The XML document to load is specified as a command-line parameter to the application (this is necessary for later on). To access the file's name, use the `ParamStr` function: `LoadDocument(ParamStr(1), FMovies, FCinemas, FScreenings);`

You make use of the string list's ability to associate an object with each string throughout the program. Each list returned from the load procedure contains the object's display name as the string value, and adds a reference to an appropriate object in the corresponding `Objects` property. As the user selects different lists, copy their contents into the list box on the form (which sorts them automatically) along with the object references. Then, when more details are requested, you have immediate access to the necessary object and its attributes.

TIP String lists are very useful in Delphi programming. They do much more than just manage a list of strings. Setting the `Sorted` property to `True` automatically orders the contents. Use the `Duplicates` property to control the handling of duplicate values in sorted lists. The `Values` property allows you to map from one string value to another, especially useful when dealing with .ini file style values. And finally, the `Objects` property lets you associate any object with a particular string value.

Information Hiding

To insulate the user interface from the source XML document, introduce a separate unit, MWObjs, which defines the classes corresponding to the objects extracted from the XML. Here you flatten out the XML tree structure, providing properties for sub-elements and attributes, and direct pointers to other objects rather than indirect ones through ID references. Compare the movie object in Listing 24-1 with the XML structure shown in Listing 2-1.

Listing 24-1: A movie object

```
{ Details about a movie }
TMovie = class(TObject)
private
  FId: string;
  FName: string;
  FRating: TMovieRating;
  FLength: TDateTime;
  FDirector: string;
  FStars: TStringList;
  FSynopsis: string;
  function GetRatingText: string;
  procedure SetRatingText(RatingText: string);
public
  constructor Create(Id: string);
  destructor Destroy; override;
  property Id: string read FId write FId;
  property Name: string read FName write FName;
  property Rating: TMovieRating read FRating write FRating;
  property RatingText: string read GetRatingText
    write SetRatingText;
```

```
    property Length: TDateTime read FLength write FLength;
    property Director: string read FDirector write FDirector;
    property Stars: TStringList read FStars write FStars;
    property Synopsis: string read FSynopsis write FSynopsis;
  end;
```

Although you could navigate through the XML tree itself and extract all the necessary details yourself, this approach makes it much easier for the application to deal with the information. You do not have to know about the structure of XML documents and what internal objects are used to represent them. Instead, you have real-world objects with familiar patterns of properties. Furthermore, having this extra layer means that you could, at some time in the future, load the data from another source or in some other way without having to change the user interface.

NOTE This hiding of implementation details is one of the mainstays of object-oriented programming, known as *encapsulation*. By reducing the knowledge of one object or module required by another, you reduce their reliance on one another. This *decoupling* of the objects makes it easier to make changes in one place without adversely affecting another area. Using interfaces is another important way to enforce decoupling.

The LoadDocument procedure declared in this unit handles all the translation for you. Just pass it the name of the XML document and three lists to use in returning the data.

To create these movie-watcher objects, parse the source XML document to generate them. Using a SAX-compliant parser makes this an easy and maintainable task.

Parsing the XML Documents

As is usually the case in using SAX for XML processing, you need to write a content handler that knows about the expected document format. Since you are not interested in any of the extra abilities provided by SAX2, you can use a SAX1 parser, which means implementing the ISAXDocumentHandler interface. Passing an instance of the handler to the SAX-compliant parser and supplying a document identifier causes the parser to invoke the events in the handler as it reads the various parts of the document.

The simplest way to define a class that implements the document handler interface is to make use of the default handler supplied by SAX. The TSAXHandlerBase class implements all of the standard SAX1 handler interfaces, supplying default behaviors for each method that generally do nothing. All these routines are declared as virtual, allowing you to easily replace them in a subclass through overriding.

This is exactly what you do with the movie-watcher document handler, as shown in Listing 24-2. To generate the movie-watcher objects, only a few of the SAX events need to be dealt with. Here you see the benefit of using the default handler as a base. All the other SAX routines, which must be implemented to satisfy the requirements of the interface, are already defined, and do not interfere with your specific processing of the document.

Listing 24-2: Declaring a movie-watcher document handler

```
{ A SAX document handler that knows about
  movie-watcher documents }
TMWDocumentHandler = class(TSAXHandlerBase)
private
  FCinema: TCinema;
  FCinemas: TList;
  FMovie: TMovie;
  FMovies: TList;
  FPrice: TPrice;
  FScreening: TScreening;
  FScreenings: TList;
  FText: string;
public
  constructor Create;
  destructor Destroy; override;
  property Cinemas: TList read FCinemas;
  property Movies: TList read FMovies;
  property Screenings: TList read FScreenings;
  { ISAXDocumentHandler }
  procedure Characters(Text: TSAXString); override;
  procedure EndElement(Name: TSAXString); override;
  procedure StartElement(Name: TSAXString;
    Attributes: ISAXAttributeList); override;
end;
```

As can be seen in the LoadDocument routine (see Listing 24-3), an instance of the customized content handler is created, along with an instance of a SAX1-compliant parser (in this case the native Delphi one). The TMWDocumentHandler class constructs three lists, corresponding to the string lists used in the client program, and fills them with the domain-specific objects it extracts from the document.

Listing 24-3: Loading the movie-watcher document

```
{ Load XML document and process into string lists
  with references to the appropriate objects }
procedure LoadDocument(URI: string;
  MoviesList, CinemasList, ScreeningsList: TStringList);
var
  Index: Integer;
  SAXParser: TSAXDelphiParser;
  Handler: TMWDocumentHandler;
begin
  { Create the XML parser }
  Handler                  := TMWDocumentHandler.Create;
  SAXParser                := TSAXDelphiParser.Create;
  SAXParser.DocumentHandler := Handler;
  try
    { And parse the document }
    SAXParser.Parse(URI);
    with Handler do
    begin
      { Are they all here? }
      if (Movies.Count = 0) or (Cinemas.Count = 0) or
         (Screenings.Count = 0) then
        raise Exception.Create(InvalidDocument + URI);
      { Step through the handler's lists and
        convert to output format }
      for Index := 0 to Movies.Count -1  do
```

```
            MoviesList.AddObject(
              TMovie(Movies[Index]).Name, Movies[Index]);
          for Index := 0 to Cinemas.Count -1 do
            CinemasList.AddObject(
              TCinema(Cinemas[Index]).Name, Cinemas[Index]);
          for Index := 0 to Screenings.Count -1 do
            ScreeningsList.AddObject(Format(ScreeningDesc,
              [TScreening(Screenings[Index]).Movie.Name,
              TScreening(Screenings[Index]).Cinema.Name]),
              Screenings[Index]);
      end;
    finally
      SAXParser.Free;
    end;
  end;
```

Once the parse process has completed, these lists are transferred to the ones supplied by the calling program. For each of the internal lists, you step through all the items and set the identifying string to an appropriate value. Movies and cinemas have their names entered, while screenings combine the names of their associated movie and cinema.

Constructing Model Objects

The first step in building the movie-watcher object model is performed by the document handler's constructor. Since the class is intended for a single use, the constructor creates the necessary lists.

Then, as each element is encountered and the handler is notified through the `StartElement` method, you prepare the model environment for later processing in the other event routines. For elements that correspond to objects within the internal model, create a new instance of them and add it to their appropriate list (see Listing 24-4). References to the most recently constructed objects are held within the object for them to be accessed later.

Listing 24-4: Preparing a new real-world object

```
  { Create objects as necessary for document elements }
  procedure TMWDocumentHandler.StartElement(Name: TSAXString;
    Attributes: ISAXAttributeList);
  { Locate the movie with the given identifier }
  function FindMovie(Id: string): TMovie;
  var
    Index: Integer;
  begin
    Result := nil;
    for Index := 0 to FMovies.Count -1 do
      if TMovie(FMovies[Index]).Id = Id then
      begin
        Result := TMovie(FMovies[Index]);
        Exit;
      end;
  end;
  { Locate the cinema with the given identifier }
  function FindCinema(Id: string): TCinema;
  var
    Index: Integer;
  begin
    Result := nil;
```

```
      for Index := 0 to FCinemas.Count -1 do
        if TCinema(FCinemas[Index]).Id = Id then
        begin
          Result := TCinema(FCinemas[Index]);
          Exit;
        end;
    end;
    { Locate the pricing scheme with the given identifier }
    function FindPrice(PriceId: string): TPrice;
    var
      Index, Index2: Integer;
    begin
      Result := nil;
      for Index := 0 to FCinemas.Count -1 do
        with TCinema(FCinemas[Index]) do
        begin
          Index2 := Pricing.IndexOf(PriceId);
          if Index2 > -1 then
          begin
            Result := TPrice(Pricing.Objects[Index2]);
            Exit;
          end;
        end;
    end;
  begin
    if Name = MWMovie then
    begin
      FMovie           := TMovie.Create(Attributes.Value(MWId));
      FMovie.RatingText := Attributes.Value(MWRating);
      FMovies.Add(FMovie);
    end
    else if Name = MWCinema then
    begin
      FCinema := TCinema.Create(Attributes.Value(MWId));
      FCinemas.Add(FCinema);
    end
    else if Name = MWPrices then
    begin
      FPrice := TPrice.Create(Attributes.Value(MWId));
      FCinema.Pricing.AddObject(Attributes.Value(MWId), FPrice);
    end
    else if Name = MWScreening then
    begin
      FScreening :=
        TScreening.Create(FindMovie(Attributes.Value(MWMovieId)),
          FindCinema(Attributes.Value(MWCinemaId)));
      FScreenings.Add(FScreening);
    end
    else if Name = MWSession then
      FPrice := FindPrice(Attributes.Value(MWPriceId));
  end;
```

Movie objects are created with their ID and rating, as extracted from the attributes of the element, before being added to the list of movies. Similarly, cinema instances are constructed and added to the cinemas list. Pricing details belong to a particular cinema, so price elements cause a new price object to be added to the current cinema's (FCinema) own list.

Screenings contain references to the movie and cinema linked together through IDREF attributes. These objects are located from their respective lists before being passed to the screening object's constructor. As before, the resulting object is added to its list. Individual sessions within a screening refer to their pricing structure via an attribute. The associated price object is located and saved for later.

Accumulating Content

Other elements appear as properties of the model objects, rather than as objects in their own right. Their content appears as text that is returned to the handler through the `Characters` event. However, this method is only invoked as the content is parsed, following the `StartElement`. Hence, these elements are dealt with in the `EndElement` event, once their content has been identified.

Within the text content event (shown in Listing 24-5), you add the new text to any existing value and save it for later. It is possible for an element's content to be made up of several text nodes, perhaps coming from different embedded elements (such as the emph element in the synopsis), or through the use of entity references or CDATA sections.

Listing 24-5: Accumulating text

```
{ Accumulate text content }
procedure TMWDocumentHandler.Characters(Text: TSAXString);
begin
  FText := FText + Text;
end;
```

TIP Some XML parsers automatically normalize text as they read it. In others, this behavior can be controlled through a property. The parser used here is fairly basic and simply returns all the text it finds, requiring the handler to do the operation itself.

Saving Properties

As described earlier, elements from the XML document that are present in the movie-watcher model as properties have their content built up within the `Characters` event. Once the end tag for those elements is encountered, you can transfer that accumulated text into the corresponding model object.

The `EndElement` routine (see Listing 24-6) uses the element name to determine which object and property to set from the text. In the case of the name element, the element name is insufficient identification since it appears in the movie, cinema, and prices elements. For this reason, you need to check which object is currently being constructed (the non-`nil` one).

Listing 24-6: Saving object model property values

```
{ Save text content to appropriate property }
procedure TMWDocumentHandler.EndElement(Name: TSAXString);
  { Replace consecutive white space with one space }
  function Normalize(Text: string): string;
  const
    Blanks = [#1..#32];
  var
    Index: Integer;
```

```
    begin
      Result := Text;
      if Length(Text) < 2 then
        Exit;
      for Index := Length(Result) downto 2 do
        if (Result[Index] in Blanks) and
            (Result[Index -1] in Blanks) then
          begin
            Result[Index -1] := ' ';
            Delete(Result, Index, 1);
          end;
    end;
    { Return the accumulated text and clear for next time }
    function ReadAndClearText: string;
    begin
      Result := Trim(Normalize(FText));
      FText  := '';
    end;
begin
  if Name = MWMovie then
    FMovie := nil
  else if Name = MWMovie then
    FCinema := nil
  else if Name = MWPrices then
    FPrice := nil
  else if Name = MWScreening then
    FScreening := nil
  else if Name = MWName then
  begin
    if Assigned(FMovie) then
      FMovie.Name := ReadAndClearText
    else if Assigned(FPrice) then
      FPrice.Name := ReadAndClearText
    else if Assigned(FCinema) then
      FCinema.Name := ReadAndClearText;
  end
  else if Name = MWLength then
    FMovie.Length := StrToInt(ReadAndClearText) / 24 / 60
  else if Name = MWDirector then
    FMovie.Director := ReadAndClearText
  else if Name = MWStar then
    FMovie.Stars.Add(ReadAndClearText)
  else if Name = MWSynopsis then
    FMovie.Synopsis := ReadAndClearText
  else if Name = MWPhone then
    FCinema.Phone := ReadAndClearText
  else if Name = MWAddress then
    FCinema.Address := ReadAndClearText
  else if Name = MWDirections then
    FCinema.Directions := ReadAndClearText
  else if Name = MWCandyBar then
    FCinema.CandyBar := True
  else if Name = MWDisabledAccess then
    FCinema.DisabledAccess := True
  else if Name = MWPeriod then
    FPrice.Period := ReadAndClearText
  else if Name = MWAdult then
    FPrice.Adult := StrToFloat(ReadAndClearText)
  else if Name = MWChild then
    FPrice.Child := StrToFloat(ReadAndClearText)
```

```
        else if Name = MWDiscount then
          FPrice.Discount := StrToFloat(ReadAndClearText)
        else if Name = MWStartDate then
          FScreening.StartDate := StrToDateTime(ReadAndClearText)
        else if Name = MWEndDate then
          FScreening.EndDate := StrToDateTime(ReadAndClearText)
        else if Name = MWNoPasses then
          FScreening.NoPasses := True
        else if Name = MWDigitalSound then
          FScreening.DigitalSound := ReadAndClearText
        else if Name = MWSession then
          FScreening.Showing.AddObject(ReadAndClearText, FPrice);
    end;
```

The supplied text must be normalized before being used. This replaces consecutive occurrences of white space characters with a single space and trims white space from the start and end of the text. The ReadAndClearText function performs this activity, as well as clearing out the FText field so it is ready for accumulating text for the next node.

Properties that are not text values are converted as necessary, such as the ticket prices and the screening dates. Some elements provide information simply through their presence, like the disabled access and candy bar settings for a cinema. Here you set the corresponding Boolean property to True when they are encountered.

The objects that are being operated on were created in the appropriate StartElement method, and the saved references are used here.

NOTE Elements that do not contribute to the object model structure, and do not have any text content can be ignored in the event handlers. Examples from the current documents include the starring element from the movies, and the facilities element from the cinemas. Although they are not used here, they are necessary when generating an HTML representation since they serve to group their sub-elements.

Client Processing

The returned lists are used within the client application for display and navigation purposes. Since they are string lists they can be assigned directly to the Items property of the list box on the left of the form. Setting the Sorted property of that list box automatically reorders the entries for display, retaining the association with the attached objects. The tabNavigationChange method of the form (see Listing 24-7) is invoked when the user selects one of the tabs on the screen (and during the initial load). It performs the necessary assignment.

Listing 24-7: Display movie items

```
{ Show selected details in listbox }
procedure TfrmMovieWatchers.tabNavigationChange(Sender: TObject);
begin
  with lbxNavigation do
  begin
    Items.BeginUpdate;
    Items.Clear;
    if tabNavigation.TabIndex = MoviesTab then
      Items := FMovies
```

```pascal
      else if tabNavigation.TabIndex = CinemasTab then
        Items := FCinemas
      else if tabNavigation.TabIndex = ScreeningsTab then
        Items := FScreenings;
      Items.EndUpdate;
    end;
    lbxNavigation.ItemIndex := 0;
    lbxNavigationClick(lbxNavigation);
    ActiveControl            := lbxNavigation;
end;
{ Select an item to display its details }
procedure TfrmMovieWatchers.lbxNavigationClick(Sender: TObject);
begin
  with lbxNavigation do
  begin
    if ItemIndex < 0 then
      ItemIndex := 0;
    if tabNavigation.TabIndex = MoviesTab then
      ShowMovie(TMovie(Items.Objects[ItemIndex]))
    else if tabNavigation.TabIndex = CinemasTab then
      ShowCinema(TCinema(Items.Objects[ItemIndex]))
    else if tabNavigation.TabIndex = ScreeningsTab then
      ShowScreening(TScreening(Items.Objects[ItemIndex]));
  end;
end;
{ Display details for a movie }
procedure TfrmMovieWatchers.ShowMovie(Movie: TMovie);
var
  Index: Integer;
begin
  with Movie do
  begin
    edtTitle.Text        := Name;
    edtRating.Text       := MovieRatingText[Rating];
    edtLength.Text       := FormatDateTime(TimeFormat, Length);
    edtDirector.Text     := Director;
    lbxStars.Items       := Stars;
    memSynopsis.Lines.Text := Synopsis;
    { Show which cinemas it is playing at }
    with lbxCinemas.Items do
    begin
      BeginUpdate;
      Clear;
      for Index := 0 to FScreenings.Count -1 do
        if TScreening(FScreenings.Objects[Index]).Movie = Movie
        then
          AddObject(TScreening(
            FScreenings.Objects[Index]).Cinema.Name,
            FScreenings.Objects[Index]);
      if Count > 0 then
        lbxCinemas.ItemIndex := 0;
      EndUpdate;
    end;
  end;
  pgcDetails.ActivePage := tshMovie;
end;
```

As items in the list are selected, it is easy to retrieve all the information to be displayed through the corresponding `Objects` entry. This is shown in the `lbxNavigationClick` routine (see Listing 24-7).

From that object, you extract the details appropriate to its type and set them into the controls on the screen. The `ShowMovie` routine is shown in Listing 24-7 as an example of the required processing. Using the power of string lists, combined with the domain-specific objects, makes displaying the details of the movies and their screenings fairly simple.

Other navigation comes from responding to user interactions with the client program. For example, double-clicking an entry in the list of cinemas showing a particular movie invokes the event handler shown in Listing 24-8, which moves to the Screening page and locates the corresponding combination. For keyboard users, another event handler reacts to pressing the Enter key while on an entry in this list (reusing the functionality of the double-click routine).

Listing 24-8: Additional navigation

```
{ Go to the screening details for a movie }
procedure TfrmMovieWatchers.lbxCinemasDblClick(Sender: TObject);
begin
  ShowList(ScreeningsTab, Format(ScreeningDesc,
    [edtTitle.Text, lbxCinemas.Items[lbxCinemas.ItemIndex]]));
end;
{ Enter acts like a double-click }
procedure TfrmMovieWatchers.lbxCinemasKeyDown(Sender: TObject;
  var Key: Word; Shift: TShiftState);
begin
  if Key = VK_RETURN then
    lbxCinemasDblClick(lbxCinemas);
end;
```

To run the program, you must supply the name of the target XML document as a command line parameter. Running from within Delphi you specify this value through the Run | Parameters menu option.

Through the Browser

So far the application has been standalone. You supply it with the name of the file to load as a command-line parameter and it opens and displays that file. But one of the advantages of XML is its delivery across the Internet. To enable a downloaded file to trigger your client automatically, all you do is define a new file type for this class of documents.

To define this type in Windows you do the following:

1. Open Windows Explorer, select **View | Options**, and select the **File Types** tab.
2. Examine the list of the registered file types and the associated programs that deal with them. Note that each has a list of file extensions that identify the type, the corresponding MIME type, and the name of the program that knows how to deal with them.
3. Add a new file type for the movie-watcher XML documents by pressing **New Type**.

Part V: Sample Applications

4. Enter a description, Movie-Watcher, the content (MIME) type, application/x-movie-watcher, and the extension, .mwx. The MIME type, application/x-???, indicates that the file is application specific.

5. Press **New** for a default action.

6. Enter its name, open, and press **Browse** to search for your application. Follow the path and filename with the text "%1" to indicate that the name of the file being opened is passed to the program (hence the need for the processing of the command-line parameter earlier). Press **OK** to save the action (see Figure 24-4).

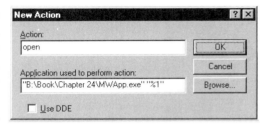

Figure 24-4: The open action for movie-watcher documents.

7. Change the associated icon if you wish. Set the other check box options if desired.

8. Save the results (see Figure 24-5) by pressing the **Close** button.

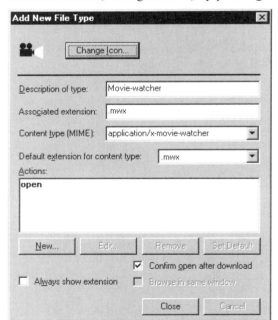

Figure 24-5: A new file type for movie-watcher documents.

Having defined the new type, you must rename the movie-watcher XML document to have an .mwx extension. Now whenever this file type is opened up within your browser, it loads directly into your application. A temporary file is created to hold the downloaded text, with the name of that file being passed to your client program as a command-line parameter.

 TIP You may need to set up your Web server to supply the correct MIME type for these documents. This process is dependent on the server that you are using, however, you need to associate the application/x-movie-watcher MIME type with the .mwx extension.

Summary

Although generic processors can handle XML in many useful ways, one of the advantages of using XML is that the information held within can also be sent to specialized applications and easily accessed. This allows for more user-friendly processing, as well as increased integrity and validations, without losing the benefits of XML in data interchange and legibility.

The application described here shows how you can write a client application in Delphi that receives and processes a particular class of XML documents. By defining a new file type in the registry specific to this type of XML document, you can have your Web browser automatically kick off the program whenever such a file is downloaded. Delivering data was never so easy.

Chapter 25

Examination XML — Delphi Client

Applications that administer exams allow you to verify that certain knowledge has been retained. Presented here is an XML scheme that allows the exam content to be created separately from any implementation of the testing environment. From this you generate objects to model the examination and a Delphi application that runs it.

The examination definitions are based on XML, allowing easy manipulation of the content of the exams without worrying about its presentation. Obviously, the document element in each document is exam (see the sample document in Listing 25-1). As attributes of this element, you have the mark (expressed as a percentage) that is required to pass the test, pass_mark, and a flag to indicate whether or not the questions must be presented in the order given, strict_order.

Listing 25-1: XML examination document

```
<?xml version="1.0" encoding="UTF-8"?>
<?xml:stylesheet type="text/xsl" href="ExamReview.xsl"?>
<!DOCTYPE exam SYSTEM "exam.dtd">
<exam pass_mark="66" strict_order="false">
  <title>Delphi Exam</title>
  <description>These questions test your knowledge of Delphi.
  </description>
  <instructions>Please answer every question.
  </instructions>
  <question id="Q1">
    <query>What is the value of i at the end of this code?
  for i := 1 to 5 do
    if i = 2 then
      Continue
    else if i = 4 then
      Break;
    </query>
    <answers type="radio">
      <answer>2</answer>
      <answer>3</answer>
      <answer correct="true">4</answer>
      <answer>5</answer>
      <answer>Undefined</answer>
    </answers>
    <explanation>The Continue causes the loop to return to the
beginning, whereas the Break causes the loop to exit.
    </explanation>
```

```xml
    </question>
    <question id="Q2">
      <query>Which of the following are components?
      </query>
      <answers type="checkbox">
        <answer>TBitmap</answer>
        <answer>TCanvas</answer>
        <answer correct="true">TImage</answer>
        <answer correct="true">TImageList</answer>
        <answer>TPicture</answer>
      </answers>
      <explanation>TImage and TImageList descend from TComponent. The
remainder are classes used internally to handle images.
      </explanation>
    </question>
    <question id="Q3">
      <query>From which class is every other class derived?
      </query>
      <answers type="text">
        <answer correct="true">TObject</answer>
        <answer correct="true">tobject</answer>
        <answer correct="true">TOBJECT</answer>
      </answers>
      <explanation>TObject is at the root of the Delphi class hierarchy.
      </explanation>
    </question>
</exam>
```

As top-level elements within the main one you have the name of the exam, `title`, a description of it, `description`, any special instructions to be followed, `instructions`, and the questions themselves. Except for the questions, these details are usually presented in an introduction to the exam.

Each question element has an `id` attribute to enable it to be referred to later. Within the question element you have the text of the question, `query`, a list of possible responses, `answers`, and an explanation for the correct answer(s), `explanation`.

Answers are identified by type with the `type` attribute of the `answers` element. This can be set to `checkbox` for multiple independent options, to `radio` for mutually exclusive options, or to `text` for text entry. Each possible answer then follows, along with an optional attribute, `correct`, to denote its validity. Note that for a text-type answer, only the valid answers should appear.

Loading an Exam

To make it easier to manipulate an exam within an application, you load the XML document and create a set of integrated classes that represents it (see Listing 25-2). For reusability reasons, you place these objects in their own unit, Exams.

Listing 25-2: Examination classes

```
{ A possible answer }
TAnswer = class(TObject)
private
  FCorrect: Boolean;
  FValue: string;
public
  constructor Create(Value: string; Correct: Boolean);
```

```
    property Correct: Boolean read FCorrect write FCorrect;
    property Value: string read FValue write FValue;
  end;
  { A single question }
  TQuestion = class(TObject)
  private
    FAnswers: TList;
    FAnswerType: TAnswerType;
    FExplanation: string;
    FId: string;
    FQuery: string;
    FValidAnswers: TStringList;
    procedure Add(Answer: TAnswer);
    function GetAnswer(Index: Integer): TAnswer;
    function GetAnswerCount: Byte;
    function GetValidAnswers: TStringList;
  public
    constructor Create(Id: string);
    destructor Destroy; override;
    property AnswerCount: Byte read GetAnswerCount;
    property Answers[Index: Integer]: TAnswer read GetAnswer;
    property AnswerType: TAnswerType read FArswerType write FAnswerType;
    property Explanation: string read FExplanation write FExplanation;
    property Id: string read FId write FId;
    property Query: string read FQuery write FQuery;
    property ValidAnswers: TStringList read GetValidAnswers;
    function IsValid(Response: string): Boolean;
  end;
  { The entire exam }
  TExam = class(TObject)
  private
    FDescription: string;
    FInstructions: string;
    FPassMark: Byte;
    FQuestions: TList;
    FStrictOrder: Boolean;
    FTitle: string;
    procedure Add(Question: TQuestion);
    function GetQuestion(Index: Integer): TQuestion;
    function GetQuestionById(Id: string): TQuestion;
    function GetQuestionCount: Byte;
  public
    constructor Create;
    destructor Destroy; override;
    property Description: string read FDescription write FDescription;
    property Instructions: string read FInstructions write FInstructions;
    property PassMark: Byte read FPassMark write FPassMark;
    property QuestionCount: Byte read GetQuestionCount;
    property QuestionById[Id: string]: TQuestion read GetQuestionById;
    property Questions[Index: Integer]: TQuestion read GetQuestion;
    property StrictOrder: Boolean read FStrictOrcer write FStrictOrder;
    property Title: string read FTitle write FTitle;
  end;
```

The primary class is TExam, which embodies the entire exam. It has properties for the title, description, and instruction elements from the XML document, as well as the pass mark and strict order attributes. It also maintains a list of questions as separate objects, with access by their numeric order and by their ID attribute.

The TQuestion class encapsulates a question. Here you have the identifier for the question, the query itself, the explanation of the correct answer, and a list of possible answers and their type. Another property, ValidAnswers, returns a list of correct answers for further use. A helper method, IsValid, compares a supplied response with the values above and returns a flag indicating its correctness.

Given that you have different answer formats, you need some common way to work with them. For a radio-type answer the correct response is a single selection, which can be represented by its index (starting from zero). With a check box-type answer, you may have several selections. For consistency, this is presented as a list of the indexes of the correct responses separated by commas. In this way, the radio result is merely a simpler form of the check box one, having only one value. With both of these as a single text value, you can now prepare a similar value based on the user's selections and compare the two in a consistent manner.

Text-type questions may have multiple correct values, representing equivalent terminologies or different capitalization. Given that some answers may be case-sensitive, no manipulation of the values is performed. The multiple values can be loaded into a string list to allow for simple validation of a response. Again, you can map the other two answer types into this format, just by having a list with a single item. Thus, you can represent correct responses for all the answer types as a string list and provide the same functionality for each (see Listing 25-3).

Listing 25-3: Listing valid answers

```
{ Return the valid answer(s) in string format }
function TQuestion.GetValidAnswers: TStringList;
var
  Index: Integer;
  ValidAnswers: string;
begin
  if FValidAnswers.Count = 0 then
  begin
    ValidAnswers := '';
    for Index := 0 to AnswerCount -1 do
      { For each correct answer}
      if Answers[Index].Correct then
        { Add complete answer if text type }
        if AnswerType = atText then
          FValidAnswers.Add(Answers[Index].Value)
        { Otherwise string together numeric positions }
        else
          ValidAnswers := ValidAnswers + ',' + IntToStr(Index);
    if ValidAnswers <> '' then
      FValidAnswers.Add(Copy(ValidAnswers, 2, Length(ValidAnswers)));
  end;
  Result := FValidAnswers;
end;
```

Finally, you have the TAnswer class. This just holds the text for each possible answer and a flag denoting whether or not it is a correct one.

A hierarchy of these objects is created with the LoadExam function (see Listing 25-4), which returns a reference to the new TExam. This function takes the name of the XML document to read as a parameter and passes it along to an instance of the Microsoft XML Document Object Model.

From this model you can step through each of the internal elements and process them appropriately. Properties of the TExam object are set from the top-level attributes and elements.

Listing 25-4: Loading an XML exam

```
{ Read an XML file containing the exam specification
  and convert it into the above objects }
function LoadExam(FileName: string): TExam;
var
  XMLDoc: IXMLDOMDocument;
  Exam: TExam;
  ExamNode: Integer;
  { Retrieve the attribute value from the element }
  function Attribute(Node: IXMLDOMNode; Attribute: string): string;
  var
    AttrNode: IXMLDOMNode;
  begin
    AttrNode := Node.Attributes.GetNamedItem(Attribute);
    if Assigned(AttrNode) then
      Result := AttrNode.Text
    else
      Result := '';
  end;
  { Extract the details for a question }
  procedure GetQuestion(QuestionNode: IXMLDOMElement);
  var
    Question: TQuestion;
    QstNode: Integer;
    AnsType: string;
    AnswerType: TAnswerType;
    { Extract the details for a series of answers }
    procedure GetAnswers(Answers: IXMLDOMElement);
    var
      AnsNode: Integer;
      Answer: TAnswer;
    begin
      if Answers.HasChildNodes then
        with Answers.ChildNodes do
          { Get each possible answer }
          for AnsNode := 0 to Length -1 do
          begin
            if Item[AnsNode].NodeName = AnswerTag then
            begin
              Answer :=
                TAnswer.Create(Item[AnsNode].FirstChild.NodeValue,
                  (Attribute(Item[AnsNode], CorrectAttr) = TrueValue));
              try
                { And add it to the question }
                Question.Add(Answer);
              except
                Answer.Free;
                raise;
              end;
            end;
          end;
    end;
  begin
    { Create the question }
    Question := TQuestion.Create(Attribute(QuestionNode, IdAttr));
    try
```

```
            if QuestionNode.HasChildNodes then
              with QuestionNode.ChildNodes do
                for QstNode := 0 to Length -1 do
                  { Get question values from child nodes }
                  if Item[QstNode].NodeName = QueryTag then
                    Question.Query := Item[QstNode].FirstChild.NodeValue
                  else if Item[QstNode].NodeName = ExplanationTag then
                    Question.Explanation :=
                      Item[QstNode].FirstChild.NodeValue
                  else if Item[QstNode].NodeName = AnswersTag then
                  begin
                    { Get type of answers }
                    Question.AnswerType := atText;
                    AnsType := Attribute(Item[QstNode], TypeAttr);
                    for AnswerType := Low(TAnswerType) to
                        High(TAnswerType) do
                      if AnswerTypes[AnswerType] = AnsType then
                      begin
                        Question.AnswerType := AnswerType;
                        Break;
                      end;
                    { Then load the actual values }
                    GetAnswers(IXMLDOMElement(Item[QstNode]));
                  end;
            { Validations }
            if Question.Query = '' then
              raise EExamException.Create(
                Format(MissingQuery, [Question.Id]));
            if Question.AnswerCount = 0 then
              raise EExamException.Create(
                Format(MissingAnswers, [Question.Id]));
            { And add the question to the exam }
            Exam.Add(Question);
          except
            Question.Free;
            raise;
          end;
      end;
    end;
begin
  { Create the exam }
  Exam := TExam.Create;
  try
    { Create the XML parser }
    XMLDoc := CoDOMDocument.Create;
    try
      try
        { And parse the XML document }
        if not XMLDoc.Load(FileName) then
          Abort;
      except
        raise EExamException.Create(
          Format(CannotParse, [Filename, XMLDoc.ParseError.Reason]));
      end;
      if XMLDoc.DocumentElement.NodeName <> ExamTag then
        raise EExamException.Create(Format(NotAnExam, [Filename]));
      { Get the exam attributes }
      try
        Exam.PassMark :=
          StrToInt(Attribute(XMLDoc.DocumentElement, PassMarkAttr));
      except
```

```
          Exam.PassMark := 100; { % }
      end;
      Exam.StrictOrder := (Attribute(XMLDoc.DocumentElement,
        StrictOrderAttr) = TrueValue);
      { Load child elements }
      if XMLDoc.DocumentElement.HasChildNodes then
        with XMLDoc.DocumentElement.ChildNodes do
          for ExamNode := 0 to Length -1 do
            { Get exam values from child nodes }
            if Item[ExamNode].NodeName = TitleTag then
              Exam.Title := Item[ExamNode].FirstChild.NodeValue
            else if Item[ExamNode].NodeName = DescriptionTag then
              Exam.Description := Item[ExamNode].FirstChild.NodeValue
            else if Item[ExamNode].NodeName = InstructionsTag then
              Exam.Instructions := Item[ExamNode].FirstChild.NodeValue
            { Process each question }
            else if Item[ExamNode].NodeName = QuestionTag then
              GetQuestion(IXMLDOMElement(Item[ExamNode]))
            else if (Item[ExamNode].NodeType = NODE_ENTITY_REFERENCE)
                and (Item[ExamNode].FirstChild.NodeName = QuestionTag)
                then
              GetQuestion(IXMLDOMElement(Item[ExamNode].FirstChild));
      { Validations }
      if Exam.QuestionCount = 0 then
        raise EExamException.Create(MissingQuestions);
    finally
      XMLDoc := nil;
    end;
  except
    Exam.Free;
    raise;
  end;
  Result := Exam;
end;
```

When a question is encountered, you branch to another routine that creates a new `TQuestion` object, fills its properties and attaches it to the exam. Similarly, multiple answers are handled in another routine. Custom exceptions are raised if structural anomalies are found, such as an examination with no questions or a question with no answers.

User Tracking

The classes established earlier provide a static view of a test, as extracted from an appropriate XML document. In conjunction with these, you need some way of tracking a user's interactions with that exam. So you create the `TUserSession` class (see Listing 25-5).

Listing 25-5: Tracking a user's progress

```
  { The user's answers to the questions }
  TUserSession = class(TPersistent)
  private
    FAnswers: TStringList;
    FExam: TExam;
    function GetAnswer(QuestionId: string): string;
    function GetAnswered: Integer;
    function GetCorrect: Integer;
```

```
    function GetIsAnswered(QuestionId: string): Boolean;
    function GetQuestionId(Index: Integer): string;
    function GetQuestionCount: Integer;
    function GetScore: Integer;
    procedure SetAnswer(QuestionId, UserAnswer: string);
  public
    constructor Create(Exam: TExam);
    destructor Destroy; override;
    property Answer[QuestionId: string]: string read GetAnswer
      write SetAnswer;
    property Answered: Integer read GetAnswered;
    property Correct: Integer read GetCorrect;
    property Exam: TExam read FExam;
    property IsAnswered[QuestionId: string]: Boolean read GetIsAnswered;
    property QuestionId[Index: Integer]: string read GetQuestionId;
    property QuestionCount: Integer read GetQuestionCount;
    property Score: Integer read GetScore;
    procedure InitialiseQuestions;
  end;
```

On creation, a user session is associated with a single test (and this cannot be changed). Then you need to add properties that record the user's responses to each question, Answer, and can provide statistics on their progress, Answered, Correct, and Score.

Although the questions that make up an exam are the same for every user, their order may be different. Once a user session is created and attached to an exam, a method is called to establish the specific order for this session, InitializeQuestions (see Listing 25-6). First, this routine clears out any existing responses and lists the questions in order. A string list keeps track of the responses (and also the order of the questions). Using the Values property of the string list allows you to associate an answer with each question ID. Since at the start there are no answers, and given that the Values property does not store anything (not even the key value) when the associated value is blank, you must introduce a special value to denote this—Unanswered.

Listing 25-6: Initializing a user session

```
{ Randomize the order of the questions (if appropriate) }
procedure TUserSession.InitializeQuestions;
var
  Index: Integer;
begin
  { Load the question ids as unanswered }
  FAnswers.Clear;
  for Index := 0 to Exam.QuestionCount -1 do
    FAnswers.Values[Exam.Questions[Index].Id] := Unanswered;
  { If cannot reorder or nothing to reorder then finished }
  if Exam.StrictOrder or (Exam.QuestionCount < 2) then
    Exit;
  { Shuffle the questions }
  Randomize;
  for Index := FAnswers.Count -1 downto 1 do
    FAnswers.Exchange(Random(Index + 1), Index);
end;
```

Next the routine checks the exam to see whether the questions can appear in any order, and exits if they must appear as given. Otherwise, you shuffle the entries in the string list to vary the question order. The Randomize procedure ensures that a new seed is chosen for the random number generator. Then you step through the list, selecting one entry at random from the remainder to swap with the current entry.

Now when you iterate through the list in index order, you find questions in a random order. The QuestionId property returns this information, and can then be used to access the corresponding question object from the exam itself.

Exam Application

Now that you have your XML document loaded into objects, you can wrap a Delphi application around them to administer the examination. Note that the objects described above only model the examination and a user taking it; they do not assume any kind of presentation, making their reuse possible in different front ends.

Your main form contains a TPageControl that shows one of three pages: an introduction, a single question, or a progress and score page. The application accepts the name of the XML document to read as a command-line parameter. It passes this to the LoadExam method and gets back the corresponding TExam object. A new user session is then created and the introductory page is populated and displayed (see Figure 25-1).

Buttons along the bottom of the screen provide navigation, with the current question being tracked by the FCurQuestion variable. For generic navigation processing you have all the buttons call a common routine, btnNextPreviousClick (see Listing 25-7), and encode the direction of movement in each one's Tag property by setting it to either –1 or +1. The Start button on the introductory page also uses this technique, functioning as a Next button.

Figure 25-1: Introduction to the exam.

Listing 25-7: Navigating the questions

```
{ Go to the next/previous question }
procedure TfrmExam.btnNextPreviousClick(Sender: TObject);
begin
  ProcessCurQuestion;
  FCurQuestion := FCurQuestion + TBitBtn(Sender).Tag;
  if FCurQuestion > FExam.QuestionCount -1 then
    ShowScore
  else
    ShowCurQuestion;
end;
```

As each question is accessed, you must first process any answer(s) to the previous question (as shown in Listing 25-8). Depending on the answer type, you construct a response by concatenating selected index values (radio or check box types) or by taking the entered text. This is given to the user session object to store against the current question ID. Of course, if the question has already been answered, no changes are allowed.

Listing 25-8: Saving an answer

```
{ Process the answers provided for the current question }
procedure TfrmExam.ProcessCurQuestion;
var
  QuestionId: string;
begin
  if FCurQuestion = -1 then
    Exit;
  QuestionId := FSession.QuestionId[FCurQuestion];
  { A question can only be answered once }
  if not FSession.IsAnswered[QuestionId] then
    ProcessQuestion(FExam.QuestionById[QuestionId]);
end;
{ Process the answers provided for the specified question }
procedure TfrmExam.ProcessQuestion(Question: TQuestion);
var
  Index: Integer;
  Answer: string;
begin
  Answer := '';
  case Question.AnswerType of
    atCheckbox:
      { Find index(es) of selected checkbox(es) }
      for Index := 0 to Question.AnswerCount -1 do
        with TCheckBox(FindComponent('cbxAnswer' +
            IntToStr(Index + 1))) do
          if Checked then
            Answer := Answer + ',' + IntToStr(Index);
    atRadio:
      { Find index of selected radio button }
      for Index := 0 to Question.AnswerCount -1 do
        with TRadioButton(FindComponent('rabAnswer' +
            IntToStr(Index + 1))) do
          if Checked then
            Answer := Answer + ',' + IntToStr(Index);
    atText:
      Answer := ',' + edtAnswer.Text;
  end;
  if Answer <> '' then
    FSession.Answer[Question.Id] :=
      Copy(Answer, 2, Length(Answer) -1);
end;
```

Using the updated value in `FCurQuestion`, you ask the session object to identify which question you are currently on. Then, you extract its details from the exam object (as shown in Listing 25-9). The question number and query text are copied directly to their corresponding fields. Display of the answers depends on their type.

Listing 25-9: Displaying a question

```
{ Present the specified question }
procedure TfrmExam.ShowQuestion(Question: TQuestion;
  CurQuestion: Integer; Response: string);
var
```

```
    Index: Integer;
  Answered, Selected: Boolean;
  Answers: string;
  { Has the user selected this checkbox/radio button? }
  function UserSelected(Index: Integer): Boolean;
  begin
    Result := (Pos(',' + IntToStr(Index) + ',', ',' +
      Response + ',') > 0);
  end;
begin
  pgcExam.ActivePage := tshQuestion;
  { Has the user answered this question? }
  Answered := (Response <> '');
  { Set page header }
  lblQuestion.Caption   := IntToStr(FCurQuestion + 1);
  memQuestion.Lines.Text := Question.Query;
  btnNext.SetFocus;
  { Set answer fields }
  case Question.AnswerType of
    atCheckbox:
      begin
        pgcAnswers.ActivePage := tshCheckBox;
        tshCheckBox.Enabled   := not Answered;
        for Index := 0 to Question.AnswerCount -1 do
        begin
          Selected := Answered and UserSelected(Index);
          { Set checkbox }
          with TCheckBox(FindComponent(
            'cbxAnswer' + IntToStr(Index + 1))) do
          begin
            Caption := Question.Answers[Index].Value;
            Checked := Selected;
            Visible := True;
          end;
          { If already answered show correctness }
          with TImage(FindComponent(
            'imgCheckbox' + IntToStr(Index + 1))) do
          begin
            Visible := Answered and Question.Answers[Index].Correct;
            Picture.Assign(
              FCorrect[Question.Answers[Index].Correct and Selected]);
          end;
        end;
        { Set focus }
        if tshCheckBox.Enabled then
          cbxAnswer1.SetFocus;
        { Hide extranous answers }
        for Index := Question.AnswerCount to FmaxAnswers -1 do
        begin
          TCheckBox(FindComponent('cbxAnswer' + IntToStr(Index + 1))).
            Visible := False;
          TImage(FindComponent('imgCheckbox' + IntToStr(Index + 1))).
            Visible := False;
        end;
      end;
    atRadio:
      begin
        pgcAnswers.ActivePage := tshRadio;
        tshRadio.Enabled    := not Answered;
        for Index := 0 to Question.AnswerCount -1 do
```

```
      begin
        Selected := Answered and UserSelected(Index);
        { Set radio button }
        with TRadioButton(FindComponent(
          'rabAnswer' + IntToStr(Index + 1))) do
        begin
          Caption := Question.Answers[Index].Value;
          Checked := Selected;
          Visible := True;
        end;
        { If already answered show correctness }
        with TImage(FindComponent(
          'imgRadio' + IntToStr(Index + 1))) do
        begin
          Visible := Answered and Question.Answers[Index].Correct;
          Picture.Assign(
            FCorrect[Question.Answers[Index].Correct and Selected]);
        end;
      end;
      { Set focus }
      if tshRadio.Enabled then
      begin
        rabAnswer1.SetFocus;
        rabAnswer1.Checked := False;
      end;
      { Hide extranous answers }
      for Index := Question.AnswerCount to FmaxAnswers -1 do
      begin
        TRadioButton(FindComponent(
          'rabAnswer' + IntToStr(Index + 1))).Visible := False;
        TImage(FindComponent('imgRadio' + IntToStr(Index + 1))).
          Visible := False;
      end;
    end;
  atText:
    begin
      pgcAnswers.ActivePage := tshText;
      tshText.Enabled       := not Answered;
      { Set text }
      edtAnswer.Text := Response;
      { If already answered show correctness }
      imgText.Visible := Answered;
      imgText.Picture.Assign(FCorrect[Question.IsValid(Response)]);
      { Set focus }
      if tshText.Enabled then
        edtAnswer.SetFocus;
    end;
end;
{ Show the explanation if already answered }
pnlExplanation.Visible := Answered;
if Answered then
begin
  Answers := '';
  if Question.AnswerType = atText then
  begin
    { List valid text answers }
    for Index := 0 to Question.ValidAnswers.Count -1 do
      Answers := Answers + ', ' + Question.ValidAnswers[Index];
    Answers := Accepted + ' ' +
      Copy(Answers, 3, Length(Answers)) + #13#10;
```

```
    end;
    memExplanation.Lines.Text := Answers + Question.Explanation;
  end;
  { Dis/enable navigation buttons }
  btnPrevious.Enabled := (FCurQuestion > 0);
end;
```

Each answer type has a corresponding tab on a second `TPageControl` embedded in the question page. They contain appropriate controls for the different answer styles. You may have up to five answers for radio and check box types, or a single edit control for text ones. The `FindComponent` method lets you locate individual controls as you process answers other than text types. Given a known base name, you just append the index for each answer and retrieve the matching component. When reviewing responses, the entire tab is disabled, preventing any further updates. See Figure 25-2 for an example question that uses radio buttons.

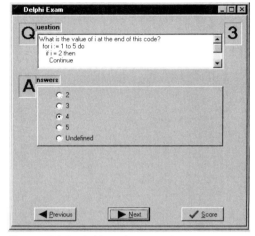

Figure 25-2: Asking the question.

Alongside each answer is an image control, which indicates the correctness of the answer. The image is only visible once the question has been answered and the user is reviewing their responses (see Figure 25-3). To manage the icons that appear here you use two invisible image controls on the form itself that are loaded at design time. These can then be assigned to the other images as required. Icons are used so that their background easily blends in with the current color scheme.

The explanation for each question is also only shown once the question has been answered. Its presence is simply set by adjusting the visibility of an underlying panel that contains all the necessary controls. For text-type answers you include a list of the valid responses at the start of the explanation, since they would otherwise never be visible.

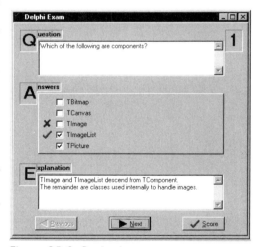

Figure 25-3: Reviewing an answer.

Finally, the score page is available on request (see Figure 25-4), allowing the user to follow their progress through the test. On the left it shows a list of all the questions in the exam and indicates their current status with an image (unanswered ones are blank). A question can be reviewed by double-clicking its entry in the list. On the right are the statistics for the exam, including the all-important measure—did I pass?

In a stricter examination, you may not allow access to previous questions nor the score page until the end of the exam. Once all the questions were answered you could show the results and allow the user to go back through the questions to review their responses. This can be easily done through setting the navigation buttons' Visible properties at appropriate times.

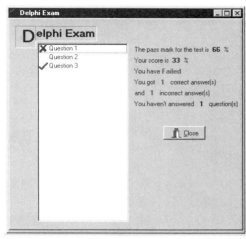

Figure 25-4: Have I passed?

NOTE The sample project described here takes the name of the exam to administer as a command-line parameter. Several exams accompany the program: DelphiExam.xml tests your knowledge of Delphi, DelphiExam2.xml has the same content but places each question in a separate XML document (DelphiQx.xml) that are recombined using entities, and PythonExam.xml is a very silly exam on *Monty Python and the Holy Grail*. Have fun!

Summary

Separating the examination content from its presentation allows you to offer different access methods to the same test. With XML it is possible to have the individual questions in separate documents, and then combine these into an integrated test using external entities. This would allow the questions to be developed separately from the test as a whole, and possibly be reused in other tests.

The Delphi application presented here demonstrates a Windows program interface to the exam. However, the underlying classes could be easily reused in a different environment, such as presenting the test over the Internet as discussed in the next chapter.

Chapter 26
Examination XML — Web Client

As mentioned in the previous chapter, XML lets you separate the content from its presentation. The examination document discussed in that chapter is read and administered by a customized Delphi client. To show how XML is reused in other situations, this chapter describes a Web-based front end to the same document (or any other exam for that matter).

Since the exam appears in a browser under this application, you can use XSL Transformations to convert the XML content directly into HTML. This simplifies the generation process as you do not have to write code to perform the substitutions necessary with Delphi's page producer components. Furthermore, you can adjust the look of the site through modifications to the stylesheets without a recompilation of the application.

The Microsoft XML package provides methods to apply XSLT stylesheets to documents (or even individual nodes), so the Web application is based around its abilities. Microsoft has also introduced additional interfaces and objects to improve the performance of the transformation process.

Exam Transformations

You need three different transformations to administer an exam: one for the introduction, one for an individual question, and one for the results. This parallels the three tabs used in the standalone Delphi version.

XSLT is a powerful language for specifying the conversion, letting you locate any section of an XML document and reformat its contents with relative ease. Recall that any content and any tags in the stylesheet that do not belong to the XSLT namespace are passed along to the output. Thus it is simple to embed the HTML tags within the transformation.

NOTE HTML tags within an XSLT document must be well-formed since they are part of an XML document. So, all tags must be closed (including ones like img and hr), and all attributes must be properly quoted.

Listing 26-1 shows the XSLT stylesheet for displaying and processing a single question from the exam. It starts with an `xsl:stylesheet` element that has a namespace declaration for the transformation tags. This namespace must appear like this (although you could alter the prefix) for the transformation engine to function correctly. After setting up the basic HTML page in the whole-document template, it selects a single question node and formats its contents into a form so that any response can be dealt with.

Listing 26-1: Transformation for a question

```xml
<?xml version="1.0" encoding="UTF-8"?>
<!-- Examination Question Stylesheet
     Show a single question with possible answers
     Written by Keith Wood, 16 June, 2000 -->
<xsl:stylesheet version="1.0"
    xmlns:xsl="http://www.w3.org/1999/XSL/Transform">
  <!-- The answer(s) selected by the examinee -->
  <xsl:param name="answer">tobject</xsl:param>
  <!-- The name of the script processing this page -->
  <xsl:param name="engine">webexam.dll</xsl:param>
  <!-- The id of the question to display -->
  <xsl:param name="qid">Q3</xsl:param>
  <!-- The question's ordinal position in the exam -->
  <xsl:param name="qno">2</xsl:param>
  <!-- Set to 'true' to show results,
       'false' for initial questioning -->
  <xsl:param name="results">true</xsl:param>
  <!-- The user's id -->
  <xsl:param name="ses">123</xsl:param>
  <!-- The overall document -->
  <xsl:template match="/">
    <html>
    <head>
    <title><xsl:value-of select="exam/title"/>–Question
      <xsl:value-of select="$qno"/></title>
    </head>
    <body>
    <xsl:apply-templates select="id($qid)"/>
    <hr/>
    <p>Written by <a href="mailto:kbwood@compuserve.com">
      Keith Wood</a>.</p>
    </body>
    </html>
  </xsl:template>
  <!-- Display text for a single question -->
  <xsl:template match="question">
    <form method="post" action="{$engine}">
      <table border="0" width="100%">
        <tr><td colspan="2"><h2>Question
          <xsl:value-of select="$qno"/></h2></td>
        </tr>
        <tr><th align="right" valign="top">Query:</th>
          <td><pre><xsl:value-of select="query"/></pre></td>
        </tr>
        <tr><th align="right" valign="top">Answer:</th>
          <td>
            <table border="0">
              <xsl:apply-templates select="answers"/>
            </table>
```

```xml
            </td>
          </tr>
          <xsl:if test="$results='true'">
          <tr><th align="right" valign="top">Explanation:</th>
            <td><p><xsl:value-of select="explanation"/></p></td>
          </tr>
          </xsl:if>
      </table>
      <div align="center" xml:space="preserve">
        <input type="hidden" name="ses" value="{$ses}"/>
        <input type="hidden" name="qno" value="{$qno}"/>
        <input type="submit" name="act" value="Previous"/>
        <input type="submit" name="act" value="Next"/>
        <xsl:if test="$results='true'">
          <input type="submit" name="act" value="Results"/>
        </xsl:if>
      </div>
    </form>
</xsl:template>
<!-- Format answers for radio button/checkbox type responses -->
<xsl:template match="answers[@type!='text']/answer">
  <tr>
    <td>
      <xsl:choose>
        <xsl:when test="$results='true' and @correct='true'">
          <xsl:choose>
            <xsl:when
                test="contains($answer,string(position() -1))">
              <img src="images/correct.gif" alt="Correct"
                height="16" width="16"/>
            </xsl:when>
            <xsl:otherwise>
              <img src="images/incorrect.gif" alt="Incorrect"
                height="16" width="16"/>
            </xsl:otherwise>
          </xsl:choose>
        </xsl:when>
        <xsl:otherwise>
          <img src="images/blank.gif" height="16" width="16"/>
        </xsl:otherwise>
      </xsl:choose>
    </td>
    <td><input name="answer" type="{../@type}"
        value="{position() -1}">
      <xsl:if test="contains($answer,string(position() -1))">
        <xsl:attribute name="checked"/></xsl:if>
      </input><xsl:value-of select="."/></td>
  </tr>
</xsl:template>
<!-- Format answers for text type responses -->
<xsl:template match="answers[@type='text']">
  <tr>
    <td>
      <xsl:choose>
        <xsl:when test="$results='true'">
          <xsl:choose>
            <xsl:when test="answer=$answer">
              <img src="images/correct.gif" alt="Correct"
                height="16" width="16"/>
            </xsl:when>
```

```
        <xsl:otherwise>
          <img src="images/incorrect.gif" alt="Incorrect"
               height="16" width="16"/>
        </xsl:otherwise>
       </xsl:choose>
      </xsl:when>
      <xsl:otherwise>
        <img src="images/blank.gif" height="16" width="16"/>
      </xsl:otherwise>
     </xsl:choose>
    </td>
    <td><input name="answer" type="text" value="{$answer}"/></td>
   </tr>
   <xsl:if test="$results='true'">
   <tr>
     <td colspan="2">Valid answers:
       <xsl:apply-templates select="answer"/></td>
   </tr>
   </xsl:if>
  </xsl:template>
  <!-- Format correct answers for text type responses -->
  <xsl:template match="answers[@type='text']/answer">
    <xsl:value-of select="."/>
    <xsl:if test="position()!=last()">,</xsl:if>
  </xsl:template>
</xsl:stylesheet>
```

Obviously, the template cannot know ahead of time what question is to be transformed for a particular call. Similarly, there are several other values that change from one question to the next of which the template has no knowledge since they cannot be placed in the XML document itself. The XSLT specification provides a way to overcome these difficulties and supply the stylesheet with additional information. Through the `xsl:param` element you can pass values into the template. You retrieve these values through the `$param-name` notation within the rest of the document. Default values appear in Listing 26-1 for testing purposes (although the declarations themselves must be present), and are overwritten by the real values at run time.

The display of possible answers for a question differs significantly if the response is text-based rather than using radio buttons or check boxes. To handle this, two templates are defined with the selection pattern controlling which one appears. All `answers` and `answer` tags are processed through the following call in the question template:

```
<xsl:apply-templates select="answers"/>
```

Non-text answers then match with the template headed:

```
<xsl:template match="answers[@type!='text']/answer">
```

which means to find any `answers` element (within the current question) that has a `type` attribute not equal to `text` and return its `answer` element children. The alternative is to locate a text-type `answers` element with the other template, which returns that element itself:

```
<xsl:template match="answers[@type='text']">
```

Thereafter, you generate each individual answer as a radio button or check box (in the first case), or as a single text entry. Any existing response appears in another of the document's parameters, allowing you to indicate its current value. Figure 26-1 shows the result of applying this transformation to a question.

Another parameter determines whether or not to show the outcome of the user's response. The results parameter is set to True or False. Initially it is False, causing the suppression of any scoring markers and of any explanation for the correct answer. When set to True, images appear next to each correct answer showing whether or not the user got it right, and any necessary explanation appears. The parameter appears in several xsl:if and xsl:when tags that test its value. Figure 26-2 illustrates the view when this parameter is set to True.

Control over the exam progress comes from the HTML form that surrounds the question content, and a number of buttons placed at its bottom. These let you move to the next or previous question, or, once all questions are answered, directly to the results page. Hidden fields in the form pass vital details back to the Web application, including a session number to identify each user and the number of the current question within the exam.

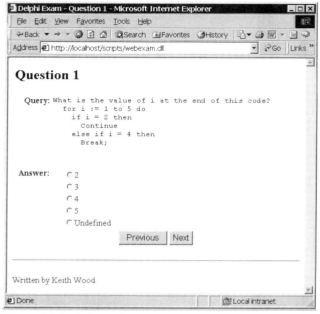

Figure 26-1: Asking the question.

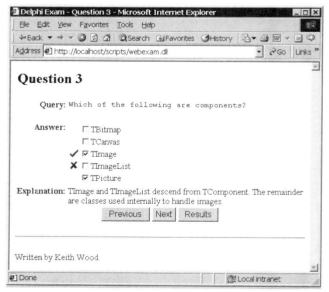

Figure 26-2: Checking your answer.

Scripting in Transformations

Since you are using the Microsoft XML package and its transformation engine, you can take advantage of some unique abilities that it provides. The engine lets you embed script within your stylesheet and invoke it in the rest of the document. Thus you can add functionality beyond the capabilities of straight XSLT. The transformation for the exam results makes use of this in scoring and presenting the list of questions for review.

To invoke the script processing you first need to declare appropriate namespaces within the xsl:stylesheet element. Following the standard XSLT namespace, you must add one for Microsoft's scripting extensions:

```
xmlns:msxsl="urn:schemas-microsoft-com:xslt"
```

then one for use with your new scripted functions:

```
xmlns:exam="urn:keith/exams"
```

These say that the msxsl prefix identifies script declarations, while the exam prefix indicates calls to those functions from the stylesheet body. Listing 26-2 shows these declarations and their use in the stylesheet.

Listing 26-2: Using scripting in the transformation

```xml
<?xml version="1.0" encoding="UTF-8"?>
<!-- Examination Results Stylesheet
     Show the outcome of the examination,
     with links back to the questions
     Written by Keith Wood, 16 June, 2000 -->
<xsl:stylesheet version="1.0"
    xmlns:xsl="http://www.w3.org/1999/XSL/Transform"
    xmlns:msxsl="urn:schemas-microsoft-com:xslt"
    xmlns:exam="urn:keith/exams">
  <!-- Are the questions answered correctly -->
  <xsl:param name="answers">Y N</xsl:param>
  <!-- The name of the script processing this page -->
  <xsl:param name="engine">webexam.dll</xsl:param>
  <!-- The user's id -->
  <xsl:param name="ses">123</xsl:param>
  <!-- Functions to count answers -->
  <msxsl:script language="JScript" implements-prefix="exam">
    <![CDATA[
    // How many answered?
    function getCount(answers) {
      var count = 0;
      for (index = 0; index < answers.length; index++)
        if (answers.charAt(index) != ' ')
          count++;
      return count;
    }
    // How many correct?
    function getScore(answers) {
      var score = 0;
      for (index = 0; index < answers.length; index++)
        if (answers.charAt(index) == 'Y')
          score++;
      return score;
```

```xml
      }
    ]]>
  </msxsl:script>
  <!-- The overall document -->
  <xsl:template match="/">
    <html>
    <head>
    <title><xsl:value-of select="exam/title"/> Results</title>
    <style>
      .passed { color=green; font-weight=bold; }
      .failed { color=red; font-weight=bold; }
    </style>
    </head>
    <body>
    <xsl:apply-templates select="exam"/>
    <hr/>
    <p>Written by <a href="mailto:kbwood@compuserve.com">
      Keith Wood</a>.</p>
    </body>
    </html>
  </xsl:template>
  <!-- Display outcome of examination -->
  <xsl:template match="exam">
    <h1><xsl:value-of select="title"/> Results</h1>
    <p><xsl:value-of select="description"/></p>
    <table border="0" width="100%">
      <tr>
        <td width="50%" valign="top">
          <p>This test has a pass mark of
          <strong><xsl:value-of select="@pass_mark"/>%</strong>.</p>
          <p>You have answered <strong>
            <xsl:value-of select="exam:getCount(string($answers))"/>
            </strong> out of <strong>
            <xsl:value-of select="count(question)"/></strong>
            questions.</p>
          <p>Your score is <strong>
            <xsl:value-of select="exam:getScore(string($answers))"/>
            </strong>.</p>
          <xsl:choose>
            <xsl:when test="(exam:getScore(string($answers))*100 div
                count(question))>=number(@pass_mark)">
              <p>You have <span class="passed">passed</span>.</p>
            </xsl:when>
            <xsl:otherwise>
              <p>You have <span class="failed">failed</span>.</p>
            </xsl:otherwise>
          </xsl:choose>
        </td>
        <td width="50%" valign="top">
          <xsl:apply-templates select="question"/>
        </td>
      </tr>
    </table>
  </xsl:template>
  <!-- Provide a link back to the question -->
  <xsl:template match="question">
    <xsl:choose>
      <xsl:when test="substring($answers, position(), 1)='Y'">
        <img src="images/correct.gif" alt="Correct"
          height="16" width="16"/>
```

```
        </xsl:when>
        <xsl:when test="substring($answers, position(), 1)='N'">
          <img src="images/incorrect.gif" alt="Incorrect"
            height="16" width="16"/>
        </xsl:when>
        <xsl:otherwise>
          <img src="images/blank.gif" height="16" width="16"/>
        </xsl:otherwise>
      </xsl:choose>
      <a href="{$engine}?ses={$ses}&amp;act=Goto&amp;qno={position()}">
        Question <xsl:value-of select="position()"/>
      </a><br/>
    </xsl:template>
</xsl:stylesheet>
```

The actual script appears within the msxsl:script element, which takes attributes denoting what language is being used and the namespace prefix to match up with. In this example, one function counts the total number of questions that have been answered, while another counts the number of correct answers. Both operate on a string passed to the stylesheet as a parameter (answers). It contains one character for each question in the exam in order. A Y indicates that the question at that position was answered correctly, an N shows an incorrect answer, and an empty string means that this question has not been answered at all.

TIP Embed all your script within a CDATA section in the msxsl:script element. This means that you do not have to worry about escaping any metacharacters that appear in the script itself.

To obtain the result of one of these functions you refer to it with the declared namespace prefix, generally within an xsl:value-of element:

```
<p>Your score is <strong><xsl:value-of
select="exam:getScore(string($answers))"/></strong>.</p>
```

The answers parameter value is also tested to determine which image to display next to each question reference. Use the standard substring function from XSLT to test the individual character corresponding to that question and include an appropriate image.

```
<xsl:when test="substring($answers, position(), 1)='Y'">
  <img src="images/correct.gif" alt="Correct" height="16" width="16"/>
</xsl:when>
```

Following the image is a link back to that question so that you can easily review your answer and any explanation. Several other parameter values for the stylesheet are included in the link. The final result is shown in Figure 26-3.

```
<a href="{$engine}?ses={$ses}&amp;act=Goto&amp;qno={position()}">
  Question <xsl:value-of select="position()"/>
</a>
```

NOTE You do not need to use the scripting available through Microsoft's XSLT engine, since doing so restricts you to using only this implementation. Instead, you can perform all the necessary calculations in Delphi and pass just the results over as further xsl:param fields. Scripting is shown here simply to demonstrate its use.

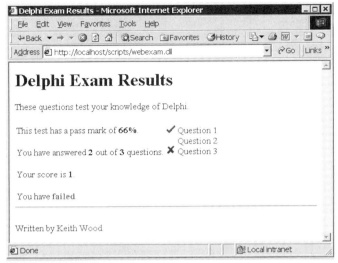

Figure 26-3: The outcome of the examination.

Web Application Initialization

To create the Web application that administers the examinations online, you generate a new ISAPI-based Web Server Application. This provides the necessary functionality to accept HTTP requests from the Web server and present them for processing within the program.

As part of the discussion of Microsoft's XML DOM package in Chapter 9, you saw the IXSLTemplate and IXSLProcessor interfaces. These provide the performance benefits mentioned earlier. Normally, when applying a transformation you load in the original XML document as a DOM structure, then load the XSLT stylesheet as another DOM, and call the TransformNode method to process the conversion. However, this involves the compilation of the stylesheet definitions before they can be used in the process.

Since the stylesheets remain fairly static, pre-compiling them and keeping the resulting object around produces a performance boost. It can then be applied to numerous XML documents without further preparation. The IXSLTemplate interface describes an object that does just that. A stylesheet is loaded into a DOM and passed to the template object, whereupon it is compiled. When you want to apply a transformation, you ask the template for an IXSLProcessor object that you supply with an XML document and from which you retrieve the formatted output.

There are three stylesheets used for the online examination application and these are applied over and over as exams are requested. So it would be useful to have these loaded and prepared when the program starts, ready for them to be called upon as needed. The best place for this type of setup is the initialization section of the Web module unit. Code in this section executes before anything else in the unit, letting you establish the environment for the main code. Listing 26-3 shows the initialization and finalization sections that load in the XSLT stylesheets.

Listing 26-3: Initialization for the transformations

```
initialization
  BaseDir  := 'c:\inetpub\scripts\';
  { Create lists for exams and user sessions }
  ExamList := TStringList.Create;
  Sessions := TStringList.Create;
  XMLDocs  := TInterfaceList.Create;
  { Create template for introduction stylesheet }
  XSLIntro                  := CoFreeThreadedDOMDocument.Create;
  if not XSLIntro.Load(BaseDir + ExamIntro) then
    MessageDlg('Couldn''t load exam intro'#13 +
      XSLIntro.ParseError.Reason, mtError, [mbOK], 0);
  XSLIntroTemplate          := CoXSLTemplate.Create;
  XSLIntroTemplate.Stylesheet := XSLIntro;
  { Create template for individual question stylesheet }
  XSLQuestion               := CoFreeThreadedDOMDocument.Create;
  if not XSLQuestion.Load(BaseDir + ExamQuestion) then
    MessageDlg('Couldn''t load exam question'#13 +
      XSLQuestion.ParseError.Reason, mtError, [mbOK], 0);
  XSLQuestionTemplate       := CoXSLTemplate.Create;
  XSLQuestionTemplate.Stylesheet := XSLQuestion;
  { Create template for results stylesheet }
  XSLResults                := CoFreeThreadedDOMDocument.Create;
  if not XSLResults.Load(BaseDir + ExamResults) then
    MessageDlg('Couldn''t load exam results'#13 +
      XSLResults.ParseError.Reason, mtError, [mbOK], 0);
  XSLResultsTemplate        := CoXSLTemplate.Create;
  XSLResultsTemplate.Stylesheet := XSLResults;
finalization
  { Release resources }
  for Index := 0 to ExamList.Count -1 do
    ExamList.Objects[Index].Free;
  ExamList.Free;
  for Index := 0 to Sessions.Count -1 do
    Sessions.Objects[Index].Free;
  Sessions.Free;
  XMLDocs.Free;
  XSLIntroTemplate    := nil;
  XSLIntro            := nil;
  XSLQuestionTemplate := nil;
  XSLQuestion         := nil;
  XSLResultsTemplate  := nil;
  XSLResults          := nil;
end.
```

A template object is created for each stylesheet through the `CoXSLTemplate` CoClass. You can use `CoXSLTemplate30` instead to tie the implementation to this version of the XML package. The stylesheet documents themselves are loaded into DOMs that are then passed to the templates through their `Stylesheet` property. Since templates are designed to share a stylesheet between many different requests, you must use a free-threading model DOM for the stylesheet document. The `CoFreeThreadedDOMDocument` CoClass creates just what you need. During the finalization processing these global objects are released by setting their references to `nil` (as mentioned before, this is not strictly necessary since Delphi will release them once their variables go out of scope anyway).

Also created in the start-up code are three lists. The first, `ExamList`, is a string list that links names of exams to `TExam` objects. This lets you cache exam definitions (from the XML documents) on their first request and reuse them subsequently. Similarly, the `XMLDocs` list contains a set of matched references to the DOMs for those exams. These are used when applying the various transformations. Finally, there is another string list, `Sessions`, which links session IDs to `TUserSession` objects. This list keeps track of what users have requested exams and where in that exam they are.

Applying the Transformations

The Web module used in this application needs no page producer or any other components on it. You perform all the output generation in code through the XSLT templates loaded above. All that is required is a single action to receive the users' requests.

1. Right-click on the Web module and select **Action Editor**.
2. Add a new action and set it to be the default.
3. Create an `OnAction` handler for the action and enter the code shown in Listing 26-4.

Listing 26-4: Transforming the exam document

```
{ Generate the appropriate HTML page from the exam and user responses }
procedure TwmdExam.wmbExamwacExamAction(Sender: TObject;
  Request: TWebRequest; Response: TWebResponse; var Handled: Boolean);
var
  CurQuestion: Integer;
  Exam: TExam;
  Fields: TStrings;
  QuestionId: string;
  ScriptName: string;
  Session: TUserSession;
  SessionId: string;
  UserAction: string;
  XMLDoc: IXMLDOMDocument;
  XSLProcessor: IXSLProcessor;
{ Save any answers from the current page }
procedure ProcessAnswers(QuestionId: string);
var
  Answer: string;
  Index: Integer;
  Question: TQuestion;
begin
  { If already answered then can't change it }
  if Session.IsAnswered[QuestionId] then
    Exit;
  { Retrieve answer(s) based on type }
  Question := Session.Exam.QuestionById[QuestionId];
  if Question.AnswerType = atCheckbox then
  begin
    Answer := '';
    { Could be multiple selections }
    for Index := 0 to Fields.Count -1 do
      if Fields.Names[Index] = AnswerField then
        Answer := Answer + ',' +
```

```
          Copy(Fields[Index], Length(AnswerField) + 2, 255);
    if Answer <> '' then
      Delete(Answer, 1, 1);
  end
  else
    Answer := Fields.Values[AnswerField];
  Session.Answer[QuestionId] := Answer;
end;
{ Initialization—extract common fields and save any answer }
procedure Initialize;
var
  ExamName: string;
  Index: Integer;
begin
  { Extract the script location }
  ScriptName := Request.ScriptName;
  { Set up a pointer to the request fields }
  if Request.Method = GetMethod then
    Fields   := Request.QueryFields
  else
    Fields   := Request.ContentFields;
  { Retrieve the current session details }
  SessionId := Fields.Values[SessionField];
  Index     := Sessions.IndexOf(SessionId);
  if Index > -1 then
  begin
    { Retrieve previous session details }
    Session := TUserSession(Sessions.Objects[Index]);
    Exam    := Session.Exam;
    XMLDoc  := XMLDocs[ExamList.IndexOfObject(Exam)] as
       IXMLDOMDocument;
  end
  else
  begin
    ExamName := Fields.Values[ExamField];
    Index    := ExamList.IndexOf(ExamName);
    if Index > -1 then
    begin
      { Retrieve existing exam }
      Exam   := TExam(ExamList.Objects[Index]);
      XMLDoc := XMLDocs[Index] as IXMLDOMDocument;
    end
    else
    begin
      { Load new exam }
      Exam   := LoadExam(BaseDir + ExamName);
      { Create XML object model for exam }
      XMLDoc := CoDOMDocument.Create;
      if not XMLDoc.Load(BaseDir + ExamName) then
        raise Exception.Create('Couldn''t load exam doc'#13 +
          XMLDoc.ParseError.Reason);
      { Cache for future reference }
      ExamList.AddObject(ExamName, Exam);
      XMLDocs.Add(XMLDoc);
    end;
    { Create a new user session }
    Session := TUserSession.Create(Exam);
    repeat
      SessionId := IntToStr(Random(SessionRange));
    until Sessions.IndexOf(SessionId) = -1;
```

```pascal
      Sessions.AddObject(SessionId, Session);
    end;
    { Extract the user requested action }
    UserAction := Fields.Values[ActionField];
    try
      { Get the current question number }
      CurQuestion := StrToInt(Fields.Values[QuestionField]);
      QuestionId  := Session.QuestionId[CurQuestion -1];
      { Do we need to save any current answers? }
      if UserAction <> GotoAction then
        ProcessAnswers(QuestionId);
    except
      { Ignore }
    end;
  end;
  { Has the exam been completed? }
  function Completed: Boolean;
  begin
    Result := (Session.Answered = Session.QuestionCount);
  end;
  { Compile a string representing the results of
    answering the questions-'Y' for correct,
    'N' for incorrect, ' ' for unanswered }
  function CompileAnswers: string;
  const
    Correct: array [Boolean] of string = ('N', 'Y');
  var
    Index: Integer;
    QuestionId: string;
  begin
    for Index := 0 to Session.QuestionCount -1 do
    begin
      QuestionId := Session.QuestionId[Index];
      if Session.IsAnswered[QuestionId] then
        Result := Result + Correct[Exam.QuestionById[QuestionId].
          IsValid(Session.Answer[QuestionId])]
      else
        Result := Result + ' ';
    end;
  end;
  { Create an XSL processor and set common properties }
  function PrepareProcessor(XSLTemplate: IXSLTemplate): IXSLProcessor;
  begin
    Result       := XSLTemplate.CreateProcessor;
    Result.AddParameter(EngineParam, ScriptName, '');
    Result.AddParameter(SessionParam, SessionId, '');
    Result.Input := XMLDoc;
  end;
begin
  try
    { Extract common fields and save any answer }
    Initialize;
    { Move to a new question }
    if UserAction = NextAction then
      Inc(CurQuestion)
    else if UserAction = PreviousAction then
    begin
      Dec(CurQuestion);
      if CurQuestion < 1 then
        CurQuestion := 1;
```

```
    end;
    { Perform the requested action }
    if (UserAction = ResultsAction) or
      (CurQuestion > Session.QuestionCount) then
    begin
      { Show the scoring page }
      XSLProcessor     := PrepareProcessor(XSLResultsTemplate);
      XSLProcessor.AddParameter(AnswersParam, CompileAnswers, '');
      XSLProcessor.Transform;
      Response.Content := XSLProcessor.Output;
    end
    else if (UserAction = NextAction) or
      (UserAction = PreviousAction) or
      (UserAction = GotoAction) then
    begin
      { Show a question page }
      QuestionId       := Session.QuestionId[CurQuestion -1];
      XSLProcessor     := PrepareProcessor(XSLQuestionTemplate);
      XSLProcessor.AddParameter(AnswerParam,
        Session.Answer[QuestionId], '');
      XSLProcessor.AddParameter(QuestionIdParam, QuestionId, '');
      XSLProcessor.AddParameter(QuestionParam, CurQuestion, '');
      XSLProcessor.AddParameter(ResultsParam, Completed, '');
      XSLProcessor.Transform;
      Response.Content := XSLProcessor.Output;
    end
    else
    begin
      { Default-show the introduction }
      XSLProcessor     := PrepareProcessor(XSLIntroTemplate);
      XSLProcessor.Transform;
      Response.Content := XSLProcessor.Output;
    end;
  finally
    Response.ContentType := 'text/html';
    Handled              := True;
    XMLDoc               := nil;
    XSLProcessor         := nil;
  end;
end;
```

Each request first goes to an initialization procedure that establishes the environment for that particular user. It extracts the session ID from the request parameters and retrieves the corresponding `TUserSession` object from the `Sessions` list. A new session is generated and added to the list if one does not currently exist. Session IDs are randomly generated numbers in a specified range to limit cross-talk between users.

If the session exists, then it has a reference to the associated exam object. From the latter you also retrieve the corresponding DOM. If there was no session, then you check the cache for the specified exam, loading it if it is not there and retrieving it otherwise.

TIP There are problems with storing DOM references (`IXMLDOMDocument`) directly in a normal list since this does not handle the reference counting properly. However, starting with Delphi 4, you can use the `TInterfaceList` class for just this purpose.

Once the necessary objects are found, processing can begin. From the request parameters you extract the current question number and any action specified by the user. If there is a current question, you also need to save away any answer from that page.

The `ProcessAnswers` procedure first checks whether or not the specified question has already been answered, since you cannot change your answer once entered. In the case of a question that has multiple possible answers (presented as check boxes), you must compile the list of choices selected to be the final answer (there may be multiple answer fields in the request parameters). Otherwise, just use the value of the single answer field. The answer value is saved to the user session object against the current question.

The user action field is then checked for a navigation request, either incrementing or decrementing the current question number. Now you must decide which transformation to apply depending on the current state of the examination. If the user asked to see the results page, or they have moved on from the last question, you generate the final page showing the exam outcome. Otherwise, if an action was supplied, you display the page for the current question. If none of these situations applies, you present the introduction page.

A transformation is initiated by creating an `IXSLProcessor` object from the appropriate template. This is a single-use object for the encapsulated transformation. Its `Input` property is set to the XML DOM that represents the exam. Pass parameters to the processor through its `AddParameter` method, supplying its base name, new value, and any namespace URI. The `Transform` method of the processor initiates the actual transformation, with the result available from the `Output` property as a string. Return this value to the browser through the `Response` object.

Finishing Up

An HTML page provides the initial access to the online examination program (see Figure 26-4). It lists each exam by a descriptive name and links that to the Web application, passing along the name of the XML document that defines the exam content. Since no other parameters appear, the program defaults to the introduction page for that exam, as shown in Figure 26-5.

```
<a href="/scripts/webexam.dll?exam=DelphiExam.xml">Delphi</a>
```

To deploy the application, you need to copy the ISAPI DLL to the `scripts` directory on the Web server. In that same location you also need to place the examination XML documents (DelphiExam.xml, PythonExam.xml), their DTD (Exam.dtd), and all the XSLT stylesheets (Exam*.xsl). To initiate the exam sessions, you copy the Exams.html page to the normal Web root (wwwroot) and invoke it with `http://localhost/Exams.html`.

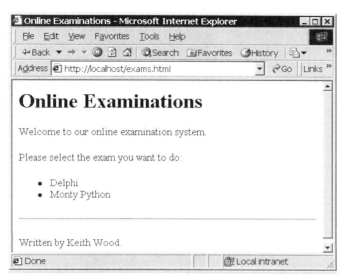

Figure 26-4: Selecting an examination.

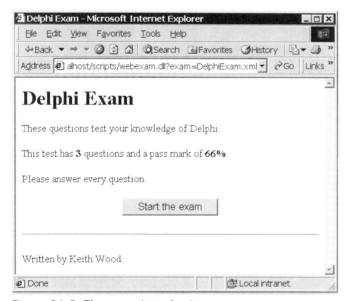

Figure 26-5: The exam introduction.

Summary

One of the prime objectives in the XML specification is to separate content from presentation. The previous chapter and this one demonstrate this ideal in action. From a single XML document that describes the content on an examination, you can build a customized Delphi application that administers it locally or a Web-based application that presents it within a browser. Both make use of a basic set of objects that encapsulate the information held in the XML document, but make it easier to work with within Delphi.

XSL Transformations provides a convenient and standardized way of converting the XML content into HTML for presentation purposes. This language has sufficient power to select any part of the original document and reformat it into a different structure. The three stylesheets used in this example each operate on the one exam definition but produce quite different results. Passing parameters to the stylesheet for each transformation lets you customize the output even further.

The Microsoft XML package supplies the means to apply these transformations, with enhancements such as `IXSLTemplate` to improve the efficiency with which it operates. Although the scripting abilities of this transformation engine are non-standard, they provide valuable extra functionality in particular situations.

Chapter 27
Simple Object Access Protocol

The Simple Object Access Protocol (SOAP) is a "lightweight protocol for exchange of information in a decentralized, distributed environment" (www.w3.org/TR/2000/NOTE-SOAP-20000508/). Based on XML, it defines a messaging framework for use in a distributed system.

The SOAP specification is currently a W3C Note as of May 8, 2000. As such, it is intended for discussion only, although several organizations are promoting its use. It details the contents of the messages that are sent between distributed objects, describes an encoding scheme for representing data within those messages, and sets out a convention for using these to facilitate remote procedure calls and responses.

SOAP may be used with a variety of underlying transport mechanisms; however, only HTTP is discussed in the specification. Using HTTP lets you establish a SOAP server as a Web application and communicate with it through the standard port. This overcomes problems in opening up other ports for a more specialized connection.

SOAP Introduction

Messages under SOAP are simple XML documents with some defined structure and some content that depends entirely on the application. Although they are basically a one-way transmission from one object to another, SOAP messages can be combined to provide a request/response pattern.

The basic structure of a SOAP message is shown in Listing 27-1. An `Envelope` document element contains the message. Its namespace must be as shown since this value defines the version of SOAP in use and a SOAP server must reject messages for versions it does not recognize. Another optional attribute of the `Envelope` may define the encoding scheme used for data within the request. It should appear like the following, which denotes the standard SOAP encoding based on the XML Schema specification:

```
SOAP-ENV:encodingStyle="http://schemas.xmlsoap.org/soap/encoding/"
```

Listing 27-1: A SOAP message

```
<?xml version="1.0"?>
<SOAP-ENV:Envelope
    xmlns:SOAP-ENV="http://schemas.xmlsoap.org/soap/envelope/">
```

```
      <SOAP-ENV:Body>
        <findMovies>
          <rating>PG-13</rating>
        </findMovies>
      </SOAP-ENV:Body>
    </SOAP-ENV:Envelope>
```

An optional Header element may appear as the first child of the Envelope (and nowhere else). It surrounds any number of elements that contain items of global interest to the main request. For example, it may define a transaction to use in database accesses. Each element in the header may have a SOAP-ENV:mustUnderstand attribute that is set to 0 (False, the default) or 1 (True). When True, the server must acknowledge and process this header element since it is assumed to affect the request in some fundamental way. If it cannot be actioned, an error must be generated.

SOAP also has the notion of an *actor*, which is the application that is destined to process the message. Each message may pass through a number of intermediaries before arriving at its final destination. A header targeted at a particular application must include a reference to it (as a URI) in the SOAP-ENV:actor attribute. The special URI http://schemas.xmlsoap.org/soap/actor/next indicates the receiving application (as does no actor specification). An application must remove and process all headers noted for it before passing the request on to another server. It is free, however, to add duplicate header elements for the next processor.

The Body element contains the actual requests, formatted as child elements. Parameters for each request appear as children of that element. Such elements may have arbitrary types (defined through an attribute) that conform to the encoding scheme established in the envelope. Additional elements may appear following the Body.

Once a SOAP application processes a request, it sends a response in the form of another SOAP message. Again, you have the SOAP Envelope and Body tags with appropriate namespace declarations. Within the body you have an element that contains the result of the request. By convention, this element is named the same as the request element with the string Response appended. It surrounds the elements that provide the actual reply. Listing 27-2 shows a possible response to the message above.

Listing 27-2: The SOAP response

```
    <?xml version="1.0"?>
    <SOAP-ENV:Envelope
        xmlns:SOAP-ENV="http://schemas.xmlsoap.org/soap/envelope/">
      <SOAP-ENV:Body>
        <findMoviesResponse>
          <movie>Entrapment</movie>
          <movie>Life is Beautiful</movie>
        </findMoviesResponse>
      </SOAP-ENV:Body>
    </SOAP-ENV:Envelope>
```

If some error condition arises, a response is still sent, but it contains a SOAP-ENV:Fault element in the body instead. Within this appear a number of predefined elements that describe the problem. The faultcode element is intended for automated use and consists of one of a small number of generic types. The SOAP specification defines those shown in Table 27-1. You may define other types as necessary.

Table 27-1: SOAP fault codes

Code	Meaning
VersionMismatch	The namespace on the SOAP Envelope is unrecognized.
MustUnderstand	A header element with the mustUnderstand attribute set to 1 is not understood or cannot be processed.
Client	The message body is badly formed or does not contain enough information to process it. Some change is required to the body before the message can be re-sent.
Server	The request could not be processed due to problems in the server. The message itself is fine and may succeed if re-sent at a later time.

In the `faultstring` element you find a human-readable description of the problem. Both of these two elements must always be present. The `faultactor` element identifies the actor that generated the error and is only required when multiple actors are used. Finally, the `detail` element must appear whenever the error results from processing the body of the request, and must not be present otherwise. It contains further details on the problem, such as internal error codes, a stack trace, etc. See Listing 27-3 for an example of an error response.

Listing 27-3: Returning a SOAP error

```
<?xml version="1.0"?>
<SOAP-ENV:Envelope
    xmlns:SOAP-ENV="http://schemas.xmlsoap.org/soap/envelope/">
  <SOAP-ENV:Body>
    <SOAP-ENV:Fault>
      <faultcode>SOAP-ENV:Client</faultcode>
      <faultstring>No movies found</faultstring>
      <detail>No movies found for rating 'NR'</detail>
    </SOAP-ENV:Fault>
  </SOAP-ENV:Body>
</SOAP-ENV:Envelope>
```

When transmitted via HTTP, any error response must be sent back with an HTTP status code of 500—Internal server error. For valid responses the return code is the usual 200—OK. Incoming SOAP requests over HTTP must also include a header field that indicates the purpose of the message. This allows firewalls to easily filter requests. The header looks like the following, with the supplied URI identifying the request. Specifying an empty string means that the HTTP URL itself denotes the call.

```
SOAPAction: "http://www.movies.com/findMovies.dll"
```

NOTE A SOAP document does not have a DTD associated with it. This is primarily due to the flexibility of the header and body content. A generic SOAP processor does not have to know about each request element, only how to extract the relevant parts of the document and invoke an action based on their content. In fact, the specification states that it is invalid for a SOAP document to contain a `DOCTYPE` declaration.

Processing SOAP

Using SOAP over HTTP is the only combination described in the specification, although other transport mechanisms could be used. HTTP requests let you easily add SOAP functionality by extending your Web server, and overcomes security problems in opening up alternate ports.

Under this scheme, you write a Web application that gets called for specific SOAP requests. The program knows how to extract the message and to direct it to an appropriate processor for evaluation. It then packages up the response (or error) and sends it back to the client. In true Delphi fashion, you can create components that encapsulate this functionality and reduce writing a SOAP processor to dropping a couple of components on a form and coding an event handler.

In normal Web applications, the request comes into a Web module that encapsulates a dispatcher for the query to one of a number of actions. When you create a Web application through the wizard you have a Web module automatically generated for you. An alternative is to replace that Web module with a standard data module and drop a TWebDispatcher component on it to handle the forwarding. Since SOAP fundamentally alters the normal dispatch of requests, the easiest way to implement it is to build a replacement for the TWebDispatcher.

This new component, the TSOAPDispatcher, derives from TCustomWebDispatcher to pick up the basic request handling mechanisms. However, it does not expose the Actions property since all queries are processed in the same manner. Internally it registers a single action, setting it to deal with any incoming request, and ties it to a customized handler. A SOAPParser property is added to connect with an XML parser that unpacks the message, while the OnHeader property lets you attach an event handler to respond to header elements. Listing 27-4 shows the declaration for the new dispatcher. This component and supporting code appear in the SOAPDispatcher unit.

Listing 27-4: A SOAP dispatcher

```
{ Event signature for SOAP headers }
TSOAPHeaderEvent = procedure(Sender: TSOAPDispatcher;
  Name, Value: string; Attrs: TStrings; MustUnderstand: Boolean;
  var Understood: Boolean) of object;
{ The customized Web dispatcher for SOAP requests }
TSOAPDispatcher = class(TCustomWebDispatcher)
private
  FName: string;
  FOnHeader: TSOAPHeaderEvent;
  FResponses: TList;
  FSOAPFault: ESOAPFault;
  FSOAPActions: TSOAPActions;
  FSOAPParser: TCustomSOAPParser;
  procedure ClearResponses;
protected
  function GetContent: string; virtual;
  procedure Notification(AComponent: TComponent;
    Operation: TOperation); override;
  procedure SetSOAPFault(Fault: ESOAPFault);
  procedure SetSOAPParser(Parser: TCustomSOAPParser);
  procedure SOAPAction(Sender: TObject; Request: TWebRequest;
    Response: TWebResponse; var Handled: Boolean); virtual;
public
  constructor Create(AOwner: TComponent); override;
  destructor Destroy; override;
```

```
    property Content: string read GetContent;
    property SOAPFault: ESOAPFault read FSOAPFault write SetSOAPFault;
    procedure DoHeader(Name, Value: string; Attrs: TStrings;
      MustUnderstand: Boolean; var Understood: Boolean);
    procedure SetResponse(Name: string; Responses: TList);
  published
    property AfterDispatch;
    property BeforeDispatch;
    property OnHeader: TSOAPHeaderEvent read FOnHeader write FOnHeader;
    property SOAPActions: TSOAPActions read FSOAPActions
      write FSOAPActions;
    property SOAPParser: TCustomSOAPParser read FSOAPParser
      write SetSOAPParser;
  end;
```

Instead of the Web actions of a standard dispatcher, the SOAP one provides the SOAPActions property. This is a collection of TSOAPAction objects, each of which matches a name with an event handler that knows how to deal with requests of that type. When an incoming message matches with one of these names, the corresponding event is triggered, passing across the action object, any parameters extracted from the message, references to the HTTP request and response, and a flag to indicate that processing was completed. See Listing 27-5 for the declarations of the collection and its event handler.

Listing 27-5: SOAP actions defined

```
{ Event signature for SOAP requests }
TSOAPInvokeEvent = procedure(Sender: TSOAPAction; Params: TStrings;
  Request: TWebRequest; Response: TWebResponse; var Handled: Boolean)
  of object;
{ A single SOAP action }
TSOAPAction = class(TCollectionItem)
private
  FName: string;
  FOnInvoke: TSOAPInvokeEvent;
protected
  function GetDispatcher: TSOAPDispatcher;
  function GetDisplayName: string; override;
public
  procedure AssignTo(Dest: TPersistent); override;
  procedure DoInvoke(Params: TStrings; Request: TWebRequest;
    Response: TWebResponse; var Handled: Boolean);
  procedure SetResponse(Name: string; Responses: TList);
published
  property Name: string read FName write FName;
  property OnInvoke: TSOAPInvokeEvent read FOnInvoke write FOnInvoke;
end;
{ The list of SOAP actions handled by a dispatcher }
TSOAPActions = class(TCollection)
private
  FOwner: TSOAPDispatcher;
  function GetItem(Index: Integer): TSOAPAction;
  procedure SetItem(Index: Integer; const Value: TSOAPAction);
protected
  function GetOwner: TPersistent; override;
public
  constructor Create(Owner: TSOAPDispatcher);
  property Items[Index: Integer]: TSOAPAction read GetItem
    write SetItem; default;
```

```
    function Add: TSOAPAction;
  end;
```

Within those event handlers you should retrieve any required parameters and process the request appropriately. A SOAP response should be generated through the `SetReponse` method on the action, passing in the name of the response element (usually the action name with `Response` appended) and a list of `TSOAPResponse` objects, each of which has a name and associated value. These are used to produce the elements and content of the returned SOAP body.

Processing the request to invoke an appropriate action is shown in Listing 27-6. The entire incoming message is retrieved based on the request method, before being passed off to the XML parser connected to the dispatcher. It returns a `TSOAPRequest` object that contains the request name and a list of parameters stored as name/value pairs in a string list. You then iterate through the list of defined SOAP actions to find a match and call its event handler. An error arises if no match is found. The HTTP response is formatted from the content established by the action handler (or an exception) and returned to the client.

Listing 27-6: Handling a SOAP request

```
{ Process a SOAP request }
procedure TSOAPDispatcher.SOAPAction(Sender: TObject; Request: TWebRequest;
  Response: TWebResponse; var Handled: Boolean);
var
  Index: Integer;
  SOAP: TSOAPRequest;
  SOAPQuery: string;
begin
  SOAP := nil;
  try
    try
      if not Assigned(FSOAPParser) then
        raise ESOAPFault.Create(SOAPFaultServer, NoParser);
      if Request.Method = 'GET' then
        SOAPQuery := Request.Query
      else
        SOAPQuery := Request.Content;
      { Parse the incoming request }
      SOAP    := FSOAPParser.ParseSOAP(Self, HTTPDecode(SOAPQuery));
      Handled := False;
      { Find a registered handler for it }
      for Index := 0 to FSOAPActions.Count -1 do
        if FSOAPActions[Index].Name = SOAP.Name then
        begin
          { And call it }
          FSOAPActions[Index].DoInvoke(SOAP.Params,
            Request, Response, Handled);
          Break;
        end;
      if not Handled then
        raise ESOAPFault.Create(SOAPFaultClient,
          Format(UnknownRequest, [SOAP.Name]));
    except on Error: Exception do
      begin
        { Trap errors and return to the caller }
        if Error is ESOAPFault then
          with ESOAPFault(Error) do
            SOAPFault :=
```

```
                    ESOAPFault.Create(FaultCode, FaultString,
                FaultActor, Detail)
            else
              SOAPFault := ESOAPFault.Create(SOAPFaultServer,
                Error.Message);
              Response.StatusCode := 500;   // Internal server error
          end;
        end;
      finally
        if Assigned(SOAP) then
          SOAP.Free;
      end;
      { Format the response }
      Response.Content     := Content;
      Response.ContentType := 'text/xml';
      Handled              := True;
    end;
```

If an error occurs, you raise an ESOAPFault exception (as shown in Listing 27-7). This has properties that map to those defined in the SOAP specification, letting you set their values during construction. The XML function formats the values as a SOAP Fault element ready for returning to the client.

Listing 27-7: The SOAP fault class

```
    { A SOAP exception }
    ESOAPFault = class(Exception)
    private
      FDetail: string;
      FFaultActor: string;
      FFaultCode: string;
      function GetFaultString: string;
      procedure SetFaultString(FaultString: string);
    public
      constructor Create(FaultCode, FaultString: string;
        Detail: string = ''; FaultActor: string = ''); virtual;
      property Detail: string read FDetail write FDetail;
      property FaultActor: string read FFaultActor write FFaultActor;
      property FaultCode: string read FFaultCode write FFaultCode;
      property FaultString: string read GetFaultString
        write SetFaultString;
      function XML: WideString; virtual;
    end;
    Parsing a Request
```

To avoid restricting SOAP processing through the TSOAPDispatcher to a single XML parser, the abstract TCustomSOAPParser class is defined (see Listing 27-8). It establishes the functionality required of a parser, namely, to take a request as an XML string and to return a TSOAPRequest object that embodies that content. The assumption is that each call contains only a single request, and that its parameters are simple string values. A subclass of this one must implement the ParseSOAP method using the abilities of a particular parser.

Listing 27-8: Abstract SOAP parser

```
    { Abstract base class for SOAP parsers }
    TCustomSOAPParser = class(TComponent)
    public
      constructor Create(AOwner: TComponent); override;
```

```
function ParseSOAP(SOAPDispatcher: TSOAPDispatcher;
    SOAPRequest: string): TSOAPRequest; virtual; abstract;
end;
```

NOTE Ideally the definition of TCustomSOAPParser would be an interface that lets you add its functionality to any object. However, during design, Delphi does not match interfaces with other components through the Object Inspector. Thus, you cannot select a parser from the drop-down list. Making TCustomSOAPParser a component instead makes it behave as expected during the design process.

As an added convenience, the constructor for the custom parser component automatically searches for a dispatcher and links itself to it (as shown in Listing 27-9). Since the dispatcher always requires the services of some parser, this should make it easier to use the combination. Merely dropping the dispatcher and parser components on the data module ties them together. To achieve this, the parser checks that it is during design time, then searches through all the components belonging to its parent (the data module) seeking a dispatcher. Once found, its SOAPParser property is assigned to the new parser (unless it had already been set). The dispatcher has similar code in its constructor to look for and connect to a parser.

Listing 27-9: Automatic linking to the dispatcher

```
{ Initialization }
constructor TCustomSOAPParser.Create(AOwner: TComponent);
var
  Index: Integer;
begin
  inherited Create(AOwner);
  { If there is a TSOAPDispatcher in the data module, attach to it }
  if csDesigning in ComponentState then
    for Index := 0 to AOwner.ComponentCount -1 do
      if AOwner.Components[Index] is TSOAPDispatcher then
        with TSOAPDispatcher(AOwner.Components[Index]) do
          { But only if not already attached }
          if not Assigned(SOAPParser) then
            SOAPParser := Self;
end;
```

In a separate unit, SOAPOXParser, you write a concrete implementation of the SOAP parser, allowing you to only include the parser you want. In this case, the Open XML parser is used. Its processing for the parse call appears in Listing 27-10. After creating the XML parser itself, the DOM is built from the incoming string. Thereafter the structure is traversed to extract the various elements.

Listing 27-10: Implementing the parser with Open XML

```
{ Actually parse the SOAP request }
function TSOAPOpenXMLParser.ParseSOAP(SOAPDispatcher: TSOAPDispatcher;
    SOAPQuery: string): TSOAPRequest;
var
  Element: TdomElement;
  Envelope: TdomElement;
  SOAPRequest: TSOAPRequest;
  XMLDoc: TdomDocument;
  { Return the next element sibling }
  function NextElement(Node: TdomNode): TdomElement;
```

```
begin
  while Assigned(Node) do
  begin
    case Node.NodeType of
      ntProcessing_Instruction_Node:
        { SOAP document cannot have processing instructions }
        raise ESOAPFault.Create(SOAPFaultClient, NoInstructions);
      ntElement_Node:
        begin
          Result := TdomElement(Node);
          Exit;
        end;
    end;
    Node := Node.NextSibling;
  end;
  Result := nil;
end;
{ Concatenate text content from this node and all its children }
function GetText(Node: TdomNode): string;
var
  Index: Integer;
begin
  Result := '';
  for Index := 0 to Node.ChildNodes.Length -1 do
    Result := Result + Node.ChildNodes.Item(Index).NodeValue +
      GetText(Node.ChildNodes.Item(Index));
end;
{ Process the headers for the request }
procedure ExtractHeader(Header: TdomElement);
var
  Attrs: TStringList;
  Element: TdomElement;
  Index: Integer;
  MustUnderstand: Boolean;
  Understood: Boolean;
begin
  Attrs := TStringList.Create;
  try
    Element := NextElement(Header.FirstChild);
    while Assigned(Element) do
    begin
      { Compile attributes }
      MustUnderstand := False;
      Understood    := False;
      Attrs.Clear;
      for Index := 0 to Element.Attributes.Length -1 do
        with Element.Attributes.Item(Index) do
          if NodeName = SOAPEnvPrefix + ':' + SOAPMustUnderstand then
            MustUnderstand := (NodeValue = '1')
          else
            Attrs.Values[NodeName] := NodeValue;
      { Invoke header handler }
      SOAPDispatcher.DoHeader(Element.NodeName, GetText(Element),
        Attrs, MustUnderstand, Understood);
      { Check that it was processed }
      if MustUnderstand and not Understood then
        raise ESOAPFault.Create(SOAPFaultUnderstand,
          Format(NotUnderstood, [Element.NodeName]));
      Element := NextElement(Element.NextSibling);
    end;
```

```
      finally
        Attrs.Free;
      end;
    end;
  { Compile the parameters for the request
    into the SOAPRequest object }
    procedure ExtractBody(Body: TdomElement);
    var
      Element: TdomElement;
      Index: Integer;
    begin
      if (Body.ChildNodes.Length <> 1) or
         (Body.FirstChild.NodeType <> ntElement_Node) then
        raise ESOAPFault.Create(SOAPFaultClient, BodyChildUnique);
      Element       := TdomElement(Body.FirstChild);
      SOAPRequest.Name := Element.NodeName;
      for Index := 0 to Element.ChildNodes.Length -1 do
        with Element.ChildNodes.Item(Index) do
          if NodeType = ntElement_Node then
            SOAPRequest.Params.Values[NodeName] :=
              GetText(Element.ChildNodes.Item(Index));
    end;
  begin
    SOAPRequest := TSOAPRequest.Create;
    try
      XMLDoc   := FXMLParser.StringToDOM(SOAPQuery);
      Envelope := XMLDoc.DocumentElement;
      { SOAP document cannot have a DOCTYPE declaration }
      if Assigned(XMLDoc.DocType) then
        raise ESOAPFault.Create(SOAPFaultClient, NoDocType);
      { SOAP document element must be Envelope }
      if Envelope.NodeName <> SOAPEnvPrefix + ':' + SOAPEnvelopeTag then
        raise ESOAPFault.Create(SOAPFaultClient, Format(
          InvalidMainElement, [SOAPEnvPrefix + ':' + SOAPEnvelopeTag]));
      { SOAP version must be correct (= namespace) }
      if Envelope.GetAttribute(NamespaceAttr + ':' + SOAPEnvPrefix) <>
         SOAPEnvNamespace then
        raise ESOAPFault.Create(SOAPFaultVersion, Format(UnknownVersion,
          [Envelope.GetAttribute(NamespaceAttr + ':' + SOAPEnvPrefix)]));
      Element := NextElement(Envelope.FirstChild);
      if Assigned(Element) and
         (Element.NodeName = SOAPEnvPrefix + ':' + SOAPHeaderTag) then
      begin
        { Optional header element }
        ExtractHeader(Element);
        Element := NextElement(Element.NextSibling);
      end;
      { SOAP document must have a body element }
      if not Assigned(Element) or
         (Element.NodeName <> SOAPEnvPrefix + ':' + SOAPBodyTag) then
        raise ESOAPFault.Create(SOAPFaultClient,
          Format(MissingElement, [SOAPEnvPrefix + ':' + SOAPBodyTag]));
      ExtractBody(Element);
      Result := SOAPRequest;
    except
      SOAPRequest.Free;
      raise;
    end;
  end;
```

Numerous checks are made in accordance with the SOAP specification: No DOCTYPE declaration or processing instruction nodes may appear, the required Envelope and Body elements must appear in the correct positions, the SOAP namespace (version) must be correct, and headers that must be understood are indeed understood. Any violation generates an ESOAPFault exception that is trapped by the dispatcher.

As header elements appear in the hierarchy, a call is made back to the dispatcher in case an OnHeader event handler is available. Upon return, the MustUnderstand and Understood flags are compared, producing an error if they are not compatible.

The contents of the Body element are compiled into the TSOAPRequest object constructed by this function. Each parameter is set as a simple string value against its element's name in a string list. The action handler then retrieves these by name from the Values property.

These components are compiled and made available to Delphi by including them in a package. A new unit, SOAPReg.pas, contains the registration calls for them, while an associated resource file, SOAPReg.dcr, supplies the icons for the component palette.

SOAP Server

To demonstrate these components in action, you can build a Web server application that responds to a findMovies request. It takes one optional parameter, the rating, and returns a list of matching movies from those in the database table. Typical request and response documents appear in Listings 27-1 and 27-2.

Create the server by following these steps:

1. Start a new Web server application based on ISAPI by selecting the Web Server Application icon in the New Items dialog (select **File | New...**).

2. Remove the generated Web module from the project without saving its contents.

3. Add a data module to the project by selecting the **Data Module** icon in the New Items dialog.

4. Place a TSOAPDispatcher and a TSOAPOpenXMLParser component on the data module. They are automatically linked together.

5. Drop a TSession and a TQuery component on the data module. Set the session's AutoSessionName property to True. Point the query at the movie-watchers database (see Chapter 16) and enter its SQL:

    ```
    SELECT *
    FROM movie
    WHERE rating = '?'
    ```

    The query must be entered on different lines as shown so that the where clause can easily be replaced later on.

6. Press the ellipsis button next to the SOAPActions property of the dispatcher in the Object Inspector.

7. Add a new SOAP action and name it findMovies. Create an OnInvoke event handler for it and enter the code shown in Listing 27-11. This procedure retrieves the rating value sent by the client (if there is one) and queries the database for matching movies. Those found are placed into TSOAPResponse objects for use in the response document. Your data module should look like the one shown in Figure 27-1.

Listing 27-11: The action handler in the SOAP server

```
{ Handle the 'findMovies' SOAP request }
procedure TdmdSOAP.SOAPFindMoviesInvoke(
  Sender: TSOAPAction; Params: TStrings; Request: TWebRequest;
  Response: TWebResponse; var Handled: Boolean);
var
  Movies: TList;
  Rating: string;
begin
  Movies := TList.Create;
  try
    Rating := Params.Values['rating'];
    with qryMovies do
    begin
      if Rating <> '' then
        SQL[2] := 'WHERE rating = ''' + Rating + ''''
      else
        SQL[2] := '';
      Open;
      while not EOF do
      begin
        Movies.Add(TSOAPResponse.Create('movie',
          FieldByName('name').DisplayText));
        Next;
      end;
      Close;
      if Movies.Count = 0 then
        raise ESOAPFault.Create(SOAPFaultClient, 'No movies found',
          'No movies found for rating ''' + Rating + '''');
      Sender.SetResponse(Sender.Name, Movies);
    end;
  finally
    Movies.Free;
  end;
  Handled := True;
end;
```

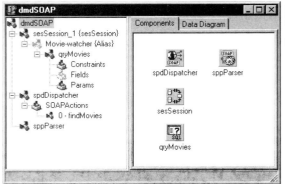

Figure 27-1: The SOAP server data module.

8. Compile and deploy your application to the Web server. Copy the resulting DLL to your executable directory on the Web server. Under PWS or IIS this is usually \inetpub\scripts. The `movie-watcher` alias should already have been established for use by the application.

SOAP Client

Next you need to create a client to talk to the server. Although you could use a simple HTML page and have the returned XML show up in the browser, a standalone client lets you more easily supply the variable rating parameter, and display the outgoing request and incoming response. Furthermore, with IE you cannot see any error response since the HTTP status of 500 overrides this and displays its own message.

The client application is very simple (see Figure 27-2). It contains a page control to allow for entry of the request, and then the display of both the SOAP request and its response. A combo box provides a selection of the standard movie ratings. Most of the processing occurs behind the Find button, whose event handler is shown in Listing 27-12.

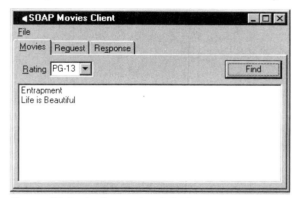

Figure 27-2: A client using SOAP.

Listing 27-12: Sending a SOAP request

```
{ Compile the SOAP request and parse the results }
procedure TfrmMovies.btnFindClick(Sender: TObject);
var
  Element: IXMLDOMNode;
  Request: string;
  { Extract the list of matching movies }
  procedure ListMovies(Node: IXMLDOMNode);
  var
    Index: Integer;
  begin
    for Index := 0 to Node.ChildNodes.Length -1 do
      with Node.ChildNodes.Item[Index] do
        lbxMovies.Items.Add(Text);
  end;
begin
  Screen.Cursor := crHourglass;
  try
```

```
    pgcSOAP.ActivePage := tshMovies;
    lbxMovies.Items.Clear;
    memRequest.Lines.Clear;
    memResponse.Lines.Clear;
    Request := '<?xml version="1.0"?>' +
      '<' + SOAPEnvPrefix + ':' + SOAPEnvelopeTag + ' ' +
      NamespaceAttr + ':' + SOAPEnvPrefix + '="' +
      SOAPEnvNamespace + '">' + '<' + SOAPEnvPrefix + ':' +
      SOAPBodyTag + '>' + '<findMovies>';
    if cbxRating.Text <> '' then
      Request := Request + '<rating>' + cbxRating.Text + '</rating>';
    Request := Request + '</findMovies>' +
      '</' + SOAPEnvPrefix + ':' + SOAPBodyTag + '>' +
      '</' + SOAPEnvPrefix + ':' + SOAPEnvelopeTag + '>';
    memRequest.Lines.Text   := Request;
    htpSOAP.Header          := SOAPActionHeader + ': findMovies';
    htpSOAP.Post(FApplication, Request);
    memResponse.Lines.Text := htpSOAP.Body;
    if ((htpSOAP.ReplyNumber <> 200) and
      (htpSOAP.ReplyNumber <> 500)) or
      (Pos('<HTML', UpperCase(htpSOAP.Body)) > 0) then
    begin
      MessageDlg('HTTP error: ' + IntToStr(htpSOAP.ReplyNumber),
        mtError, [mbOK], 0);
      Exit;
    end;
    if not FXMLDoc.LoadXML(htpSOAP.Body) then
    begin
      MessageDlg(FXMLDoc.ParseError.Reason, mtError, [mbOK], 0);
      Exit;
    end;
    Element := FXMLDoc.DocumentElement.FirstChild.FirstChild;
    if Element.NodeName = SOAPEnvPrefix + ':' + SOAPFaultTag then
      MessageDlg('Error in request'#13 +
        Element.ChildNodes.Item[1].Text, mtError, [mbOK], 0)
    else
      ListMovies(Element);
  finally
    Screen.Cursor := crDefault;
  end;
end;
```

First, the list box, request, and response memo controls are cleared, followed by the construction of the SOAP XML as a string value and its copying to the first memo field. A `TNMHTTP` component supplies the connectivity to the Web application. After setting the required SOAP header, its `Post` method is called to send the SOAP request out. Any response appears in its `Body` property, which is copied into a memo field and loaded into a DOM for interpretation. Microsoft's DOM is used in this case.

If an error response is found, it produces a dialog box showing the reason. Otherwise, each entry in the response (a movie title) is added to the main list box. To generate a SOAP error, just pick a rating that has no matching movies, such as `NR`.

By default the client looks for your local Web server and an application named `scripts/SOAPServer.dll`. The two menu options on the form let you change these settings.

Summary

The Simple Object Access Protocol, being based on XML, provides a platform- and operating system-independent way of communicating between distributed objects. Part of its design goals are simplicity and extensibility. It does not take the place of more robust schemes such as CORBA as it provides no additional services. There is no distributed garbage collection and no passing of objects by reference.

The development of the SOAP components in this chapter let you easily create a Web application that offers SOAP functionality. Just drop the `TSOAPDispatcher` onto a data module, connect a SOAP parser, hook up the actions, and compile.

SOAP can provide a simple entry point into using remote procedure calls, letting you decouple the client and server, which may be using different environments and programming languages. Instead of the Delphi client shown here, you could just as easily use Java, C++, or JavaScript. Watch for more development in this arena.

Glossary

ASCII	The American Standard Code for Information Interchange. A 7-bit encoding of the standard English letters, numbers, punctuation, and assorted control characters.
Attribute	Additional information attached to an **element** in **XML**. These are declared as `name=value` pairings within an element's opening **tag**. Attribute values must appear within quotes in XML.
Byte order mark	A series of bytes at the start of a document that indicate which **encoding scheme** is used in the document. Typically it is only used to distinguish between **UTF-16BE** and **UTF-16LE**.
CDATA	Character Data. Used in **DTD**s, this denotes an attribute that can have a textual value.
CDATA section	A special section of character data in an **XML** document in which the **XML processor** does not interpret any markup. Thus, it can contain XML metacharacters (<, &, etc.) without them being escaped.
CGI	Common Gateway Interface. An early specification for the way that an external program can be invoked in response to a request to a Web server. A newer alternative, **ISAPI**, offers better performance.
Character encoding	See **Encoding scheme**.
Complex type	In an **XML Schema**, these are built up from **simple types** by defining structures and/or adding **attributes**.
CORBA	Common Object Request Broker Architecture. A distributed object computing infrastructure being standardized by the **OMG**.
CSS	Cascading Style Sheets. A language for describing the formatting of **HTML/XML** elements. The "cascading" part comes from the fact that multiple styles may apply and are combined.
CSS2	A later version of **CSS**.
Decoupling	The limiting of knowledge of one class by another. The fewer interactions between them, the more stable the application.
Document fragment	A portion of a **DOM** hierarchy that is separate from the main structure. It is used to construct parts before being added to the main tree, or to transfer sections between positions within the hierarchy.

DOM	Document Object Model. An object-oriented model of the structure and contents of an **XML** (or other structured) document.
DTD	Document type definition. The definition of the allowable structure of a particular class of documents. DTDs may appear as an integral part of an **XML** document or externally to be shared among many documents.
Element	A structural piece within an **XML** document. As content, an element may contain simple text, other elements, or combinations of the two. Elements may have additional values associated with them through **attributes**.
Empty tag	A **tag** that has no content, neither text nor other tags, although it may have **attributes**.
Encapsulation	An object-oriented term denoting the hiding of the way an object works. All you need to interact with it are the definitions of its **interfaces**.
Encoding scheme	The way that characters are mapped to a byte stream. Common encodings include **ASCII**, **ISO-8859-1**, **UTF-8**, **UTF-16**, and **Unicode**.
Entity	An entity is a reference to further content, either as inline text or as an external **URI**, within a **DTD**. Include the entity's contents with an **entity reference**.
Entity reference	A reference to an **entity** within the body of an **XML** document. The name of the entity is prefixed by & and followed by ;. It is effectively replaced by the content indicated by the entity declaration.
External entity	An **entity** whose content resides outside the current document.
FOP	Formatting Objects to PDF. A free Java program that converts documents marked up with **XSL** formatting objects into **PDF** documents.
GIF	Graphics Interchange Format. A bitmapped graphics format widely recognized by browsers.
HTML	Hypertext Markup Language. The standard markup language for displaying information on the Web.
HTTP	Hypertext Transfer Protocol. The standard protocol used on the Internet to deliver Web pages.
IDL	Interface Definition Language. A programming language-neutral way of describing interfaces developed by the **OMG**. These can then be implemented by specific languages.

Glossary

IIS	Internet Information Server. A Windows-based Web server package from Microsoft.
Interface	In programming terms, this is a definition of the interactions supported by a class that implements the interface.
Internal entity	An **entity** whose content is specified within the current document.
ISAPI	Internet Server Application Programming Interface. An alternative to **CGI** that provides better performance since the requested applications run within the Web server process itself.
ISO-8859-1	One of a group of related 8-bit encoding schemes. This corresponds to standard **ASCII** and the accented Latin characters that are used in many Western European languages.
JavaScript	A scripting language based on Java which is often used within Web pages to orchestrate activities therein.
JPEG	Joint Photographic Experts Group. This group defined a graphics format that encodes photographic-like images. It allows the images to be compressed, based on perceptual research, in a way that loses detail but that is generally not noticeable.
Local name	The portion of an **element** or **attribute** name that does not include any **prefix** for a **namespace**. For example, the template in xsl:template.
MathML	Mathematical Markup Language. An **XML** application that describes the presentation and content of mathematical equations.
MIDAS	Multi-tier Distributed Application Services. A framework developed by Borland for multi-tier applications that communicate database information.
Namespace	A notional domain that serves to distinguish **element** and **attribute** names that would otherwise be identical. Namespaces associate a **prefix** with an identifier (usually a **URI**), and that prefix appears with the element or attribute name, such as xsl:template.
Normalization	In **XML** terms, this has two meanings. The first is the process of standardizing spacing within text fields (changing all white space to spaces, combining multiple spaces, trimming the text). The second is the process of combining adjacent text nodes within a **DOM**.
Notation	A notation defines the data content of an **attribute**, **entity**, or **processing instruction** within an **XML** document.
OASIS	Organization for the Advancement of Structured Information Standards. A non-profit, international consortium that creates

Glossary

	interoperable industry specifications based on public standards such as **XML** and **SGML**.
OMG	Object Management Group. An organization that develops specifications for object-oriented usage, including **CORBA** and **IDL**.
Parameter entity	An **entity** that is only used within a **DTD**. References to them use a % as the prefix instead of the usual &.
Parsed entity	An **entity** that refers to **XML** content (either externally or internally). Its content is included in the document and is parsed along with its surrounding nodes (usually text or elements).
PCDATA	Parsed Character Data. Used in **DTD**s, this identifies an **element** that may contain textual content.
PDF	Portable Document Format. A document format produced by Adobe Systems that describes layout in a transportable manner.
PICS	Platform for Internet Content Selection. A **W3C Recommendation** for exchanging descriptions of the content of Web pages and other material.
PNG	Portable Network Graphics. A graphics format similar to **GIF**. It was designed as a replacement for GIF since the latter contains patented algorithms.
Prefix	A mnemonic associated with a **namespace** that precedes an **element** or **attribute** name to uniquely identify it. For example, the xsl in xsl:template.
Pre-order traversal	Stepping through the nodes in a **DOM** in the same order that they appear in the text version of the **XML** document.
Processing instruction	A command embedded within an **XML** document. It is targeted at a particular application.
Prolog	The declaration at the start of an **XML** document or external entity that defines the contents as XML and may specify the **encoding scheme** used and whether or not the document can be used **standalone**.
PWS	Personal Web Server. A simplified version of **IIS** for personal use.
Qualified name	An **element** or **attribute** name that includes a **namespace prefix**, such as xsl:template.
RDF	Resource Description Framework. An **XML** application that lets you describe the resources available at a Web site.

SAX	Simple API for XML. An event-based API for parsing **XML** documents.
Schema	See **XML Schema**.
SGML	Standard Generalized Markup Language—ISO 8879. A specification for describing documents and their contents. The foundation for **XML**.
Simple type	In an **XML Schema**, these are the fundamental data types (strings, numbers, etc.), or straightforward restrictions of these. They can form the basis for **complex types**.
SMIL	Synchronized Multimedia Integration Language. An **XML** application that lets you define how various multimedia resources interact to create a presentation.
SMTP	Simple Mail Transfer Protocol. A standard for sending e-mail messages.
SOAP	Simple Object Access Protocol. An **XML** application that encodes remote procedure calls.
Standalone	A document is standalone if it does not refer to any **external entities**. A declaration to this effect can appear in the **prolog** to the **XML** document.
SVG	Scalable Vector Graphics. An **XML** application that describes 2D graphics constructs.
Tag	The markup denoting a particular **element** within a document.
UCS-2	A 16-bit character encoding, equivalent to **Unicode**.
UCS-4	A 32-bit character encoding that extends **UCS-2**. Currently only the UCS-2 part is defined.
Unicode	A 16-bit character encoding that encompasses most of the world's major written languages. The first 128 characters correspond to the more common **ASCII** encoding.
Unparsed entity	An **entity** that refers to resources that are not included in the current document. These entities are always external and may include non-**XML** resources such as **HTML** pages, images, etc.
URI	Uniform Resource Identifier. A reference to an external document or document fragment, often on the Internet.
URL	Uniform Resource Locator. A reference to an external document, often on the Internet.

Glossary

UTF-8	A multi-byte character **encoding scheme** for **Unicode** or **UCS**. It uses a single byte for standard **ASCII** characters, and two or three bytes for other **Unicode** characters. Thus, any ASCII file is also a UTF-8 file.
UTF-16	A 16-bit character encoding scheme for **Unicode** or **UCS**. It comes in two flavors: **UTF-16BE** and **UTF-16LE**.
UTF-16BE	**UTF-16** with big-endian byte order where the most significant byte appears first.
UTF-16LE	**UTF-16** with little-endian byte order where the least significant byte appears first.
Valid	A valid **XML** document is one that is both **well-formed** and conforms to its **DTD** or **schema**.
W3C	World Wide Web Consortium. A vendor-neutral organization dedicated to the definition of standards for use on the World Wide Web.
W3C Candidate Recommendation	This stage in the **W3C** process is a published report that invites feedback on implementing the proposal, and follows any **W3C Working Drafts**.
W3C Last Call Working Draft	The stage following **W3C Working Draft**, indicating that the specification is considered ready and is available for review both within the wider **W3C** community and by the outside public.
W3C Proposed Recommendation	Following **W3C Candidate Recommendation** status, this stage demonstrates that the specification is workable and incorporates any final changes.
W3C Recommendation	The end result of the **W3C** specification process, this stage indicates that the ideas or technology described therein are appropriate for widespread deployment.
W3C Working Draft	A work in progress at the **W3C** that represents a commitment to pursue developments in this area by a Working Group. This is the first stage towards a new W3C specification.
Well-formed	An **XML** document that adheres to the basic rules of XML: must have a single top-level element, and all elements must be closed and in the reverse order to that in which they were opened.
XDR	See **XML Data Reduced**.
XHTML	Extensible Hypertext Markup Language. A reformulation of **HTML** as an **XML** application.
XLink	**XML** Linking Language. A specification for defining links between resources (**URIs**).

Glossary

XLL	Extensible Linking Language. An overall term for linking in **XML**. It includes **XLink** and **XPointer**.
XML	Extensible Markup Language. A subset of **SGML** that is easier to use and allows for the definition of markup languages for use in specific projects.
XML Data	An early proposal for defining **XML** content that fed into the **XML Schema** specification.
XML Data Reduced	A subset of **XML Data** that is supported by Microsoft in its **XML** package.
XML processor	A software module that can handle an **XML** document. They come in two basic types: validating (those that check that the document conforms to its **DTD** or **schema**) and non-validating (those that check only for **well-formedness**).
XML Schema	An alternative to **DTDs** for specifying the valid content of an **XML** document. Schemas are XML documents themselves.
XPath	**XML** Path Language. A specification for identifying individual parts of an XML document. It is used in **XSLT** to identify nodes to be selected.
XPointer	**XML** Pointer Language. A specification for identifying individual parts or ranges within an XML resource (**URI**). It extends **XPath** and is intended for use with **XLink**.
XQL	XML Query Language. A work in progress for specifying a query against an **XML** document.
XSL	Extensible Stylesheet Language. A formatting language for presenting **XML** documents.
XSLT	Extensible Stylesheet Language Transformations. A language for transforming **XML** documents into other formats.

Index

A
Adapter pattern, 354
ASCII encoding, 30
ATTLIST, 37
Attr interface, 91-92
    in CUESoft DOM, 172
    in Microsoft DOM, 124-125
    in Open XML DOM, 211-213
attributes, 23
    declarations, 37, 71
    under DOM, 91
    under SAX, 280, 289
Attributes interface, 280-281
    in Delphi SAX, 323-324
    in Microsoft SAX, 296-298

C
CDATASection interface, 94
    in CUESoft DOM, 174
    in Microsoft DOM, 127-128
    in Open XML DOM, 215
CDATA sections, 28
    under DOM, 94
    under SAX, 288
CGI,
    converting to ISAPI, 430
    with Web modules, 377
    with XMLBroker, 426
character reference, 27
CharacterData interface, 92-93
    in CUESoft DOM, 172-173
    in Microsoft DOM, 125-127
    in Open XML DOM, 213-214
comma-separated values, *see* CSV
Comment interface, 94
    in CUESoft DOM, 174
    in Microsoft DOM, 128
    in Open XML DOM, 215
comments, 26
    under DOM, 94
    under SAX, 288
Common Gateway Interface, *see* CGI
complex types, 69
components
    TCustomSOAPParser, 501-502
    TDCOMConnection, 426
    TdomImplementation, 244-247, 261, 392
    TMidasPageProducer, 425
    TNMHTTP, 321, 508
    TNMSMTP, 445
    TPageProducer, 376, 381
    TReconcilePageProducer, 425
    TRecordPageProducer, 381
    TShowDeltaButton, 425
    TShowXMLButton, 425
    TSOAPDispatcher, 498
    TSOAPOpenXMLParser, 502
    TWebModule, 376
    TXMLBroker, 425
    TXmlDomImplementation, 181-182
    TXmlObjModel, 182-184, 189, 391
    TXmlParser, 185-189
    TXmlToDomParser, 252, 261
conditional sections, 40
    under Open XML DOM, 220
content models
    in DTDs, 36
    in XML Schemas, 69
    under Open XML DOM, 228
ContentHandler interface, 282-283
    in Delphi SAX, 326-328
    in Microsoft SAX, 298-300, 314
CSV, 416
CUESoft DOM, 157
    creation, 189
    example, 189
    generating XML, 391
    parsing a document, 184, 189
    TDomException, 158-159
    TXmlAttribute, 172
    TXmlCDataSection, 174, 191
    TXmlCharacterData, 172-173
    TXmlComment, 174, 191
    TXmlDocument, 179-181, 191, 391
    TXmlDocumentFragment, 178
    TXmlDocumentType, 175-176, 191
    TXmlDomImplementation, 181-182
    TXmlElement, 169-171, 191, 391
    TXmlEntity, 176-177, 192
    TXmlEntityReference, 177
    TXmlNamedNodeMap, 167-168
    TXmlNode, 160-165, 190
    TXmlNodeList, 165-167
    TXmlNotation, 177-178, 192
    TXmlObjModel, 182-184, 189, 391
    TXmlParser, 185-189, 359
    TXmlParserError, 159-160
    TXmlProcessingInstruction, 175, 191
    TXmlText, 173-174, 191
    wrapped in SAX, 359

517

Index

D
database,
    generating XML, 377, 386, 403
    mapping to XML, 367
    movie-watcher, 368-369
    updating with MIDAS, 422
declaration-handler property, 289, 305, 333, 348
DeclHandler interface, 289
    in Delphi SAX, 333
    in Microsoft SAX, 305-306, 313
DefaultHandler class, 293
    in Delphi SAX, 340-341
Delphi SAX, 317
    ESAXException, 319
    ESAXNotRecognizedException, 319
    ESAXNotSupportedException, 319
    ESAXParseException, 320-321
    examples, 345, 354, 359, 453
    ISAXAttributes, 323-324
    ISAXContentHandler, 326-328, 349
    ISAXDeclHandler, 333
    ISAXDocumentHandler, 453
    ISAXDTDHandler, 328-329
    ISAXEntityResolver, 329
    ISAXErrorHandler, 330
    ISAXLexicalHandler, 331-332
    ISAXLocator, 322-323
    ISAXXMLFilter, 336
    ISAXXMLReader, 334-335
    parsing a document, 334, 335, 348
    SAX2RDR, 339
    SAXPSR, 339
    TCustomParser, 341-343
    TSAX2DelphiReader, 341
    TSAX2MSReader, 355
    TSAXAttributes, 324-326
    TSAXCuesoftParser, 360
    TSAXCustomParser, 359
    TSAXCustomXMLFilter, 336
    TSAXCustomXMLReader, 335, 354
    TSAXDefaultHandler, 340-341
    TSAXHandlerBase, 453
    TSAXInputSource, 321-322
    TSAXLocator, 323
    TSAXParserAdapter, 336-337, 363
    TSAXXMLReaderAdapter, 336-338
    TSAXXMLReaderFactory, 338-340
    TXMLParser, 341-345
    wrapper for CUESoft DOM, 359
    wrapper for Microsoft SAX, 354
delta, 432
DOCTYPE, 35
Document interface, 98-101
    in CUESoft DOM, 179-181
    in Microsoft DOM, 133-139
    in Open XML DOM, 235-244

Document Object Model, *see* DOM
Document Type Definition, *see* DTD
DocumentFragment interface, 98
    in CUESoft DOM, 178
    in Microsoft DOM, 132-133
    in Open XML DOM, 234-225
DocumentHandler interface, 282, 453
documents
    under DOM, 98
    under SAX, 282
DocumentTraversal interface, 106
    in Microsoft DOM, 143
    in Open XML DOM, 247
DocumentType interface, 95-96
    in CUESoft DOM, 175-176
    in Microsoft DOM, 129-130
    in Open XML DOM, 216-219
DOM, 75
    Attr, 91-92, 124-125, 172, 211-212
    CDATASection, 94, 127-128, 174, 215
    CharacterData, 92-93, 125-127, 172-173, 213-214
    Comment, 94, 128, 174, 215
    comparison to SAX, 269
    CUESoft's DOM, 157, 189, 391
    Document, 98-101, 133-139, 179-181, 235-244
    DocumentFragment, 98, 132-133, 178, 234-235
    DocumentTraversal, 106, 143, 247
    DocumentType, 95-96, 129-130, 175-176, 216-219
    DOMException, 81-82, 158-159, 195, 197-198
    DOMImplementation, 101-102, 143, 181-183, 244-247
    DOMString, 78
    Element, 89-91, 122-124, 169-171, 208-211
    Entity, 96-97, 130-131, 176-177, 221-223
    EntityReference, 97, 131, 177, 224-225
    examples, 149, 189, 261, 440, 467, 502, 508
    features, 101
    generating XML, 386
    Microsoft's DOM, 108, 149, 386, 440, 467, 508
    NamedNodeMap, 87-88, 120, 167, 206
    Node, 82-87, 111, 160, 198
    NodeFilter, 102-103, 247
    NodeIterator, 103-104, 248
    NodeList, 87, 119, 165, 205
    Notation, 97-98, 132, 177, 225
    Open XML's DOM, 195, 261, 392, 502
    ProcessingInstruction, 94-95, 128, 175, 216
    Text, 93-94, 127, 173, 214
    TreeWalker, 104-106, 250
    XSL Transformation, 407
DOMException exception, 81-82
    in CUESoft DOM, 158-159
    in Open XML DOM, 195, 197-198
DOMImplementation interface, 101-102
    in CUESoft DOM, 181-182
    in Microsoft DOM, 143
    in Open XML DOM, 244-247

DTD, 33
    attributes, 37
    ATTLIST, 37
    CDATA, 37
    comparison with XML Schema, 66
    conditional sections, 40
    content models, 36
    CUESoft DOM, 175
    declarations, 35, 95
    DOCTYPE, 35
    DocumentType interface, 95
    ELEMENT, 36
    elements, 36
    entities, 38, 39
    ENTITY, 39
    example, 33
    external subset, 35
    FIXED, 38
    generating XML, 393, 403
    ID, IDREF, 38
    internal subset, 35
    links, 54, 56
    Microsoft DOM, 129
    Microsoft SAX, 403
    mixed content, 36
    NOTATION, 39
    notations, 38, 39
    Open XML DOM, 216
    PCDATA, 36
    under DOM, 95
    under SAX, 287
DTDHandler interface, 284
    in Delphi SAX, 328-329
    in Microsoft SAX, 301

E
e-mail, 437
EDomException exception, 195, 197-198
ELEMENT, 36
Element interface, 89-91
    in CUESoft DOM, 169-171
    in Microsoft DOM, 122-124
    in Open XML DOM, 208-211
elements, 23
    declarations, 36, 72
    document element, 23
    empty, 23, 36, 70
    under DOM, 89
    under SAX, 283, 289
encoding schemes, 29-31
entities, 26, 39
    as attribute values, 38
    character references, 27
    declarations, 39
    Entity interface, 96-97, 130
    EntityReference interface, 97, 131

    EntityResolver interface, 285
    external, 27, 40, 477
    internal, 27, 40
    parameter, 40
    parsed, 27, 40
    under DOM, 96, 97
    under SAX, 283, 284, 285, 288, 289
    unparsed, 28, 40
ENTITY, 39
Entity interface, 96-97
    in CUESoft DOM, 176-177
    in Microsoft DOM, 130-131
    in Open XML DOM, 221-223
EntityReference interface, 97
    in CUESoft DOM, 177
    in Microsoft DOM, 131
    in Open XML DOM, 224-225
EntityResolver interface, 285
    in Delphi SAX, 329
    in Microsoft SAX, 302
ErrorHandler interface, 285-286
    in Delphi SAX, 330
    in Microsoft SAX, 302-303
ESAXException exception, 319
ESAXNotRecognizedException exception, 319
ESAXNotSupportedException exception, 319
ESAXParseException exception, 320-321
examinations
    Delphi client, 464
    example XML, 464-465
    Web client, 478
Extensible HTML, *see* XHTML
Extensible Linking Language, *see* XLL
Extensible Markup Language, *see* XML
Extensible Stylesheet Language, *see* XSL
Extensible Stylesheet Language Transformations, *see* XSLT
extensions to SAX, 286, 330
external entities, 27, 40, 477
external-general-entities feature, 287, 300, 331
external-parameter-entities feature, 287, 300, 331
external subset, 35

F
Façade pattern, 445, 446
facets, 69
features, 101, 286, 290
    exceptions, 319
    external-general-entities, 287, 300, 331
    external-parameter-entities, 287, 300, 331
    in Delphi SAX, 331, 335, 348
    in Microsoft SAX, 307, 313
    namespace-prefixes, 287, 299, 331, 348
    namespaces, 287, 299, 331, 348
    normalize-line-breaks, 308
    parameter-entities, 288, 304, 332
    server-http-request, 308

setting, 290, 307, 313, 335, 348
validation, 287, 308, 331, 348
FindComponent, 473

G
generating XML
  as text, 370
  using DOM, 386
  using SAX, 397
  using Web module, 376
  using XSLT, 407

H
HandlerBase class, 293
  in Delphi SAX, 453
hasFeature, 101, 106
  in CUESoft DOM, 182
  in Microsoft DOM, 143
  in Open XML DOM, 245
HTML
  as Extensible HTML, 6
  comparison with XML, 4
  comparison with XLink, 54
  from XSLT, 42, 48, 408, 411, 413, 478
  with InternetExpress, 422
HTTP, 376, 497
  using TNMHTTP, 321, 508
HyperText Markup Language, *see* HTML
HyperText Transfer Protocol, *see* HTTP

I
IMXAttributes interface, 399-401
IMXWriter interface, 397-399
  XML generation, 401
InputSource class, 277-278
  in Delphi SAX, 321-322
  in Microsoft SAX, 295
internal entities, 27, 40
internal subset, 35
Internet Server API, *see* ISAPI
Internet transmission, 376
InternetExpress, 422, 425
  TMidasPageProducer, 425
  TReconcilePageProducer, 425
  TShowDeltaButton, 425
  TShowXMLButton, 425
  TXMLBroker, 425
ISAPI,
  converting from CGI, 430
  examination example, 486
  SOAP example, 505
  with XMLBroker, 430
ISAXAttributes interface, 323-324
ISAXContentHandler interface, 326-328, 349
ISAXDeclHandler interface, 333
ISAXDocumentHandler, 453
ISAXDTDHandler interface, 328-329

ISAXEntityResolver interface, 329
ISAXErrorHandler interface, 330
ISAXLexicalHandler interface, 331-332
ISAXLocator interface, 322-323
ISAXXMLFilter interface, 336
ISAXXMLReader interface, 334-335
ISO-8859-1 encoding, 30
IVBSAXAttributes interface, 296-299, 399
IVBSAXContentHandler interface, 298-300, 314, 355, 404
IVBSAXDeclHandler interface, 305-306, 313, 358
IVBSAXDTDHandler interface, 301, 355, 403
IVBSAXEntityResolver interface, 302, 355
IVBSAXErrorHandler interface, 302-303, 355
IVBSAXLexicalHandler interface, 303-304, 312, 358, 403
IVBSAXLocator interface, 295-296
IVBSAXXMLFilter interface, 309
IVBSAXXMLReader interface, 306-309
IXMLDOMAttribute interface, 124-125, 151
IXMLDOMCDATASection interface, 127-128, 151, 389
IXMLDOMCharacterData interface, 125-127
IXMLDOMComment interface, 128, 151, 387
IXMLDOMDocument interface, 133-139, 147, 387
IXMLDOMDocument2 interface, 139-140
IXMLDOMDocumentFragment interface, 132-133
IXMLDOMDocumentType interface, 129-130, 151
IXMLDOMElement interface, 122-124, 150, 388
IXMLDOMEntity interface, 130-131, 151
IXMLDOMEntityReference interface, 131
IXMLDOMImplementation interface, 143
IXMLDOMNamedNodeMap interface, 120-122
IXMLDOMNode interface, 111-119, 150, 152
IXMLDOMNodeList interface, 119-120
IXMLDOMNotation interface, 132, 152
IXMLDOMParseError interface, 110-111, 149
IXMLDOMProcessingInstruction interface, 128-129, 151, 387
IXMLDOMSchemaCollection interface, 140-141
IXMLDOMSelection interface, 141-143
IXMLDOMText interface, 127, 150, 389
IXSLProcessor interface, 145-147, 486
IXSLTemplate interface, 144, 486

J
JavaScript, 422

L
language, *see* xml:lang
lexical-handler property, 288, 304, 332, 348
LexicalHandler interface, 287-288
  in Delphi SAX, 331-332
  in Microsoft SAX, 303-304, 312
links, *see* XLink
Locator interface, 279
  in Delphi SAX, 322-323
  in Microsoft SAX, 295-296

M

Mathematical Markup Language, *see* MathML
MathML, 8-10
Microsoft DOM, 108
   creation, 147
   examples, 149, 440, 467, 508
   generating XML, 386
   installation, 108
   IXMLDOMAttribute, 124-125, 151
   IXMLDOMCDATASection, 127-128, 151, 389
   IXMLDOMCharacterData, 125-127
   IXMLDOMComment, 128, 151, 387
   IXMLDOMDocument, 133-139, 147, 387
   IXMLDOMDocument2, 139-140
   IXMLDOMDocumentFragment, 132-133
   IXMLDOMDocumentType, 129-130, 151
   IXMLDOMElement, 122-124, 150, 388
   IXMLDOMEntity, 130-131, 151
   IXMLDOMEntityReference, 131
   IXMLDOMImplementation, 143
   IXMLDOMNamedNodeMap, 120-122
   IXMLDOMNode, 111-119, 150, 152
   IXMLDOMNodeList, 119-120
   IXMLDOMNotation, 132, 152
   IXMLDOMParseError, 110-111, 149
   IXMLDOMProcessingInstruction, 128-129, 151, 387
   IXMLDOMSchemaCollection, 140-141
   IXMLDOMSelection, 141-143
   IXMLDOMText, 127, 150, 389
   IXSLProcessor, 145-147, 486
   IXSLTemplate, 144, 486
   parsing a document, 137, 148
   schemas, 140
   threading, 155
   transformations, 407, 478
Microsoft SAX, 295
   creation,
   example, 309
   exceptions, 295
   features, 307, 313
   generating XML, 397
   IMXAttributes, 399-401
   IMXWriter, 397-399
   IVBSAXAttributes, 296-298, 399
   IVBSAXContentHandler, 298-300, 314, 355, 404
   IVBSAXDeclHandler, 305-306, 313, 358
   IVBSAXDTDHandler, 301, 355, 403
   IVBSAXEntityResolver, 302, 355
   IVBSAXErrorHandler, 302-303, 355
   IVBSAXLexicalHandler, 303-304, 312, 358, 403
   IVBSAXLocator, 295-296
   IVBSAXXMLFilter, 309
   IVBSAXXMLReader, 306-309
   normalize-line-breaks, 308
   parsing a document, 306, 308, 313
   properties, 308, 312
   server-http-request, 308
   wrapped in Delphi SAX, 354
   xmldecl-encoding, 308
   xmldecl-standalone, 308
   xmldecl-version, 308
MIDAS, 422
mixed content, 36
movie-watcher, 21
   customized client, 450
   database, 368-369
   DTD, 33
   SOAP example, 505
   XML fragment, 22, 79
   XML generation, as text, 370
   XML generation, using DOM, 386
   XML generation, using SAX, 397
   XML generation, using Web module, 377
   XML Schema fragment, 72
MSXML, *see* Microsoft DOM *and* Microsoft SAX
msxml:script, 483
Multi-tier Distributed Application Services, *see* MIDAS

N

name tokens, 24
NamedNodeMap interface, 87-88
   in CUESoft DOM, 167-168
   in Microsoft DOM, 120-122
   in Open XML DOM, 206-208
namespace-prefixes feature, 287, 299, 331, 348
namespaces, 24
   examples, 11, 15, 16, 43, 52, 67
namespaces feature, 287, 299, 331, 348
Node interface, 82-87
   in CUESoft DOM, 160-165
   in Microsoft DOM, 111-119
   in Open XML DOM, 198-204
NodeFilter interface, 102-103
   in Open XML DOM, 247-248
NodeIterator interface, 103-104
   in Open XML DOM, 248-249
NodeList interface, 87
   in CUESoft DOM, 165-167
   in Microsoft DOM, 119-120
   in Open XML DOM, 205
normalization
   of DOM, 86, 124, 171, 204
   of text, 25
normalize-line-breaks feature, 308
NOTATION, 39
Notation interface, 97-98
   in CUESoft DOM, 177-178
   in Microsoft DOM, 132
   in Open XML DOM, 225-226
notations, 39
   as attribute values, 38

Index

under DOM, 97
under SAX, 284

O
Open XML DOM, 195
    character functions, 257
    conversion functions, 258
    creation, 261
    examples, 261, 502
    generating XML, 392
    EDomException, 195, 197-198
    namespace functions, 256
    OnExternalSubset, 254, 261
    parsing a document, 254, 261
    TdomAttr, 211-213
    TdomAttrDefinition, 231-232, 265
    TdomAttrList, 230-231, 265
    TdomCDATASection, 215, 263, 394
    TdomCharacterData, 213-214
    TdomChoiceParticle, 229
    TdomComment, 215, 264, 394
    TdomConditionalSection, 220-221
    TdomDocument, 235-244, 264, 392
    TdomDocumentFragment, 234-235
    TdomDocumentType, 216-219, 264, 393
    TdomElement, 208-211, 263, 393
    TdomElementParticle, 230
    TdomElementTypeDeclaration, 227-228, 265
    TdomEntity, 221-223, 394
    TdomEntityDeclaration, 223-224, 264, 394
    TdomEntityReference, 224-225, 263
    TdomExternalSubset, 219-220
    TdomImplementation, 244-247, 261, 392
    TdomInternalSubset, 219, 393
    TdomNamedNodeMap, 206-208
    TdomNametoken, 232-233
    TdomNode, 198-204, 263
    TdomNodeFilter, 247-248
    TdomNodeIterator, 248-249
    TdomNodeList, 205
    TdomNotation, 225-226
    TdomNotationDeclaration, 226, 265, 393
    TdomParticle, 228
    TdomPcdataChoiceParticle, 229
    TdomProcessingInstruction, 216, 264, 394
    TdomSequenceParticle, 229
    TdomText, 214, 263, 394
    TdomTextDeclaration, 234
    TdomTreeWalker, 250-251
    TdomXmlDeclaration, 233, 264, 393
    token functions, 257
    tokenizing functions, 259
    TXmlToDomParser, 252-256, 261

P
parameter entities, 40
parameter-entities feature, 288, 304, 332

parsed entity, 27, 40
ParserAdapter class, 292
    in Delphi SAX, 336-337
parsing
    under DOM, 137, 184, 254
    under SAX, 290, 291
processing instructions, 26
    under DOM, 94
    under SAX, 283
ProcessingInstruction interface, 94-95
    in CUESoft DOM, 175
    in Microsoft DOM, 128-129
    in Open XML DOM, 216
prolog, 29
properties, 286, 291
    declaration-handler, 289, 305, 333, 348
    in Delphi SAX, 335, 348
    in Microsoft SAX, 308, 312
    lexical-handler, 288, 304, 332, 348
    setting, 291, 308, 312, 335, 348
    xmldecl-encoding, 308
    xmldecl-standalone, 308
    xmldecl-version, 308

R
randomize, 471
RDF, 15-19
Resource Description Framework, *see* RDF
Rich Text Format, *see* RTF
RTF, 418

S
SAX, 269
    Attributes, 280-281, 296, 323
    comparison to DOM, 269
    ContentHandler, 282-283, 298, 326
    CUESoft's parser, 359
    DeclHandler, 289, 305, 333
    DefaultHandler, 293, 340
    Delphi SAX, 317
    DocumentHandler, 282, 453
    DTDHandler, 284, 301, 328
    EntityResolver, 285, 302, 329
    ErrorHandler, 285-286, 302, 330
    examples, 309, 345, 354, 359, 453
    extensions, 286-287, 330
    features, 286, 288, 290, 307, 331
    generation, 397
    HandlerBase, 293, 453
    InputSource, 277-278, 295, 320
    LexicalHandler, 287-288, 303, 331
    Locator, 279, 295, 322
    Microsoft's SAX, 295
    ParserAdapter, 292, 336
    properties, 286, 288, 289, 291, 308, 335
    SAXException, 275-276, 295, 319
    SAXNotRecognizedException, 276, 286, 319, 330

Index

SAXNotSupportedException, 276, 286, 319, 330
SAXParseException, 276-277, 320
XMLFilter, 291-292, 309, 336
XMLReader, 290-291, 306, 334
XMLReaderAdapter, 292, 336
XMLReaderFactory, 293, 338
SAX2RDR variable, 339
SAXException exception, 275-276
    in Delphi SAX, 319
SAXNotRecognizedException exception, 276
    in Delphi SAX, 319
SAXNotSupportedException exception, 276
    in Delphi SAX, 319
SAXParseException exception, 276-277
    in Delphi SAX, 320
SAXPSR variable, 339
Scalable Vector Graphics, *see* SVG
Schema, *see* XML Schema
scripting XSLT, 483
server-http-request feature, 308
SGML, 3
Simple API for XML, *see* SAX
Simple Mail Transfer Protocol, *see* SMTP
Simple Object Access Protocol, *see* SOAP
simple types, 68
SMIL, 13-15
SMTP, 437, 445
SOAP, 495
    client, 507
    example XML, 495
    faults, 496
    server, 505
    TCustomSOAPParser, 501-502
    TSOAPDispatcher, 498
    TSOAPOpenXMLParser, 502
standalone, 29
Standard Generalized Markup Language, *see* SGML
SVG, 10-13
Synchronized Multimedia Integration Language, *see* SMIL

T

tags, 23
TCustomParser class, 341-343
TCustomSOAPParser component, 501-502
TDCOMConnection component, 426
TdomAttr class, 211-213
TdomAttrDefinition class, 231-232, 265
TdomAttrList class, 230-231, 265
TdomCDATASection class, 215, 263, 394
TdomCharacterData class, 213-214
TdomChoiceParticle class, 229
TdomComment class, 215, 264, 394
TdomConditionalSection class, 220-221
TdomDocument class, 235-244, 264, 392
TdomDocumentFragment class, 234-235
TdomDocumentType class, 216-219, 264, 393
TdomElement class, 208-211, 263, 393
TdomElementParticle class, 230
TdomElementTypeDeclaration class, 227-228, 265
TdomEntity class, 221-223, 394
TdomEntityDeclaration class, 223-224, 264, 394
TdomEntityReference class, 224-225, 263
TDomException exception, 158-159
TdomExternalSubset class, 219-220
TdomImplementation component, 244-247, 261, 392
TdomInternalSubset class, 219, 393
TdomNamedNodeMap class, 206-208
TdomNametoken class, 232-233
TdomNode class, 198-204, 263
TdomNodeFilter class, 247-248
TdomNodeIterator class, 248-249
TdomNodeList class, 205
TdomNotation class, 225-226
TdomNotationDeclaration class, 226, 265, 393
TdomParticle class, 228
TdomPcdataChoiceParticle class, 229
TdomProcessingInstruction class, 216, 263, 394
TdomSequenceParticle class, 229
TdomText class, 214, 263, 394
TdomTextDeclaration class, 234
TdomTreeWalker class, 250-251
TdomXmlDeclaration class, 233, 264, 393
templates, 43
text content, 25
    CDATA sections, 28
    in XSLT, 45
    under DOM, 93
    under SAX, 283
Text interface, 93-94
    in CUESoft DOM, 173-174
    in Microsoft DOM, 127
    in Open XML DOM, 214
TMidasPageProducer component, 425
TNMHTTP component, 321, 508
TNMSMTP component, 445
TPageProducer component, 376, 381
transformations, *see* XSLT
traversal, 106
    in Microsoft DOM, 143
    in Open XML DOM, 247
    NodeFilter, 102-103, 247-248
    NodeIterator, 103-104, 248-249
    TreeWalker, 104-106, 250-251
TReconcilePageProducer component, 425
TRecordPageProducer component, 381
TreeWalker interface, 104-106
    in Open XML DOM, 250-251
TSAX2DelphiReader class, 341
TSAX2MSReader class, 355
TSAXAttributes class, 324-326
TSAXCuesoftParser class, 360
TSAXCustomParser class, 359

TSAXCustomXMLFilter class, 336
TSAXCustomXMLReader class, 335, 354
TSAXDefaultHandler class, 340-341
TSAXHandlerBase, 453
TSAXInputSource class, 321-322
TSAXLocator class, 323
TSAXParserAdapter class, 336-337, 363
TSAXXMLReaderAdapter class, 336-338
TSAXXMLReaderFactory class, 338-340
TShowDeltaButton component, 425
TShowXMLButton component, 425
TSOAPDispatcher component, 498
TSOAPOpenXMLParser component, 502
TWebModule component, 376
TXmlAttribute class, 172
TXMLBroker component, 425
TXmlCDataSection class, 174, 191
TXmlCharacterData class, 172-173
TXmlComment class, 174, 191
TXmlDocument class, 179-181, 191, 391
TXmlDocumentFragment class, 178
TXmlDocumentType class, 175-176, 191
TXmlDomImplementation component, 181-182
TXmlElement class, 169-171, 191, 391
TXmlEntity class, 176-177, 192
TXmlEntityReference class, 177
TXmlNamedNodeMap class, 167-168
TXmlNode class, 160-165, 190
TXmlNodeList class, 165-167
TXmlNotation class, 177-178, 192
TXmlObjModel component, 182-184, 189, 391
TXmlParser component, 185-189, 359
TXMLParser class, 341-345
TXmlParserError class, 159-160
TXmlProcessingInstruction class, 175, 191
TXmlText class, 173-174, 191
TXmlToDomParser component, 252, 261

U
Unicode encoding, 25, 30
unparsed entities, 28, 40
UTF-8 encoding, 30
UTF-16 encoding, 31

V
valid, 23, 35
validation feature, 287, 308, 331, 348
version, 29

W
W3C, 3
    Recommendation process, 3
Web module, 376
Web server application
    CGI with Web modules, 377
    CGI with XMLBroker, 426
    ISAPI with examination XML, 486
    ISAPI with SOAP, 505
    ISAPI with XMLBroker, 430
well-formed, 23
white space, 25, 114, 137, 183
    under SAX, 283
World Wide Web Consortium, *see* W3C

X
XDOM, *see* Open XML DOM
XHTML, 6-8
XLink, 52
    extended links, 55
    out-of-line links, 57
    simple links, 54
    xlink:actuate, 53
    xlink:arcrole, 53
    xlink:from, 54
    xlink:href, 53
    xlink:label, 54
    xlink:role, 53
    xlink:show, 53
    xlink:title, 53
    xlink:to, 54
    xlink:type, 53
xlink:actuate, 53
xlink:arcrole, 53
xlink:from, 54
xlink:href, 53
xlink:label, 54
xlink:role, 53
xlink:show, 53
xlink:title, 53
xlink:to, 54
xlink:type, 53
XLL,
    XLink, 52
    XPointer, 58
XML
    attributes, 23, 37, 91, 280, 289
    CDATA sections, 28, 94, 288
    character reference, 27
    comments, 26, 94, 288
    configuration file example, 439
    customized client, 450
    datapacket example, 430
    document element, 23, 99
    documents, 98, 282
    DTD, 33, 95, 287
    elements, 23, 36, 89, 283, 289
    empty elements, 23, 36, 70
    encoding schemes, 29
    entities, 26, 39, 96, 283, 284, 285, 288, 289, 477
    examination example, 464
    generation, as text, 370
    generation, using DOM, 386
    generation, using SAX, 397

Index

generation, using Web module, 376
goals, 3-4
history, 3-4
Internet transmission, 376
mapping from database, 367
MathML, 8
mail-out template example, 440
movie-watcher client, 450
movie-watcher example, 22
name tokens, 24
namespaces, 24, 283
notations, 39, 97, 284
parameter entities, 40
processing instructions, 26, 94, 283
processors, 31
prolog, 29
RDF, 15
SMIL, 13
SOAP, 495
standalone, 29
SVG, 10
syntax, 22
tags, 23
text content, 25, 93, 283
valid, 23, 35
well-formed, 23
white space, 25, 283
XHTML, 6
XML Schema, 66
xml:lang, 25, 62
xml:space, 25, 114, 137, 183
XML Linking Language, *see* XLink
XML Path Language, *see* XPath
XML Pointer Language, *see* XPointer
XML processors, 31
XML Schema, 66
    attributes, 70, 71
    comparison with DTDs, 66
    complex types, 69
    elements, 69, 72
    examples, 72
    facets, 69
    in Microsoft DOM, 139, 140
    linking to documents, 68
    simple types, 68
    xs:all, 70
    xs:annotation, 68
    xs:any, 70
    xs:attribute, 71
    xs:attributeGroup, 71
    xs:choice, 70
    xs:complexType, 69
    xs:element, 72
    xs:enumeration, 69
    xs:extension, 70
    xs:group, 70
    xs:restriction, 69
    xs:sequence, 70
    xs:simpleType, 68
xml:lang, 25, 62
xml:space, 25, 114, 137, 183
XMLBroker, 422
    delta, 432
    reconciliation, 432
xmldecl-encoding property, 308
xmldecl-standalone property, 308
xmldecl-version property, 308
XMLFilter interface, 291-292
    in Delphi SAX, 336
    in Microsoft SAX, 309
XMLReader interface, 290-291
    in Delphi SAX, 334-335
    in Microsoft SAX, 306-309
XMLReaderAdapter class, 292
    in Delphi SAX, 336-338
XMLReaderFactory class, 293
    in Delphi SAX, 338-340
XPath, 58
    in XSLT, 43
XPointer, 58
    axis, 59
    examples, 64
    functions, 61
    locations, 61
    points, 61
    predicates, 60
    ranges, 61
    shorthand form, 59, 63
xs:all, 70
xs:annotation, 68
xs:any, 70
xs:attribute, 71
xs:attributeGroup, 71
xs:choice, 70
xs:complexType, 69
xs:element, 72
xs:enumeration, 69
xs:extension, 70
xs:group, 70
xs:restriction, 69
xs:sequence, 70
xs:simpleType, 68
XSL, 42
xsl:apply-templates, 44, 413
xsl:attribute, 45, 412
xsl:call-template, 45
xsl:choose, 47, 412
xsl:comment, 46
xsl:copy, 46
xsl:element, 45
xsl:for-each, 46, 411, 419
xsl:if, 47, 412

Index

xsl:otherwise, 47, 412
xsl:output, 43, 411, 416, 419
xsl:param, 146, 479
xsl:processing-instruction, 46
xsl:sort, 46, 411, 414
xsl:stylesheet, 43, 411
xsl:template, 43, 413
xsl:text, 45
xsl:value-of, 45, 412
xsl:when, 47, 412
XSLT, 42, 407
    comma-separated values example, 416
    conditional processing, 47
    functions, 417
    HTML examples, 48, 411, 413, 479, 483
    IXSLProcessor interface, 145-147, 486
    IXSLTemplate interface, 144, 486
    loops, 46, 411
    Microsoft DOM, 118, 407
    modes, 45, 413
    named templates, 45
    parameters, 146, 479, 492
    patterns, 43
    rich text format example, 418
    scripting, 483

templates, 43, 413
text content, 45
transform, 146
transformNode, 118, 407
transformNodeToObject, 118, 408
xsl:apply-templates, 44, 413
xsl:attribute, 45, 412
xsl:call-template, 45
xsl:choose, 47, 412
xsl:comment, 46
xsl:copy, 46
xsl:element, 45
xsl:for-each, 46, 411, 419
xsl:if, 47, 412
xsl:otherwise, 47, 412
xsl:output, 43, 411, 416, 419
xsl:param, 146, 479
xsl:processing-instruction, 46
xsl:sort, 46, 411, 414
xsl:stylesheet, 43, 411
xsl:template, 43, 413
xsl:text, 45
xsl:value-of, 45, 412
xsl:when, 47, 412

Extend Your Power.

Borland Solution Partner Resource Guide provides an opportunity for vendors of software products and services designed to extend the power of Borland developer tools and technologies to reach developers and IT professionals at the point of purchase.

The primary means of distribution of *Borland Solution Partner Resource Guide* is its placement into every North American box of Delphi (for both Linux and Windows), C++Builder, JBuilder, Application Server, VisiBroker, and AppCenter from Borland Software Corporation. In addition, Borland Software Corporation and Informant Communications Group will distribute *Borland Solution Partner Resource Guide* at a number of leading industry trade shows.

When you advertise in *Borland Solution Partner Resource Guide*, you will also receive a FREE advertisement in the electronic version at www.BorlandSolutions.com. Traffic will be directed to this site from both the Borland and Informant Communications Group Web sites. Advertisements in the electronic version may be updated each month. Visitors to your online advertisement will be linked directly to your Web site. Your electronic advertisement will appear until the next edition of *Borland Solution Partner Resource Guide* is published.

No other publication will reach as many Borland development and IT professionals more quickly or efficiently.

2 Great Ways to Get Your Delphi Fix!

Delphi Informant Magazine: FREE Issue, FREE Web Site

Receive **one free issue** of **Delphi™ Informant® Magazine**, and a **FREE** 30-day **DelphiZine.com** Web site membership. If you choose to subscribe, you'll get 12 additional issues (13 in all) and a one-year Web site membership for the super low price of **$49.99**. If you don't, simply write "cancel" on the invoice and owe nothing.

With the first issue, you'll discover why **Delphi Informant Magazine** is the world's leading publication covering Delphi development. And you'll see why **DelphiZine.com** is the most comprehensive and valuable information resource on Delphi development in the world.

- ► Complete Delphi 6 coverage
- ► Ready-to-run code examples
- ► Real-world solutions
- ► Tips, tricks, and techniques
- ► Web and database development
- ► COM+, MTS, LDAP, and more

Delphi Informant Magazine Complete Works CD ROM

(1995-2000)

Get a jump on your Delphi skills with this comprehensive reference. The **Delphi Informant Magazine Complete Works CD-ROM** contains all content published in **Delphi Informant Magazine** from 1995-2000, including all supporting code and sample files. Order this unbelievable collection for only **$49.99** (additional charges apply for shipping & handling).

The must-have ultimate reference source for Delphi developers *features*:

- ► Over 500 technical articles, product reviews, book reviews, and other content appearing in **Delphi Informant Magazine** from 1995 through 2000
- ► All supporting code, sample files, and utilities from each article
- ► Fast text searching across all articles contained on the CD-ROM
- ► Bookmarks for easy navigation
- ► ... And much more

CALL NOW!
800-884-6367 x10
Outside the US dial (916) 686-6610

YES! *I want to sharpen my Delphi™ programming skills...*

INFORMANT
COMMUNICATIONS GROUP

About the CD

The companion CD-ROM contains the code listings from the book, XML and related specifications, third-party software, and links to relevant Internet sites.

The files are arranged in three folders: BookCode, Software, and Specifications. These folders are accessible through the links in the Index.html document on the root or by using Windows Explorer. Each of the three main folders contains an additional Index.html file that serves as a link to the contents within that folder and to other resources.

 WARNING: Opening the CD package makes this book non-returnable.

CD/Source Code Usage License Agreement

Please read the following CD/Source Code usage license agreement before opening the CD and using the contents therein:

1. By opening the accompanying software package, you are indicating that you have read and agree to be bound by all terms and conditions of this CD/Source Code usage license agreement.
2. The compilation of code and utilities contained on the CD and in the book are copyrighted and protected by both U.S. copyright law and international copyright treaties, and is owned by Wordware Publishing, Inc. Individual source code, example programs, help files, freeware, shareware, utilities, and evaluation packages, including their copyrights, are owned by the respective authors.
3. No part of the enclosed CD or this book, including all source code, help files, shareware, freeware, utilities, example programs, or evaluation programs, may be made available on a public forum (such as a World Wide Web page, FTP site, bulletin board, or Internet news group) without the express written permission of Wordware Publishing, Inc. or the author of the respective source code, help files, shareware, freeware, utilities, example programs, or evaluation programs.
4. You may not decompile, reverse engineer, disassemble, create a derivative work, or otherwise use the enclosed programs, help files, freeware, shareware, utilities, or evaluation programs except as stated in this agreement.
5. The software, contained on the CD and/or as source code in this book, is sold without warranty of any kind. Wordware Publishing, Inc. and the authors specifically disclaim all other warranties, express or implied, including but not limited to implied warranties of merchantability and fitness for a particular purpose with respect to defects in the disk, the program, source code, sample files, help files, freeware, shareware, utilities, and evaluation programs contained therein, and/or the techniques described in the book and implemented in the example programs. In no event shall Wordware Publishing, Inc., its dealers, its distributors, or the authors be liable or held responsible for any loss of profit or any other alleged or actual private or commercial damage, including but not limited to special, incidental, consequential, or other damages.
6. One (1) copy of the CD or any source code therein may be created for backup purposes. The CD and all accompanying source code, sample files, help files, freeware, shareware, utilities, and evaluation programs may be copied to your hard drive. With the exception of freeware and shareware programs, at no time can any part of the contents of this CD reside on more than one computer at one time. The contents of the CD can be copied to another computer, as long as the contents of the CD contained on the original computer are deleted.
7. You may not include any part of the CD contents, including all source code, example programs, shareware, freeware, help files, utilities, or evaluation programs in any compilation of source code, utilities, help files, example programs, freeware, shareware, or evaluation programs on any media, including but not limited to CD, disk, or Internet distribution, without the express written permission of Wordware Publishing, Inc. or the owner of the individual source code, utilities, help files, example programs, freeware, shareware, or evaluation programs.
8. You may use the source code, techniques, and example programs in your own commercial or private applications unless otherwise noted by additional usage agreements as found on the CD.